Microsoft® Project 2007 All-in-One Desk Reference For Dummies®

Cheat Sheet

Checklist for Creating a Project Plan

You can use Project Guide to walk through building a project. However, if you prefer to do things yourself, here's a handy checklist that you can follow to build a Project schedule.

- ✔ Enter project information (such as the start date).
- ✔ Set up your work calendar.
- ✔ Create tasks, entering information about durations.
- ✔ Create milestones (tasks of zero duration) in your project.

- ✔ Organize your tasks into phases, using Project's outline structure.
- ✔ Establish dependencies among tasks, adding constraints if appropriate.
- ✔ Create resources, assigning cost/rate and resource calendar information.

- ✔ Assign resources to tasks.
- ✔ Resolve resource conflicts.
- ✔ Review the total duration and cost of the project, making adjustments if necessary.
- ✔ Set a baseline.

After you complete the preceding list, you're ready to start the project and track any progress on it, reporting progress to management by using Project reports or by simply printing your schedule or sharing it on the Web.

Checklist for Resolving Problems

Here's a checklist of things to try when a resource is overallocated in your project or your schedule is running overlong. Your ability to use any of these suggestions depends on the circumstances of your project. For example, you can add resources only if your budget allows it and you can drop tasks from your project only if doing so still allows you to reach your overall goal.

- ✔ Revise a resource's availability to the project. For example, change the person's availability from 50 percent to 100 percent.
- ✔ Modify assignments to take a resource off some tasks during the timeframe of the conflict.
- ✔ Move a task to which the resource is assigned to a later date, or modify the task's dependency relationships.
- ✔ Replace one resource with another on some tasks. See the Resource Substitution Wizard for help with this.

- ✔ Make changes to the resource base calendar to allow the resource to work more time in a week.
- ✔ Modify dependencies so that some tasks can start sooner.
- ✔ Create overlapping dependencies where appropriate.
- ✔ Add resources to effort-driven tasks to enable them to finish sooner.
- ✔ Outsource a phase of your project.

D1402523

For Dummies: Bestselling Book Series for Beginners

Microsoft® Project 2007 All-in-One Desk Reference For Dummies®

Cheat Sheet

Project Management Web Sites

Here are some useful project management–oriented Web sites as well as a few sites where you can access Project templates or third-party add-ins for Project:

Microsoft Template Gallery
http://officeupdate.
microsoft.com/template
gallery

Microsoft Enterprise Project Management Solutions
www.microsoft.com/
office/project/prodinfo/
epm/overview.mspx

Project Management Institute
www.pmi.org

Project Management
www.projectmanagement.
com

American Society for the Advancement of Project Management
www.asapm.org

allPM, International Institute for Learning, The Project Manager's Homepage
www.allpm.com

International Project Management Association
www.ipma.ch

Checklist for Setting Up to Use Project Server

Using Project Server takes more upfront work than simply installing the software. If you plan the implementation, it will go more smoothly and end-users will be happier with the results. Here's a checklist of things to consider before implementing a Project Server installation.

- Identify the people who will approve the Project Server database design.
- Identify the team members, resource managers, project managers, portfolio managers, executives, and administrators who will use the Project Server database.
- Interview the people who will use the Project Server database to determine how they work; you'll succeed at identifying requirements best if you create a questionnaire for the interviews from existing reports your company uses to monitor project performance.
- Set up a plan that phases in the use of Project Server; for example, start with only one project in your organization and use Project Server to manage it. Then, you can learn from your successes and resolve issues you faced before managing the next project with Project Server.
- Assess existing technology to determine whether it will meet the infrastructure, hardware, and software requirements of Project Server.
- Determine whether your organization needs the collaborative tools provided by Windows SharePoint Services.
- Establish organizational standards for Project elements such as custom fields, outline codes, views, and calendars.
- Set up the enterprise resource pool.
- Provide training to those who will use the Project Server database; make sure you focus the training on the needs of each particular group, because day-to-day users need to know different things than project managers.

For Dummies: Bestselling Book Series for Beginners

Microsoft® Office
Project 2007
ALL-IN-ONE DESK REFERENCE
FOR
DUMMIES®

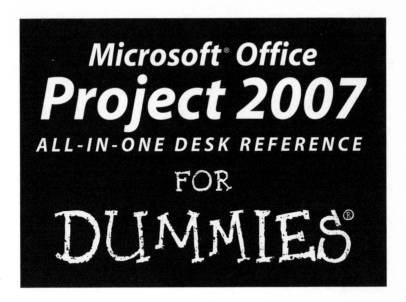

Microsoft® Office
Project 2007
ALL-IN-ONE DESK REFERENCE
FOR
DUMMIES®

by Elaine Marmel,
Nancy C. Muir

Wiley Publishing, Inc.

Microsoft® Office Project 2007 All-in-One Desk Reference For Dummies®

Published by
Wiley Publishing, Inc.
111 River Street
Hoboken, NJ 07030-5774

www.wiley.com

For general information on our other products and services, please contact our Customer Care Department within the U.S. at 800-762-2974, outside the U.S. at 317-572-3993, or fax 317-572-4002.

For technical support, please visit www.wiley.com/techsupport.

Wiley also publishes its books in a variety of electronic formats. Some content that appears in print may not be available in electronic books.

Library of Congress Control Number: 2007931548

ISBN: 978-0-470-13767-3

Manufactured in the United States of America

10 9 8 7 6 5 4 3 2 1

WILEY

About the Authors

Elaine Marmel is President of Marmel Enterprises, LLC, an organization that specializes in technical writing and software training. Elaine left her native Chicago for the warmer climes of Arizona (by way of Cincinnati, Ohio; Jerusalem, Israel; Ithaca, New York; Washington, D.C., and Tampa, Florida) where she basks in the sun with her PC, her dog Josh, and her cats, Cato, Watson, and Buddy, and sings barbershop harmony with the 2006 International Championship Scottsdale Chorus. Elaine spends most of her time writing; she has authored and co-authored over 50 books about Microsoft Project, QuickBooks, Peachtree, Quicken, Microsoft Excel, Microsoft Word for Windows, Microsoft Word for the Mac, Windows, 1-2-3 for Windows, and Lotus Notes. From 1994 to 2006, she also was the contributing editor to monthly publications *Peachtree Extra* and *QuickBooks Extra*.

Nancy C. Muir is the author of over 50 books on topics including project management, desktop applications, the Internet, distance learning, and e-commerce. She is the author of *Microsoft Project For Dummies,* and *Microsoft Project For Dummies Quick Reference*. She has also written or contributed to several textbooks for middle-school students. Her books have won awards for excellence and have been translated into over a half-dozen languages. Prior to her writing career, Ms. Muir trained Fortune 500 companies in project management software, and taught technical writing at the university level. Her company, The Publishing Studio, specializes in writing, editing, and consulting services for the publishing industry.

Dedication

To my brother and sister-in-law for always being there for me, and to my co-author, Nancy Muir — working with you inspires me, and you're fun when we're not working, too.

— Elaine Marmel

To Earl for his ongoing love and support, and to my co-author, Elaine Marmel, for being as great a friend as she is a writer.

— Nancy Muir

Authors' Acknowledgments

Special thanks to Kyle Looper for thinking up this project and trusting us to take it on. Our editor, Blair Pottenger, has made this book a delight to work on, as he always does. Thanks also to copy editor Virginia Sanders and technical editor Thuy Le for making sure our work is accurate and literate. We also want to acknowledge the Microsoft Project team and their product manager, Adrian Jenkins, for the help they provided during the beta testing of Microsoft Project 2007.

Publisher's Acknowledgments

We're proud of this book; please send us your comments through our online registration form located at www.dummies.com/register/.

Some of the people who helped bring this book to market include the following:

Acquisitions, Editorial, and Media Development

Project Editor: Blair J. Pottenger

Acquisitions Editor: Kyle Looper

Copy Editor: Virginia Sanders

Technical Editor: Thuy Le

Editorial Manager: Kevin Kirschner

Media Development and Quality Assurance: Angela Denny, Kate Jenkins, Steven Kudirka, Kit Malone

Media Development Coordinator: Jenny Swisher

Media Project Supervisor: Laura Moss-Hollister

Editorial Assistant: Amanda Foxworth

Sr. Editorial Assistant: Cherie Case

Cartoons: Rich Tennant (www.the5thwave.com)

Composition Services

Senior Project Coordinator: Kristie Rees

Layout and Graphics: Claudia Bell, Stacie Brooks, Denny Hager, Shane Johnson, Stephanie D. Jumper, Barbara Moore, Melanee Prendergast, Erin Zeltner

Proofreaders: Aptara, Christy Pingleton

Indexer: Aptara

Anniversary Logo Design: Richard Pacifico

Publishing and Editorial for Technology Dummies

    Richard Swadley, Vice President and Executive Group Publisher

    Andy Cummings, Vice President and Publisher

    Mary Bednarek, Executive Acquisitions Director

    Mary C. Corder, Editorial Director

Publishing for Consumer Dummies

    Diane Graves Steele, Vice President and Publisher

    Joyce Pepple, Acquisitions Director

Composition Services

    Gerry Fahey, Vice President of Production Services

    Debbie Stailey, Director of Composition Services

Contents at a Glance

Table of Contents

Introduction

*P*roject management has been around as long as there have been people coming together trying to get things done. Some ancient fellow with a lot of ambition probably took the lead as the very first project manager. He carved diagrams in stone tablets to help his team members understand his strategy and actually talked to them to communicate progress (no e-mail in those days!). Unlike you, this early project manager had no senior management to report to, no formal budget, and no cubicle, but the fundamental spirit of a project was there.

Over the years, project management has evolved into a sophisticated discipline that involves standardized methodologies and techniques. Project managers have a toolkit that includes detailed analyses and projections, tools to track time and money, and highly visual reports to impress management. Project management software — which has been around only about 25 years or so — has brought a new face and functionality to project management that would have left our ancient project managers speechless.

About This Book

Microsoft Office Project 2007, the most recent version of the world's most popular project management software, provides a treasure trove of functionality; it makes the features of your average word processing software look like child's play in comparison.

All that functionality can be wonderful, but if you've never used project management software, those features can also be a bit overwhelming. One key to making the leap from your traditional project management methods to project management software is to understand how its features relate to what you do every day as a project manager. Another is to get a book like this one that tells you all about Project's features and how to use them. Even if you have used project management software or Project itself before, this book offers a wealth of advice and information on Project 2007 features that can help you get productive right away.

In *Microsoft Office Project 2007 All-in-One Desk Reference For Dummies,* our goal is to help you explore all that Project offers, providing information on relevant project management concepts in handy modules (called minibooks) while also offering specific procedures to build and track your Project plans. But more importantly, we offer advice on how to make all these features and procedures mesh with what you already know as a project manager to make the transition easier.

How This Book Is Organized

This book is organized into digestible chunks of chapters contained in ten minibooks. Each minibook covers an important topic you need in order to use Project, such as basic project management concepts, resources, and tracking. If you're new to Project, you might want to read each book in sequence, but if you've used Project before, you can simply refer to the mini-book that you need at the moment.

In addition, we include case studies throughout this book to help you see how Project works in action. Files that go along with those case studies are on the book's companion Web site, located at www.dummies.com/go/project 2007aiofd.

The following sections offer a quick synopsis of what each book contains.

Book I: Project Management

This book gives you a firm grounding in project management concepts and the Microsoft Project 2007 environment. You discover what typical tasks go into a project, as well as how using Project to manage your tasks and resources can save you time and money. Finally, in Chapter 5, we explore what's new in Project 2007, particularly some neat features such as Change Highlighting and Task Drivers.

Book II: Project Basics

Some of the basic building blocks of Project include the overall structure of a project plan, which we discuss in Chapter 1, and the tasks that make up that plan. It's in this minibook that you create your first task and explore the many views Project offers to help you review and analyze your project data. In Chapter 4, we cover calendars, very important tools in building your project's timing. Finally, in Chapter 5, we explore Project's help system so you can use it to find topics of interest easily.

Book III: Getting Your Plan in Order

This is the minibook where you explore the outline structure of a Project plan, made up of summary tasks and subtasks, and how to assign outline codes. Chapter 3 introduces you to the work breakdown structure (WBS) code, used by many organizations to uniquely identify tasks in a project plan. Finally, in Chapter 4 you discover the ins and outs of inserting and linking projects so that a task within one project can represent the timing of another project.

Book IV: Establishing Task Timing

Task timing is determined by a number of factors, several of which are reviewed in the chapters of this minibook. Chapter 1 explores the basics of timing. Chapter 2 provides an introduction to what drives task timing, including the start and finish dates of a project and the setting for how Project schedules tasks. In Chapter 3, you explore dependencies, timing relationships between tasks that control their timing in relation to each other. Finally, Chapter 4 deals with constraints, settings such as Start No Later Than that force a task's timing in some fashion.

Book V: Working with Resources and Costs

Resources are the people, equipment, and materials that you use to get things done on your project. There are various kinds of resources, which you discover in Chapter 1, "Creating Resources." Chapter 2 shows you how resources relate to costs in your project. Chapter 3 is where you discover how to assign resources you've created to tasks in your project. The last chapter in this minibook explores how Project totals up costs resulting from resource assignments.

Book VI: Communicating Project Information

When you input data about tasks and resources into Project, it returns a wealth of information about your schedule and costs. In this minibook, you look more closely at all the views Project offers for reviewing that information, as well as tables of data you can display in those views and even customize. This minibook ends with two chapters about reporting, one covering traditional Project reports and one covering a Visual Reports feature that's new in Project 2007.

Book VII: Resolving Problems in Your Plan

When you have created a Project plan, before you put it into action it's a good idea to review it and fix any problems. In this minibook, we introduce filters and groups that help you spot trends and problems. Chapter 2 helps you through several methods for resolving resource conflicts, which might include resources who are overbooked at some point during the life of your project or whose assignments are causing delays in your schedule. Chapters 3 and 4 show you how to spot and resolve problems with timing in your project, including how you can use Project to help you convince your management that you need more time to get everything done.

Book VIII: Tracking

The project has started, tasks are being worked on, resource costs are tallying up. Now comes the tracking phase, when you set a baseline against which you can record progress. In this minibook, we discuss recording actual activity on tasks and reviewing what that activity is doing to your budget.

Book IX: Advanced Project Topics

Project is a very sophisticated piece of software, and it provides you with several more advanced tools to make your life easier. Book IX is where you find out how to customize the interface that Project shows you and the look of the various elements in your project plan. You also discover how to use macros to automate procedures and how to both import and export data in Project.

Book X: The Basics of Project Server

Project Professional can be used in conjunction with Project Server to create an enterprise-wide project management solution. Chapter 1 of this book gives you an overview of Project used with Project Server. Chapters 2 through 4 approach enterprise project management using Project and Project Server from the perspective of the Project Server administrator, the project manager, and the project team member.

Glossary

Project management and Project itself involve a lot (and we mean a lot) of terms and acronyms that you need to know to input and analyze data. This glossary is a good place to go when an unfamiliar word or string of letters pops up.

Conventions Used in This Book

We use a few conventions in this book that you ought to know about.

Web site addresses, or URLs, and other items such as filenames are highlighted like this: www.microsoft.com and IAmAFile.mpp.

Menu commands are given in the order in which you select them; for example, Choose Tools➪Resource Sharing➪Share Resources.

Options in dialog boxes use initial caps even if they aren't capitalized on your screen. This makes it easier for you to identify them in sentences. For example, what appears as "Show summary tasks" in the Options dialog box appears as Show Summary Tasks in our chapters.

Foolish Assumptions

We've made some assumptions in writing this book. First, we've assumed that you are computer literate — that you've used software and know what a menu and dialog box are. We assume you know how to use a mouse to select objects and text. We assume you have good file management skills and know that you should keep copies of your files and save frequently.

We have *not* assumed that you have used Project before, though you might have used a previous version and simply want to find out more about some area of it.

We haven't assumed that you manage multimillion dollar projects; whether you deal with small projects or large projects, the information and concepts in this book help you manage them better.

In case you're new to project management, we've provided the first minibook to give you a grounding in some key project management concepts.

Icons Used in This Book

Putting little pictures in the margins of tech books to call your attention to certain types of information has become a standard, and *For Dummies* books use the neatest little pictures around. Here's what they mean:

Tips are the advice columns of computer books. They offer wise advice from those of us who have been in the Project trenches, a bit more information about a topic under discussion, or a different way to achieve some results.

Remember icons offer a relevant fact or reminder of a key concept. These juicy tidbits are likely to be useful to you repeatedly, so don't forget them.

Warning icons alert you to potential problems, so don't ignore them. If you don't take the advice in warnings, you might end up with lost data, a faulty project plan, or a really bad day.

This icon marks Project information that goes beyond the basics.

Throughout this book, we have included case studies that help you envision how Project works in a real world (well, a pretend real world) setting. The files for these case studies are also included on the companion Web site (www.dummies.com/go/project2007aiofd).

Where to Go from Here

If you know a bit about Project and want to explore some aspect of it further, just jump to the relevant book and have at it. If you want to start by checking out what's new in Project 2007, Book I, Chapter 5 is the place to go. If you need to start from square one, start with Chapter 1 of Book I and work your way through each minibook to get a logically organized introduction to all that project management with Project has to offer.

Wherever you dive in, you'll find what you need to make your experience with Project more productive.

Book I

Project Management

The 5th Wave   By Rich Tennant

"Okay people, remember — use your project management software. It's customizable, so those of you collecting 'juice' will use a slightly different entry from those of you doing shakedowns or fencing stolen goods."

Contents at a Glance

Chapter 1: A Project Management Overview

In This Chapter

✔ Examining the project life cycle

✔ Looking at project roles

✔ Understanding the triple constraint, critical path, and slack

✔ Exploring the basics of resource management

Microsoft Project 2007 is a wonderful tool for managing projects. However, a tool is only as good as the person wielding it. Understanding how Project fits in the context of a typical project is important to using it successfully.

In this chapter, we look at what occurs during the life of a project and how Microsoft Project fits within that life cycle; the typical roles in a project and how people in each of those roles might interact with Project; and some basic project management concepts.

The Life of a Project

You handle projects day in and day out. Some take a few hours to complete, such as that shed you built in your yard last Saturday. Others might take years from beginning to end to complete the work and reach your goals. However, most projects that you handle will have several things in common.

So, just what is a project?

Microsoft Project has certain features that help you deal with all the elements of a typical project. So what is a typical project? All projects have

✦ An overall goal

✦ A project manager

✦ Individual tasks to be performed

✦ Timing for those tasks to be completed (such as three hours, three days, or three months)

✦ Timing relationships between those tasks (For example, you can't launch a space shuttle until you fill it with fuel.)

✦ *Resources* (people, equipment, facilities, and supplies, for example) to accomplish the work

✦ A *budget* (the costs associated with the people, equipment, facilities, and supplies)

Project management is simply the process of managing all the elements of a project, whether that project is large or small.

Taking a closer look at the project life cycle

You can typically expect to work through several phases of a project, and in each phase, you'll perform different activities in Microsoft Project. Projects typically break down into the following phases:

1. **Planning:** Whether it takes hours, days, or months, this is a very important phase. This is when you identify your goal or goals (see Chapter 2 of this minibook for more about this process), get management support for the project, and line up your internal and external resources, including people, facilities, equipment, and so on. In Project you can start to sketch out your Project plan by adding tasks that, at this point, might or might not have timing (see Figure 1-1) and entering information about resources that you'll use.

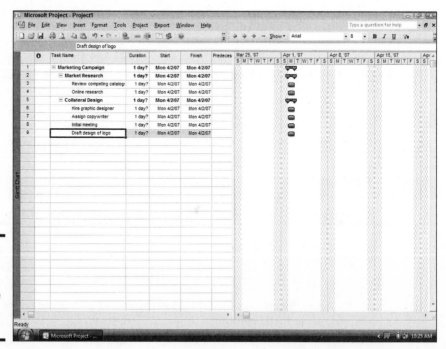

Figure 1-1:
A Project plan in its early phase of development.

2. **Finalizing the plan:** After you've gathered all your resources and thought through the steps of your project in the planning phase, it's time to dot your *i*'s and cross your *t*'s so you're ready to launch the project. In Project, this means making sure all the logical timing relationships between tasks have been accounted for (see Figure 1-2), all the cost information for resources is correct, and that you resolve any resource conflicts. (An example of a *resource conflict* is when one person is booked to work 16 hours in one day, for example.) This is also the time to present your final plan to management and get their approval. (Project's reporting capabilities come in handy here.) When your plan is approved, you save a baseline project against which you can track actual progress after your project begins.

See Book IV for information about task timing, Book VII about resolving problems in your plan, and Book VIII, Chapter 1 for information about setting a baseline.

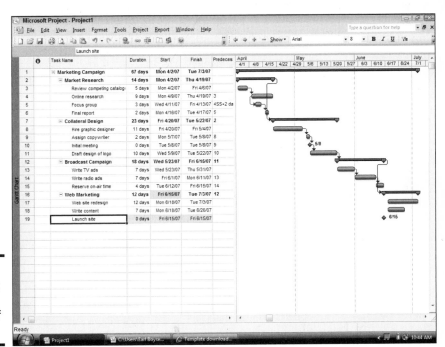

Figure 1-2:
Timing built into the workflow of tasks.

3. Launching the project: With an approved plan in hand, you can officially launch the project. Make sure your entire team has information about individual responsibilities and that you've set up channels of communication either online, using printed reports, or through regular in-person meetings. Also make sure you have set up reporting mechanisms for your team members to report their work hours on tasks and progress. Be sure to instruct your team in how to use those mechanisms, such as the Timesheet feature built into Project Web Access (see Figure 1-3). See Book X, Chapter 4 for more about this.

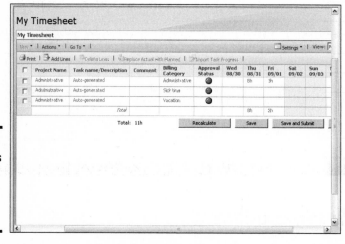

Figure 1-3: Timesheet is an easy-to-use time-reporting feature.

4. Tracking and revising your plan: When your team starts working on tasks and reporting progress, you or somebody you designate has to track that progress in Project. With information on tasks and resource time added into your project plan, you'll find that actual work is likely to differ from your projections. When that happens, you might have to make adjustments to the remainder of your plan to meet your deadline, budget limits, or goals. You can also use Project's reporting capabilities (see Figure 1-4) to keep your management, clients, and other project stakeholders current on the status of your project. See Book VIII for details about tracking activity on a project.

5. Ending the project and debriefing: If you've established a clear set of goals and deliverables, you'll know when the project is over. When that moment comes, your job isn't quite finished. It's important that you send out final reports or accountings to management and clients, thank your team members for their efforts and communicate with them about the project's success, and hold a meeting to debrief the team about the project so you can learn from both your failures and successes along the way.

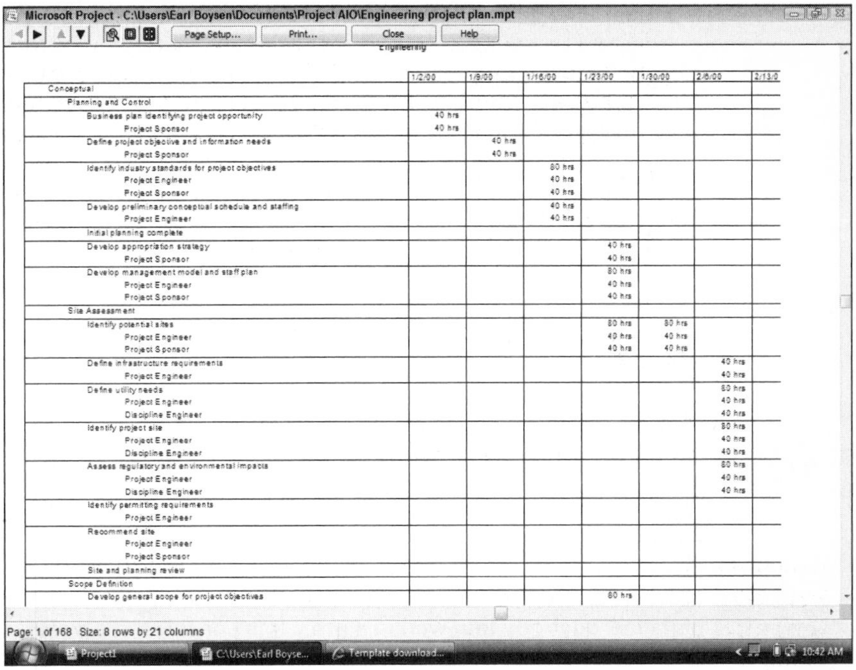

Figure 1-4:
Project
reports can
hold a
wealth of
information.

Everybody Plays a Role

Projects are driven by people, and just as everybody on a sports team plays a particular role, everybody in a project has unique responsibilities. From the project manager to the folks who do work on tasks and even the client or customer who will benefit from the final results, you need to understand how each person in your project fits in. What does a project manager do?

A *project manager* could be described as somebody who knows how to wear many hats. A project manager is a scheduler, a budget maker, a facilitator of communications, a resolver of conflicts, a troubleshooter, a counselor, and much, much more.

A project manager isn't always the highest authority in a project; often, that role belongs to the project manager's own manager, up to and including members of senior management. Rather, the project manager is the person on the front lines who puts together a plan, gathers resources, makes sure that the tasks in the project happen, and records project activity in Project.

Ideally, a project manager should have some experience in managing people and processes and to some degree should be familiar with the type of work that resources will be asked to perform.

A project manager supervises these essential pieces of a project:

✦ **The project plan or schedule:** This is what you create with Microsoft Project. It includes the estimated steps and associated timing and costs involved in reaching the project goal.

✦ **Resources:** Managing resources involves assigning resources and tracking their activities on the project as well as resolving resource conflicts and building consensus. This part of the job also involves managing the use of nonhuman resources, such as materials and equipment.

✦ **Communication with the project team, management, and customers:** Communicating the project's status to everyone who has a legitimate stake in its success *(stakeholders)* is a key responsibility.

As a project manager, it's your job to keep all stakeholders informed, get appropriate approvals, and involve the right people at the right time.

Stakeholders of all types

In addition to a project manager and the resources who perform tasks, others will have an interest in the project and its outcome. In project management parlance, anybody involved in a project is considered a *stakeholder*.

✦ The person who champions (and has the ultimate responsibility for) a project is the *project sponsor.* This person usually belongs to higher-up management and should support the project manager by helping to get key approvals, providing input on larger organizational priorities, and obtaining funding from management.

✦ Although a project manager might work for a project sponsor, the project often also has a *customer* for whom the end product is produced. That customer can be outside the project manager's own company or within. A customer generally gets final approval of the deliverables of a project and pays the costs of a project.

✦ A project might have a whole slew of additional stakeholders in the form of vendors, contractors, or consultants who will work on the project along with internal resources.

Getting a Few Project Management Concepts under Your Belt

As you work with Microsoft Project, you'll deal with all-important timing details to try to make your deadline. You need to understand some concepts behind scheduling in order to make intelligent choices as you build a Project plan.

The dreaded triple constraint

You've seen the signs at the copy store or the auto repair place: "You can have it fast, cheap, or right; pick two." That, good friend, is the triple constraint of project management in a nutshell.

In a project, you have timing, resources (which are essentially costs), and the quality of the product or service you want to produce at the end of the project. Microsoft Project helps you to manage the resources and timing of your project. Still, the quality of your project is often affected directly by how well you manage these other two elements. If you add time, costs increase because resources are working longer hours at a certain wage. If you take away resources, you save money, but this can affect quality.

Creating a balance among time, money, and quality is the juggling act you will perform throughout the life of a project. Project offers the following tools to help you do this:

✦ **Change Highlighting** helps you see how one change (say, in timing) affects other aspects (such as cost). See Book I, Chapter 5 for more about Change Highlighting.

✦ **Resource leveling** is a calculation that moves your schedule out to free up overtaxed resources. Of course, in this case you sacrifice time, but with less-stressed resources, you probably improve the quality of your outcome. See Book VII, Chapter 2 to discover how to use this handy feature.

✦ You can **set priorities on tasks** so that you can keep tabs on changes that occur on tasks that ensure quality (for example, quality testing or QA tasks).

Keeping on track: Critical path and slack

If you look at all the tasks in a project, you find a series of tasks that, if delayed, would delay the project. This is called the *critical path*. The simplest example of a critical path is a project with two tasks, one of which takes two weeks to complete and one of which takes one week to complete. If those tasks can happen simultaneously, the longer path is on the critical path, but the shorter task could be delayed several days and not delay the end date of the project. If the shorter task is delayed, say, eight days, it then becomes the critical task in the project.

Staying aware of what the critical path of your project is at any point in time (and it will shift around, trust us) is vital to staying on schedule. Project provides filters and reports that help you spot your critical path easily (see Figure 1-5).

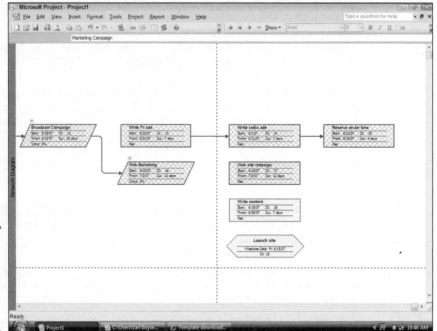

Figure 1-5:
Follow the
critical path
in Network
Diagram
view.

Tasks that aren't on the critical path in your project have some *slack* — that is, some time that they could be delayed without delaying the entire project. Ideally, every task in your project *should* have slack because things can come up that you never expected (shortages of vital materials, asteroid strikes, or management turnover that places you in an entirely different department). It's up to you to build slack into your schedule as you build in task timing in Project (see Book IV for more about how to do this).

See Book VII, Chapter 4 for more about working with slack.

Using tried-and-true methodologies

Microsoft Project incorporates some scheduling and tracking tools that are the result of many years of developing project management methods. A few of these are worth noting:

✦ A **Gantt chart** (shown in Gantt Chart view in Figure 1-6, which is the main view of Project), shows you a spreadsheet with columns of data along with a graphical representation of the tasks in the project arranged along

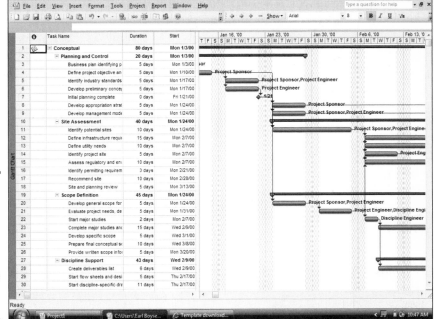

Figure 1-6:
The Gantt
Chart
method of
project
scheduling
as it appears
in Microsoft
Project.

a horizontal timeline. By using the data in the columns (such as task name, start date, finish date, and resources assigned to tasks), you can understand the parameters of each task and see its timing in the graphical area. Being able to view all this information on one page helps you understand what's happening in your project in terms of time and costs. If you're a history buff, you'll be interested to hear that the Gantt chart was created in 1910 by Henry Gantt, a mechanical engineer, and the idea was first published in *The Engineering Magazine.*

See Book II, Chapter 3 for more about working with and changing Project views.

✦ The **Network Diagram** (also called a **logic diagram**), shown in Figure 1-7, is essentially the Microsoft version of a PERT chart. PERT *(Program Evaluation and Review Technique)* was developed during the construction of the Polaris submarine in the 1950s. This mostly graphical representation of the tasks in your project reflects the flow of work in your project rather than the literal timing of tasks. This view helps you to see how one task flows into another and to get a sense of where you are — not so much in time, but rather in terms of the work you have to accomplish.

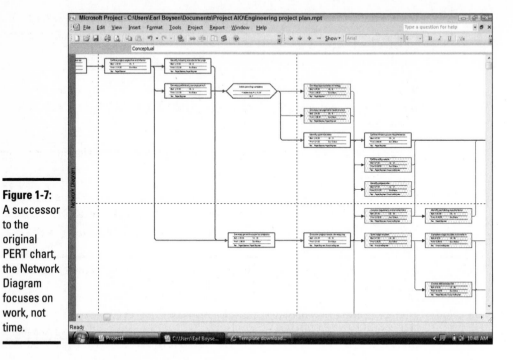

Figure 1-7:
A successor to the original PERT chart, the Network Diagram focuses on work, not time.

Resource Management Basics

If you asked us to do so, we could write an entire book about resource management. This is one of the most important skills a project manager can acquire because resources are the way things get accomplished in any project. But we have much more to cover, so here's the ten-cent tour of resource management.

How Project sees resources

Resource management consists of using your resources wisely. This involves not only managing people, but also strategically selecting the right resource and making the right assignments.

In Microsoft Project, resources are also the method used to accrue costs. Resources, in Project's terms, can be people, equipment, facilities that you rent, or fixed costs such as a consultant's fee or an airplane ticket; in short, a resource is anything or anybody you use to perform the tasks in your project.

All resources have a defined amount of availability. You might have to ensure that there is enough material on hand to complete a task, that a meeting room is available when you need it, that an in-demand piece of scientific testing equipment isn't offline, or that a key human resource isn't on vacation or assigned to another project.

What it takes to manage people

When dealing with human resources, a good project manager can do the following:

✦ Find the right resource for the job, taking into account skill level and cost.

✦ Provide any required training for resources.

✦ Assign the resource a reasonable workload, which sometimes means negotiating with other project managers for that person's time.

✦ Stay alert for shifts in the schedule that cause the resource to be overbooked.

✦ Make adjustments during the life of the project that keep all resources most productive.

In Project, tools are available, such as a *resource graph* (traditionally called a *histogram*) and the resource usage chart (shown in Figure 1-8), to help you track resource workload. You can see how overbooked the Systems Analyst is.

Project allows you to assign codes for resources that you can use to designate skill levels or abilities so that finding the right resource for each job is as simple as performing a search.

Do I always need resources?

Resources in Project are there to accrue costs and to help you monitor overbooked resources, which might cause delays in your schedule. Some project managers choose not to assign resources to tasks in Project if those resources have no associated cost and their time doesn't need to be tracked. For example, if an administrative assistant does some work for the department that includes project work, but nobody allocates his or her time to the project budget, there's no need to assign that person to individual tasks. If you use a meeting room but there is no charge to use it and the hours you use it don't need to be tracked for any reason, you don't need to create, assign, or track such a resource.

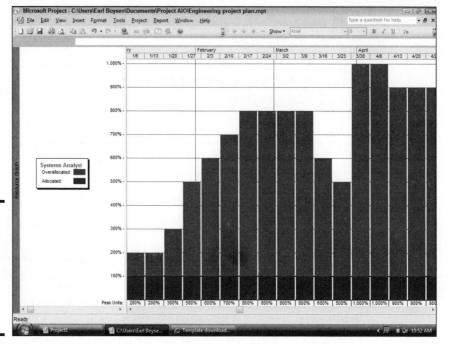

Figure 1-8:
A resource usage chart helps you spot resource-scheduling problems.

It's especially hard to anticipate resource assignments in a lengthy project because it's difficult to know who will be available a year or two from now. To deal with that, consider creating generic resources, such as "Engineer," and fill in the appropriate individual's information later in the project.

Chapter 2: The Ins and Outs of Using Project

In This Chapter

✔ Exploring what you need to put into Project

✔ Understanding tasks, timing, and resources

✔ Using tracking to update a project

✔ Getting useful reports out of Project

Welcome to the world of computerized project management with Microsoft Project. If you've never used project management software, you're stepping into a whole new era of project management. You'll be leaving the world of the handwritten to-do list and entering a world teeming with hi-tech calculations and sophisticated project data.

Everything you ever did with handwritten to-do lists, word processors, and spreadsheets all magically comes together in Project. However, the transition into computerized project management doesn't happen in seconds. First you need a basic understanding of what project management software can do, what it demands of you, and what results it can provide.

If you've used previous versions of Project, this little overview can help you refresh your memory as well as ease you into a few of the new features of Project 2007.

The Basics of Computerized Project Management

If you've scanned this book's Table of Contents, you're probably shaking your head and saying, "Boy, handwritten to-do lists look pretty good right now. Beats having to key in tons of data about tasks, schedules, and resources," right?

Well, you're right *and* wrong about that. You do have to enter a lot of information into Project to get the benefit of its features. But after you provide Project with some data, you can also get a lot out of it.

Making the leap to Project

"So," you ask, "what exactly can Project do for me?" The following list describes the payoff that you get for investing time to understand and use Project to manage your work.

With Project, you enjoy the following benefits:

✦ **Automatic calculations:** Project automatically calculates costs and timing for you based on your input. This gives you an instant snapshot of your status at any point during your project. See Book VII for more about automatic versus manual calculations.

✦ **Ability to try out what-if scenarios:** You can quickly have Project recalculate what-if scenarios to solve resource conflicts, get your costs within budget, or meet your final deadline.

✦ **Views and reports:** Project offers views and reports that, with the click of a button, make a wealth of information available to you and those you report to. No more manually building a report on total-costs-to-date to meet a last-minute request from your boss. If she wants to know total-costs-to-date, you can just print your Tracking Gantt view with the Tracking table displayed. See Book VI for information about reporting.

✦ **Templates:** You can use built-in templates to get a head start on your project. Project *templates* are prebuilt plans for a typical business project, such as commercial construction, an engineering project, a new product rollout, software development, or an office move (see Figure 2-1 for an example). See Book II, Chapter 1 for more about using templates.

You're likely to do similar types of projects all the time. After you create one project, make it a custom template for future projects. See Book II, Chapter 1 for information about how to save a file as a template.

✦ **Resource management:** You can create resources for your project based on information that already exists in your Outlook Address Book. Your company could create one set of resources and give access to them to every project manager in the company. This not only saves you time in building resources from scratch, but it also helps you track resource time across multiple projects. See Book V for more about working with resources.

✦ **Calculation of project data:** A number of tools in Project employ complex algorithms (that we couldn't even begin to explain) to help you resolve problems or view data, such as leveling resource assignments to solve resource conflicts, filtering tasks by various criteria, and calculating in dollars (or francs, or whatever) the value of work performed to date. See Book V, Chapter 4 for information about how Project calculates costs, and Book VII, Chapter 1 to discover how filters help you focus on certain types of information in your project.

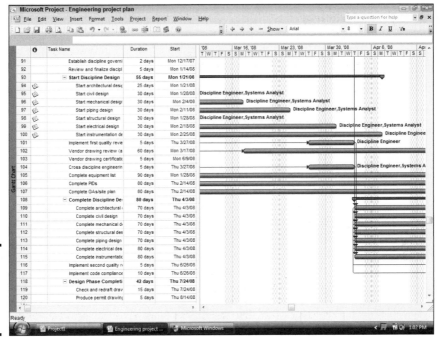

Figure 2-1:
An
engineering
project
template.

Connecting with your team online

You can hop onto the Internet and communicate with your project team by using Project collaboration features. In fact, using Project 2007 you can enter the world of Enterprise Project Management (EPM), where it becomes possible for you to easily share ideas, information, and documents across your entire enterprise.

You can do a number of useful activities online; for example, Project allows you to request updates on a task's progress from team members via e-mail. You can post documents to a SharePoint site and ask for team input. You can even publish your project on the Web so those without Project can view it.

The Professional version of Project includes Project Server and Project Web Access, which enable many of the workgroup collaboration features in Project. With these tools, you can take advantage of an online project center and resource center with areas for discussions, progress tracking, document exchange, and more.

Book X looks at how to take advantage of the enterprise-wide features of Project Server and Project Web Access.

What You Have to Put Into Project

Project can give a lot back, but it depends on the information you put in to produce its calculations, reports, and so on.

Though there are a few other pieces of information you can provide to Project, by far the two biggest chunks of data it requires of you are the tasks, or steps, to be completed to reach your project goal and the resources you will use to accomplish those tasks.

Tasks and their timing

A *task* is simply one of those items you used to scribble on your handwritten to-do lists, such as *Write final report* or *Apply for permits*. Tasks are typically organized into *phases* (appropriate stages) in Project, arranged in an outline-like structure, as you can see in the project shown in Figure 2-2.

The length of tasks (their *duration*) and the sequence of tasks together create the timeline for your project. Project allows you to create that sequence by building in timing relationships among tasks.

Figure 2-2:
You'll probably spend most of your time in Project in the outline-like Gantt Chart view.

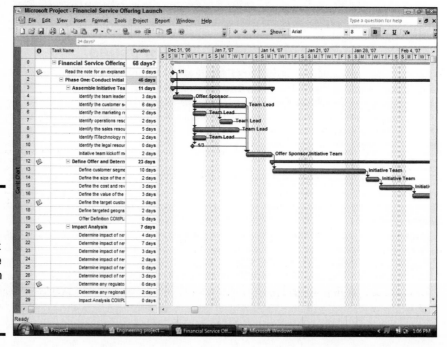

Mastering tasks

A task can be as broad or as detailed as you like. For example, you can create a single task to research your competition, or you can create a project phase that consists of a *summary task* and various *subtasks* below it (see Figure 2-3).

In a project phase involving researching your competition, the summary task might be Competitive Research, which includes the subtasks Researching Online Business Databases, Assembling Company Annual Reports, and Reviewing Competitive Product Lines.

REMEMBER

A project can have as many tasks and as many phases as you like. You simply use the outlining structure in Project to indent various levels of tasks. The more deeply indented in an outline a task is, the more detailed the task. However, don't overdo it: If you're tallying up task 2,503, consider whether you need to make your project less granular or start to break up this behemoth into a few smaller projects.

Book I
Chapter 2

The Ins and Outs of Using Project

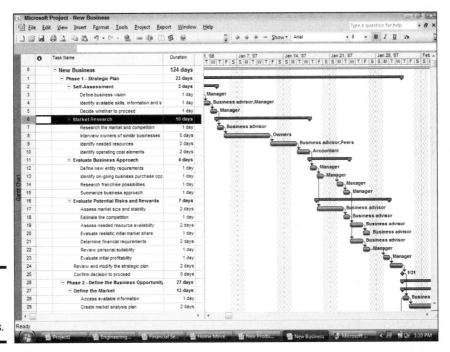

Figure 2-3:
A project
broken up
into phases.

One handy thing about Project's outlining structure is that you can roll up all the timing and cost data from the subtasks within your phases into summary-level tasks. Three sequential subtasks that take two days each to complete and cost you $500 apiece result in a summary task that spans six days and costs $1,500. You can view your project at various levels of detail. If you view only summary tasks, you get automatic tallies of timing and costs, and if you display deeper levels of detail, you get an accounting of every last dime and minute in your project.

For more about organizing your tasks and outlining, see Book III.

It's all in the timing

They say that timing is everything: Knowing when to sell that hi-tech stock, buying real estate before the boom hits, and finding the best time to pop the question come to mind. The importance of timing applies to Project tasks, as well. Almost all tasks have timing — referred to as *duration*. Duration is simply the amount of time it takes to complete the task.

The only tasks without duration are called milestones. A *milestone* is a task of zero duration; in essence, it simply marks a moment in time that you need to account for in your Project outline. Typical milestones are the approval of a proposal and an assembly line startup. Figure 2-4 shows a project with several important milestones, indicated by a diamond-shaped icon.

Unfortunately, you can't ask Project to come up with accurate durations: You assign duration based on your own experience and judgment. Does printing a product package take three days or three weeks? Will getting senior management approval take a day or a month? (Don't forget to pad this task in proportion to how many of those senior types have to buy in.) Project can't come up with these estimates: You have to provide facts, figures, and educated guesses to build your Project schedule. After you enter that information, though, Project can do some wonderful things to help you maintain your schedule and monitor your progress.

How tasks depend on each other

One very important determining factor in how long your project will take involves the concept of *dependencies,* or the timing relationships among tasks. If you have a schedule that includes ten 2-day tasks that all begin at the same time, your entire project will take as long as the longest task, which in this case is two days (see Figure 2-5). However, after you define and implement timing relationships among tasks, ten 2-day tasks could take as long as 20 days to accomplish.

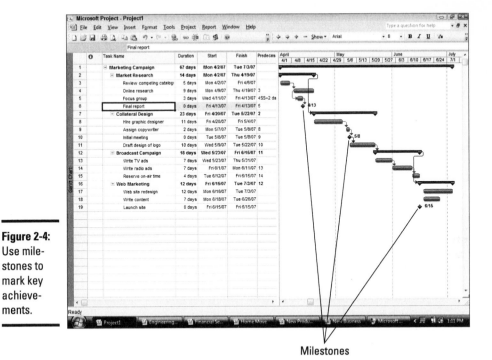

Figure 2-4:
Use mile-
stones to
mark key
achieve-
ments.

Milestones

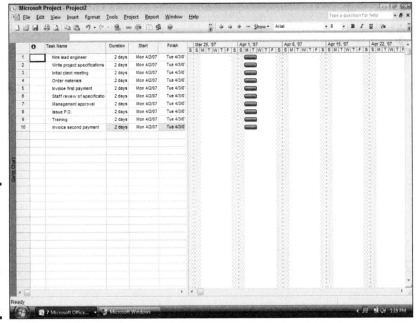

Figure 2-5:
This
schedule
includes
tasks with
timing but no
dependen-
cies.

Here's how this works. On the simplest level, if each of ten 2-day tasks happens in sequence — that is, each task can't begin until the task before it is completed — it will take 20 days to complete them. But dependencies are often more complex. For example, one task might begin only after another is finished, but another task can start halfway through the preceding task. The second task cannot start until a week after the first task is finished. Only after you start to assign these relationships can you begin to see a project's timing as related not just to each task's duration but also to the specific ways in which the tasks relate to each other.

Here are some examples of dependencies:

✦ You can't begin to use a new piece of equipment until you train people in how to use it.

✦ You must wait for a nuclear reactor to get online before you can begin to generate energy.

✦ You can't start to ship a new food product until the FDA approves it.

Figure 2-6 shows a project plan where each task's duration and the dependencies among tasks have been established. Note the resulting overall timing of the project.

You can find out more about the fine art of managing dependencies in Book IV, Chapter 3.

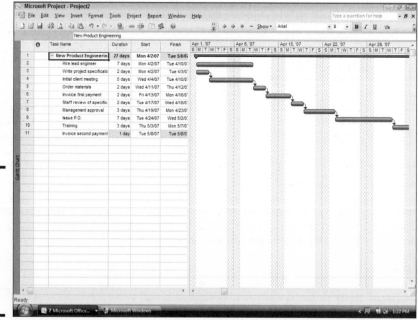

Figure 2-6:
This schedule includes tasks with both timing and dependencies.

Built-in constraints count, too

There's one other thing you should know about the timing of tasks: In addition to applying dependencies to tasks, you can apply *constraints*. For example, say you don't want to start shipping your new toy until you get the ad for it in your Christmas catalog, so you set a dependency between those two events. You can also set a constraint which says that you must start manufacturing the toys no later than November 3. In this case, if you don't make the catalog deadline, the product will still ship on November 3; that task won't be allowed to slip its constraint because of this dependency relationship.

You can find out more about constraints in Book IV, Chapter 4.

Lining up resources

When you're new to Project, it's easy to get a bit confused about what a resource is. Resources aren't just people: A *resource* can be a piece of equipment you rent, a meeting room that you have to pay an hourly fee to use, or a box of nails or a software program you have to buy. Essentially, a resource is anything or anybody you need to get your tasks done, and though they don't always have costs associated with them, they usually do. Resource costs are, in fact, how Project accounts for your project budget.

Project allows for three kinds of resources: work resources, material resources, and cost resources. A *work resource* is charged by how many hours or days the resource (often human) works on a task. A *material resource,* such as baking supplies or steel, is charged by a per-use cost or by a unit of measurement (such as pounds of flour or tons of steel). A *cost resource* has a set cost, such as a conference fee of $250; this fee doesn't vary by how much time you spend at the conference, nor by how many events you attend.

Some resources, typically people, perform their work according to a working calendar (see Figure 2-7). Say the calendar includes 5 workdays in a working week. If a person works an 8-hour day and you assign him to a task that takes 24 hours to complete, that person has to put in 3 workdays to complete the task. In comparison, someone with a 12-hour workday takes only 2 days to complete the same task.

In addition to establishing the workdays in a typical week, you can set working and nonworking days for your human resources to accommodate variations such as 4-day weeks or shift work.

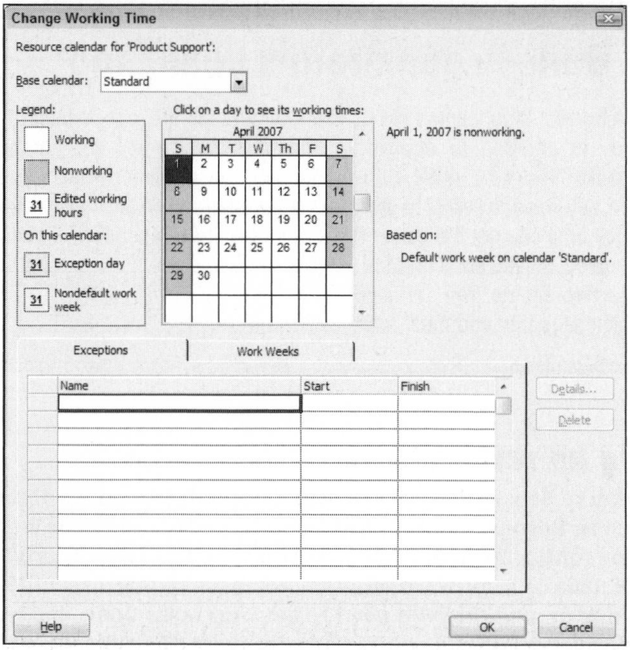

Change Working Time

Resource calendar for 'Product Support':

Base calendar: Standard

Legend:

Click on a day to see its working times:

April 2007   April 1, 2007 is nonworking.

	S	M	T	W	Th	F	S
	1	2	3	4	5	6	7
	8	9	10	11	12	13	14
	15	16	17	18	19	20	21
	22	23	24	25	26	27	28
	29	30					

Working

Nonworking

31 Edited working hours

On this calendar:

Based on:
Default work week on calendar 'Standard'.

31 Exception day

31 Nondefault work week

Exceptions | Work Weeks |

Name	Start	Finish		Details...
				Delete

Help   OK   Cancel

Figure 2-7:
A resource's
working
calendar.

You can set different rates for resources, such as a standard hourly rate and an overtime rate. You can even indicate that the resource rate changes at certain times of the year over the life of the project. Project applies the appropriate rate based on each resource's calendar and work assigned. For more about resources and costs, see Book V.

Resource assignments have an impact on both the cost of your project and its timing. In addition, several views in Project let you see information about resources and how their assignment to tasks affects your project. Figure 2-8 shows you the Resource Sheet, which has columns of information about resources and their costs.

Here's another important thing you should know about resources: They tend to have schedule conflicts. When assigned resources become overallocated for their available work time because they're assigned to too many tasks at once, Project will alert you to the fact.

For example, if you assign one poor guy to three 8-hour tasks that must all happen on the same day — and in the same eight hours — Project has features that do everything but jump up on your desk and whistle *Dixie* to alert you to the conflict (see Figure 2-9). Happily, Project also provides tools that help you resolve those conflicts, which are covered in Book VII, Chapter 2.

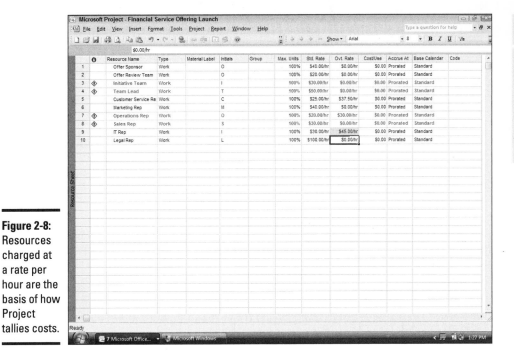

Figure 2-8:
Resources
charged at
a rate per
hour are the
basis of how
Project
tallies costs.

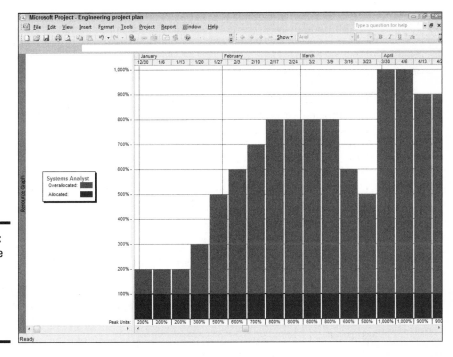

Figure 2-9:
A resource
graph
showing a
very over-
allocated
resource.

Keeping a Project on Track

Projects aren't set in stone: They typically go through a lot of changes over their lifetime. Tasks run late, costs go over budget, and sometimes the whole scope of your deliverables changes. That's why Project's capability to make changes to your project data on the fly is so useful. And the ability to track those changes against your original plan can be invaluable.

After you complete your original plan, build all your tasks, give them durations and dependencies, and assign all your resources and costs, you set a baseline. A *baseline* is a snapshot of your project at the moment you feel your plan is final and you're ready to get started on that first task.

Because Project saves both sets of data in a single schedule, after you set a baseline and record actual activity on your tasks, you can then compare that actual activity against your baseline (see Figure 2-10).

The recording of actual activity in a project is called *tracking*. Tracking activity in your project involves recording the actual timing of tasks and the time that your resources spend on those tasks, as well as entering any actual material costs that accrue. You can then display Project views that show you how far off you are at any time (compared with your baseline) in terms of the actual timing of tasks and cost of your project.

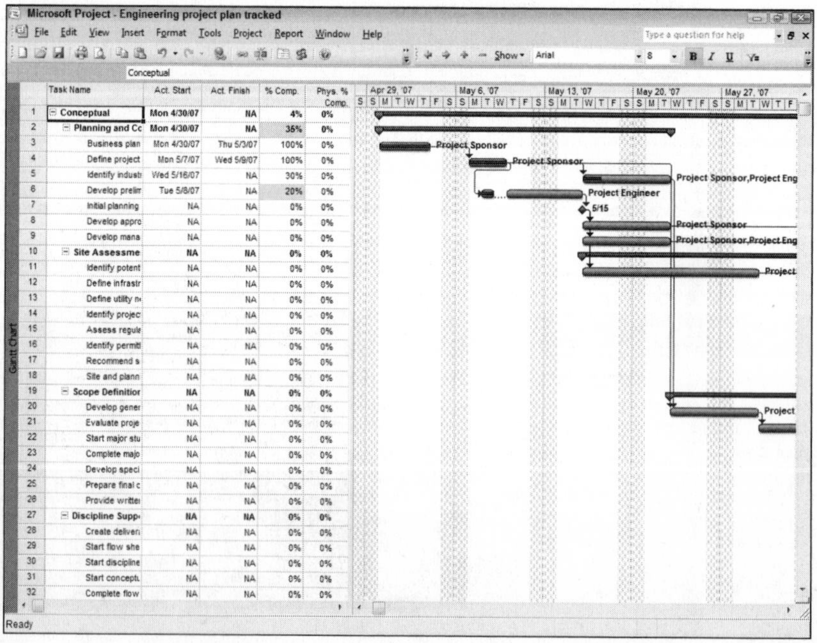

Figure 2-10: Actual activity displayed against a baseline.

Tracking allows you to make adjustments when you see that your schedule or costs are getting out of hand. In addition, when you track activity to date, you can easily generate reports that help you show your bosses the status of your project.

Keeping Others in the Loop

One of the big payoffs for entering all that information about tasks and resources into Project is the ability it offers you to share that information in reports. Reports help you document progress, beg for additional funding, or even motivate your team members by showing them all they've accomplished.

Project offers a wealth of reporting options to help you view your project and communicate your progress to your project team, clients, and management.

You can generate predesigned reports based on information in your schedule or simply print any of the views you can display in Project. Project 2007 offers a set of Basic Reports and a new feature called Visual Reports.

You must have the Microsoft .NET Framework installed, which is free and downloadable from www.microsoft.com/downloads, in order to use Visual Reports.

Figures 2-11 and 2-12 show you just two of the reporting options available in Project.

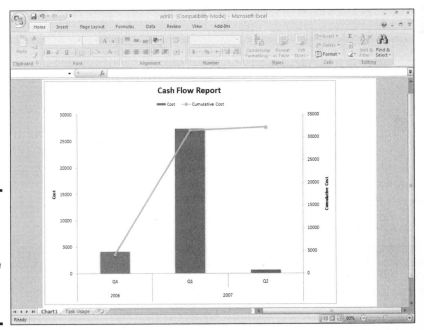

Figure 2-11:
Study resource hours by task with the graphical Task Usage view.

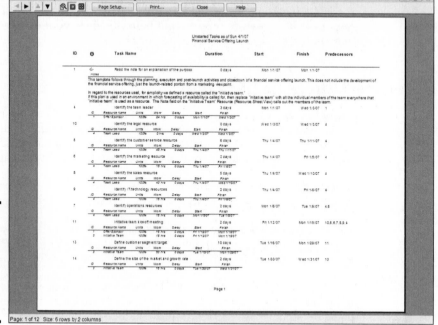

Figure 2-12: An Unstarted Tasks report shows work that still has to be done.

Chapter 3: Just What Tasks Should You Include?

In This Chapter

✔ Determining your business need

✔ Writing a goal statement

✔ Establishing your project's scope

✔ Writing a scope statement

✔ Deciding on project phases

✔ Choosing how detailed your tasks should be

✔ Determining when a phase is a project

*O*ne of the trickiest parts of putting your project down on paper (or in a computer file) is knowing exactly what tasks to include in it. Too much detail and you'll spend more time creating tasks than getting the work of your project done. Too broad a vision and you might miss crucial tasks because nobody defined them along the way.

Some useful tools that are available to project managers can help them focus their projects at the outset to lay a foundation for eventual success. These tools include establishing a *clear-cut* goal and defining the scope of your project. After you've taken these steps, you can start to outline the various phases of your project and begin to fill in the tasks you need to get to your goal.

In this chapter, we walk you through setting your project goal and scope, including writing a goal statement and a scope statement. Then, we take a look at some general rules that help you make choices about building your project phases.

First Things First: Define the Business Need

Good project management practice requires that you start at the beginning, considering what business need your project is fulfilling. Before you begin a project to upgrade your computer network at a branch office, you should be sure that your company will continue to invest in that division and won't be downsizing the staff that will use the network. You should be sure the technology you're installing today will meet the technology needs of the staff in the future.

Too often in companies, projects are launched without anybody considering the greater organizational goals. One good way to ensure that there's a match is to get senior management buy-in up front. If your senior management folks have a cohesive vision of the short- and long-term goals of the company, it's their job to put a stamp of approval on your project goals within that context. (If your senior management doesn't have a cohesive vision, we can't help you.)

Don't assume your managers have given approval because you copied them on a memo about the project launch. Get approval, get it in writing, and file it away.

In looking at the overall fit of your project in your organization, consider factors such as

✦ **Future budget and cash flow issues:** Does the cost of your project fit in with overall budgetary constraints?

✦ **Risk tolerance:** For example, is your company being conservative or aggressive in its growth projections, and does your project fit within risk parameters?

✦ **Target customer base:** Will your project meet the needs of internal or external customers, or is your company intending to target new sets of customers in the future?

Another good idea is to measure your project's goal against your company's mission statement. If the fit isn't good, your project might be doomed to fail. For example, if your company's mission statement includes the phrase "to service a small, select clientele with high-quality products" and your project is to launch a Web site offering low-priced products to a wide customer base, think again!

Target Practice: Project Goal Setting

You can't hit a target if you don't know what it looks like. Similarly, you can't possibly reach your project's goal if you don't know what it is. When you understand how your project fits in with the broader company direction, it's time to really pin down your goal.

"But," you say, "I know exactly what my goal is, because my boss told me." However, a set of deliverables isn't necessarily a goal.

On first consideration, you might say the goal of expanding the railroad westward in the United States was to enable a train to go from coast to coast. But was it? Perhaps the goal of those railroad barons was not to get a train to go cross country, but to open up opportunities for commerce in the West.

It's time to put the same kind of thought to your project's goal.

Getting your goal straight

Say your project involves training new employees in a new software system. Your goal in training them on this software could be to

+ Make employees more productive in their jobs.

+ Enable employees to better serve customers.

+ Create a prototype program with reduced training costs that can be used to reduce overall training costs across the company.

+ Increase employee retention by providing useful on-the-job skills.

These goals suggest different priorities as well as different measurements for gauging the degree to which your project has succeeded in meeting its goal.

How, exactly, do you go about determining your goal? First, go back to the person who asked you to take on the project and grill him or her about what's expected of this project. Should the training have a measurable impact on job performance, customer satisfaction, employee retention, or cost of delivery?

The answer you get might be that the project should do all of these things. But think about whether that's realistic and whether one of these goals should be paramount in guiding you and your project team. If overall training-program cost reduction is the biggest goal factor, for example, employee productivity might have to take a back seat when you're making choices along the way. If customer satisfaction is the real goal, training costs might have to be adjusted accordingly.

Writing a goal statement

After you get more specifics about your project's goal, it's a good idea to put your goal in writing in a goal statement.

A *goal statement* outlines why you're doing this project and what you hope to accomplish at the end. You don't get down to specific deliverables and parameters in a goal statement (you tackle that in the next section on the project's scope). For now focus on the why and the desired result.

Here are a few sample goal statements:

+ The goal of the project is to upgrade the shopping cart feature on our Web site to be easier to use so we can increase online sales by 25 percent.

+ Our goal is to reduce human resource workload by 10 percent by offering self-service information on job benefits on the company intranet.

Using the example of a training project, consider for a moment what such a project might involve. Are you supposed to write new training materials, hire staff to deliver classes, analyze the training's effectiveness, update training materials as needed, and promote the training internally? In that case, the scope of your project involves managing the entire creation, delivery, and maintenance of a training program.

Or is your goal to simply create the training materials? Or should your focus be limited to launching the new training, including promoting it to management and staff? These goals indicate very different projects, each with its own set of deliverables, tasks, resources, schedule, and costs. Writing a goal statement helps you focus on such a project from the outset.

Taking a Look at Your Project's Scope

When you understand your goal, you can begin to define the specific parameters of the project. This is often referred to as a project's *scope*.

A scope is not a goal

Though some confuse them, a goal is not a definition of scope. Here's how they differ. Take a look again at this goal statement from the previous section:

> The goal of the project is to upgrade the shopping cart feature on our Web site to be easier to use so we can increase online sales by 25 percent.

A scope statement for this same project might look something like this:

> This project will involve all the steps involved to design and implement a new shopping cart feature (but does not include maintaining or refining it once launched). The cost of the project will not exceed $25,000 and implementation must be completed before October 1 to accommodate holiday sales traffic. The new shopping cart feature should help to increase sales by allowing customers more options to review their orders, give them more frequent opportunities to shop for more items after they have added a product to the cart, and allow them to save their cart contents and come back to complete the sale at a future date. The new feature must function on our existing Web technology infrastructure.

Writing a scope statement

Scope statements define both what a project will involve and what it will not involve. In our example here, the scope statement specifies that the maintenance and refining of the shopping cart feature, once launched, will be handled by some other project team.

You typically get into specifics about the project budget, timeframe, and deliverables in a scope statement. You shouldn't include every single detail, but you should have enough information that a project team can understand the most important parameters of the project. Together, a goal statement and a scope statement are two valuable tools for focusing yourself and your team and keeping you on track as you proceed.

If you take the next logical step in pinning down your project at the outset, at this point you would create what's called a project charter. This would include specifying a project name, getting authorization in writing to begin the project as of a certain date and to draw on a specified budget, creating a list of responsibilities, and having those with an interest in the project (called stakeholders) sign off giving you authority to run the project. You can use your goal and scope statements to help you obtain the various pieces of your project charter.

Breaking Your Project into Phases

How does all this goal and scope analysis relate to Project? We're glad you asked.

When you start a new project schedule in Project, one of the first things you will do is begin to enter individual tasks. Knowing your goal and scope helps you to identify the steps you should be performing to accomplish them.

Thinking things through

Before you create your first task, you should probably begin to think beyond the scope of your project to more detailed project parameters. These parameters help you determine what tasks to include in your project.

For example, you might consider

+ **Deliverables:** These are tangible products, services, or results that you'll produce during your project. Somewhere in your project should be tasks that reflect the delivery of each deliverable.

+ **Key Dates:** In addition to the project end date, do you have to meet other key dates along the way? A rough timeline might help you figure out the general order of tasks.

+ **Completion Criteria:** How will you know when you're done? Do you start up the new service and that's it, or do you have to test it for a week before your job is done? Knowing your completion criteria gives your team something specific to aim for and helps you create the last phase of your project.

+ **Expectations:** Knowing what you expect from your team, management, and yourself can help you identify some tasks. If you expect your team to hold a quarterly debriefing meeting and submit a progress report, you might include such a task in your project. If you expect management to sign off on a prototype, a task such as Prototype Approval is logical.

✦ **Potential Risks:** Identifying potential problem areas can help you build in some checks and balances to help avoid or minimize them. For example, you may create tasks that contain terms such as Q&A, Testing, Review, Debrief, and Revise to monitor or fix problems along the way.

It's just a phase

Many people prefer to start at the upper level of detail in the project by defining the major *phases*. Within each phase are the detailed tasks that are essentially steps to complete the phase.

Figure 3-1 shows the major phases of a Web site implementation project. With the scope of your project in mind, be sure you know what your last phase is; in the earlier example of adding a shopping cart feature, the last phase might be to hand off the project to a team that will handle the maintenance and refinement of the feature after it's implemented.

Book III covers specifics about how to organize a project into major phases and subtasks.

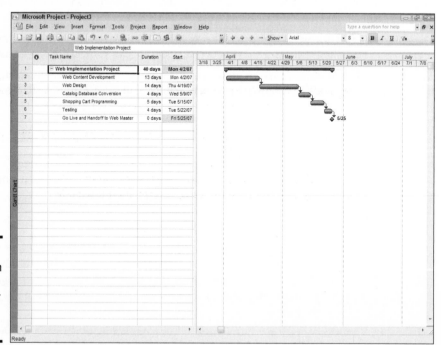

Figure 3-1:
Phases form the upper level of your project outline.

Choosing how granular to make your tasks

When you have the major phases of your project in place, you can begin to add tasks. People who are new to project management or to Project sometimes overdo it at this stage, creating a task for just about every activity they can imagine. Others don't put down enough detail to ensure that all requirements for the project are met. So how much detail is enough?

We wish we could tell you it's a science, but it's not. However, here's some guidance about how to identify tasks. You should include tasks that indicate

✦ **The start of a phase:** For example, the first step in hiring a vendor might be to send out a request for proposal.

✦ **Key milestones:** These can be points in time such as approvals, completed reviews, or confirmation of a deliverable. Milestones help you measure your achievements in a project.

✦ **Action steps that must be completed before a next step can occur:** If you have to obtain a permit before you can begin to build a house, don't skip the permit task!

You *don't* have to include steps that are either too detailed or not project specific, such as

✦ Tasks that your team members should keep track of themselves as they manage their own time to produce a result (it's the result you need to track)

✦ Everyday work tasks such as frequent staff meetings, refilling the copy machine with paper, or booking travel arrangements

Figure 3-2 shows a project outline for a marketing project. This schedule is too general to be very useful.

Figure 3-3 shows a project that has way too much detail. You would spend all day every day tracking the progress on such tiny tasks.

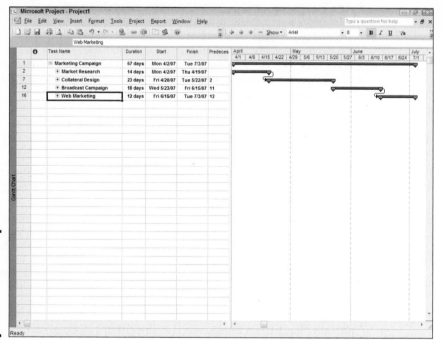

Figure 3-2:
With no specific steps, this project isn't very useful.

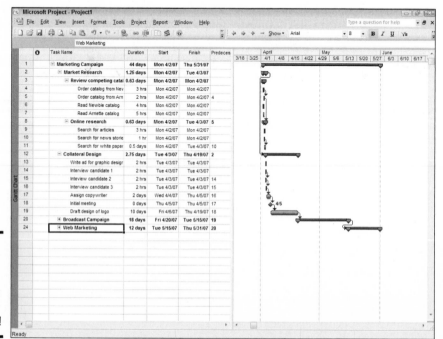

Figure 3-3:
Imagine tracking progress on each of these steps!

Figure 3-4 shows a much better level of task detail, with enough tasks to keep track of progress and be sure all bases are covered, without micromanaging people or activities.

As you work on projects using Project, you will get better and better at defining the level of task detail you should create. One good rule is to not create more tasks than you have the means or the time to track in your Project schedule.

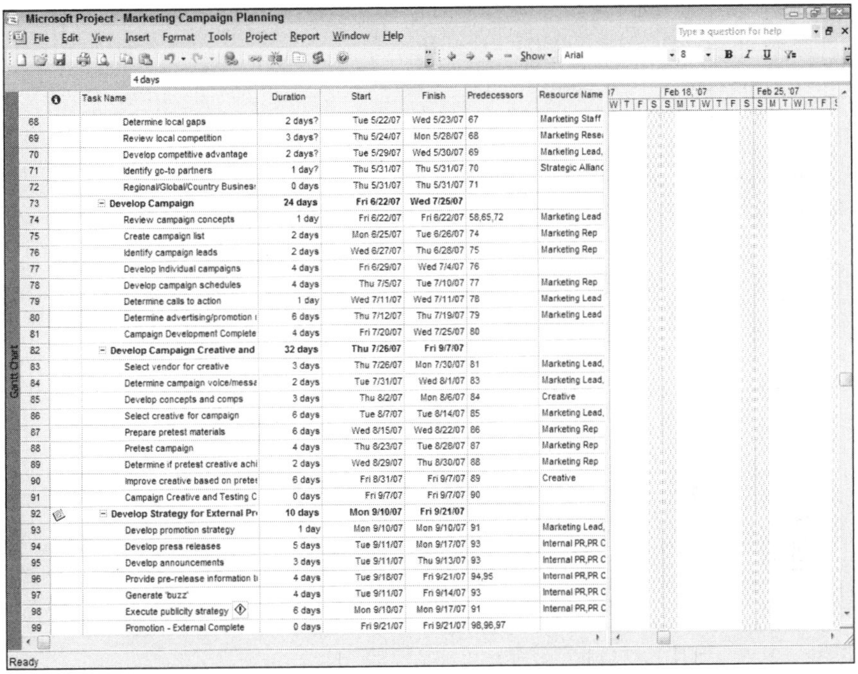

Figure 3-4:
This one is
just right!

Chapter 4: Exploring the Project Environment

In This Chapter

✔ **Looking at menus and toolbars**

✔ **Navigating Project**

✔ **Exploring Project views**

✔ **Modifying views**

✔ **Displaying various tables of data**

✔ **Displaying task panes**

✔ **Working with Project Guide**

*I*n 2007, Microsoft launched a dramatically new interface for selected products in the Microsoft Office family, of which Microsoft Project is a part. However, Microsoft Project wasn't one of the Office family products to get this new interface-lift, so it sports a very similar look to the previous edition, based on menus and toolbars that are familiar to most folks.

In this chapter, you get a glimpse of Project 2007 menus and tools, as well as the various views that make up Project. These views offer you different perspectives on data that can help you manage your projects efficiently. In addition, Project Guide offers a wizardlike interface that can walk you through the development of a new project. Finally, task panes such as New Project allow you to work with handy sets of tools to complete certain activities.

This chapter helps to familiarize you with all that the Project environment has to offer.

Exploring Menus and Toolbars in Project

Menus and toolbars have been the way to get work done in software for the last several years. Here's a quick overview of the menus and toolbars that Project 2007 offers.

Menu basics

If you've ever used a computer, you know what a menu is. Menus such as the one shown in Figure 4-1 contain sets of commands that might perform a function or display a dialog box.

In Project 2007 menus, tool icons are displayed to the left of any command that has a corresponding tool. Also, in the View menu, a check mark appears to the left of any items that are currently displayed in the view, such as Gantt Chart, or the View bar (which you read more about later). Some menu commands also display keyboard shortcuts (such as Ctrl+X) to their right.

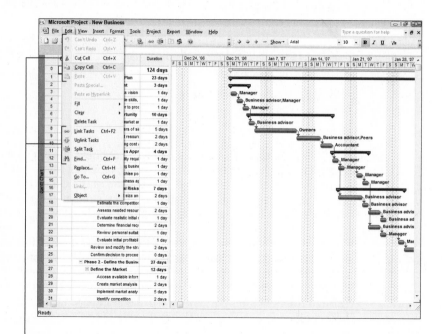

Figure 4-1:
The Edit menu of Project 2007.

Corresponding tool icons

If you use Project Standard, you have ten menus available to you, as described in Table 4-1.

Table 4-1		Overview of Project Menus
Menu	**Purpose**	**Typical Commands**
File	Common file operations	Save, Open, Print, Send to
Edit	Modify project entries	Cut, Copy, Paste, Clear, Go To
View	Switch or customize views	Calendar, Gantt Chart, Toolbars

Menu	Purpose	Typical Commands
Insert	Insert objects, resources, or tasks	New Resource, Project, Drawing
Format	Modify the format of project elements	Font, Bar, Timescale, Text Styles
Tools	Perform various operations	Resource Sharing, Tracking, Spelling
Project	Make overall project settings	Sort, Filtered for, Outline, WBS
Report	Generate reports for your project	Visual Report, Reports
Window	Organize display	New Window, Arrange All, Hide
Help	Access the Project Help system	Microsoft Office Project Help, Microsoft Office Online

If you use Project Professional, you also have a Collaborate menu available, which lets you interact with others via Project Web Access or a SharePoint site. Book X explores these collaborative capabilities in more detail.

Displaying and using toolbars

Toolbars (which vary slightly depending on the version of Project you're working with) are simply another way of invoking commands. You can display several built-in toolbars in Project 2007, such as the Resource Management toolbar shown in Figure 4-2.

Figure 4-2:
Tools for working with resources are all together on this toolbar.

Follow these steps to display or hide a toolbar:

1. **Right-click in the toolbar area.**

2. **In the list of toolbars that appears, click the one you want to display.**

   The toolbar appears near the top of the screen.

3. **To hide a toolbar, right-click the toolbar area.**

4. **In the list of toolbars that appears, click a selected toolbar to deselect it.**

   The toolbar is hidden.

To save space on your screen, you might want to show toolbars on one row instead of two. To do this, click the arrow at the far right of a toolbar and choose Show Buttons On One Row from the list of commands that appears.

Navigating Project

Project 2007 offers a wealth of views that provide different perspectives on your project. Throughout this book, we advise you on which view to display to get certain types of work done most efficiently. But first things first: Here we tell you the basics about how to display and change views.

Getting to a view

You can move from one view to another in Project by using the View bar or the View menu. The View bar runs along the far left side of every view, as shown in Figure 4-3. Simply click any view icon there to display that view.

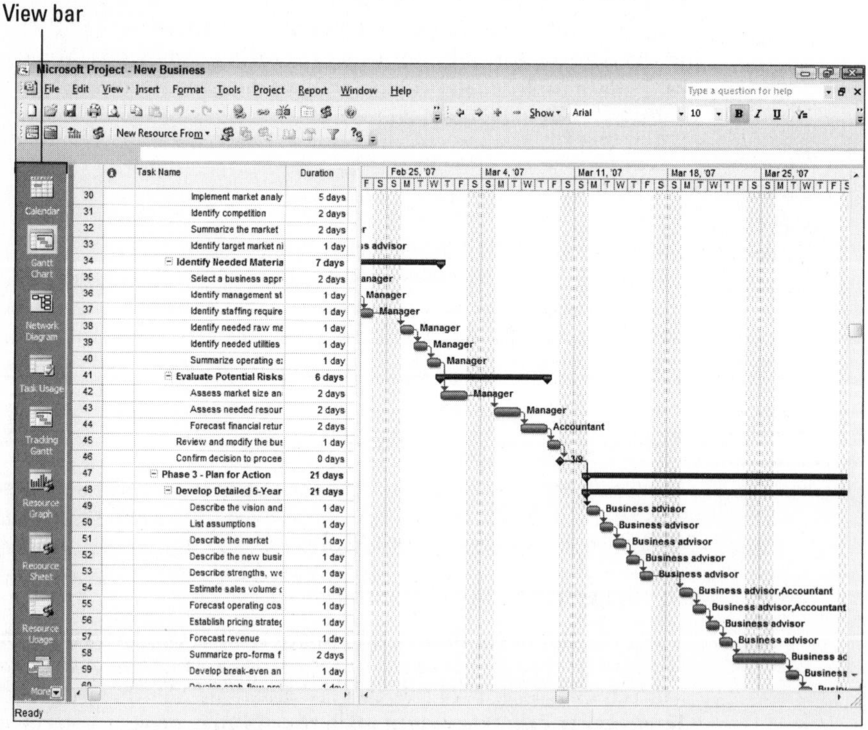

View bar

Figure 4-3: When displayed, the View bar is located along the left in every Project view.

If the View bar doesn't appear on your screen, choose View⇨View Bar to display it.

Eight commonly used views are already displayed on the View bar: Calendar, Gantt Chart, Network Diagram, Task Usage, Tracking Gantt, Resource Graph, Resource Sheet, and Resource Usage. In addition to these views, you might want to use any of the few dozen other views available. To display views not shown on the View bar, follow these steps:

1. **Click the arrow at the bottom of the View bar to scroll down to the bottom.**

2. **Click the More Views icon.**

The More Views dialog box appears, as shown in Figure 4-4.

You can also access the More Views dialog box by choosing View⇨More Views.

Figure 4-4:
Dozens of views are available for display in Project.

3. **Use the scroll bar to locate the view you want.**

4. **Select the view you want and click Apply.**

Scrolling to get a better view

The simplest views, such as Calendar view, have a single pane with horizontal and vertical scroll bars. Other views, such as Resource Usage view (see Figure 4-5), sport two panes. Each pane has its own horizontal scroll bar, but they share the vertical scroll bar, so the panes move up and down together.

In views with two panes, the pane on the left is referred to as the *sheet.* This is a spreadsheetlike interface that contains columns of information. The pane located on the right of this view is called the *chart.* The chart uses bars, symbols, and lines to represent each task in your project and the dependency relationships among them.

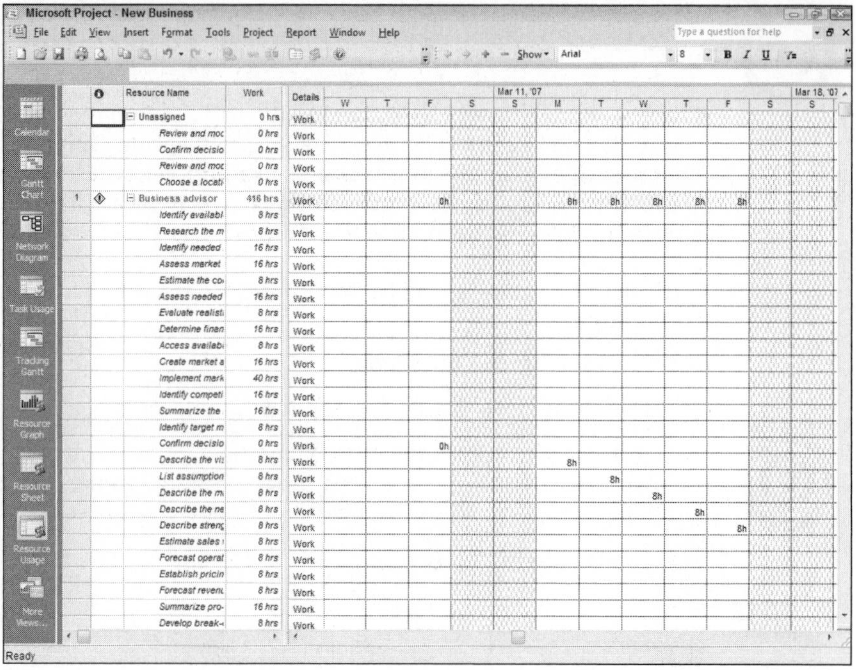

Figure 4-5:
Multiple
panes of
information
maximize
space in
many views.

At the top of the chart area is the *timescale*. This tool is used as a scale against which you can interpret the timing of the taskbars. To see your plan in greater or lesser timing detail, you can modify the time units used in the timescale. For example, you can look at your tasks in detail over hours or in a broader overview in weeks or months. Figure 4-6 shows a two-pane view with a sheet, chart, and timescale.

See the "Changing the timescale" section, later in this chapter, to find out how to change the time increments displayed in the timescale.

You can click and drag the horizontal scroll bars in either pane to view additional columns or additional time periods in any pane that includes a timescale. Timescale panes cover the life of the project; in longer projects, you can find yourself scrolling through years of time.

Use these different methods to work with horizontal scroll bars:

✦ **Click the scroll box and drag it until you reach the location in the pane that you want to look at.** When you click and drag the scroll box to move through a timescale display, the date display indicates where you are at any time in your scrolling calendar. Release the mouse button when the date display matches the date you want to view.

✦ **Click to the left or right of the horizontal scroll box to move one page at a time.** Note that a page in this instance is controlled to some extent by how you resize a given pane. For example, with a timescale pane and a timescale set to weeks, you move one week at a time. In a sheet pane displaying three columns, you move to the next (or preceding) column.

✦ **Click the right or left arrow at either end of a scroll bar to move in smaller increments.** With a sheet pane, you move about one-half column per click. In a timescale view with weeks displayed, you move about one day at a time.

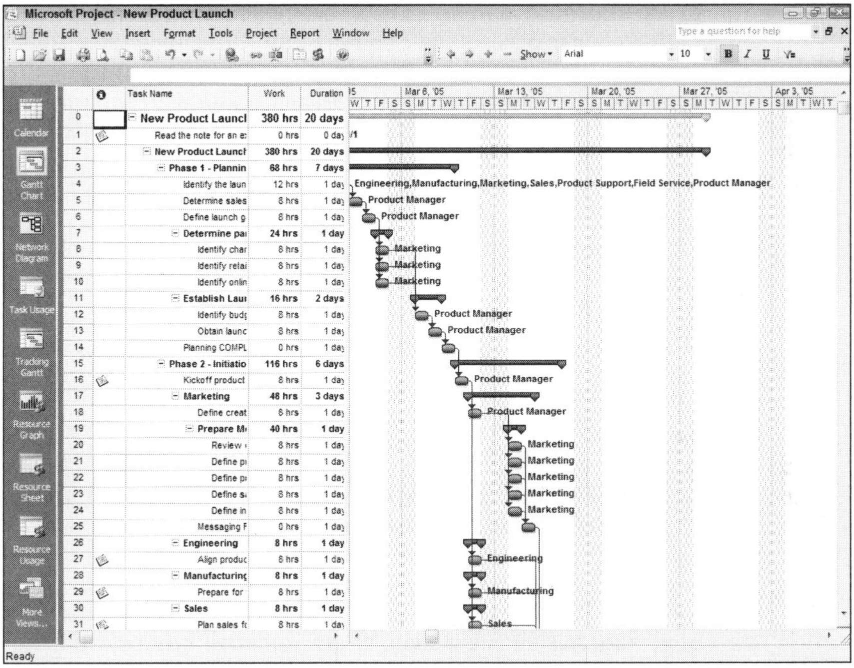

Figure 4-6:
The sheet, chart, and timescale of Gantt Chart view.

Jumping to a particular point in time

To reach a specific timeframe in your Project plan, you can also use the Go To command on the Edit menu. In the Go To dialog box, you can enter one of two criteria to find a task:

✦ **A task date** you select from a drop-down calendar.

✦ **A task ID,** which is assigned automatically when you create tasks. This number provides a unique identifier for tasks in the plan. See Book III for more about the structure and organization of tasks in a project.

You can also click the Go To Selected Task tool (or press Ctrl+Shift+F5) to scroll the timescale to show the taskbar for a selected task in the sheet pane.

You can use the View➪Zoom command to change the timescale that is displayed in the Chart pane. For example, you can show a week of tasks or the entire project.

Finding Another View

Views are a way to organize information in the software so that you can find useful information in logical ways. A typical Project plan contains a lot of data. The many views offer you a way to examine logical subsets of data. You need these many views because, if an average spreadsheet document is as complex as a calculator, your average Project plan is more like a souped up master computer that tracks and controls our national debt.

For example, in a typical Project plan, you can find data about the following:

+ **Resources:** The resource name, resource type, rate per hour, overtime rate, assignments, department, cost per use, and more

+ **Tasks:** The task name, duration, start and finish dates, assigned resources, costs, constraints, and dependencies, for example

+ **Project timing and progress:** Several types of calendars, project start and finish dates, percentage of tasks completed, resource hours spent, baseline information, critical path information, and more

+ **Financial information:** Earned value, time and cost variance, and projected costs for uncompleted work, for example

You might mostly work in two or three views, but still, finding out how to use the many Project views to enter, edit, look at, and analyze Project data is an important basic Project skill. When you know what's available and how to display it, you can pick and choose what you need.

For more about modifying the format of elements displayed in a view, see Book VI, Chapter 1.

A popular view: Gantt Chart

Gantt Chart view is like your comfortable neighborhood hangout, the cafe where most people end up and like to linger. It's the view that appears first when you open a new project. This view, shown in Figure 4-7, is a combination of spreadsheet data and a graphical representation of tasks. Gantt Chart view is popular because it offers a wealth of information in one place.

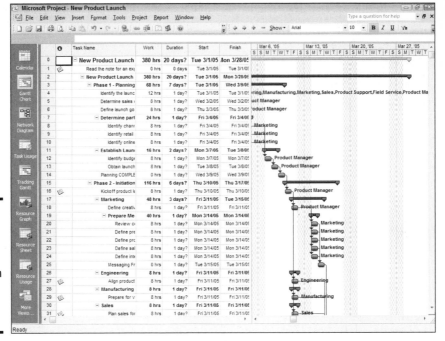

Figure 4-7:
Gantt Chart
view can
display any
combination
of columns
of data that
you want.

Gantt Chart view is one of those two-sided views, so it has two major sections: the sheet pane and the chart pane.

Gantt charts were first developed by engineer Henry L. Gantt in 1917 to deal with production-control projects in manufacturing. Today they're used in all kinds of industries to organize all kinds of projects.

Following the (work)flow: Network Diagram view

Network Diagram view, which is shown in Figure 4-8, is a more visual representation of data. The organization of information in this view represents the workflow in your project with a series of task boxes.

Lines run between these boxes to reflect the sequence of tasks as well as dependency relationships between them (see Book IV, Chapter 3 for more about dependency relationships).

In Network Diagram view, the earlier tasks are on the left, and later tasks and subtasks are to the right. Tasks that happen in the same timeframe are aligned vertically above each other. Tasks with an X through them have been marked as complete.

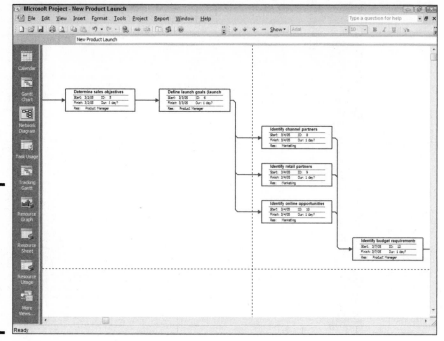

Figure 4-8:
Network
Diagram
view puts
important
task
information
in a visual
context.

More history: Traditionally called a *PERT chart,* this method of diagramming workflow was developed by the United States Navy in the 1950s to help build the Polaris submarine, a pretty hefty project by anybody's standards.

Note that there is no timescale in this view. That's because the view isn't used to see specific timing but rather to see the general order and flow of tasks in your project. However, you can set up task boxes to hold specific timing information about each task, such as the start date, finish date, and duration. (Customizing the information in the task boxes is described in Book VI, Chapter 2.

Controlling time with Calendar view

Look at just about any workplace in the world and you'll find a calendar. Calendars are one of the most familiar tools for managing our time, and therefore, logically, Calendar view is one of the many views offered in Project. Calendar view, as shown in Figure 4-9, resembles your wall calendar, representing each week of the month as a row on the calendar.

Calendar view can be set up to display from one to six weeks (or more, by using a Custom setting in the Zoom dialog box). Calendar view sports a timescale, which you can change to show a 7-day or 5-day week. If you display a 5-day week, shading indicates working and nonworking days based on the base or resource calendar you've selected.

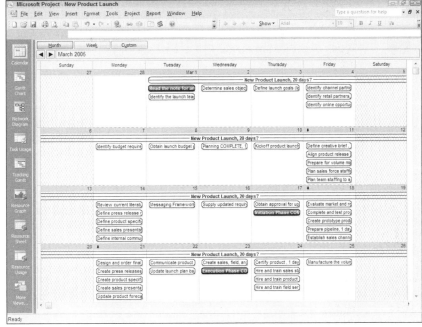

Figure 4-9:
Note that
one task
can straddle
several days
(or even
weeks).

Changing Views

The array of views in Project is impressive, but consider this: Every one of those views can be customized to show a variety of information. Given this, the possible view variations become astronomical.

For example, you can choose to show different columns of information in spreadsheets, different labels on the task boxes in Network Diagram boxes or taskbars in Gantt Chart view, or different sets of data in graph views. You can modify the size of panes in certain views and adjust the timescale to reflect different time periods in your project.

This flexibility helps you focus on different aspects at various times over the life of your project. If you're having a problem with costs, for example, you might take a look at Resource Usage view and insert several columns of cost information, such as resource rates and total actual costs. If your project is taking a lot — we mean *a lot* — more time than you expected, you might want to display Tracking Gantt view and look at a bunch of columns with timing and dependency data or examine the project's critical path in the chart pane. If you need to display more of the sheet area so that you can read columns without having to scroll, you can do that, too.

This is the section where you find out how to show a variety of information in each view.

These sections cover some of the most-often used views in Project, but many more views are available. As you work through specific elements of Project in this book, keep an eye out for views that are useful for certain types of project management activities.

Modifying view panes

Several views besides Gantt Chart view also include two panes. These include Task Usage, Tracking Gantt, and Resource Usage views. You can modify the information that you see in the sheet pane as well as the scale for timing in the chart pane. You can also display information near taskbars in the chart pane.

Resizing a pane

In views that include more than one pane, you can reduce or enlarge the size of each pane. This allows you to see more information in one area, to suit your focus at the time.

The overall area taken up by the two panes is constant, so when you enlarge one pane, you reduce the size of the other.

Follow these steps to change the size of a pane in a view:

1. **Place your cursor over the edge of a pane.**

2. **When you see a cursor that's a line with two arrows (one pointing left and one pointing right), click and drag.**

   • Dragging to the left enlarges the pane on the right.

   • Dragging to the right enlarges the pane on the left.

3. **Release the mouse button.**

   The panes are resized.

Note that if you display the Project Guide or another task pane, such as New Project, Project automatically resizes the sheet and chart panes to accommodate the additional pane.

Project Guide and the View bar take up valuable on-screen space, so a quick way to see more of any of the project information in any view is to hide the Project Guide or View bar. The Project Guide toolbar includes a Hide/Show Guide button that you can click to hide or display it. Choose View➪View Bar to turn the View bar on and off.

Changing the timescale

At times during the life of your project, you might want to focus on the details or switch to the big picture. The ability to modify the timescale to display your plan in larger or smaller time increments is a handy feature to help you get the focus you need.

A timescale consists of a possible total of three tiers, as you can see in Figure 4-10. You can use them to display different time increments. For example, the top tier could mark off months, whereas the middle tier could mark off weeks, and the bottom tier could mark off days. This variety of detail lets you easily observe overall task length as well as points in time during the life of the task. You can use all three tiers, only the middle tier, or the middle and bottom tiers.

You can customize the timescale in several ways. You can

✦ Modify the units of time and the alignment of each tier.

✦ Include tick lines to mark the beginning of each increment on the timescale.

✦ Include nonworking time on the timescale. For example, if you include an indication of nonworking time on a project for which weekends are nonworking, Saturdays and Sundays are indicated by a shaded area in the display, which can help you visually differentiate between weeks.

✦ Display text labels near taskbars. Labels can be placed above, below, inside, or to the left or right of the taskbars.

✦ Change what data is included in text labels.

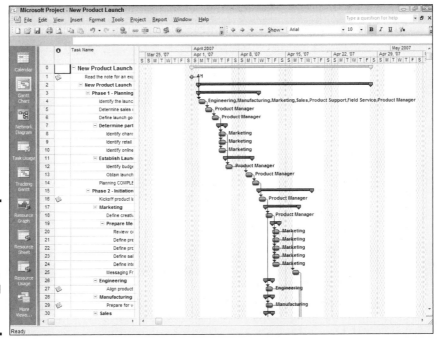

Figure 4-10:
The timescale allows you to view time from several perspectives.

Especially in projects where you display many columns of data and a lengthy schedule, a taskbar can be placed far to the right of the sheet pane data, making it hard to track which task the taskbar is associated with. In that case, it can be useful to include information, such as the task name or start date, alongside the taskbar to help you read your plan more easily.

To modify the timescale, follow these steps:

1. **Right-click the timescale in any view that contains one and then choose Timescale.**

   The Timescale dialog box appears. (See Figure 4-11.)

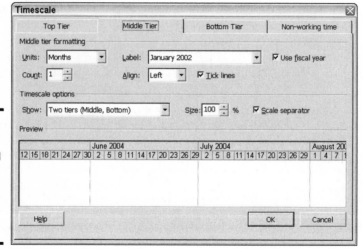

Figure 4-11:
The Time-
scale dialog
box allows
you to
customize
the time-
scale.

2. **Click a tier tab and select styles for Units, Label, and Align.**

3. **Set the count.**

   For example, if your Units choice is weeks and you change the Count option to 2, the timescale appears in two-week increments.

4. **If you don't want to display a certain tier, select One Tier or Two Tiers from the Show drop-down list (under the Timescale Options section).**

5. **If you want Project to use fiscal year notation in the timescale, select the Use Fiscal Year check box.**

   For example, if your 2006 fiscal year begins July 1, 2006, 2007 is used on all months in the fiscal year. The fiscal year is set in the Options dialog box on the Calendar tab.

6. **To show marks at the beginning of each unit of time, select the Tick Lines check box.**

7. **Repeat Steps 2–6 for each tier you want to modify.**

8. **Click the Non-Working Time tab.**

9. **In the Draw options, select the one you prefer.**

   Your choices are to have the shaded area for nonworking time appear behind or in front of taskbars or just not appear.

10. **In the Color or Pattern list, select different options for the shading format.**

11. **Click the Calendar setting and select a different calendar to base the timescale on.**

   You can find out more about calendar choices in Book II, Chapter 4.

12. **Click OK to save your new settings, which apply only to the timescale for the currently displayed view.**

You can use the Size setting on the three tier tabs to shrink the display proportionately to get more information on your screen or the printed page.

Choosing to display different columns

Each spreadsheet view has certain default columns of data that are stored in something called *tables,* which are described in the next section. In addition to displaying predefined tables of columns, you can also modify any spreadsheet table to display any columns you like.

Follow this procedure to show selected columns of data:

1. **Right-click the column heading area and then choose Insert Column.**

   The Column Definition dialog box appears, as shown in Figure 4-12.

Figure 4-12:
You can select any one of a number of columns to insert.

2. **In the Field Name list, select the field that contains the information you want to include.**

3. **If you want to enter a different title for the field, type it in the Title box.**

   The title in the current view appears in the column heading for this field.

Zooming in and out

One way to modify your display for any Project view is to use the Zoom In and Zoom Out buttons on the Standard toolbar. This feature shows you a longer or shorter period of time in your project without you changing the timescale settings. When you need to see several years at a time in your project, for example, click Zoom Out several times until you fit as many months or years as you like in the view. You can also choose View⇨Zoom and specify periods of time to display in the Zoom dialog box, or even choose to have the entire project appear on-screen.

4. Use the Align Title, Align Data, and Width options to modify the column format.

5. Click OK to insert the column.

To hide a column, right-click its heading in the sheet pane and then choose Hide Column.

Changing tables

In any view with a sheet pane, such as Gantt Chart view, you can change what information is shown in the sheet by using tables. *Tables* are preset combinations of columns of data. Displaying the appropriate table helps you deal with certain tasks, such as using the Tracking table for recording activity on tasks or the Entry table for entering new task information.

You can easily display a different table by following these steps:

1. Choose View⇨Table.

2. Select a table (such as Entry or Cost) from the submenu that appears.

3. To view more tables, click More Tables from the submenu.

4. Click a table and then click Apply.

The columns for the selected table are displayed.

You can also customize the column display for any table by displaying or hiding individual columns of data one by one. (See Book VI, Chapter 2 for more about customizing tables.)

Displaying task panes

Project 2007 has a couple of task panes. *Task panes* display a side panel of tools and text boxes you can use to work on a particular type of task.

A New Project task pane (see Figure 4-13) displays when you choose File⇨ New, and a Document Management task pane appears when you choose Tools⇨Document Management, for example.

Figure 4-13:
The New Project task pane offers various options for getting started.

Displaying and Hiding Project Guide

Project Guide is a special task pane that offers you a great way to get a new project going. It walks you through a series of steps that ask you to enter certain project information. Based on your choices and entries, Project Guide then takes care of the creation of various aspects of your project, such as tasks and resources.

Book II, Chapter 4 provides detailed information about using Project Guide.

To display or hide Project Guide:

1. If the Project Guide toolbar isn't showing, right-click the toolbar area and choose Project Guide from the menu that appears.

2. Click the Show/Hide Project Guide icon to the far left of the toolbar.

The Tasks pane appears (see Figure 4-14).

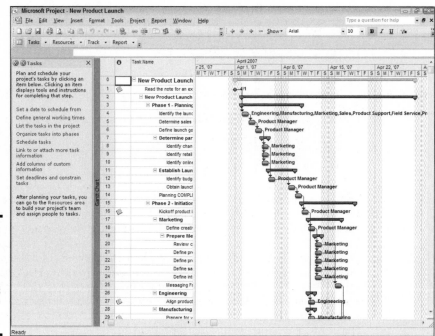

Figure 4-14: The Tasks section of Project Guide offers several options.

Chapter 5: What's New in Project 2007

In This Chapter

✓ **Understanding the different versions of Project 2007**

✓ **Using the Multiple Undo feature**

✓ **Turning on Change Highlighting**

✓ **Identifying task drivers**

✓ **Appreciating the value of Visual Reports and report templates**

✓ **Making use of Cost resources**

✓ **Defining and tracking budgets**

*I*f you're one of those people who have to be in on anything new, or if you used Project 2003 and need a heads up about what new features in Project 2007 are worth checking out, this chapter is for you.

In this chapter, we offer a rundown of the various versions of Project 2007 that are available to help you choose the right one for your needs. We also provide an overview of new features, including Multiple Undo, Change Highlighting, task drivers, Visual Reports, Cost resources, and budget tracking. Each of these features will make your Project experience a little more fruitful.

Each of these features is covered in more detail in individual chapters throughout this book. Check the index to find additional coverage!

Exploring the Many Versions of Project

Microsoft has, for some time, offered several different versions of Project based essentially on the size of your organization and projects. Project 2007 is no exception, with two individual user packages and what Microsoft calls the *EPM*, or Enterprise Project Management Solution.

Enterprise Project Management simply means project management that takes place in an organization that is large enough to have departmental and geographical boundaries across which people must work on projects. Collaborative tools, most of which are hosted online on a company intranet or the Internet using Microsoft SharePoint, are vital for enterprises. Book X covers Enterprise Project Management in more detail.

Here's the rundown of Project products available to you, starting with the two individual user offerings:

✦ **Project Standard is the meat and potatoes version of Project, with lots of the core functionality, but some of the fancier features are omitted.** These core tools help you manage schedules and resources, but with less ability to share your project information with others. The product integrates well with Microsoft Office 2007 products such as Excel and Word.

✦ **Project Professional 2007 contains all that Standard does but adds some collaborative tools for sharing resources and information with others.** Professional is integrated with Microsoft Office Project Server 2007; when your IT person sets this up, you can keep folks updated and keep your project updated by using Project Web Access tools.

✦ **Enterprise Project Management (EPM) Solution helps an entire organization manage a portfolio or projects and standardize their project practices.** This solution requires that you own several products, including Project Professional, Project Server, Project Server Client Access, and more. At this level, your organization is probably working directly with a Microsoft salesperson to buy licenses for these many products, and your IT people have to get involved to set the whole thing up.

Getting out of Hot Water with Multiple Undo

Multiple Undo has been a requested feature in Project for years. Though an undo feature sounds simple, it can have a lot of value when working with a project because individual changes to timing in your project plan can cause hundreds of changes in a large schedule. For that reason, undoing several actions in a row in Project was a major technology challenge.

Many project managers find that the ability to try out different scenarios that involve several changes to a project is extremely useful. In the past, you had to do an action and then undo it, then do the next action and undo it, and so on, which is time-consuming and doesn't really enable you to see cumulative effects.

With Multiple Undo, you can try out several changes and then undo the whole list of changes or a portion of them at once. Because you often want to try out several changes when finalizing or making adjustments to a project — for example, changing the timing of a set of tasks — Multiple Undo can be very handy.

Be aware that you have to undo all changes in order. For example, if you made six changes and you want to undo the fourth change, you have to undo changes four through six.

Here's how to undo more than one change:

1. **Make all the changes you want to your schedule but don't save the schedule yet.**

2. **Click the down arrow to the right of the Undo icon on the Standard toolbar.**

You see a list of changes you've made (see Figure 5-1), starting with the most recent action at the top.

3. **Click the change you want to undo.**

That change and all others you performed subsequent to it are undone.

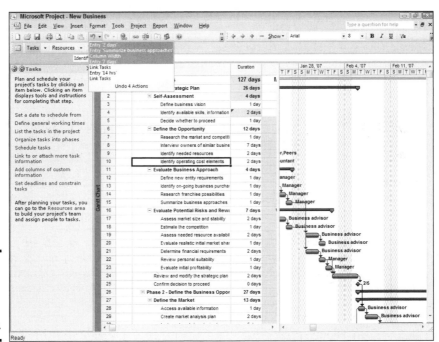

Figure 5-1:
Undo more
than one
task,
sequentially.

Spotting Changes with Change Highlighting

You can use the brand-new Change Highlighting feature to see how the changes you make affect your project. When you turn on Change Highlighting and take any action that changes your project's schedule, a highlight appears on every task that has been affected (see Figure 5-2). Because it's easy to miss how a single change can impact dozens of other tasks, Change Highlighting provides a visual clue to help you avoid surprises down the road.

You can toggle this feature on and off by choosing View➪Show Change Highlighting/Hide Change Highlighting.

Change Highlighting shows you only the results of the last change you made and works only on changes that have an impact on the timing of tasks in your schedule.

Figure 5-2:
Change
Highlighting
lets you see
just what
effect your
changes will
have.

Knowing What's Driving Your Tasks

When you create a task such as Print Brochure in a project, several factors might affect its timing. It might have a constraint causing it to start no later than a certain date or a dependency relationship with the earlier task, Design Brochure. A new feature called Task Drivers helps you understand all the settings that are affecting the timing of a task.

The Task Drivers feature helps you recognize the many possible settings that might affect your tasks, which can include

✦ **Actual Start Date or Assignments:** You've entered an actual start date, or you have made a resource assignment to a task and the resource isn't available.

✦ **Leveling Delay:** If you turned on leveling to deal with resource overallocations, it might have caused a delay on a task.

✦ **Constraints:** You apply a constraint to a task, such as forcing it to finish on a certain date.

✦ **Summary Tasks:** Summary tasks' timings are driven by the timing of their child tasks or subtasks.

✦ **Dependency Relationships:** A predecessor task can cause changes in a task's timing.

To display task driver information, follow these steps:

1. **Scroll to the task in your project that you want to review.**

2. **Click the Task Drivers icon on the Standard toolbar. (It looks like a taskbar with an arrow and question mark above it.)**

   The Task Drivers pane appears (see Figure 5-3), explaining the various conditions driving a task's timing.

3. **Click another task to display its drivers.**

4. **Click the Close button in the Task Drivers pane to close it when you're done.**

See Book IV, Chapter 1 for more about how task drivers can help you fine-tune task timing in your project.

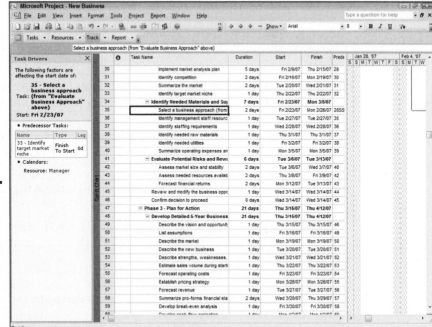

Making Reports More Visual

Many people swear by PivotTable reports in Excel and Visio because they allow you to compare data from a variety of perspectives. Pivot tables offer perspectives that are especially useful for data analysis. If you're a PivotTable fan, you'll be glad to know that the same capability has come to Project 2007 in the form of Visual Reports. Pivot tables allow you to view data from a variety of perspectives beyond the standard Project report capabilities.

The Visual Reports feature allows you to select the fields you want to view and compare and to modify your reports in a variety of ways (see Figure 5-4).

Project offers six categories of Visual Reports as well as custom reports that you can build yourself. Some of these categories are based on *timephased data* (that is, data distributed over time, such as allocations of resource time or costs).

Visual Report categories include

✦ **Task Usage:** Based on timephased data for tasks, this category of report gives you a peek at information such as cash flow and earned value over time.

✦ **Resource Usage:** Based on timephased resource data, these reports include cash flow, resource availability, resource costs, and resource work data.

✦ **Assignment Usage:** Also based on timephased data, this category of reports provides information in areas such as baseline versus actual costs and baseline versus actual work.

✦ **Task Summary, Resource Summary, and Assignment Summary:** These three categories of reports provide diagram views of a variety of work and cost data and are not based on timephased data.

See Book VI, Chapter 4 for in-depth information about working with Visual Reports.

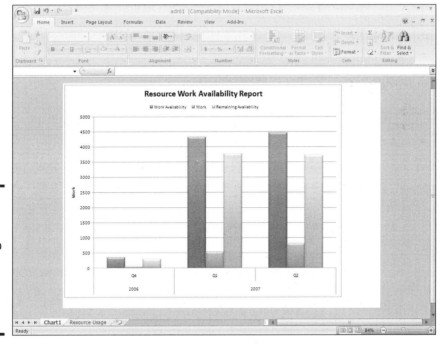

Figure 5-4:
Visual Reports allow you to choose among several fields to display.

A New Resource: Cost

If you've used Project in earlier versions, you worked with material and work resources. *Material resources* might include tons of steel or yards of fabric; the units of these resources have an associated cost and the more units you use, the more it costs you. *Work resources* are typically people who get paid so much per hour that they put in on a task; the more hours they work, the more it hits your budget.

In Project 2007, there's a new resource in town called the Cost resource. *Cost resources* have a set cost associated with them that you create in the Task Information dialog box, which displays when you double-click a task name in any view (see Figure 5-5). Unlike material resources that affect your budget by the number of units you use and work resources whose hourly costs tally up dollars, Cost resources have a fixed cost that you assign.

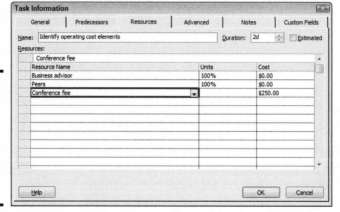

Figure 5-5: Choose the type of resource you need in the Task Information dialog box.

Here's an example of how you would use Cost resources: Say you're managing a construction project to build 20 cottages. Each cottage requires a building permit with a cost of $250. You can create a Cost resource called Permit and assign it to each of the 20 subprojects in your overall project. No matter how long each cottage takes to build or how many resources work on them, your permit cost remains the same. (That is, unless you run over the allotted time allowed by the permits for building and final inspection on each of the cottages, in which case you'd better have a Penalty Cost resource ready to apply!)

See Book V, Chapter 1 for more about various resource types.

Working with Budgets

In Project 2007, budget resources can help you track your budget against your actual costs.

You can specify a resou rce as a budget resource by selecting the Budget check box in the Resource Information dialog box, which displays when you double-click a resource name in a view such as Resource Sheet (see Figure 5-6). You then assign these resources to the project's single summary task. For example, you might create a budget resource called Travel Budget and associate costs with it. You can then assign this resource to the project summary task so that it's applicable to the entire project.

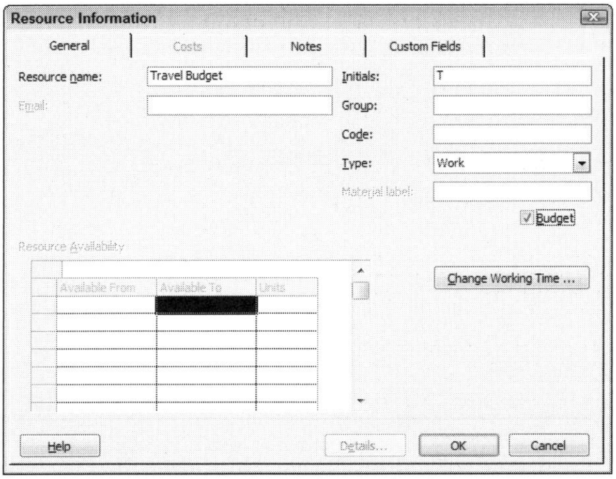

Figure 5-6:
Creating a budget resource.

Using budget resources, you can display fields that allow you to compare your budgeted cost with your planned cost. (Unfortunately, there's often a difference.)

For example, you might have $10,000 budgeted for travel, and in creating your individual tasks you might have applied $11,450 in costs for individual business trips associated with the project. The budget setting can help you compare these amounts as you add and delete resources to or from various tasks.

If you assign a budget resource, you can then view budgeted work at any time by displaying the Budget Work field. Note that this field reflects only material and work resource costs.

Book II

Project Basics

The 5th Wave   By Rich Tennant

"Look you've got Project Manager, Acct. Manager, and Opportunity Manager, but Sucking Up to the Manager just isn't a field the program comes with."

Contents at a Glance

Chapter 1: Building a Project Plan

In This Chapter

✔ **Opening a new, blank project**

✔ **Opening project templates**

✔ **Opening a schedule based on an existing project**

✔ **Entering basic project information**

✔ **Saving projects**

*W*hen you're ready to begin your first project using Microsoft Project 2007, you start by opening a file. You can use a blank template or get a head start by opening a template that includes sample tasks for a certain category of project.

After you open a project, your first step is to enter certain global project information, such as the scheduling method for the project. Finally, you should know how to save and close a project so that it's ready for you to work on it another day.

In this chapter, you get going with the creation of your very first Project schedule.

Creating That First Project

You can create a new project in three ways: You can open a new, blank project; open a project template that contains sample tasks; or open a project based on an existing project. In the following sections, you get a feel for the pros and cons of each method.

Starting from scratch

If you want a clean slate to work with when you begin a new project, opening a blank template is your best bet. You can start building your new project directly in this blank schedule, which contains no tasks, resources, or other settings except default project settings. Starting a project from the blank template requires you to do more work inputting information, but if your project is somewhat unique, this might be the best way to go.

Whenever you open Project 2007, you see a blank project file on-screen along with the Project Guide task pane. You can also open a new, blank project schedule at any time by choosing File➪New and then clicking the Blank Project link in the New Project task pane (see Figure 1-1).

TIP

Project Guide can help you build a project. Project Guide reminds you of the typical steps you should take in entering project, task, and resource data. Discover more about this method of creating tasks in Chapter 5 of this minibook.

Getting a head start with templates

You don't have to start from scratch if your project is typical of those in your industry, because Microsoft provides some convenient project templates to get you going. These include projects by type: for example, an engineering project or office move. Templates include many tasks appropriate to your project to save you time and help you to think through your plan when you are new to Project.

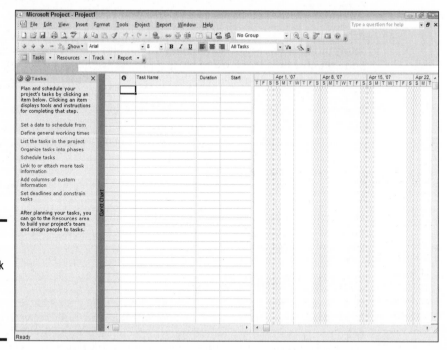

Figure 1-1:
The New Project task pane with a blank schedule open.

Figure 1-2 shows the Project Office template. Templates typically contain sample tasks broken down into logical phases, with task durations and dependencies in place. The templates from Microsoft sometimes include generic resources, but you can create your own resources as well as use, edit, or delete the ones provided.

You can open a template from the New Project task pane. To do so, follow these steps:

1. **Choose File⇨New.**

The New Project task pane appears, as shown in Figure 1-3.

2. **Click the On Computer link.**

The Templates dialog box opens. You can also use the On Web Sites link and the Templates on Office Online link to access online templates.

3. **Click the Project Templates tab, which is shown in Figure 1-4.**

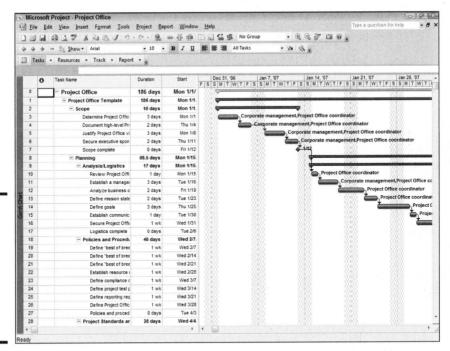

Figure 1-2:
Templates provide a great head start in building common business projects.

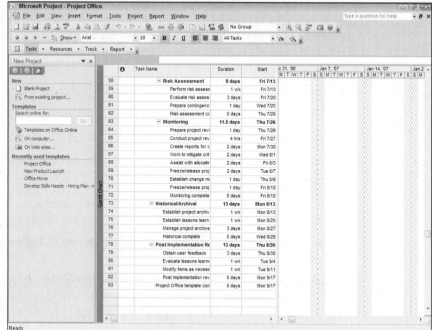

Figure 1-3:
Open a
template
from the
New Project
task pane.

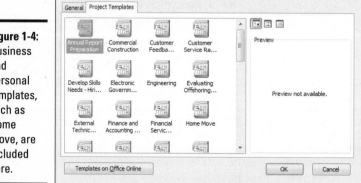

Figure 1-4:
Business
and
personal
templates,
such as
Home
Move, are
included
here.

4. **Click a template to display a preview.**

5. **When you find the template you want to use, click OK.**

   The template opens in Microsoft Project document format (MPP). You
   can then save the file with a new name. You can also delete tasks, move
   them around, or add tasks as necessary for your project.

After you open a template, be sure to check its project information (choose Project⊅Project Information) to make sure that the Start Date and Calendar options are set as you want. See the next section for more about this.

If you modify a template and want to use that set of tasks again for future projects, consider saving the file as a custom template. Just choose File⊅ Save As and then select Template in the Save As Type list. You might also consider having organizational templates that are saved on your network or in a shared folder for other project managers to access.

If you have an existing project with similarities to a new project but you neglected to save it as a template, you can simply open the existing Project file, save it with a new name, and voila — you have a head start on building your new plan.

Making Global Project Settings

When you start a new project and find yourself staring at that blank project schedule, a logical first step is to enter some general project information. This information mostly affects the general timing of your project.

Entering settings

To enter general project information, choose Project⊅Project Information. The Project Information dialog box appears, as shown in Figure 1-5.

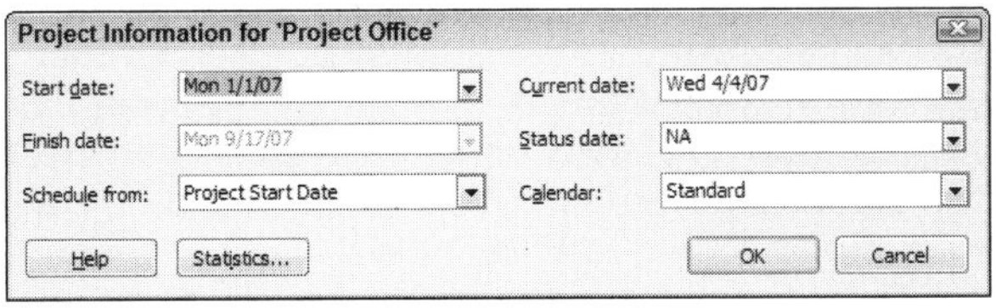

Figure 1-5:
Use the
Project
Information
dialog box
for some
basic
project
settings.

Project Information for 'Project Office'			
Start date:	Mon 1/1/07	Current date:	Wed 4/4/07
Finish date:	Mon 9/17/07	Status date:	NA
Schedule from:	Project Start Date	Calendar:	Standard
Help	Statistics...		OK Cancel

Here's what you can do in this dialog box:

✦ **Use the Start Date setting to specify the start date for the project.** If you're not sure when the project will start, set the start date about a month from today. Then, after you build some tasks and have a better handle on the entire length of your project, you can come back and set a real start date. Project automatically recalculates all dates when you do.

✦ **Use the Finish Date setting to specify the finish date for the project.** Especially if you have a *drop-dead date* (an attention-getting term!) beyond which the project cannot wander and still reach completion, you can set the finish date. In such a case, be sure to look at the next setting in this list — and change it accordingly.

✦ **Schedule from the start or finish of the project.** Most projects work forward from the start date. However, if you have an absolute drop-dead date for the end of your project (for example, if you're organizing a sports event that must occur on New Year's Day next year), you might want to set the finish date and then work backward to fit all your tasks into the allotted length of time. If you change this setting to Project Finish Date, the Finish Date field becomes available.

✦ **Set the current date.** You can fill in the current date according to your computer calendar. Or, you can choose another date if you like, but that usually doesn't make much sense unless you're in a different time zone from where the project will occur.

✦ **Set a status date.** By default, no status date is set for the project. You use a *status date* when you're tracking the progress of your project at regular intervals. If you set a status date, your computer assumes that any activity you record in your project is being tracked as of this date. You can find out more about settings for tracking in Book VIII.

✦ **Set the working calendar for your project.** You have three choices: Standard, Night Shift, and 24 Hours. Base your choice on the working habits of your organization. For example, if your company uses resources in three shifts per day — a total of 24 hours of straight working time — and all those shifts would contribute work to your project, choose 24 Hours. If you use a day shift and a night shift, choose Night Shift. If you work a standard 8-hour day, choose Standard. (Most projects use a standard calendar with a typical 8-hour workday.)

Calendars can be a little complex. A project calendar that you set in this dialog box indicates what the usual workday is at your company, but you can set up individual calendars for each task you create. The Task calendar then takes precedence over the project calendar. See Book II, Chapter 4 for more about Task calendars.

✦ **Assign a priority to your project.** Assigning a priority can be especially useful if you use the same resources across several projects and want to use the Resource Leveling feature. With your priorities set on all projects, Project tools can then automatically reallocate resources. A priority of 1 would cause Resource Leveling to assume it is just fine to delay a task, where a priority of 1000 would cause Resource Leveling to avoid moving such a task at any cost.

You can also create custom project information fields for your organization in the Enterprise Custom Fields section of this dialog box. For example, you might want a field that explains which department in the company is running the project.

Click the Statistics button in this dialog box to get an overview of your project, as shown in Figure 1-6.

Figure 1-6: You can review a summary of the information you entered.

You need to enter much more information in addition to general project information and tasks in order to build a complete project, as you discover in the next few chapters. However, entering general project information is a logical starting point.

Using start and finish dates

It's important at this point to give you some advice about how to use start and finish dates in Project. Many people new to project management software attempt to use it like a paper-based schedule, pinning down every known date, setting the start and finish dates while still in the planning stages.

However, one of the most useful aspects of Project is that it can show you what a shift in timing does to your project instantly. If you nail down specific dates, you have to go in and reset them whenever a change occurs. This is true on the task level, where making settings that force a task to happen on a certain day undermines the abilities of Project to move tasks based on their timing relationships. For example, suppose you build in a relationship that says you can't send out the brochure until you receive the brochure from the printer. If the printer is late, the ship date of the brochure moves out automatically, providing you with valuable real-world information.

Setting the start or finish date of a project while still in the planning stage can have similar issues. If you don't really know the very day things can start rolling, you don't have to set a start date until you're further along in your planning. You can still observe the overall length of time it will take for the project to run its course. Then when you have better information about a real start date or you want to propose a few different start dates and see the results in your schedule (see Figure 1-7), use the Start Date setting to do so.

One final word of advice: It usually makes sense to set a start date or a finish date, but you cannot set both. By setting a start date, the tasks and timing relationships you create reveal to you what a realistic finish date will be. If you don't like the results, make changes to tasks, relationships between them, or resource assignments to tighten things up. (See Book VIII for more about how to do this.) Setting a finish date lets you see when you must start (or have already started) by to complete your project on time.

Conversely, if you decide to schedule back from a finish date, don't set the start date as well. Setting a drop-dead finish date and creating your tasks then lets you see exactly when you have to start (or when you should have started) to realistically complete your project (see Figure 1-8). Again, when you see what Project shows you about your start date, you can adjust your tasks if necessary to obtain a start date you can live with.

Figure 1-7:
Setting a start date in this project reveals the finish date in the summary task.

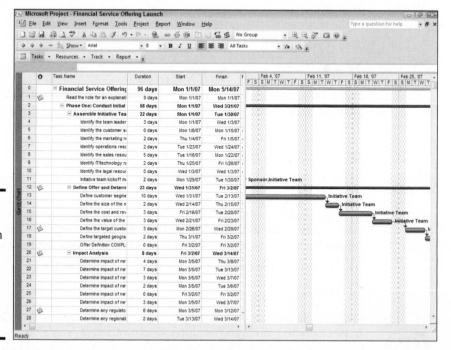

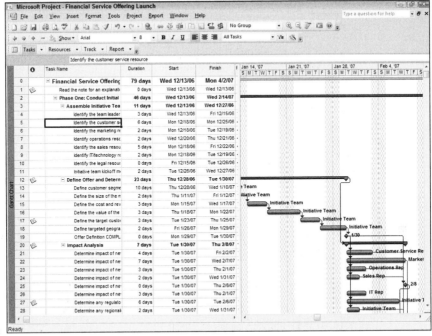

Figure 1-8:
You had to
have started
a while ago
to hit this
finish date.

Save That Project!

You can save a project just as easily as you do in any other software, or you
can save a Project Workspace. You can also save a project in various other
file formats. Here's the lowdown on how you save all the work you've done.

Saving a project

To save a Project file that you haven't saved before, follow these steps:

1. **Choose File⇨Save As.**

2. **Use the Save In drop-down list at the top (see Figure 1-9) to locate the
   folder where you want to save the file; then click to select it.**

3. **In the File Name text box, type a name for the project.**

4. **Click Save.**

It's a good idea to create a folder for your project either on your local hard
drive or on your company network where you save in one place not only
your Project files but also supporting documents, e-mails, and other items.
You can create a new folder from within the Save As dialog box by clicking
the New Folder button.

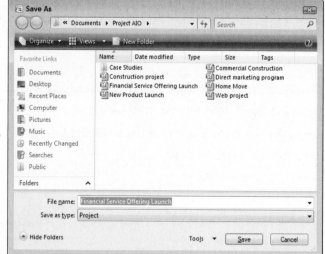

Figure 1-9:
You can
review a
summary of
the informa-
tion you
entered.

Saving in other formats

As with most software, Project allows you to save a file in other formats.
When in the Save As dialog box, use the Save as Type field to choose one of
these other formats:

✦ **Project 2000–2003:** If you want to share this file with folks who have an
earlier version of Project, this could be a logical format to save in.

✦ **Template:** To create a template from a file, save in the Template format.

✦ **Excel:** There are two options here: You can save a project as an Excel
Workbook or an Excel PivotTable. If you want to share your data in
Excel, choose one of these formats.

✦ **Text, CSV:** Text saves your file in formats that don't include a lot of
formatting bells and whistles. When you choose these formats or any
Excel formats (see previous bullet), an Export Wizard appears to help
you choose which fields of data will export and how to export.

✦ **XML:** This is similar to the MPV format in older versions of Project, in that
it allows you to exchange data with programs other than Project 2007.
XML stands for Extensible Markup Language, and is used especially over
the World Wide Web to deliver structured data in a consistent format.

You can save a file to a workspace. A project in a workspace offers an easy
way for members to access and work on related files in one central location.
Just choose File➪Save as Workspace to do so.

Chapter 2: Creating That First Task

*T*asks are the essential building blocks of any project. They're like the items on your old-fashioned to-do list for your project. When you create a task, you build in the What, When, Who, and Where information of your plan.

But tasks serve other roles. For example, resources work on a project when you assign them to tasks. The timing of tasks and the relationships between them form the overall schedule for your project. By tracking the activity on tasks, you can see the progress of your project over time.

You can create tasks in a few different ways: by typing information in the sheet area of Gantt Chart view (or any other view that displays information in columns) or by using the Task Information dialog box. You can also import tasks from Outlook or Excel. You can even use a hyperlink to create a task in your project that represents data in another project.

In this chapter, you find out all about the various ways to create tasks, entering task basics in the process.

Tackling Task Basics

Before you can start to build tasks, you have to identify the individual steps required to complete your project. When you know what steps you need to take to accomplish your project goal, you can create each of those steps as individual tasks in Project.

Chapter 1 in this minibook gives you a lot of advice about how to figure out which tasks to include in your project and how to identify your project scope and goal.

In a longer project, you might find that your tasks number in the hundreds or even thousands. As you create tasks, you might find it useful to organize those tasks in a logical way by creating phases consisting of summary tasks with subtasks below them. This structure is essentially Project's version of an outline (see Figure 2-1). For example, you might have a summary task named Product Brochure with three subtasks: Design Brochure, Write and Approve Copy, and Print Brochure. It's up to you to decide how much detail each phase of your project requires.

You can find out how to organize tasks into outlines in Book III, Chapter 2. All you have to focus on in this chapter is how to create tasks.

Identifying what makes up a task

Creating a task is a bit more complicated than writing an item on a to-do list. Think of each task in your project as a record — like a database record that lists a person's name, address, e-mail, and birthday. In a similar way, a task in Project contains data about that task: not only a task name but also other vital data about how that task fits into your project.

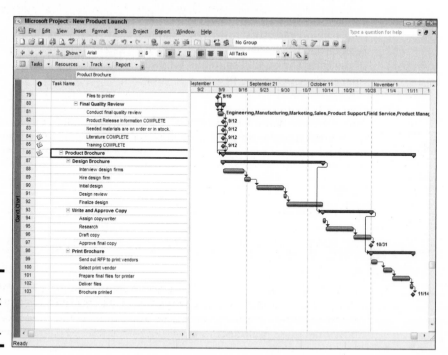

Figure 2-1:
A large task organized into phases.

To create a task, you enter information such as

✦ Task name

✦ Task duration

✦ Task type

✦ Task priority

✦ Constraints for scheduling the task

At a basic level, all you have to do to create a task is enter a task name. However, a task record can contain much more information than that. You can add all task information up front or, if you haven't obtained or figured out all the task settings, enter more and more data over time.

What task settings control

You have to make some choices when you create tasks, which we don't go into detail about here because our goal in this chapter is to simply have you create a task. However, you see several task settings in the Task Information dialog box that you use in this chapter (see Figure 2-2), so we briefly address them.

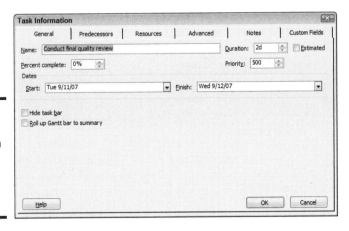

Figure 2-2:
The Task
Information
dialog box
contains a
wealth of
data.

Some settings, such as task type (fixed duration) and priority (none), can often be left at default settings. Others, such as task duration (how long the task will take to complete), almost always require some input from you. Book IV provides details about how to make each task setting and how they drive task timing.

For now, remember that pretty much everything that you enter about a task (except the task name and resources assigned to the task) involves how the task timing is controlled. Several of these settings work in combination, with

Project performing complex algorithms to set the timing of the task according to the value of each setting. Other elements, such as the task finish date, don't determine timing but rather cause Project to display a symbol in the Indicator column (the column to the right of the task number column with a small blue circle containing an *i* at the top) to alert you when a task has moved beyond its estimated finish date.

You can also specify a unique Task calendar in the Task Information dialog box; calendars are covered in Chapter 4 of this minibook.

The Many Different Ways to Create a Task

You can create a task by entering a name for it. You can fill in the details of task duration and task type, for example, at the same time or later.

However detailed you want to get in your task settings, you can create tasks by using a few different methods:

✦ Enter task data in a Gantt Chart view sheet pane.

✦ Enter data in a Task Information dialog box.

✦ Import tasks from Excel or Outlook.

✦ Link to a task in another project.

Creating a task in Gantt Chart view

Many people who work on lengthy projects find that entering all task names in the sheet pane of Gantt Chart view is the quickest and easiest way to go. You can actually use any view that includes columns of data, such as Task Usage or Tracking Gantt.

You don't have to use a spreadsheet view to enter a new task, though it is perhaps the quickest way to create tasks. You can also enter a new task in Network Diagram or Calendar view by displaying the view and choosing Insert➪New Task. A new task box or calendar entry opens and is ready for you to type a task name. However, in Resource views, the New Task command isn't available to you on the Insert menu at all.

Follow these simple steps to enter a task in Gantt Chart view:

1. **In the Task Name column, click a blank cell.**

2. **Type a task name.**

You can edit what you type by clicking in the entry box above the sheet and pressing the Backspace or Delete key to clear characters (see Figure 2-3). You can also click the X and check mark buttons to the left of the entry box to clear or accept your entry.

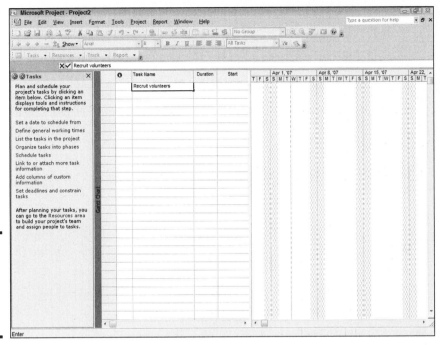

Figure 2-3:
You can
clear or
accept text
in the entry
field.

3. Press the down-arrow key to move to the next cell in the column and then type the next task name.

When you move to the next cell, Project automatically assigns a sequential task number in the far-left column. This number is a handy way to identify tasks in larger schedules.

4. Repeat Step 3 until you enter all task names.

You can display other columns in Gantt Chart view to quickly enter additional task information, such as duration, type, start date, and finish date. To display additional columns, right-click any column heading, choose Insert Column, and then select the column you want to display from the Field Name list.

Try displaying the Entry table (choose View➪Table➪Entry). This table offers the most common task information columns.

Going the Task Information dialog box route

Dialog boxes offer the advantage of a centralized information form that allows you to make more than one entry or setting at a time. The form also serves to remind you about all the possible settings you have at your disposal. If this approach appeals to you, consider using the Task Information dialog box to enter task information. A series of tabs in this dialog box contain all the information that can possibly exist about a task.

Follow these steps to create a task by using the Task Information dialog box:

1. **In the Task Name column, double-click a blank cell.**

The Task Information dialog box appears, as shown in Figure 2-4. The General and Advanced tabs in this dialog box contain various timing settings for the task.

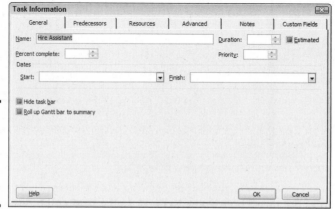

Figure 2-4:
Determine
various task
timing
settings
here.

2. **In the Name field, type a task name.**

3. **Click OK to save the new task.**

The task name appears in Gantt Chart view in the cell you clicked in Step 1.

4. **Press the down-arrow key to move to the next cell.**

5. **Repeat Steps 2–4 to add as many tasks as you like.**

Try to keep the task names in your project both descriptive and unique so you and others reviewing your project don't get confused. However, if you can't make all the names unique (for example, you want to have three tasks in three different phases named Hire Staff), you can use the automatically assigned task number or the work breakdown structure (WBS) code (see Book III, Chapter 3 for more about WBS) to identify tasks. These numbers are always unique for each task.

Importing tasks from Outlook

Just as you might start roughing out a project with a handwritten to-do list, you might start thinking about your project as a series of simple to-do tasks that you enter in Outlook. When that list of tasks becomes the basis of a project, you don't have to lose the list and start from scratch. Microsoft provides an easy-to-use import feature that puts the tasks you create in Outlook into Project.

When you bring data in from one application to another, you use something called import-mapping. For example, you can map a spreadsheet field labeled Staff to the field labeled Resources in Project. The Project import-mapping feature allows you to map fields in a file created in another application to fields in Project to import data. However, the import-mapping process can be tedious at best and confusing at worst. The *Import Outlook Tasks* feature in Project is essentially an import map that's preset to work with mapping Outlook task fields to Project task fields.

Book II
Chapter 2

**Creating That
First Task**

Follow these steps to import Outlook tasks into Project:

1. **Open the plan that you want to insert tasks into or open a new project (choose File⇨New).**

2. **Choose Tools⇨Import Outlook Tasks.**

The Import Outlook Tasks dialog box appears, as shown in Figure 2-5.

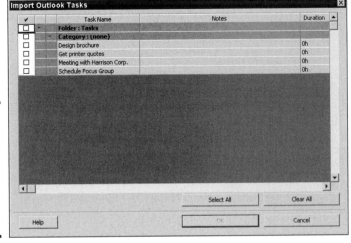

Figure 2-5:
Task names, notes, and durations entered in Outlook all come along for the ride.

3. **Select the options for the tasks you want to import or click Select All to import all Outlook tasks.**

By default, Outlook keeps tasks in a Tasks folder. Selecting the check box for the Folder: Tasks item is another way to select all tasks in Outlook.

4. Click OK.

The tasks are imported and appear at the end of your list of tasks with Change Highlighting applied (see Figure 2-6).

When you import tasks from Outlook, the task name, task duration, and any task notes are brought over. If a task in Outlook has no duration, Project creates the task with an estimated one-day time frame.

Project 2007 can integrate your schedule in various ways with Outlook via Project Web Access. See Book X, Chapter 4 for more information about this.

Getting your tasks from Excel

If you're a devoted Excel fan, you might like to create your task list for a project in Excel. At some point, when you're ready to move that list into Project, you'll be glad to hear that Microsoft has provided the Project Plan template that makes the process simple. You can open this template, located in the Microsoft Office template 1033 folder, from within Excel.

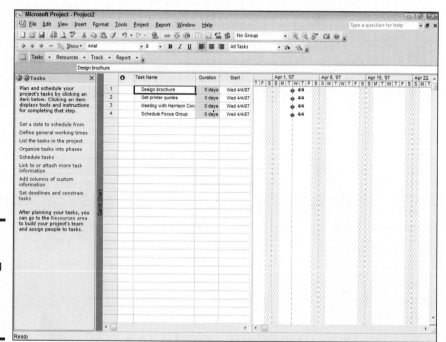

Figure 2-6: Change Highlighting flags the newly imported tasks.

The template provides four Excel worksheets, as shown in Figure 2-7. You can enter information about tasks, resources, and resource assignments on three of them and then easily export that data from Excel to Project.

Follow these steps to use this template:

1. **In Excel, open the template called ProjPlan.**

2. **Fill in information about tasks, resources, and dates in the appropriate columns on the appropriate worksheets and then save the file.**

3. **Open Project and choose File⇨Open.**

The Open dialog box appears.

4. **Locate the ProjPlan file you just saved and then click Open.**

The Import Wizard appears.

5. **Click Next to begin the wizard.**

6. **Choose the second option, Project Excel Template, for the format of the data you're importing. Then click Next.**

**Book II
Chapter 2**

Creating That
First Task

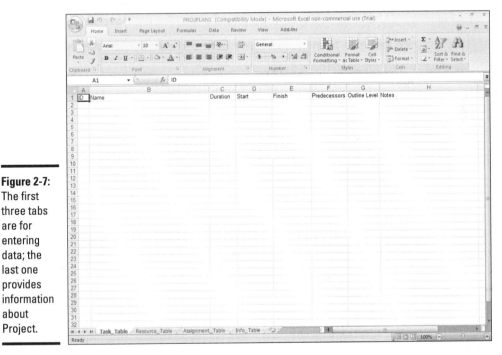

Figure 2-7:
The first three tabs are for entering data; the last one provides information about Project.

7. **On the next wizard screen (see Figure 2-8), choose the method for importing the file.**

You can import the file As a New Project, to Append the Data to the Active Project, or to Merge the Data into the Active Project. If you choose the third option, you have to create a *merge key* that delineates how the data should merge with existing tasks.

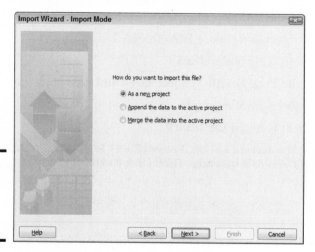

Figure 2-8:
Choosing how to import the file.

8. **Click Next and then click Finish.**

The project appears with whatever tasks, resources, and assignment information you entered in a project plan format.

Creating a task that represents another project

When you and your co–project managers handle a lot of projects, it's often useful to create a task in one project that represents the timing of the sum of tasks in another project. For example, if you're driving the network installation project, having a task that indicates the completion of your new office building construction can be very helpful.

To accomplish this, you can insert a hyperlink in a project outline. This creates a task that not only reflects the overall timing of another project, but also provides a handy way to quickly open the other project from within yours, assuming it's available on your company network or intranet. After you create the task, you can move it around in your project and even create timing relationships, called *dependencies,* to it (see Book IV, Chapter 3 for more about dependency relationships).

To insert a hyperlink to another Project file in your project, follow these steps:

1. Click to select the blank task name cell where you want the hyperlinked task to appear.

2. Choose Insert⇨Hyperlink.

The Insert Hyperlink dialog box appears, as shown in Figure 2-9.

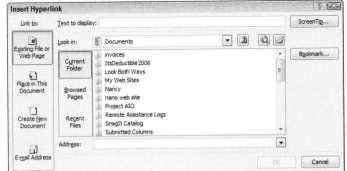

Figure 2-9:
Choose a
linking
destination.

3. In the Text to Display box, type a name for the hyperlinked file.

Make sure that this text indicates what information is being summarized.

4. In the Link To area, click the Existing File or Web Page icon.

You can link to a document, an e-mail address, or a Web page.

5. In the Look In list, locate and select the file to which you want to insert a hyperlink.

6. Click OK.

The link text is inserted, and a hyperlink symbol appears in the Indicator field (see Figure 2-10). You can simply click that link symbol to open the other file.

If you need to, use the Indent and Outdent tools on the Formatting toolbar (arrows pointing to the left and right, respectively) to place tasks at the appropriate level in your project. You can find out more about how to organize tasks into outlines in Book III, Chapter 2.

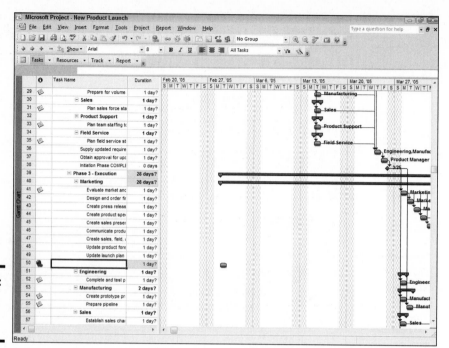

Figure 2-10:
A hyper-
linked task
in Project.

Chapter 3: Exploring Task Views

In This Chapter

✔ **Getting an overview of views**

✔ **Choosing the best view for your needs**

✔ **Displaying combination views**

✔ **Exploring various task views**

✔ **Making use of resource views**

✔ **Discovering great views for tracking progress**

*I*n real estate, they say a view is worth thousands. In Project, the right view could easily help save you thousands. That's because views are the way you get at all the valuable data you need to keep your project on track and within budget.

Essentially views in Project provide you with different perspectives on your Project plan. Some help you focus on resources. Others help you get your tasks in line. There are views that make data entry quick and easy, and others that help you track progress on your project.

In Book I, Chapter 4 we discuss the three most commonly used views — Gantt Chart, Network Diagram, and Calendar. In this chapter, we go deeper into views, showing you some of the more esoteric but very useful views Project makes available to you.

A View for Every Need

Think about it: After you enter all the project, task, and resource data for a big project of, say, 1,000 tasks, you've created a powerful database of information. Add to that, Project automatically performs complex calculations on that data to make information about schedules, costs, dependencies, and more available, and you have a huge chunk of data at your disposal. The way you get at that data is through views.

Many people spend the majority of their time in Gantt Chart view (see Figure 3-1), which is fine. Gantt Chart view provides columns of data in a variety of tables that you can display and modify, as well as a graphical depiction of your task timing.

But Project has a great deal more to offer, namely 25 different built-in views. Some views let you examine your data in unique ways that might help you spot problems or opportunities. Some, such as Milestone Rollup (see Figure 3-2), summarize information; others enable you to enter data you can't enter elsewhere. Still others, such as Multiple Baselines Gantt, can display several saved baselines side by side, or let you view sets of data that you can find in other views.

Book I, Chapter 4 is where you can find steps for changing from one view to another and for making basic modifications to views such as displaying different tables of columns in the sheet pane and modifying the timescale in chart panes. Book VI offers some more-advanced advice on using views to communicate information about your project.

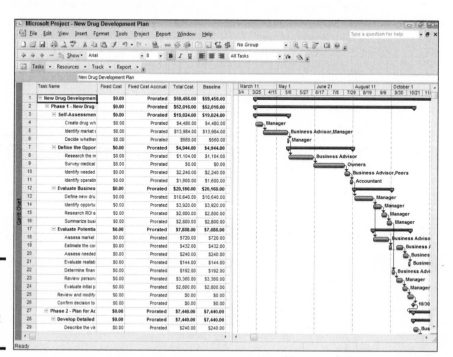

Figure 3-1:
The ever-popular Gantt Chart view.

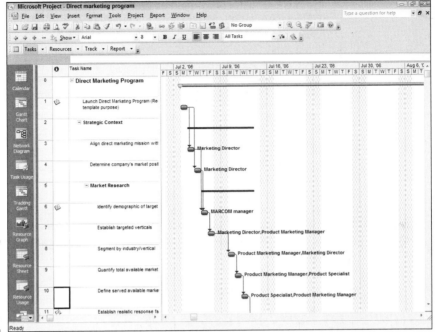

Figure 3-2:
Some views
summarize
data in
useful ways.

Finding Just the Right View for You

The view you need is likely to depend on what you're trying to accomplish
with your Project plan at the moment. Some views are useful in building your
task list, whereas others work well for entering resource data. Certain views
are wonderful for resolving problems or tracking data. How do you know
which view will work best? Here are some guidelines to help you out.

First, Project offers a few different types of views. To see the entire list, you
can click the More Views icon at the bottom of the View bar. This displays
the More Views dialog box shown in Figure 3-3.

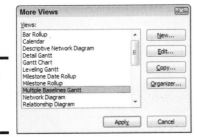

Figure 3-3:
Select a
view to
display.

Scanning this list, you can see views that include the term Resource or Task in their names, which gives you a clue what they're about. Beyond that, views fall into one of these categories:

✦ **Graph views** such as Resource Graph present information in a visual way. If you want a quick impression of what's going on or of a trend, rather than the detailed numbers, a graph view might be for you.

✦ **Chart views** such as Gantt Chart view include a sheet pane and a chart pane. The sheet includes columns of data, whereas the chart displays a graphical representation of that data.

✦ **Combination views** quite logically combine two views, displaying them one above the other. If you need to analyze one set of data, such as information about tasks, along with another set of data, such as information about resources, a combination view might fit the bill.

Beyond understanding the basic types of views, the best way to find the ones that are useful to you is to look at them and see what each has to offer.

Discovering Various Task Views

Most views contain some information about tasks; even resource views might offer resource data listed by task. However, some views are useful for working with task data. Here's a quick survey of some interesting task views:

✦ **Task Details,** shown in Figure 3-4, is a handy view for reviewing task essentials. Though much of this information is available on the various tabs of the Task Information dialog box, this view offers both a one-page summary of the most important settings and an option to open the dialog box for changing those settings.

✦ **Task Entry** is a combination view (see Figure 3-5). Gantt Chart view is shown on top, and the Task Details view is shown on the bottom. This is a great way to be able to review detailed task settings alongside your entire project plan to see how that task fits in the larger scheme of things.

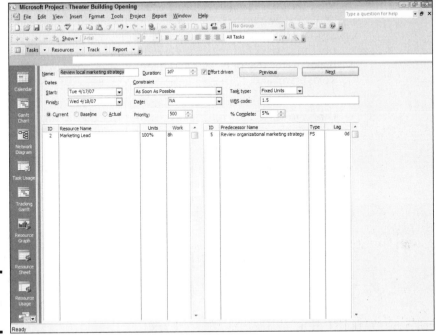

Figure 3-4:
Task Details view.

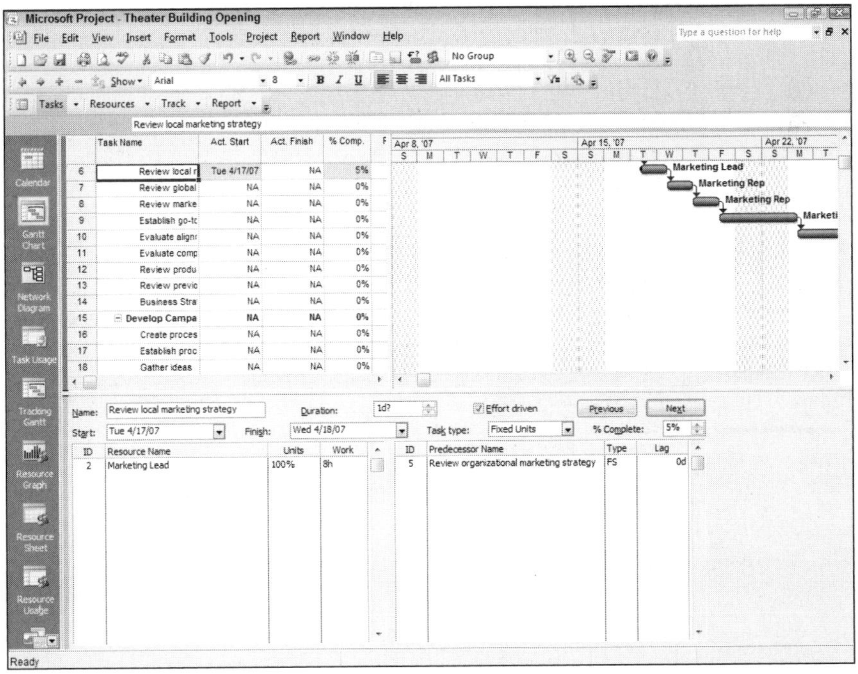

Book II
Chapter 3

Exploring Task Views

Figure 3-5:
Task Entry view.

✦ **Task Usage,** shown in Figure 3-6, is a useful view for spotting the amount of work going on in your project task by task over a period of time such as a week or month. This overview of work hours can help you spot potential work bottlenecks, slow times when it might be a good idea to make better use of resource downtime, and times when resources might be overworked.

✦ You may have used Network Diagram view, but **Descriptive Network Diagram** view adds information about whether a task is critical or non-critical (that is, whether the task can be delayed without delaying the overall deadline of the project).

✦ **Relationship Diagram** is a simple graphical view that shows you each task in your project, one by one, with all the dependency relationships to each task shown in a simple diagram with the type of relationship noted next to each task (see Figure 3-7).

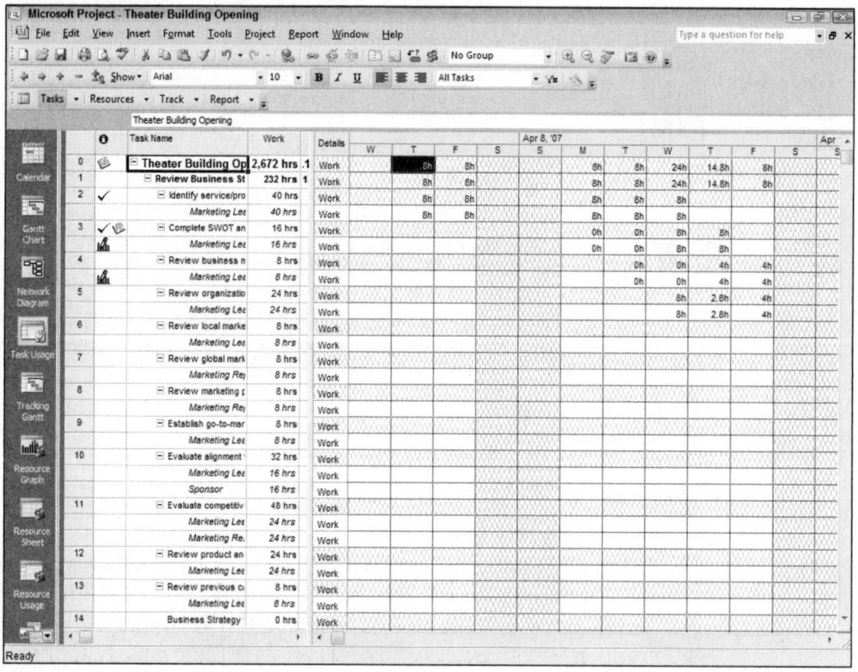

Figure 3-6:
Task Usage view.

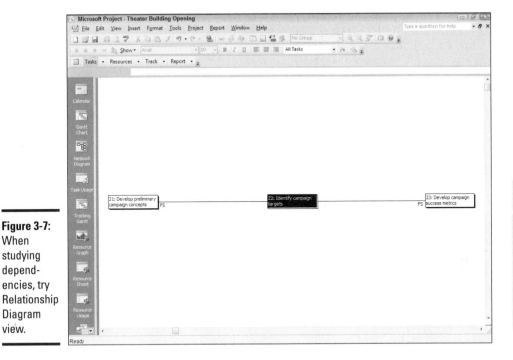

Figure 3-7:
When
studying
depend-
encies, try
Relationship
Diagram
view.

What Resource Views Tell You

Resource information also pops up in many views, but some resource-specific views could help you manage your resources more effectively. Here are a few to consider:

✦ **Resource Graph** view (see Figure 3-8) offers a visual way to review work-load, resource by resource. You can easily spot when resources are over-booked by looking at the peak units (often this is 100%) and the bars that show when a resource is booked over peak time.

✦ **Resource Allocation** is a combination view (see Figure 3-9) that allows you to view all the tasks to which a resource is assigned, both as a work hours listing at the top and a Gantt chart with task bars on the bottom. This helps you see both workload and task timing within your schedule, simul-taneously, so you can resolve resource conflicts or fine-tune assignments.

✦ **Resource Form** view (see Figure 3-10), like the Task Entry view, is a sum-mary of all of a resource's settings on a single page. Use this view to review resource assignments, calendars, and rates of pay. It's a one-page alternative to the various tabs of the Resource Information dialog box.

✦ **Resource Sheet** (see Figure 3-11) is a great view for entering resource information, including the type of resource, maximum units of work, standard and overtime rates, cost, and calendar.

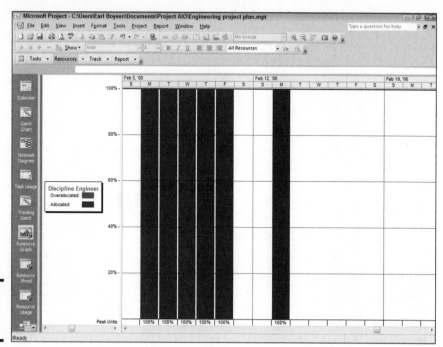

Figure 3-8:
Resource
Graph view.

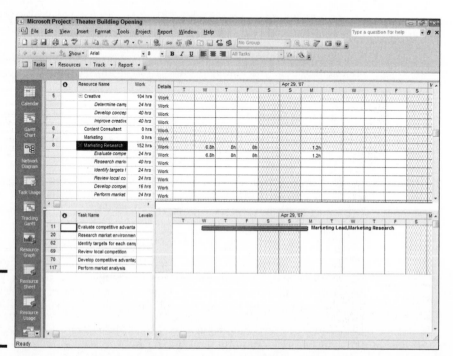

Figure 3-9:
Resource
Allocation
view.

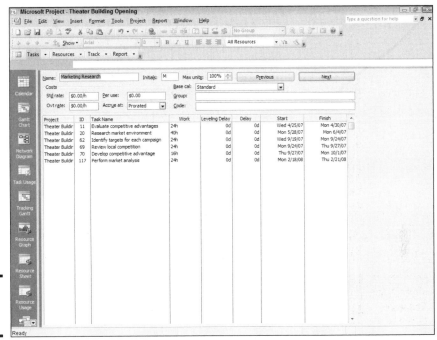

Figure 3-10:
Resource
Form view.

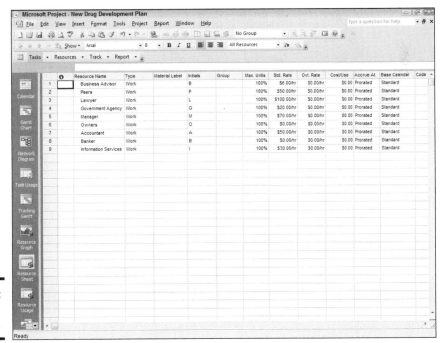

Figure 3-11:
Resource
Sheet view.

The Best Views for Tracking Progress on Your Project

After you save a baseline copy of your project plan, you can begin to track progress against that baseline. Tracking usually involves a combination of two things: entering information about actual versus planned activity, and finding ways to resolve problems that occur with your schedule and resources. Several views work very well for helping you to track and make changes to your plan.

Turn to Book VIII for a wealth of information about tracking activity on your projects.

✦ **Leveling Gantt** view (see Figure 3-12) allows you to see what delays leveling has caused in your schedule if you use Project's Resource Leveling feature (a calculation you can apply to delay tasks to avoid resource overallocations) to work out resource issues.

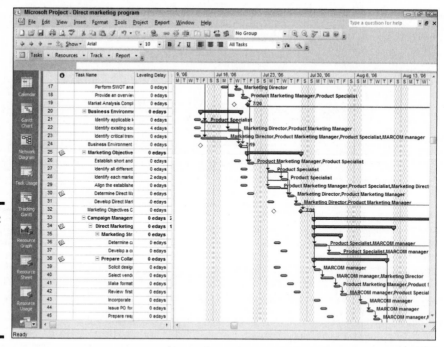

Figure 3-12: Leveling Gantt view helps you figure out your resource challenges.

TIP

If you find that delays due to Resource Leveling are unacceptable, you can turn it off and use other methods to solve resource problems. See Book VII, Chapter 2 for more about this.

✦ **Tracking Gantt** (see Figure 3-13) is a great place to go to enter actual start and end dates for your tasks and to mark tasks as finished in the columns of the sheet area. You can then view your tracked activity against the baseline by looking at the taskbars in the chart pane.

✦ **Multiple Baselines Gantt** (Figure 3-14) is useful if you've had occasion to save several baselines over the life of your project. This can occur when serious changes to your project come up — for example, if you have to stop your project midway because of a materials shortage and start it up again months later. By setting a new baseline, you're tracking against an iteration of your plan that makes sense against future actual activity. This view displays, side by side, all baselines you have saved in your project so you can see (or explain) how things changed overtime.

**Book II
Chapter 3**

Exploring Task
Views

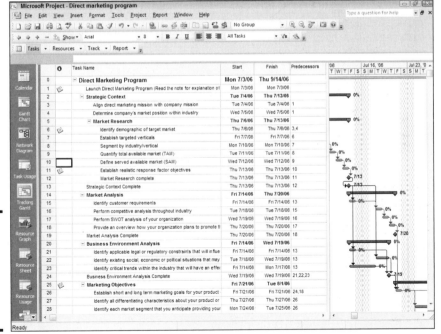

Figure 3-13:
Tracking
Gantt view
makes it
easy to
track
progress.

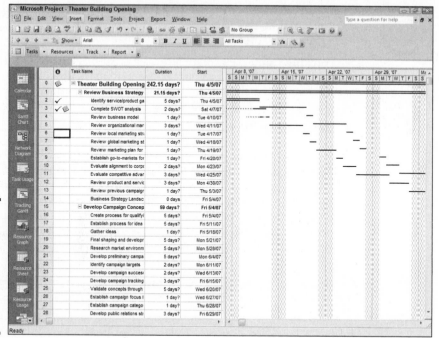

Displaying Combination Views

Looking at two views side by side (or more accurately, one on top of the other on your computer screen) can be useful when you're comparing two aspects of your project. That's where combination views come in.

For example, you might display Network Diagram view along with Gantt Chart view to get columns of data about your tasks and a graphic representation of project workflow. You can also display a combination view and then print the view, packing lots of data into your printout.

To display a combination view, follow these steps:

1. **Display the first view you want to use by using the View bar or View menu.**

2. **Choose Window⇨Split.**

A second copy of the currently displayed view appears.

3. **Click within the view you want to change.**

4. **Click the view you want in the View bar. Alternatively, choose View⇨ More Views, select the other view from the list of views, and click OK to apply it.**

   The combination view is displayed (see Figure 3-15).

If the second view you want to display is listed on the View bar, a quicker method for displaying it is to display the first view and then press the Shift key and click the View icon.

To remove the bottom view at any time, choose Window⇨Remove Split or click on the line dividing the panes and drag down to close the bottom pane. You can also change the views that appear by simply clicking another view in the View bar; it replaces the active view in the combination view.

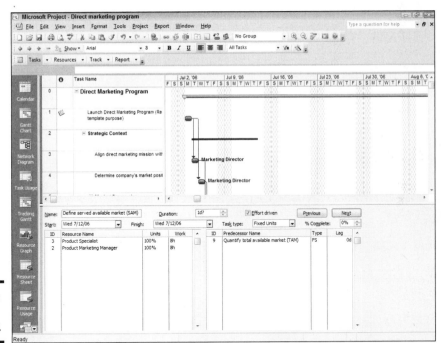

Figure 3-15:
A combi-
nation view.

Chapter 4: Working with Calendars

In This Chapter

✓ Exploring the Base, Project, Resource, and Task calendars

✓ Understanding how calendars work together

✓ Setting calendar options, working times

✓ Creating the Project calendar

✓ Using Project Guide to make calendar settings

✓ Working with Task calendars

✓ Using Resource calendars

✓ Creating your own calendar templates

✓ Copying calendars to another project

Time: There's never enough of it, so using what you've got wisely can make the difference between a successful project and a disaster. In Microsoft Project, one of your most useful tools for getting your project timing right is calendars. Calendars allow you to define working and non-working time, such as your average workday or workweek, and specify exceptions such as holidays.

It's not difficult to define your company's typical workday, whether everybody works from 9 to 5 or particular jobs call for people to work from midnight to 8 a.m. Project 2007 calendars allow you to set standards for typical working time and then allow for variation. But to make life interesting, Project 2007 has several types of calendars you have to deal with.

The Big 4: Base, Project, Resource, and Task Calendars

Mastering the four calendars in Project 2007 takes a little time. However, understanding how calendars work in Project 2007 is essential to mastering the software. You schedule tasks and assign resources based on the calendar settings that you make. The costs accumulated by resource work hours won't be accurate if you don't understand your calendar settings from the get-go.

Because the use of the term "project" can get confusing as it refers to the software, your project plan, and one of the calendar types (the Project calendar), we need to explain the terminology we use in this chapter. We use *Project 2007* when referring to the software itself, *Project calendar* when referring to the calendar settings in the software, and just plain old *project* when talking about your project plan or schedule.

How calendars work

Project 2007 has four calendars that you have to deal with. Each takes precedence over others in a very specific way, which we cover in the next section.

The four Project calendars are

✦ **Base calendar:** This is the calendar template that all other calendars are built on top of. Three Base calendars are available: Standard, 24 Hours, and Night Shift.

Not everybody in a company works the same schedule, and not every task can be performed in the same eight-hour workday. To deal with the variations in schedules that occur in most workforces, Project, Resource, and Task calendars can be set to use one of three Base calendar templates built into Project 2007.

The three Base calendar templates are as follows:

• *Standard:* The default setting. It sets a working day as 8 a.m.–5 p.m. with an hour for lunch and a five-day, Monday–Friday workweek.

• *24 Hours:* Allows work to go on around the clock every day of the week.

• *Night Shift:* Sets Sunday as a nonworking day, three shifts Tuesday through Friday, two shifts on Saturday, and one on Monday. Working times for a Night Shift calendar are shown in Figure 4-1.

The legend in Figure 4-1 explains how different hours are shaded to help you identify them in the calendar display.

You can modify the three Base calendar templates and create new templates from them. See the section "Creating Your Own Custom Calendar Template," later in this chapter.

✦ **Project calendar:** This is the default calendar for scheduling. This is where you choose which Base calendar template this particular project should use.

✦ **Resource calendar:** This combines the Base calendar settings with any exceptions (nonworking times) that you set for a particular resource.

✦ **Task calendar:** This is where you can set exceptions for a particular task.

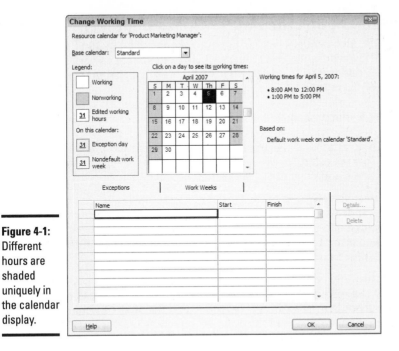

Figure 4-1:
Different hours are shaded uniquely in the calendar display.

When you create tasks and assign resources to work on them, Project 2007 has to base that work on a timing standard. For example, if you say that a task should be completed in one workday, you also have to tell Project that a *workday* means 8 hours (or 12 hours or whatever). That's why you have to set up a standard workday in your Project calendar.

In a similar way, suppose that you assign a resource to put in two weeks of work on a task in a company that uses a standard five-day workweek. If that resource is part-time and their calendar is set for a standard three-day work-week, the two weeks of work put in by that resource defer to the timing of the Resource calendar for a total of only six workdays.

Several variables affect the timing of tasks in Project. Some settings you make when you create a task can also have an effect on resource time. A two-week, effort-driven task isn't complete until its resources have put in two weeks (according to the Project or Task calendar) of effort. You can set other tasks to finish in two weeks no matter how much effort has been expended. Find out more about settings, such as the effort-driven setting, in Book IV, Chapter 2.

How does one calendar relate to another?

By default, all calendars in your project are controlled by the Project calendar setting. However, when you change a Task or Resource calendar (this type of change is referred to as an *exception*), it's important that you understand which setting takes precedence.

Here's how this precedence works:

✦ With no other settings made, the Base calendar template you select for the Project calendar when you first create the project controls the working times and days of all tasks and resources.

✦ If you make changes in the working hours for a resource assigned to a task, those settings take precedence over the Project calendar for that resource and the Task calendar. Likewise, if you assign a different Base calendar for a task, that calendar takes precedence over the Project calendar for that task.

✦ If you apply one calendar to a resource and a different calendar to a task that the resource is assigned to, Project 2007 uses only common hours to schedule the resource. For example, if the Task calendar allows work from 8 a.m.–5 p.m. and the Resource calendar allows work from 6 a.m.–2 p.m., the resource works from 8 a.m.–2 p.m., which is the only period the calendars have in common.

✦ You can set a task to ignore Resource calendar settings by opening the Task Information dialog box (double-click the task name in Gantt Chart view) and selecting the Scheduling Ignores Resource Calendars check box on the Advanced tab. (This setting isn't available if the Task calendar is set to None.) You might select this setting if you know that all resources are required to be involved in a task, such as a quarterly company meeting, regardless of their usual work hours.

Understanding Calendar Options and Working Times

Just when you thought you were beginning to get a handle on calendars, we throw two more timing elements at you — calendar options and working times. These aren't that hard to grasp, so just hang in there!

You use *calendar options* to change the standards for a working day, week, and year. For example, if you set a Project calendar to Standard (by default, 8 a.m.–5 p.m., five days a week), the Calendar tab of the Options dialog box is where you can designate which five days are working days or modify the working hours to 9 a.m.–6 p.m.

You use *working time* to adjust the time available for work on a particular date or days. Suppose you make a change to the calendar options so that you have 8-hour days and 32-hour workweeks. You should also check your working time and be sure that you specify that three days of the seven-day week should be nonworking to jibe with the 32-hour week. If you want to set a certain date, such as your company offsite meeting day, as *nonworking* for your project, you can do that with the working time settings.

If you use Project Server to implement enterprise-wide project management, you can make settings in the Enterprise Global Template. This template sets the working time for all projects across your company. See Book X, Chapter 2 for more about the Enterprise Global template.

Setting calendar options

When you make changes to a Resource or Task calendar, you simply adjust the times that a resource is available to work or the time during which a task can occur. You don't change the length of a typical workday for your company. A day is still eight hours long if that's the Project calendar setting, even if you say that a task that takes place on that day uses the 24-hour Base calendar template.

To change the length of a typical workday to ten hours rather than eight, for example, use the Calendar tab of the Options dialog box.

Follow these steps to modify the calendar options:

1. **Choose Tools⇨Options.**

The Options dialog box appears.

2. **Click the Calendar tab, as shown in Figure 4-2.**

You can also display these settings by clicking the Options button in the Change Working Time dialog box. Read about the settings there in the following section.

3. **From the Week Starts On drop-down list, select a day.**

4. **To modify the start of your fiscal year, select the month you want from the Fiscal Year Starts In drop-down list.**

5. **To change the working hours for a typical day, type new times in the Default Start Time and Default End Time fields.**

If you change the Default Start Time or Default End Time setting, you should also change the corresponding working times. See the following section to discover how to do this.

6. **Modify the Hours Per Day, Hours Per Week, and Days Per Month fields as needed.**

7. **Click OK to save the settings.**

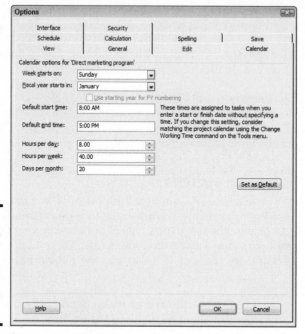

Figure 4-2:
Define your typical working day, week, month, and year.

> If your company uses the settings you specified in the previous steps for most projects, you can click the Set As Default button on the Calendar tab of the Options dialog box. Then, whenever you create a new project, these are set by default.

Making exceptions

If you want to change the available working hours for a particular day (for example to take the day before a holiday off), you use the working time settings. For example, if you want the day before Christmas to be a half day, you can modify the working time settings for that day; then any resources assigned to a task on this date put in only one-half day of work. You also use these settings to specify global working and nonworking days to match the calendar options settings.

Here's how to change working times:

1. **Choose Tools⇨Change Working Time.**

 The Change Working Time dialog box appears, as shown in Figure 4-3.

2. **In the Click On a Day to See Its Working Times calendar section, click the day you want to change.**

3. **Click the Exceptions tab to display it; then click a blank row and type a name for the exception.**

4. **Click the Details button.**

   The Details dialog box for this calendar appears (see Figure 4-4).

5. **Select either the Nonworking or Working Times radio button.**

**Book II
Chapter 4**

**Working with
Calendars**

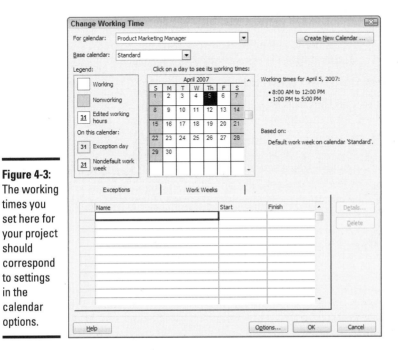

Figure 4-3: The working times you set here for your project should correspond to settings in the calendar options.

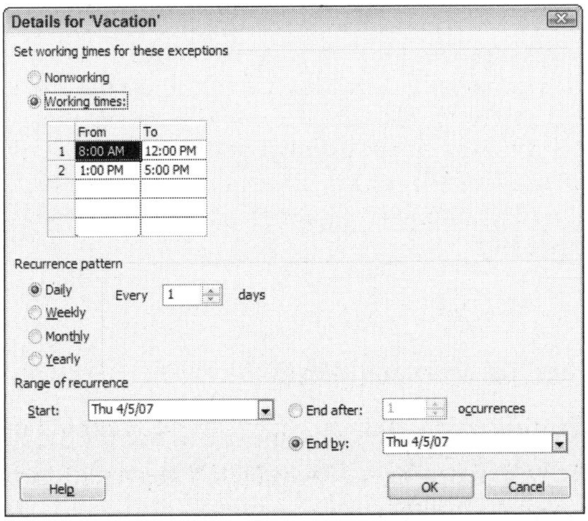

Figure 4-4: Modify the settings for the default calendar.

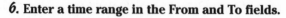

6. Enter a time range in the From and To fields.

If you want to set nonconsecutive hours (for example, to allow for working mornings, taking a lunch break, and then including afternoons), you can. Simple enter two or more sets of numbers in the time range fields, such as 8 to 12 and 1 to 5.

7. Select a recurrence pattern and then set an interval in the Every *X* field.

For example, if you select Weekly and click the arrows to set the interval field to 3, this pattern recurs every three weeks.

8. Set the range of recurrence.

You can do this step by entering Start and End By dates or by selecting the End After radio button and setting the number of occurrences there.

9. Click OK twice to close the dialog boxes and save your changes.

Use the Nondefault Work Week legend item in the Change Working Time dialog box (refer to Figure 4-3) to specify a working time that varies from the working time established by the Base calendar template for this calendar.

Getting the Project Calendar Set Up

The first calendar that you should set up for your project is the Project calendar, which sets up overall defaults. You set the Project calendar in the Project Information dialog box (shown in Figure 4-5). You can display this dialog box by choosing Project⇨Project Information.

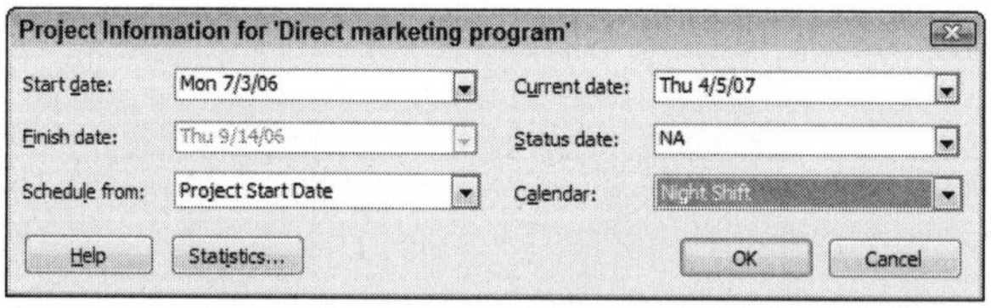

Figure 4-5:
Your choice
of calendars
includes
one of these
three Base
calendar
templates.

Project Information for 'Direct marketing program'	
Start date: Mon 7/3/06	Current date: Thu 4/5/07
Finish date: Thu 9/14/06	Status date: NA
Schedule from: Project Start Date	Calendar: Night Shift
Help Statistics...	OK Cancel

Here are the settings that you can make in the Project Information dialog box:

✦ **Calendar:** Select the Base calendar template to use for the Project calendar from this drop-down list. We list this setting first because it's the only one you *have* to deal with when you start a new project.

✦ **Start Date and Finish Date:** You might want to wait to set these dates until you build in most of your tasks and resources. Then, when you really know when you can start work, set the start date and let Project 2007 calculate the finish date based on your tasks' timing and dependencies. See more about these settings in Book IV, Chapter 1.

✦ **Schedule From:** You can choose to have tasks scheduled backward from the finish date or forward from the start date. Most folks go forward from the start date.

✦ **Current Date:** By default, this setting matches your computer clock setting. However, you can change this so that it doesn't match your computer clock setting. Changing this date is useful for looking at what-if scenarios or for tracking progress as of a certain date in the past.

✦ **Status Date:** You typically set this to the current date to track progress on your project. When tracking, you usually want to see the status of your project as of now, so you don't really need to deal with this setting. However if you want to track as of the end of a fiscal period or another timeframe, you can change this to track the status of your tasks as of any other date.

✦ **Priority:** This field is useful if your organization has many projects and you create links among them. If you use a tool such as Resource Leveling to resolve conflicts (see Book VII, Chapter 2 for more about this topic), it can consider this project's priority setting when making its calculations about what to delay and what to keep on track.

Book II Chapter 4

Working with Calendars

Letting Project Guide Make Calendar Settings For You

Project Guide includes a useful Calendar Wizard that can help you set both calendar options and working time settings. This guided procedure can be very useful when you're new to Project.

Follow these steps to make calendar options and Project calendar settings using this wizard:

1. **If Project Guide isn't already visible, you can display it at any time by choosing View⇨Toolbars⇨Project Guide.**

If the Project Guide toolbar is displayed and you want to hide it, you can click the Show/Hide Project Guide button on the Project Guide toolbar to hide it.

2. **Click the Task button if the task pane isn't already displayed.**

3. **Click the Define General Working Times item listed in the Project Guide task pane.**

The Preview Working Time calendar appears, as shown in Figure 4-6.

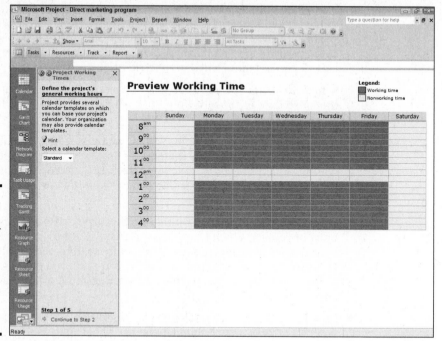

Figure 4-6:
You can choose your Base calendar and see a graphical view of it here.

4. **From the Select a Calendar Template drop-down list, select the Base calendar that you want your project to use.**

   The Calendar setting offers the three Base calendar templates: Standard, Night Shift, and 24 Hours, as described in the "How calendars work" section, earlier in this chapter; if you or an administrator has created any custom calendars, they are also listed here.

5. **Click the Continue to Step 2 option at the bottom of the Project Guide pane.**

   The task pane contents change to show check boxes for each day of the week (see Figure 4-7). If you want to change the working days in your calendar for this project, click to select or deselect any day.

6. **Click the Continue to Step 3 option, and then click Change Working Time in the task pane.**

   The Change Working Time dialog box, described in the preceding section, appears. Refer to that section to find out about changes you can make here.

7. **Click OK to close the Change Working Time dialog box and then click the Continue to Step 4 option.**

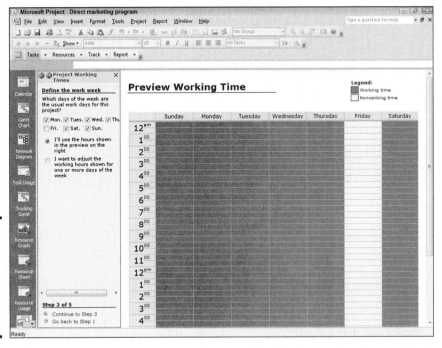

Figure 4-7:
Click and
choose
which days
you want
resources
to work.

8. **Use the three text boxes that appear in the task pane to change the Hours Per Day, Hours Per Week, and Days Per Month settings, if you want.**

9. **Click the Continue to Step 5 option.**

   A message appears in the task pane to say that the Project calendar is now set. If you want to work with other calendars at this point, you can click the Define Additional Calendars option.

10. **Click Save and Finish.**

When you choose a Base calendar template, it sets the typical working time for your company. If a few resources on your project work the night shift but the majority of your resources work a standard workday, you might want to choose the Base calendar template that applies to the majority of your resources (in this case, Standard). You can make changes to specific Resource and Task calendars later (see the next two sections).

Making Changes to Task Calendars

You can set a Task calendar to use a different Base calendar template than the one you selected for the Project calendar. When you change a Task calendar, it takes precedence over the Project calendar for that task.

Suppose that you select the Standard calendar template for a project and a 24 Hours Task calendar template. If you then specify that the task has a duration of one day, it's a 24-hour day. But remember, Resource calendar settings take precedence over the Task calendar!

To modify settings for a Task calendar, follow these steps:

1. Double-click the task name.

The Task Information dialog box appears.

2. Click the Advanced tab.

3. From the Calendar drop-down list, choose a different Base calendar, as shown in Figure 4-8.

Figure 4-8:
You can apply any of the three calendar types to tasks in your project.

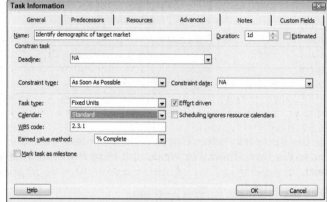

4. Click OK to save your new calendar setting.

If a resource assigned to this task has a modified calendar, that resource works only during the specific hours that the Task calendar and Resource calendar have in common.

Setting Up Resource Calendars

Even the most productive resources have only so many hours in a day to work. When you have to deal with variations in resource schedules, you can modify Resource calendars.

Calendars for different types of resources

Remember that projects can have three types of resource: Work, Material, and Cost, which you can read more about in Book V. For now, you should know that only one resource type — the Work resource — has its own calendar. That's because Material resources are charged not by time worked but rather by units used, and a Cost resource gets assigned a set cost that also doesn't relate to the amount of time worked on a task.

You can change the Base calendar template for each Work resource and set specific dates as working or nonworking. These exceptions take precedence over your Project and Task calendars, and control when a specific resource can work.

Book II
Chapter 4

Working with
Calendars

We have one word of caution about modifying Resource calendars: Unless a resource truly has a unique working schedule, don't change its Base calendar template. For example, if a resource usually works a day shift but works a night shift for only a few days during the life of the project, don't change that resource's Base calendar template to Night Shift. If one person works from 10 a.m.–7 p.m. because the company allows him to, you probably don't have to vary his schedule from the typical 8-to-5 work schedule that's set in the Project calendar because he puts in eight hours a day like everyone else. Unless your project deals with the most detailed level of time, where hours and not days are the typical units of measure for tasks, making these types of changes is more work than it's worth.

If you are trying to use a resource that is part of an enterprise pool, you will need permission to make changes to a resource. See Book 10, Chapter 3 for more about this topic.

Making changes to Resource calendars

To modify a resource's calendar settings, follow these steps:

1. **Display a view that includes a resource column, such as the Resource Sheet.**

   Just click the view in the View bar. Book I, Chapter 4 covers how to display different views.

2. **Double-click a resource name.**

   The Resource Information dialog box appears.

3. **Click the Change Working Time button to display the Change Working Time dialog box, shown in Figure 4-9.**

   The Exceptions and Work Weeks tabs have settings identical to the ones in the Change Working Time dialog box for tasks, but changes made here affect this resource rather than the task.

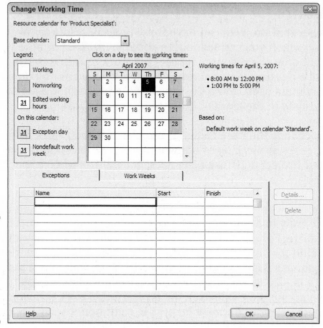

Figure 4-9:
Making
changes
here affects
this
resource.

4. **In the Click On a Day to See Its Working Times calendar section, click the day that you want to change.**

5. **Click the Work Weeks tab to display it; then click a blank row and enter a name for the exception.**

6. **Click the Details button.**

   The Details dialog box for this calendar appears (see Figure 4-10).

7. **Select either the Nonworking or the Working Times radio button.**

8. **Enter a time range in the From and To fields.**

   If you want to set nonconsecutive hours (for example, to build in a lunch break), you have to put two or more sets of numbers here, such as 8 to 12 and 1 to 5.

9. **Select a recurrence pattern and then set an interval in the Every *X* box.**

   For example, if you choose Daily and click the arrows to set the interval field to 3, this pattern recurs every three days.

10. **Set the range of recurrence.**

   You can do this by entering Start and End By dates or selecting the End After radio button and setting the number of occurrences.

11. **Click OK twice to close the dialog boxes and save your changes.**

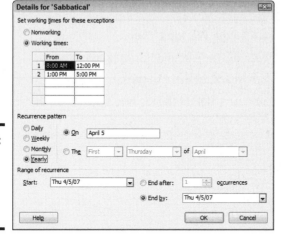

Figure 4-10:
Modify the
default
calendar
settings
here.

Resources can work overtime even if their calendars say that their regular hours are, say, 8 to 5, but you have to tell Project 2007 to schedule overtime work. You can also set a different rate to be charged for overtime work for that resource. To find out more about overtime, see Book V, Chapter 3.

Creating Your Own Custom Calendar Template

What do you do if you've got a very unique situation, calendar-wise? Although Project 2007's three Base calendar templates probably cover most working situations, you might want to create your own calendar template. For example, if your project involves a telemarketing initiative and most project resources work six hours, from 4 p.m.–10 p.m. (that's when they all call us!), it might be useful to create a new calendar template and give it a name like Telemarketers.

You can save some time when creating a custom template by starting with the existing Base calendar that most closely fits your needs. Then modify it as you like by making changes to the working times and calendar options (see the section "Understanding Calendar Options and Working Times," earlier in this chapter) to make sure that they're in agreement. After you create a new calendar template, it's then available for you to use when setting up any of the other three calendar types: Project, Task, and Resource.

Because the Project calendar is the basis of your entire project, it should represent the most common working schedule in your project. If only some resources in your project work odd hours, change the Resource calendars and not the Project calendar.

Follow these steps to create a new calendar template:

1. **Choose Tools⇨Change Working Time.**

The Change Working Time dialog box appears.

2. **Click the Create New Calendar button.**

The Create New Base Calendar dialog box appears, as shown in Figure 4-11.

Figure 4-11:
Start your
new
calendar
here.

3. **In the Name box, type a unique name for the new calendar.**

4. **Select either the Create New Base Calendar or the Make a Copy Of** *X* **Calendar radio button. Then select an existing Base calendar from the list to base your calendar template on.**

In Step 4, if you choose Create New Base Calendar, Project creates a copy of the Standard calendar with a new name. If you choose Make a Copy Of and select 24 Hours or Night Shift, your new calendar is based on that choice. Whichever you choose, it's your starting point, and you can make changes to make the calendar unique after making this choice.

5. **Click OK to return to the Change Working Time dialog box.**

Now you can make changes to the working time for the new calendar template.

6. **Click Options.**

The Options dialog box appears with the Calendar tab displayed.

7. **Make changes to the start of the week or year, the start and end times for a workday, and the hour or day settings.**

8. **Click OK twice to save the new calendar settings.**

Sharing Calendars with Other Projects

You can make a calendar available for all projects in two ways:

✦ **Set a calendar as the default for all new projects by making that choice in the Change Working Time dialog box.**

✦ **Make calendars from one project available for use in another project.**

This second method is especially useful when you want to share calendars with other project managers in your company and don't want to change your own default calendar.

To copy a calendar from one project to another, follow this procedure:

1. **Open the project to which you want to copy a calendar.**

2. **Choose Tools⇨Organizer.**

The Organizer dialog box appears.

3. **Click the Calendars tab, as shown in Figure 4-12.**

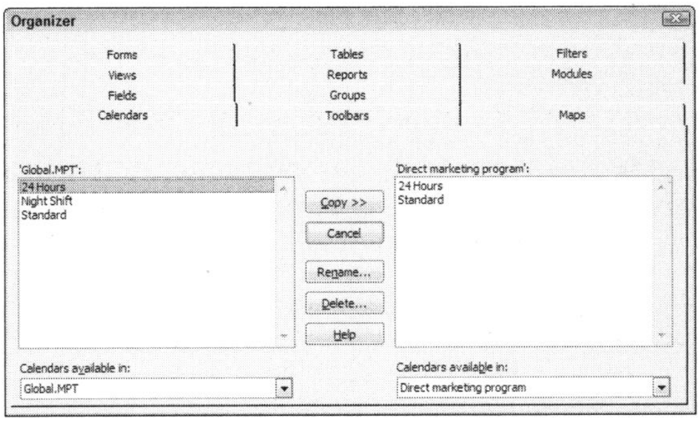

**Book II
Chapter 4**

**Working with
Calendars**

Figure 4-12:
You can
copy your
calendar
to other
projects.

4. **From the Calendars Available In drop-down list (lower left), select the Project 2007 file that contains the calendar you want to copy.**

5. **In the Calendars Available In drop-down list (lower right), choose whether you want to make the calendar available in another currently open project or the Global template.**

6. **In the list on the left, click the calendar you want to copy and then click the Copy button.**

The calendar is copied to the current project.

7. **If you want to give the calendar a different name, click the Rename button, type a new name in the Rename dialog box that appears, and then click OK.**

8. **Close the Organizer by clicking the close button (the X) in the upper-right corner.**

Here are a few pointers about copying calendars from project to project:

✦ **Make sure that the name you give the calendar is descriptive.**
   Providing an appropriate name helps you remember the calendar's general parameters.

✦ **If your company has standard calendars, try having one resource create and disseminate them.** If ten versions of a management calendar float around and you grab the wrong one, it can cause problems.

✦ **Put the project manager's initials in each calendar template name you create.** That way, you know which ones you created.

Chapter 5: Getting Help

Microsoft Office Project 2007 is a complex product that offers a wealth of functionality. But all that functionality comes at a price: It's not always perfectly obvious how the many tools at your disposal work or how to find the information about your project that you need.

That's where Project's Help feature comes in. In Project Help, you can look up information or get answers to questions; go online and tap into a wider range of information and advice; run Diagnostics that tell you what to do if you're having problems with the Project software; or let a guide take you through the process of creating a project.

Entering the Universe of Project Help

Because you probably use software day in and day out, you probably have used a Help feature before. Though they all have similarities, they all are slightly different, as well. Project 2007 Help relies heavily on online resources, though it also contains a built-in knowledge base of help topics, accessed through a Table of Contents.

Here's a rundown of the type of help you can find in Project 2007 when you click the Help icon on the Standard toolbar. As you can see from this list, you have several ways to get to help in Project:

✦ **Microsoft Office Project Help:** This option displays the full Help feature with a Browse feature, Table of Contents, and a Search field.

✦ **Microsoft Office Online:** Because Project is part of the Office family of products, this link to the Office Online Assistance Center is provided.

✦ **Microsoft Office Diagnostics:** This option automatically identifies errors and tries to correct them. Use it if you have serious problems using the software (for example, if the software continually shuts down or displays error messages).

One helpful option not accessed from the Help menu, Project Guide, offers step-by-step guidance to help you build a new project (see the last section of this chapter for more about Project Guide).

Exploring Microsoft Office Project Help

Though this portion of Help sports some new features and a look that differs from Project 2003, it offers similar functionality. Essentially you can click on the links in the Browse Project Help list to display articles of information, locate a help topic in a Table of Contents, or use a search tool to search the Help knowledge base.

Click the Help menu and choose the Microsoft Office Project Help option, or simply click the Microsoft Office Project Help button on the Standard toolbar to display the window shown in Figure 5-1.

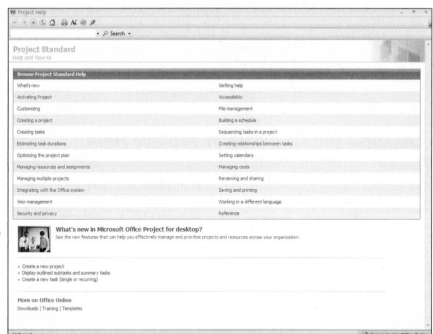

Figure 5-1:
The main
Microsoft
Office
Project Help
window.

Browsing topics

Home in the Microsoft Office Project Help window consists of a list of topics labeled Browse Project Help (refer to Figure 5-1). By clicking a topic, you can drill down to articles of information related to a major topic.

For example, if you click a topic such as Estimating Task Durations, you see a further list of subtopics like the one shown in Figure 5-2.

By clicking one of these subtopics, you can display an article about the topic, which often includes step-by-step instructions (see Figure 5-3). Here are a few guidelines for getting the most out of these subtopics:

**Book II
Chapter 5**

Getting Help

+ A blue arrow pointing to the right indicates that additional detail is hidden there. Click the arrow to display the information.

+ A word formatted in color displays a further explanation or definition of the term when you click it.

+ To show every definition and any hidden text, click the Show All icon at the top of the page.

+ In longer articles, take advantage of the Top of Page and In This Article links to move quickly around the information.

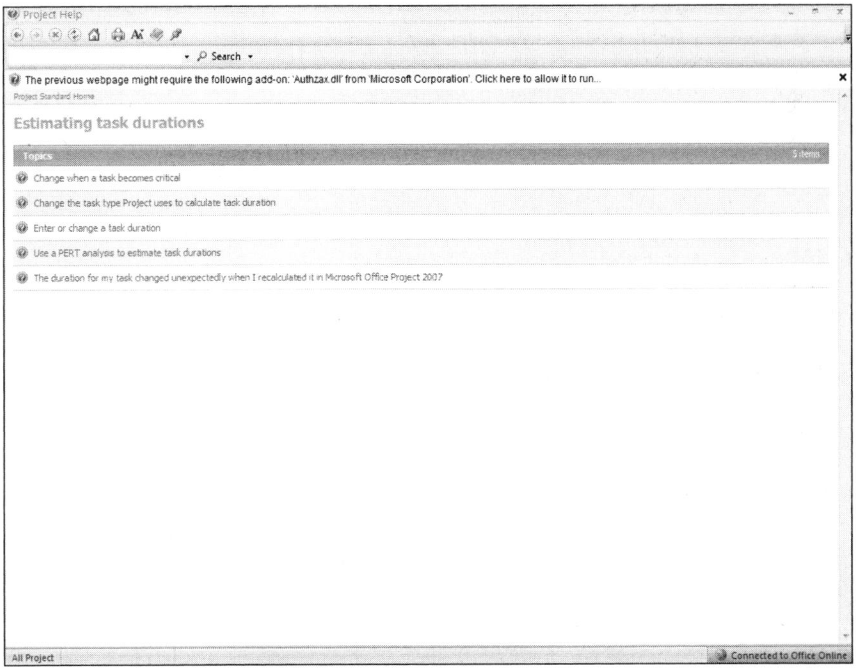

Figure 5-2:
Browsing through subtopics in Help.

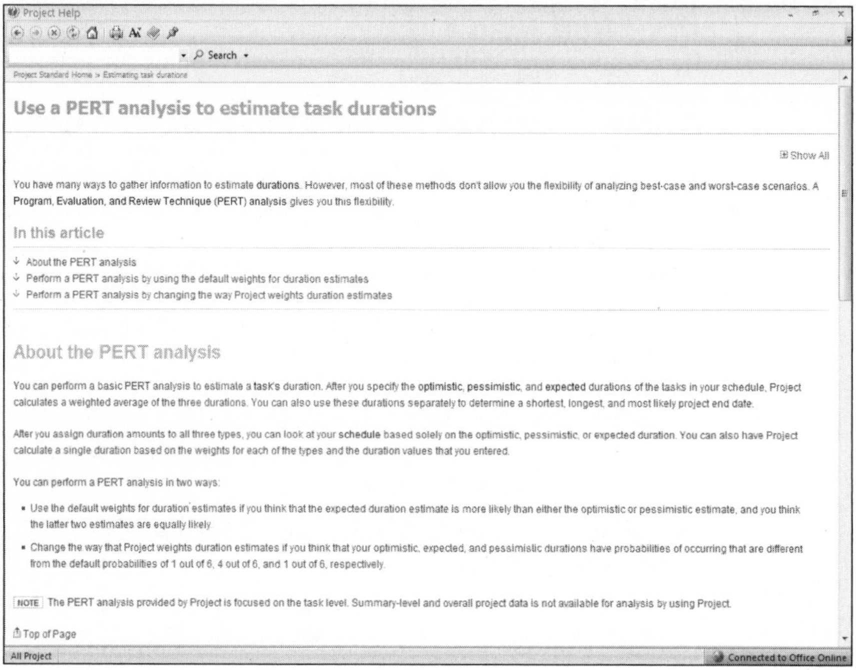

Figure 5-3:
Help articles cover a wide variety of topics.

Using the Table of Contents

When you display the Help window (click the Microsoft Office Project Help button on the Standard toolbar), note the set of tools at the top. One of these, shaped like a little blue book, is the Show Table of Contents button. When you click this button, a pane opens on the left of the window that shows a list of all Help topics. You can click a book icon to the left of a major topic to display its subtopics (see Figure 5-4).

The topics and subtopics listed in the Table of Contents are the same as those listed in the Browse Project Help section to the right of this pane. However, by displaying the Table of Contents, you can display all subtopics in a single list, rather than going to a new window to view each set of subtopics as you do when you use the Browse feature. This capability might help you spot the subtopic you need more easily.

Searching for Help

You can search for help in two ways. One method is to simply enter a question in the Ask a Question box on the Project page and press Enter (see Figure 5-5). This brings up the Help window with suggested topic matches. Click a topic to view it.

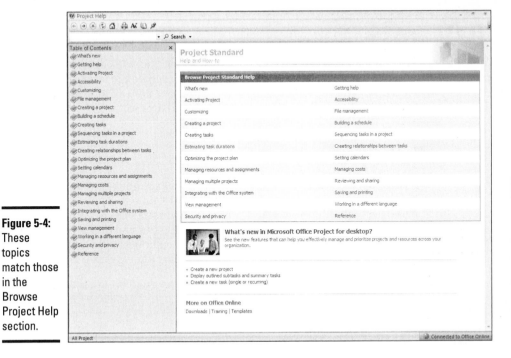

Figure 5-4:
These
topics
match those
in the
Browse
Project Help
section.

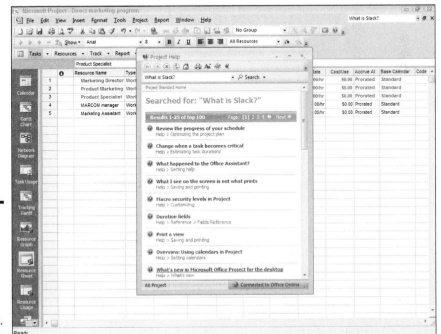

Figure 5-5:
If your
search
returns lots
of results,
click the
Next button
to see more.

Microsoft advises that searches with two to seven words in them get the best results. So avoid using single words and avoid getting too wordy!

The second place to search from is within the Microsoft Office Project Help window. Enter words or a question in the Search box located there (refer to Figure 5-5) and then click Search. Again, results appear, and you can browse through them or click one to read the related article.

Going Online to Find the Answer

If you want a broader universe of answers to explore and to be sure you have the most up-to-date help information, it's time to leave the knowledge database built into Project and wander around the Internet. When you take this trip through the Microsoft Office Online command in the Help menu, you end up at the Microsoft Office Online site shown in Figure 5-6. Here you find downloadable clip art, templates, training, and advice.

Figure 5-6:
Microsoft Office's online resource for templates, training, help, and more.

When you go to the Microsoft Office Online site, follow these steps to get help with Project:

1. **Click the Products tab.**

2. **Click the Project link in the list of desktop products on the left.**

The Microsoft Office Project 2007 page appears (see Figure 5-7).

At this point, you find a variety of links that offer you options, which might change slightly over time, but which might include

- Getting help on specific tasks such as creating a new task

- Taking an online test drive of product features

- Exploring advice via the Ask the Experts feature that enables you to communicate with the Project community

- Running Project training courses (see Figure 5-8) and demos

- Clicking a Product Support link that takes you to how-to and troubleshooting articles

3. **When you're done working online, simply click the Close button to close your browser and return to Project.**

Figure 5-7: The Project 2007 page of the Microsoft Office Online site.

Figure 5-8:
A free
online
training
course.

Running Diagnostics

Sometimes the problem isn't that you can't figure out how to do something in Project; sometimes the problem is that Project itself isn't working correctly. When that happens, you can run Diagnostics, which test your computer to see why you might be experiencing crashes while using Project.

Diagnostics check for a few possible problems, including those caused by

✦ Hard drive errors

✦ Conflicting Office programs

✦ Missing updated service packs for Office that might correct bugs or errors

✦ Memory

Running Diagnostics can take about 15 minutes, so be prepared to take a break from your work. Also, it's a good precaution to close all other programs while running Diagnostics.

You can follow these steps to use Diagnostics:

1. **Choose Help⇨Microsoft Office Diagnostics.**

2. **In the dialog box that appears, click Continue**.

The Start Diagnostics dialog box shown in Figure 5-9 appears.

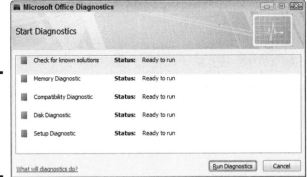

Figure 5-9:
A list of possible diagnostics appears here.

3. **Click Run Diagnostics.**

The tests run and display progress and results. When the tests are complete, a window might appear telling you whether any repairs were made.

4. **Click the Detailed Results link to get more information about the repairs.**

Putting Project Guide to Work

Project Guide is a wizard-like tool that helps step you through the process of building a project. If you've never used project management software (or Project itself), you might find it helpful to run through Project Guide when you're faced with a new project. Project Guide helps you work through the entire life of your project, helping you to enter task information at the start, add resources, track the project, and even generate your final report.

Where Project Guide can lead you

Project Guide is divided into four sections: Tasks, Resources, Track, and Report. Within each of those categories are ten or so links for you to click to initiate an action. When you do so, you might have to choose a variety of subactions, depending on what you need to do to create your particular project.

To know how to make intelligent choices in Project Guide, you need some basic understanding of how a project is built, which we provide starting in this minibook. Our advice is to walk with us through many of the steps in this book and then use Project Guide to practice building your first project. Then you make intelligent choices about how to use the various options Project Guide offers.

Getting to work with Project Guide

A Project Guide toolbar displays by default as the bottommost of the toolbars at the top of your Project screen (see Figure 5-10). The toolbar includes an icon you click to show or hide Project Guide, so if Project Guide doesn't appear on the left side of your screen, just click the Show/Hide Project Guide button.

Figure 5-10:
The Project
Guide
toolbar.

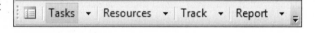

To use the Project Guide, you click a category on the Project Guide toolbar (such as Tasks) and then click a link in the drop-down list of items (such as List the Tasks in the Project). This displays additional information in the Project Guide pane (see Figure 5-11) asking you to enter data or choose or accept a setting and move through a series of screens. When you finish working through one set of screens, you return to the Project Guide pane and can click another task or category to proceed.

Microsoft laid out these categories and tasks in the logical order in which you should tackle them to build most projects. Therefore it's a good idea, when you start to use Project Guide, to just click the categories and the tasks within them in sequence. Each item serves to remind you of all the things you should consider (and even a few things you might have forgotten you need to do), even if you choose to skip a few steps here and there for your particular project.

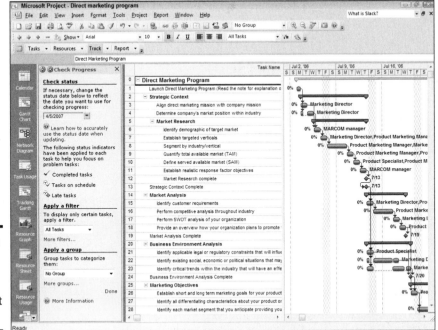

Figure 5-11:
A typical
information
request
from Project
Guide.

Book III

Getting Your Plan in Order

The 5th Wave   By Rich Tennant

Ned Beally, of Beally Construction Co., helps his children with a Lego® Mindstorms™ robotics project.

@RICHTENNANT

"Oh, big surprise — another announcement of cost overruns and a delayed completion date."

Contents at a Glance

Chapter 1: Organizing the Structure of a Project Plan

In This Chapter

✔ Understanding a project's outline structure

✔ Promoting and demoting tasks

✔ Reorganizing the outline

There's nothing stopping you from creating a project schedule that simply lists your tasks and subsequently creating links that identify which tasks depend on other tasks. But, if you take advantage of Project's outlining capabilities, you establish additional visual cues that help you easily identify related tasks and help you organize both your project and your thoughts.

Project provides several ways to organize tasks in the schedule; in this chapter, you work with the basic ways Project can outline tasks in a schedule.

A To-Do List . . . or a Project Schedule?

If you simply type tasks into a project schedule, you end up with a schedule that looks just like a to-do list. Even when you later add dependencies, the titles of the tasks still look just like a to-do list (see Figure 1-1).

Although there's nothing wrong with a to-do list, an *organized* to-do list is typically more useful. From an organized to-do list, you can get a sense of which tasks are related to other tasks by simply looking at the list. Using the outlining features available in Project, you can look at the table portion (the spreadsheet-like interface in the left pane that contains columns of information) of Gantt Chart view to identify related tasks without looking at the chart portion (the right pane) of the view to study dependencies (see Figure 1-2).

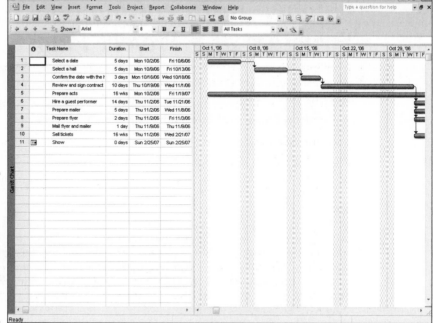

Figure 1-1:
When you don't organize your project schedule, your task list resembles a to-do list.

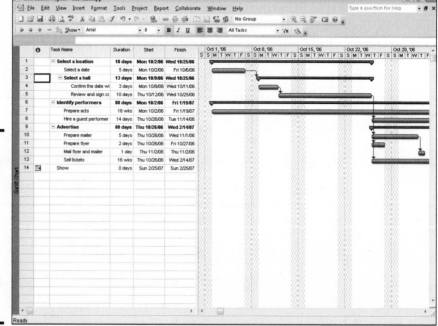

Figure 1-2:
When you take advantage of outlining, you get a sense of related tasks from the table portion of any view.

Building an outline

So, how do you actually go about building an organized outline? No hard and fast rules exist, so just use the approach that works best for you:

✦ Some people like to list all the major headings first and then fill in more detailed information below each major heading.

✦ Other people like to list everything they can think of and then focus on sorting those items in orderly and logical groups.

✦ Still other people work on one phase at a time, listing its major heading and then the tasks associated with it.

✦ And then there's the group of people who use combinations of all of these methods.

"I've got a little list . . ."

One of the major questions facing a project manager is, "What should I include and what should I exclude?" A sketchy project schedule has holes that can threaten the integrity of the schedule, leaving you late on delivery and overbudget. A schedule filled with excessive detail can make you lose focus of the project's purpose.

When you're making that list of tasks to include in your project, help yourself focus by defining both the goal and the scope of your project. Lack of a clearly defined goal and scope is among the top five reasons that projects fail. So, don't set yourself and your project up for failure; before you dive into entering data in a project management software package, settle the matters of goal and scope for your project.

To identify your goal, ask yourself, "What will my project achieve? What will have changed when I complete my project?" Will you, for example, have put on a conference, built a building, or trained a staff?

To define the scope of your project, ask yourself questions like these:

✦ What is my project's budget?

✦ Who will be affected by my project — my entire company, the IT department, or my workgroup in Human Resources?

✦ How many people will work on or have input into my project?

✦ Does my project have a deadline date and, if so, what is it?

For more on a project's scope and goal, see Book I, Chapter 3.

Book III Chapter 1

Organizing the Structure of a Project Plan

A typical project outline

Whether you're writing a paper or preparing a project schedule, an outline is an outline. It contains higher-level headings that summarize the topics of the lower-level headings below. Yep, just like your English teacher taught you.

If you look closely at the project outline shown back in Figure 1-2, you notice that it organizes the tasks into three levels, and each level represents a collection of tasks that you can consider a phase of your project. A task that has other tasks indented below it is called a *summary task,* and the indented tasks are called *subtasks.* Summary tasks appear in boldface type, and you can easily identify them because a plus sign (+) or a minus sign (–) appears beside the task name. When you see a plus sign beside a summary task, its subtasks are hidden. The subtasks are visible when a minus sign appears beside the summary task name.

You can have just about as many levels of detail as you want in a schedule, but before you get "level-happy," consider that tracking a very detailed project can be difficult. In addition, if you find yourself building a project schedule with four, five, or six levels, you might actually be building several projects. When you find yourself with many levels, you might want to consider taking a group of tasks and turning it into a separate project, with a separate project manager. By dividing that many-level project into several smaller projects, managing the projects should be easier. And, even if the phases relate and seem to be part of the same project, you can still break them into separate projects and then consolidate the smaller projects when you need to view the big picture.

You can read more about consolidating projects in Chapter 4 of this minibook.

Summary tasks are special

A summary task isn't one to which you assign resources to accomplish; it's a placeholder task in Project that you can use to get a feel, at a glance, for the duration and cost of a set of tasks — a phase — of your project.

In addition to appearing in boldface type, a summary task has no duration, start date, or finish date of its own. Instead, the duration, start date, and finish date of the summary task all summarize the information of the subtasks indented below the summary task. And, by default, Project changes the appearance of the bar in the chart portion of Gantt Chart view to a solid black bar with downward-pointing arrows at the beginning and ending dates of the period covered by the subtasks that the summary task summarizes.

In Figure 1-3, the Select a Location summary task is expected to take 18 days to complete, and 18 days is the sum of the durations of the subtasks shown below Select a Location. The start date and finish date for the summary task are, respectively, the start date of the earliest subtask and the end date of the latest subtask.

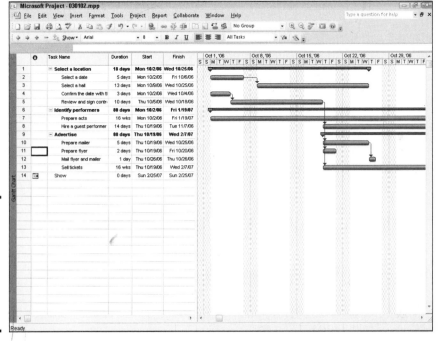

Figure 1-3:
A summary task summarizes the information shown for its subtasks.

Book III Chapter 1

Organizing the Structure of a Project Plan

In addition to summarizing duration information, a summary task, by default, has no cost of its own. However, you can assign a cost to a summary task by assigning a resource to the summary task. The cost of a summary task includes the cost of the resource you assigned to it plus the cost of the subtasks below it.

The most special task of them all — the project summary task

Ideally, you'd like one more summary task — one for the entire project. This is called the *project summary task*. Take the easy way to achieve this and let Project insert the project summary task for you. Follow these steps:

1. **Choose Tools⇨Options.**

2. **Click the View tab.**

3. **Click Show Project Summary Task.**

4. **Click OK.**

Project adds, on Row 0, a summary task at the top of your schedule, naming the task with the name you assigned to the file in which you saved your schedule. I like the name of the project summary task to match the project name, and that's what happens by default if I name the file using the project name.

5. **(Optional) Change the name of the project summary task and press Enter.**

If, however, you prefer to name the file something different than the project name and you want the summary task to reflect the project name, no problem. Just edit the Task Name of the summary task by clicking in the Task Name column and pressing F2. Then type a new name and press Enter. In Figure 1-4, you see a project file with a name that's different from the project's summary task name.

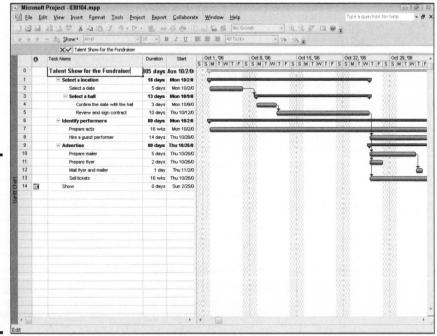

Figure 1-4:
You can change the name Project assigns to the summary task by editing the Task Name.

Although you might think that setting the option to display the project summary task applies to all projects, it doesn't. If you want to display a project summary task, you need to set this option in each project file you create.

Creating Structure in the Schedule

After you identify the tasks that you want to include in the outline, you can add structure to the outline — and obtain peace of mind — by grouping the tasks into phases of your project and establishing summary tasks for each phase. Adding structure enables you to easily identify, at a glance, related tasks, helping you organize both your project and your thoughts.

Selecting tasks

Many of the activities involved in adding structure to your outline require that you select a task. You can use any of the techniques in Table 1-1 to select tasks, depending on what you want to select.

Table 1-1	Selecting Tasks
To Select This . . .	*Do This . . .*
A single task	Click its Gantt bar or its ID number.
Several contiguous tasks	Select the first task. Then hold down Shift and click the last task that you want to select.
Several noncontiguous tasks	Hold down Ctrl as you click the ID numbers or Gantt bars of the tasks that you want to select.

Promoting and demoting tasks

You use the Indent and Outdent buttons on the Formatting toolbar in Project to create an outline of summary tasks and subtasks. Select the task you want to indent or outdent and then click the appropriate button. To indent or outdent several tasks, select all of the tasks and then click the appropriate button.

When you indent a task, Project makes that task a subtask of the task that precedes it in the Task Name column, and that preceding task becomes a summary task. Outdenting a task moves the task to a higher level in the outline and can change the status of a summary task to a task or subtask if you outdent the only subtask of a summary task.

In Figure 1-5, Select a Location is a summary task and Select a Date is a subtask of the Select a Location summary task. To change Select a Location from a summary task to a regular task, we would need to outdent the task that appears immediately below the summary task, eliminating both the conceptual and visual status of the summary task.

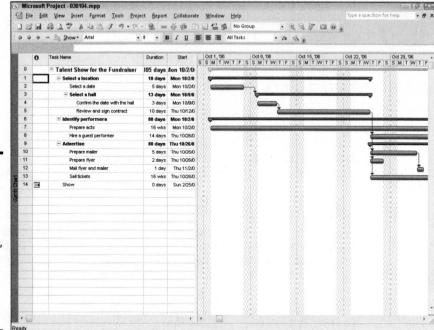

Figure 1-5:
To change any summary task to a regular task, outdent the task that appears on the line below it.

Expanding and collapsing the outline

Outlining is the tool of choice for organizing your thoughts. In writing, outlining helps you identify major topics and topics subordinate to the major topics. You not only identify what you want to write about, but you also identify an order in which to write. Also, you can easily focus on one area of the outline.

Outlining in software products adds some delightful capabilities. In Project, you can hide all tasks except the most major ones — the ones at the left edge of the outline. You also can display the subtasks of only one major heading. Or you can hide all subtasks but display the major headings of your choice. To take advantage of these delightful capabilities, you need only to have indented some tasks, creating summary tasks and subtasks.

You can use outlining to help you focus your attention. You might want to display only summary tasks for a project while talking to your boss. During a meeting, you might want to collapse all portions of the outline except the portion being discussed in the meeting. You also can close most of the outline so that you can easily jump to a later phase in the project without scrolling endlessly.

For any summary task, you can use the Show Subtasks and the Hide Subtasks buttons on the Formatting toolbar to expand or collapse the outline. Select a summary task and click the appropriate button. If a plus sign (+) appears beside a summary task, Project has collapsed that portion of the outline and hidden the subtasks below the summary task. If a minus sign (–) appears beside a summary task, Project expands that portion of the outline and displays the subtasks of that summary task. In Figure 1-6, we've collapsed the entire schedule except the subtasks below the Identify Performers summary task.

In addition to the Show Subtasks and Hide Subtasks buttons on the Formatting toolbar, you can click the plus and minus symbols beside the name of each summary task to collapse or expand that portion of the outline.

 You also can use the Show button to control which levels of tasks appear as you view the schedule. When you click the Show button, Project displays a list, as shown in Figure 1-7; choose the outline level to display. For example, display Outline Level 1 to see only the highest level tasks in the schedule.

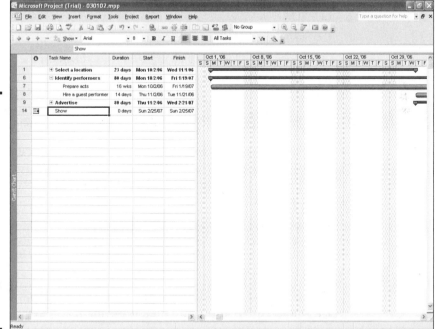

Figure 1-6: You can identify expanded and collapsed portions of the project outline from the plus or minus symbol beside each summary task.

Book III Chapter 1

Organizing the Structure of a Project Plan

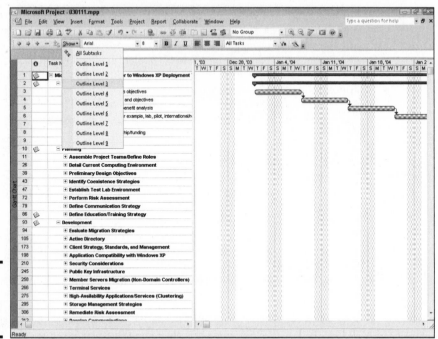

Figure 1-7:
Select an
outline level
to display.

You can choose the All Subtasks command from the Show list to display all
tasks in your schedule.

So, What Happens When You Reorganize the Outline?

You can easily reorganize a schedule after you initially set it up. You can add,
delete, move, and copy tasks.

Adding tasks

As you created your list of tasks, you might not have thought about adding
tasks that serve as summary tasks. Or, you might have simply forgotten a
task. No worries — you can easily add a task. To add a task, follow these
steps:

1. **Position the cell pointer on the task that should appear below the new
task you intend to insert and then press the Insert key.**

Project inserts a blank row in the sheet pane (see Figure 1-8), renumbering the rows of the tasks that fall below the new row.

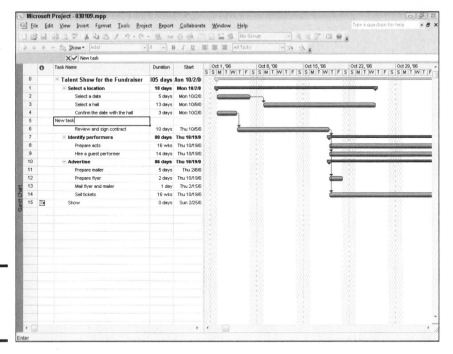

Figure 1-8:
Inserting
a task is
simple.

2. **Type a title for the task and, if you're creating a new task for the project, supply a duration.**

If you're creating a summary task for a phase, you can skip entering the duration because Project calculates the summary task's duration as the sum of the durations of its subtasks.

3. **Press Enter to finish the process.**

For more on setting up any task as a summary task, read the section "Promoting and demoting tasks," earlier in this chapter.

Deleting tasks

It happens — you set up a task and then realize that you don't need it. You can easily delete it by following these steps:

1. **Select the task by using any of the techniques described earlier in this chapter and press the Delete key.**

Because deleting a summary task has ranging effects, Project displays a dialog box after you press the Delete key to confirm that you really want to delete the summary task and all of its subtasks (see Figure 1-9).

If you delete a summary task, Project also deletes all of the summary task's subtasks. Make sure this is what you really want to do before deleting any summary tasks.

2. **Select Continue or Cancel and then click OK.**

   If you choose to continue, Project deletes the task.

Figure 1-9:
If you delete a summary task, you also delete all of its subtasks.

"Doing it over and over again . . ."

You might need to include tasks in your project that occur at some regular interval — what Project calls a *recurring task*. For example, perhaps you need to review some work daily. You can avoid the drudge of setting up these tasks and let Project set them up for you. Use the Recurring Task feature by following these steps:

1. **Select the task that you want to appear below the recurring task.**

2. **Choose Insert➪Recurring Task to open the Recurring Task Information dialog box, as shown in Figure 1-10.**

Figure 1-10:
Use this dialog box to create a task that occurs at regular intervals.

3. **Type a name for the recurring task.**

4. **Set the task duration in the Duration field.**

5. **Set the pattern for the occurrence of the task by selecting one of the Recurrence Pattern option buttons: Daily, Weekly, Monthly, or Yearly.**

   Depending on the recurrence that you select, the timing settings to the right of the control buttons change. Figure 1-10 shows daily settings.

6. **Select the appropriate settings for the recurrence frequency.**

   If you choose Weekly, place a check mark next to the day(s) of the week on which you want the task to occur. If you choose Monthly, select either the date of each month or the day, such as the third Wednesday. If you choose Yearly, select a specific date or a day, such as the second Thursday in March.

7. **In the Range of Recurrence section, set the period during which the task should recur by entering Start and End After or End By dates.**

8. **Click OK.**

Project creates the appropriate number of tasks above the task you selected in Step 1 and displays them as subtasks under a summary task with the name that you supplied in Step 2. In Figure 1-11, you can see the recurring daily task we created; the symbol in the Indicators column identifies the task as a recurring task. If you hover the cursor over the Indicators column, Project displays the number of times the task occurs between its start and end dates. When you expand the task, you see that Project adds the number of the occurrence to the task name of each recurring task.

Moving tasks

Moving tasks and subtasks isn't a difficult proposition; you just need to be aware of the effects that moving summary and subtasks can have on the schedule's outline:

✦ When you move a summary task, its subtasks move with it. To move a summary task only (without moving any of its subtasks), you must first promote all its subtasks so that the summary task is no longer a summary task.

✦ If you move a task at the highest level of the outline to a new location just below a task with subtasks, Project demotes the task that you move.

✦ If you move a subtask so that it appears below a task at the highest level of the outline, Project promotes the subtask that you move.

To move tasks in an outline, you can drag and drop or you can cut and paste.

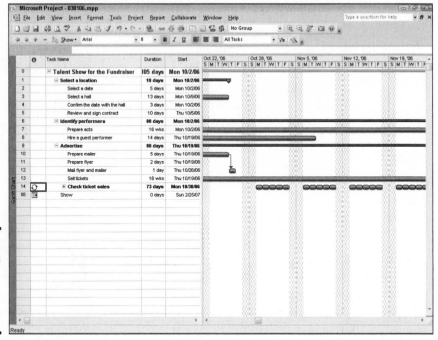

Figure 1-11:
Project uses an indicator to identify a recurring task.

Moving by dragging

You can easily move a task by dragging it to a new location using these steps:

1. **Display a view that contains a table, such as Gantt Chart view.**

2. **Select the task(s) you want to move using any of the techniques described in the preceding section.**

   If you select a summary task, Project automatically selects its subtasks for the move.

3. **In the row number column, drag the task to the place in the task list where you want it to appear.**

   A gray line appears, identifying the place where the task will appear (see Figure 1-12).

4. **When the gray line appears where you want the task to appear, release your mouse button.**

   Project moves the task from its original location to the new one; you can change the task's level in the outline by indenting or outdenting it.

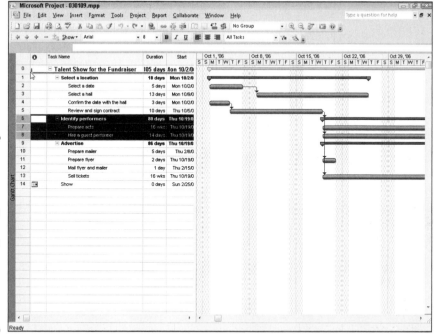

Figure 1-12:
The gray line running across the table portion of the view identifies the proposed position of the task you're moving.

Moving by cutting

If you're not dealing with a lot of tasks in a project schedule, dragging works well. But, if your project contains lots of tasks, dragging to find the target location can be difficult; and, if you're like us, you run the risk of accidentally releasing that mouse button earlier than you intended (we can be clumsy with the mouse). So, consider using the Cut and Paste tools on the Standard toolbar to move your tasks. Follow these steps:

1. **Display a view that contains a table, such as Gantt Chart view.**

2. **Select the task(s) you want to move using any of the techniques described earlier in this chapter.**

3. **Click the Cut tool on the Standard toolbar.**

   Project removes the task from the outline and places the task information on the Windows Clipboard. If you selected a summary task, Project asks whether you really want to remove the summary task and all its subtasks.

4. **Scroll to the place in the task list where you want the task to appear.**

5. **Click the task that appears below the place where you want the task you're moving to appear.**

6. Click the Paste tool.

Using the information stored on the Windows Clipboard, Project displays the task(s) you cut in the new location.

You might need to adjust the task's position in the outline by using the Indent and Outdent buttons.

Copying tasks

Copying tasks in a schedule is a simple matter. To copy a single task, follow the steps in the preceding section, but select the Copy tool in Step 3 instead of the Cut tool.

Planning for a regular meeting

Company: A law firm with more than 75 employees that depends on word-processing software

Project: Upgrade the word-processing software on all computers in the firm to Word 2007

Challenge: Meet regularly to monitor team progress during the planning phase of the project

Because the law firm depends on word processing, migrating to a new word-processing package is a huge project. To effectively manage the project, the project manager has set up a separate project for the planning phase. The project manager is concerned about communication during the planning phase, which will impact all other phases. During the planning phase, several resources will be performing a variety of tasks. Existing hardware and operating systems must be identified and assessed to ensure that they can support the new software. Existing documents and templates must be evaluated and assessed to determine which will be converted, which will be used "as-is," and which will be redone. Compatibility issues must be examined with other software used by the firm and by other

firms with which the firm interacts. Potential customization issues need to be identified. Network, browser, and Internet profiles need to be established. Security and Training needs must be addressed.

Because the findings of one team member can affect the analysis of other team members, the project manager has decided to include weekly meetings in the project plan during the planning phase to exchange findings. The meetings will be held every Thursday, and team members can place this meeting on their calendars.

Solution: To include this weekly meeting in the project schedule, the project manager sets up a recurring task that will last over the life of the planning phase of the project, which is projected to last approximately 53 days, as shown in the duration column for the summary task in the figure. The project manager uses the summary task bar of the Planning phase to identify the starting and ending dates of the Planning phase, determining that the phase is scheduled to begin on December 26, 2006 and end on March 8, 2007.

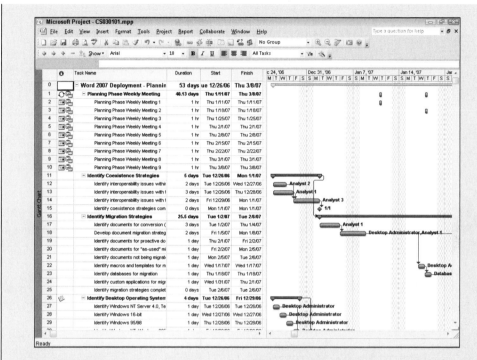

If you open the project file for this case study on our book's Web site, you can hover the cursor over the Indicators column to see the information stored about each occurrence of the recurring task. You also can double-click the summary task for the recurring task to view the settings we used to create this weekly recurring task.

Suppose, though, that you have a series of tasks that you need to repeat in the outline. For example, when planning to install new software company-wide, you typically set up test environments that mirror the conditions under which the new software will run, and then you test the software repeatedly. So, the test plan portion of your project plan might include tasks like Run Test Case, Record Results, Revise Test Case, Rerun The Test, and Record Revision Case Results for each test case you devise. Instead of typing these tasks repeatedly, you could enter them once and then use the Fill handle — a small black square that appears in the lower-right corner of a selected cell — to copy them repeatedly. When all the repeated tasks appear in the project plan, you can simply insert summary tasks that represent each of the test cases and therefore distinguish the groups of repeated tasks from each other.

WARNING! The Fill handle copies tasks into a contiguous range. If the range already contains information, using the Fill handle to copy overwrites the existing information. To avoid this problem, insert blank rows in the project before using the Fill handle. Select the task that you want to appear beneath the new row and press the Insert key on your keyboard. To insert several blank rows, select the number of rows that you want to insert before pressing the Insert key.

To copy a contiguous group of repeated tasks using the Fill handle, follow these steps:

TIP

1. **Select the tasks by using any of the techniques described earlier in this chapter.**

   If you include both the task name and the duration in the selection, Project copies both the task name and the duration.

2. **Place the mouse pointer over the Fill handle in the lower-right corner of the selection.**

   The mouse pointer changes to a plus sign (+).

3. **Drag the fill handle down until you have selected the group of rows that you want to contain the repetitive tasks (see Figure 1-13).**

Fill handle

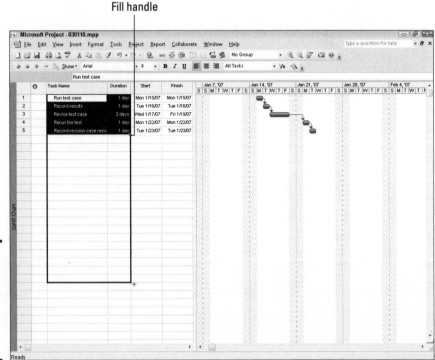

Figure 1-13:
Take advantage of the fill handle to copy tasks that repeat.

4. **Release the mouse button when you have selected the rows you want to fill.**

   Project copies the tasks into the selected range (see Figure 1-14).

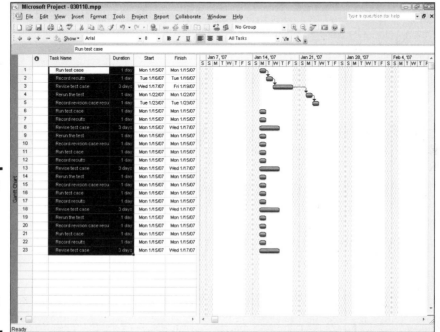

Figure 1-14:
The tasks you selected appear in the range you selected using the fill handle.

Chapter 2: Assigning Outline Codes to Tasks

In This Chapter

✔ **Understanding outline numbers**

✔ **Assigning outline numbers**

✔ **Understanding outline codes**

✔ **Creating customized outline codes**

✔ **Adjusting outline codes and renumbering**

*Y*ou have a couple of options that you can consider if you want to assign outline numbers to the tasks in your schedule. In addition to the WBS (work breakdown structure) codes described in Chapter 3 of this minibook, you can use automatic outline numbering, or you can use outline field codes.

Make the choice between outline numbers and outline codes based on whether you want the value to remain static when you make changes to the project's outline structure. When you use outline numbers, Project automatically updates the numbers if you change your project's outline structure. When you use outline codes, Project doesn't make any changes to the value when you change your project's outline structure.

Understanding Outline Numbers

Project can assign outline numbers to the tasks in your schedule based on the task's level in the outline; the *outline numbers* help you identify, visually, each task's hierarchical position in the outline. In addition, you can easily and clearly refer to tasks by using their outline number.

Project uses an outline numbering system that's similar to the numbering system you find in most legal documents. You usually find a whole number preceding each major heading in a legal document. Headings subordinate to the major heading are numbered with the major heading's whole number, a period, and then a subordinate paragraph number. So, the first paragraph under the first major heading is numbered 1.1, and the second paragraph under the first major heading is numbered 1.2.

By default, Project uses the same numbering scheme, assigning whole numbers to tasks that aren't indented at all. Subtasks are assigned outline numbers based on what task they fall under and how many times they are indented from the left edge of the outline.

Letting Project Assign Outline Numbers

You can let Project assign outline numbers that identify each task's level in the outline, as shown in Figure 2-1. Project adds a number that you *can't* edit to the task's name. Like the legal numbering scheme described in the previous section, Project assigns whole numbers to the tasks at the left edge of the outline, which are tasks at the top level of the outline. To each subtask of a task at the left edge of the outline, Project assigns the whole number, followed by a period, and then a sequential number for each subtask. Project continues to follow this pattern for any subtasks that appear beneath other subtasks. So, in Figure 2-1, the tasks at the left edge of the outline — the highest level in the outline — display numbers 1, 2, 3, and 4. Below Select a Location, which is Task 1, each subtask displays a number that includes its parent number and a sequential number for its place in the outline. The Sell Tickets task, with outline number 3.4, is the fourth subtask under the third top-level task.

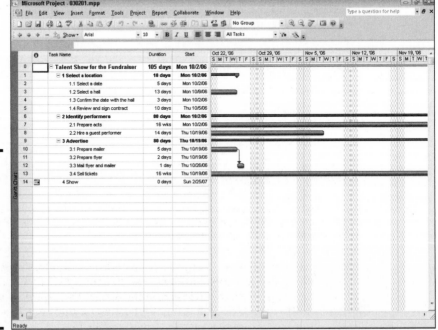

Figure 2-1:
When Project assigns outline numbers, each task's number reflects its level in the outline.

To display outline numbers, follow these steps:

1. **Choose Tools⊅Options to display the Options dialog box.**

2. **Click the View tab.**

3. **Select the Show Outline Number check box in the Outline Options section (see Figure 2-2).**

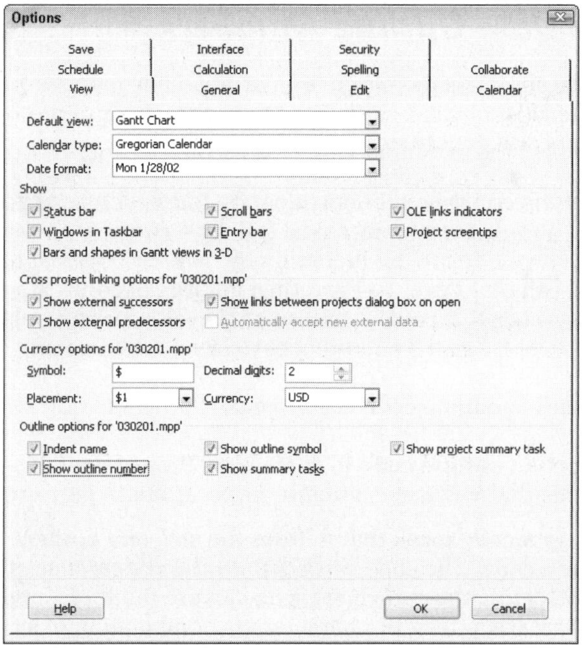

Figure 2-2:
Use the
Show
Outline
Number
check box
to add
outline
numbers to
task names.

4. **Click OK.**

Understanding Outline Codes

When you use the technique described in the preceding section to assign outline numbers, you can't edit the outline numbers. You must simply accept the outline numbers Project assigns.

Suppose, though, that you want to assign codes to your tasks that reflect the way your organization does business. For example, you might have developed accounting codes that use an outline format and you want to assign these codes to each task. You can use a custom outline code field to create your accounting codes and assign them to each task.

Project's automatic outline codes and custom outline codes aren't mutually exclusive — you can assign both to your tasks. They differ in that you can control the appearance of custom outline codes but not the appearance of Project's automatic outline numbers. In addition, outline codes aren't tied to the hierarchical structure of your project like outline numbers are but can be set up to use a hierarchical structure that you define. And, outline numbers and outline codes behave differently when you move a task.

Designing Your Own Outline Numbers

You can enter outline code information in an ad hoc manner, but most people create a list of valid outline codes so that the outline codes assigned are meaningful and consistent.

Although outline codes aren't dependent on the structure of your project outline, they do work in a hierarchical fashion — hence the name *outline code*. However, you define the hierarchy by defining codes at the highest level — we'll call that Level 1 — and then additional codes at various subordinate levels — Level 2, Level 3, and so on. Level 2 codes would appear subordinate to Level 1, Level 3 subordinate to Level 2, and so on.

Defining a custom outline code is a three-part process:

1. **You select an outline code to customize.** Project contains ten outline code fields that you can customize for a variety of purposes.

2. **You set up a code mask that defines the size and content of each portion of the code.** The *code mask* defines the appearance of the code, and when you define the code mask, you can use numbers, uppercase letters, lowercase letters, or characters (a combination of letters and numbers).

3. **You set up a lookup table for the outline code.** The *lookup table* contains the valid values for the outline code that you can assign to tasks. By using a lookup table to assign outline code values, you ensure that the outline code values you use are both valid and consistent.

Although Project won't limit you, try not to get carried away defining subordinate levels of outline codes; stacking codes deeply makes them harder to use.

Selecting an outline code to define

To complete the first part of the process of defining an outline code, follow these steps to select an outline code to define:

1. **Choose Tools⇨Customize⇨Fields.**

Project displays the Custom Fields dialog box (see Figure 2-3).

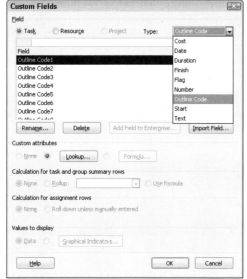

**Book III
Chapter 2**

**Assigning Outline
Codes to Tasks**

Figure 2-3:
Use this
dialog box
to define
the type of
custom field
you want
to set up.

2. **Open the Type drop-down list and select Outline Code.**

3. **Select an Outline Code from the Field section to customize.**

4. **Click the Rename button and type the new name (see Figure 2-4).**

Figure 2-4:
Renaming
the outline
code makes
it easier
for you to
remember
its purpose.

5. **Click OK to redisplay the Custom Fields dialog box.**

Continue reading the next section to define a code mask for the outline code.

Defining the code mask

We didn't ask you to close the dialog box in the previous section because you haven't finished the process of defining an outline code. When you use a code mask, you define the format of the code — the number of characters in each part of the code, and whether the characters are numbers, letters, or a combination. To define the code mask, follow these steps:

1. **Click the Lookup button.**

Project displays the Edit Lookup Table dialog box. In Figure 2-5, we've collapsed the dialog box so that you can focus on the pertinent part at this point — the code mask.

Figure 2-5: Use the options in this dialog box to define the allowable lookup codes.

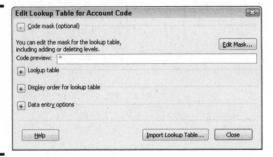

2. **To define a mask for the lookup table, click the plus sign (+) beside Code Mask.**

The plus sign changes to a minus sign (–) and displays the top portion of the Edit Lookup Table dialog box.

3. **Click the Edit Mask button.**

Project displays the Code Mask Definition dialog box, shown in Figure 2-6. As you define the code mask, Project displays filler characters in the Code Preview box.

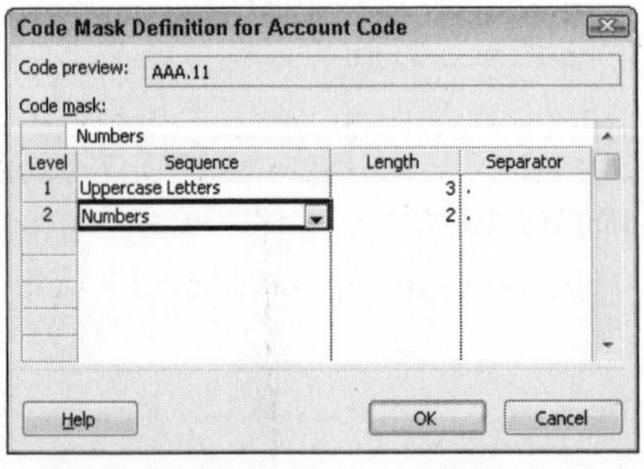

Figure 2-6: The Code Mask Definition dialog box.

4. **Click the first blank row in the Sequence column to display a drop-down arrow and select the type of character that you want to use for the first part of the outline code.**

   If you choose Characters, Project initially displays asterisks for that part of the code mask in the Code Preview box, indicating that you can replace those asterisks with any characters that you want when you define values in the Lookup Table.

5. **Click the first blank row in the Length column and then specify a length for that portion of the outline code.**

6. **Click in the first blank row of the Separator column and select a character to separate the parts of your WBS code.**

   You can choose a period (.), dash (–), plus (+), slash (/), or type any character that isn't a number or a letter (such as =).

7. **Repeat Steps 4 through 6 for each level you want to define in your outline code.**

8. **Click OK to redisplay the Edit Lookup Table dialog box.**

In the next section, you see how to create valid values that can appear as the task's outline code.

Defining values for the lookup table

Finally, to complete the process of defining an outline code, define a list of acceptable entries to use when assigning the outline code to tasks in the project. Follow these steps with the Edit Lookup Table dialog box still open:

1. **Click the plus sign beside Lookup Table.**

   Project expands the Edit Lookup Table dialog box so that you can define lookup table values (see Figure 2-7).

2. **On Row 1 of the Value column, type a permissible value for the first level of your outline code — think of it as Level 1 — and press Enter.**

   You can optionally type an explanation of the value in the Description column.

3. **On the next line, type an outline code for the second level that is permissible under Level 1 and press Enter.**

4. **Move the pointer back into the row in which you typed a Level 2 outline code and click the Indent button (the right arrow) at the top of the dialog box to indent the value.**

5. **On subsequent lines, type other acceptable Level 2 values.**

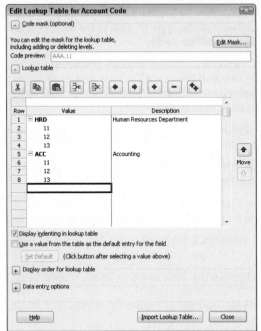

6. **If you need a Level 3 outline code under a Level 2 outline code, simply type the code on a blank line below the Level 2 outline code, press Enter, move the pointer back to the line on which you just typed the code and click the Indent button.**

7. **To supply another Level 1 code, type the code on a blank line, place the pointer on the code's row, and click the Outdent button (the left arrow) as many times as necessary, depending on the last code that you entered.**

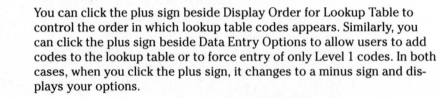 If you forget to include a code, highlight the code that you want to appear *below* the code that you'll add, and then click the Insert Row button at the top of the dialog box. And, if a code becomes invalid at some later date, reopen this dialog box, highlight the code, and click the Delete Row button.

 You can click the plus sign beside Display Order for Lookup Table to control the order in which lookup table codes appears. Similarly, you can click the plus sign beside Data Entry Options to allow users to add codes to the lookup table or to force entry of only Level 1 codes. In both cases, when you click the plus sign, it changes to a minus sign and displays your options.

8. **Click Close to redisplay the Custom Fields dialog box.**

9. **Click OK to save your outline code settings.**

Entering outline codes

After you define an outline code, you need to insert a column in a table to display outline codes. Follow these steps:

1. **Display a view that includes a table, such as Gantt Chart view.**

2. **Right-click the name of the column that you want to appear to the right of the column that will display the outline code.**

3. **Choose Insert Column from the shortcut menu that appears.**

   The Column Definition dialog box appears (see Figure 2-8).

Figure 2-8:
Use this dialog box to insert a column in the table that displays an outline code.

Book III
Chapter 2

Assigning Outline Codes to Tasks

4. **From the Field Name list, select the outline code you customized.**

   After you open the list, you can type the first letter of the name you assigned to the outline code to see the first choice in the list that begins with that letter.

5. **Click OK.**

   Project displays a column for the outline code you customized. No codes appear in the column yet because you need to use the lookup list that you defined to assign a code to each task.

6. **Enter values in the custom outline code column by clicking in the outline code column.**

   Project displays a list box arrow.

7. **Open the list to display the entries from the lookup table and select a code (see Figure 2-9).**

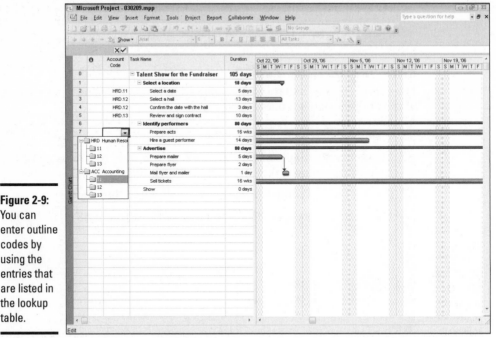

Outline Numbers and Codes and Renumbering

What happens to outline numbers and outline codes when you move tasks? Insert new tasks? Delete tasks? Well, that depends.

If you're using the outline numbers, Project renumbers affected outline numbers automatically if you move a task, insert a new task, or delete a task. In Figure 2-10, we've hidden all the subtasks except for those in the Select a Location phase. When we switch the first two subtasks, Project automatically renumbers them, as you can see in Figure 2-11. We also added a new task — cleverly named New Task — just above the Review and Sign Contract task. Project renumbered the Review and Sign Contract task from 1.4 to 1.5 to accommodate the new task's number, 1.4, and place in the outline.

Although Project automatically renumbers outline numbers, Project *doesn't* automatically renumber outline codes when you move tasks, insert new tasks, or delete tasks. Outline codes are static values you assign. Although you can create a hierarchical structure for an outline code, Project doesn't read the outline codes as values that can be sorted in any particular order. Further, Project doesn't associate the outline codes with the level of the task in your project schedule outline. So, Project doesn't renumber outline codes when you make structural changes to the tasks in your outline.

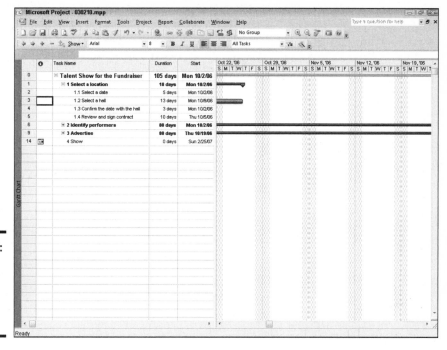

Figure 2-10:
A project schedule that uses outline numbers.

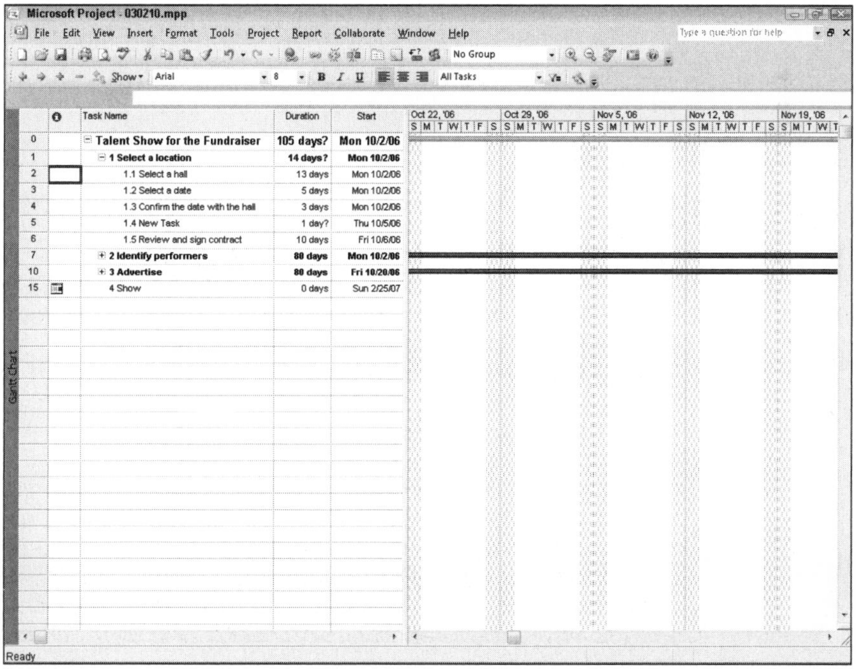

Figure 2-11:
We moved the first subtask so that it appears below the second subtask, and Project automatically renumbered them.

In Figure 2-12, we've displayed the customized outline code we created earlier in this chapter. In Figure 2-13, we've once again switched the first two tasks and added a new task above Review and Sign Contract. As you can see, the outline codes assigned to each task stayed with the task, and the new task has no outline code assigned automatically.

Use outline numbers if you want Project to automatically update the numbers based on changes to your project's outline structure. Use outline codes if you want the value you assign to the task to remain static, regardless of the changes you make to your project's outline structure.

For a combination approach, consider using WBS codes; you can read about them in the next chapter of this minibook.

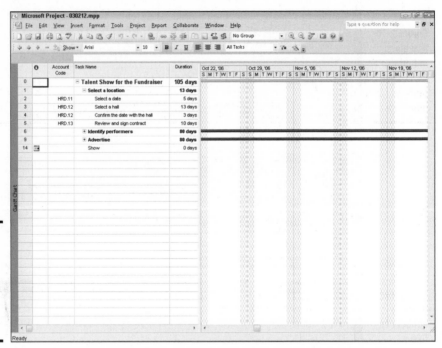

Figure 2-12:
A project schedule that uses customized outline codes.

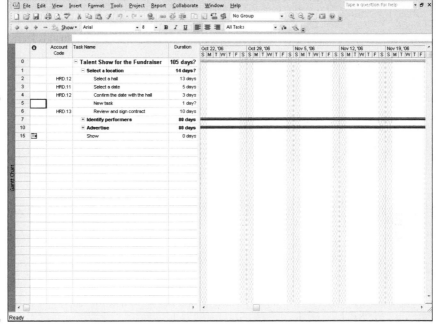

Figure 2-13:
Project doesn't automatically renumber tasks that use customized outline codes when you change the project outline.

Chapter 3: Using WBS Coding

In This Chapter

✔ Understanding WBS codes

✔ Creating WBS codes

✔ Creating a WBS chart

✔ Customizing WBS codes

✔ Understanding WBS codes and renumbering

*L*ike outline numbers and codes, WBS codes provide a way to number tasks in a project; the structure of the WBS code helps the reader identify the phase of the project in which the task occurs. You can use WBS codes instead of or in addition to outline numbers and outline codes.

WBS stands for *work breakdown structure*. WBS codes were originally developed by the United States defense establishment to help identify tasks in a project based on the phase in which the task occurs. So, you can use WBS codes as another way to organize tasks in a project. In this chapter, you explore Project's support for WBS codes.

What's a WBS Code?

The United States defense establishment designed a numbering system, reminiscent of the paragraph numbering used in legal documents, to help a person viewing a list of project tasks quickly and easily identify the phase in which the task occurs and its relationship to other tasks in the phase. When working with the government, unique WBS codes are often assigned to each task in a project, and the tasks are often referred to by their WBS codes.

In Figure 3-1, you see a common view of a WBS chart, which probably reminds you of a company organization chart. Notice how each task's WBS code identifies the phase in which it occurs and the phase's hierarchical relationship in the project; for example, the third task in the first phase of the project has a WBS code of 1.3.

Although Project doesn't produce a WBS chart picture, you can assign WBS codes to the tasks in your project.

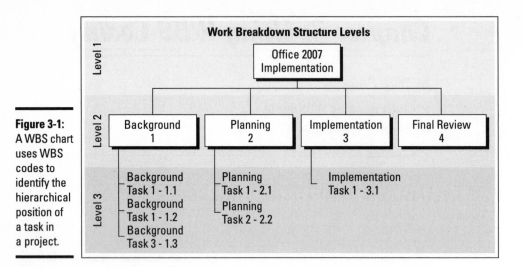

Figure 3-1:
A WBS chart
uses WBS
codes to
identify the
hierarchical
position of
a task in
a project.

Creating WBS Codes

You don't have to create WBS codes; you can use the default codes that Project assigns to your tasks. Project assigns WBS codes based on a task's position in the outline structure. So, you start by setting up your outline so that it displays the summary task and subtasks with which you want to work, as described in Chapter 1 of this minibook. Then follow these steps to display the WBS codes that Project has already assigned to each task:

1. **Display a view that includes a table, like Gantt Chart view.**

2. **Right-click the name of the column that you want to appear to the right of the column that will display WBS codes.**

3. **Select Insert Column from the shortcut menu that appears.**

 The Column Definition dialog box appears (see Figure 3-2).

4. **From the Field Name drop-down list, select WBS.**

 After you open the list, you can type a W to see the first choice in the list that begins with W.

5. **Click OK.**

 Project displays WBS codes for each task in the WBS column, as shown in Figure 3-3. The WBS code that Project assigns to each task is based on the task's level in the outline; tasks at the highest level of the outline have whole numbers for WBS codes.

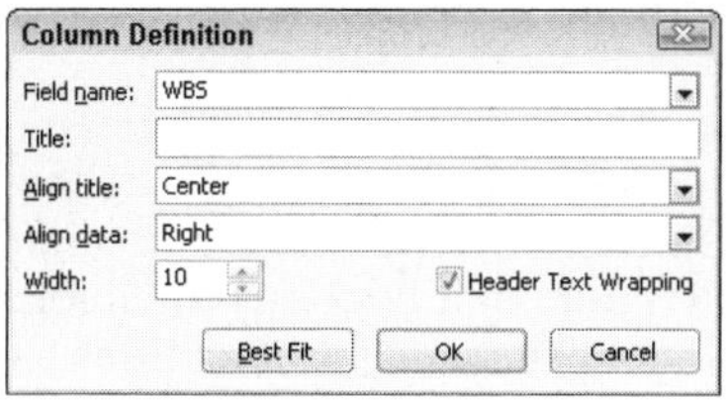

Figure 3-2:
Use this
dialog box
to insert a
column in
the table
that displays
WBS codes.

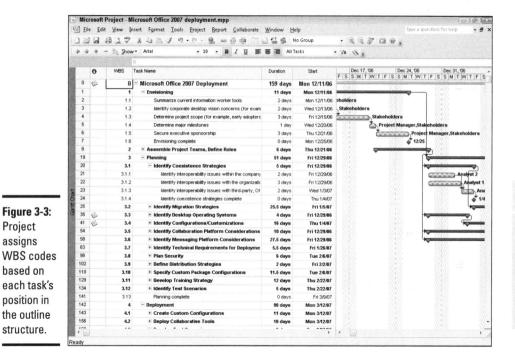

Figure 3-3:
Project
assigns
WBS codes
based on
each task's
position in
the outline
structure.

Creating a WBS Chart

Project doesn't contain a view of your project as a WBS chart, but you can create a WBS chart from your project data in two ways:

✦ **Using Visio,** as we describe in this section

✦ **Using WBS Chart Pro,** a software add-on that takes Project files and creates WBS charts

Visit www.criticaltools.com to find out more about WBS Chart Pro.

To use Visio to create a WBS chart from Project data, you need Visio 2007 installed on your computer. You create a WBS chart using the visual reports in Project, which are new to Project 2007. To create a WBS chart with Project data in Visio, you create a visual report that contains the information you want to view in Visio. In Visio, you make some modifications to display WBS numbers. Follow these steps to create a Visio report in Project, send the data to Visio, and modify the Visio report to display WBS numbers:

1. **Open the project for which you want to create the WBS chart.**

The project doesn't need to display WBS codes.

2. **Choose Report⇨Visual Reports.**

The Visual Reports – Create Report window appears (see Figure 3-4).

3. **On the All tab, click a report to use as a foundation for your template; for this example, we chose Task Status Report (US).**

4. **Click the View button.**

Visio opens on your computer, displaying the visual report you selected using the data found in the project you opened in Step 1. The WBS numbers don't appear by default.

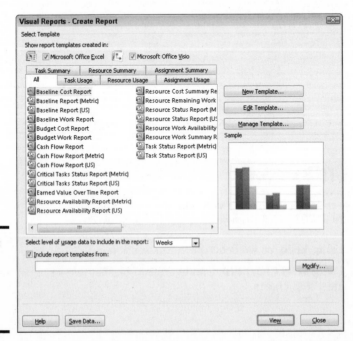

Figure 3-4: Use this window to select a visual report.

5. **Right-click any graphic on the Visio report and choose Data⇨Edit Data Graphic (see Figure 3-5).**

   Visio displays the Edit Data Graphic dialog box (see Figure 3-6).

6. **Click New Item and choose Text.**

   Visio displays the New Text dialog box (see Figure 3-7).

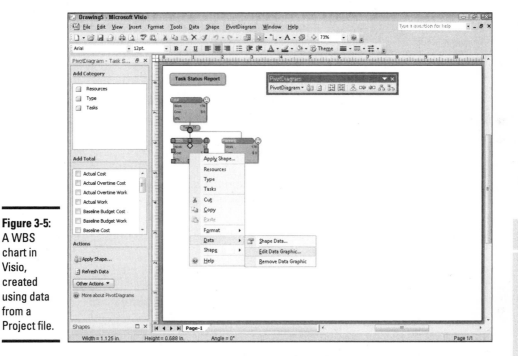

Figure 3-5: A WBS chart in Visio, created using data from a Project file.

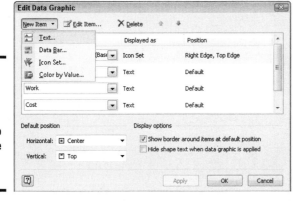

Figure 3-6: Use this dialog box to add a new field to each shape on a Visio diagram.

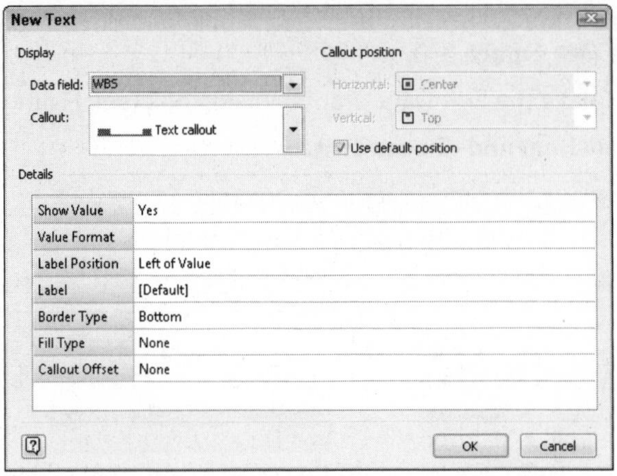

Figure 3-7:
Use this
dialog box
to select the
WBS field
as the new
field on the
Visio
diagram
shape.

7. **Open the Data Field list box and select WBS.**

8. **Click OK twice.**

   Visio redisplays the report and the WBS code appears at the bottom of
   each shape on the diagram (see Figure 3-8).

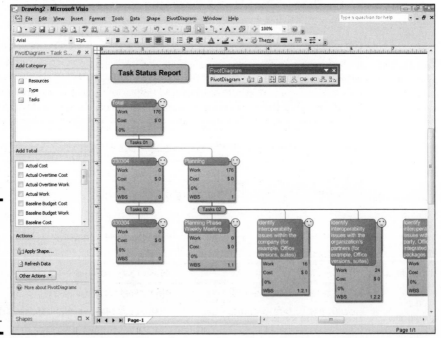

Figure 3-8:
A Visio
diagram
report of
Project
information
displaying
WBS codes.

We displayed more tasks in the project by selecting both tasks (using Ctrl+Click) at the bottom of the Visio diagram and then clicking Tasks in the Add Category section on the left side of the Visio screen.

If you use custom WBS codes and you've assigned them to tasks so that they don't match the hierarchical structure of your project, the Visio report won't be a true WBS chart; it will display your custom WBS codes but it will present the report hierarchically using Project's built-in WBS codes, which *do* match the hierarchical structure of your project.

Customizing WBS Codes

By default, Project assigns WBS codes using numbers only, and it bases the assigned number on each task's position in the project schedule's outline. Project assigns whole numbers to the tasks at the left edge of the outline, which are tasks at the top level of the outline. To each subtask of a task at the left edge of the outline, Project assigns the whole number, followed by a period, and then a sequential number for each subtask. Project continues to follow this pattern for any subtasks that appear beneath other subtasks.

You can think of the whole number as identifying a phase of the project; tasks within that phase start with the phase's whole number followed by a period and a sequential number. So, the third task in the second phase of the project would have the number 2.3.

Often, those default numbers work just fine. However, you might find yourself in a situation where you want to modify the appearance of the WBS code to incorporate information that's meaningful to you and your client. For example, you might want to include the project name or a client number as a prefix for the WBS code. Further, you might want to include letters in the WBS code along with numbers, as does the project shown in Figure 3-9.

You can customize the WBS codes that Project assigns by establishing your own *code mask;* the code mask defines the appearance of the code. When you define the code mask, you define the length of the code. You can use any or all of the types of information listed in Table 3-1.

**Book III
Chapter 3**

Using WBS Coding

Table 3-1	WBS Code Mask Elements
Code Mask Element	*Displays*
Numbers (ordered)	Numbers in sequential order
Uppercase Letters (ordered)	Capital letters in alphabetical order
Lowercase Letters (ordered)	Lowercase letters in alphabetical order
Characters (unordered)	Numbers or letters in no order

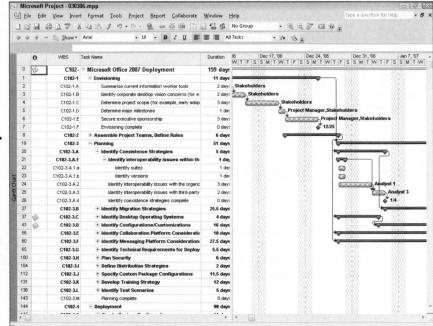

Figure 3-9:
Customized WBS codes can display more information than just the task's hierarchical position in the project outline.

The first three elements are fairly self-explanatory, but the last element, Characters (unordered), deserves a little more attention. If you include Characters (unordered) in your code mask, Project initially displays asterisks for that part of the code mask, and you can replace those asterisks with any characters that you want. For example, suppose that you use a mask of Numbers (ordered) with a length of one, Characters (unordered) with a length of 3. For any second-level task, you can enter any three characters that you want for the second part of the WBS code. In this example, when you enter a second-level task, you initially see a WBS of 1.***. However, you can change it to something like 1.x%7.

To create your own custom WBS codes, follow these steps:

1. **Choose Project⇨WBS⇨Define Code.**

Project displays the WBS Code Definition dialog box (see Figure 3-10).

The Code preview box shows you the format of the WBS code that you're designing as you design it, so it appears blank until you make selections.

2. **In the Project Code Prefix box, type a prefix that you want to appear at the beginning of all WBS codes.**

For example, you might want to use the initials of the project name or a client number.

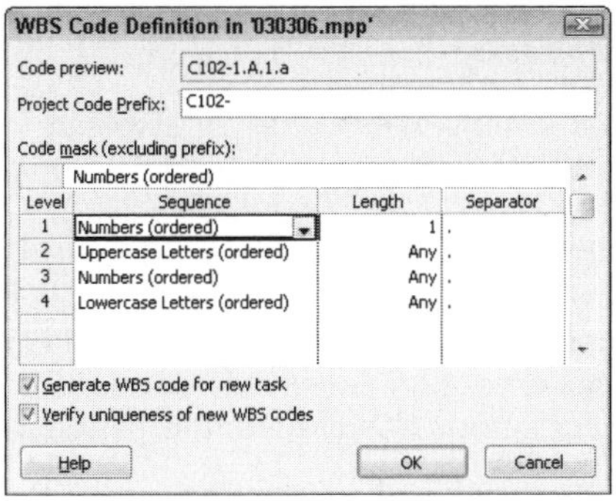

Figure 3-10:
Use the
WBS Code
Definition
dialog box
to define the
appearance
of the
WBS code.

> **WBS Code Definition in '030306.mpp'**
>
> Code preview: C102-1.A.1.a
>
> Project Code Prefix: C102-
>
> Code mask (excluding prefix):
>
> | Level | Sequence | Length | Separator |
> |---|---|---|---|
> | | Numbers (ordered) | | |
> | 1 | Numbers (ordered) | 1 | . |
> | 2 | Uppercase Letters (ordered) | Any | . |
> | 3 | Numbers (ordered) | Any | . |
> | 4 | Lowercase Letters (ordered) | Any | . |
>
> ☑ Generate WBS code for new task
> ☑ Verify uniqueness of new WBS codes
>
> Help   OK   Cancel

3. **Click the first blank row in the Sequence column to display a drop-down arrow and select the type of character that you want to use for the first part of the WBS code.**

4. **Click the first blank row in the Length column and then specify a length for that portion of the WBS code.**

   You can type a number, choose Any, or choose a number between 1 and 10. If you choose 3 for the first level of your WBS code, the WBS code for all tasks in the first phase of your project begins with your project code prefix followed by 001, and the WBS code for all tasks in the second phase of your project begins with your project code prefix followed by 002.

   Choosing Any, the default choice, is a safe bet because Project then automatically expands the WBS code to accommodate the task's position in the outline.

   In case you care, I tested the number 100, and Project accepted it. But using a 100-digit number in a WBS code isn't particularly practical.

5. **Click in the first blank row of the Separator column and select a character to separate the parts of your WBS code.**

   You can choose a period (.), dash (–), plus (+), or slash (/), or you can type any character that isn't a number or a letter (such as =).

6. **Repeat Steps 3 through 5 for each level in your outline.**

7. **Click OK to save your customized WBS code.**

You might have noticed that the two boxes at the bottom of the WBS Code Definition dialog box in Figure 3-10 were both checked. Project selects these boxes by default; leaving them selected ensures that new tasks you insert in the project are assigned WBS codes and that all WBS codes are unique. When might WBS codes not be unique? If you insert a subproject, it's possible that the subproject might contain WBS codes that duplicate those that already exist in your project.

Read more about inserting subprojects in Book 4 of this minibook.

WBS Codes and Renumbering

What happens to WBS codes when you move tasks? Insert new tasks? Delete tasks? Well, that depends.

If you're using the default WBS codes that Project inserts (that is, if you haven't customized WBS codes), Project renumbers affected WBS codes automatically if you move a task, insert a new task, or delete a task. In Figure 3-11, we've hidden all the subtasks except for those in Phase 1. When we switch the first two subtasks, Project automatically renumbers them, as you can see in Figure 3-12.

If, however, you use a custom code mask for WBS codes, Project *doesn't* automatically renumber the subtasks. In Figure 3-13, we customized the WBS codes for the same project shown in Figure 3-11. We made sure that both check boxes at the bottom of the WBS Code Definition dialog box were selected to ensure that Project would generate a new WBS code for any new task we insert and that the WBS code would be unique.

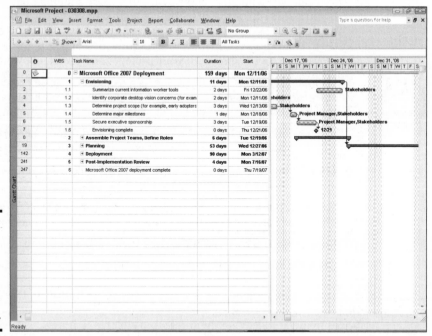

Figure 3-11:
A project schedule that uses outline numbers for WBS codes.

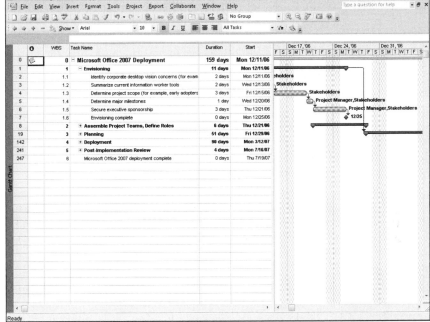

Figure 3-12:
We moved the first sub-task so that it appears below the second sub-task, and Project automatically renumbered them.

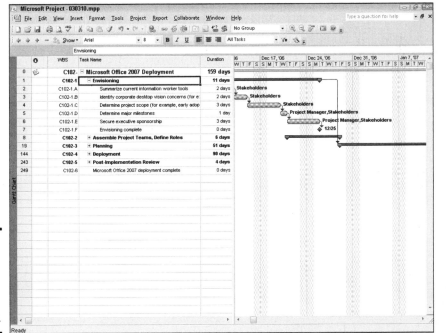

Figure 3-13:
A project schedule that uses customized WBS codes.

In Figure 3-14, we once again switched the first two subtasks. As you can see, the WBS codes appear to be out of sequential order; Project lists the task with WBS code C102-1.B before the task with WBS code C102-1.A.

We also inserted a new subtask before the first subtask; notice that its WBS code of C102-1.G is unique, but again, out of sequential order.

Project uses this behavior with custom WBS codes because there are circumstances under which you don't want to renumber the WBS codes in your project. However, for those times when you *do* want to renumber WBS codes, you can. Choose Project➪WBS➪Renumber. Project displays the WBS Renumber dialog box, shown in Figure 3-15. Click OK, and Project renumbers the WBS codes in the project schedule.

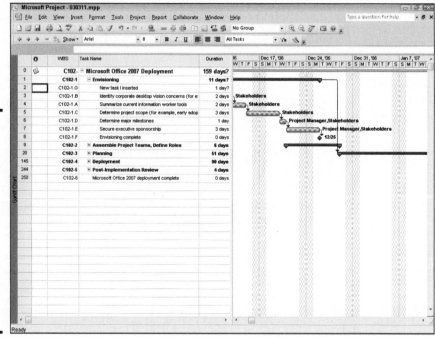

Figure 3-14: Project doesn't automatically renumber tasks that use customized WBS codes when you change the project outline.

Figure 3-15:
Use this
dialog box
to renumber
customized
WBS codes
after chang-
ing the tasks
included in
your project
schedule.

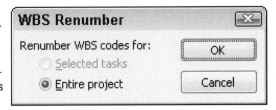

If you want to renumber the WBS codes for only some tasks, select those
tasks before you open the WBS Renumber dialog box. Project then offers you
the option of renumbering only the selected tasks or the entire project.

Chapter 4: Linking and Consolidating Projects

In This Chapter

✔ Linking projects

✔ Consolidating projects

✔ Understanding consolidation and dependencies

✔ Viewing a consolidated project

✔ Following the critical path in a consolidated project

✔ Using a resource pool

In this chapter, we look at different ways to link and insert projects. For example, you can include a link in a project to backup documentation stored in an Excel spreadsheet, or you can create several project files that cover different phases of the same project and then consolidate them to look at the big picture. As you read about these techniques, you also see how they can affect the structure of your project.

Connecting Projects with Hyperlinks

You can link one project to another by using a *hyperlink*. A hyperlink enables you to jump from the currently displayed document to another document on your hard drive, a computer network, or the Internet — useful when, for example, you'd like your Project schedule to reference some backup information stored in a Word document, an Excel spreadsheet, or even another Project file.

Creating a hyperlink

When you insert a hyperlink in a project schedule, you can link an existing task to another project or create a new task that you can use to represent the timing or costs of another project. The hyperlink contains information about the physical location of the other Project file, but it doesn't contain any of the timing or cost information, so you have to add that information to the task formed by the hyperlink.

To create a hyperlink to another Project file, follow these steps:

1. **Select a blank cell in the Task Name column where you want the hyperlinked task to appear.**

2. **Choose Insert➪Hyperlink or click the Insert Hyperlink button on the Standard toolbar.**

The Insert Hyperlink dialog box appears (see Figure 4-1).

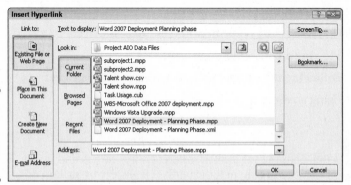

Figure 4-1:
Use this dialog box to set up the hyperlink.

3. **In the Text to Display box, type text that represents the hyperlinked file.**

This text should explain to viewers what they'll see if they click the link.

4. **In the Link To area on the left, select the Existing File or Web Page option.**

5. **Use the Look In drop-down list to select the file or Web page to which you want to link.**

6. **Click OK.**

Project inserts the hyperlink. A hyperlink icon, like the one shown in Figure 4-2, appears in the Indicator field to the left of the selected task.

When you move the mouse pointer over the icon and pause, Project displays a ScreenTip containing the text you supplied in Step 3. If you click the hyperlink icon in the Indicators column, Project opens the file associated with the hyperlink.

To remove a hyperlink, right-click the task for which you created the link and then choose Hyperlink➪Remove Hyperlink. No warning appears; Project simply removes the hyperlink.

Hyperlink icon

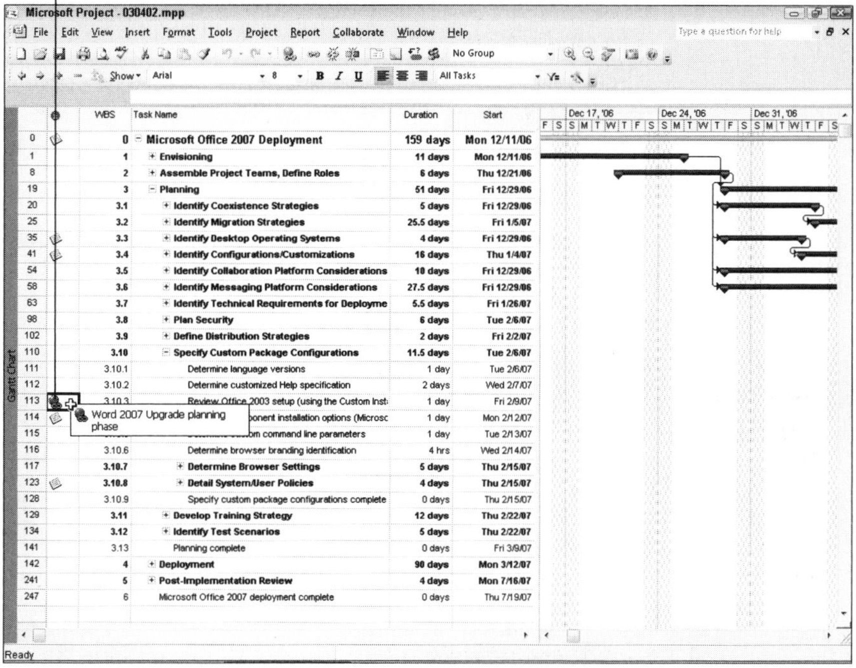

Figure 4-2:
When a task contains a hyperlink, you see the hyperlink icon in the Indicator field.

What happened? My hyperlinks don't work

Typically, when a hyperlink doesn't work, the file to which you created the link no longer exists in the location you specified when you created the link, which can happen for two reasons:

✦ **The linked file was deleted.** If the file has been deleted, you can't link to it any longer.

✦ **The linked file was moved to a new location.** Here's some good news: You can avoid hyperlinks that don't work because files moved. To prevent such a calamity, simply use relative addressing whenever possible when you create hyperlinks. For example, `g:\project.mpp` is an absolute address. If your server drive changes from `G:` to `H:`, the link won't work. However, if you use `\\servername\share\project.mpp`, a relative address, your server drive can change from `G:` to any other letter, and the relative address to your server will still work.

Editing hyperlinks

If you create a lot of hyperlinks, using the Project ScreenTip that appears when you hover the mouse pointer over each link to review hyperlink information can be tedious. You might find it easier to display hyperlinks in one of Project's built-in tables by following these steps:

1. Begin in any view that includes a table, such as Gantt Chart view.

2. Choose View⇨Table⇨Hyperlink.

The Hyperlink table shown in Figure 4-3 displays columns of information relevant to any links that you've created for your project.

You can edit the hyperlink by using the Edit Hyperlink dialog box. Right-click the link and choose Hyperlink⇨Edit Hyperlink to reopen the dialog box (shown previously in Figure 4-1) and make changes.

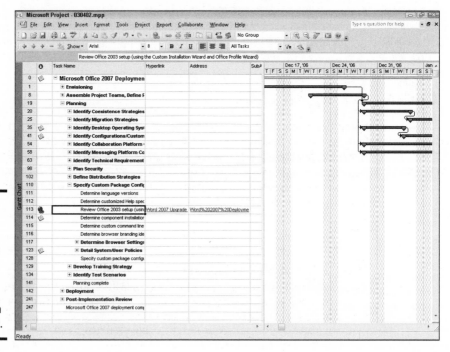

Figure 4-3: Using the Hyperlink table gives you easy access to hyperlink information at a glance.

Moving or copying hyperlinks

If the information in the hyperlinked file becomes pertinent to a different task or more than one task, you can move or copy the hyperlink from one task to another by using the Hyperlink table. Follow these steps:

1. **Select the hyperlink cell by clicking its task name and then using the right-arrow key to select the hyperlink cell.**

   Clicking a cell in the Hyperlink, Address, or SubAddress column of a task containing a hyperlink activates the link.

2. **Press the Shift key and the right-arrow key to also select the address and, if appropriate, the subaddress of the hyperlink.**

3. **Do one of the following:**

   - *To move the link:* Click the Cut button on the Standard toolbar, click the hyperlink cell next to the task where you want to move the link, and then click the Paste button.

   - *To copy the link:* Click the Copy button, click the hyperlink cell next to the task where you want to place a copy of the link, and then click the Paste button.

Consolidating Projects

Sometimes you have a really complex project to manage, and although you can expand and collapse the outline for the schedule, you feel you'd work better if you could just focus on one piece with no other distractions — including collapsed portions of the outline. Setting up separate projects for each phase would help you focus, but what do you do about dependencies across phases? And resource allocations?

The answer: Use consolidation.

What is consolidation?

Consolidating is a useful way to break a complex project down into smaller projects — referred to as *subprojects* — and then combine the smaller projects into one large project when you need to look at the big picture. Consolidating projects can help you manage the following situations:

✦ A project might be so complex that breaking it into smaller pieces can help you to organize it. You can use consolidation to combine the subprojects to view the big picture.

✦ Suppose that you have tasks in a project that are managed by different people and those tasks are interdependent. By creating subprojects and using consolidation techniques, you can allow independent project management and still create the correct dependencies between the schedules of the various subprojects and assign the necessary resources.

✦ If you use the same resources for several projects, you can consolidate those projects so that you can level the resources and avoid overallocations — and surprises.

See Book VII, Chapter 2 for more information on handling resource overallocations.

When you use Project's consolidation features, you create subprojects that contain the tasks that constitute one portion of your project, and you save the subproject as a separate project file. You assign resources and set up each subproject with links and constraints, just as if you were working with the entire project.

While working in the consolidated project, you can focus on any portion of the project. Subprojects appear as summary tasks in the consolidated project, and you can use Project's outlining tools to hide all tasks that are associated with any subproject. You can view, print, and change information for any subproject, just as if you were working with a single project. Figure 4-4 shows you a consolidated project.

You can review outlining techniques in Chapter 1 of this minibook. And, the numbering techniques described in Chapters 2 and 3 of this minibook also apply to consolidated projects and their subprojects.

Best of all, when you work in a consolidated project file, you have the option to save changes you make to any subproject to that subproject's source file. Similarly, if you open the subproject file and make changes, Project asks whether you want to update the consolidated project file. So, you don't have to face the nightmare of recording changes twice; Project tracks all the changes for you, and Project updates the consolidated file if you want it to.

Do I need to use consolidation?

"My company uses Project Server with Project Professional. Do I need to read this section?" you ask. Although Project Server can provide Project

Professional users with much of the information you can get from consolidating, Project Server can't show you one *critical path* (the series of tasks in your project that must happen on time for the project to meet its final deadline) across a consolidated project. In the section "The Critical Path in a Consolidated Project," later in this chapter, you see how consolidation affects the critical path. So, even Project Professional users have a reason to use consolidation.

In Book X, you can read about Project Server, a product used in conjunction with Project Professional in environments that manage many projects using the same set of resources. Project Server provides your organization with a database in which all projects are stored. Users with the proper credentials and a browser can use Project Web Access, a browser-based interface, to view and work with projects stored in the Project Server database.

When you use consolidation, you also want to use resource pooling, covered later in this chapter in the section "Sharing Resources Using a Resource Pool," to assign the same resources across projects and avoid overallocations.

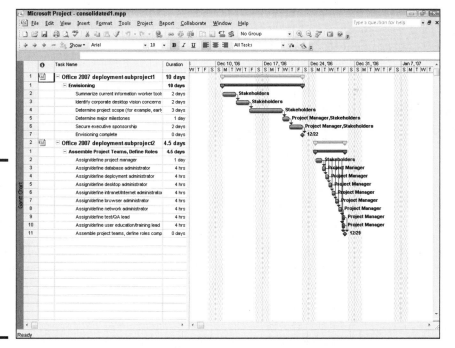

Figure 4-4:
A consolidated project looks just like any other project with summary tasks and subtasks.

Creating subprojects

It doesn't really matter when, in the project schedule setup process, you decide to use consolidation. For example, you might realize right away that the project is too large to handle in a traditional way; in this case, start by saving each phase of the project as a subproject file.

If you discover that consolidation would work for you after you start working on a project, no problem. Suppose, for example, that you're working on setting up a project plan to migrate your organization to Word 2007, and then management decides to also migrate to Excel 2007 and Outlook 2007 at the same time. Adding these two software packages to the upgrade process changes the scope of the project and adds tasks and dependencies that didn't exist previously. In this case, you can easily break the original project down into subprojects and create additional subprojects to accommodate the new tasks.

If you decide to use consolidation at the outset, create separate Microsoft Project files for various portions of the project that will serve as subprojects when you consolidate. Set up each subproject file so that it's independently complete and create any necessary links within each subproject file.

If you start a project and then find that you want to use consolidation, you can create subprojects by following these steps:

1. **Save your original project file.**

2. **Select all the tasks that you want to save in your first subproject file (see Figure 4-5).**

Use the Show button on the Formatting toolbar to display only Outline Level 1 headings. Then select the heading for the set of tasks you want to save in a subproject; Project selects the heading and all of its subtasks.

 3. **Click the Copy button.**

4. **Click the New button to start a new project.**

5. **If necessary, click Blank Project in the New Project task pane.**

Project displays the Project Information dialog box (see Figure 4-6).

If Project doesn't automatically display the Project Information dialog box when you start a new project, choose Project⇨Project Information to display it.

6. **Establish basic information for the subproject, such as the start date and scheduling method.**

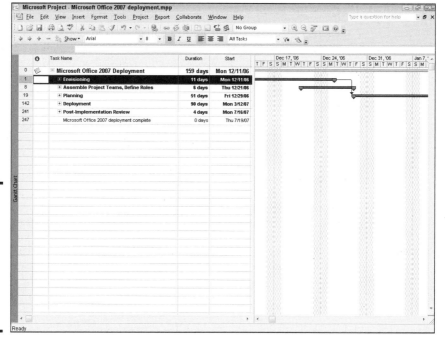

Figure 4-5:
In your
original
project file,
select the
tasks you
want to
include in a
subproject.

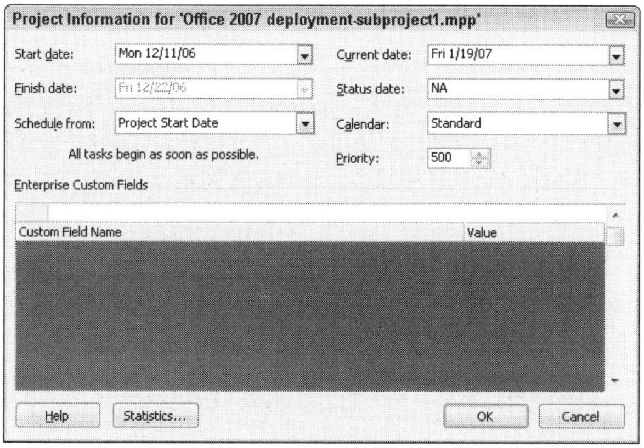

Figure 4-6:
In this
dialog box,
establish
basic
information
for the
subproject.

TIP

To make the Project Information dialog box appear each time you start a
new project, choose Tools➪Options, click the General tab, and select
the Prompt for Project Info for New Projects check box.

7. Click the Paste button.

Project pastes the information you copied from the original project into the new Project file (see Figure 4-7).

8. Save the subproject and close it.

9. Repeat Steps 2 through 5 until you've saved several separate files that contain portions of your original project.

In our example, we included the last Outline Level 1 heading, a milestone to mark the end of the project, in our last subproject file. So, we created five subproject files from the original file shown in Figure 4-5.

10. Close the original file.

You're now ready to edit each subproject file that you create to make it an independently complete project. For example, establish task durations and dependencies and assign resources in each subproject file. Don't worry about connecting tasks in one subproject to another; you can use the techniques in the following sections to consolidate the subprojects and link them together.

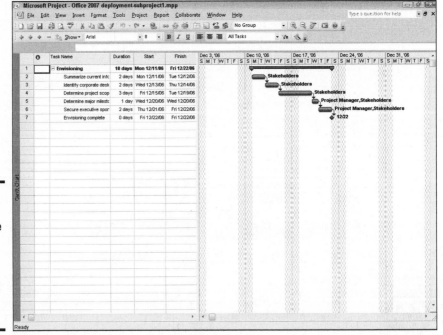

Figure 4-7:
Project displays the set of tasks you copied from your original project in a new file.

Creating a consolidated project

To consolidate subprojects, you insert them into another project file; being the clever folks we are, we call that project file the *consolidated project file.* Each subproject that you insert appears as a summary task in the consolidated project file, and Project calculates inserted projects like summary tasks. An icon in the Indicator field identifies an inserted project (see Figure 4-8).

You might notice, in Figure 4-8, that the task numbers appear a bit odd. Project assigns the equivalent of a project number to each inserted project, with task numbers following that run sequentially for each inserted project. So, the summary task for the first inserted project appears on Row 1, followed by its first task, also assigned a row number of 1. After Task 7, the last task in the first inserted project in Figure 4-8, the summary task for the second inserted project appears on what seems to be Row 2, but it's actually the inserted project's project number. The tasks of the second inserted project follow, beginning again with Row 1 for the first task of the second inserted project.

**Book III
Chapter 4**

Linking and
Consolidating
Projects

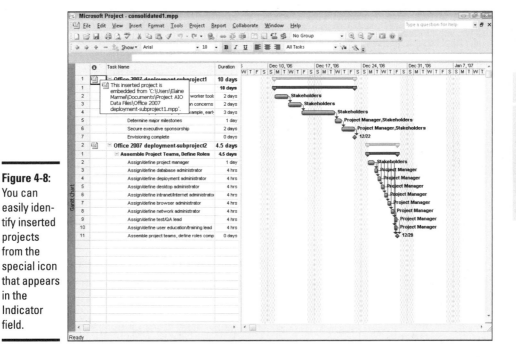

Figure 4-8:
You can easily identify inserted projects from the special icon that appears in the Indicator field.

To insert a project, follow these steps:

1. **Start a new project or open the project you want to use as the consolidated project.**

2. **Switch to Gantt Chart view.**

3. **Click in the row of the Task Name column where you want the inserted project to begin.**

When you insert a project, Project places the project immediately above the selected row. So, if your consolidated project already contains tasks, click the task in the Task Name column that you want to appear below the subproject.

4. **Choose Insert⇨Project.**

Project displays the Insert Project dialog box (see Figure 4-9).

Figure 4-9:
The Insert Project dialog box looks and works like the Open dialog box.

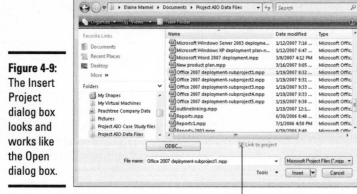

Link to Project check box

5. **Navigate to the folder that contains the project that you want to insert.**

6. **Highlight the file that you want to insert.**

7. **Click the Insert button.**

Project inserts the selected file into the open project. The inserted subproject file appears as a summary task, and its subtasks are hidden (see Figure 4-10).

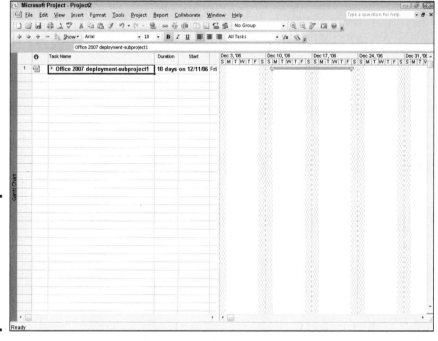

Figure 4-10:
Inserted
projects
appear as
summary
tasks, with
subtasks
hidden.

When you insert a project, you have a couple of options you can set:

✦ By default, a check mark appears in the **Link to Project check box** (refer to Figure 4-9). When the projects are linked, Project retains all of the information stored in the inserted file, including the information you provided in the Project Information dialog box (the information you set concerning how to calculate the project schedule). If you remove the check mark, Project doesn't connect the inserted project to its source project. You don't see the icon in the Indicators column, and Project ignores the information you stored in the subproject's Project Information dialog box. If you make changes to the subproject while working in the consolidated project file, Project doesn't prompt you to update the inserted project's source file.

✦ **The Insert button** has a drop-down arrow beside it. If you click that button, you can choose either Insert or Insert Read-Only. If you choose Insert Read-Only from the Insert drop-down menu, Project still treats the subproject as an inserted project for purposes of calculating the project schedule, but if you make changes to the subproject in the consolidated file, Project doesn't let you save the changes to the subproject file.

Because linking the files makes updating easy, why wouldn't you want to link the files? Well, you might want to create a consolidated file just so you can generate a report quickly.

The link you create when you insert a project works like any link that you create between two files in the Windows environment. For example, if you rename the subproject file or move it to a different folder, the link won't work anymore unless you update it. To update a link, display the consolidated project in Gantt Chart view and double-click the inserted project. Project displays the Inserted Project Information dialog box for the inserted project; this dialog box is the equivalent of the Task Information dialog box for any task (see Figure 4-11).

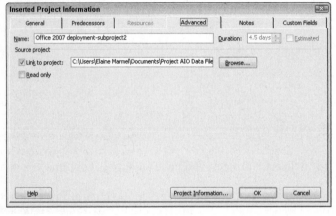

Figure 4-11:
Update links
for inserted
projects
from the
Advanced
tab of the
Inserted
Project
Information
dialog box.

In addition to using the Browse button to navigate to the new location for an inserted project, you can unlink subprojects from their source files by removing the check mark from the Link to Project check box.

If you attempt to expand the outline of an inserted project in a consolidated project file and the inserted project's location isn't valid any longer, Project automatically displays a dialog box that looks like the Open dialog box. Use this dialog box to navigate to the new location of the file and click OK after you finish. This process also re-establishes the link between the files.

Inserted projects and the outline

You can hide or show tasks of a subproject in the consolidated project file the same way you hide or show tasks in any project file. Click the outline symbol — the plus or minus sign next to the task name — of the inserted project's summary task.

You can insert projects at any level in the project outline, and the outline level assigned to the inserted project depends on the level of the tasks above and below the inserted project in the consolidated project.

CASE STUDY

A shortcut to consolidate projects

Company: Medium-sized company with more than 75 employees.

Project: Upgrade all computers from Office 2003 to Office 2007.

Challenge: To monitor overall progress on a project being managed by several different managers.

In this situation, when several different people within the organization will be managing different phases of a large project, each manager will want to create and manage a project schedule for his or her phase of the project. However, dependencies exist between phases, so viewing the "big picture" is just as important as managing the phases. The company wants to be able to quickly and easily produce a consolidated project for analysis.

Solution: There's a quick and easy way to consolidate projects, but to make sure that the subprojects appear in the correct order when you consolidate, naming the subproject files becomes important. To take advantage of this shortcut, name your subprojects with a number at the end that represents the order in which it should appear when you consolidate. For example, name the first phase Subproject1, the second phase Subproject2, and so on.

Then use this very cool shortcut to create a consolidated project:

1. **Open all the subprojects that you want to consolidate.**

2. **Choose Window⇨New Window.**

Project opens the New Window dialog box shown in the figure.

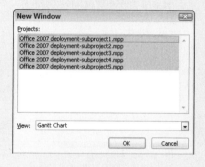

3. **Press and hold down Ctrl as you click each project that you want to consolidate.**

4. **Click OK.**

Project creates a new consolidated project that contains the projects that you selected in the New Window dialog box. Project inserts the subprojects as linked files into the consolidated project file in the order in which the subprojects appear in the New Window dialog box, so naming the subprojects as we describe sets the order in which they consolidate. On this book's Web site, you'll find five subproject files: `Office 2007 deployment-subproject1.mpp` through `Office 2007 deployment-subproject5.mpp`. Open all five subprojects in any order, select some or all of them, and see the results. And, using this approach, any changes made to any subproject update the consolidated project file and vice versa.

When you insert a project, you select the task that you want to appear below the inserted project. Project assigns the outline level of the inserted project at the same level in the outline as either of the following:

✦ The selected task

✦ The task above the selected task

In most cases, Project inserts the project at the same outline level as the task above the selected task. But there's one exception (isn't there always at least one?): If the task above the selected task is at the same outline level or outdented farther than the selected task, the inserted project appears in the outline at the same level as the selected task, not the task above the selected task.

To really get a handle on this behavior, compare Figures 4-12, 4-13, and 4-14. In Figure 4-12, we selected the Secure Executive Sponsorship task when we inserted Subproject2. This subproject appears at the same outline level as the Determine Major Milestones task, the task above the selected task.

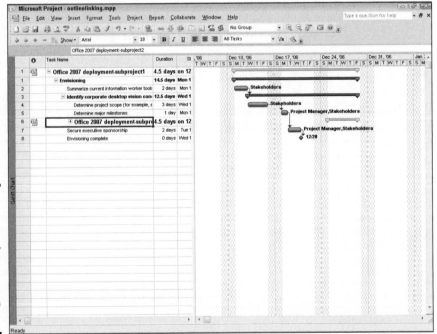

Figure 4-12: When we inserted Subproject2, we selected the Secure Executive Sponsorship task.

In Figure 4-13, we collapsed the Identify Corporate Desktop Vision task, selected the Secure Executive Sponsorship task, and then inserted Subproject2. Although the Identify Corporate Desktop Vision task contains indented subtasks, they're hidden, so Project inserts the subproject at the same level as the Identify Corporate Desktop Vision task, which is the task above the selected task.

In Figure 4-14, we selected the Determine Project Scope task when we inserted Subproject2. This subproject appears at the same outline level as the Determine Project Scope task we initially selected because the task above it is outdented farther than the selected task.

To produce a consolidated project in which the inserted projects line up at the highest outline level, make sure that you collapse the preceding inserted project so that you can't see its tasks when you insert the next subproject.

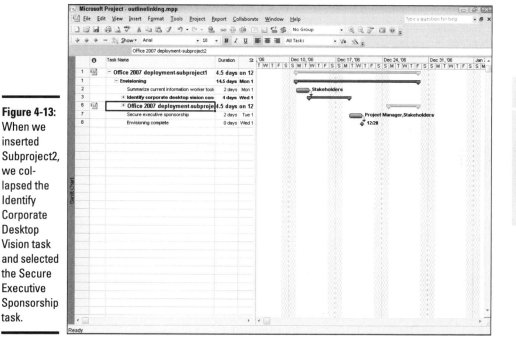

Figure 4-13: When we inserted Subproject2, we collapsed the Identify Corporate Desktop Vision task and selected the Secure Executive Sponsorship task.

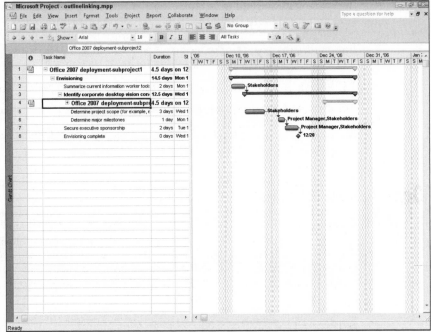

Figure 4-14:
When we inserted Subproject2, we selected the Determine Project Scope task.

Moving subprojects within a consolidated project

You can easily move subprojects around in the consolidated project by following these steps:

1. **Select the row of the summary task for the subproject.**

2. **Click the Cut tool on the Standard toolbar.**

Project opens the Planning Wizard dialog box (see Figure 4-15).

Figure 4-15:
The Planning Wizard dialog box appears when you cut a subproject summary task.

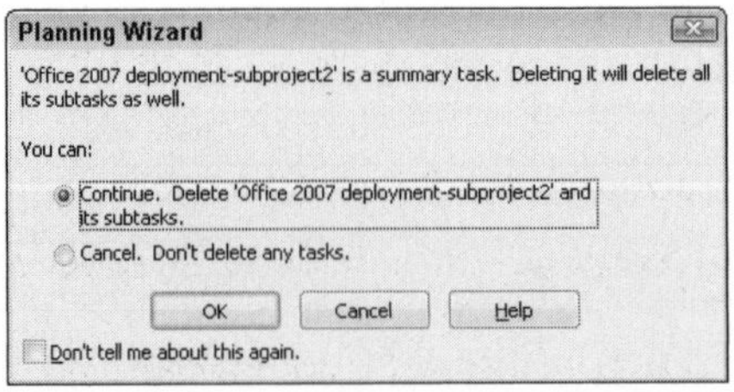

Planning Wizard

'Office 2007 deployment-subproject2' is a summary task. Deleting it will delete all its subtasks as well.

You can:

○ Continue. Delete 'Office 2007 deployment-subproject2' and its subtasks.

○ Cancel. Don't delete any tasks.

[OK] [Cancel] [Help]

☐ Don't tell me about this again.

3. **Select the Continue option.**

4. **Click OK.**

The summary task that represents the subproject disappears, along with all of its subordinate tasks.

5. **Select the row you want to appear below the last task of the subproject.**

6. **Click the Paste button on the Standard toolbar.**

Project reinserts the subproject at its new location, immediately above the row you selected in Step 5.

Dependencies in Consolidated Projects

Like tasks in any project, tasks in a consolidated project depend on other tasks in the project. Most likely, a task within one phase of the project depends on a task in another phase of the project. Essentially, you need to create dependencies that reflect how you work, even if the dependencies cross phases that you've divided into subprojects, which isn't a problem.

Creating dependencies across projects

You find out about dependencies in great detail in Book IV, Chapter 3. So, in this section, we focus on showing you how to create dependencies across subprojects.

In Project, you can create the same four types of dependencies between subprojects as you can create between tasks: finish-to-start, start-to-start, finish-to-finish, and start-to-finish. And, you can add lag or lead time to links between subprojects, just like you can to links between tasks.

Create a consolidated project and then follow these steps to link a task stored in one subproject to a task stored in another subproject:

1. **Click Gantt Chart on the View bar.**

2. **Select the tasks that you want to link (see Figure 4-16).**

To select noncontiguous tasks, press and hold down Ctrl as you click each task name.

3. **Click the Link Tasks button on the Standard toolbar.**

Project creates a finish-to-start link line between the two tasks.

In the consolidated project, the link line between tasks across subprojects looks just any other link line. Things look normal.

Link line

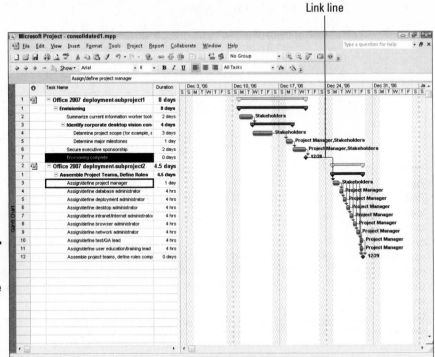

Figure 4-16:
You can link
a task in one
subproject
to a task in
another
subproject.

But, in either of the subproject files, an external task appears. You can iden-tify an external task because both its task name and Gantt bar are light gray (see Figure 4-17). If you point at the bar in Gantt Chart view, Project displays information about the task, including the fact that it is an external task. If you double-click the task name of the external task, Project opens the subproject to which the external task is linked.

From a subproject file, you can create an external link to another subproject file using the Predecessors field on the Entry table of Gantt Chart view (see Figure 4-18).

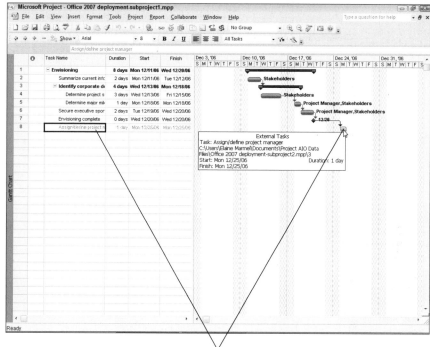

Figure 4-17:
Project
identifies
external
tasks when
you point the
mouse at the
Gantt bar of
an external
task.

External tasks identified in light gray

In the Predecessors field, type a path to the subproject file and ID number of the task to which you want to link. Separate the path to the location of the subproject file from the ID number of the task with a backslash (\). In Figure 4-18, the Assign/Define Project Manager task, which is Task 3 in a subproject file named `Office 2007 Deployment-Subproject2.MMP`, is linked to the Envisioning Complete task, which is Task 7 in a subproject file called `Office 2007 Deployment-Subproject1.MPP`. You can see the complete pathname of a linked task in the Entry bar (just below the toolbars) when you select the task's information in the Predecessors column.

Entry bar

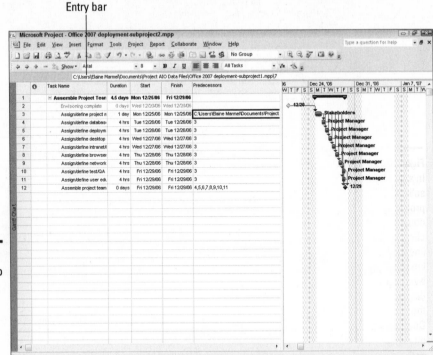

Figure 4-18:
You can also
create
external
links from
subproject
files.

Changing cross-project dependencies

After you link tasks across subprojects, you might need to change information about the link. For example, you might want to add lag time or assign a different type of dependency.

You can modify a link between tasks in different subprojects from the subproject or from the consolidated project using pretty much the same technique. About the only advantage to working in the subproject is that you can change the path to the subproject.

In the consolidated project, double-click the line that links the two tasks (see Figure 4-19). In the subproject, double-click the line that links an internal task to the external task (see Figure 4-20). In both cases, Project displays the Task Dependency dialog box.

Double-click this arrow

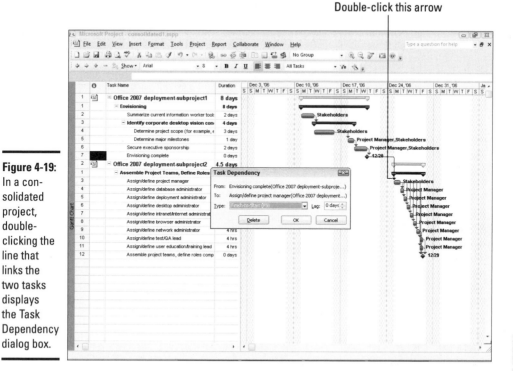

Figure 4-19:
In a con-
solidated
project,
double-
clicking the
line that
links the
two tasks
displays
the Task
Dependency
dialog box.

Book III
Chapter 4

Linking and
Consolidating
Projects

As you can see, the two versions of the dialog box differ slightly. In both
versions, you can use the Type list box to change the type of link and the
Lag box to change the amount of lag time between the linked tasks. If you
work from within the subproject, you can update the path of the link, but if
you work from within the consolidated project, you can't update the path of
the link.

Saving a consolidated project

You don't need to save consolidated project files unless you want them,
because you can easily re-create the consolidated project file. But, as you'd
expect, Project prompts you to save a consolidate project when you close it.
No problem; choose Yes or No as appropriate. But, because the project
you're closing is a consolidated project, Project's behavior changes slightly.

Double-click this arrow

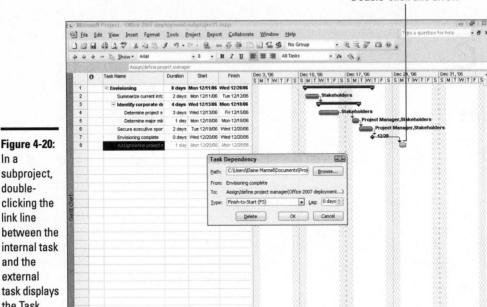

Figure 4-20:
In a subproject, double-clicking the link line between the internal task and the external task displays the Task Dependency dialog box.

When you close the consolidated project, Project first asks whether you want to save the consolidated project. Whether you save the consolidated project doesn't change Project's behavior; Project next asks whether you want to save changes that you made to inserted projects (see Figure 4-21).

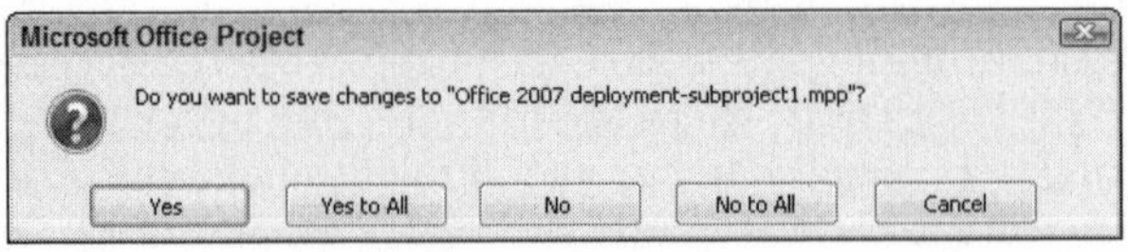

Figure 4-21:
When you close a consolidated project, Project asks whether you want to save changes that you made to each subproject.

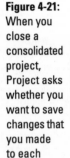

Project treats a subproject file like any other Project file; when you close a subproject, Project asks whether you want to save changes to the file.

Here's a cool thing: If you save the changes to the subprojects — even if you don't save the consolidated project — Project saves external tasks, such as the one that you saw previously in Figure 4-18, in the subproject files.

The Critical Path in a Consolidated Project

In a regular project, Project automatically calculates the *critical path* (the series of tasks in your project that must happen on time for the project to meet its final deadline) for the entire project using the late finish date of the project to make calculations. And, by default, when you consolidate projects, Project calculates inserted projects like summary tasks and calculates the critical path by using the finish date of the consolidated project to show you the overall critical path across all the projects. This behavior can make subprojects look like they don't have critical paths of their own. In Figure 4-22, the critical path has a hatched pattern and is driven by Subtask 7 in Subproject2.

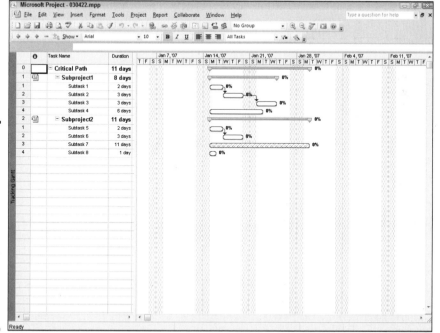

Figure 4-22:
By default, Project treats inserted projects like summary tasks, and you see only one critical path for the consolidated project.

But suppose that you want to see each subproject's critical path while viewing the consolidated project. No problem.

Although you might be tempted to turn on the Project setting to view multiple critical paths while working in the consolidated project, you probably won't see any change to the project. Why? Because multiple critical paths apply only to tasks that are owned by the project, and a consolidated project doesn't own the tasks of the subprojects you insert — the subprojects own those tasks.

To view the critical path of each inserted project, tell Project to stop treating subprojects as summary tasks. If you do, Project uses the late finish dates that the subprojects pass along to the consolidated project to determine the critical path, and you're likely to see each subproject's critical path. When you turn off this setting, you see critical paths in the consolidated project as they appear in each subproject. In Figure 4-23, the critical path for Subproject1 is driven by Subtask1, Subtask2, and Subtask3, and the critical path for Subproject2 is driven by Subtask7.

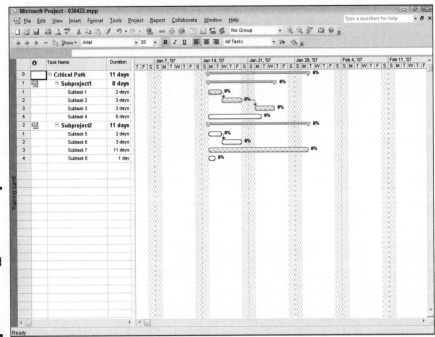

Figure 4-23:
Critical paths appear in a consolidated project for each inserted project.

To view a critical path for each subproject in a consolidated project, follow these steps:

1. Open the consolidated project.

2. Choose Tools⇨Options.

The Options dialog box appears.

3. Click the Calculation tab.

4. Deselect the Inserted Projects Are Calculated Like Summary Tasks check box (see Figure 4-24).

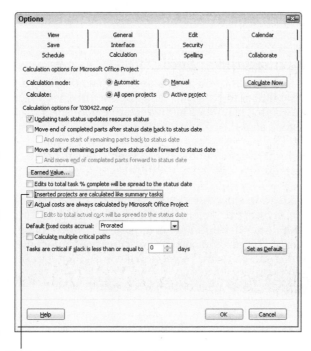

Figure 4-24:
You can view the critical paths for each subproject in the consolidated project by changing this setting.

The Inserted Projects Are Calculated
Like Summary Tasks check box

**Book III
Chapter 4**

Linking and
Consolidating
Projects

5. Click OK.

Critical paths for each subproject appear in the consolidated project.

Sharing Resources Using a Resource Pool

If you work in an environment in which several project managers use the same set of resources on multiple projects, a *resource pool* can be useful. A resource pool is pretty much what its name implies: a set of resources that are available to any project. When you set up a resource pool in Project, you can open it and view resource assignments across all projects using the pool.

The resource pooling techniques we describe in the following sections apply more to Project Standard users than Project Professional users who also use Project Server. Project Professional users using Project Server can use the Enterprise Resource Pool in Project Server to accomplish the same things that resource pooling does.

Creating a resource pool

To use resource pooling, you need a project that contains all the available resources you intend to share. To really be effective, we suggest that you include all available resources in the resource pool, even if you intend to share resources across two projects and use only some of those resources. By including all your resources in the resource pool, you eliminate the need to create several resource pools and to keep straight which ones contain which resources.

You create a resource pool by simply setting up the resources in a Project file and then saving that Project file. The Project file doesn't have to contain tasks, but if it does, that won't affect anything. To keep things clean and avoid confusion, we recommend that you create a Project file that contains only resources and no tasks. To get details on setting up resources, See Book V, Chapter 1.

Sharing resources

If you intend to share the resources in the resource pool, don't bother to set up any resources in your project. Instead, connect your project to the project file that contains the resource pool by following these steps:

1. **Open the project that serves as the resource pool file.**

Ours is cleverly named `resource pool.mpp`.

2. **Open the project that will share resources.**

Both projects appear on the Windows taskbar.

3. **Choose Tools⇨Resource Sharing⇨Share Resources.**

   Project displays the Share Resources dialog box (see Figure 4-25).

4. **Select the Use Resources option.**

5. **Open the From drop-down list to select the resource pool project.**

   You can choose any open project when you identify the resource pool. So, if you have any projects open besides the resource pool project and the project that will share resources, those additional projects appear as candidates for the resource pool project when you open the From list box.

6. **Select an option to tell Project how to handle calendar conflicts.**

   If you select the Pool Takes Precedence option, the Resource calendars in the resource pool file take precedence when conflicts arise. If you select the Sharer Takes Precedence option, the Resource calendars in the file that's sharing resources take precedence over the Resource calendars in the resource pool file when conflicts arise.

7. **Click OK.**

Figure 4-25:
Use this dialog box to connect your project to the resource pool.

If you switch to Resource Sheet view of the project that you just set up to share resources, Project displays all the resources that appear in the resource pool file. And, although those resources appear to be in your project file, they aren't until you actually make an assignment.

If you ignored our advice and set up resources in a project that you then set up to share resources, the resource pool resources appear along with any resources that you set up in your project file, which could cause some confusion.

You can now continue working in your project, or you can save your project and close it. You can also close the resource pool file.

Opening a project

Okay, you saved and closed your file that shares resources and now you want to open it again. You open this file the same way that you open any file, but you might be wondering whether you need to open the resource pool file first. The answer, in a word, is no. Instead, when you open a file that you have set up to share resources, Project displays the Open Resource Pool Information dialog box (see Figure 4-26).

Figure 4-26:
The Open
Resource
Pool
Information
dialog box
helps you
work in your
project file
that shares
resources.

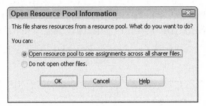

So, which option do you choose? When you select the Open Resource Pool to See Assignments Across All Sharer Files option, Project opens your file and the resource pool, but the resource pool opens as a read-only file. If you make changes that involve resources, you need to update the resource pool to reflect the changes — you can read more about updating the resource pool in the next section.

The "read-only" thing happens so that multiple users can work with the resource pool file simultaneously.

If you select the Do Not Open Other Files option, Project opens only your file. If you haven't previously assigned resources and you check Resource Sheet view, you don't see any resources — remember, they are stored in the resource pool. When Resource Sheet view is blank, you can't make any changes involving resources to your project.

When in doubt, choose the first option to open the resource pool.

Updating the resource pool

Remember, letting multiple project managers working in different projects share a finite set of resources is the whole idea behind the resource pool. While you're working, if you change resource information, you need to update the resource pool file so that others who are using the resource pool have the most up-to-date information.

To update the resource pool, it has to be open. Choose Tools⇨Resource Sharing⇨Update Resource Pool (see Figure 4-27).

 "But the Update Resource Pool command isn't available," you say. That happens when you open your project file but you choose not to also open the resource pool. And, you lose your changes if you save and close your file and then reopen it along with the resource pool. So, to get around the problem, click the Open tool on the Standard toolbar to open the resource pool file. Project then displays the dialog box you see in Figure 4-28.

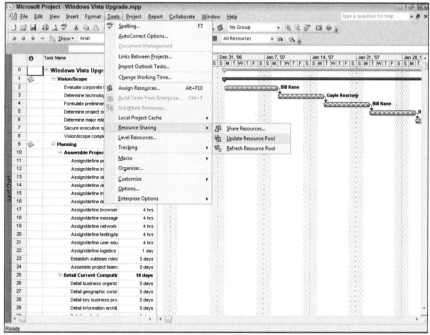

Figure 4-27: Use the Update Resource Pool command to store resource changes in your project while the resource pool file is open.

Figure 4-28:
When you open the resource pool separately, Project asks you to make some choices about the way you open it.

If you select the first option, Project opens the resource pool file so that you can update it with the changes you made to your project, and others can continue to use the resource pool. (The second and third options in the Open Resource Pool dialog box are discussed in the next section.)

If you forget to update the resource pool after you make a change in your project that affects the resource pool, Project displays a message, shown in Figure 4-29, when you save your project. If you click OK, Project updates the resource pool for you.

Figure 4-29:
Project reminds you to update the resource pool when you save your project.

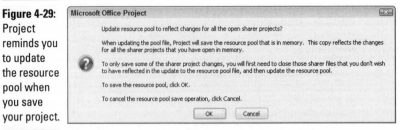

Viewing resource assignments when you share resources

If you're sharing resources, it's important to monitor resource allocations, and the resource pool makes that task easy.

Use the Open tool on the Standard toolbar to open the resource pool file. Project displays the Open Resource Pool dialog box shown previously in Figure 4-28.

To get a good handle on resource assignments across projects, choose the third option. Project opens the resource pool file *and* creates a consolidated project that includes all the files that are sharing the resource pool file. Switch to the consolidated file by using the Windows taskbar or the Window menu in Project (see Figure 4-30). You can make updates, and other users can work at the same time in the files that share the resource pool; other users see updates you make as you work.

Choose View⇨Resource Usage to review the resource assignments.

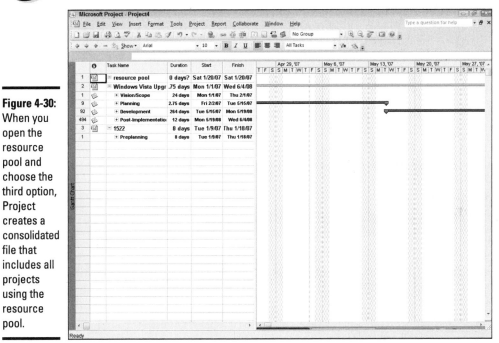

Figure 4-30: When you open the resource pool and choose the third option, Project creates a consolidated file that includes all projects using the resource pool.

**Book III
Chapter 4**

Linking and
Consolidating
Projects

You might be wondering what the second option in the Open Resource Pool dialog box does. If you want to update cost or availability information, the second option lets you open the resource pool and make those changes. However, others won't be able to update the pool with new information; that is, when they choose Tools➪Resource Sharing, the Update Resource Pool command you saw in Figure 4-27 isn't available until you close the resource pool. If Project prompts you to save any of the files that share the resource pool, save them.

Stop sharing resources

You don't have to continue to use the resource pool after you connect a project file to it. You can disable the resource pool for your project if you follow these steps:

1. **Open the project that you want to disconnect from the resource pool.**

When prompted, you can open the resource pool or not — it doesn't matter.

2. **Choose Tools➪Resource Sharing➪Share Resources.**

Project displays the Share Resources dialog box (see Figure 4-31).

Figure 4-31: Use this dialog box to disconnect a project from the resource pool.

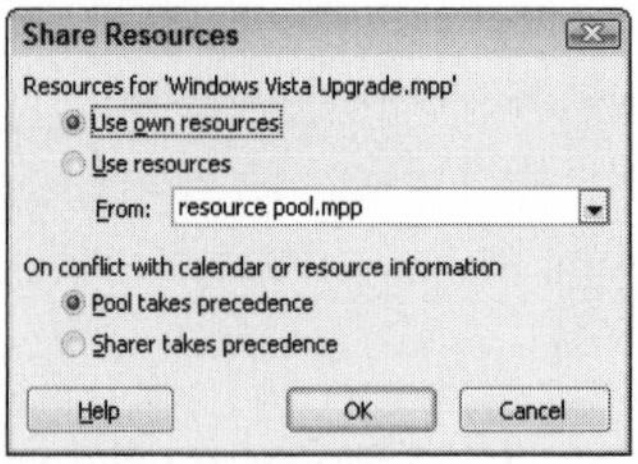

3. **Select the Use Own Resources option.**

Project displays a message, asking you to confirm that you want your project to now use its own resources instead of the resource pool.

4. **Click Yes.**

Project redisplays the Share Resources dialog box.

5. **Click OK.**

Project closes the Share Resources dialog box and your project now must use its own resources.

Do you want to disable the resource pool in general? No problem. You *don't* need to open each file and disable resource sharing. Follow these steps to disable the resource pool file:

1. **Click the Open tool on the Standard toolbar and open the resource pool file the same way that you would open any file.**

   Project displays the Open Resource Pool box (refer to Figure 4-28).

2. **Choose either the middle option or the last option.**

   Either option works because both options open the resource pool as a read-write file.

3. **Choose Tools➪Resource Sharing➪Share Resources.**

   Project displays the Share Resources dialog box (see Figure 4-32).

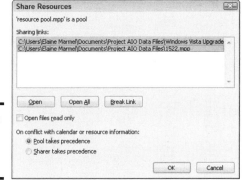

Figure 4-32:
The Share
Resources
dialog box.

4. **Select the project(s) that you want to exclude from the resource pool.**

   Press and hold Ctrl as you click to select multiple noncontiguous projects or press and hold Shift as you click the first and last projects to select contiguous projects.

   If you choose to break the links of *all* files to the resource pool and other project managers use the pool, you could become a *very* unpopular person. Make sure you select files for which you have responsibility.

5. **Click the Break Link button.**

   Project closes the Share Resources dialog box and disconnects all the projects you selected from the resource pool.

6. **Save the resource pool file.**

Book IV

Establishing Task Timing

The 5th Wave   By Rich Tennant

"This isn't a quantitative or a qualitative estimate of the job. This is a wish-upon-a-star estimate of the project."

Contents at a Glance

Chapter 1: Looking at Timing

In This Chapter

✔ Understanding what drives timing

✔ Using scheduling from start or finish dates

✔ Understanding the nature of backward scheduling

✔ Saving time

*A*fter you have created tasks, given them durations, added dependencies, and designated any constraints, you have effectively set up the timing for your project. At this point, it's important to take a look at the timing information Project is returning to you and what it means for your project's overall schedule.

In this chapter, we sit back and take a look at timing, review what drives timing, and look at the options available for scheduling.

Understanding What Drives Timing

Consider the way your typical day goes. The timing of all the tasks you perform, all the errands you run, and all the work you get done is affected by a number of factors. It's not just the times you set up to get to work, run to a doctor's appointment, or have dinner that drives your day's timing. Your schedule is also affected by whether your partner showed up to help you prepare dinner, whether your co-worker finished the draft of the report you were supposed to finalize, and whether you got a late start because your alarm clock didn't go off.

The timing of tasks in a Project plan also isn't determined by a single factor, but by a combination of factors.

Timing factors

Timing of tasks in a Project schedule might be influenced by several things, including

✦ A task duration you specify (for example, 3 days)

✦ The start or finish date of the project

✦ Dependencies with other tasks that must be started or completed before this task can begin or finish (see Figure 1-1)

✦ Constraints that you have set such as starting on a certain date or finishing no sooner than a certain date

✦ Resource availability, especially if you have turned on the Resource Leveling feature

✦ Project, Task, and Resource calendars

One other point you should understand is that Project assigns weight to the various timing influences in a complex calculation to set final task timing. So, for example, a constraint that a task must start on a certain date takes precedence over dependencies with other tasks. A Resource calendar takes precedence over the project calendar in determining when a task can take place.

You have some control over the rules of precedence that Project follows. For example, you can make task dependencies override the more inflexible constraints that you have set for tasks. In the Tools menu, click Options, and then click the Schedule tab. In the Scheduling options section, deselect the Tasks Will Always Honor Their Constraint Dates check box.

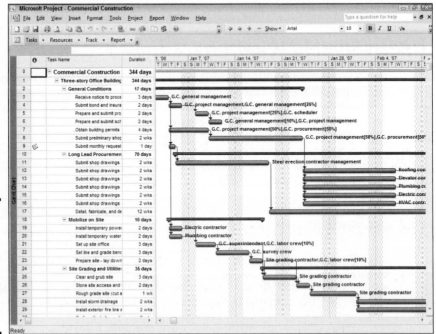

Figure 1-1:
You can see the flow of dependency relationships among tasks in this project.

You can also cause Project to ignore Resource calendars by selecting the Ignore Resource Calendars setting on the Advanced tab of a task information dialog box.

Your first look at your project's timing

If you've left the start date for your project at the default, it stays set at the current day (whatever date it was when you first created your project). We suggest you leave this setting (which you find in the Project Information dialog box) alone while entering the details of your project plan. When you've made all the settings for your tasks, you can see how long completing your project will take either by looking at a project summary task which summarizes all the timing of your tasks in one line item, or by looking at the start date of the first task and finish date of the last task.

You can read more about creating a project summary task in Book V, Chapter 4.

If, for example, your project is starting today and today is March 1, and your overall project duration is six months, you can figure that if you started today you would be done around August 31, depending somewhat on holidays, working days, and so on. If you then calculate that the work on the project won't actually start till you get your plan approved and get funding, which could take about a month, you can figure that you'll actually get done closer to the end of September.

At this point, you can really begin to see whether your schedule is going to fit your timing needs. You can start to play around with setting different start dates (see the next section for more about this process) or tweaking any of the timing factors in the previous list to try to shorten your schedule to meet a more aggressive deadline (see Book VII, Chapters 3 and 4 for more about the process of finalizing your schedule).

Project 2007 has a feature called Task Drivers. This feature allows you to open a pane that displays all the drivers for a selected task. Book VII, Chapter 2 goes into detail about using task drivers.

Scheduling Backwards or Forwards

When you're content that your project plan is complete and you're ready to begin work, that's the moment when you freeze your plan in time by setting either a start date or a finish date, which is dealt with in Book VII. For now, it's important that you understand how Project schedules tasks so you can understand the timing information it shows you.

How scheduling works

One reason using Project is a lot handier than entering tasks on your calendar or to-do list is that Project works with your built-in scheduling logic to make your plan flexible. So, if you change your project start date or add a new task, Project automatically adjusts your schedule. That's why you should avoid putting in specific constraints on tasks, but instead let them start as soon as possible. If you set a specific date and things change, you just have to manually change all those set dates, just as you had to do when you worked with a calendar program.

In most cases, people schedule from the beginning of a project so that all the task timing flows from the beginning date of the schedule. After you build all your tasks, Project in effect tells you when the project will finish, based on your start date.

However, in some cases, the finish date is such a driving factor (think of a project such as planning an event for the opening day of fishing season) that scheduling from the finish makes the most sense. Scheduling from the finish is one way to let Project tell you when you have to start to get things done by a certain date.

Here are the three settings in the Project Information dialog box (see Figure 1-2) that you need to understand regarding scheduling:

✦ **Set the start date for the project.** When you set the start date for your project, the first task in the project (assuming it's set at the default constraint of as soon as possible) starts on that date, with all subsequent task timing being driven by all the timing factors Project takes into account. Project automatically recalculates all dates when you select this setting.

✦ **Set the finish date for the project.** You can set the finish date. This option is especially handy if you have a drop-dead date beyond which the project cannot wander and still reach completion. In such a case, be sure to look at the next setting in this list — and change it accordingly.

✦ **Schedule from the start or finish of the project.** If you change this setting to Project Finish Date, the Finish Date field becomes available. All tasks occur by default as late as possible in the schedule. This is sometimes referred to as backward scheduling of backward estimating.

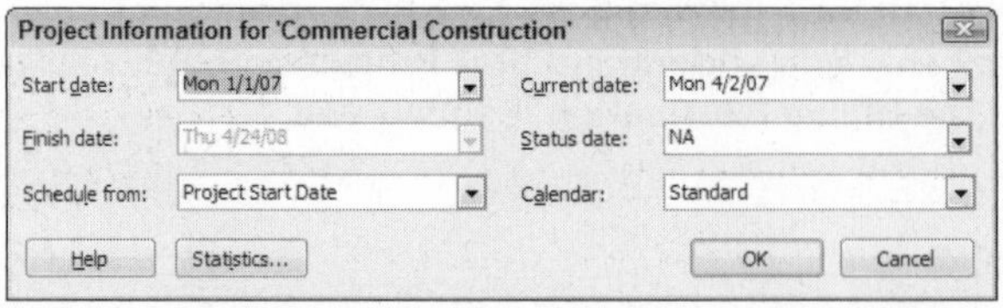

Figure 1-2:
The Project
Information
dialog box.

Project Information for 'Commercial Construction'				
Start date:	Mon 1/1/07	Current date:	Mon 4/2/07	
Finish date:	Thu 4/24/08	Status date:	NA	
Schedule from:	Project Start Date	Calendar:	Standard	
Help	Statistics...		OK	Cancel

A word of warning about backward scheduling

If you leave the default setting in the Project Information dialog box to schedule from the start date, all tasks you create have the As Soon As Possible (ASAP) constraint. If you change this setting to schedule from the finish date, all tasks you create have the As Late As Possible (ALAP) constraint applied.

Here's where this gets tricky. If you don't change this setting at the outset, create your schedule, and then change to the Schedule from Finish of Project setting, tasks you already created stay set at ASAP and tasks you create subsequent to changing the setting are created with the ALAP setting.

This situation causes ASAP tasks to start only when you enter an actual start date, which can cause some unnecessary down times (or slack) in your schedule. For that reason, you must modify this one setting before you even begin to enter information for your project. However, you can wait to set the actual start or finish date till your project planning is complete.

If you find out after the fact that you have to use backward scheduling, you have to go in and change the ASAP setting on tasks manually. However, you can display the Constraint Type column in any Gantt Chart view table (see Figure 1-3) to speed up your changes, or you can even create a macro to go down this column changing all settings in sequence. See Book IX, Chapter 3 for more about using macros.

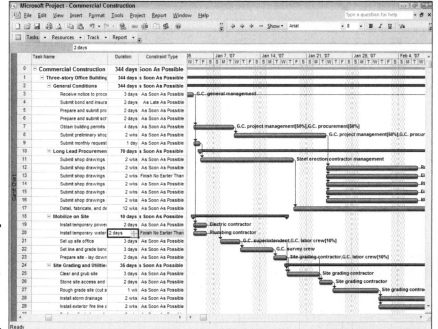

Figure 1-3: Quickly viewing task constraints in Gantt Chart view.

Book IV Chapter 1

Looking at Timing

Surviving Schedule Shock

Most people panic when they first see the length of the schedule they've created in Project. But take a step back for a moment. If you have entered correct information about your tasks, dependencies, and resources, what Project tells you should be realistic, if a bit frightening.

The first thing you should do upon seeing the total duration of your schedule is go back and make sure you were accurate in the information you gave Project. Check dependencies and constraints to see whether they're really logical. Is Resource Leveling on and therefore pushing tasks out to accommodate resource schedules? (See Figure 1-4 and 1-5, which show the total duration of a project with Resource Leveling turned on and turned off.) Did you move a task in your schedule in such a way that a former dependency no longer makes sense?

A timing case study

Company: A large Canadian pharmaceutical company.

Project: Direct marketing campaign for a new drug launch.

Challenge: Make sure that the launch of the marketing campaign happens as soon as the drug has been approved for sale.

This project involves the creation and delivery of e-mail, regular mail, and telemarketing campaigns to educate doctors about the release of a new drug product for the treatment of hypertension.

The key to the timing of this large direct-marketing campaign is the final approval of the drug by the Canadian government. The project manager wants to ensure that much of the work is done so she can move quickly on the final push.

The following factors need to be considered here:

✔ It is probably logical to schedule this project from the start, because the finish date is not set yet and won't be set until later in the project when the drug is approved.

✔ Tasks should therefore, for the most part, use the ASAP constraint.

✔ The task of actually launching the campaign should have a dependency such that it cannot start until an approval task is complete.

✔ The project manager has to judge how much time, effort, and money should be put in before the company is absolutely sure the drug will be approved. He might therefore build in checkpoints at the end of each phase to get formal internal approval for proceeding.

Solution: One tactic the project manager could use is to break up the project into two parts, the first one including all the tasks that can be performed before the launch, and the second part including the tasks that are part of the launch, as shown in this figure. That way, she won't delay the first part of the project because of constraints or dependencies in the second. She can also anticipate how long from the approval it will take to complete the launch by looking at the duration of that second project. As soon as the launch is approved, she can set the start date of that second project and get going.

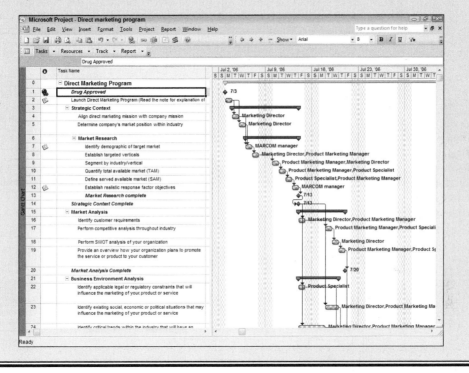

See Book VII for more about Resource Leveling and how it affects your project.

It's part of your role as project manager to take that second swing at your schedule to make it more realistic and still fit your needs. In Book VII, we go into the various techniques you can use to resolve problems in your schedule and tighten up that timing.

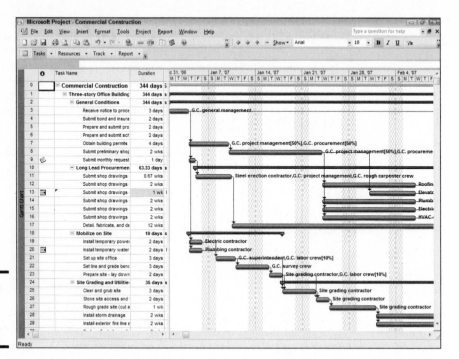

Figure 1-4:
Resource
Leveling is
turned on.

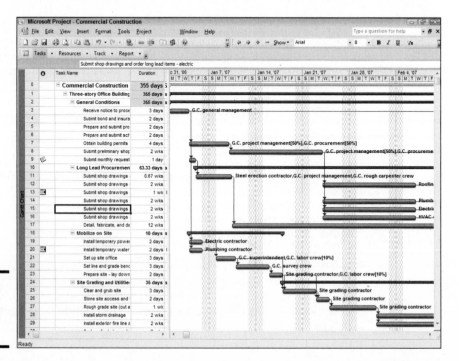

Figure 1-5:
Resource
Leveling is
turned off.

Chapter 2: Defining What Drives Task Timing

The timing of tasks is at the heart of all projects. Task timing in Microsoft Project is driven by a combination of factors, which is what this entire minibook is about. In this chapter, we explore some of the basic settings you can make when creating tasks that have an effect on timing.

First, you choose a task type that specifies what affects a task's timing, such as whether the task has a fixed duration or a duration that changes based on how much work has been accomplished. You can enter a *duration* for each task, which is simply the length of time you think it will take to complete the task. You can also enter a start date or finish date, or you can even insert a pause in the middle of the task. Finally, the Effort Driven setting has to do with how the work performed on a task affects its timing.

Be sure to also take a look at Book II, Chapter 4 to brush up on Project, Resource, and Task calendars. See Chapters 3 and 4 in this minibook to discover how dependencies and task constraints further determine the timing of tasks.

Finding Just the Right Task Type

When you perform a task, the time it takes to complete it might be a set time (for example, when you take a test in school, it might end in 30 minutes whether you're done or not), or the task might not finish until all the work is done. What constitutes a finished task varies slightly depending on the task type.

The big three: Task types

Task types define the relationship that balances a task's duration, the work required to complete the task, and resource availability. This is known as *the golden triangle*.

Before you begin to enter task durations, you need to be aware of the three task types. These types have an effect on how Project schedules the work of a task.

Essentially, your choice of task type determines which element of the task doesn't vary when you make changes to the task:

✦ **Fixed Units:** This is the default task type. With this task type, when you assign resources to a task with a certain number of *units* (hours of work expressed as a percentage of the working day), the resources' assignments don't change even if you change the duration of the task and the work amount.

✦ **Fixed Duration:** This task type takes a set amount of time to complete, no matter how many resources you add to the mix. For example, a test on a substance that requires that you leave the test running for 24 hours has a fixed duration even if you add 20 scientists to oversee the test.

✦ **Fixed Work:** The number of resource hours assigned to the task determines its length. If you set the duration of a Fixed Work task at 40 hours, for example, and you assign two resources to work 20 hours each (simultaneously) at units of 100 percent, the task will be completed in 20 hours. If you take away one of those resources, the single resource must put in 40 hours at units of 100 percent to complete the task. Understanding how the choice of task type causes your task timing or resource assignments to fluctuate is an important part of creating an efficient project.

Be sure to review Book V, Chapter 3 for information about assigning resources to tasks to get the full picture of how resource assignments can affect task length.

Specifying task type

After you figure out what type of task you're dealing with, setting the task type is simple to do through the Task Information dialog box.

Follow these steps to set the task type:

1. **Double-click a task.**

The Task Information dialog box appears.

2. **Click the Advanced tab, if necessary, to display it (see Figure 2-1).**

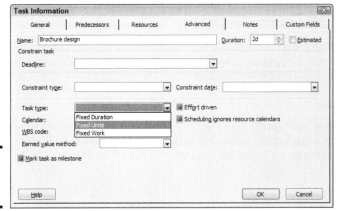

3. **Choose one of the three choices from the Task Type list (see the list of choices in the preceding section).**

4. **Click OK.**

You can also display the Type column in a Gantt Chart sheet and make this setting there.

Task types in practice

Your selection of task type — in combination with a setting that determines whether a task is effort driven, which is covered at the end of this chapter — has an effect on the timing of your tasks relative to your resource assignments.

Essentially, task types control what remains constant in a task when you add or remove work resources to it after making the initial resource assignment. Although this whole work and duration and resource assignment percentage calculation can be complicated, you need to understand it if you want Project to accurately determine task durations in your plan according to resource assignments.

**Book IV
Chapter 2**

**Defining What
Drives Task Timing**

Here's what happens when you're working with different task types in your project:

+ **The default task type is fixed units.** With a fixed-units task, the task duration you enter and the resource effort (work) assigned to that task jointly determine the timing of the task. With this task type, the assignment units you specify for your resources don't change even if the number of hours required to complete the task shrinks or grows.

  With a fixed-units task, if you increase the duration of Task A from two to three days, your resources will continue to work on it at the assigned units for the specified duration; Project increases the Work amount accordingly. When you add or take away resources, Project changes the task duration accordingly, based on the assignment units you specify.

+ **The fixed-work task type takes a specified number of work units to be completed.** A one-day task requires eight hours to be completed (assuming a Standard calendar). This type of task changes its duration in response to the number of resource units you assign.

  With a fixed-work task, resource assignments may change in response to a work change. For example, suppose Task A takes four days to complete when one person is assigned; with a fixed-work task, the same task takes only two days when two people are assigned. Project doesn't modify the hours of work required to complete the task, but it does modify resource assignment units to complete that work within the specified timeframe. Thus, if you up the duration of Task A, resource assignment units shrink in response. If you reduce the time to complete Task A, resource assignments increase to complete the unchanged amount of work hours in less time.

+ **A fixed-duration task doesn't vary its length, no matter what resource assignments you make.** Suppose that Task A takes four days. If you assign additional resources or remove resources, the task still takes four days, but the resource-assignment units will change.

Figure 2-2 shows the same task with the three different types specified. Each task was created with a four-day duration and one resource at 100 percent. Then an additional resource was added at 100 percent. Note the resulting change — or lack of change — with each type. The fixed-duration task didn't change duration but *did* reduce resource assignments. The fixed-units task kept resource assignments constant at 100 percent — but reduced the task duration. The fixed-work task was accomplished faster, and the work (32 hours) stayed constant.

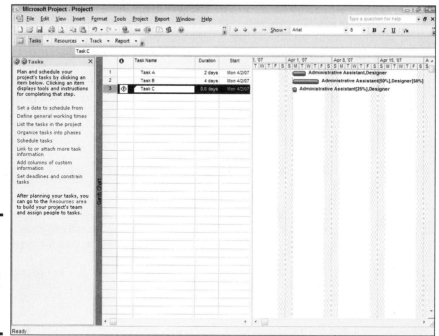

Figure 2-2:
Select the
task type
that reflects
what is
variable on
your task.

Setting Task Duration

Project can produce some wonderful calculations and reports, but it can't
tell you how long each task in your project will take. That's up to each project manager to figure out.

Estimating the duration of tasks isn't a science. A task's duration is usually
based on your experience with similar tasks and your knowledge of the
specifics of your project.

If you often do projects with similar tasks, consider saving a copy of your
schedule as a template that you can use in the future. Using this template
will save you the effort of re-estimating durations every time you start a similar project. Find out about working with templates in Book II, Chapter 1.

Determining the right duration

Most tasks in a project have a duration, whether it's ten minutes or ten months
or anything in between. (For milestone tasks, which have no duration, see
the next section.)

Deciding how finely to break down your tasks can affect how efficiently you're able to track progress on those tasks: Tasks that linger over an entire year are probably too broad, and a schedule full of tasks that take ten minutes each will force you to track progress 24 hours a day just to keep up with them.

For example, if your project is to run a half-day event, getting to the level of ten-minute tasks might make sense, although more from a planning perspective than a tracking perspective. In most projects, however, such finely detailed timing doesn't make sense because it defeats the point of all the tracking and reporting features of Project.

On the flip side, creating a 12-month-long task suggests that you might be defining your project too broadly to accurately keep track of all that can happen in a year. How do you track your progress every week, in a meaningful way, on a task that will take 12 months to complete? Is the task 1.5 percent complete in the first week, and how useful is that information? Consider breaking up tasks that linger longer than a few weeks into smaller tasks.

The Project Management Institute provides a suggestion that task durations range from 4 to 80 hours, as a rule of thumb.

Entering duration

Whatever your best guess at a task's duration is, Project makes it easy to add it to your task. As with all task information, you can enter a duration in a Gantt Chart sheet or in the Task Information dialog box.

Follow these steps to enter a duration by using the Task Information dialog box:

1. **Double-click a task to display the Task Information dialog box.**

2. **If necessary, click the General tab to display it (refer to Figure 2-1).**

3. **In the Duration box, use the spinner arrows to increase or decrease the duration.**

4. **If the current duration units aren't appropriate (for example, days when you want hours), type a new duration in the Duration box.**

New tasks are created with an estimated duration of one day unless you change the duration. You can use the following abbreviations for various time units:

- *m:* Minutes
- *h:* Hours

- *d:* Days
- *w:* Weeks
- *mo:* Months

Don't assume that changing the start and finish dates of a task changes its duration, because it doesn't. You have to manually change the duration; if you don't, your project plan won't be what you intend it to be.

5. Click OK to accept the duration setting.

If you're not sure about the timing of a particular task and want to let people know the duration is just a guess, or if you need a way to search for such tasks and enter more solid timing when you have better information, select the Estimated check box on the General tab of the Task Information dialog box. Then apply a filter for tasks with estimated durations (see Book VII, Chapter 1 for more about using filters). Tasks for which you have not set any duration will be considered estimated by default and you will see a question mark by their durations in the Duration field.

Working with tasks with no duration: Milestones

We mention in the preceding section that almost all tasks have durations; the exception is a *milestone* — a task with no duration. Milestones are perhaps less like tasks than they are like signposts that mark moments in time. Examples of milestones are the approval of a new product design (although the deliberations to make that decision might have taken months) and the completion of a network installation.

What does priority do to timing?

One other tool on the General tab of the Task Information dialog box is the Priority field. You might think establishing task priority might have an impact on timing, but think again.

Setting a high or low priority on your task doesn't influence timing of the task at all. In fact, this field is essentially there to help you enter your own ranking of the importance of tasks in your project. You can use that ranking to filter tasks by priority or to display a priority column in a view with a sheet area so you can scan tasks that have high importance and stay abreast of major shifts in your schedule. Though not part of the timing calculation Project uses, it can be a useful tool for flagging your own priorities in a project.

You can use the Priority field either in the Task Information dialog box or in a column on a sheet pane to set a priority from 0 (lowest) to 1000 (highest).

Book IV
Chapter 2

Defining What
Drives Task Timing

Some people include tasks such as Design Complete or Testing Complete at the end of each phase of their projects. They can then create timing relationships to the moment of completion (for example, allowing production of a drug to proceed after the testing and approval is complete). Such milestones also alert you and your team members to a moment of progress in your project that can help to keep the team motivated.

New tasks are created with an estimated duration of one day unless you enter a duration. To create a milestone, you indicate that the task has zero duration. The quickest way to do that is to simply type **0** in the Duration column in Gantt Chart view. Or, you can perform these steps:

1. **Double-click a task to open the Task Information dialog box.**

2. **Click the Advanced tab.**

3. **Set the Duration to 0.**

Project marks the Mark Task as Milestone check box.

4. **Click OK.**

When you return to Gantt Chart view, the milestone is designated with a black diamond shape rather than a taskbar.

They keep showing up: Recurring tasks

Some tasks occur again and again in projects. For example, attending a monthly project debriefing or generating a quarterly project report is considered a recurring task.

No one wants to create all the tasks for the monthly debriefing in a project that will take a year to complete. Instead, you can designate the recurrence, and Project automatically creates the 12 tasks for you.

Here's how you create a recurring task:

1. **Choose Insert⇨Recurring Task.**

The Recurring Task Information dialog box appears, as shown in Figure 2-3.

2. **In the Task Name box, type a name for the task.**

3. **In the Duration box, click the spinner arrows to set a duration or type a duration, such as** 10d **for 10 days.**

You can read about the abbreviations you can use for units of duration — such as *d* for days — in the earlier section, "Setting Task Duration."

Figure 2-3:
When you
enter this
information,
Project
creates
multiple
occurrences
of a task
automat-
ically.

Recurring Task Information	
Task Name: Staff Meeting	Duration: 1d

Recurrence pattern

○ Daily   Recur every 1 ⇳   week(s) on:
⦿ Weekly
○ Monthly   ☐ Sunday   ☐ Monday   ☐ Tuesday   ☐ Wednesday
○ Yearly   ☐ Thursday ☐ Friday   ☐ Saturday

Range of recurrence

Start: Mon 4/2/07 ▾   ○ End after: 0 ⇳ occurrences

                          ⦿ End by: Thu 4/5/07 ▾

Calendar for scheduling this task

Calendar: None ▾   ☐ Scheduling ignores resource calendars

[Help]   [OK] [Cancel]

4. **Select a recurrence pattern by selecting the Daily, Weekly, Monthly, or Yearly option.**

   What you select here provides different options for the rest of the recurrence pattern.

5. **Depending on the selections offered to you, make choices for the rest of the pattern.**

   For example, if you select the Weekly option, you must choose a Recur Every *X* Week(s) On setting, and then choose one or more days such as Wednesday and Friday. Or, if you select Monthly, you must specify which day of every month the task will recur.

6. **In the Range of Recurrence area, type a date in the Start box. Then select and fill in either the End After or End By option.**

   For example, you might start on January 1 and end after 12 occurrences to create a task that occurs every month for a year.

7. **Click OK to save the recurring task.**

If your settings cause a task to fall on a nonworking day (for example, if you choose to meet on the eighth day of every month and the eighth day is a Sunday in one of those months), a dialog box appears, asking you how to handle this situation. You can choose not to create the task, or you can let Project adjust the task to fall on the next working day in that period.

When you're ready to assign resources to a recurring task, you have to assign them to each incidence of the recurring task in Gantt Chart view; the Recurring Task Information dialog box doesn't have a Resources tab.

**Book IV
Chapter 2**

**Defining What
Drives Task Timing**

Starting and Pausing Tasks

When most people start using Project, one of the first things they try to do is enter a start date for every task in their project. This is largely a matter of habit: You always include dates when you write up a to-do list, right?

The problem is that setting every task in your project in stone from the get-go means you're missing out on one of the great strengths of project management software: the capability to schedule tasks for you according to sometimes-complex combinations of factors, such as dependencies between tasks and task constraints. When you allow Project to determine the start date of a task, you enable it to give you a realistic picture of your project's schedule. You also allow it to make adjustments automatically when changes occur.

To retain this flexibility, enter a task duration and don't enter a start date for the task. That task will then start by default as soon as possible after the project start date you set in the Project Information dialog box, based on any dependencies you set up between tasks.

In general, you establish a task's start date with dependencies (which you hear more about in the next chapter). You look for something in the project that would dictate its timing; for example, if you don't want construction to begin until you obtain permits, set a dependency between the permits task and the construction task in such a way that construction can't start before the permit task ends.

Certain tasks, however, must start on a specific date. Examples are a holiday sale, an annual meeting, or the start of the baseball season.

Project sets the finish date of a task based on when that task starts as well as the task duration. If a task must finish on a certain date, however, you can set a finish date and let Project determine the start date.

Entering the task start date

Setting a start date or a finish date for a task applies a kind of "soft" constraint on it that can override dependency relationships or other timing factors. A Must Start/Finish On task constraint, discussed in Chapter 4 of this minibook, is the way to force a task to start or end on a certain day. In many cases you do not have to set a start or finish date at all because the project start date and task dependencies will set the logical timing of the task for you. If you determine, however, that a particular task must begin or end on a set date no matter what, you can enter a specific start or finish date.

Setting the start or finish date is simple. To enter a start or finish date for a task, simply follow these steps:

1. **Double-click a task.**

The Task Information dialog box appears.

2. **Click the General tab if it's not already displayed; refer to Figure 2-1.**

3. **Click the arrow on the Start or Finish box.**

A calendar appears.

4. **Click a date to select it or click the forward or backward arrow to move to a different month and select a date.**

If the current date is the date you want, use the shortcut of clicking the Today button on the drop-down calendar.

5. **Click OK.**

Note that setting a start date isn't quite as strong a factor in how Project determines timing as applying the Must Start On constraint. You can find out more about how constraints work in Chapter 4 of this minibook.

Taking a break: Splitting tasks

Did you ever start something — building that garden shed, for example — and find that you just had to drop everything before you were done and go do something else?

It's the same in projects. Sometimes tasks start, and then you have to put them on hold until they can start again later (for example, if you experience a work shutdown due to labor negotiations). Or, perhaps you can anticipate a delay in the course of a task and want to structure it that way when you create it. In that case, you can use Project's Split Task feature to split a task so that a second or third portion starts at a later date, with no activity in between. You can place as many splits in a task as you like.

Follow these steps to split a task:

1. **Click the Split Task button on the Standard toolbar (it looks like a little taskbar with a jagged cut down the middle).**

A box appears, as shown in Figure 2-4. The box provides a readout to guide you as you set the start date for the continuation of the task.

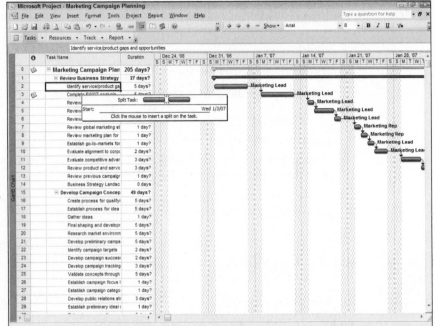

Figure 2-4:
Check out
this guide to
setting the
start date
for the
continuation
of the task.

2. **Click the task at the date where you want to split the task and then drag until the box contains the date on which you want the task to begin again.**

3. **Release the mouse button.**

   The task is split.

You can rejoin a split task by placing your cursor over the taskbar until the move cursor appears. Then click the split taskbar and drag it back to join with the other portion of the taskbar. If you need to, zoom out to make it easier for you to maneuver the pieces of the taskbar.

Don't use the split-task approach to put an artificial hold on a task until some other task is complete. Suppose that you start testing a product but then have to wait for final approval before finalizing the test results. In that case, you should create a Testing task, a Final Approval milestone, and a Finalize Test Results task, and then you must create dependency relationships among them. That way, if one task runs late, your final task shifts along with it instead of being set in stone (as a split task is).

Understanding Effort-Driven Tasks

Project's complex calculation of work, task duration, and assignment units involves not only task types and task durations, but also the Effort Driven setting. This setting, which is on by default when you create a new task, relates to the impact that work done on a task has on task durations.

How effort-driven tasks work

When you hear the word *effort* in Project, you can equate it with *work*. When you create a task, by default it is *effort driven,* which means that if you adjust resource assignments, the duration might change, but the number of hours of effort (work) you need to put in to complete the task stays the same. When you add or delete a resource on an effort-driven task, work is spread around equally among resources.

With the Effort Driven setting active, if you add resources to a task, Project distributes the specified work equally among them and might change the task duration according to the total resource effort, depending on the task type.

Suppose that you have a two-day task to install modular furniture in a new office. With one resource assigned to the task, working 8 hours a day, it will take 16 hours to complete the work (two 8-hour days). If you assign a second resource, the task no longer takes two days because the hours of effort required will be completed more quickly by the two people working simultaneously — in this case, in one 8-hour period.

An example of a task that isn't effort driven is attending a three-day workshop. No matter how many people attend or how many people are present, the workshop still takes three days to complete. With the Effort Driven setting turned off on a task, no matter how much effort your resources put in, the task won't be completed sooner.

When effort rules timing

With all three task types, by default Project makes each task effort driven. You can turn off the Effort Driven setting if you choose the fixed-duration or fixed-units task type. With the fixed-work task type selected, the Effort Driven setting isn't only turned on automatically, but in fact it can't be turned off.

Follow these steps to change the settings for an effort-driven task:

1. **Double-click a task.**

The Task Information dialog box appears.

2. Click the Advanced tab, as shown in Figure 2-5.

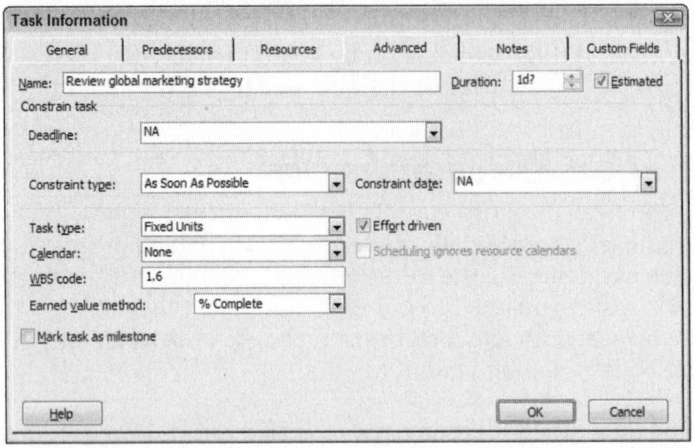

Figure 2-5:
The Effort
Driven
setting is
selected
and unavail-
able if you
select a
fixed-work
task.

Task Information					
General	Predecessors	Resources	Advanced	Notes	Custom Fields

Name: Review global marketing strategy   Duration: 1d?   ☑ Estimated

Constrain task

Deadline: NA

Constraint type: As Soon As Possible   Constraint date: NA

Task type: Fixed Units   ☑ Effort driven

Calendar: None   ☐ Scheduling ignores resource calendars

WBS code: 1.6

Earned value method: % Complete

☐ Mark task as milestone

Help   OK   Cancel

3. To turn off the Effort Driven setting, select the Effort Driven check box to remove the check mark.

The Effort Driven setting is on by default.

4. Click OK to save the new setting.

TIP

If you want to see the effect an Effort Driven setting makes on the timing of your task, display a Gantt chart and add an Effort Driven column in the table. Change the setting and view how start/finish dates and the taskbar length are affected.

Chapter 3: Adding Dependencies

In This Chapter

✔ **Exploring how dependency links affect timing**

✔ **Discovering the different kinds of dependency relationships**

✔ **Allowing for lag and lead time**

✔ **Establishing dependency links**

✔ **Reflecting the timing of external tasks in your project**

✔ **Viewing dependencies in Gantt Chart and Network Diagram views**

*I*f you create 100 tasks and don't change their default settings, they all start as soon as possible after the project start date. In the absence of timing relationships, called *dependencies,* all those tasks not only start on the project start date, but they occur simultaneously. That means that a project consisting of 100 tasks takes exactly as long to complete as the longest task.

Of course, that's not a very realistic scenario for a project. Typically, tasks don't happen at the same time. It might be impossible for certain activities to happen before others are complete, or you might not have the resources to perform two tasks at once. For that reason, you have to incorporate timing relationships that spread those tasks out through the life of your project.

Why Dependencies Are Needed

The reality is that tasks in a project can't all start at the same time. To reflect that reality in a Project plan, you have to build in a timing logic. You build that logic into your plan by setting dependency links between tasks. *Dependencies* are timing relationships between tasks (for example, when one task can't start before you complete another, or one task can't end before another task ends).

Dependencies can be driven by

✦ **The nature of the tasks:** You can't mail a brochure, for example, until it's printed.

✦ **A lack of available resources:** Your CEO can't give new product launch keynote speeches in two cities simultaneously.

Understanding Dependencies

In Chapter 2 of this minibook, we tell you that you shouldn't set task start dates very often because projects are *fluid* — that is, they change and grow — and if you set every date in stone, those dates have to be manually adjusted if a change occurs. If, instead, you build in timing logic rather than assign specific dates, Project can reflect changes by adjusting your project automatically based on that logic.

With the right dependencies in place in Project, if the Receipt of Training Materials task is delayed by a week, for example, the dependent task of Start Training moves out a week automatically. When you note a change in the timing of one task while you're tracking activity in your plan, Project makes adjustments accordingly.

The alternative to building in dependencies is to go in and manually change the start date of just about every task in your schedule *every time a task runs late*. Given the way things change in a typical project, not using dependencies will leave you with many late nights at the office and a disaster in the making.

Identifying the players in a dependency relationship

A task in a dependency relationship is either a predecessor or a successor. You might think the *predecessor* comes first and the *successor* follows, and that is usually true. However, two tasks with a timing relationship will be a *predecessor-successor pair,* even if the timing of the two tasks overlaps or they're set to happen concurrently.

Figure 3-1 shows you how the taskbars in Gantt Chart view graphically depict the predecessors and successors in dependency relationships. Notice how taskbars fall before or after another task in the relationship or when a task starts during the life of another task. Also notice the lines drawn between tasks: These lines indicate *dependency links.*

Generally speaking, you set dependencies between one task and another but not between a task and a summary task. If you set a dependency to a summary task and the specific action that had to be complete before your task could start finishes early, you may introduce unneeded delay in your schedule.

When to set a dependency and when to leave well enough alone

We want to offer one very important piece of advice about dependencies: You can have more than one dependency link to a task, but don't overthink this. Many people who are new to Project make the mistake of building every logical timing relationship that could exist. If your project timing changes or the dependencies have to be modified (for example, to shorten a schedule), you're stuck with changing the huge web of dependencies, which can easily get out of hand.

For example, say that you have to complete the tasks of designing and printing a brochure before you can mail it. You could set up a dependency between designing and mailing, designing and printing, and printing and mailing, but why bother? If you set up a dependency between designing and printing, set a dependency between printing and mailing that ensures that you can't mail the brochure before it's designed.

If you use a dependency to delay a task and then change the resources assigned to the task, you've built in a false delay. There is another and perhaps better method than dependencies to prevent resources from working on two tasks simultaneously: You can set the availability for resources and assign them to tasks. You can then use tools such as Resource Leveling, which forces one task to be delayed if there are resource conflicts. See Book VII, Chapter 2 for more about how resource conflicts affect task timing.

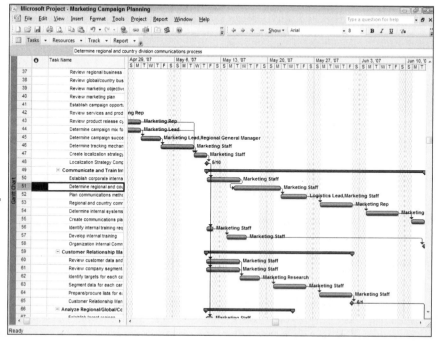

Figure 3-1:
In this view, dependency relationships are shown by the lines between taskbars.

**Book IV
Chapter 3**

**Adding
Dependencies**

All types of dependencies

You can establish four types of dependency links: finish-to-start, start-to-finish, start-to-start, and finish-to-finish. Using these types efficiently can help you to build a tightly structured timing logic into your schedule that can help keep your project moving along.

In Book IV, Chapter 4 we cover task constraints. These settings and task priorities work in concert with dependencies to determine the ultimate timing of tasks in your project.

Here are the four dependency types:

✦ **Finish-to-start:** A finish-to-start dependency is the most common type of dependency link. In this relationship, the predecessor task must be completed before the successor task can start. When you create a dependency, the default setting is finish-to-start.

An example of a finish-to-start dependency is when you must complete the Write Annual Report task before you can begin the Send Out Annual Report task. Figure 3-2 shows two tasks with the finish-to-start relationship indicated by a successor taskbar that starts where the predecessor taskbar leaves off. When one task ends, the other begins.

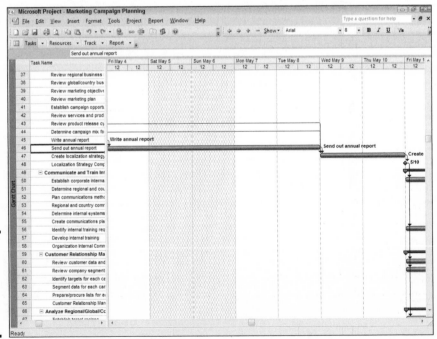

Figure 3-2:
The finish-to-start relationship between two tasks.

✦ **Start-to-finish:** In a start-to-finish dependency, the successor task can finish only after the predecessor task has started. If the predecessor task is delayed, the successor task can't finish.

Suppose that you're planning the opening of a new theater building. You might start selling tickets for the theater's first production while the building is being built, and you don't want to stop selling tickets until opening night. So, the predecessor task is Theater Building Complete (a milestone or task of no duration), and the successor task is Sell Tickets for Opening Night. If the theater isn't ready on time, you can keep selling tickets. When the theater is ready to go, the ticket windows close, and that task can finish. Break a leg!

✦ **Start-to-start:** Start-to-start means what it says: Two tasks exist in a parallel relationship and therefore start simultaneously. For example, even though posters and invitations for your blockbuster event are being created by different designers, you might want to ensure that you send the posters and invitations to the printer at the same time for cost efficiency.

Figure 3-3 shows the start-to-start relationship between the two tasks.

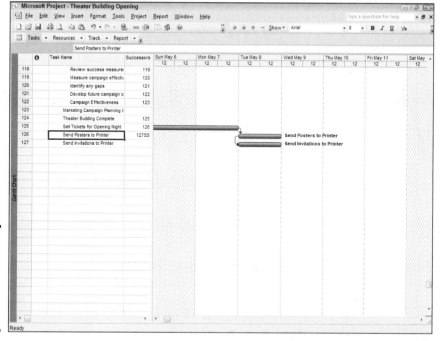

Figure 3-3: The start-to-start relationship between two tasks.

✦ **Finish-to-finish:** Finish-to-finish means that (you guessed it) two tasks must finish at the same time.

Suppose that you're preparing an advertisement for your adventure-travel company. You have to obtain photographs of travel destinations and have the ad copy laid out. You need both items in hand before you can forward the ad to travel magazines. If you set a finish-to-finish dependency between these two tasks, you allow both tasks the greatest length of time to be completed. (Why have the photos been sitting around for four weeks, for example, when the copy isn't ready?) However, keep in mind that if one task finishes late, they both finish late.

More complex dependencies: Lag and lead time

Dependencies can be more complex than simply establishing the four types of dependency links we describe in the preceding section. You can use lag time or lead time to fine-tune your timing relationships in the following ways:

✦ **Lag time** occurs when you add time to the start or finish of a predecessor task; lag time causes a gap in timing.

✦ **Lead time** is created when you subtract time from the start or finish of the predecessor task; lead time causes an overlap between two tasks.

You might use lag time to reflect that a task such as Run Focus Group might have to wait a week or two after you distribute sample materials to the group members so that they have time to study them. On the other hand, you could use lead time to allow one task to begin part way through another task. For example, you could begin to train people on new equipment when only half of the new pieces of equipment have been received.

See the Case Study at the end of this chapter for a study of the use of lag and lead time in a sample project.

Setting Dependencies

Establishing dependency relationships is easy to do. You simply create a dependency, make settings to select the dependency type, and build in any lag or lead time.

What's more complex is understanding how each type of dependency affects your plan when your project starts and you begin to record actual activity that resources perform on individual tasks.

This section provides guidance on establishing dependencies and understanding more about how they function in a real-world project.

Setting up dependency links

When you create a dependency, by default, it's a finish-to-start relationship: One task must finish before another can start. If your situation calls for that kind of simple scenario, you can set a dependency between two tasks by using a simple click-and-drag method, and you're done.

To establish a simple finish-to-start link, follow these steps:

1. Display Gantt Chart view and make sure that the two tasks you want to link are visible.

You might have to collapse some tasks in your project or use the Zoom command on the View menu to fit more tasks on your screen.

2. Move your cursor over a taskbar until it changes to a four-headed arrow.

3. Click the predecessor taskbar and drag your cursor to the successor taskbar.

As you drag, a box appears, as shown in Figure 3-4, and your cursor changes to the shape of a little chain link.

4. When the readout indicates the task number you want to link to, release your mouse button.

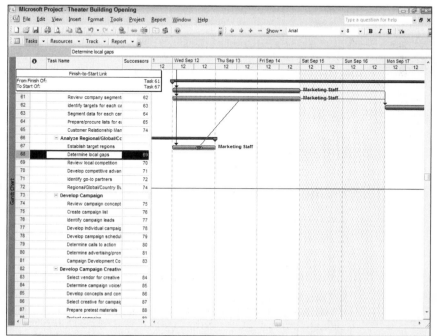

Figure 3-4:
This box lets you know when your cursor is resting over the task to which you want to link.

**Book IV
Chapter 3**

**Adding
Dependencies**

You can also use the following method to establish a finish-to-start relationship between two tasks: Click the predecessor task, press Ctrl, click the successor task, and then click the Link Tasks button on the Standard toolbar.

If you have to refine your dependency after you create a dependency link, you can edit that link to change the dependency type or to build in lag or lead time.

To establish a link in the Task Information dialog box or to modify an existing relationship, make note of the task ID number (you can find it in the far-left shaded column in the Gantt Chart sheet pane) of the predecessor task and then follow these steps:

1. **Double-click the successor task.**

The Task Information dialog box appears.

2. **Click the Predecessors tab, shown in Figure 3-5.**

On this tab, you can build as many dependency relationships as you like.

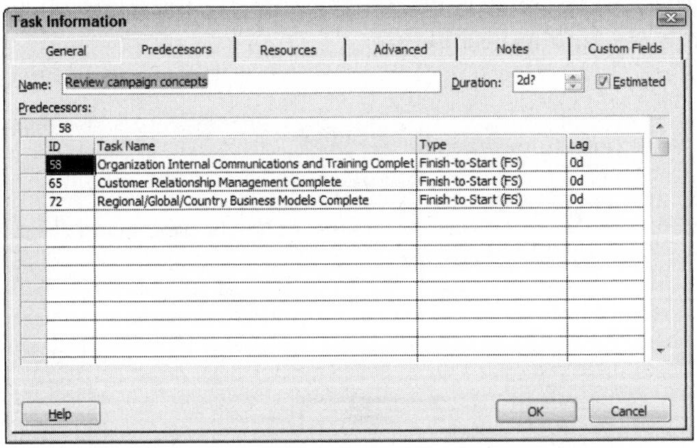

Figure 3-5:
Build
dependency
relationships
here.

Task Information					
General	Predecessors	Resources	Advanced	Notes	Custom Fields

Name: Review campaign concepts   Duration: 2d? ☑ Estimated

Predecessors:

58

ID	Task Name	Type	Lag
58	Organization Internal Communications and Training Complet	Finish-to-Start (FS)	0d
65	Customer Relationship Management Complete	Finish-to-Start (FS)	0d
72	Regional/Global/Country Business Models Complete	Finish-to-Start (FS)	0d

Help   OK   Cancel

3. **In the ID field, type a task ID number for the predecessor task.**

Alternatively, you can select the task from the Name drop-down list.

4. **Press Tab.**

The task name and the default finish-to-start dependency type with 0d (no days, the default unit of time) of lag time are entered automatically.

5. **Click the Type field and click the arrow to display the dependency types and then click the appropriate dependency for your situation.**

6. If you want to add lag or lead time, click the Lag field and use the spinner arrows to set the amount of time.

Click up to a positive number for lag time or down to a negative number for lead time.

7. Repeat Steps 3–6 to establish additional dependency relationships.

8. When you're finished, click OK to save the dependencies.

The Gantt chart displays your dependencies with lines and arrows, as shown in the project displayed in Figure 3-6.

Most dependency links exist between tasks that are close to each other in your schedule. However, sometimes dependencies exist between tasks that are weeks or months apart. In that case, the click-and-drag method can be difficult to use. For this type of situation, you can use the successor task's Task Information dialog box to create the relationship by entering the predecessor task ID number or name and by defining the lag or lead time in the appropriate fields.

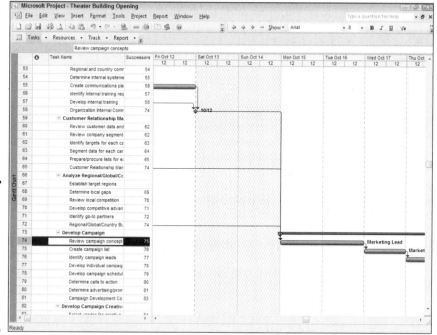

Figure 3-6: The more complex the project and its timing relationships, the more lines you see.

Connecting to other projects with external dependencies

Few projects in organizations exist in a vacuum. Many times, another project you're managing or another project going on somewhere else in your organization affects your project. Perhaps you share resources or equipment with others, or perhaps the timing of tasks in other projects affects the timing of tasks in yours.

If your project is to launch a Web site, you might have to create a dependency from your Launch Web Site task to the New Product Release task in someone else's project so you're sure you can offer the new product line on the Web site.

To deal with this cross-project coordination, you can create a hyperlinked task that represents the timing of the other project (or of a particular task in the other project). Enter a start date and duration for the external task as a task in your project. You can then create dependencies between that task and other tasks in your project to connect your activities to the external timing. Use the hyperlink to jump quickly to the other project whenever you want to update your timing information. (See Book III, Chapter 4 for information about hyperlinking tasks in projects.)

You can also insert an entire project and add a link to it so that updates to the other file are reflected in your plan automatically.

Things change: Deleting dependencies

Over the life of a project, you're likely to find that timing relationships among tasks change. For example, sometimes you no longer need a dependency you created to avoid resource conflicts because of a shift in resources or overall project timing.

When you need to get rid of a dependency, you can undo what you did in either Gantt Chart view or the Task Information dialog box.

With Gantt Chart view displayed, follow these steps:

1. **Select the two tasks whose dependency you want to delete.**

   - *For two adjacent tasks:* Click and drag to select their ID numbers.

   - *For nonadjacent tasks:* Click one task, press and hold the Ctrl key, and then click a nonadjacent task.

2. **Click the Unlink Tasks button on the Standard toolbar (it looks like a chain link with a break in the middle).**

Be careful when you use this method: If you click a single task and then click the Unlink Tasks button, all dependency relationships for that task are removed.

To remove dependency relationships in the Task Information dialog box, here's the drill:

1. **Double-click a successor task name.**

The Task Information dialog box appears.

2. **Click the Predecessors tab to display it.**

3. **Click the Type box for the dependency that you want to delete.**

A list of dependency types appears, as shown in Figure 3-7.

Figure 3-7:
You can use this tab to create and delete dependency links.

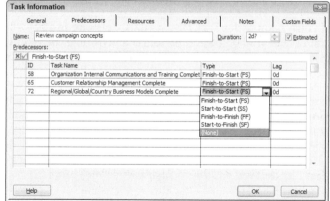

4. **Select None.**

5. **Click OK to save the change.**

The dependency line on the Gantt chart is gone. The next time you open that Task Information dialog box, you find that the dependency is no longer listed there.

Book IV
Chapter 3

Adding Dependencies

If you turn on the Change Highlighting feature, you can see how making this kind of change to dependencies affects your schedule. To turn on Change Highlighting, choose View➪Show Change Highlighting. Any tasks affected by subsequently adding or deleting a dependency have either their start or finish date column highlighted in the spreadsheet pane, depending on which date was affected.

Visualizing Task Dependencies

Being able to get a look at the dependency structure in your project can be very useful, especially when you're trying to solve a problem or refine the details in your project to save time or money.

Project provides several ways to view dependencies in your project. This involves displaying various views that represent dependencies by using text to describe them or lines that run between graphical representations of tasks.

You might have already seen the dependency link lines that appear in the Gantt chart (refer to Figure 3-6). Another great way to see the flow of dependencies is in Network Diagram view. This workflow view uses similar lines and arrows to reveal dependency relationships, but it allows you to get a different perspective on them.

You can also display the Task Drivers pane (choose Project➪Task Drivers) to see a list of everything in the schedule that's driving the timing of a selected task. For more about the Task Drivers feature, see Book I, Chapter 5.

Figure 3-8 depicts a Network Diagram view of an IT project. Notice that each task is represented by a node that contains data about the task. Between the nodes run lines that represent dependency relationships among the tasks. Although you can't see the effect in this black-and-white image, any task dependency links on the critical path are displayed in red by default, and noncritical tasks are displayed in blue. (Critical-path tasks have no slack: They can't be delayed without delaying the entire project.)

One way to help you remember what's going on with dependencies in Network Diagram view is to edit the layout to show link labels. Here are the steps to do this:

1. **Right-click anywhere outside the task nodes.**

2. **Choose Layout.**

3. **Select the Show Link Labels check box.**

A code, such as FS for finish-to-start, is displayed to explain the type of dependency that each dependency line represents, as shown in Figure 3-8.

You can also display a view that contains columns to view by task ID number, successors or predecessors for each task, or the dependencies for a task. You can do this in any view with a sheet area, such as Gantt Chart view. Figure 3-9 shows a Gantt Chart view for an engineering project with Predecessors and Successors columns displayed.

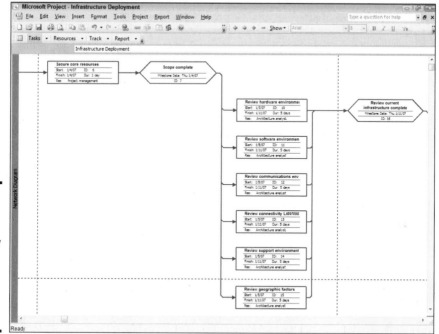

Figure 3-8:
Following the flow of dependency lines is a bit easier in Network Diagram view.

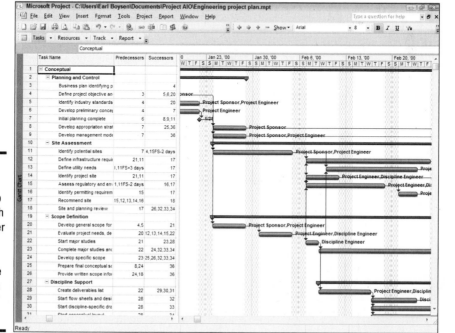

Figure 3-9:
Of course, you have to know which task number is which before you can use the information in these columns!

Training new staff efficiently

Company: Large science museum.

Project: Staff and train a new set of volunteer docents to give museum tours.

Challenge: Organize training as quickly as possible to handle upcoming peak season. In the first version of this plan there was a finish-to-start relationship between the two tasks Locate Recruits and Train Recruits. That meant that no training could begin until the last docent recruit was on board. With this dependency in place, the project couldn't meet the required deadline.

Solution: To get some docents trained and working more quickly, the project manager decided to incorporate a week of lead time — that is, allow the training of the earliest hires to start before all the recruits are hired. To do this, he essentially deducted time from the finish-to-start relationship between Locate Recruits and Train Recruits. This change allows the training to start a week before the finish of the Locate Recruits predecessor, as shown in this figure.

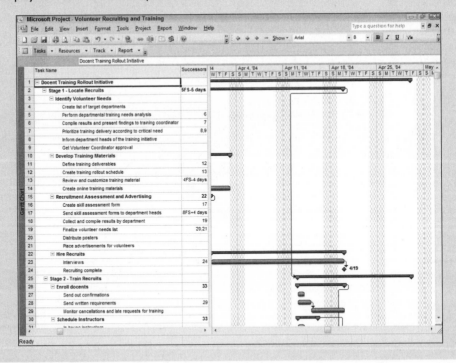

Another way to achieve this would be to break the recruiting and training into two pieces. To do this, you could have two recruiting and two training tasks. Say you have to recruit ten people. The first task could be Recruit Half of Docents and the second task Recruit Second Half of Docents. Create finish-to-start relationships between the first recruiting task and the first training task; then create the same relationship between the second recruiting task and a second training task. If there's a delay in hiring the second set of docents, the first half of the docents can still proceed with their training.

These columns also include a notation of any type of dependency other than the default finish-to-start type and any lead or lag time using percentages or lengths of time. For example, 71SS+50% is a start-to-start link to task 71, with lag time set so that the successor task begins halfway through the predecessor task. Similarly, 71SS+2 days is a start-to-start link to task 71, with lag time set so that the successor task begins two days after the predecessor task starts.

Note that you can also edit the contents of Network Diagram nodes to include predecessor and successor data.

**Book IV
Chapter 3**

**Adding
Dependencies**

Chapter 4: Working with Constraints and Deadlines

In This Chapter

✔ Looking at how constraints control timing

✔ Understanding different constraint types

✔ Assigning constraints

✔ Understanding constraints in combination with dependencies

✔ Setting a deadline

*W*hen you build a project, each task in it gains its timing from a variety of influences with a sometimes-complex set of priorities. You may give a task a specific start date, set dependency relationships that drive the task's timing, or even set up a project calendar that dictates how much work can go on in a given day or week.

In addition to all these influences and more, you can apply constraints to individual tasks. A *constraint* is a restriction that you place on a task to control when it can start or finish. In combination with other factors, a constraint can be a powerful force for determining the timing of your tasks and project.

Deadlines, on the other hand, are more informational and are used to alert you when you're running late, but they don't control the timing of tasks in any real sense.

Beginning with the Start and Finish Dates

Every task has a start date and a finish date. You can set fixed start or finish dates, or (and this is the preferred method) you can let Project schedule them based on several criteria. In the absence of a fixed start or finish date, Project schedules a task based on the task duration, calendars (including the Project calendar and assigned Resource calendars), dependencies with predecessor and successor tasks, constraints applied to predecessor and successor tasks, and a task's own calendar and constraints.

Brush up on calendar settings in Book II, Chapter 4, and on dependencies in Chapter 3 of this minibook.

The weight that Project gives each of these factors is a rather complex thing to understand, and frankly, it's not going to help you that much. Rather than dissect the complex algorithm Project uses, what you should know is that the more you change default settings to apply constraints, set a fixed start date, or modify each task's calendar, the more settings you have to track down when a problem occurs. That's one reason why you should use constraints sparingly and only when absolutely necessary (more about when that might be shortly).

So how, exactly, does a task constraint work? We're glad you asked. . . .

Understanding How Constraints Work

Though constraints are only one of the criteria used to establish task timing, when Project performs calculations to try to save you time in a project that's running late, it considers constraints to be the most sacred timing settings. For example, if you set a constraint that a task must finish on a certain date, Project doesn't do anything to change that date when recalculating timing of tasks in your project.

Default constraints

When you create a task, depending on the scheduling method that you set in the Project Information dialog box shown in Figure 4-1 (see Book II, Chapter 1 for more about scheduling methods), you can apply two default constraints:

✦ **If you're scheduling your project to be calculated from the start date, the As Soon As Possible constraint is selected by default.** In other words, the task starts as soon as the project starts, assuming that no dependencies with other tasks exist that would delay its start.

✦ **If you're scheduling your project to be calculated from the finish date, the As Late As Possible (ALAP) constraint is applied by default.** In this case, the task occurs as late as it possibly can while still meeting the finish date of the entire project.

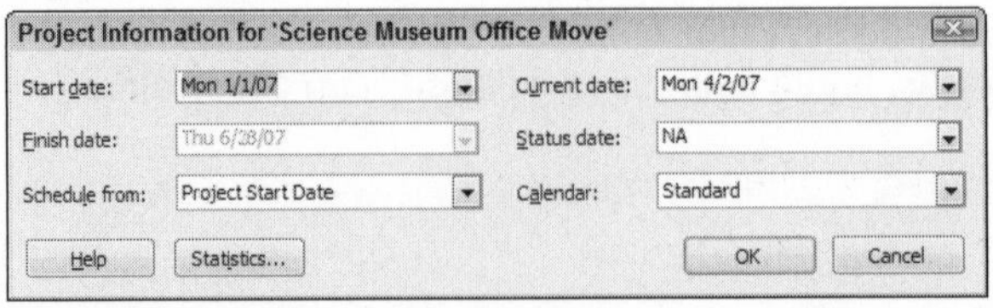

Figure 4-1:
The Project
Information
dialog box.

Project Information for 'Science Museum Office Move'

Start date:	Mon 1/1/07	Current date:	Mon 4/2/07
Finish date:	Thu 6/28/07	Status date:	NA
Schedule from:	Project Start Date	Calendar:	Standard

Help   Statistics...   OK   Cancel

You can create a task by clicking and dragging within the chart area in Gantt Chart view. When you create a task using this method, Project applies the Start No Earlier Than constraint if you have set up your project to schedule from the start date. If you're using the finish date scheduling method, such a task has the Start No Later Than constraint applied.

Constraint types

Table 4-1 lists all the constraints and an explanation of their effects on your task's timing.

Table 4-1	Task Constraints
Constraint	**Effect**
As Late As Possible	The task occurs as late as possible in your schedule, based on dependencies and the project finish date.
As Soon As Possible	The default setting; the task starts as early in the schedule as possible based on dependencies and the project start date.
Finish No Earlier Than	The end of the task can't occur any earlier than the date you specify.
Finish No Later Than	The end of the task can't occur any later than the date you specify.
Must Finish On	The task must finish on an absolute date.
Must Start On	The task must start on an absolute date.
Start No Earlier Than	The task can't start any earlier than the date you specify.
Start No Later Than	The task can't start any later than the date you specify.

Flexible versus inflexible constraints

It's helpful to understand that the constraints Project offers fall into two categories: flexible and inflexible (also known as soft and hard constraints).

Flexible constraints allow Project to move the task start and end dates based on other factors in the project such as dependencies with other tasks that are delayed. A typical flexible constraint is As Soon As Possible. A task could start, for example, as soon as possible when all other elements (such as the project start date, dependency relationships, and assigned Resource calendars) are satisfied. Flexible constraints include

✦ As Soon As Possible

✦ As Late As Possible

✦ Finish No Earlier Than

✦ Finish No Later Than

✦ Start No Earlier Than

✦ Start No Later Than

An *inflexible constraint* never allows the start or end date (depending on the constraint) to be moved because it essentially sets that date in stone. Inflexible constraints include:

✦ Must Finish On

✦ Must Start On

Constraints and dependencies

Most tasks have some dependency relationships with other tasks. When a dependency is in place, it's important that you know how constraints affect a task. Here's one example.

If you create a task called Wire House and another task called Wiring Inspection, you might put a finish-to-start dependency between them so that the inspection can't happen until the wiring is complete. If the wiring is completed early, the inspection could happen earlier. If the wiring task runs late, the inspection task is pushed back.

But if you know that inspections are done every two weeks on Thursdays and you really want the inspection to occur in a certain week of the project, you might decide to put a Must Start On constraint to force the inspection task to happen in the week you want wiring to be complete. If you set that constraint, here's what happens:

If the wiring finishes two weeks early, your schedule shows that you have to sit around for two weeks until the inflexible Must Start On constraint date rolls around. If you don't notice the problem and manually move the inspection up by removing the constraint, that could cost you valuable time in your schedule.

If you're late on the predecessor task when you track the earlier start date, Project displays a Planning Wizard dialog box like the one shown in Figure 4-2. This warning notes that the pushing back of the predecessor task causes a conflict with a successor task that cannot move. At this point, you can choose to cancel the tracking activity or allow the conflict. If you allow the conflict, the successor task falls behind the predecessor task (see Figure 4-3).

Instead of setting the Must Start On constraint, consider using a deadline (see "Setting a Deadline," later in this chapter) to flag the date you think the inspection should happen. If the deadline passes and the inspection hasn't happened, Project displays an indicator in the Indicator field for that task, alerting you to the fact that you're running late. By not using the constraint if the earlier task finishes ahead of schedule, the inspection task is allowed to move up, saving you time overall.

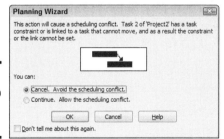

Figure 4-2:
You woke up
Planning
Wizard!

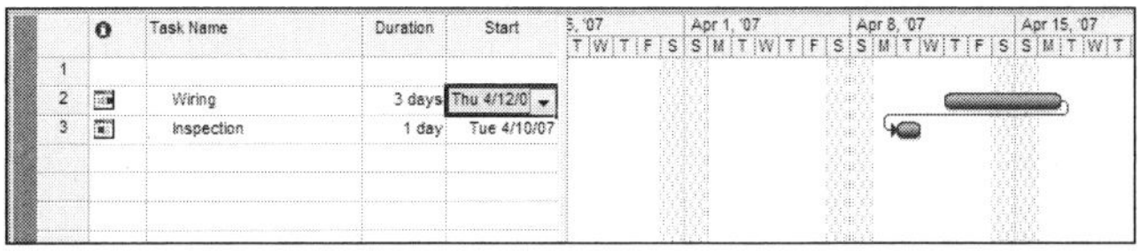

Figure 4-3:
The succes-
sor has
become the
predecessor.

Establishing Constraints

You can set only one constraint for a task. Setting a constraint involves selecting the type of constraint you want in the Task Information dialog box. Some constraints work together with a date you choose. For example, if you want a task to start no later than a certain date, you need to select a date by which the task must start. Other settings, like As Soon As Possible, work off a different date — in this case, the start date you set for the whole project or any dependency relationships you set up with other tasks. (See Chapter 3 of this minibook for more about dependency relationships.)

To set a task constraint, follow these steps:

1. **Double-click a task.**

The Task Information dialog box appears.

2. **Click the Advanced tab (see Figure 4-4).**

3. **Select a constraint from the Constraint Type list.**

4. **If the constraint requires a date, select one from the Constraint Date list.**

5. **Click OK to save the settings.**

**Book IV
Chapter 4**

**Working with
Constraints and
Deadlines**

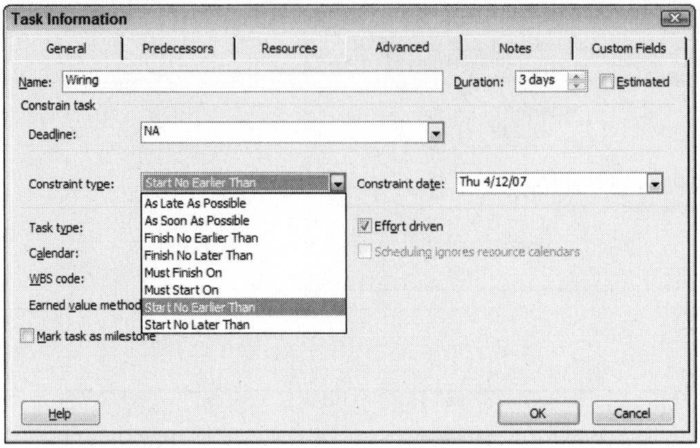

Figure 4-4:
The Task
Information
dialog box,
Advanced
tab.

Setting a Deadline

Strictly speaking, deadlines aren't constraints (although the setting for the deadline is in the Constraint Task area of the Task Information dialog box, on the Advanced tab). Deadlines differ from constraints in that they don't force the timing of your tasks in any sense.

If you set a deadline, it simply causes Project to display a symbol in the Indicator column if the task has run past the deadline to alert you so that you can panic (we mean, take appropriate action). Using a deadline is often preferable to setting an inflexible constraint because a deadline allows a task to shift with other changes in your schedule, yet keeps you aware when you're going to miss a target date.

To set a deadline, follow these steps:

1. **Double-click a task.**

The Task Information dialog box appears.

2. **Click the Advanced tab.**

3. **Click the arrow in the Deadline field to display a calendar (see Figure 4-5), and then select a date.**

If necessary, use the forward or backward arrow to move to a different month.

4. **Click OK to save the deadline setting.**

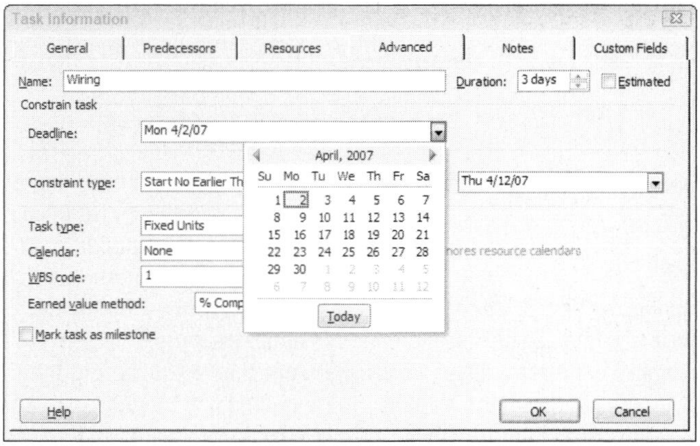

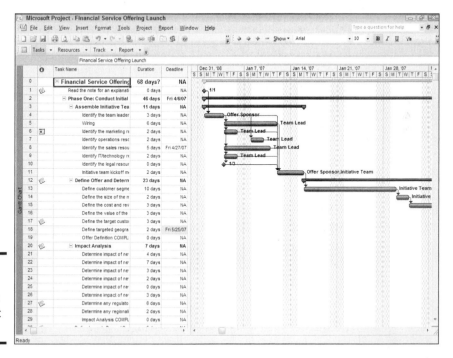

Figure 4-5:
The
Deadline
field
calendar.

You can also display a deadline column in your Gantt Chart sheet pane (see Figure 4-6) to enter the deadline or to show yourself and others what your targeted deadline date is.

Figure 4-6:
Entering a
deadline in
Gantt Chart
view.

Waiting till the last minute

Company: Home office of a large retail clothing chain.

Project: Office move.

Challenge: Training employees on the new phone system should happen as late as possible in the move so they can begin working on a day-to-day basis, with minimal down time, with the phones in their new office space right after training.

The main office of a company that runs dozens of retail clothing stores is moving to new office space. The staff in the office includes the customer support group that provides support via phone and e-mail. Part of the move involves installing a new phone system with some sophisticated features, and the staff needs training to use those features.

The project manager has been charged by the VP of Operations with arranging the training on the phone system to occur as close as possible to the end of the project — the last milestone task named "Move Complete." This ensures that employees are trained in the phone system no more than a day before they move into the new offices and begin to use the system.

Solution: To achieve this result, the project manager applies an As Late As Possible constraint to the training task and then creates a finish-to-start dependency between it and the Move Complete task. With these settings, the task appears just before the move-in but no earlier, as shown here.

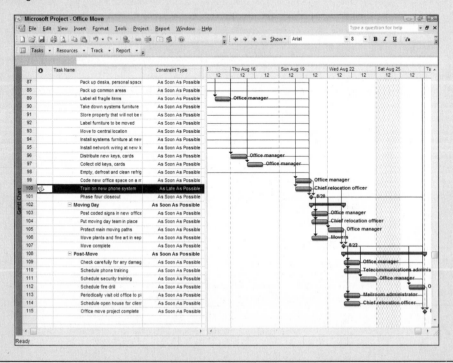

Book V

Working with Resources and Costs

The 5th Wave   By Rich Tennant

ANY AMOUNT WILL HELP

" And tell David to come in out of the hall. I found a way to adjust our project budget estimate."

Contents at a Glance

Chapter 1: Creating Resources

In This Chapter

✔ **Discovering resources**

✔ **Understanding resource types**

✔ **Estimating resource requirements**

✔ **Entering resource information**

✔ **Using the Resource Information dialog box**

✔ **Working with consolidated resources**

*P*rojects typically involve people to get the work done. Projects also use equipment and materials. Those people, equipment, and materials are your project *resources*.

Resources are the means by which Project adds up the costs in your plan. For example, when you assign a resource to work for ten hours on a task and give that resource an hourly rate of $30, you've just added a $300 cost to your project.

Because resources affect timing and costs, they're an important element of Project. Many tools are available to help you create resources, make settings for how and when they'll work, assign them to tasks, manage their costs, and manipulate their workload. The first step in working with resources is to create them in Project and enter certain information about them. That's what this chapter is all about.

What Exactly Is a Resource?

It's natural to think of a resource as a person. After all, companies have human resources who work on projects, right? Well, people are indeed a frequently used project resource, but they're not the only type of resource. Resources can also be equipment that you rent or buy (such as a truck), as well as materials (such as paper clips or scrap iron).

You can even create resources that represent facilities you have to rent by the hour, such as a laboratory or a meeting space, or travel costs. For example, you could create a resource named Conference and assign it a unit cost of $900, which covers the average cost for attending a professional conference, including airfare, hotel, and the conference fee.

Here are some typical and not-so-typical project resources:

✦ Lab technicians

✦ Trade show booth

✦ Office supplies

✦ Offsite meeting facility

✦ Administrative assistants

✦ Rocket fuel

✦ Consultant fees

✦ Service call

✦ Computer software

✦ Printing services

✦ Web designer

✦ Prototype design

Essentially, a resource is anything or anyone who adds to the bottom line cost of your project or whose time or involvement you need to track.

All Kinds of Resources

Typically after you create and organize the tasks in your project, the next step is to create resources. Before you start creating resources, however, you should understand how they affect not only your project costs, but also the timing of tasks.

Understanding resources

The key to understanding resources is to realize that costs in Project are accumulated by assigning resources. If you want to account for costs in your project — such as a person putting in hours of work on a task, materials that you have to buy to make a product, or your monthly office space rent — you have to create resources and assign them to one or more tasks. When you do, you can see the resulting costs in the Total Cost column of the Gantt Chart spreadsheet, as shown in Figure 1-1.

You can create resources with no associated costs. You might do that so you can track only that resource's time. Some people use Project strictly as a scheduling tool, so watching the time people are spending on tasks is their only interest, not what the time is costing. That's okay as long as you know that if you don't assign costs to resources, you get no cost or budget information back from Project.

Total Cost column

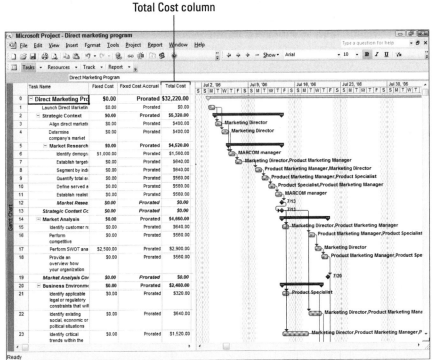

Figure 1-1:
Tasks with
assigned
resources
show the
associated
total costs in
the Total
Cost column.

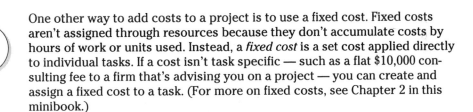

One other way to add costs to a project is to use a fixed cost. Fixed costs aren't assigned through resources because they don't accumulate costs by hours of work or units used. Instead, a *fixed cost* is a set cost applied directly to individual tasks. If a cost isn't task specific — such as a flat $10,000 consulting fee to a firm that's advising you on a project — you can create and assign a fixed cost to a task. (For more on fixed costs, see Chapter 2 in this minibook.)

After you create the resources, you need to manage the workflow for any resource that has limited time availability for your project. You can track the time being used for any type of resource with limited availability by creating resources that are available so many hours per day and so many days per week. For example, one person might be available to work on your project 50 percent of the time, or 20 hours in a 40 hour workweek, whereas another might be available full-time (40 hours). A supercomputer might be available to your project only 10 hours a week, or you might be able to book a meeting room for only an hour a day.

When you assign limited-availability resources to your project, you can then use various views, reports, and tools to see whether any resource is over-booked at any point during your project. You can also see whether people are sitting idle when you might be able to make use of them on another task. You can even account for resources that work on multiple projects across your organization and make sure that they're being used efficiently.

See Chapter 3 in this minibook and Book III, Chapter 4 for more about resources used in multiple projects.

Views such as Resource Usage view (as shown in Figure 1-2) help you visual-ize resource working time in your project.

Resource types: Work, Material, and Cost

The number of resources you assign to work on a task usually has an effect on the duration of that task. Think about it: If you have a certain number of hours of work to do but few people to do that work, a typical task takes longer to finish than if you had all the resources in the world.

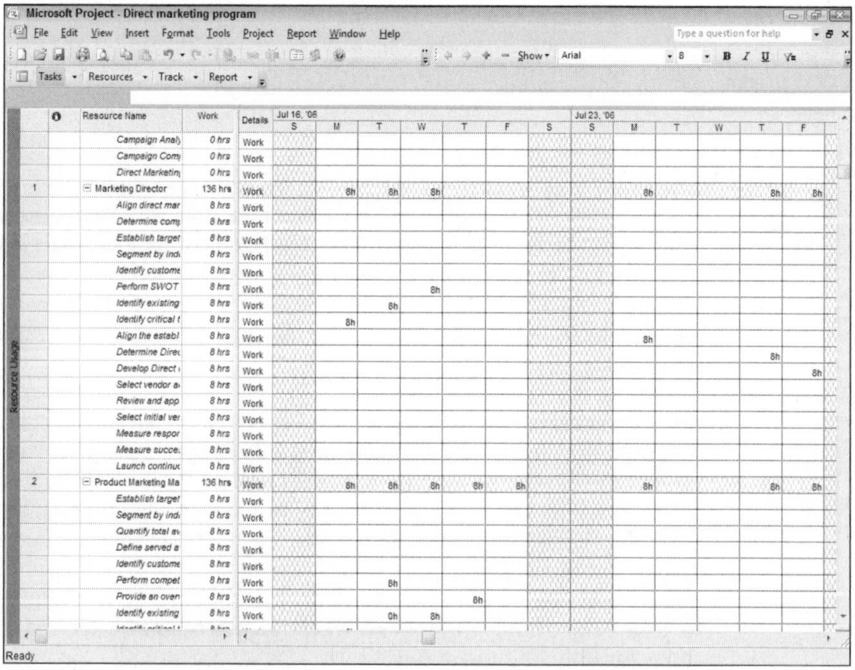

Figure 1-2:
You can see total hours on the project by resource and an itemization of the hours assigned task by task for that resource.

The task type determines whether a task's duration changes based on the number of resources assigned to it. See Book IV to explore more about tasks and timing.

Although people and things come in all shapes and sizes, only three types of resources exist as far as Project is concerned:

✦ **Work resources** are typically (but not always) people. They can't be depleted but can be reassigned. Their costs are associated with the amount of work time they put in, usually at an hourly rate or a cost per use. Work resources are assigned to tasks based on a Working Time calendar (as shown in Figure 1-3), where you specify their working and nonworking hours. You can select one of three base calendars and then modify specific working hours.

A typical Work resource is a person working eight hours a day at a standard rate of $20 per hour and an overtime rate of $30 per hour. Another example of a Work resource is a meeting facility available only eight hours a day at an hourly rate. Even though it's not a person, the meeting facility would probably be created as a working resource because it has limited "working" hours.

Figure 1-3:
Work resources are assigned to tasks based on a Working Time calendar.

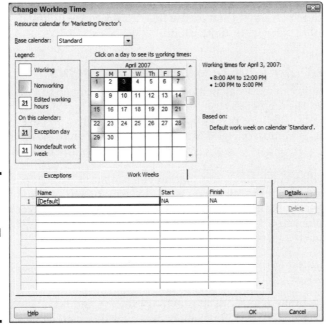

The number of hours a resource can work is determined by the calendars. The three kinds of calendars are Project, Task, and Resource. Calendars, their settings, and how those settings interact are discussed at some length in Book II, Chapter 4.

✦ **Material resources** can have an hourly rate or a unit cost, and they also have an unlimited working time. This type of resource has no calendar, no overtime, and you make no settings for working and nonworking time.

A typical Material resource is any material — such as steel, rubber, paper, chairs, or shoes — assigned to a task with an associated unit cost. For example, a resource called *Books* with a unit price of $12.95, assigned to a task called *Computer Training* at ten units, accrues a cost of $129.50 to the task. Another example of a material cost is anyone performing a service for a fee in a situation where working time isn't an issue. A facilitator who runs an offsite meeting for a fee of $1,000, but whose working calendar and time aren't your concern, could be created as a Material resource with a unit cost of $1,000.

✦ **Cost resources** have a set cost associated with them. Calendars and units of work or unit costs have nothing to do with the amount such resources deduct from the bottom line of your project.

An example of a Cost resource is a consultant working for a set fee. The cost to set up your network might be $25,000, for example, and wouldn't change based on the time it took to set up the network or the volume of hours or units used.

Estimating your resource requirements

You usually can use a calculation to estimate how much of a Material resource you need to complete a task: In most cases, you can calculate the number of pounds of sugar, tons of steel, yards of fabric, and so on based on previous projects and industry standards. But how do you know how much effort it will take on the part of Work resources to complete the tasks in your project?

As with many aspects of information you put into a Project plan, this judgment rests to a great degree on your own experience with similar tasks and resources. One approach is to start with an educated guess at how long it might take you to complete such a task, and then factor in variables for an individual resource. Consider the following guidelines:

✦ **Consider skill levels.** A less skilled or inexperienced resource is likely to take more time to finish something.

✦ **Look to the past.** Look at previous projects and tasks. If you've tracked people's time, you can probably see how much effort was required to complete various types of tasks on other projects and draw parallels to your project. If you've worked with a particular resource before, check your notes about his or her performance and use that as a guide.

✦ **Go to the source.** Ask the resources themselves how long they think it will take. Then add 10 percent to that time in case the resources were being overly optimistic!

Committed versus proposed resources

Last time you asked somebody whether he was available to work on your project, did you get a half-hearted, "Well, maybe, if I have time, if my manager says it's okay, if it falls on a Leap Year . . ."? You may well ask: So is that resource available or not? You can't always be positive about a resource's commitment in the planning stages of your project. How can Project help? Project has the capability to designate a resource as either *proposed* or *committed.* You can use the Booking Type field in the Resource Information dialog box to make this setting.

What does this setting do? Well, it's pretty much a field you can use to keep track of resource status. If you're not quite sure about a resource's commitment to your project, you call that resource *proposed.* Then you can display the Booking Type column in a resource view (such as the Resource Sheet) and keep track of resources you might have to firm up as you get closer to finalizing your project plan.

Creating Resources

Creating a resource in Project essentially involves filling out a form with some vital statistics about the resource. On the Resource Information form, you enter information such as the resource name, rate per hour or cost per use, and availability. You can also enter optional information. Entering a resource's e-mail address helps you stay in touch, and entering a setting such as proposed (see the previous section) gives you a field you can search or filter to locate certain resources by those criteria.

You can create a resource to represent an individual person; a thing such as a telescope used for scientific study; a generic resource (that is, a skill set with no person attached, such as Assistant or Engineer); and even a group of several resources that work together.

Creating one resource at a time

Whether your resource is a person, a piece of equipment, or a material, you can begin to create these individual resources by entering information in the Resource Information dialog box.

Another method for entering resource information is to display Resource Sheet view and enter information in the columns included there for each individual resource. This is often a faster way to enter information about several resources one after the other.

When you create a resource, you must, at a minimum, type the Resource Name. You can also include as much information as you want on the several tabs of the Resource Information dialog box. Some people prefer to create all the resources first and deal with details such as contact and cost information at a later stage.

They say the devil is in the details! If you create resources with only bare-bones information, be sure to go back later in your planning to add the details. The details, such as rate per hour or working time settings, can make the difference between an accurate schedule and one that bears no resemblance to reality.

Note that to create a resource using the Resource Information dialog box, which allows you access to every single detail of a resource, you have to first display a view that includes a Resource Name column. Follow these steps to create a resource via the Resource Information dialog box:

1. **Click Resource Sheet view on the View bar.**

2. **Double-click a blank Resource Name cell.**

The Resource Information dialog box appears, as shown in Figure 1-4.

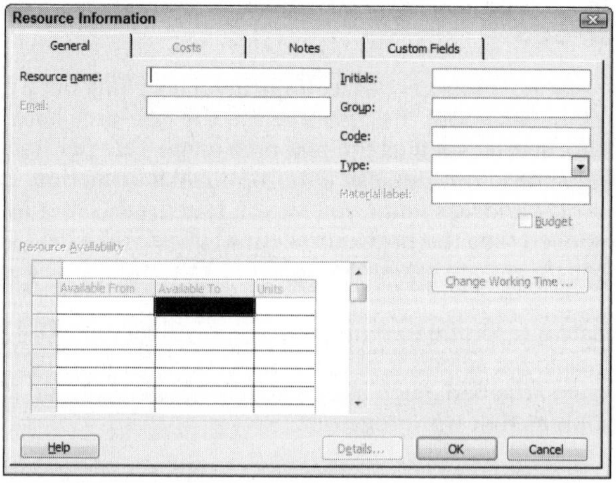

Figure 1-4: These four tabs can hold a wealth of information about any resource.

3. **In the Resource Name text box, type a name.**

4. **In the Initials box, type an abbreviation or initials for the resource.**

These shorthand versions of the names can be displayed in the Resource Initials column and can be a useful reference if you have many resources assigned to a task. If you don't enter anything here, the first letter of the resource name is inserted when you save the resource.

5. **From the Type drop-down list, select Work, Material, or Cost.**

   The settings available to you differ slightly depending on what you choose. For example, a Material resource won't have the Email box available, and a Work or Cost resource won't have the Material Label box available.

6. **Continue to enter any information you want to include for the resource.**

   That information might include

   - *Email:* Just what it seems

   - *Group:* A department, division, or workgroup, for example

   - *Code:* Such as a cost center code

   - *Material Label:* For example, pounds for food coloring or tons for steel

   If you enter information in the Group text box, you can then use filters, sorting features, and the Group feature to look at sets of resources. See Book VII, Chapter 1 for more about filtering and working with groups.

7. **Click OK to save the new resource.**

If you use Project Server (a feature that you can use along with Project Professional for online collaboration, covered in Book X), the Resource Information dialog box will include a Workgroup field. You or the administrator who sets up your enterprise-wide resource pool can choose the Microsoft Project Server option in the Workgroup field. You can also use the Windows Account option in the Resource Information dialog box to specify how you'll communicate with the team. See Book X, Chapter 2 for more about enterprise resources.

Identifying resources you don't know

In the planning stages of a project, you might find that all your resources aren't identified. Sometimes even well into the project, you don't know what resource you'll be using; you know only that you need a resource with a certain skill set to complete upcoming tasks. In that case, you might be better off creating some generic resources.

If you want to create a generic resource, you should give it a name that describes its skill, such as Engineer, or Designer, or even Meeting Space (as opposed to a specific resource named Conference Room B). Then, in the Resource Information dialog box, be sure to select the Generic check box.

You can display a column titled *Group* to identify these resources (see Figure 1-5). You can then create a resource filter to find resources with a Generic entry in the Group column when it's time to update these resources with more specific information.

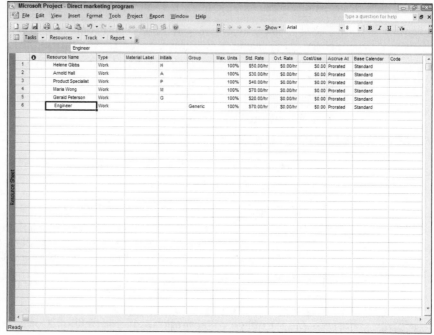

Figure 1-5:
Identifying
generic
resources in
your project.

No formula takes the Generic setting into account in recalculating your schedule based on resource availability. However, many people find this setting useful in long-range planning and in situations where they aren't responsible for specific resource assignments (for example, if you have to assign a temporary worker to a task when the specific individual will be chosen by the temp agency).

Resources that work in groups

Although you probably have little use for a chain gang in your project, it exemplifies the principle of a resource that represents multiple resources. Rather than assigning people one by one to some tasks, you want to assign a group of people who typically work together. Being able to make one assignment of a *consolidated resource* rather than several separate resources and assignments can be a timesaver in larger projects.

Here's an example of a consolidated resource: Suppose that you're managing a project to get a new office site up and running. You have four office planners of equal skill at your disposal, so you create a resource named Office Planners. You can assign Office Planners to a task at 400 percent (see Figure 1-6) and have all four planners working at once. Or you can assign the Office Planners resource to work on a task at 100 percent, thereby assigning one resource to it.

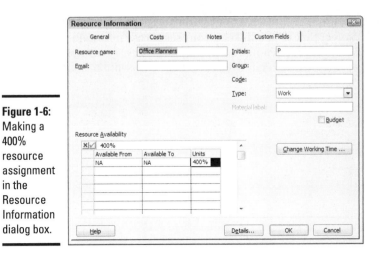

Figure 1-6:
Making a
400%
resource
assignment
in the
Resource
Information
dialog box.

See Chapter 3 in this minibook for making resource assignments such as
the 400 percent maximum units assignment mentioned in the preceding
example.

There is no special setting to designate a multiple resource: However, you
might want to include some indication of the number of resources in the
resource name. For example, you could name your planner resource *Four
Office Planners* (if you know the office planner group consists of four people)
or *Office Planner Group.* What really defines this type of resource is the maximum assignment units; 400 percent would indicate four resources in the
group each working 100 percent of the time.

Resource management: An art, not a science

When you start creating resources, you almost
immediately have to start managing them.
Here's the nickel tour of the art of managing the
people who will make your project happen.

Conflict resolution is a necessary skill for project
managers. It involves creating an environment
of cooperation and respect, building consensus
(agreement) among team members, and encour-
aging honest communication.

As a project manager, you can set up well-
designed communications tools (such as frequent
status meetings or reports) so people stay in
touch throughout your project. You can also make
a point of staying alert to conflict — and nipping
it in the bud. (A conflict ignored only festers and
becomes something worse.) Try to keep the focus
of any project discussions on the project goal,
and not on personalities. See Book I, Chapter 1
for more about project management concepts.

In Book VI, Chapters 3 and 4, we tell you all about designing and generating reports in Project that help you keep your resources informed. Book X also offers some ways to help resources communicate clearly with each other in an online enterprise environment, which can help you avoid misunderstandings.

Chapter 2: Understanding Costs

In This Chapter

✔ **Understanding how costs accrue**

✔ **Establishing Work resource rates**

✔ **Specifying unit costs**

✔ **Adding fixed costs**

✔ **Allowing for overtime**

✔ **Estimating resource availability**

These days, not much in life is free — and if you use Project to track costs, there's no such thing as a free resource. That's because Project uses resources assigned to tasks as a way of calculating most of the costs accruing to your project.

When you create a resource, you specify a Work resource rate (by default, this rate is tallied up per hour) or a per-use cost for a Material resource. You can also create *Cost resources;* that is, a set cost that you can apply to a task that isn't calculated using a per-use or hourly rate. An example of a Cost resource is a fee for your trade show booth.

Other factors can come into play in determining your project costs, such as how many hours a day a resource is available to work and overtime rates. As you tally your bottom line, all these settings come together to put you over or under budget.

In this chapter, you explore the relationship between resources and costs. You find out how to set resource standard and overtime rates, create fixed costs, and set the availability of resources on individual tasks in your project.

Accruing Costs All Over the Place

Project helps you to account for costs on your various tasks with a combination of costs per hour, costs per unit, and fixed costs. Before you begin to assign cost information to your resources, it's important to understand how these cost calculations work.

Tallying costs

The best way to understand how costs add up in your project is to look at an example. Jane Doe (that's not her real name) is managing a project involving the building of a new candy-packaging plant. Jane has created a task called *Install Candy Mixers*. Here are the costs Jane anticipates for that task and how they add up:

✦ **About ten person-hours of effort to do the installation**

The ten hours of effort will be expended by Work resources. The total cost for the ten hours is a calculation: 10 × the resource rate. If the resource rate is $20, this cost totals $200. If two resources work on the task, one at a rate of $20 and one at a rate of $30, then (by default) Project splits the ten hours of effort between them, and the resulting cost is $250.

✦ **A fixed cost of $500 paid to the mixer manufacturer to oversee the installation and train workers on the machine**

The fixed cost of $500 for a fee to the manufacturer is created as a Cost resource. When you assign this resource to a task, you enter a cost for that resource on that task. This cost won't change based on the number of resources or the time involved.

✦ **Twenty pounds of ingredients to test the mixers**

The cost for 20 pounds of sugar for the test candy is calculated as 20 × the unit cost of the ingredients. If the unit cost is $2, this cost is $40.

And that's how costs are assigned and how they add up on your projects.

Not all resources have associated costs. For example, if you want your vice president (VP) to review status reports on your project but your company doesn't require that the VP's time be charged to your project, you can simply use her resource assignment to remind you about the need for the VP's availability on a particular day or week.

Your project has two main perspectives on your budget: one perspective at the moment you freeze your original plan (a *baseline plan*) and one perspective of the ongoing picture of actual costs that comes from the activity and material usage you record as your project moves along. You record a certain amount of work effort on tasks, and tasks with resources assigned to them then run up costs based on the effort expended or units of materials used.

The sound of costs hitting the bottom line

Wouldn't it be nice if you could choose when all your costs hit your pocket book? Well, in Project, you can choose when your costs hit your budget.

You can set up resources to accrue costs at the start or end of the task that they're associated with or to be prorated throughout the life of the task. So, if a three-month-long task begins April 1, a $90 Cost resource could be added to your actual costs to date on day 1, on day 90, or at $1 per day until the end of the task.

Now, this isn't exactly a realistic reflection of when you have to pay for costs, because most bills come due 30–60 days after they arrive, long after the task is finished. It's more a factor of when you want that cost to show up for the purposes of tracking costs and reporting expenses on your project.

Assigning Costs to Resources

You have to do your homework before you can assign resources to tasks. Most projects involve a combination of the three cost types: Cost, Work, and Material. That means that you have to find out the fixed costs as well as the hourly or unit rates for all your resources.

In the early stages of your project planning, you might not be able to find out exactly what a particular cost will be or know every resource's rates. If you have to, build the resource or fixed cost with your best estimate. That way, at least some cost will be reflected in your plan, and you can go back to enter more accurate information as soon as you know it. Don't worry; Project updates everything when you enter a change.

Use a field in your Resource Sheet, such as Code, to designate resources for whom you have estimated rates or costs. Then apply a filter or display the column so you can easily go back to those tasks and update the estimates as your plan progresses.

Fixed costs you can count on

Maybe you have to pay a huge fee to a design company to redesign your product logo, including all your collateral marketing materials. Or perhaps you have to buy yourself a $2,000 laptop so you can manage your oil exploration project with three drilling sites in different states when you're on the road. Whatever it is, it's a cost that won't change no matter how many hours the task goes on or how many people work on the task. It has no unit cost or rate per hour. It's a *fixed cost.*

You can specify fixed costs by creating a resource with a Cost type. Every time you assign the resource to a task, you specify the cost associated with it.

You can also simply enter a fixed cost associated with a task without having to create and assign a Cost resource to it. To do so, you can use the Cost Table in any view with a spreadsheet pane, such as Gantt Chart view.

REMEMBER

Tables are preset column combinations that make entering certain information in a sheet pane easier. See Book VI, Chapter 2 for more about customizing tables.

Follow these steps to view the Cost Table and enter a fixed cost for a task:

1. **Display the project in Gantt Chart view (click Gantt Chart in the View bar).**

2. **Choose View⇨Table⇨Cost.**

The table of columns appears, as shown in Figure 2-1.

3. **Click the Fixed Cost column for the task to which you want to assign the cost and then enter the amount.**

Cost Table

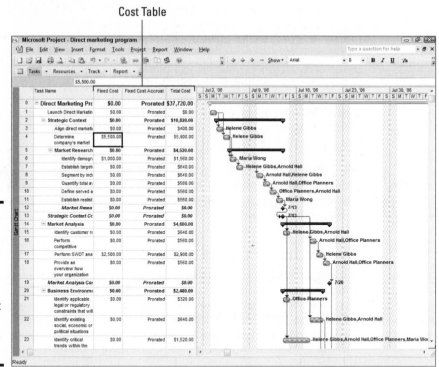

Figure 2-1: You can insert the Fixed Cost column in any sheet, but the Cost Table already includes it.

You can enter only one fixed-cost amount for a task by using the Fixed Cost column. You can total your fixed costs and enter that number here, but in that case, you should also enter a task note where you can itemize fixed costs if you have more than one. The option if you have a lot of fixed costs is creating fixed Cost resources and assigning them to the task one by one.

Note also that the default fixed-cost accrual method is prorated. If you prefer to have your fixed costs hit your budget at the start or end of a task, use the Fixed Cost Accrual column in this table to select another option.

Paying per hour

Whether a resource gets minimum wage or charges a hefty billable hourly rate every time you make a phone call, most people get paid something per hour. To represent most people involved in your project, you create Work resources and charge them to your project with a specific hourly rate.

After you set a resource hourly rate and enter an estimate of how many hours that person will work on each task that he's assigned to, Project totals the cost of using that resource on your project. These estimates form the budget for your project in the planning stage.

When you track actual effort expended on tasks, a calculation of actual effort × the hourly rate returns your actual costs.

By comparing estimated costs and actual costs, you get an ongoing picture of whether your project is financially on track. See Book VIII for more about tracking costs in a project.

To set resource rates per hour, follow these steps:

1. **Display Resource Sheet view by clicking the Resource Sheet item in the View bar (see Figure 2-2).**

2. **Click the Std. Rate column for the resource to which you want to assign a cost.**

3. **Type a dollar amount.**

   If you're entering a rate for a unit other than hours, type a slash (/) and then the unit (for example, **minute** or **month**).

4. **Press Enter.**

   The entry is saved.

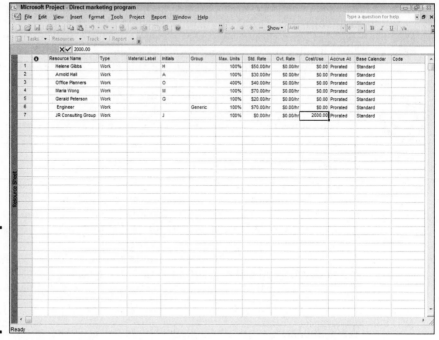

Figure 2-2:
Entering a
resource
rate in
Resource
Sheet view.

Setting alternative rates

Note that you can also make cost-rate entries in the Resource Information
dialog box (to get to this dialog box display a view with a Resource Name
column such as Resource Sheet view and double-click the resource name).
The Costs tab of this dialog box, which is shown in Figure 2-3, offers a
Standard Rate, an Overtime Rate, and a Per Use Cost.

Even more options for setting rates are available in the Resource Information
dialog box; five tabs labeled A through E allow you to enter several different
rates for any resource during different time periods of your project. Tab A is
the default rate, but by using the Effective Date column in the other tabs to
specify the start date of a new rate, a resource could work for several
months at one rate and then start working at a different rate on a preset
date. This helps you account for periodic raises or seasonal shifts in rates
(for example, paying a premium for construction resources in months with
better weather when they are more in demand).

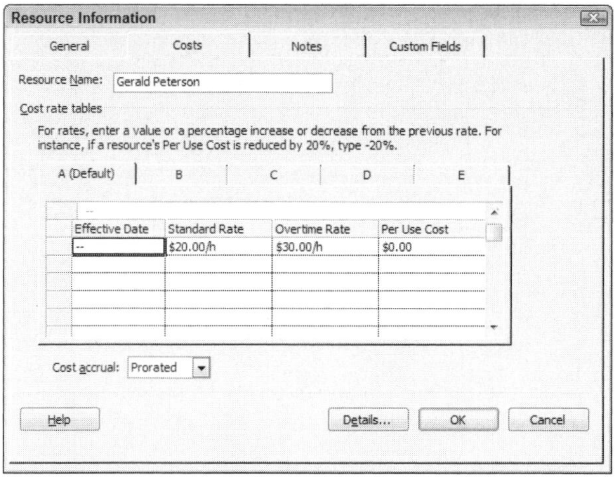

Resource Information

General | Costs | Notes | Custom Fields

Resource Name: Gerald Peterson

Cost rate tables

For rates, enter a value or a percentage increase or decrease from the previous rate. For instance, if a resource's Per Use Cost is reduced by 20%, type -20%.

A (Default) | B | C | D | E

Effective Date	Standard Rate	Overtime Rate	Per Use Cost
--	$20.00/h	$30.00/h	$0.00

Cost accrual: Prorated

Help | Details... | OK | Cancel

Figure 2-3:
You can set
several
rates for a
resource.

The cost-per-use scenario

Project allows you to enter a *cost per use*. With a cost-per-use scenario you assign a cost for a single unit (per yard, ton, or gallon, for example), and assign so many units to each task. Project calculates the cost based on the number of units × the cost per use.

Technically speaking, you can have a cost per use for either a Work or Material resource. You could, for example, have a consultant who costs $500 per use (that is, each time you use her to consult on a task, you get hit with a $500 fee). More commonly, you use a cost per use for a Material resource such as steel or sugar.

To assign a cost per use, follow these steps:

1. **Display Resource Sheet view.**

2. **Click the Cost/Use column for the resource you want to set and then type an amount for the per-use cost.**

3. **Click the Material Label column for that resource and then type a unit name (such as Tons, as shown in Figure 2-4).**

4. **Press Enter to accept your entry.**

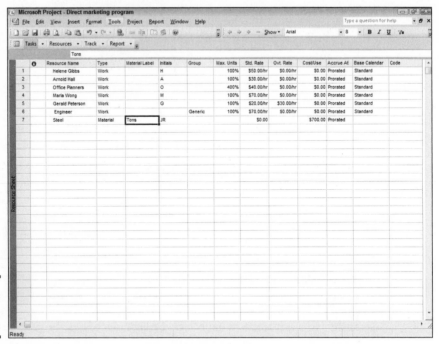

Figure 2-4:
Entering a
cost per use.

Note that you can use the Resource Information dialog box to enter up to five per-use costs with effective dates. You might do this to deal with fluctuations in unit cost because of inflation or seasonal variations over the life of your project.

Oops . . . you're into overtime!

Overtime is a fact of working life for many people: It can be helpful for those who earn it but hard on the project manager paying and tracking it. If you have resources that shift into time and a half after so many working hours, Project makes it easy for you to enter an overtime rate for them. With the rate in place, overtime automatically kicks in when that resource's calendar indicates that her regular day is over but her task assignment still has her working.

For example, a resource with a standard eight-hour-day calendar who puts in ten hours on a one-day task is charged by Project with eight hours at the standard rate and two hours at the overtime rate.

To enter an overtime rate for a resource, follow this procedure:

1. **Display Resource Sheet view.**

2. **Click the Ovt. Rate column for the resource.**

3. **Type an amount (see Figure 2-5).**

4. **Press Enter.**

The entry is saved.

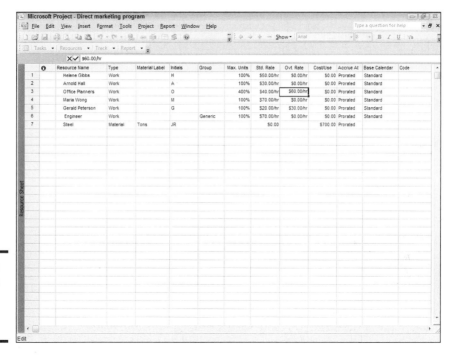

Figure 2-5:
Setting the
overtime
rate for a
resource.

Chapter 3: Assigning Resources to Tasks

In This Chapter

- ✔ Locating just the right resource
- ✔ Assigning resources to tasks
- ✔ Choosing the percentage of availability
- ✔ Applying a contour setting
- ✔ Creating a resource pool
- ✔ Modifying resource working time
- ✔ Communicating assignments to your team

So you've created dozens of resources available to work on your project. Now you must find the right resources for each task and assign them. It's important that you understand how to make those assignments and how they affect the timing of tasks and ultimately your entire project.

Sometimes you need to finesse resource assignments to make them work. For example, you might find that assigning resources as groups rather than one by one saves you time. In other cases, you might want to tell Project when resources put in different amounts of effort over the life of a task to avoid resource overallocations. Finally, you might need to modify the time that a resource puts in on any task.

In this chapter, you discover the vagaries of assigning resources to tasks, and even how to let your resources know their assignments.

Locating the Right Resource for the Job

If you were coaching a basketball team, you probably wouldn't bring in just anybody in the fourth quarter with one minute to go to sink the winning basket. It has to be Reggie or nobody. In projects, sometimes the same principle is true, and you have to have a specific person for a task.

However, if just about anybody with a certain skill level (or a certain rate per hour or the availability) will work, you can use Project features to find the right resource and make sure he or she has enough time to take on just one more task.

Finding resources

You've probably used the Find feature in other software to find a word or phrase or number. Project's Find feature is all that plus a bag of potato chips. After all, Project's Find feature can find you anything from a corporate jet to a person.

You can use Project's Find feature to look for resources with a wide variety of criteria. You might search for resources who are assigned certain pay rates or who come from a particular workgroup. You can search for resources by their initials, their maximum assignment units, their standard or overtime rate, and so on.

For example, you might need to find a resource whose standard rate is less than $50. Or you might want to find someone who can put in extra hours on a task, so you search for any resource whose maximum units are greater than 100 percent. (In other words, the resource can put in a longer-than-usual day before he or she is considered *overallocated*.)

Perhaps you need to find a Material resource that consists of a metal alloy measured in tons, but you can't remember the exact name of the alloy. In that case, you can search for resources whose material label includes the word *tons* and locate the resource you need.

To use the Find feature with resources, first display any resource view and then follow these steps to find resources in Project:

1. **Choose Edit➪Find.**

The Find dialog box appears, as shown in Figure 3-1.

2. **In the Find What text box, type the text you want to find.**

For example, type **50** if you want to search for a resource with a standard rate of $50, or **laboratory** if you want to find a resource whose material label contains that word.

Figure 3-1:
Searching
combines
looking for
some ele-
ment in a
particular
field that
meets a
certain
criterion.

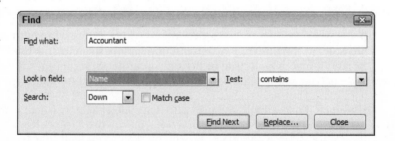

3. **From the Look in Field drop-down list, select the name of the field you want to search in.**

   For example, to search for resources that have a maximum unit assignment percentage of more than 100 percent, choose the Max Units field here.

4. **From the Test drop-down list, select a criterion.**

   For maximum units of more than 100 percent, for example, this choice would be Is Greater Than. There are a total of eleven criteria, such as contains, equals, is less than, is within, and does not contain.

5. **(Optional) If you prefer to search backward from your current location (that is, the currently selected cell in the task list) instead of forward, select Up from the Search drop-down list.**

6. **(Optional) If you want to match the case of the text, select the Match Case check box.**

7. **To begin the search, click Find Next.**

8. **Continue to click Find Next until you find the instance you're looking for.**

You can also use the Find feature to find and replace an entry. For example, if your Human Resources department (HR) changes its name to Human Capital Management (HCM), you can take these steps:

1. **Search the Group field for the code *HR*.**

2. **In the Replace dialog box that appears, click the Replace button, and type the letters HCM, as shown in Figure 3-2.**

3. **Click the Replace button to replace each instance one by one or click the Replace All button to replace every instance of that entry in that field, wherever it occurs in your project.**

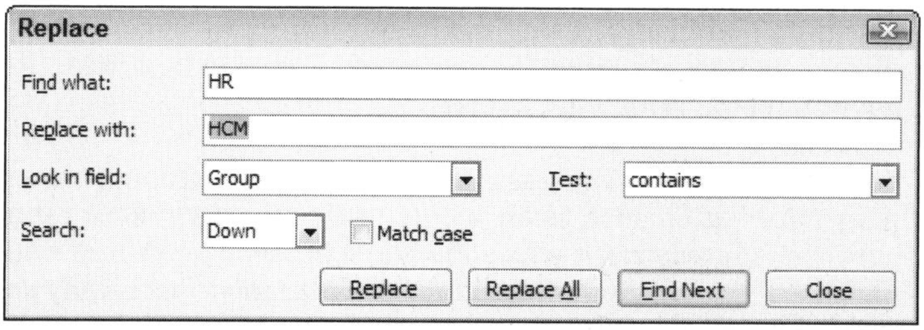

Figure 3-2:
Use Replace With to quickly change every instance of specified text in your project field by field.

Creating custom fields

When you assign resources to tasks, it's often important to take a person's skill set into account. If you absolutely have to have someone who can type 110 words a minute, it would be handy to have a way to locate such a keyboard wizard. If a person with less skill or experience could work on a particular task (and save you money because he or she has a lower rate per hour), wouldn't it be nice to be able to find such resources easily?

Project doesn't include a Skill field, but it does allow you to add fields of your own called *custom fields*. After you create them, you can use these fields for anything, but one great way to use them is to code your resources by skill level. You can use a rating system such as A, B, and C, or use terms such as *Exp* for an experienced worker and *Beg* for a beginning-level worker.

Consider using custom fields for information about tasks, as well. You can create a field to identify tasks that require your boss's input, tasks that involve another department's approval, or tasks that have to have their results reviewed by your legal department, for example.

Here's how to add a custom field:

1. **Choose Tools⇨Customize⇨Fields.**

2. **Click a field name.**

3. **Click Rename.**

4. **In the Rename Field dialog box, type a name for the field.**

5. **Click OK twice to save the change.**

You can now go to any view with a sheet pane, right-click the column headings, and choose Insert Column. In the Column Definition dialog box that appears, choose the newly named field and click OK to display it.

After you create a custom field, you can enter whatever you like in this column for each resource in your project. Then you can search for specific entries in that field by using the Find feature, or you can turn on a filter to display only resources with a certain skill level in that field. (Read more about filters in Book VII, Chapter 1.)

Some organizations designate enterprise-wide custom fields for certain company information such as an accounting code or a vendor rating. If you have a project administrator who's in charge of these enterprise-wide standards, check with him or her before you choose to modify a locally saved custom text field.

Acquiring the right resources

If you find the right resources for your tasks, the task of resource management becomes much easier. But how do you know who will work best on a given task?

What makes a good resource choice is a combination of factors. The right resource for a task is somebody who has

✦ The right skills for the task at hand (or who is trainable, if training is included in your budget)

✦ Enough time available to complete the task according to your schedule

✦ The ability to commit to the project (which sometimes involves getting not only the resources but also their manager's buy-in)

✦ A cost that fits in your budget

Although the preceding list covers some basics, it's important that you consider other details, such as whether the resource is set up to communicate with the project team and whether the technology to communicate and share documents is available (see Book X for more about this). Also, give some thought to how well each resource you choose will work as part of the team and whether the resource is considered dependable.

In Project, you have several ways to flag and find resources, categorizing them by skill or other criteria:

✦ **Use the Resource Notes area** to record information about a resource's skills and abilities. Then use the Find feature to search note fields for words such as *highly skilled, dependable,* and *trainable.*

✦ **Use the Code field in the Resource Information dialog box** to rank resources by skill, cost, or ability to work well with others.

✦ **Create Custom Fields for resources** to note specific skills and search for resources by those skills.

Sometimes it's worthwhile to consider using a less experienced, cheaper resource to save money. However, if you do, just be sure to factor in the time and money needed to train or mentor that resource.

Keeping resource workload balanced

Another important part of resource management is managing the assignment of resources so that nobody is excessively overbooked. Although occasional overtime is expected of most workers, constant overtime causes people to burn out and work to suffer.

Also keep in mind that a less skilled worker takes longer to perform a task than a skilled worker. Take that into account when scheduling the time a resource might need to complete his or her work.

The following techniques can help you stay aware of resource workload when working with Project:

✦ **Keep an eye on your Project plan.** Various tools such as Resource Graph view (as shown in Figure 3-3) allow you to spot overbooking on tasks.

✦ **Track the workload of individual resources.** When tracking activity on tasks, you will receive an account from resources (see Book VIII for information on tracking) about the actual time they're spending on tasks. Notice the people who have to constantly put in overtime to keep their heads above water, and keep an eye on those who are falling behind.

✦ ***Talk* to people.** That's right. This isn't a feature of Project, so stop looking for the Talk to People button. It's an old-fashioned communications device that works amazingly well. Check in with resources often and ask whether things are going well — and don't forget to ask whether your human resources are running on empty. Then help those who are overworked by modifying your schedule or adding other resources to help.

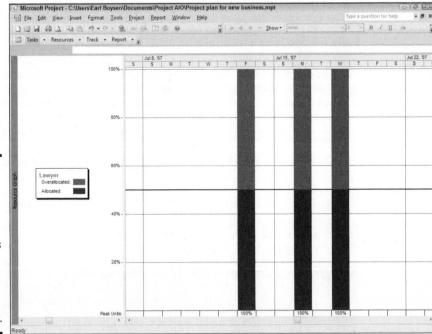

Figure 3-3: Resource Graph view shows resource assignments and helps you see problem times in your project.

Your Assignment Is . . .

After you've located the right resources, assigning resources to tasks is just the software equivalent of filling out paperwork. However, it's useful to understand a few things before you begin making assignments.

First, it's important that you understand how resource assignments affect task timing. That knowledge helps you to understand how to handle assignment units, which differ slightly between Work resources and Material resources.

Finally, you can use a couple of methods to assign resources to tasks.

Of course, you have to create resources before you can assign them, so make sure you've covered that by reading Chapter 1 of this minibook.

How resources affect task timing

For a fixed-unit or fixed-work task type, the addition or removal of resources assigned to the task has an impact on the time it takes to complete the task. In essence, the old saying that "two heads are better than one" might be modified to "two heads are faster than one."

Here's an example: Suppose that one person is assigned to the Clean Up task, which should take four hours of effort. Two people assigned to the Clean Up task will finish the job in two hours because two hours are being worked by each resource simultaneously, which achieves four hours of effort in half the time.

One *big* word of warning here: Assigning additional people to tasks doesn't always cut work time down proportionately even though that's how Project calculates it. When you have more people, you have more meetings, more memos, some duplicated effort, personality conflicts, and so on. If you add more resources to a task, you might consider upping the amount of effort required to complete that task to account for inevitable workgroup inefficiencies.

Determining Work, Material, and Cost resource assignment units

You assign Work resources, which are typically people, to a task by using a percentage: for example, 100 percent, 50 percent, or 150 percent. When you assign a resource at a percentage, the assignment is based on the Resource calendar.

A resource with a Standard calendar will put in eight hours a day if you assign it at 100 percent assignment units. Theoretically, a resource with a 24-hour calendar will work a grueling 24 hours a day at 100 percent (and quit the next day) or 12 hours at 50 percent. (If such a resource were not a human but a machine in your plant, such an assignment might work just fine.)

A Material resource is assigned in units such as gallons, consulting sessions, yards, or tons. When you assign a Material resource to a task, you designate how many units of that resource will go to that task.

Note that Work resource units are part of the entire work-unit-duration calculation that can cause Work resource assignments to change task durations.

A Cost resource is one that incurs a certain cost every time you assign it. For example, if you create a Cost resource called Permit Fee and assign a cost of $100, every time you assign a permit fee to a task, it is assigned at $100.

Making assignments

You have four ways to make resource assignments in Project. You can select resources from the Resources tab of the Task Information dialog box, enter resource information in the Resource column in the Entry table (displayed in Gantt Chart view), split the window and use the Resources and Predecessors form in a pane, or use the Assign Resources dialog box.

Which method you use depends to some extent on your own preferences, but generally speaking, here are some parameters for using each:

+ **Use the Resource Column** to assign a default 100 percent assignment. If you want to assign a different percentage, don't use this method.

+ **Use the Assign Resources dialog box** if you want to replace one resource with another (a handy Replace feature is available in this dialog box) or if you want to filter the list of available resources by a criterion (for example, resources with a rate or unit cost of less than a specified amount). This dialog box is very useful for making multiple resource assignments.

+ **Work in the Task Information dialog box** if you want to have task details (such as task type or the constraints contained on other tabs of this dialog box) handy when you make assignments.

Choosing resources in the Resource column

You can add resources in a Resource column, whether you access it from Gantt Chart view or Tracking Gantt view. (See Book I, Chapter 4 for information about displaying additional columns or tables of columns in views.)

Even though it lists tasks in its sheet pane and can even display a Resource column, you can't use Task Usage view to add resource assignments.

Follow these steps to assign resources at a default percentage:

1. **Display Gantt Chart view by clicking it on the View bar.**

2. **Choose View⇨Table⇨Entry.**

3. **Click in the Resource Names column for the task on which you want to make a resource assignment.**

An arrow appears at the end of the cell.

4. **Click the arrow to display a list of resources.**

5. **Click the resource you want to assign.**

The resource name appears in the Resource column, assigned at 100 percent.

You can create assignments at the default level and then change the assignment units later by opening the Task Information dialog box and making the change on the Resources tab.

Using the Assign Resources dialog box

To assign a Work or Material resource to a task, you can select a task and then use the Assign Resources dialog box to make assignments. To do so, follow these steps:

1. **Click a task to select it.**

2. **Click the Assign Resources button on the Standard toolbar.**

The Assign Resources dialog box appears, as shown in Figure 3-4.

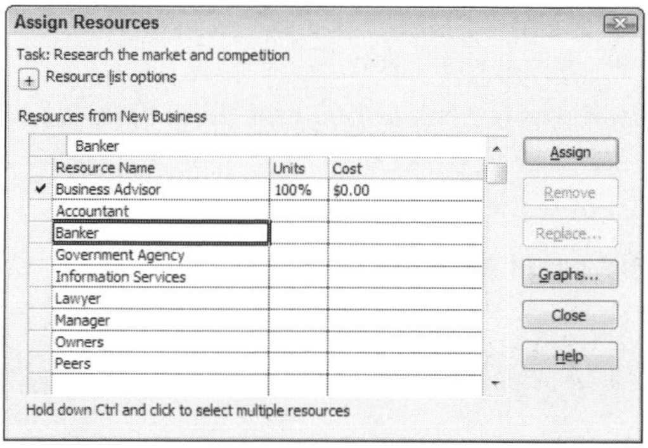

Figure 3-4:
Every resource you've created is shown in this list.

Assign Resources			
Task: Research the market and competition			
⊞ Resource list options			
Resources from New Business			
Banker			
Resource Name	Units	Cost	Assign
✔ Business Advisor	100%	$0.00	Remove
Accountant			
Banker			Replace...
Government Agency			
Information Services			Graphs...
Lawyer			
Manager			Close
Owners			
Peers			Help
Hold down Ctrl and click to select multiple resources			

3. **Click a resource to select it and then click the Assign button.**

   A check mark appears next to the assigned resource in the Resource Name column.

4. **Click the Units column for the resource you just assigned.**

   If it's a Work resource, the default assignment of 100% appears. If it's a Material resource, the default is one unit.

5. **Specify a percentage of assignment units for the resource.**

   Click the spinner arrows in the box to increase or decrease the setting. For a Work resource, change the percentage units in 50-percent increments by clicking the arrows; or, you can simply type a percentage. For a Material resource, use the spinner arrows in the Units column to increase or decrease the unit assignment; or, you can type a number of units.

6. **Repeat Steps 3–5 to add all resources.**

7. **(Optional) If you want to replace one resource with another, click an assigned resource (indicated with a check mark), click Replace, select another name on the list, set its units, and click OK.**

8. **Click Close to save all the assignments.**

You can also open the Assign Resources dialog box from the Resource Management toolbar. This toolbar offers handy tools for adding resources to your project, from sources such as your Outlook Address Book, and tools for managing overallocated resources.

Adding assignments in the Task Information dialog box

You can assign resources on the Resources tab of any Task Information dialog box by following these steps:

1. **Double-click a task name in Gantt Chart view.**

   The Task Information dialog box appears.

2. **Click the Resources tab to display it.**

3. **Click in a blank Resource Name box and then click the arrow that appears at the right side of the box.**

   A drop-down list of resources appears.

4. **Click the resource you want to assign.**

5. **Click the Units column and use the spinner arrows to set an assignment percentage.**

6. **Repeat Steps 3–5 to assign additional resources.**

7. **Click OK.**

If you're assigning a Material resource, the Units default is a single unit. (For example, if your units are pounds, the default assignment is 1 lb.) Use the spinner arrows in the Unit field to assign additional material units.

Contours set the level of work

When you make a Work resource assignment, Project spreads the work evenly over the life of the task. Even if work effort isn't identical every single day, if it averages out across the life of the task, this default setting is probably fine.

However, there are times, especially on longer tasks, that it's useful to specify that more work goes on at some point in the task. This can help you free up resources that have a conflict with another task, for example.

To deal with a variable workload, you can modify the level of work that goes on during the life of the task — called a *work contour* — so that more work takes place near the beginning, middle, or end of the task.

Look at an example: Suppose that you know that the people assigned to set up a new enterprise-computing database will have to spend some time up front studying the software manuals and customizing templates before they can begin to make measurable progress on the task. In this case, you might use a late-peaking contour. Or, if you know that people are likely to put in a lot of work up front on a survey and then sit back and wait for the results to come in, you might choose an early peaking contour.

Using a different contour on a particular resource's task assignment could free up that resource to work on a second task that occurs during the life of the first task. This can help you resolve a resource conflict.

The contour you select will have slightly different effects depending on the task type, some of which can throw your schedule entirely out of whack. This is a complex equation not worth your while to try to analyze. My advice is to simply try a different contour and see whether it solves your problem and doesn't make too dramatic a change to your task duration or other resource assignments.

To set a task's contour, follow these steps:

1. **Display Task Usage view.**

   This view shows resource assignments by task.

2. **Double-click a resource.**

   The Assignment Information dialog box appears, as shown in Figure 3-5.

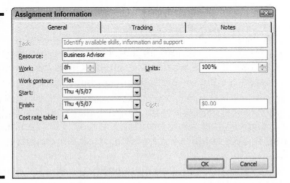

Figure 3-5: This dialog box is a handy summary of all assignment information for a resource on a task.

3. **From the Work Contour drop-down list, select one of the preset patterns.**

   The default choice is Flat, with work spread out evenly throughout the task. Other options include the self-explanatory Backloaded and Frontloaded; Early Peak and Late Peak with spike of work in the first or last half of the project, respectively; Double Peak, which ups the work-load twice over the life of the task; and the Bell and Turtle Curves, which you can visualize by thinking of their namesakes.

4. **Click OK to save the setting.**

   A symbol for the contour pattern is displayed in the Indicator field for the resource.

If none of the contour patterns fits your situation, you can manually modify a resource's work. You do this by changing the number of hours the resource puts in day by day on a task in Task Usage view. Remember that if you do this painstaking manual work to deal with resource availability, if tasks shift timing you may have to undo all this and redo it all over again.

Before you save a contour setting, make sure your modifications add up to the number of hours you want the resource to work, or you could inadvertently change the resource's assignment.

Resource Allocation view is useful for reviewing resource assignments at this stage. This view provides a side-by-side comparison between a single resource's workload and all the tasks going on during a particular time period in your project.

Making Sure of Availability

By default, a resource is assigned to a task at 100 percent availability, but you can modify that if you know a resource will be assigned to several tasks and is likely to put in only part of that person's time over the course of a task.

How you assign availability is important to managing your resources successfully. Consider that many Project features that deal with resources help you to spot resource overallocation. *Overallocation* is a calculation involving the resource's calendar and availability that tells you when a resource is overbooked on one or more tasks.

Here's an example: Charlie Ruiz is a graphic designer who works a standard, eight-hour day based on his calendar. Charlie is assigned to the Create Design Budget task at 50 percent of his availability and to the Create Design Specs task — which occurs at the same time as the budget task — at 100 percent of his availability. Charlie is now working at 150 percent of his availability, or 12 hours per day. Charlie is definitely overallocated, and one way to solve that is to make sure you've dealt with availability correctly.

Setting availability

Availability is easier to estimate for some resources than for others. A manager isn't likely to give an entire day over to any single task because he has to deal with all the people who report to him, or he has to sign authorizations, go to meetings concerning various projects, work on budgets, and so on. With a production worker, it might be simpler to pin down availability to a single task: If one manufacturing job is going through the line for three days and one person is working on the line all that time, it's closer to the mark to say that he or she is working on that task full-time.

One big mistake that new users of Project make is to microthink availability. Of course, no one actually spends eight hours every day on a single task in one project. People spend part of their days reading e-mail about company holidays, chatting with co-workers, and blogging about their latest vacations. A resource might spend seven hours on a task one day but only three the next. Don't get hung up on a day-by-day resource schedule in estimating availability. If over the life of a task the person is pretty much devoted to it, 100 percent availability is a good setting. If that person puts in only, say, five days of work on a ten-day task, that's 50 percent availability whether she works four hours per day for ten days or five full days at any point.

The Availability setting exists to help you spot overbooking of a resource who might work on multiple tasks at the same time in a project schedule.

To set resource availability, follow these steps:

1. **Display Resource Sheet view.**

2. **Double-click a resource.**

The General tab of the Resource Information dialog box appears, as shown in Figure 3-6.

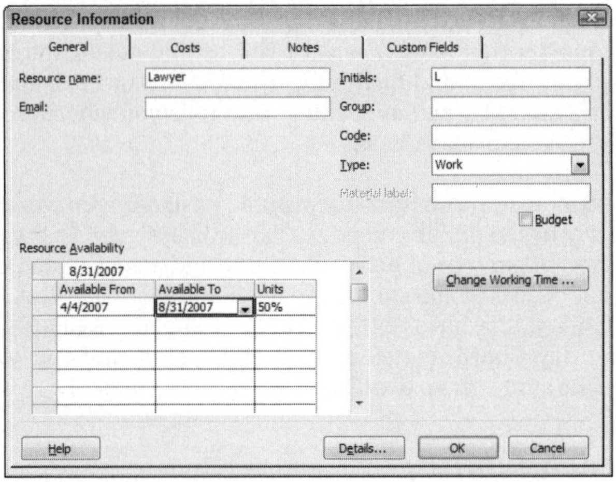

Figure 3-6: You can enter any number you like in the Units box.

3. **In the Units column (in the Resource Availability area), either click the arrows to raise or lower the availability in 50-percent increments or type a number.**

The most common entry here (the default entry) is 100% for a single resource working full-time on the task.

4. **Click OK to save the setting.**

Here's an example of how you might use the Units column for assignments; type **33** for a resource available one-third of the time, or **400%** for a pool of four resources all available full-time.

When resources appear and disappear

In addition to being available only a certain percentage of the time on any task or project, a resource might be available for only a certain period of time during the life of the task or project.

On the other hand, you might have a resource that's available half-time for the first few days of the project and then full-time for the rest of the project.

In either case, you can enter a date range in the Available From and Available To columns of the Resource Availability area in the Resource Information dialog box (refer to Figure 3-6) to specify the variations in the resource's availability.

Sharing Resources

Most organizations have several projects going on simultaneously. Sometimes a project, such as managing company acquisitions, is the only project of its type happening in a company. Others, such as setting up PR campaigns in an advertising company, will happen at the same time as several other similar projects and draw on many of the same resources, such as market researchers and copywriters.

If your organization has projects of a similar nature going on at the same time, creating centralized resources is useful. This can save you time because you don't have to create resources again and again for each project. It can also help you to track resources across projects.

You can also pull existing resources from a company address book or your own Address Book in Outlook. See Book IX, Chapter 4 for information about importing information into Project.

This collection of enterprise resources is called a *resource pool.* By using a resource pool, you can save everybody the time of re-creating the same resources again and again.

Don't confuse a resource pool with *enterprise resources,* which require that you have Project 2007 Professional, Project Server 2007, and Microsoft Office Project Web Access set up. With all this in place (see Book X for more about enterprise projects), you can track and assign resources across an entire enterprise. A *resource pool,* on the other hand, is simply a list of resources, saved on your company server, that several people can assign to projects. A resource pool saves everybody the trouble of creating these resources again and again in their individual projects.

Both individual and consolidated resources can be created in a blank project as a resource pool and saved to an accessible location on your company server. Then any project manager can call on those resources for his or her own projects; those projects are then referred to as *sharer files* because they share resources with the resource pool. For example, if you have a pool of maintenance people that everyone in your manufacturing company assigns to projects, create a project called *Resource Pools* and then create all your enterprise resources in this project. Or you could create a resource called *CEO* and let all the people managing projects that require the CEO's involvement assign him or her from that central location. Then use the resource-sharing tools in Project to assign these resources to your plan.

When anyone makes resource assignments in a sharer file, that information is also saved in the resource pool file. Then anyone can use that file to look at resource allocations across all projects in the organization.

To access a resource that's available to your entire organization, follow this procedure:

1. **Choose Tools⇨Resource Sharing⇨Share Resources.**

The Share Resources dialog box appears, as shown in Figure 3-7.

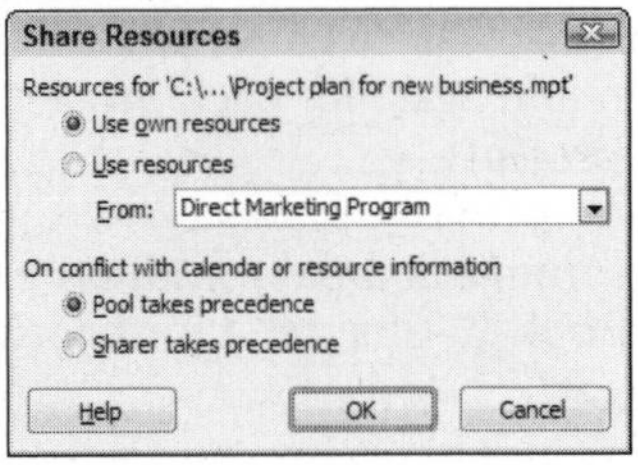

Figure 3-7:
When many people pull on the same resources in a company, sharing resources becomes a good idea.

2. **Specify the resources for the project.**

If you want to specify that a project will use only its own resources (the default), select the Use Own Resources option. If you want to share resources, select the Use Resources option and then choose a project in the From list.

3. **Specify what Project should do when a conflicting resource setting, such as a different calendar setting in the shared resources and your project, exists.**

If your project's setting should take precedence, select the Sharer Takes Precedence option. If you want the pool setting to rule, select Pool Takes Precedence.

4. **Click OK to complete the process.**

All resources in the specified resource pool are added to your own project's resource list, ready to be assigned to tasks.

After you add a shared resource to your project, you should periodically update shared resource information. You want to do this in case the person who maintains those shared resources has made a change, such as upping the resource's rate per hour. To do this, choose Tools⇨Resource Sharing⇨ Refresh Resource Pool.

If you combine separate projects into one master project at any point, Project allows you to have duplicate resources. But be careful: If you link the combined projects and then delete a duplicate resource in the master project, it's deleted in the subproject, as well.

If you share resources across an enterprise, see Book X, Chapter 2 for more about how to set these up.

When Do My Resources Work?

In Book II, Chapter 4, we cover calendars, including Project, Task, and Resource calendars. Now that you're in the thick of working with resources, take a closer look at how Resource calendars work.

First, be aware that Resource calendar settings take precedence over your Project and Task calendar settings. You create your Resource calendar based on a base calendar template that can be Standard, Night Shift, or 24 Hours. (You can also create custom calendars.)

+ **Standard** is a typical 9-to-5 workday and five-day workweek.

+ **Night Shift** is an eight-hour workday, scheduled between 11 p.m. and 8 a.m., with an hour off for a meal, from Monday through Friday.

+ The **24 Hours** base calendar shows just what it says: 24 hours per day, 7 days per week.

After you specify a base template for your Resource calendar, you can specify working hours, such as 9 a.m. to 12 p.m. and 1 p.m. to 5 p.m. for a standard eight-hour day, or 8 a.m. to 12 p.m. and 1 p.m. to 4 p.m. for a variation on that eight-hour day. Finally, you can select specific days when a resource isn't available (for example, when someone will be on vacation, at an offsite conference, or busy on another project) and mark him or her as nonworking.

Avoid micromanaging nonworking time for your resources because that could drive you crazy. For example, if someone is taking off half a day to go to the dentist, it's probably not necessary to set that half day as nonworking, because you figure the resource will make up the time on the task overall. However, if a resource is taking a two-week vacation or a three-month sabbatical, it's probably a good idea to modify that resource's Working Time calendar.

To make changes to the Resource calendar and available working times, you can click the Change Working Time button on the General tab of the Resource Information dialog box. The Change Working Time dialog box opens (see Figure 3-8).

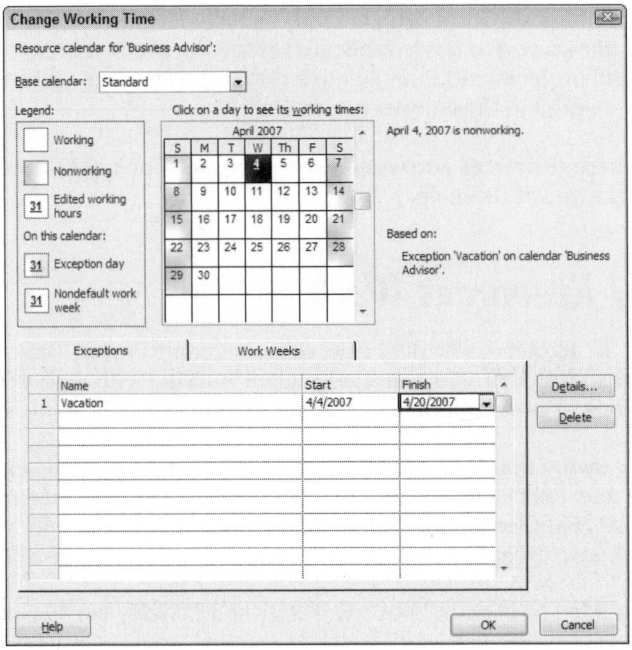

Figure 3-8:
The legend on the left explains how non-working and working days appear.

To make changes to a resource's calendar, follow these steps:

1. **Display the Resource Sheet.**

2. **Double-click a resource name.**

   The Resource Information dialog box appears.

3. **Click the Change Working Time button on the General tab.**

   The Change Working Time dialog box opens.

4. **In the Base Calendar box, select a base calendar.**

5. **If there will be an exception to the default base calendar hours, enter the Name, Start, and Finish for the exception on the Exceptions tab. Then click the Details button.**

   The Details for *'Exception'* dialog box opens (see Figure 3-9).

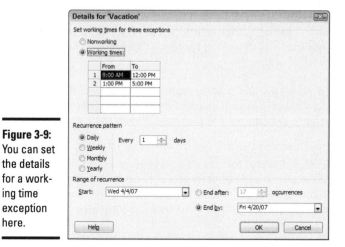

Figure 3-9:
You can set
the details
for a work-
ing time
exception
here.

6. **Select a day. Then click in the From and To boxes and type new times.**

Note that to build in a break or lunch hour, you must enter two sets of numbers.

7. **Click OK when you're finished and then click OK twice more to close the remaining dialog boxes.**

To change a day to nonworking time, select it in the Change Working Times dialog box and click the Details button. Click the Set Day(s) to These Specific Working Times radio button and then clear any working times from the From and To fields and click OK. To change all instances of a particular day (for example, all Wednesdays) as nonworking, choose the day in the Details dialog box and then click Set Days to Nonworking Times and click OK.

E-mailing an Assignment to Your Team

After you work out all your resource assignments on paper, see whether your ideas will work for your resources' schedules.

Of course, you should check to see who is available for your project. And because things can change in the time it takes to work out your plan and make assignments, make sure that your resources are committed to you before you commit yourself to a final plan.

TIP

If you use Project Server and Project Web Access with Project, you can use collaborative tools to publish assignments to a server, where people can review them and accept or decline. For more on Project Web Access, see Book X, Chapter 3.

You can send your entire project plan to resources as an e-mail attachment or just send selected tasks. You can also generate a resource assignment report and send that to people so that they can review their assignments in detail.

E-mail can be a very useful tool for any project manager. You can use it to communicate throughout the life of your project and to send your project plan for review at various stages. One of those stages is the point at which you want your resources to commit to their task assignments.

You can send your project as an e-mail attachment or as a *schedule note,* which is an e-mail with only updated tasks attached; you might send a schedule note after the project has started when you change or make a new assignment. You also have the choice of sending an entire plan or just selected tasks from it.

To send a project as an e-mail attachment, follow these steps:

1. Choose File⇨Send To⇨Mail Recipient (as Attachment).

An e-mail form is displayed.

2. Fill in a subject and your e-mail message.

3. Click Send to send the message.

If you want to send a schedule note, follow these steps:

1. Choose File⇨Send To⇨Mail Recipient (as Schedule Note).

The Send Schedule Note dialog box, as shown in Figure 3-10, appears.

Figure 3-10: Use this dialog box to specify who will receive your note.

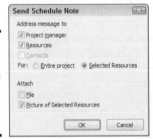

2. **Choose any intended recipients of the message from among Project Manager, Resources, and Contacts.**

3. **Select either Entire Project or Selected Resources to specify what to include in the schedule note.**

4. **In the Attach area, select what to attach to the e-mail message.**

   If you select the File option, Project attaches the entire file. If you instead select the Picture of Selected Resources option, Project attaches a bitmap picture of the selected tasks in the view you had active when you started the Send procedure.

   Note: If you were in a Resource view when you began this process, this option reads Picture of Selected Resources, and the resources you had selected are sent.

5. **Click OK.**

   An e-mail form is displayed.

6. **Fill in a subject and your e-mail message.**

7. **Click Send to send the message.**

To help you make sure that e-mails to resources on your project arrived, set your e-mail program to provide return receipts when messages are received or read. Check your e-mail client help program to find out how to do this.

Chapter 4: Tallying Costs

In This Chapter

✔ Reviewing what affects costs

✔ Determining how Project calculates costs

✔ Viewing cost data

✔ Customizing cost fields

✔ Creating a project summary task

After you've created and assigned some resources to your project, you begin to see your costs mount up at the summary task level. Understanding what affects those costs, how Project calculates those costs, and what cost information Project makes available helps you to understand what constitutes your Project budget.

In this chapter, we provide a good grounding in the hows and whys of costs and your Project plan.

How Your Settings Affect Your Budget

In Chapters 2 and 3 of this minibook, you explore costs and assigning resources to tasks. To help round out this discussion of costs, you should review all the factors that drive costs. In addition to a resource cost per hour and a resource base calendar and availability, you assign resources to tasks at certain percentages. Project uses all these factors to calculate the cost of a resource assigned to a task. (See the next section to understand how those calculations work.)

Here's the real beauty of entering information in Project: After you make settings for your resources, Project does the work of tallying and showing total costs to you in views, such as the Cost Table of Gantt Chart view shown in Figure 4-1.

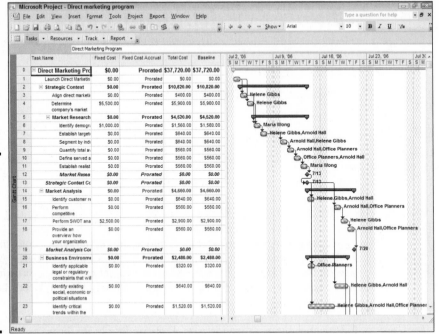

Figure 4-1:
Total costs
at the
summary-
task level
give you a
quick idea
of your total
budget and
costs in
this table.

For example, suppose you want to assign a production worker to a task. Here are the specifics:

> **Base calendar:** Night Shift (8 hours, 6 days per week, between 11 p.m. and 8 a.m.)
>
> **Cost per hour:** $20
>
> **Overtime cost:** $30
>
> **Availability:** 100 percent
>
> **Assigned to a two-day task:** 50 percent

What's the cost of this resource? Here's how it works: Two days at half-time availability based on an 8-hour calendar is a total of 8 hours (4 hours per day). The resource incurs no overtime, so the cost is 8 × $20, or $160.

Change one setting for the same resource, and see what you get:

> **Assigned to a two-day task:** 150 percent

Now the resource is working 12 hours per day (150 percent of 8 hours) over 2 days. With 16 total hours at the standard rate ($20) and 8 hours of overtime ($30), this person costs $560.

How Project Calculates Costs

While you enter resource information and assign resources to tasks, Project is busy making calculations that can shift around task timing and resource workload in your plan. These calculations relate to how Project updates tasks, determines the critical path, and calculates earned value. You can, to some extent, control how Project goes about making these calculations.

Earned value is a calculation that occurs after you have begun your project and recorded actual work on it. It's essentially the value of work completed. A task with $1,000 of costs has an earned value of $750 when the task is 75 percent complete. See Book VIII, Chapter 3 for more about earned value.

Letting Project calculate or doing it yourself?

By default, Project performs calculations automatically. When you make a change to your plan, Project recalculates totals, the critical path, and so on without you having to do a thing. However, you can change that default setting and have Project wait for you to initiate calculations manually. You make this setting on the Calculation tab of the Options dialog box (Tools⇨Options). Figure 4-2 shows the settings available there.

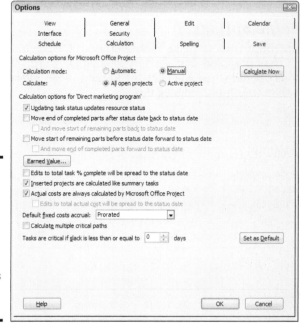

Figure 4-2:
Click the Calculate Now button to make Project perform calculations on your command.

If you change the Calculation mode to Manual, you must either press F9, or click the Calculate Now button in this dialog box any time you want Project to perform all its calculations. You also have the choice of affecting All Open Projects or only the Active Project.

So why would you choose to use manual calculation? One reason might be that you want to make a lot of changes and not have Project take the milliseconds required to recalculate between each change, slowing down your entry work. You can put things on Manual, make all your changes, and then use the Calculate Now button to make all the changes at once.

In addition, even with Change Highlighting on it's not always easy to spot all the items that have been recalculated when you make a series of changes. So, it might be easier to make all the changes in Manual mode, print your Gantt Chart view, and *then* recalculate and compare the two. This approach shows you the cumulative calculations that occurred when all your changes were made so you can see whether you're happy with the revised plan. (This feature is especially useful for trying out what-if scenarios.)

In Project 2007, you can also take advantage of the Multiple Undo feature. This means you can leave your calculations on automatic, make changes, and then undo them, thereby undoing the calculations in sequence. For more on Multiple Undo, see Book VII, Chapter 2.

Earned-value options

What do the settings you can make to the earned-value calculation do to your project? To understand that, start by looking at Figure 4-3, which shows you the options offered when you click the Earned Value button on the Calculation tab of the Options dialog box.

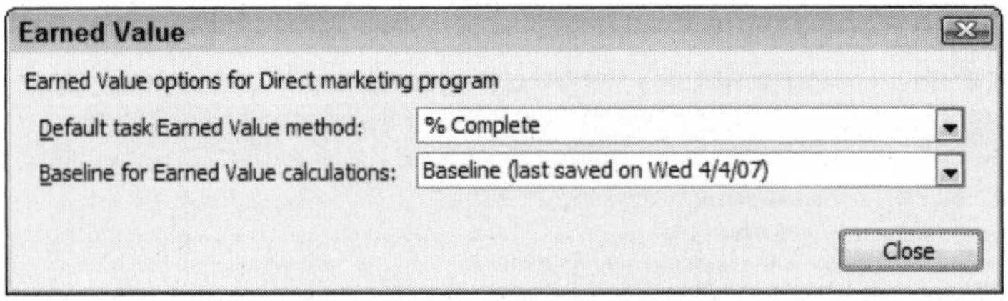

Figure 4-3:
Here are two simple settings to use for calculating earned value.

Earned Value	⬜⬛
Earned Value options for Direct marketing program	
Default task Earned Value method:	% Complete ▾
Baseline for Earned Value calculations:	Baseline (last saved on Wed 4/4/07) ▾
	Close

The Default Task Earned Value Method setting provides two choices:

✦ **% Complete:** This setting calculates earned value using the percent complete that you record on each task. This assumes that for a task that's halfway complete, half the work hours have been used.

✦ **Physical % Complete:** Use this setting if you want to enter a percent of completion that isn't based on a straight percent-complete calculation. For example, if you have a four-week task to complete a mail survey, 50 percent of the effort might happen in the first 25 percent of the duration of the project: designing, printing, and mailing the survey. Nothing happens for two weeks while you wait for responses, and then there's a flurry of activity when the responses come back. So a straight calculation that 50 percent of the task is completed 50 percent of the way through wouldn't be accurate. If your projects have a lot of tasks like this, you might consider changing your settings to use this method. Then, you can display the Physical % Complete column in your Gantt Chart sheet pane and enter what you consider more accurate percent-complete information for each task.

The second setting in the Earned Value dialog box is the Baseline for Earned Value Calculations drop-down list. As we mention earlier, *earned value* is the value of work completed, expressed in dollars, according to the baseline: A $2,000 task at 50 percent complete (for example) has a $1,000 earned value of work performed. Therefore, the baseline against which you calculate this value is hugely important. Choose any of the 11 possible baselines you might have saved in your project here. After you make these two choices, click Close to close the Earned Value dialog box.

You should explore one more option in the Options dialog box that concerns earned-value calculations. The Edits to Total Task % Complete Will Be Spread to the Status Date option, which isn't selected by default, affects how Project distributes changes in your schedule. If you leave this option deselected, calculations go to the end of the duration of tasks in progress, rather than up to the status date or the current date. If you select this option, calculations spread changes across your plan up to the status date or the current date, and no further. Selecting this choice helps you see changes to your project in increments of time, rather than across the life of tasks in progress.

Our advice is to leave the Edits to Total Task % option not selected for the most accurate reflection of progress on your project.

Examining Cost Data

After you assign all your resources to tasks and set all your fixed costs, it's time for sticker shock. Project will tally all those costs and show you the project's budget. First you have to look at your bottom line, which Project lets you do from several perspectives. Then you might have to get out a sharp knife and trim those costs down.

Viewing cost information

Several views give you a good idea of what your project will cost and where those costs are coming from:

✦ Gantt Chart view with the Cost Table displayed shows you total cost by task and a fixed cost column. Several of the columns in this table come in handy when you begin to track spending on your project and need to compare actual costs to projected costs.

✦ Network Diagram view can also display the Cost Table, showing you a neat snapshot of each task's costs within its own task box (see Figure 4-4).

✦ Resource Sheet view helps you to review the hourly and overtime rates of resources currently assigned to your project.

✦ Try using filters to display the highest-priced tasks in your project, a logical place to start trimming your budget. (See Book VII, Chapter 1 for information about using filters.)

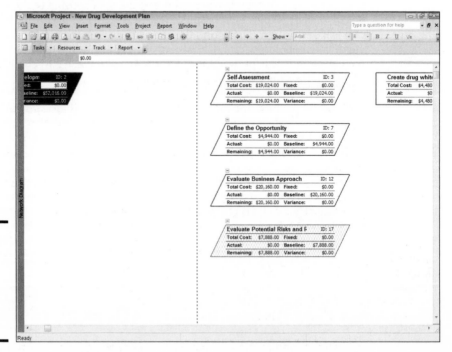

Figure 4-4:
Network Diagram view with the Cost Table displayed.

Customizing cost fields

When you display the Cost Table with fields, such as the Standard Resource Rate, you can click in any cost column and enter a rate for each resource. A neat shortcut is to customize those fields with a lookup table.

A *lookup table* allows you to create a drop-down list of values in a field to select from. So, if your company has a few standard hourly rates or per-use costs for materials, customizing these fields can make your information entry faster and also help prevent data-entry mistakes that can occur when you enter all rates manually.

To customize a field, follow these steps:

1. **Display a table with the column you want to customize.**

   You display tables by choosing View⇨Table and selecting one from the list that appears.

2. **Right-click the column heading and choose Customize Fields from the shortcut menu that appears.**

   The Custom Fields dialog box appears, as shown in Figure 4-5.

Figure 4-5: You can use the Rename button in this dialog box to rename a cost field if you like.

3. **Click the Lookup button.**

   The Edit Lookup Table dialog box appears, as shown in Figure 4-6.

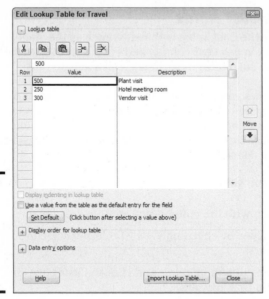

Figure 4-6:
Create
preset
values for
the field by
building a
Value list.

4. **Enter a value (if you're filling in a cost field, this is a dollar amount) in the Value column.**

5. **Enter a description (for example,** plant worker **or** engineer **for the category of resource charged at this rate) in the Description column.**

6. **Repeat Steps 4 and 5 to enter additional values for this field.**

7. **If you want to restrict the field to accept only the values in this list, make sure the Data Entry option Allow Additional Items to be Entered into the Fields check box is not selected.**

   You might have to click the plus symbol to the left of Data Entry Options to see this check box.

8. **Click a radio button to select an order for the list (you might have to click the plus sign to the left of Display Order for Lookup Table to see these options):**

   • *By Row Number:* Lists the items as you've listed them in this dialog box

   • *Ascending:* Lists them in ascending value order, lowest value first

   • *Descending:* Lists them in descending value order with the highest value first

9. **Click Close and then click OK to save the list and close all dialog boxes.**

A good view to use if you want to see all of a resource's work assignment information is Resource Allocation view. You can display it by clicking the Resource Allocation View button on the Resource Management toolbar, or you can select it from the More Views dialog box.

The Value of a Project Summary Task

Just as a ship can have only one captain, only one task can summarize all other tasks in each project. We strongly suggest that you create a *project summary task,* which represents the highest (least detailed) level of information and is often simply the title of the project, such as New Product Rollout or Space Shuttle Launch.

A project summary task is created when every task in the project falls under it in the outline, as shown in Figure 4-7. You can see in the figure that all project phase summary tasks are subordinate to the project summary task.

See Book III, Chapter 1 for more about the outline structure of a project plan.

Project summary task

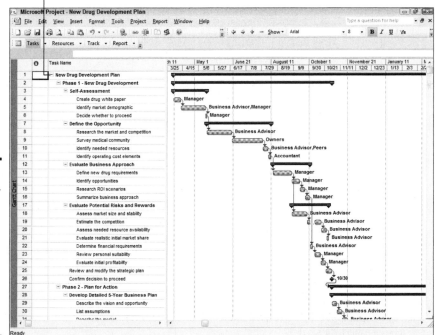

Figure 4-7:
The highest-level task in the outline with all tasks indented below it is the project summary task.

Working with budgets

Company: A medium-sized capital venture company.

Project: Planning for an office move.

Challenge: The project manager has to budget the cost of an office move. He wants a way to track the entire budgeted cost for moving against several individual costs that are tallying up as he adds resources to individual tasks.

Solution: The project manager can specify a resource as a budget resource by selecting the Budget check box in the Resource Information dialog box, shown in the following figure. He can then assign these resources to the project's single summary task. Using budget resources, he can display fields that allow him

to compare budgeted work with planned work. (Believe us, there's often a difference.) For example, he might have $10,000 budgeted for mover time, and he might have planned to use $11,450 of resource work for the move. The budget setting can help him compare these amounts as you add and delete resources from various tasks.

If you assign a budget resource, you can use Task Usage view or Resource Usage view to enter a work amount for that resource. You can view budgeted work by displaying the Budget Work field. Note that this field reflects only Material and Work resource type costs. You can use the Budget Cost field to view the budgeted amount for Cost resource types.

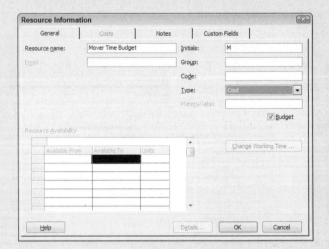

The highest-level headline in an outline reflects the sum of all the items below it. The project summary task rolls up all the actual data from other tasks into one line item. Thus, the project summary task's duration reflects the duration of the entire project. From a cost angle, the project summary task's total cost reflects the total costs for the entire project. Being able to see your total bottom line costs at a glance is one of the things that make a summary task so useful.

The length of your summary task can be a bit confusing. Remember that the *summary task duration* is the difference between the earliest task start date and latest task end date. However, nonworking days aren't counted in the summary task duration. The length of the summary task, therefore, equals the number of days of work over the course of the subtasks, not the number of calendar days between the start of the first task and end of the last.

Not everyone uses project summary tasks. You can simply create tasks that summarize tasks within project phases — with subphases and subtasks below them — and not create a project summary task. However, there are two good reasons for creating a project summary task:

✦ **You can quickly view totals for both time and money for the project at a glance in the columns of data in Gantt Chart view and other views.**

✦ **You can place a link to your project summary task in another project so that all data for one project is reflected in another.** For example, if you create five schedules for new product launches in your company, you can easily create a master schedule for all company product launches by linking to the project summary tasks in each of the projects.

As you build your project, you can easily create a project summary task yourself by simply indenting other tasks beneath it. But if you neglect to do this till later in your planning, you can use a Project feature to generate this summary task automatically at any time — even after you build all the phases of your project.

To have Project automatically create a project summary task, follow these steps:

1. **Choose Tools⇨Options.**

The Options dialog box appears.

2. **Click the View tab to display it (see Figure 4-8).**

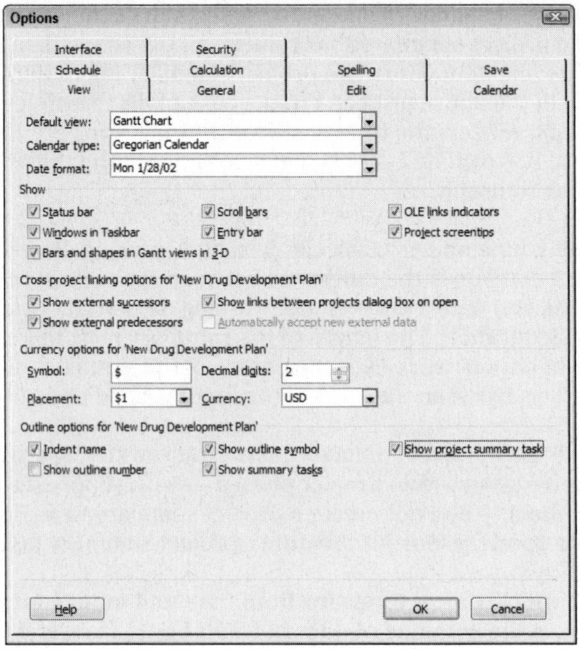

Figure 4-8:
The View
tab of the
Options
dialog box.

3. Select the Show Project Summary Task check box.

4. Click OK to insert the Project Summary task.

Book VI

Communicating
Project Information

Contents at a Glance

Chapter 1: Working with Views

In This Chapter

✔ Understanding views

✔ Changing the default view

✔ Adding views to the View bar and the View menu

✔ Sorting, filtering, and grouping tasks in views

✔ Displaying a combination view

✔ Creating a view

✔ Creating a combination view

✔ Printing views

*V*iew is the term Project uses to describe a way for you to look at project information; a view offers you a perspective of your project. As the project manager, you're actually going to want to look at your project from many different perspectives, and Project contains a wealth of views to accommodate you. If you can't find what you want using one of the built-in views, you can always create your own view. Project also lets you sort, filter, and group information in views, which helps you focus on different issues.

Network Diagram view and Calendar view behave a little differently than all the other Project views; you can customize these two views using techniques described in Book IX, Chapter 2.

What's a View?

When it comes to looking at the information in your project, you're going to want to look at it in a variety of ways so you can focus on particular issues. For example, you'll want to view the tasks in your project without concern for the resources assigned to the tasks. Then you're going to want to focus on the resource assignments for the project. Also, you'll find that you want to look at different information concerning tasks; for example, you might want to look at baseline information, and then you might want to review task costs. Similarly, you'll want to look at different types of information for resources.

Of course, you can try to look at all the information using only one view, but that would result in confusion instead of clarity. So, Project provides 28 built-in views to let you look at your project from a variety of perspectives. If one of these built-in views doesn't meet your needs, you can create your own view.

Book II, Chapter 3 contains a lot of really good information that should help you decide what view to use, depending on the circumstances.

You can classify the views in Project into three types:

✦ **Chart or graph views**

✦ **Form views**

✦ **Table or sheet views**

Chart or graph views present information by using pictures. Relationship Diagram view, shown in Figure 1-1, is a chart view.

Form views present information the same way that a paper form presents information. A form displays information about a single item (or task) in your project. The Task Form shown in Figure 1-2 is a form view.

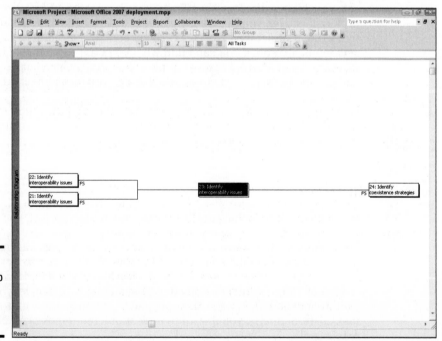

Figure 1-1:
Relationship
Diagram
view is a
chart view.

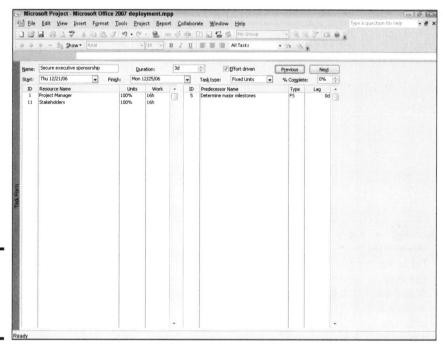

Figure 1-2:
Task Form
view is a
typical form
view.

Table or sheet views present information in rows and columns, similar to the way that a spreadsheet program presents information. Resource Sheet view, shown in Figure 1-3, is a table view. Each row of the table contains all the information about one resource in your project, and each column represents a field that identifies the information that you're storing about the resource.

Shortcut menus are available in many views; right-click anyplace on the view to see a shortcut menu.

Each table view actually comprises a variety of tables, and you can easily switch to any of these variations. In Chapter 2 of this minibook, you find out more about tables.

Finally, Project contains combination views, like the Task Entry view shown in Figure 1-4, that combine two of the types of views just described. In a combination view, one view appears in the top half of the screen while another appears in the bottom half. Later in this chapter, you discover how to work with combination views.

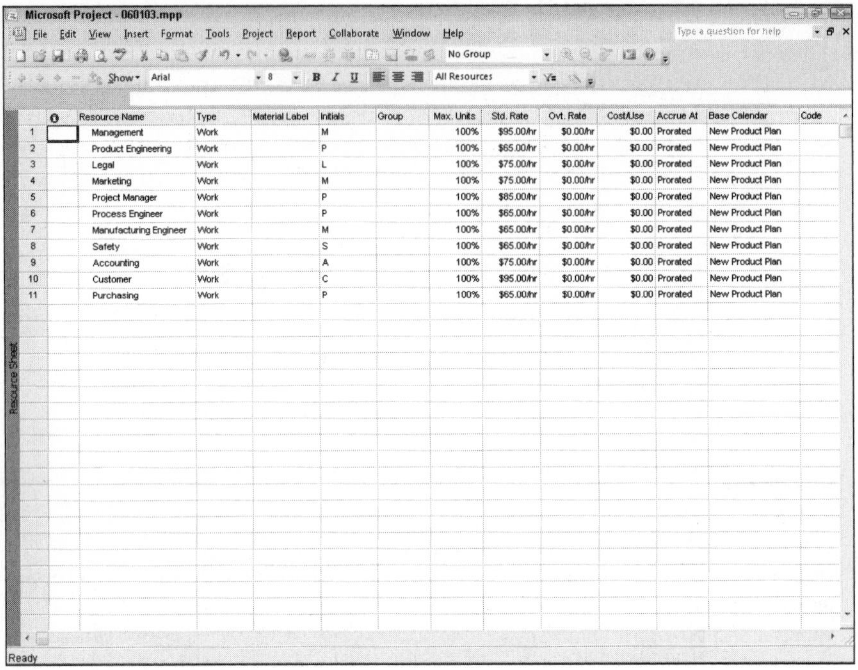

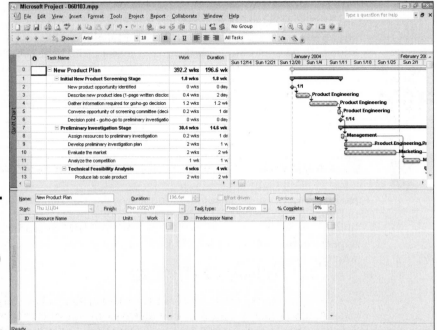

Figure 1-3:
Resource
Sheet view
is a typical
table view.

Figure 1-4:
Task Entry
view is a
combination
of Gantt
Chart view
and Task
Form view.

Selecting the Startup View

By default, the first view you see when you open Project is Gantt Chart view. But suppose, after working in Project awhile, that you discover you really work most in Task Usage view. Can you make that view appear when you open Project? Yes. Follow these steps:

1. **Choose Tools⇨Options.**

2. **Click the View tab shown in Figure 1-5.**

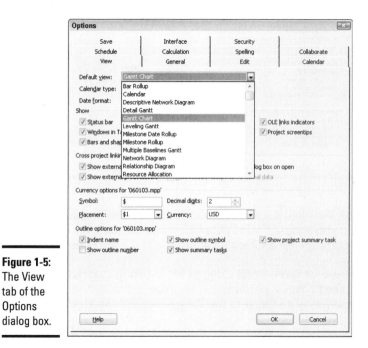

Figure 1-5:
The View tab of the Options dialog box.

3. **In the Default View drop down list, click the view you want to use as your default view.**

4. **Click OK.**

Project displays the view you select the next time you open Project.

Making a View Handy to Display

Even though you can select a default view, you probably have several views that you use regularly, and you want an easy way to display those views. You can easily add those views to the View menu or the View bar that can appear down the left side of the Project window (see Figure 1-6).

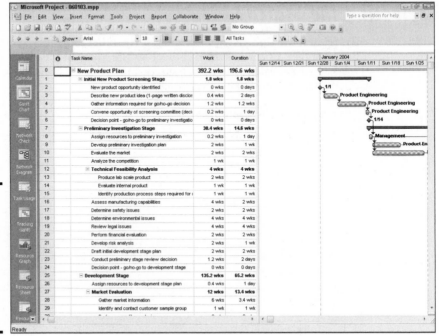

Figure 1-6:
When you
display the
View bar,
the name
of the view
doesn't
appear on-
screen.

Displaying the View bar is a matter of personal preference; the View bar appears when you choose View➪View Bar. When you hide the View bar, the name of the current view appears on a thin bar at the left edge of the view.

Suppose that you've taken a real liking to Relationship Diagram view because you like its visual presentation of predecessor and successor tasks. To easily display it by adding it to the View menu and the View bar, follow these steps:

1. **Choose View➪More Views.**

The More Views dialog box appears (see Figure 1-7).

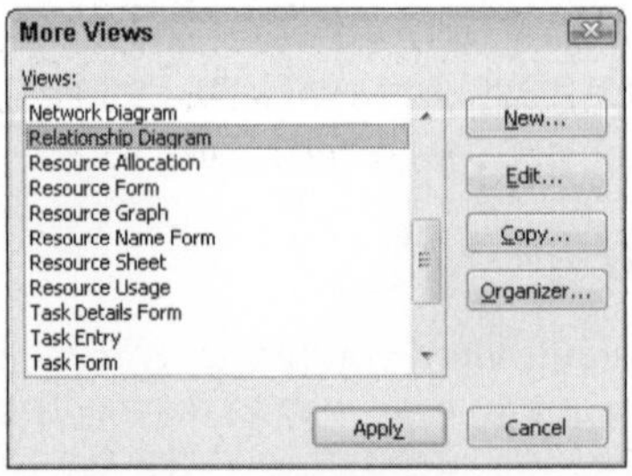

Figure 1-7:
Select the
view to
which you
want easy
access from
this dialog
box.

2. Click the view you want to add in the Views list.

3. Click Edit.

The View Definition dialog box appears (see Figure 1-8).

4. Select the Show in Menu check box.

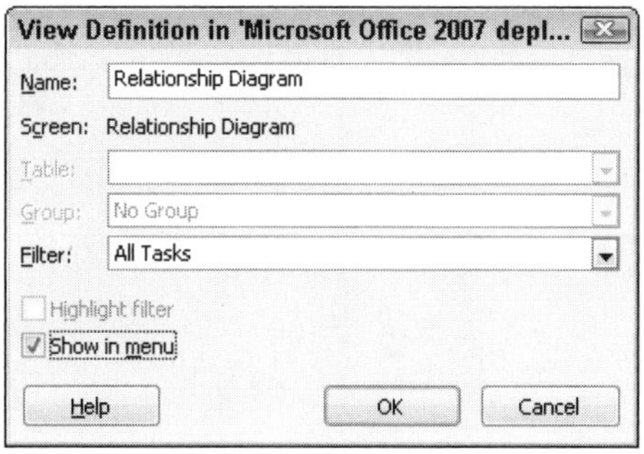

Figure 1-8:
In the View
Definition
dialog box,
select the
Show in
Menu
check box.

View Definition in 'Microsoft Office 2007 depl...	
Name:	Relationship Diagram
Screen:	Relationship Diagram
Table:	
Group:	No Group
Filter:	All Tasks

☐ Highlight filter
☑ Show in menu

Help   OK   Cancel

5. Click OK.

The view you selected appears on the View menu and the View bar.

You can remove any views you seldom use from the View menu and the View bar. To remove a view from the View menu and the View bar, repeat this procedure but deselect the Show in Menu check box.

Sorting Tasks in a View

Different people find different techniques work well when they're trying to organize large sets of information. And, planning a project can be an exercise in organizing large sets of information.

Sorting tasks in your project schedule is one technique you can use to organize a project's information to help you focus on particular aspects of the project. You can sort a project from most views in almost any way that you want. For example, in Gantt Chart view, Project automatically sorts tasks by ID (see Figure 1-9). But you might find it easier to view your project information if you sort by cost. Choose Project⇨Sort⇨By Cost, and Project reorders Gantt Chart view so that tasks are ordered by cost, and row numbers become nonsequential (see Figure 1-10).

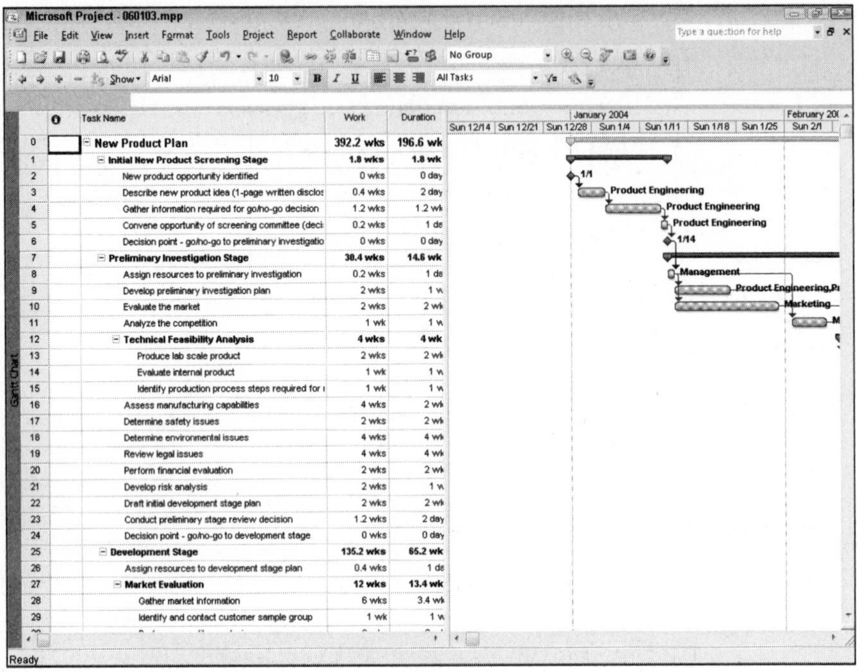

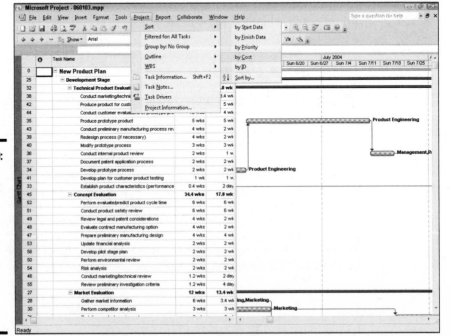

Figure 1-9:
By default, Project sorts Gantt Chart view in Task ID order, so row numbers are sequential.

Figure 1-10:
Using commands from the Sort submenu, you can select a different sort order for a project.

The five most common sort keys appear when you choose Project⇨Sort, but if you choose the Sort By command at the bottom of the submenu, the Sort dialog box appears (see Figure 1-11). From this dialog box, you can select from a wide variety of fields on which to sort your project. And, you can set up three sort keys so that Project can break any "ties" it finds while sorting. For example, if Project finds a tie at the first level, it uses the second sort that you specify to break the tie. Project uses the third sort key to break ties at the second level.

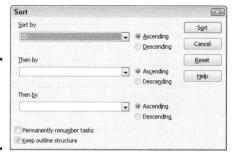

Figure 1-11:
Sort your project by almost any field.

**Book VI
Chapter 1**

*Working with
Views*

Using the check boxes at the bottom of the dialog box, you can make your sort choices permanent by reassigning Task IDs, and you can choose to retain the outline structure of the project.

Filtering a View

Filtering is another technique you can use to help you focus on a particular aspect of your project. When you *filter,* you specify criteria, and Project either limits the information that appears in the view or highlights the information that meets the criteria. For example, you can view only the tasks assigned to a certain resource, or you can highlight the tasks on the critical path of your project.

The filters available to you in a particular view are dependent on the view's primary purpose. For example, Gantt Chart view is primarily a task-oriented view, so you can apply task-related filters to the view. On the other hand, the Resource Sheet is a resource-oriented view, so the only filters available to you are resource filters. Table 1-1 lists alphabetically each task filter and the information Project displays when you apply one of these filters. Table 1-2 lists similar information for the available resource filters.

Table 1-1	Task Filters
Filter	*Purpose*
All Tasks	Displays all the tasks in your project.
Completed Tasks	Displays all finished tasks.
Confirmed	Displays the tasks on which specified resources have agreed to work.
Cost Greater Than	Displays the tasks that exceed the cost you specify.
Cost Overbudget	Calculated filter that displays all tasks with a cost that exceeds the baseline cost.
Created After	Displays all tasks that you created in your project on or after the specified date.
Critical	Displays all tasks on the critical path.
Date Range	Interactive filter that prompts you for two dates and then displays all tasks that start after the earlier date and finish before the later date.
In Progress Tasks	Displays all tasks that have started but haven't finished.
Incomplete Tasks	Displays all tasks that haven't finished.
Late/Overbudget Tasks Assigned To	Prompts you to specify a resource. Then Project displays tasks that meet either of two conditions: the tasks assigned to that resource that exceed the budget you allocated for them, or the tasks that haven't finished yet and will finish after the baseline finish date. Note that completed tasks don't appear when you apply this filter, even if they're completed after the baseline finish date.
Linked Fields	Displays tasks to which you have linked text from other programs.
Milestones	Displays only milestones.
Resource Group	Displays the tasks that are assigned to resources that belong to the group you specify.
Should Start By	Prompts you for a date and then displays all tasks not yet begun that should have started by that date.
Should Start/Finish By	Prompts you for two dates: a start date and a finish date. Then Project uses the filter to display those tasks that haven't started by the start date and those tasks that haven't finished by the finish date.
Slipped/Late Progress	Displays two types of tasks: those that have slipped behind their baseline scheduled finish date and those that aren't progressing on schedule.
Slipping Tasks	Displays all tasks that are behind schedule.
Summary Tasks	Displays all tasks that have subtasks grouped below them.

Filter	*Purpose*
Task Range	Shows all tasks that have ID numbers within the range that you provide.
Tasks with Attachments	Displays tasks that have objects attached or a note in the Notes box.
Tasks with Deadlines	Displays all tasks to which you have assigned deadline dates.
Tasks with Estimated Durations	Displays all tasks to which you have assigned an estimated duration.
Tasks with Fixed Dates	Displays all tasks that have an actual start date and tasks to which you assign some constraint other than As Soon As Possible.
Tasks/Assignments with Overtime	Displays the tasks or assignments that have overtime.
Top Level Tasks	Displays the highest-level summary tasks.
Unconfirmed	Displays the tasks on which specified resources have not agreed to work.
Unstarted Tasks	Displays tasks that haven't started.
Update Needed	Displays tasks that have changes, such as revised start and finish dates or resource reassignments, and that need to be sent to resources for update or confirmation.
Using Resource	Displays all tasks that use the resource that you specify.
Using Resource in Date Range	Displays the tasks that are assigned to a specified resource that start after the first date you specify and finish before the second date you specify.
Work Overbudget	Displays all tasks with scheduled work greater than baseline work.

Book VI
Chapter 1

Working with Views

Table 1-2	**Resource Filters**
Filter	*Purpose*
All Resources	Displays all the resources in your project.
Confirmed Assignments	Available only in Resource Usage view; displays only those tasks for which a resource has confirmed the assignment.
Cost Greater Than	Displays the resources that exceed the cost that you specify.
Cost Overbudget	Calculated filter that displays all resources with a cost that exceeds the baseline cost.
Date Range	Interactive filter that prompts you for two dates and then displays all tasks and resources with assignments that start after the earlier date and finish before the later date.
Group	Prompts you for a group and then displays all resources that belong to that group.

(continued)

Table 1-2 *(continued)*

Filter	Purpose
In Progress Assignments	Displays all tasks that have started but haven't finished.
Linked Fields	Displays resources to which you have linked text from other programs.
Overallocated Resources	Displays all resources that are scheduled to do more work than they have the capacity to do.
Resource Range	Acts as an interactive filter that prompts you for a range of ID numbers and then displays all resources within that range.
Resources with Attachments	Displays resources that have objects attached or a note in the Notes box.
Resources/Assignments	Displays the resources or assignments that have overtime.
Should Start By	Prompts you for a date and then displays all tasks and resources with assignments not yet begun that should have started by that date.
Should Start/Finish By	Prompts you for two dates: a start date and a finish date. Then Project uses the filter to display those tasks or assignments that haven't started by the start date and those tasks or assignments that haven't finished by the finish date.
Slipped/Late Progress	Displays two types of resources: those that have slipped behind their baseline scheduled finish date and those that aren't progressing on schedule.
Slipping Assignments	Displays all resources with uncompleted tasks that are behind schedule because the tasks have been delayed from the original baseline plan.
Unconfirmed Assignments	Displays the assignments for which requested resources haven't yet agreed to work.
Unstarted Assignments	Displays confirmed assignments that haven't yet started.
Work Complete	Displays resources that have completed all their assigned tasks.
Work Incomplete	Displays all resources with baseline work greater than scheduled work.
Work Overbudget	Displays all resources with scheduled work greater than baseline work.

Applying a filter to a view

Because you can apply task filters to task views only and resource filters to resource views only, the filters you can select depend on the view that you display before starting these steps:

1. **Display the view that you want to filter.**

2. **Choose Project⇨Filtered For.**

Project displays a list of the most commonly used filters.

3. Choose the filter that you want to apply.

Project applies the filter you selected.

You can quickly determine that Project is filtering information by looking at the ID column. The ID numbers for hidden tasks or resources don't appear.

To apply a filter that doesn't appear on the list or to apply a highlighting filter, follow these steps:

1. Display the view that you want to filter.

2. Choose Project⇨Filtered For⇨More Filters.

Project displays the More Filters window (see Figure 1-12).

Book VI
Chapter 1

Working with Views

Figure 1-12:
You can use the More Filters window to apply, well, more filters.

3. Select a filter name from the list.

4. Click Apply to apply the filter or click Highlight to apply a highlighting filter.

If the filter that you want to apply requires additional information, such as a date range, type the information Project requests.

5. Click OK.

Project applies the filter.

If you highlight tasks or resources that meet the criteria, Project displays the information that meets the criteria in blue.

To turn off a filter, choose Project⇨Filtered For. Then choose All Tasks or All Resources, as appropriate for the filtered view.

Creating custom filters

Yes, you guessed it: You can create a new filter or modify an existing filter. Because creating and editing a filter are very similar activities, follow these steps to edit an existing filter, and after the steps, we tell you the changes to make to create a new filter:

1. **Display the view that you want to filter.**

2. **Choose Project⇨Filtered For⇨More Filters.**

   Project opens the More Filters window.

3. **Highlight the filter that you want to modify.**

4. **Click the Copy button.**

   Project displays the Filter Definition dialog box (see Figure 1-13).

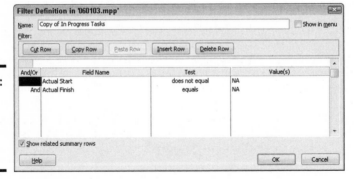

Figure 1-13: Use this dialog box to edit an existing filter.

Any changes that you make to a filter are permanent. For this reason, we suggest that you click the Copy button to make a copy of a filter that you want to modify, rather than clicking the Edit button to edit the original filter.

5. **Click in the Name box and type a new name for your filter.**

6. **Click in the Field Name column.**

   Project displays a list box arrow to the right of the field.

7. **Select a field from the list.**

8. **Click in the Test column and select a comparison operator from the list.**

9. **Click in the Value(s) column and supply a filtering value.**

10. **Repeat Steps 6 through 9 for each criterion that you want to create.**

Also supply an And/Or operator if you supply additional criteria.

If you use "And," Project displays information only if the task or resource meets *all* criteria. If you use "Or," the filter displays information if a task or resource meets *any* of the criteria.

11. Click OK.

Project redisplays the More Filters window.

12. Click Apply.

Project closes the More Filters window and applies the filter.

To create a new filter, click the New button in Step 4 above. In the Filter Definition dialog box, the name Filter 1 appears in the Name box and no information appears at the bottom of the box. Type a name for the new filter and enter some filtering criteria using the techniques described in Steps 5–10. To have your new filter appear in the Filtered For list, select the Show in Menu check box.

Each line that appears in the Filter Definition dialog box is called a *statement*. To have Project evaluate certain statements together, but separate from other statements in your filter, group the statements into a set of criteria by leaving a blank line between sets of criteria. On the blank line, select either operator in the And/Or field.

If your filter contains three or more statements within one criteria group, Project evaluates all And statements before evaluating Or statements. Across groups, Project evaluates And statements in the order in which they appear.

Using AutoFilters

AutoFilters are a way to filter information on any table view by selecting a value for any table column directly on the table. When you turn on Auto-Filters, Project displays a list box arrow at the right edge of each column heading (see Figure 1-14). You can turn on AutoFilters by clicking the AutoFilters button on the Formatting toolbar.

When you click an arrow, Project displays a list of values available for that column. When you select a value, Project filters the information in the table to display only those tasks that meet the filter's criteria. In Figure 1-13, we filtered by a Finish Date of This Week, and Project displayed only those tasks scheduled to finish during the current week. First, notice that the task numbers are no longer in numerical order. Then look at the timescale in the Gantt Chart portion of the window; you can see that all the tasks end within a short window of time.

List box arrow   AutoFilters button

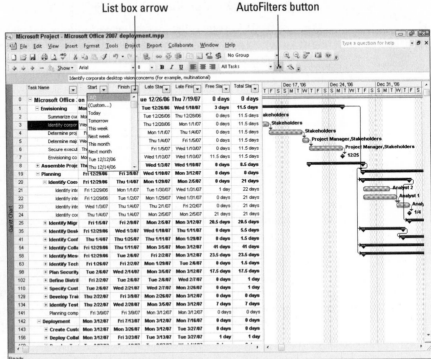

Figure 1-14:
When you
turn on
AutoFilters,
Project
displays list
box arrows
beside each
column
heading.

Project displays the column heading by which you're filtering in blue,
whereas other column heading titles are black — the difference is difficult to
see in this black-and-white book.

If you decide that you really like AutoFilters, you can have Project display
them automatically for each new project you create. Follow these steps:

1. **Choose Tools⇨Options.**

2. **Click the General tab.**

3. **Select the Set AutoFilter On For New Projects check box (see**
Figure 1-15).

4. **Click OK.**

The next time you create a new project, AutoFilter list box arrows automatically appear.

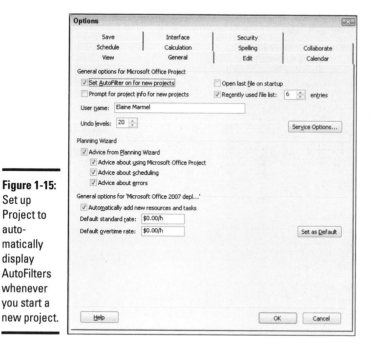

Figure 1-15:
Set up
Project to
auto-
matically
display
AutoFilters
whenever
you start a
new project.

Grouping Information

Grouping is a variation on sorting and filtering. When you use *grouping* in Project, you tell Project to group tasks based on criteria you select. Grouping differs from sorting because grouping doesn't assign an order to the tasks or hide any tasks from view.

Using a predefined group

You can group tasks in a variety of predefined ways, but the predefined groups are based on the type of view; that is, the available predefined groups differ, depending on whether you start in a task view or a resource view. To group tasks based on whether they're on the critical path, follow these steps:

1. **Display a task view that you want to use to group tasks.**

2. **Choose Project➪Group By.**

Project displays a list of predefined groups (see Figure 1-16). By default, Project doesn't group tasks, so No Group is selected.

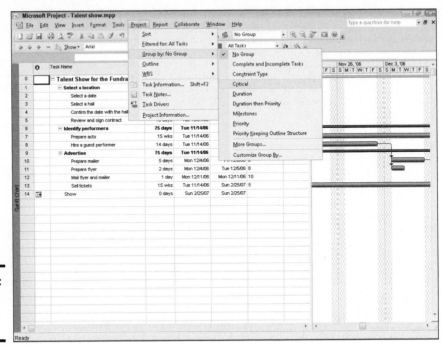

Figure 1-16:
Select a predefined group.

You also can open the Group By list on the Standard toolbar.

3. Click the group that you want to apply.

In this example, we chose Critical.

When you establish groups, Project adds headings for each group in yellow highlighting that you can't see in this black-and-white book; in Figure 1-17, we've grouped the tasks based on whether they're critical in the project.

To turn off grouping, choose Project➪Group By. Then choose No Group. Alternatively, select No Group from the Group By list on the Standard toolbar.

Grouping and usage views

If you start in a usage view, you also can group on assignment fields. In the steps that follow, we started working from Resource Usage view, where you have the option of grouping by assignment or by resource. If you start working from Task Usage view, the names of some of the options change to refer to tasks instead of resources. In addition, you have the choice of grouping by assignment or by task.

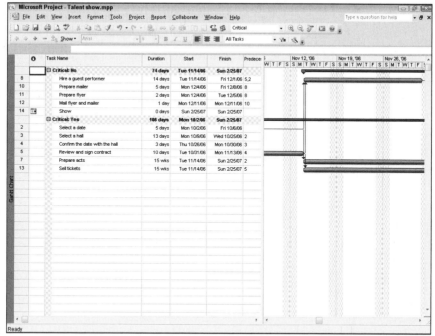

Figure 1-17:
You can
group tasks
based on
whether
they're
critical.

Follow these steps to group by assignment in a usage view:

1. **Display either Task Usage view or Resource Usage view.**

2. **Choose Project⇨Group By⇨Customize Group By.**

   The Customize Group By dialog box appears (see Figure 1-18).

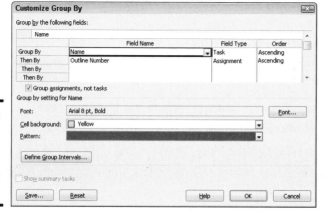

Figure 1-18:
Use this
dialog box
to group by
assignment
fields.

3. **Select the fields by which you want to group.**

4. **Select the Group Assignments, Not Tasks check box.**

5. **In the Field Type column, select whether to group by assignment or by task.**

6. **Click OK.**

Project groups the usage view by assignments (see Figure 1-19).

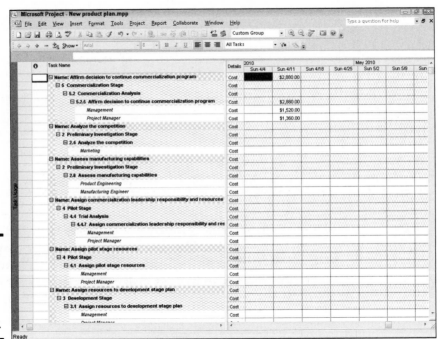

Figure 1-19: On a usage view, you can group by assignment.

Do-it-yourself groups

As you might suspect, you're not limited to using the groups that come pre-defined with Project; you can create your own groups. Follow these steps:

1. **Display the view that you want to use to group tasks.**

2. **Choose Project⇨Group By⇨More Groups.**

Project displays the More Groups dialog box (see Figure 1-20).

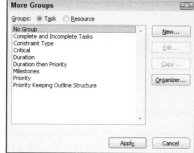

Figure 1-20:
From this dialog box, you can create your own group.

3. **Select the Task option button or the Resource option button, depending on the type of group you want to create.**

   Project doesn't let you apply a task grouping to a resource view or a resource grouping to a task view.

4. **Select a group name from the list.**

5. **Click Copy.**

   Project displays the Group Definition dialog box (see Figure 1-21), which contains a copy of the settings of the group you selected in Step 4.

   Because any changes that you make to a group are permanent, we suggest that you make a copy of a group and modify the copy instead of editing the original group.

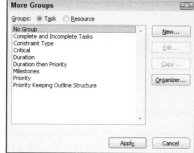

Figure 1-21:
Editing a copy of an existing group is the easiest way to create a new group.

6. **Assign a name to the group that you're creating.**

Select the Show in Menu check box if you want the group to appear on the Group By menu.

An ampersand (&) in the group name indicates that you can type the letter to the right of the ampersand to select the group from a menu.

7. Open the Field Name list box and select a field on which you want Project to group.

8. In the Order column, choose Ascending or Descending.

You can select a font for the grouping title information and change the cell background and the pattern that Project displays for the field. You also can include summary tasks in the grouping by selecting the Show Summary Tasks check box.

9. Click the Define Group Intervals button.

Project displays the Define Group Interval dialog box (see Figure 1-22).

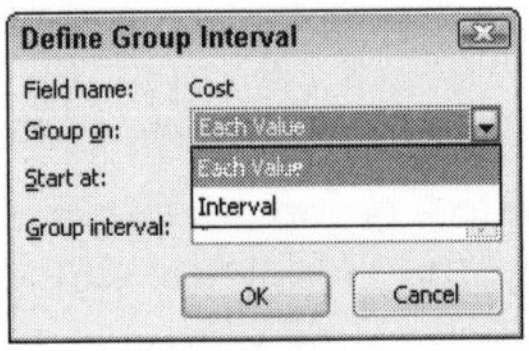

Figure 1-22: From this dialog box, identify the intervals at which you want Project to group the fields.

Define Group Interval		
Field name:	Cost	
Group on:	Each Value	
Start at:	Each Value	
Group interval:	Interval	
	OK	Cancel

10. Set the grouping intervals that Project uses.

11. Click OK.

Project redisplays the Group Definition dialog box.

12. Click OK.

Project saves your choices and redisplays the More Groups window.

13. Click Apply to apply the group you just defined or click Close.

Using Combination Views

In addition to the 28 views that exist in Project, you can create combination views, where Project splits the screen horizontally and displays one view in the top pane and another in the bottom pane. In fact, Task Entry view, shown in Figure 1-23, is a combination view by default.

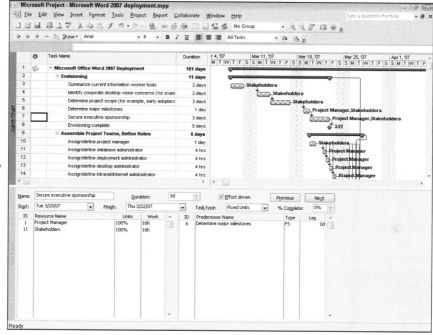

Figure 1-23:
Task Entry
view shows
Gantt Chart
view in the
top pane
and Task
Form view in
the bottom
pane.

When you work in a combination view, the bottom pane displays the information about the task or resource you select in the top pane. So, click a task or resource in the top pane to select it; then, click the bottom pane to make it the active pane and make changes to the task or resource as needed.

The name of the view appears in a bar that runs down the left side of the screen; the active pane's bar is darker than the inactive pane's bar.

You can easily display a combination view by following these steps:

1. Display the first view you want to see by using the View bar or View menu.

2. Choose Windows➪Split.

Project splits the window (see Figure 1-24), displaying either Task Form view or Resource Form view in the bottom pane.

Project selects the appropriate form for the bottom pane based on the view in the top pane. If the view in the top pane is a task view, Project displays Task Form view in the bottom pane. Similarly, if a resource view appears in the top pane, Project displays Resource Form view in the bottom pane.

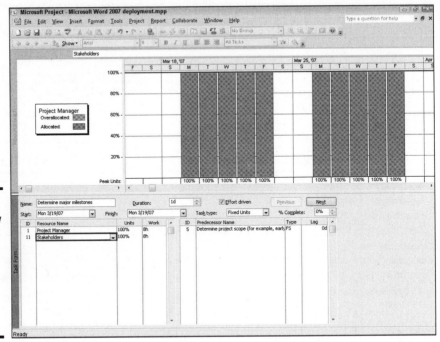

Figure 1-24: The window in Project is split, showing different views in different panes.

3. **Click anywhere in the bottom pane.**

4. **Choose View⇨More Views.**

   The More Views dialog box appears (see Figure 1-25).

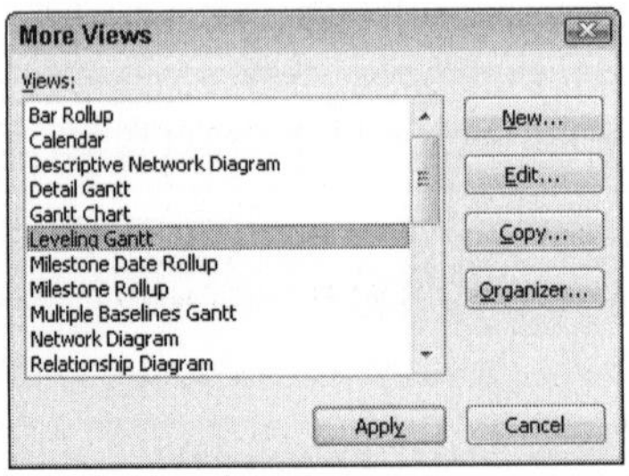

Figure 1-25: Select a view for the bottom pane.

5. **Click Apply.**

   The view you selected appears in the bottom pane.

Shortcut to display a combination view

Are you the type of person who prefers to avoid menus? Here's a quick and easy way to create a combination view. Move your pointer to the split bar, which is in the lower-right corner of the Project window, just below the vertical scroll bar. When the pointer becomes two horizontal lines with arrows, the way it appears in the figure, double-click. Or, you can also drag the split bar toward the top of your screen. You can return to a single view by double-clicking the split bar again.

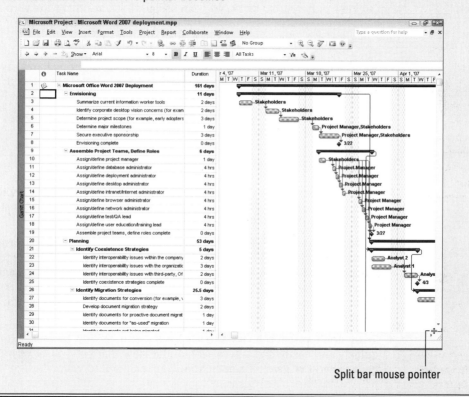

Split bar mouse pointer

While you work in a combination view, Project assumes you want to continue working in a combination view. So, if you switch views, Project displays the view you select in whichever pane was active at the time you made the switch.

To return to viewing only one view on-screen, choose Window⇨Remove Split. Project hides the view in the bottom pane and fills the screen with the view that appears in the top pane.

Customizing a View

Suppose that you work regularly in the default Gantt Chart view, but you find that you really want to see the Baseline table instead of the Entry table the majority of the time that you use Gantt Chart view. You can change the default table that Project displays for the view each time you display the view. You also can change the grouping and filtering displayed with the view. For example, if you know you always want tasks grouped as complete and incomplete, you can assign that grouping to the view. Or, if you know you want to view only critical tasks, you can assign that filtering to the view.

You can approach this process from two perspectives:

✦ You can make changes to one of the default views in Project and save those changes so that they appear each time you select that default view.

✦ You can make a copy of a default view, give it a name that describes what it shows, and then make the changes to the copy.

We prefer the second approach for the following reasons:

✦ The default views continue to display the information designed by the folks who wrote the program — and they tend to be folks who consider what most people need most of the time.

✦ You can create several versions of the same view and use the appropriate version when needed. For example, you might want to be able to quickly view both the default Gantt Chart view and a version of Gantt Chart view that uses the Baseline table. If you assign your new version to the View menu and View bar, you can quickly switch between the two versions of Gantt Chart view.

✦ If you don't assign the views to the View menu or View bar, you can quickly and easily find the version of the view that you want to use, because you've given it a name that is meaningful to you.

So, in the steps that follow, we show you a hybrid process that you can use to create a new view by making changes to a copy of an existing view:

1. **Choose View➪More Views.**

The More Views dialog box appears.

2. **Click the view you want to change.**

3. **Click Copy.**

The View Definition dialog box appears (see Figure 1-26).

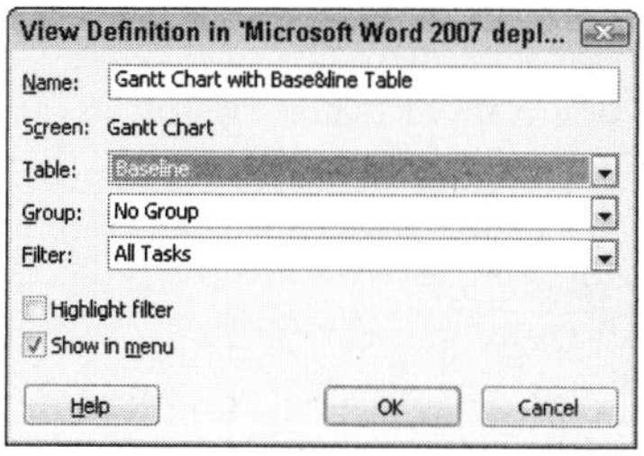

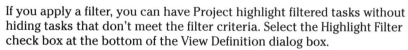

Figure 1-26:
Select a
view on
which to
base a new
view.

4. **Type a name for the new view in the Name box.**

Choose a name that describes the information that you'll show in the
view.

You can include an ampersand (&) in the name to identify the letter to
the right of the ampersand as the letter you can press on your keyboard
to select the view from the View menu. Be careful not to select any of the
letters that Project already uses on the View menu: C, G, D, K, N, A, S, U,
M, O, B, T, V, H, and Z.

5. **If the view you copied permits, select a table from the Table list box.**

6. **From the Group list box, select a group to apply to the view.**

7. **From the Filter list box, select a filter to apply to the view.**

If you apply a filter, you can have Project highlight filtered tasks without
hiding tasks that don't meet the filter criteria. Select the Highlight Filter
check box at the bottom of the View Definition dialog box.

8. **Select the Show in Menu check box to add the view to the View menu
   and the View bar.**

9. **Click OK.**

Project adds the view to the list in the More Views window.

10. **Click Apply to use the view.**

Project displays the open project using the view you just created.

Creating a New Combination View

Suppose that you find yourself setting up the same combination view over
and over, and you think to yourself, "This would be so much easier if I could
just select my personalized combination view from the View menu or the
View bar." Well, you can, if you follow these steps to create a new view:

1. **Choose View⇨More Views.**

The More Views dialog box appears.

2. Click New.

The Define New View dialog box appears (see Figure 1-27).

Figure 1-27:
When you
create a
new view,
you can
create a
single or
combination
view.

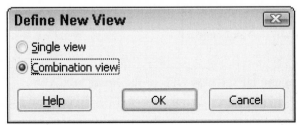

Define New View

○ Single view

◉ Combination view

[Help]   [OK]   [Cancel]

3. Select the Combination View option and click OK.

The View Definition dialog box appears (see Figure 1-28).

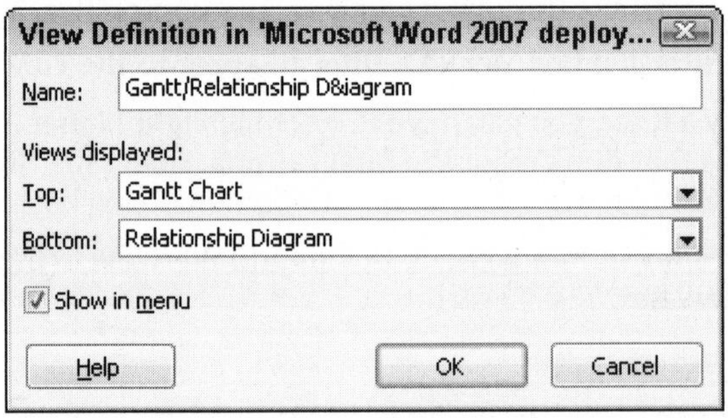

Figure 1-28:
Use this
dialog box
to select the
views you
want to
include
in the
combination
view.

View Definition in 'Microsoft Word 2007 deploy...

Name: Gantt/Relationship D&iagram

Views displayed:

Top: Gantt Chart

Bottom: Relationship Diagram

☑ Show in menu

[Help]   [OK]   [Cancel]

4. Type a name for the new view in the Name text box.

Choose a name that describes the information that you'll show in the view.

You can include an ampersand (&) in the name to identify the letter to the right of the ampersand as the letter you can press on your keyboard to select the view from the View menu. Be careful not to select any of the letters that Project already uses on the View menu: C, G, D, K, N, A, S, U, M, O, B, T, V, H, and Z.

5. From the Top list box, select the view you want Project to display in the top pane of the combination view.

6. **From the Bottom list, select the view you want Project to display in the bottom pane of the combination view.**

7. **Click the Show in Menu check box.**

8. **Click OK.**

   Project adds the view to the list in the More Views window.

9. **Click Apply to use the view.**

   Project displays the open project using the combination view you just created.

Printing Your Project

Project contains many reports that you can print that format the information in your project in a variety of ways. However, many times, you simply want to print what you're looking at on-screen. Well, here's some good news: You can print any view of your project.

If you're printing a sheet view, the number of columns that you see on-screen determines the number of columns that print. If your project view doesn't fit on one page, Project prints down first and then across; that is, the entire left side of your project prints before the right side prints.

 To print a particular view, display that view on-screen. Then click the Print button on the Standard toolbar to print using default settings.

And what are the default settings? They appear in two dialog boxes that appear if you *don't* use the Print button.

 You can also preview before printing by clicking the Print Preview button on the Standard toolbar.

Choose File⇨Print to open the Print dialog box. From the Print dialog box, shown in Figure 1-29, you can

✦ **Select a printer to use.**

✦ **Specify the number of copies you print.**

✦ **Select pages to print.**

✦ **Specify portions of the timescale to print.**

✦ **Indicate whether Project should recognize and use manual page breaks.**

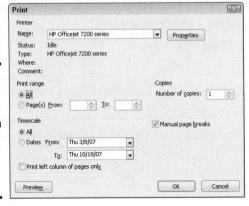

Figure 1-29:
From the Print dialog box, you can control the number of copies that you print.

When you save the project file, Project saves the settings that you make in the Print dialog box.

The Page Setup dialog box controls a wide variety of print settings for a view. You can display the dialog box by choosing File➪Page Setup. From the Page tab, shown in Figure 1-30, you can set orientation and scaling. Using scaling, you might be able to fit the printed text onto one page.

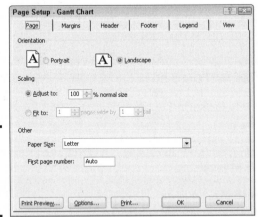

Figure 1-30:
The Page tab of the Page Setup dialog box.

Suppose that your project is ten pages long, but you intend to print only pages 5 and 6. Typically, you want to number those pages as 1 and 2. To do that, enter 1 in the First Page Number box.

From the Margins tab, shown in Figure 1-31, you can change the margins for your printed text and specify whether a border should appear.

Views and pagination

Project automatically inserts page breaks in a view based on the amount of information in the view and the paper size you select. However, sometimes you might want to insert a manual page break. For example, you might want to insert a manual page break to start each summary task and its subtasks on a new page.

You can insert manual page breaks by following these steps:

1. **Select the task (or resource) that should appear at the top of a new page.**

2. **Choose Insert➪Page Break.**

   Project inserts a manual page break, which appears as a dotted line in the view.

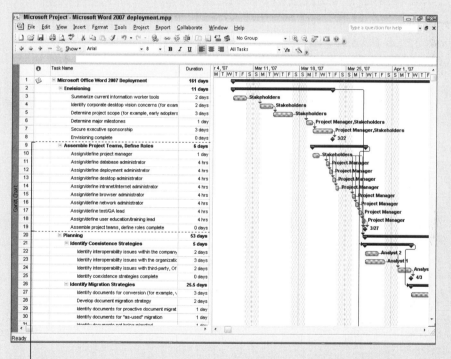

Page breaks

To make sure that Project uses these manual page breaks, select the Manual Page Breaks check box in the Print dialog box.

You can remove manual page breaks by selecting the task below the page break and choosing Insert➪Remove Page Break.

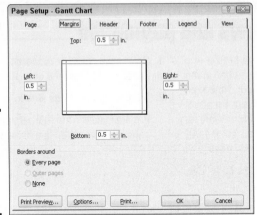

Figure 1-31:
The
Margins tab
of the Page
Setup
dialog box.

Using the Header tab, shown in Figure 1-32, you can define and align information to appear on the top of every page. Use the General list box at the bottom of the Header tab to add information that Project updates automatically, such as page numbers. Using the Project Fields list box, you can include Project fields in the header.

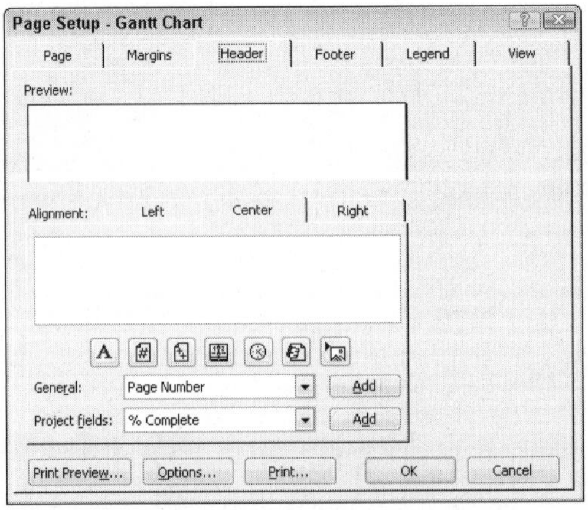

Figure 1-32:
The Header
tab of the
Page Setup
dialog box.

The Footer tab looks and works just like the Header tab. You can align and include the Project fields and updating information such as page numbers in the footer on each page of your printed text.

The Page Setup dialog box changes just slightly, depending on the view that you displayed before opening the dialog box. For example, the Legend tab, shown in Figure 1-33, is available only when you're printing a Calendar, Gantt Chart, or Network Diagram view. The Legend tab works just like the Header and Footer tabs; you can align and include Project fields and information that updates such as page numbers, and you can specify how and where the legend prints.

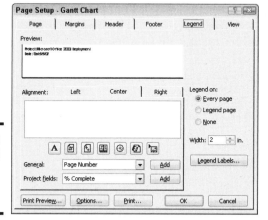

Figure 1-33:
The Legend
tab of the
Page Setup
dialog box.

The View tab, shown in Figure 1-34, enables you to control what Project prints; for example, you can choose to print all or only some columns.

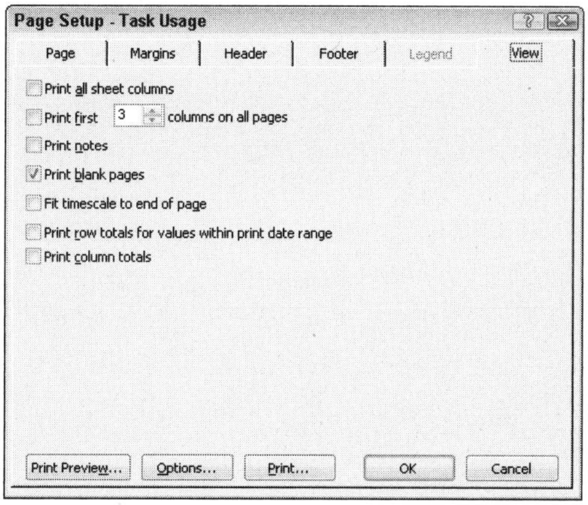

Figure 1-34:
The View
tab of the
Page Setup
dialog box.

The Print Row Totals For Values Within Print Date Range and Print Column Totals check boxes appear on the View tab in Task Usage view and Resource Usage view; the boxes are unavailable in all other views. When you select the Print Column Totals check box, Project calculates totals in memory and adds a row to the printed page showing totals for timephased data as well as for sheet data. Selecting the Print Row Totals For Values Within Print Date Range check box tells Project to add a column to the printed page that shows totals for the timephased data within the date range that you specify in the Print dialog box. These "total" lines print on the same page as the last rows or columns of data, before any Notes pages.

In many cases, you can add a column to a table that gives you the same information that you can get in the row totals. The column prints where you place it, whereas the row totals print on a separate page.

Chapter 2: Working with Tables

In This Chapter

↙ **Understanding tables and indicators**

↙ **Modifying tables**

↙ **Customizing tables**

↙ **Working with the Details portion of usage views**

*T*ables are part of most views in Project, providing project information in a columnar format. But you aren't limited to the table that appears when you display a view; you can switch to a different table to see different information. You also can control the fields that Project displays in a table and even create your own tables.

Understanding Tables

If you use a spreadsheet program like Excel, tables should remind you of a spreadsheet. Project presents information in a row/column format, and you make changes to project information by using the fields on the table. Each table in Project helps you focus on and change different kinds of information. The default table that appears in Gantt Chart view, for example, is the Entry table (see Figure 2-1). Using the Entry table, you can set up basic information (such as the task name and estimated duration) as you add tasks to your project.

Take a look at some of the commonly used task tables. The Cost table, shown in Figure 2-2, helps you focus on the estimated, baseline, actual, and remaining costs associated with your project.

Use the Schedule table (see Figure 2-3) when you're trying to resolve allocation issues. The Schedule table helps you identify tasks with slack that can afford to slip; you might be able to change those tasks to help alleviate over-allocation issues.

Use the Tracking table (see Figure 2-4) to record information that describes when tasks start and finish. As you record information in some of the fields in this table, Project calculates the other fields for you. Project also uses the "actual" information that you record to calculate the actual cost of a task.

Microsoft Project - Microsoft Word 2007 deployment.mpp

	❶	Task Name	Duration	Start	Finish	Predecessors	Resource Names
1	✎	**Microsoft Office Word 2007 Deployment**	**161 days**	**Thu 3/8/07**	**Thu 10/18/07**		
2		**Envisioning**	**11 days**	**Thu 3/8/07**	**Thu 3/22/07**		
3		Summarize current information worker tools	2 days	Thu 3/8/07	Fri 3/9/07		Stakeholders
4		Identify corporate desktop vision concerns (for exam	2 days	Mon 3/12/07	Tue 3/13/07	3	Stakeholders
5		Determine project scope (for example, early adopters	3 days	Wed 3/14/07	Fri 3/16/07	4	Stakeholders
6		Determine major milestones	1 day	Mon 3/19/07	Mon 3/19/07	5	Project Manager,Stal
7		Secure executive sponsorship	3 days	Tue 3/20/07	Thu 3/22/07	6	Project Manager,Stal
8		Envisioning complete	0 days	Thu 3/22/07	Thu 3/22/07	7	
9		**Assemble Project Teams, Define Roles**	**6 days**	**Tue 3/20/07**	**Tue 3/27/07**		
10		Assign/define project manager	1 day	Tue 3/20/07	Tue 3/20/07		Stakeholders
11		Assign/define database administrator	4 hrs	Thu 3/22/07	Thu 3/22/07	10	Project Manager
12		Assign/define deployment administrator	4 hrs	Thu 3/22/07	Thu 3/22/07	10	Project Manager
13		Assign/define desktop administrator	4 hrs	Fri 3/23/07	Fri 3/23/07	10	Project Manager
14		Assign/define intranet/Internet administrator	4 hrs	Fri 3/23/07	Fri 3/23/07	10	Project Manager
15		Assign/define browser administrator	4 hrs	Mon 3/26/07	Mon 3/26/07	10	Project Manager
16		Assign/define network administrator	4 hrs	Mon 3/26/07	Mon 3/26/07	10	Project Manager
17		Assign/define test/QA lead	4 hrs	Tue 3/27/07	Tue 3/27/07	10	Project Manager
18		Assign/define user education/training lead	4 hrs	Tue 3/27/07	Tue 3/27/07	10	Project Manager
19		Assemble project teams, define roles complete	0 days	Tue 3/27/07	Tue 3/27/07	18,17,11,12,13,16,15,14	
20		**Planning**	**53 days**	**Wed 3/28/07**	**Fri 6/8/07**		2
21		**Identify Coexistence Strategies**	**5 days**	**Wed 3/28/07**	**Tue 4/3/07**		9
22		Identify interoperability issues within the company	2 days	Wed 3/28/07	Thu 3/29/07		Analyst 2
23		Identify interoperability issues with the organizatic	3 days	Wed 3/28/07	Fri 3/30/07		Analyst 1
24		Identify interoperability issues with third-party, Of	2 days	Mon 4/2/07	Tue 4/3/07	23,22	Analyst 3
25		Identify coexistence strategies complete	0 days	Tue 4/3/07	Tue 4/3/07	24	
26		**Identify Migration Strategies**	**25.5 days**	**Wed 4/4/07**	**Wed 5/9/07**		21
27		Identify documents for conversion (for example,	3 days	Wed 4/4/07	Fri 4/6/07		Analyst 1
28		Develop document migration strategy	2 days	Mon 4/9/07	Tue 4/10/07	27	Desktop Administrato
29		Identify documents for proactive document migrat	1 day	Fri 5/4/07	Mon 5/7/07	28	Desktop Administrato
30		Identify documents for "as-used" migration	1 day	Mon 5/7/07	Tue 5/8/07	28	Desktop Administrato
31		Identify documents not being migrated	1 day	Tue 5/8/07	Wed 5/9/07	28	Desktop Administrato

Figure 2-1:
The Entry table helps you focus on setting up tasks or resources.

Microsoft Project - Microsoft Word 2007 deployment.mpp

	Task Name	Fixed Cost	Fixed Cost Accrual	Total Cost	Baseline	Variance	Actual	Remaining
1	**Microsoft Office Word 2**	**$0.00**	**Prorated**	**$72,840.00**	**$72,840.00**	**$0.00**	**$0.00**	**$72,840.00**
2	**Envisioning**	**$0.00**	**Prorated**	**$5,200.00**	**$5,200.00**	**$0.00**	**$0.00**	**$5,200.00**
3	Summarize current	$0.00	Prorated	$800.00	$800.00	$0.00	$0.00	$800.00
4	Identify corporate d	$0.00	Prorated	$800.00	$800.00	$0.00	$0.00	$800.00
5	Determine project s	$0.00	Prorated	$1,200.00	$1,200.00	$0.00	$0.00	$1,200.00
6	Determine major mik	$0.00	Prorated	$800.00	$800.00	$0.00	$0.00	$800.00
7	Secure executive s	$0.00	Prorated	$1,600.00	$1,600.00	$0.00	$0.00	$1,600.00
8	Envisioning complet	$0.00	Prorated	$0.00	$0.00	$0.00	$0.00	$0.00
9	**Assemble Project T**	**$0.00**	**Prorated**	**$2,000.00**	**$2,000.00**	**$0.00**	**$0.00**	**$2,000.00**
10	Assign/define proje	$0.00	Prorated	$400.00	$400.00	$0.00	$0.00	$400.00
11	Assign/define datal	$0.00	Prorated	$200.00	$200.00	$0.00	$0.00	$200.00
12	Assign/define deplc	$0.00	Prorated	$200.00	$200.00	$0.00	$0.00	$200.00
13	Assign/define desk	$0.00	Prorated	$200.00	$200.00	$0.00	$0.00	$200.00
14	Assign/define intrar	$0.00	Prorated	$200.00	$200.00	$0.00	$0.00	$200.00
15	Assign/define brow	$0.00	Prorated	$200.00	$200.00	$0.00	$0.00	$200.00
16	Assign/define netw	$0.00	Prorated	$200.00	$200.00	$0.00	$0.00	$200.00
17	Assign/define test/	$0.00	Prorated	$200.00	$200.00	$0.00	$0.00	$200.00
18	Assign/define user	$0.00	Prorated	$200.00	$200.00	$0.00	$0.00	$200.00
19	Assemble project te	$0.00	Prorated	$0.00	$0.00	$0.00	$0.00	$0.00
20	**Planning**	**$0.00**	**Prorated**	**$32,360.00**	**$32,360.00**	**$0.00**	**$0.00**	**$32,360.00**
21	**Identify Coexiste**	**$0.00**	**Prorated**	**$2,240.00**	**$2,240.00**	**$0.00**	**$0.00**	**$2,240.00**
22	Identify interope	$0.00	Prorated	$640.00	$640.00	$0.00	$0.00	$640.00
23	Identify interope	$0.00	Prorated	$960.00	$960.00	$0.00	$0.00	$960.00
24	Identify interope	$0.00	Prorated	$640.00	$640.00	$0.00	$0.00	$640.00
25	Identify coexiste	$0.00	Prorated	$0.00	$0.00	$0.00	$0.00	$0.00
26	**Identify Migratior**	**$0.00**	**Prorated**	**$3,320.00**	**$3,320.00**	**$0.00**	**$0.00**	**$3,320.00**
27	Identify docume	$0.00	Prorated	$960.00	$960.00	$0.00	$0.00	$960.00
28	Develop docume	$0.00	Prorated	$600.00	$600.00	$0.00	$0.00	$600.00
29	Identify docume	$0.00	Prorated	$280.00	$280.00	$0.00	$0.00	$280.00
30	Identify docume	$0.00	Prorated	$280.00	$280.00	$0.00	$0.00	$280.00
31	Identify docume	$0.00	Prorated	$280.00	$280.00	$0.00	$0.00	$280.00

Figure 2-2:
The Cost table helps you determine how much your project will cost and whether it's on track to stay within the estimated costs.

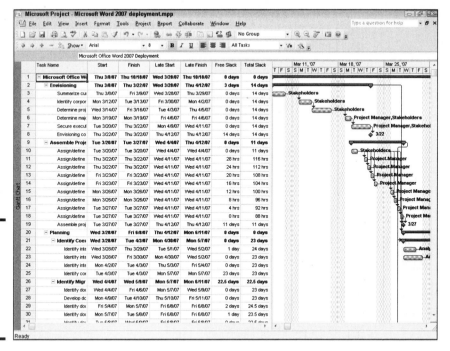

Figure 2-3:
The Schedule table helps pinpoint tasks that have slack.

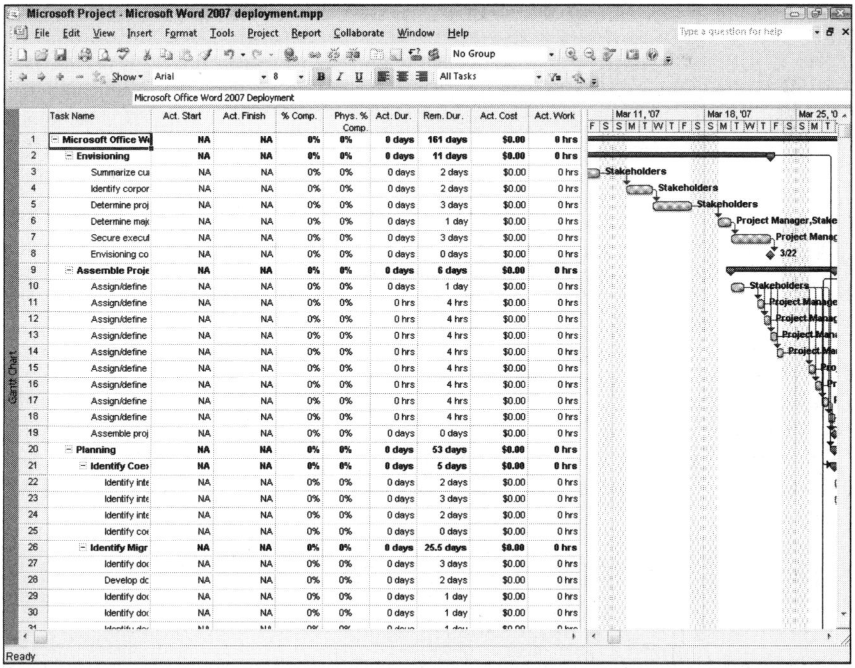

Figure 2-4:
Use the Tracking table when work on your project gets underway.

The Variance table (see Figure 2-5) helps you compare baseline start and finish dates with actual start and finish dates; using this table can help you determine when a project fell behind schedule (or got ahead of schedule!).

The Summary table (see Figure 2-6) gives you a great overview of project information, including estimated duration, start and finish dates, percent complete, cost, and work for each task.

You can easily switch to the most commonly used tables for any particular view if you right-click the Select All button, which is the gray square that appears just above Row 1 in any view with a table (see Figure 2-7). The list of "most commonly used tables" that appears for task views is different than the list that appears for resource views. To switch to a different table, simply click the table you want.

Clicking (instead of right-clicking) the Select All button selects all information in the table portion of the view.

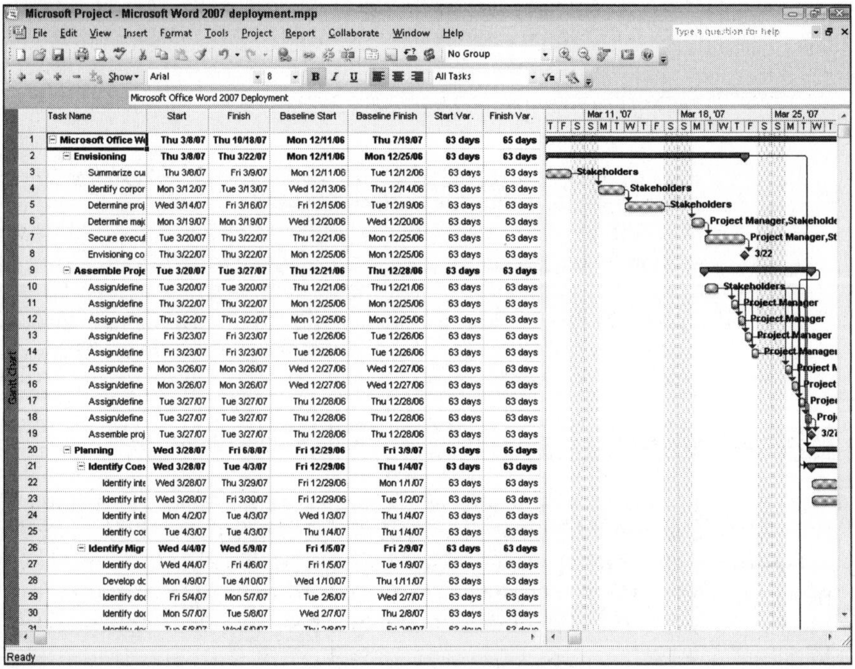

Figure 2-5:
The Variance table helps you compare baseline with actual information.

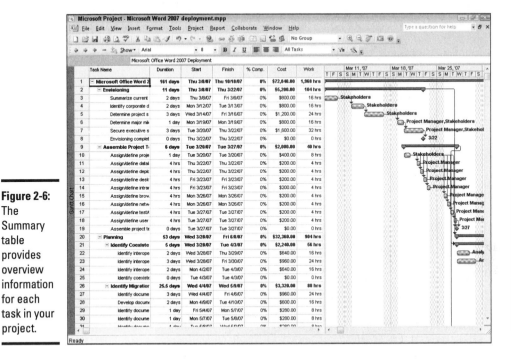

Figure 2-6:
The
Summary
table
provides
overview
information
for each
task in your
project.

As you would expect, Project contains more tables than those shown when
you right-click the Select All button. In fact, Project contains 17 tables that
you can use when viewing task information and 10 tables that you can use
when viewing resource information. If the table you want to use isn't on the
menu that appears when you right-click the Select All button, choose More
Tables. Project opens the More Tables dialog box (see Figure 2-8). Click the
Resource option button to see the tables available in resource views.

Understanding Indicators

In the Entry table shown earlier in Figure 2-1, notice the Indicators column,
the second column in the table, appearing to the right of the ID column.
Indicators represent additional information about the row in which they
appear. For example, a Notes indicator like the one shown in Figure 2-9
appears in the Indicators column if you assign a note to a task or resource.

Select All button

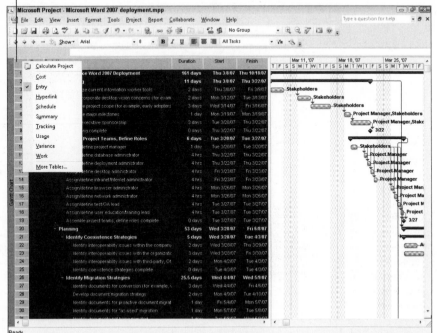

Figure 2-7:
Use the
Select All
button to
quickly and
easily
switch to
the most
commonly
used tables.

Figure 2-8:
The More
Tables
dialog box
shows all of
the tables in
Project.

To determine the purpose of an indicator, point the mouse pointer at it. Project tells you what the indicator means or displays additional information to remind you of important details. See the Project Help topic, "About Indicators," for a complete list of each indicator icon and its meaning. The following is a list of some of the more common indicators you'll run across:

✦ **Constraint indicators identify the type of constraint that's assigned to a task.** You see a constraint indicator if you assign any constraint to a task other than As Soon As Possible. You also see a constraint indicator if the task hasn't been completed within the timeframe of the constraint.

Indicators column

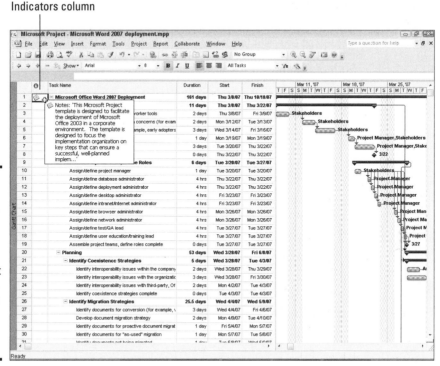

Figure 2-9:
When you
see an
indicator
in the
Indicators
column, rest
the mouse
pointer on it
to see the
indicator's
purpose.

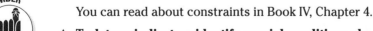

You can read about constraints in Book IV, Chapter 4.

✦ **Task type indicators identify special conditions about a task, such as whether the task is recurring or whether it has been completed.** Task type indicators also identify the inserted projects.

You can find out more about recurring tasks in Book III, Chapter 1 and inserted projects in Book III, Chapter 4.

✦ **Workgroup indicators provide some information about the task and its resources.** For example, a workgroup indicator can tell you that a task has been assigned but that the resource hasn't yet confirmed the assignment.

✦ **Contour indicators identify the type of contouring that is used to distribute the work assigned to the task.**

✦ **Miscellaneous indicators identify items, such as a note or a hyperlink, that you created; calendars that have been assigned to a task; or resources that need leveling.**

Making Changes to a Table

In addition to using the various tables, you can change tables by adding or deleting fields, moving columns to different positions, and changing the width of columns or the height of rows.

Inserting and hiding table fields

Each column in a table represents a field of project information. You can temporarily remove a column from a table by hiding it.

To hide a column, place the mouse pointer on the right boundary of the column heading. When the mouse pointer changes to a vertical bar with left- and right-pointing arrows, drag the right column boundary to meet the left column boundary. When you release the mouse button, the column disappears. In Figure 2-10, we're going to hide the Predecessors column.

When you hide a column, Project doesn't remove the data in the column from the file; instead, Project simply hides the data from view.

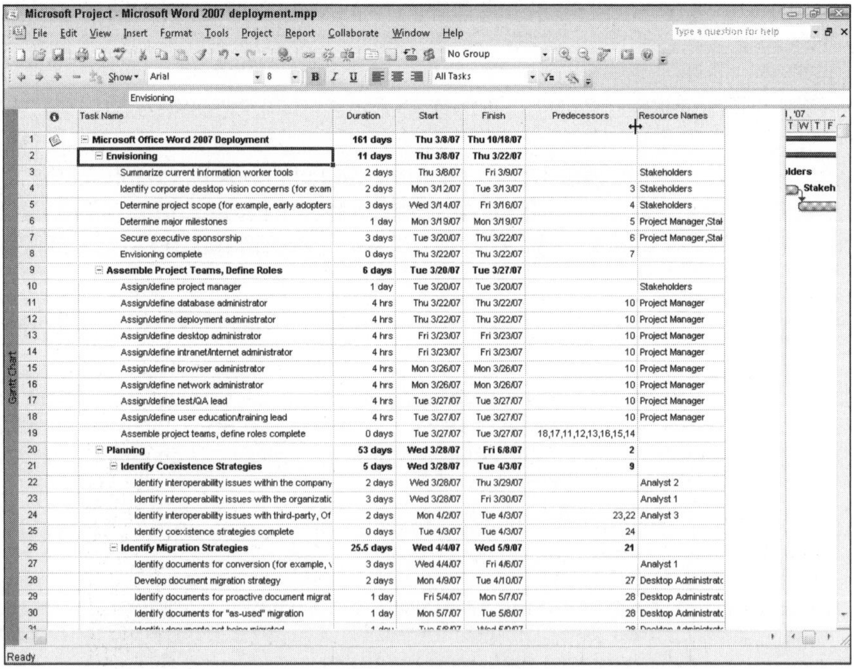

Figure 2-10: You can hide a column by dragging its right boundary to meet its left boundary.

To see the column again or to add a different column to your table, follow these steps:

1. **Right-click the column heading that you want to appear to the right of the column that you're going to insert.**

In Figure 2-11, we're going to add the Predecessor column back into the Entry table so that it appears to the left of the Resource Names column.

2. **Choose Insert Column from the shortcut menu that appears.**

The Column Definition dialog box appears (see Figure 2-12).

3. **In the Field Name list box, select the name of the column that you want to add.**

If you leave the Title box blank, Project assigns the field name to the column. You can supply a title for the column if you prefer something other than the field name.

4. **Click the Best Fit button.**

Project inserts the column to the left of the selected column, and because you clicked the Best Fit button, Project makes the column wide enough to accommodate the column title. (If you don't feel the need for a neat and tidy column, click OK instead of Best Fit.)

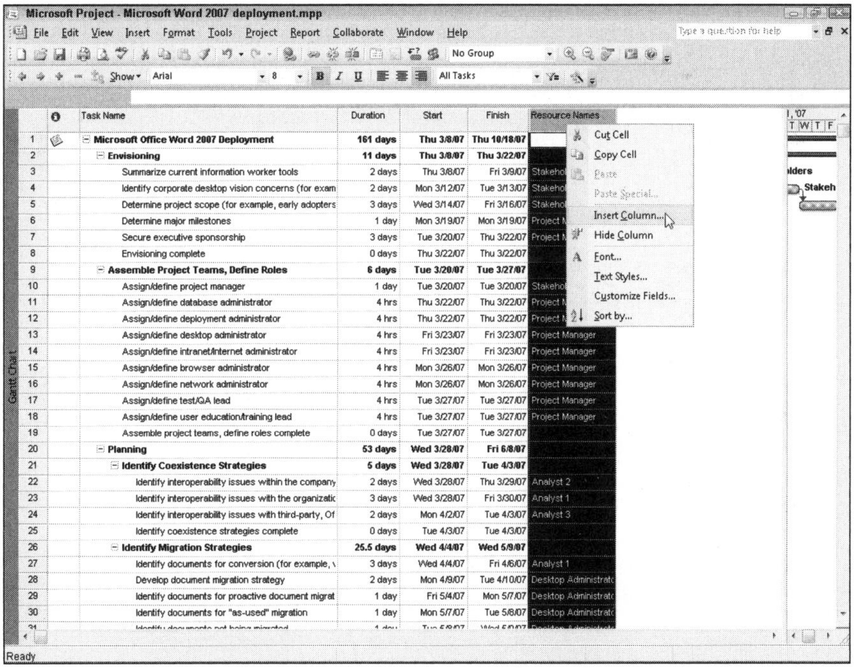

Book VI
Chapter 2

Working with Tables

Figure 2-11: Project inserts new columns to the left of the selected column.

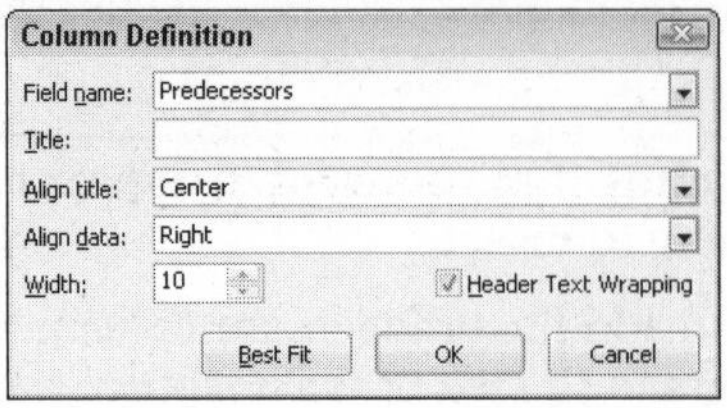

Figure 2-12:
Use this
dialog box
to add a
column to
your table.

Column Definition

Field name:	Predecessors
Title:	
Align title:	Center
Align data:	Right
Width:	10

☑ Header Text Wrapping

Best Fit   OK   Cancel

Changing column width

In some cases, you might not be able to see all the information in a column. In particular, if pound signs (#) fill a column, as they do in the Start column in Figure 2-13, the column isn't wide enough to display the information that appears in it.

You can widen the column by dragging the right edge of the column heading boundary to the right. When you move the mouse pointer over the column heading boundary, it changes to a vertical bar with left- and right-pointing arrows, as shown earlier in Figure 2-10.

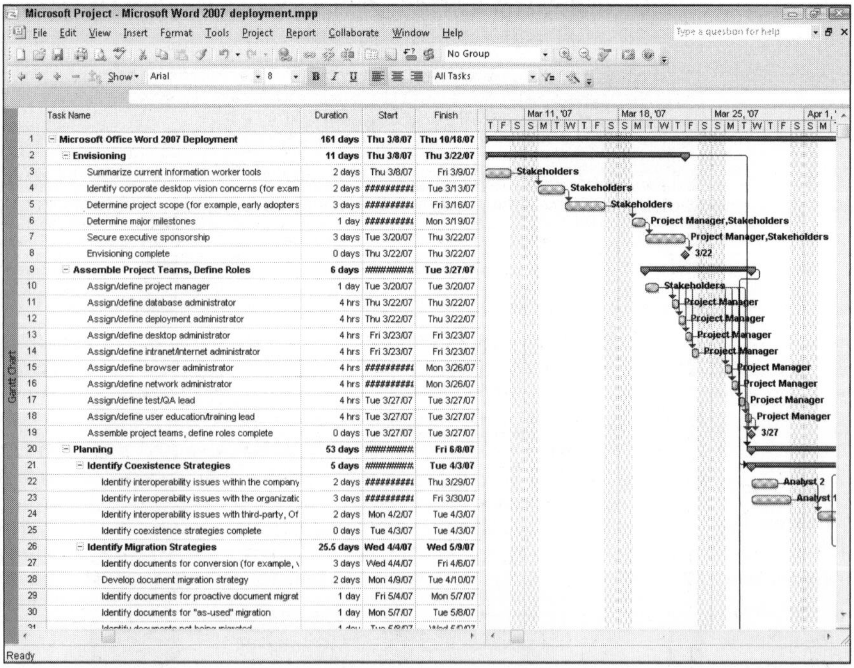

Figure 2-13:
When you
see pound
signs (#) in
a field,
the column
isn't wide
enough to
display the
information
in the field.

To quickly and easily make a column wide enough to accommodate the longest entry in the column, place the mouse pointer over the right boundary of the column heading and double-click. Project automatically adjusts the size of the column to display the longest entry in the column.

You might be tempted to try this technique on the Task Name column, but we recommend, instead, that you read the next section. If you widen the Task Name column to accommodate the longest entry in it, you might have trouble viewing any other information.

Changing row height

Unless you're using a wide monitor, it isn't really practical to widen the Task Name column to accommodate the longest entry in the column, because you'll have to scroll back and forth to see information. However, to see Task Name information, you can increase the height of rows. When you change the height of a row, Project wraps the data in the row to fit within the taller row. In many cases, increasing row height makes all the information in the Task Name column visible.

You can't read the complete names of many of the tasks in Figure 2-13. But, if you increase the row height, task names wrap so that they're visible. In Figure 2-14, we increased the height of all rows in the file.

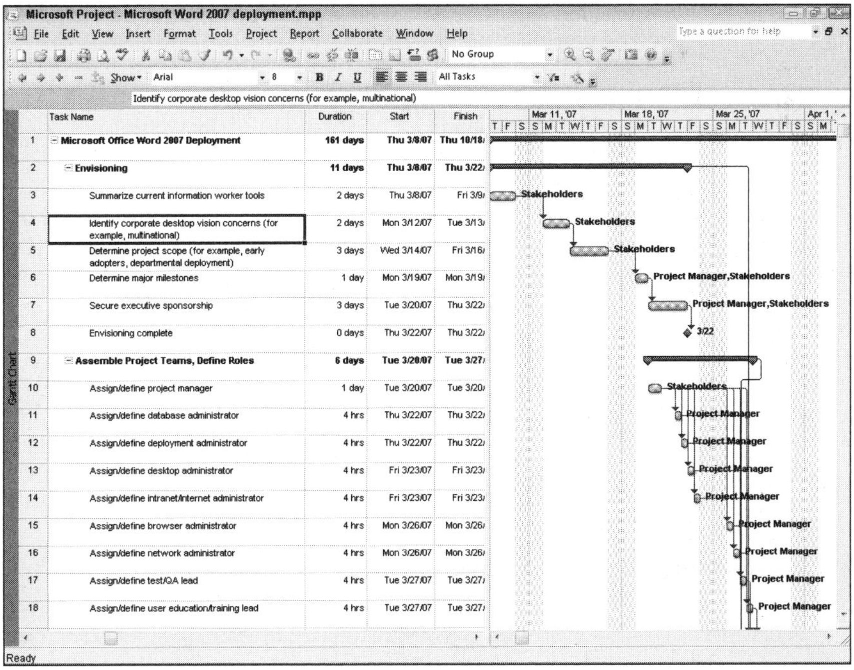

**Book VI
Chapter 2**

**Working with
Tables**

Figure 2-14:
When you increase row height, Project wraps information in columns.

To change row height, follow these steps:

1. **Move the mouse pointer into the Task ID number column at the bottom of the row you want to change.**

   The mouse pointer changes to a pair of arrows pointing up and down (see Figure 2-15).

   To change the height of more than one row, select each row that you want to change. Use Windows selection techniques to select the rows. For example, to select two noncontiguous rows, click the ID of the first row and then press and hold Ctrl while you click the ID of the second row. To change the height of all rows, click the Select All button.

2. **Drag down.**

3. **Release the mouse button.**

   Project increases the height of the selected row and wraps text in that row to fill the new row space.

You can change row heights only in full row increments. That is, you can make a row twice its original size but not one and a half times its original size.

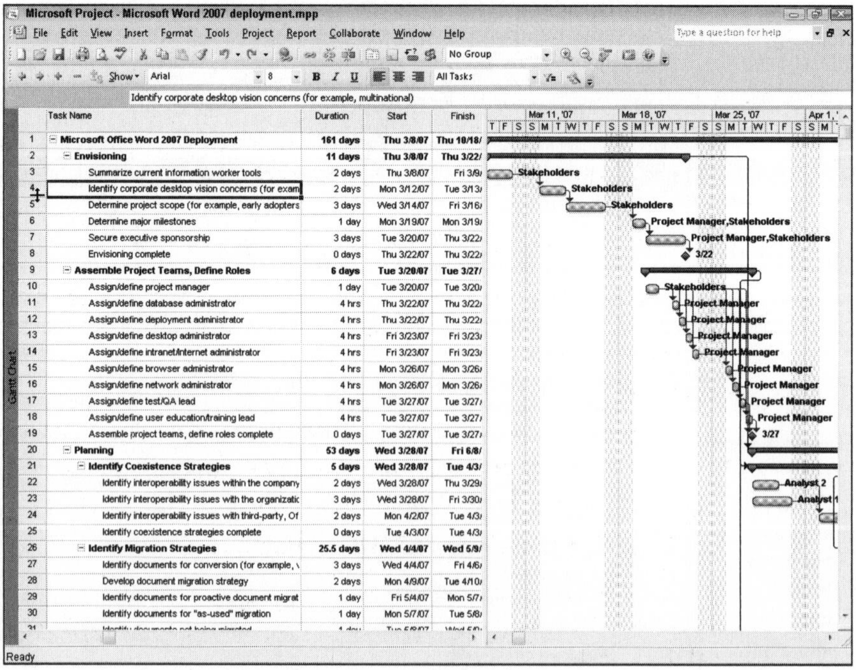

Figure 2-15:
In this figure, we're about to change the height of Row 4.

Customizing Tables

Suppose that you want a table that compares baseline and actual information, but you want the columns in the table to appear in the order of Baseline Start, Actual Start, Baseline Finish, and Actual Finish. The tables you've reviewed tend to list the information in the order of Baseline Start, Baseline Finish, Actual Start, and Actual Finish. You can create your own table that will display the information in the order you want it to appear. And, you can make your table — or any table — appear on the shortcut menu that appears when you right-click the Select All button.

As with views, you can approach this process from two perspectives:

Book VI
Chapter 2

Working with Tables

✦ You can make changes to one of the default tables in Project and save those changes so that they appear each time you select that default table.

✦ You can make a copy of a default table, give it a name that describes what it shows, and then make the changes to the copy.

We prefer the second approach for the following reasons:

✦ The default tables continue to display the information designed by the folks who wrote the program — and they tend to be folks who consider what most people need most of the time.

✦ You can create several versions of the same table and use the appropriate version when needed.

✦ If you don't assign your table to the shortcut menu that appears when you right-click the Select All button, you can quickly and easily find the version of the table that you want to use, because you've given it a name that is meaningful to you.

So, in the steps that follow, we show you a hybrid process that you can use to create a new table by making changes to a copy of an existing table:

1. **Choose View➪Table➪More Tables.**

Project displays the More Tables dialog box, shown in Figure 2-16.

2. **Click the Task or Resource option buttons at the top of the window to display the type of table that you need.**

3. **Select a table from the list of tables.**

4. **Click the Copy button.**

The Table Definition dialog box appears (see Figure 2-17).

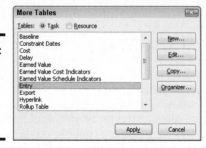

Figure 2-16: Select a table to copy from this dialog box.

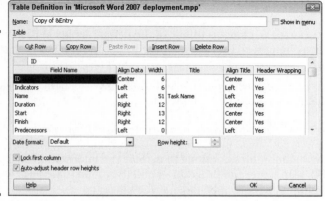

Figure 2-17: Use the Table Definition dialog box to make changes to the appearance of a table.

If you clicked New in Step 4, no information appears in the bottom portion of the dialog box.

5. **Supply a meaningful name for the table in the Name text box.**

6. **Select the Show in Menu check box.**

   If you select this check box, Project lists this table in the shortcut menu that appears when you right-click the Select All button.

7. **To replace an existing field, click that field in the Field Name column.**

   You see an arrow on the right side of the field.

8. **Click the arrow to display the drop-down list and select a field name.**

   To add a field to the table, click a blank space in the area under the Field Name column. To add a field between existing fields, click the field below the field that you want to add and click Insert Row. To delete a field, click that field in the Field Name column and click Delete Row.

9. **For the field you're replacing or adding, click in the Align Data column to display an arrow on the right side of the field.**

10. **Select Left, Center, or Right alignment for the data in the column.**

11. **Click OK.**

Project redisplays the More Tables dialog box.

12. **Click Apply and then close the More Tables dialog box.**

A few other options in the Table Definition dialog box bear mentioning:

✦ Enter a title for the column if you don't want to use the default field name.

✦ If you have any columns that include dates, such as Start or Finish information, you can modify the date format by using the drop-down list of choices in the Date Format list box.

✦ You can modify the height of all the rows in the table by using the Row Height spinner box.

✦ The Header Wrapping field, a Yes or No choice, controls whether long titles wrap within the column heading. If you set the Header Wrapping field to No, Project hides the portion of a column title that doesn't fit within the allotted space for the column.

✦ You can select the Lock First Column check box if you want the first column of your table to remain on-screen while you scroll across your page.

Book VI
Chapter 2

Working with Tables

If you want a table that you create or change to be available in all Project files, click the Organizer button in the More Tables window to copy the table to the Global.mpt file. See Book IX, Chapter 1 for more information about using the Organizer.

Working with the Details of Usage Views

Project contains two usage views: Task Usage view and Resource Usage view. Both views display assignment information that's distributed over time, and Project refers to this information as *timephased* information. The left side of both views contains a table like the ones presented earlier in this chapter. The right side of both views contains the timephased information; Project refers to the right side of the view as the Details section. In Figure 2-18, you see Task Usage view, and in Figure 2-19, you see Resource Usage view.

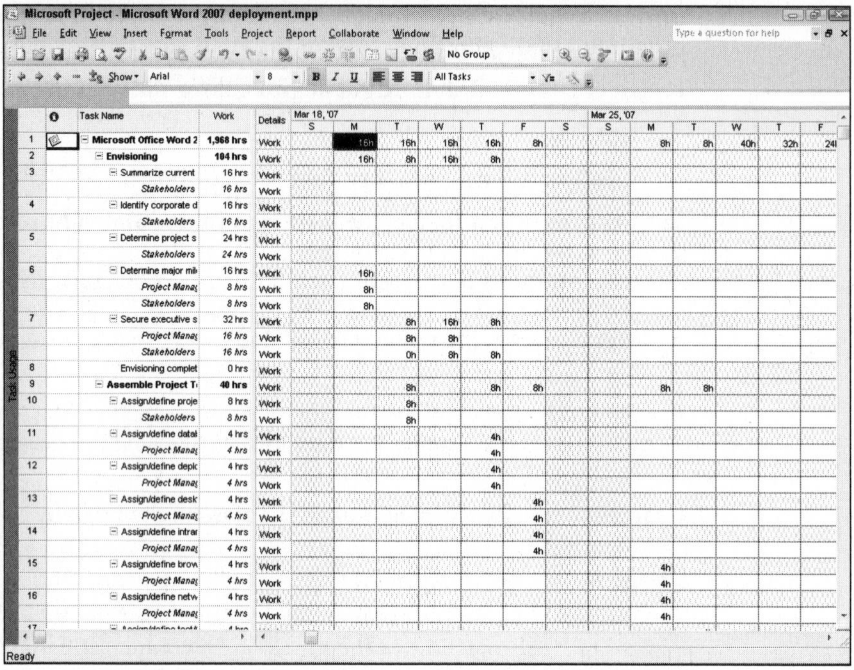

Figure 2-18:
Task Usage
view
organizes
assign-
ments by
task.

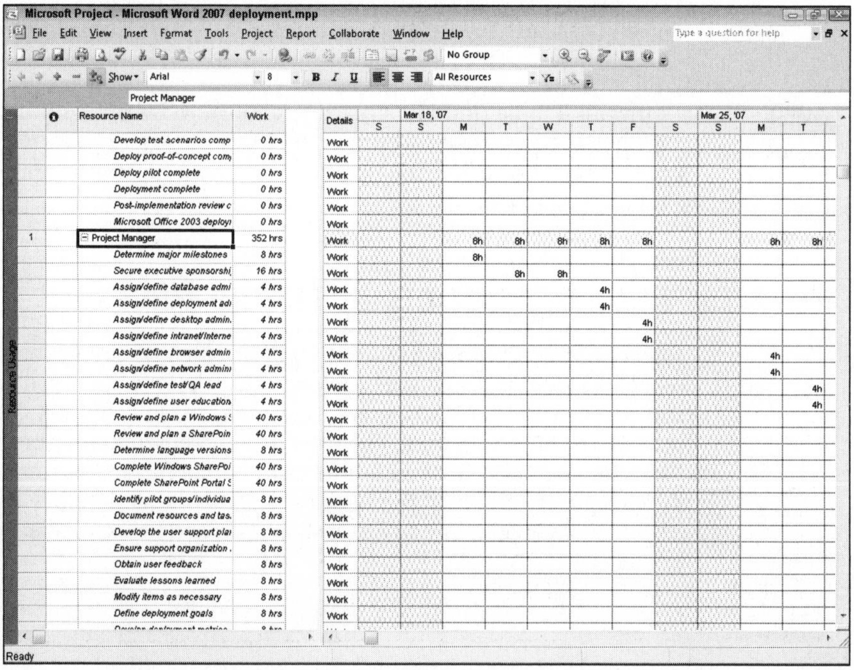

Figure 2-19:
Resource
Usage view
organizes
tasks by
resource
assignment.

The tables on the left side of these views function just like the tables in any other view; the Details portion of the view, however, is a slightly different kind of table. You can display additional information in the Details section by adding rows (instead of adding columns, like you do in other tables).

By default, the Work field appears in the Details section of both usage views. As with other tables, you can add some commonly used fields to the Details section if you right-click anywhere in the Details section and then choose the appropriate field from the shortcut menu that appears (see Figure 2-20).

TIP

Instead of right-clicking the Details section, you can Choose Format⇨Details to display the commonly used fields.

Each field you add to the Details section of a usage view increases the size of all of the rows in the table on the left side of the view.

Adding new fields to the Details section

In addition to the commonly used fields, you can add many other fields to the Details section of a usage view. If you find yourself adding a particular field on a regular basis, you can add that field to the shortcut menu that displays the list of commonly used fields.

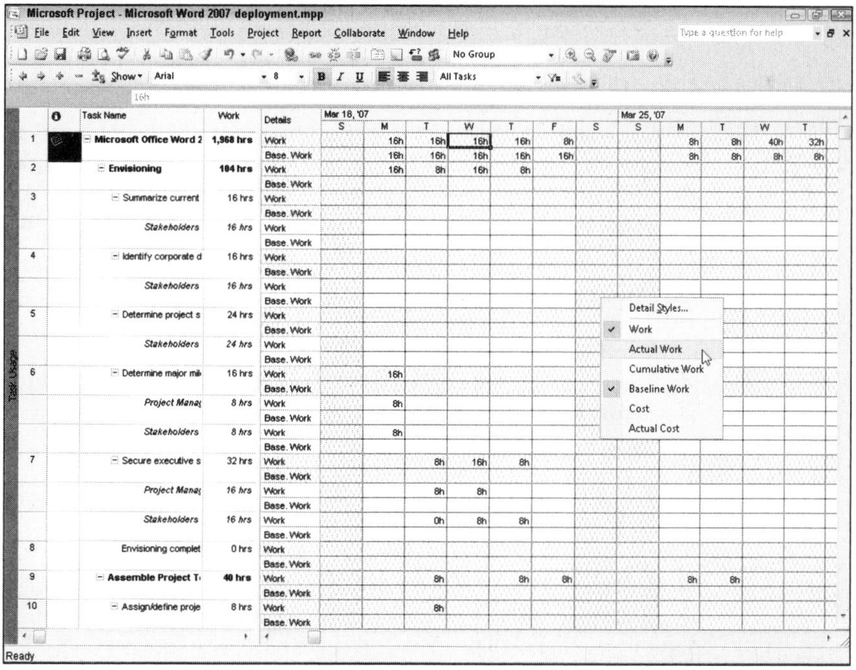

**Book VI
Chapter 2**

Working with Tables

Figure 2-20:
When you right-click the Details section, commonly used fields appear.

You enter values for a budget Work resource or a budget Cost resource by using a usage view. You can add these fields to the shortcut menu to have easy access to them.

To add a field to the Details section that doesn't appear on the shortcut menu, follow these steps:

1. **From either usage view, choose Format➪Detail Styles.**

Project displays the Detail Styles dialog box (see Figure 2-21).

Figure 2-21:
Use the
Detail Styles
dialog box
to display
other fields
in the
Details
section of a
usage view.

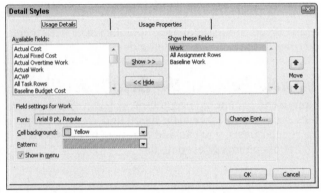

2. **In the Available Fields list, click a field.**

You can use Windows selection techniques to select more than one field simultaneously. To select noncontiguous fields, click the first field and then press and hold Ctrl while you click another field. To select contiguous fields, click the first field and then press and hold Shift while you click the last field.

3. **Click the Show button.**

The field then appears in the Show These Fields list.

4. **Select the Show in Menu check box to make these fields appear on the shortcut menu.**

5. **Click OK.**

Project displays a row for the field in the Details portion of the view.

Hiding fields in the Details section

You hide fields in the Details section of a usage view the same way you display them: Right-click anywhere in the Details section and click the field you want to hide. Project removes the field from the Details portion of the view. Remember, the information remains in your Project file; it's just hidden from view.

The Work, Actual Work, Cumulative Work, Overallocation, Cost, and Remaining Availability fields remain available from the shortcut menu even after you hide them.

Other fields you add to the Details section of a usage view by using the Detail Styles dialog box might behave differently, and their behavior is determined by whether you select the Show in Menu check box mentioned in Step 4 in the preceding section. If you select the Show in Menu check box, Project adds the field to both the Details section and to the shortcut menu. If you then hide the field, you can redisplay it by using the shortcut menu.

But, if you don't select the Show in Menu check box when you add the field to the Details section, Project adds the field to the Details section but *not* to the shortcut menu. If you then hide the field in the Details section, you can't use the shortcut menu to redisplay it; you need to follow the steps in the preceding section again to redisplay the field.

Chapter 3: Preparing Traditional Reports

In This Chapter

✔ Preparing and printing reports

✔ Reviewing summary reports

✔ Looking at task status reports

✔ Reviewing cost reports

✔ Understanding assignment reports

✔ Working with workload reports

✔ Looking at custom reports

✔ Modifying reports

*W*hat do we mean by "traditional" reports? Will you hear Tevye from *Fiddler on the Roof* singing "Tradition" when you print them? Although it's a novel idea, we haven't managed to convince Microsoft that the musical accompaniment would be the way to go. We'll keep working on that.

Meanwhile, we call them "traditional" reports only because they resemble the types of reports you're used to viewing. The reports you see in this chapter are text-based reports, typically presenting information in rows and columns. In the next chapter of this minibook, you see the visual reports available in Project; visual reports present information by using pictures. Both types of reports have a place in the reporting process; the text-based reports you see in this chapter present details that aren't obvious in visual reports.

Preparing and Printing Reports

Project organizes text reports into categories of reports that are related to the same subject; for example, all the cost reports cleverly fall into the Costs category.

You can print all the reports in Project by using the same basic technique. Follow these steps:

1. **Open the Project file on which you want to report.**

2. **Choose Report⇨Reports.**

Project opens the Reports dialog box (see Figure 3-1).

Figure 3-1: Initially, you select a category of reports.

3. **Click the category of the report that you want to produce.**

4. **Click Select.**

Project displays the reports that are available in that category.

5. **Select a report.**

6. **Click Select.**

Project displays the report on-screen in Print Preview mode (see Figure 3-2).

Use the scroll arrows to move around the report. The Zoom button enlarges the image so that you can read the report's content on-screen. To zoom out again, click the Full Page button or click again on the report.

You can click the portion of the report that you want to enlarge. To zoom out again, click the report again.

To display more than one page at a time, click the Multiple Pages button.

7. **Click the Page Setup button.**

Project displays the Page Setup dialog box (see Figure 3-3) so that you can review the page settings before printing. You can set orientation, scaling, margins, and header and footer information for the report from the Page Setup dialog box.

Zoom button Full Page button

Scroll arrows Multiple Pages button

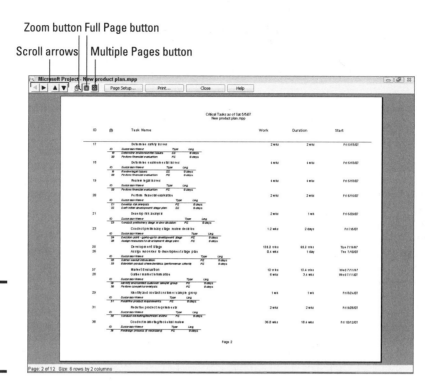

Figure 3-2:
A report
in Print
Preview
mode.

Figure 3-3:
The Page
Setup dialog
box.

The Page Setup dialog box works the same way when you print reports
and views. You can read about the settings in this dialog box in detail in
Chapter 1 of this minibook.

8. Click the Print button.

Project displays the Print dialog box (see Figure 3-4).

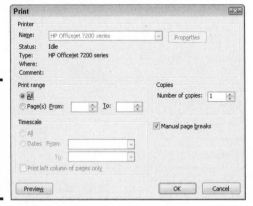

Figure 3-4: In the Print dialog box, select a print range for the report.

From the Print dialog box, you can

- Specify the number of copies you print.

- Select pages to print.

- Indicate whether Project should recognize and use manual page breaks.

9. Click OK to print.

You can select a printer from the Print dialog box if you choose File⇨Print to open the dialog box. Also, Timescale options aren't relevant for text reports, so you can't set them.

If you decide not to print the report, you can return to Project by clicking the Close button.

Preparing Big Picture Reports

The Overview category of reports in the Reports dialog box (refer to Figure 3-1) provides information about what's happening in your project in a "big picture" way. Figure 3-5 shows the Project Summary report, which provides information about the start and finish dates of your project, along with duration, work, and cost information. At the bottom of the report, you see an overall status for tasks and resources.

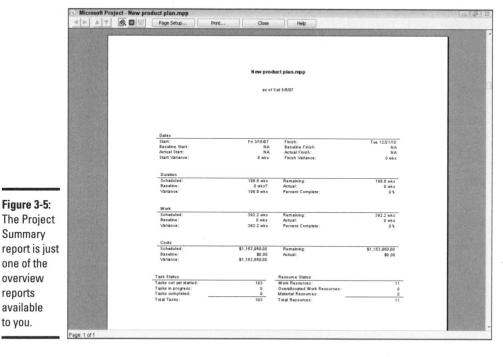

Figure 3-5:
The Project Summary report is just one of the overview reports available to you.

In Table 3-1, you see a description of each report available in the Overview category.

Table 3-1	Overview Reports
Report Name	*Shows*
Project Summary	Summarized information about dates, duration, work, costs, task status, and resource status.
Top Level Tasks	Summary tasks at the highest level in your project outline, the scheduled start and finish dates, the percentage complete, the cost, and the work required to complete the task as of today.
Critical Tasks	Status information for tasks that make the project late if you don't complete them on time, including each task's planned duration, start and finish dates, the resources that are assigned to the task, and the predecessors and successors of the task.
Milestones	The planned duration, start and finish dates, predecessors, and resources that are assigned to each milestone. If you marked summary tasks to appear as milestones in the Task Information dialog box, summary tasks also appear on this report as milestones.
Working Days	The base calendar information for your project, including the name of the base calendar and the working hours you established for each day of the week, along with any exceptions that you defined.

Reporting on Task Status

The reports in the Current Activities category in the Reports dialog box (refer to Figure 3-1) focus on the timing of your project. For example, the Unstarted Tasks report shown in Figure 3-6 lists the tasks that haven't yet started, sorted by the scheduled start date.

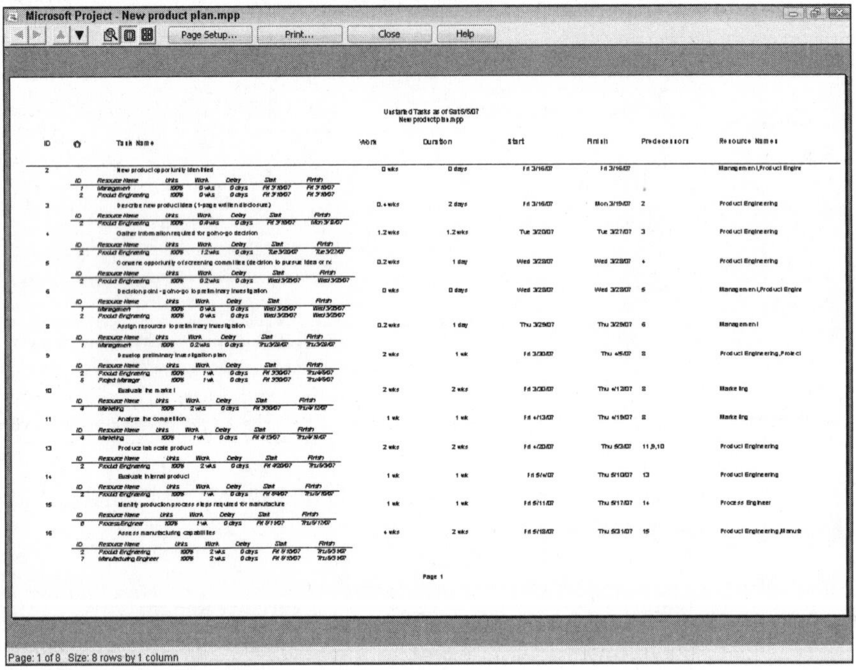

Figure 3-6: The Unstarted Tasks report shows tasks that haven't started yet.

Table 3-2 gives a description of each report available in the Current Activities category.

Table 3-2	Current Activities Reports
Report Name	*Shows*
Unstarted Tasks	The work, duration, start and finish dates, predecessor, and resource information assigned to each task. For each resource, Project displays the units, work, delay, planned start dates, and planned finish dates.

Report Name	Shows
Tasks Starting Soon	Tasks that start or finish between two dates that you specify in the Date Range dialog boxes that appear when you print the report. For each task, Project displays work, duration, start and finish dates, predecessor, and resource information assigned to each task. You can identify completed tasks on this report by the check mark that appears in the Indicators column on the report.
Tasks in Progress	The duration, start and planned finish dates, predecessors, and resource information for tasks that have started but not yet finished.
Completed Tasks	The actual duration, actual start and finish dates, percent complete, cost, and work hours of tasks that have completed. The percent complete is always 100%; partially completed tasks don't appear on this report.
Should Have Started Tasks	The planned start and finish dates, baseline start and finish dates, and variances for start and finish dates and successor task information. You supply a date by which tasks should have started.
Slipping Tasks	Planned start and finish dates, baseline start and finish dates, and variances for start and finish dates and successor task information for tasks that have been rescheduled from their baseline start dates.

Reporting on Costs

As you'd expect, the reports in the Costs category in the Reports dialog box (refer to Figure 3-1) focus on costs associated with your project. For example, the Budget report shown in Figure 3-7 lists fixed cost, fixed cost accrual, total cost, baseline cost, variance, actual cost, and remaining cost for each task, in the order of the highest total cost to lowest total cost.

In Table 3-3, you see a description of each of the reports in the Cost category.

Table 3-3	Cost Reports
Report Name	Shows
Cash Flow	The weekly costs for each task. You can change the timeframe increment from weeks to days, months, or quarters if you customize this report. For details, see the section "Adapting Reports to Suit Your Needs," at end of this chapter.

(continued)

Table 3-3 *(continued)*

Report Name	Shows
Budget	The budgeted costs, the variance between budgeted and actual costs, and the remaining budget amounts for each task. This report is meaningful only if you've saved a baseline and then recorded work on tasks.
Overbudget Tasks	Cost, baseline, variance, actual, and remaining information about tasks that exceed their budgeted amounts.
Overbudget Resources	Resources whose costs are going to exceed baseline estimates, based on the current progress of the project.
Earned Value	The status of each task's costs when you compare planned to actual costs. To understand the mysterious column headings in this report, read about earned value in Book 8, Chapter 3.

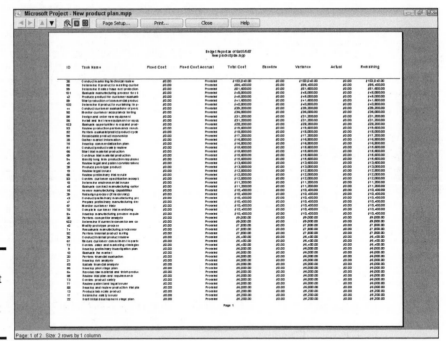

Figure 3-7:
The Budget report shows task costs.

Reporting on Assignments

The Assignments category in the Reports dialog box (refer to Figure 3-1) contains reports on, well, assignments . . . there really isn't a better way to describe them! You find reports like the Who Does What report shown in Figure 3-8, which lists each resource and then the tasks to which the resource is assigned. For each task, you see the number of units of the resource assigned to the task, the amount of planned work and delay, and the task's start and finish dates.

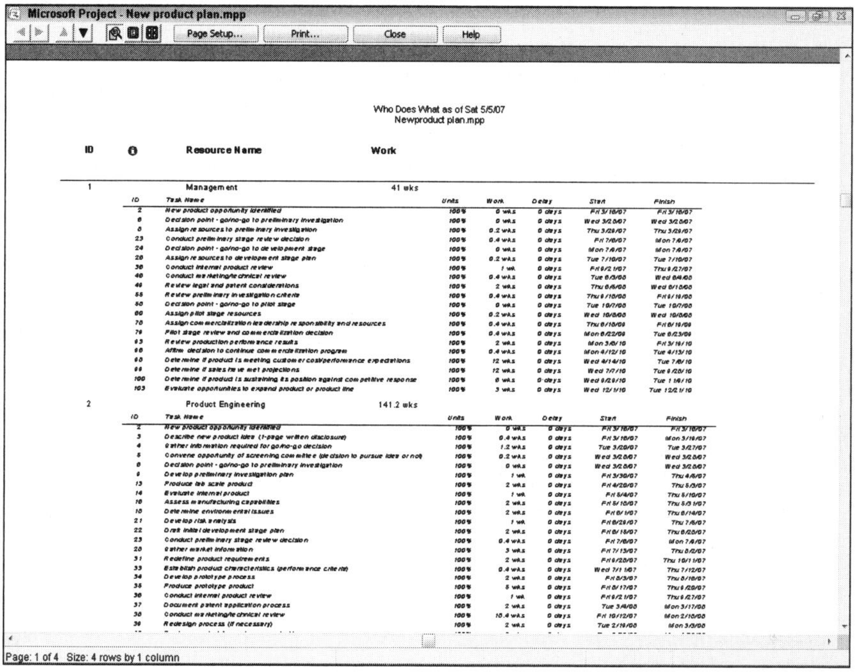

Figure 3-8:
The Who
Does What
report.

Table 3-4 describes each report in this category.

Table 3-4	Assignment Reports
Report Name	*Shows*
Who Does What	For each resource, the tasks to which the resource is assigned, and the planned units, work, delay, and start and finish dates for the task.
Who Does What When	In grid format, the daily work scheduled for each resource on each task.
To Do List	A list of tasks assigned to a selected resource on a week by week basis; each entry includes task ID number, duration, start and finish dates, predecessors, and a list of all of the resources that are assigned to the task.
Overallocated Resources	Overallocated resources, the tasks to which they're assigned, the total hours of work, delay, and the task start and finish dates.

Preparing Workload Reports

The reports in the Workload category in the Reports dialog box (refer to Figure 3-1) help you focus on task and resource usage in your project. The Task Usage report (see Figure 3-9) lists tasks and the resources that are assigned to each task, including the amount of work assigned to each resource in weekly time increments.

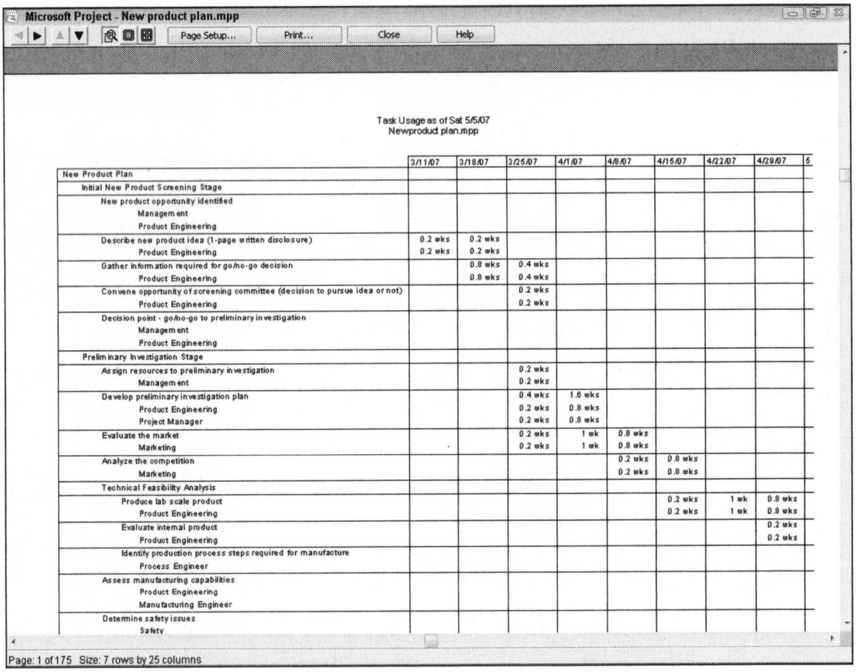

Task Usage as of Sat 5/5/07
Newproduct plan.mpp

	3/11/07	3/18/07	3/25/07	4/1/07	4/8/07	4/15/07	4/22/07	4/29/07	5
New Product Plan									
Initial New Product Screening Stage									
New product opportunity identified									
Management									
Product Engineering									
Describe new product idea (1-page written disclosure)	0.2 wks	0.2 wks							
Product Engineering	0.2 wks	0.2 wks							
Gather information required for go/no-go decision		0.8 wks	0.4 wks						
Product Engineering		0.8 wks	0.4 wks						
Convene opportunity of screening committee (decision to pursue idea or not)			0.2 wks						
Product Engineering			0.2 wks						
Decision point - go/no-go to preliminary investigation									
Management									
Product Engineering									
Preliminary Investigation Stage									
Assign resources to preliminary investigation			0.2 wks						
Management			0.2 wks						
Develop preliminary investigation plan			0.4 wks	1.6 wks					
Product Engineering			0.2 wks	0.8 wks					
Project Manager			0.2 wks	0.8 wks					
Evaluate the market			0.2 wks	1 wk	0.8 wks				
Marketing			0.2 wks	1 wk	0.8 wks				
Analyze the competition					0.2 wks	0.8 wks			
Marketing					0.2 wks	0.8 wks			
Technical Feasibility Analysis									
Produce lab scale product						0.2 wks	1 wk	0.8 wks	
Product Engineering						0.2 wks	1 wk	0.8 wks	
Evaluate internal product								0.2 wks	
Product Engineering								0.2 wks	
Identify production process steps required for manufacture									
Process Engineer									
Assess manufacturing capabilities									
Product Engineering									
Manufacturing Engineer									
Determine safety issues									
Safety									

Figure 3-9: The Task Usage report.

The Resource Usage report (see Figure 3-10) lists the same information as the Task Usage report, but it focuses your attention on resources because it lists resources and the tasks to which they're assigned.

Viewing Custom Reports

In addition to the reports described so far in this chapter, Project contains some reports available in the Custom category in the Reports dialog box (refer to Figure 3-1). The Custom Report dialog box contains the following reports:

- The Resource Usage (Material) report
- The Resource Usage (Work) report

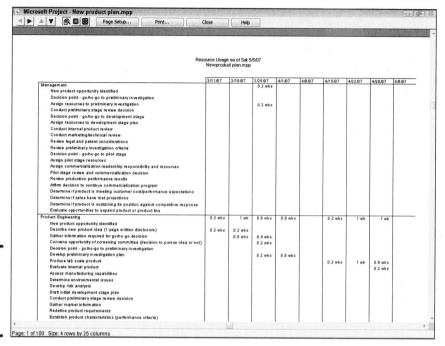

Figure 3-10:
The
Resource
Usage
report.

   ✦ The Task report

   ✦ The Resource report

   ✦ The Crosstab report

The Resource Usage (Material) and Resource Usage (Work) reports are both variations on the Resource Usage report.

The Task report (see Figure 3-11) shows task information, such as the ID number, task name, indicator icons, task duration, planned start and finish dates, predecessors, and (if resources have been assigned) resource names.

The Resource report shows similar information for resources, including resource ID numbers; indicator icons; resource names, types, labels, initials, and groups; maximum units; standard, overtime, and cost/use rate information; accrual information; base calendar information; and code information.

The Crosstab report is a tabular report that shows task and resource information in rows and time increments in columns. Much of the information on the Crosstab report also appears on the Task Usage report and the Resource Usage report, and the Task Usage and Resource Usage reports give you more formatting options, such as the period that's covered by the report and the table that's used in the report.

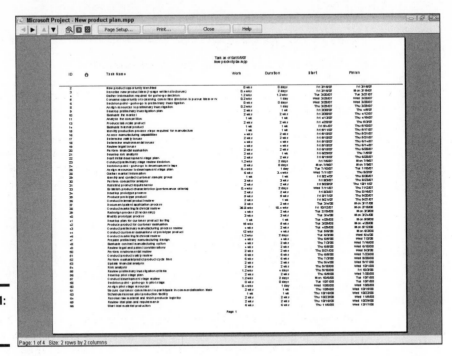

Figure 3-11:
The Task report.

To view and print these reports, follow these steps:

1. Choose Report⇨Reports.

The Reports dialog box appears.

2. Click the Custom category.

3. Click Select.

Project opens the Custom Reports dialog box (see Figure 3-12). This dialog box displays entries for all of the reports described earlier in this chapter, along with the custom reports described in this section.

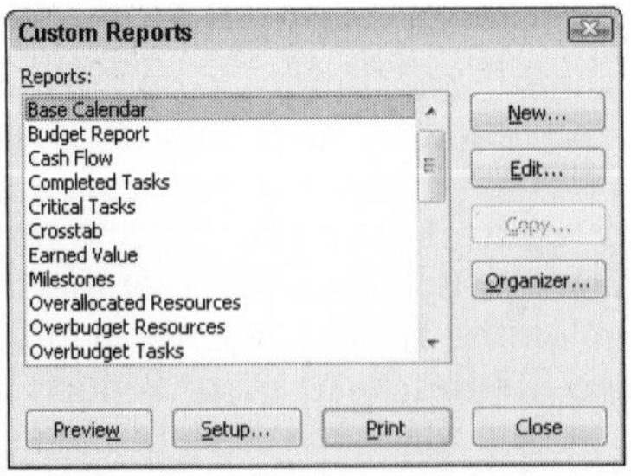

Figure 3-12:
Use this dialog box to print custom reports.

4. **Scroll to select the report you want to print.**

5. **Click Print or Preview.**

Project prints or previews the selected report.

Click Setup to display the Page Setup dialog box, described in detail in Chapter 1 of this minibook.

You can print any of the reports found in the categories described previously in this chapter either from this dialog box or by using the method described in the section, "Preparing and Printing Reports," earlier in this chapter. Remember, though, that you must use the Custom Reports dialog box to print the custom reports.

Adapting Reports to Suit Your Needs

You can make changes to any of the reports described previously in this chapter, and you can create new reports.

When would you modify a report? Well, for example, you can edit the Who Does What report to select a filter for resources on the Definitions tab; the default filter is for Work resources, but you can produce the same report for Cost resources or Material resources. Or, you might want to edit the Definition tab for the Cash Flow report to select the information that you want to appear on each row; the default information is Tasks and Cost. You also can change the time increments; the default is one week.

Because the Cash Flow report is a Crosstab report, Project displays the Crosstab Report dialog box when you edit the Cash Flow report.

You also might want to edit the Who Does What When report to change the timescale from daily to some other increment, such as weekly. And, if you see pound signs (###) in your report, you also might want to change the date format on the Details tab to a wider format.

Although you can modify a report by using the Edit button that appears in the report's category window, you can create a new report only from the Custom Report dialog box. Also, you also can modify an existing report from the Custom Report dialog box.

To modify any report, follow these steps:

1. **Choose Report⇨Reports.**

The Reports dialog box appears.

2. **Click the Custom category.**

3. **Click Select.**

   Project opens the Custom Reports dialog box.

4. **Click the report you want to modify.**

5. **Click Edit.**

   What you see next depends on the report you chose to modify.

For a few reports, such as the Base Calendar report, the only item that you can change is the font information that Project uses to print the report. In this case, Project displays the Report Text dialog box (see Figure 3-13).

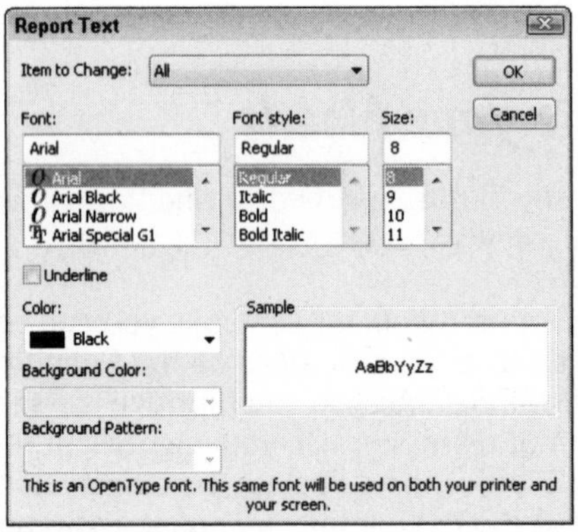

Figure 3-13:
You can change font information only for some reports.

For other reports, however, you can change the table or the task or resource filter to change the content of the report. For example, if you edit the Slipping Tasks report, Project opens the Definition tab of the Task Report dialog box (see Figure 3-14).

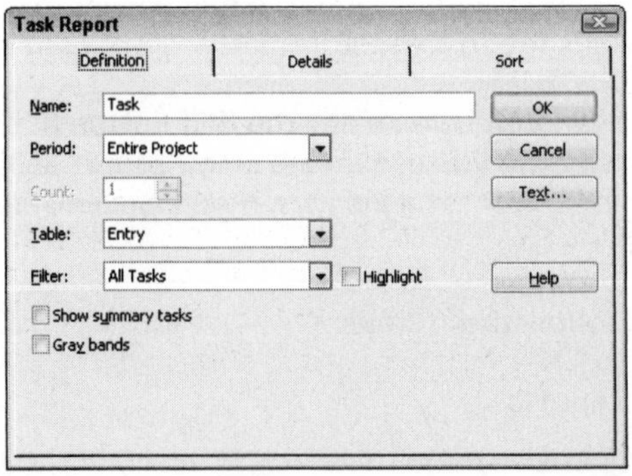

Figure 3-14:
Use the Definition tab to change a report's period, table, or filter.

From the Details tab (see Figure 3-15), you can select the information that you want to include on the report. The options on the Details tab change from report to report.

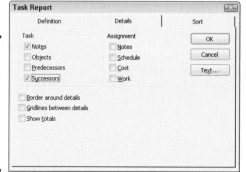

Figure 3-15:
Use the Details tab to identify details that you want to include on the report.

From the Sort tab (see Figure 3-16), you can specify fields by which to sort the report.

Figure 3-16:
Select fields to use to sort the report.

You also can create your own reports by clicking the New button in the Custom Reports dialog box. When you define a new custom report, Project offers you four formats (see Figure 3-17). Three formats are based on the Task, Resource, and Crosstab reports discussed in the section, "Viewing Custom Reports" earlier in this chapter. When you choose one of these formats, Project displays a dialog box that contains Definition, Details, and Sort tabs like the ones shown in Figures 3-15, 3-16, and 3-17.

When you select the Monthly Calendar format, Project displays the Monthly Calendar Report Definition dialog box shown in Figure 3-18.

Figure 3-17:
You can
create a
new report
based on
one of four
formats.

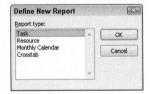

Figure 3-18:
Use this
dialog box
to create
a report
based on
the Monthly
Calendar
format.

Supply a name for the report, select a filter, and select a calendar. Use the other options in the dialog box to describe how you want the calendar to appear. If you accept the defaults Project suggests, your calendar report resembles the one shown in Figure 3-19.

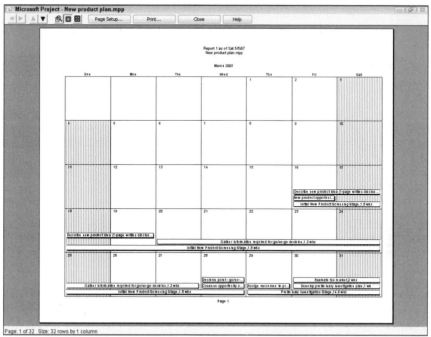

Figure 3-19:
A report based on the Monthly Calendar format that used the defaults Project suggested.

Chapter 4: Creating Visual Reports

In This Chapter

✔ **Creating a visual report**

✔ **Visually reporting on tasks and task usage**

✔ **Visually reporting on resources and resource usage**

✔ **Visually reporting on assignments and assignment usage**

✔ **Customizing visual reports**

*I*f you install Excel 2007 and Visio Professional 2007 along with Project 2007, you can produce visual reports — graphic representations of information in a Project file. Visual reports help you focus on the overview of the situation, rather than on the details. And, often, a picture can drive home a point better than the columns of numbers used to generate the picture.

Project contains a collection of Excel and Visio templates that you can use to produce a variety of visual reports. Project uses Excel PivotTables and Visio PivotDiagrams to present the information. After you produce a report, you can modify the report in Visio or Excel; changes you make to the report don't affect Project data.

And, of course, if you dream up a report that you don't find in Project, you can create your own report template.

Preparing a Visual Report

You prepare all the visual reports in Project by using the same technique:

1. **Open the Project file on which you want to report.**

It doesn't matter whether you open Excel or Visio before you create a visual report.

2. **Choose Report➪Visual Reports.**

Project displays the Visual Reports – Create Report dialog box (see Figure 4-1).

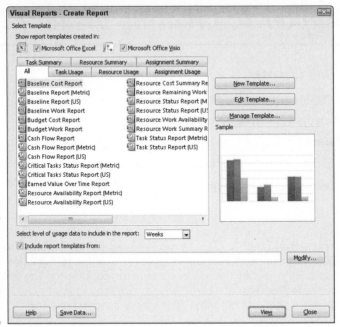

Figure 4-1:
Use this dialog box to select a visual report template.

3. **Select the tab for the type of report you want to prepare.**

4. **Click the template for the report you want to prepare.**

5. **Click View.**

Project prepares the report and displays it in the appropriate program — Excel or Visio.

Working with an Excel visual report

We're not going to spend a lot of time showing you how to fiddle with a visual report in Excel; we're just going to provide basics. Most of what you need to know revolves around Excel PivotTables, so, we recommend that you take a look at *Excel 2007 Bible,* by John Walkenbach (Wiley Publishing, Inc.).

In Figure 4-2, you see a typical Excel-based visual report. Initially, you see the chart Excel prepares using the project's data, but if you look at the bottom of the screen and figure, you'll notice two tabs in the Excel file.

On the second tab, shown in Figure 4-3, you see the PivotTable that forms the foundation of the chart displayed in Figure 4-2. On this sheet, you also see the PivotTable Field List at the right side of the screen; using this pane of information, you can change the information that appears in the chart.

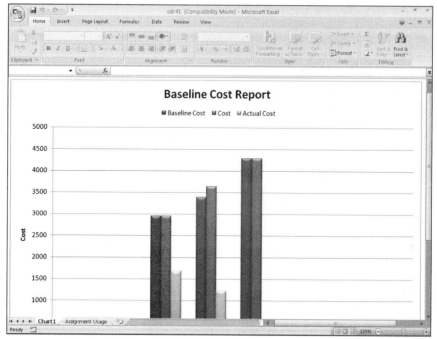

Figure 4-2:
A sample
visual report
in Excel.

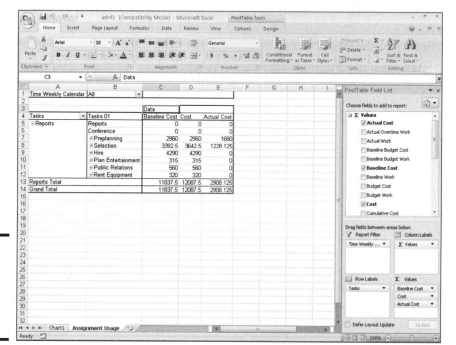

Figure 4-3:
The
underlying
data for
the visual
report.

For example, you can add or remove fields by selecting or deselecting fields in the top portion of the pane. Using the information in the lower portion of the pane, you can rearrange the information that appears in the chart. And, using any list boxes that appear in the table portion of the chart, you can filter the report to display less information.

Working with a Visio visual report

Once again, we're not going to spend a lot of time showing you how to fiddle with a visual report in Visio; we're just going to provide basics. Most of what you need to know revolves around Visio PivotDiagrams, so we recommend that you take a look at *Visio 2007 Bible,* by Bonnie Biafore (Wiley Publishing, Inc.).

In Figure 4-4, you see a typical Visio-based visual report in Print Preview that we've enlarged by zooming.

Because the chart is a PivotDiagram, when you display the regular Visio window, you also see the PivotDiagram tools in the left pane (see Figure 4-5). You can use these tools and the PivotDiagram toolbar that Visio automatically displays to add categories or totals to the PivotDiagram and modify it in other ways.

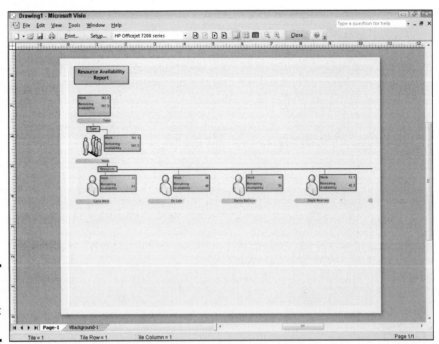

Figure 4-4:
A sample visual report in Visio.

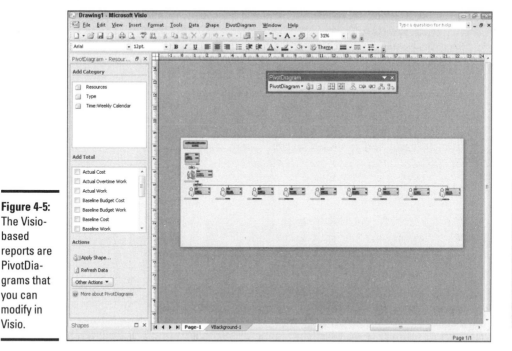

Book VI
Chapter 4

Creating Visual
Reports

Figure 4-5:
The Visio-
based
reports are
PivotDia-
grams that
you can
modify in
Visio.

Visually Reporting on Task Usage

The Task Usage visual report category contains only one report template:
the Cash Flow Report. This Excel-based visual report template uses timephased data to show Cost and Cumulative Cost over time (see Figure 4-6).

Visually Reporting on Resource Usage

Using the report templates in this category, you can focus on various
aspects of resource usage. For example, the Resource Work Availability
Report shown in Figure 4-7 is an Excel-based visual report that shows work,
work availability, and remaining availability information over time.

In Table 4-1, you see a description of each report template available in the
Resource Usage category.

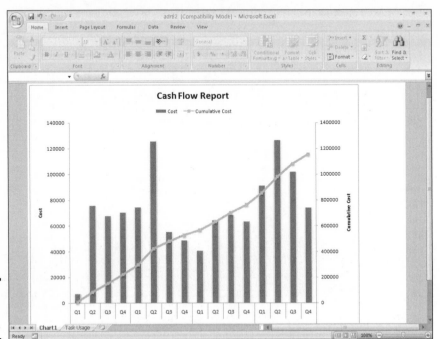

Figure 4-6:
The Cash
Flow Report.

Table 4-1		Resource Usage Reports
Report Template Name	**Excel or Visio**	**Shows**
Cash Flow	Visio	Planned and actual costs for Work, Material, and Cost resources in your project over time. This report is available in two versions: Metric and US.
Resource Availability	Visio	Total capacity, work, and remaining availability for work resources.
Resource Cost Summary	Excel	Resource costs divided in a pie chart among resource types — Work, Cost, and Material.
Resource Work Availability	Excel	Work, work availability, and remaining availability information over time.
Resource Work Summary	Excel	Work, remaining availability, and actual work for each work resource in the project.

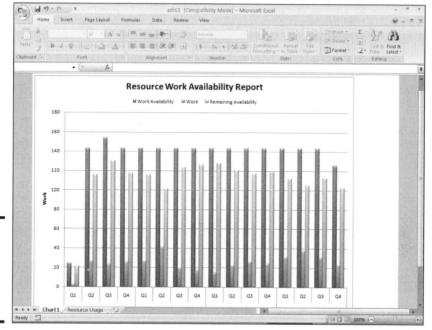

Figure 4-7:
The
Resource
Work
Availability
Report.

Visually Reporting on Assignment Usage

Using the report templates in this category, you can focus on various aspects of assignment usage. For example, the Baseline Report shown in Figure 4-8 is a Visio-based visual report that shows baseline and actual work and costs for your project over time. The report flags tasks where planned work exceeds baseline work and where planned cost exceeds baseline cost. You can find both a metric and a U.S. version of the Baseline Report.

In Table 4-2, you see a description of each report template available in the Assignment Usage category.

Table 4-2	Assignment Usage Reports	
Report Template Name	*Excel or Visio*	*Shows*
Baseline Cost	Excel	A comparison of baseline cost, planned cost, and actual cost.
Baseline	Visio	Baseline and actual work and costs for your project over time. This report identifies tasks where planned work exceeds baseline work and where planned cost exceeds baseline cost.
Baseline Work	Excel	A comparison of baseline work, planned work, and actual work.

(continued)

Table 4-2 *(continued)*

Report Template Name	Excel or Visio	Shows
Budget Cost	Excel	A comparison of budget cost, baseline cost, planned cost, and actual cost.
Budget Work	Excel	A comparison of budget work, baseline work, planned work, and actual work.
Earned Value Over Time	Excel	Actual cost of work performed (ACWP), Planned Value – PV (BCWS), and Earned Value – EV (BCWP) plotted over time.

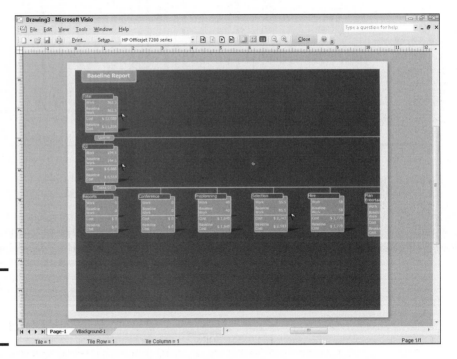

Figure 4-8:
The
Baseline
Report.

The Earned Value Over Time Report replaces the Analyze Timescaled Data Wizard found in earlier versions of Project. For more information on earned value, see Book VIII, Chapter 3.

Preparing Visual Task Summary Reports

This category contains two versions of one report template: the Critical Tasks Status Report (see Figure 4-9). This Visio-based visual report organizes tasks by whether they're critical and shows the work and remaining work for both types of tasks, along with the percent of work complete.

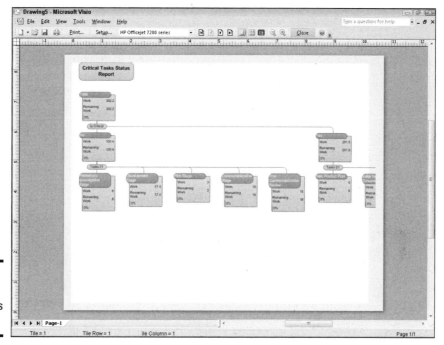

Book VI
Chapter 4

Creating Visual
Reports

Figure 4-9:
The Critical
Tasks Status
Report.

Preparing Visual Resource Summary Reports

You'll find only one report template in the Resource Summary category: the Resource Remaining Work Report (see Figure 4-10). This Excel-based visual report shows, as a stacked bar chart, work, remaining work, and total work for each work resource on your project.

Preparing Visual Assignment Summary Reports

In the Assignment Summary category, you'll find two Visio-based visual report templates, and each report template comes in both a metric and a nonmetric (U.S.) version.

The Resource Status Report (see Figure 4-11) shows work and cost values for each of your project's resources.

The Task Status Report (see Figure 4-12) shows work and percent of work complete for tasks at the highest level in your project outline.

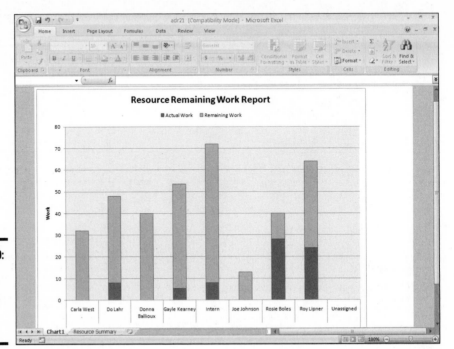

Figure 4-10:
The
Resource
Remaining
Work
Report.

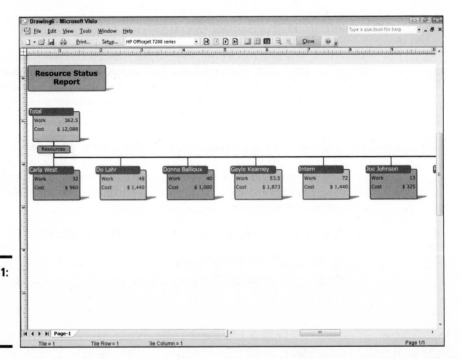

Figure 4-11:
The
Resource
Status
Report.

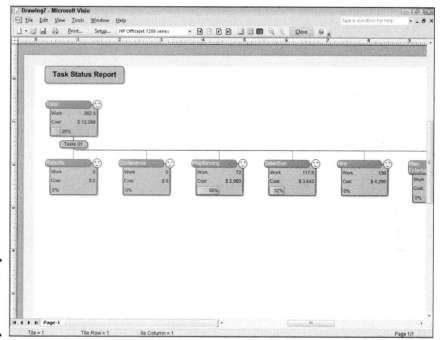

Figure 4-12:
The Task
Status
Report.

Customizing Visual Reports

Although Project provides you with a fairly good variety of visual reports, it's just possible that you won't find the one you want. Or, you might want to modify an existing visual report. The process you follow to modify an existing report is part of the process you follow to create a new report, so we walk through creating a new report.

When you create a new report template, you base it on an existing template, and you include the fields that you want to appear on your report. Each time you run the report, it displays the fields you include on the report template, but the information on the report might change because the data in your Project file has changed.

To create a new visual report template, follow these steps:

1. **Choose Reports⇨Visual Reports.**

Project displays the Visual Reports – Create Report dialog box (see Figure 4-13).

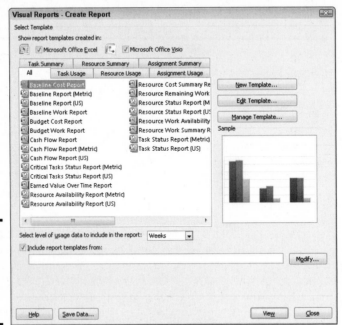

Figure 4-13:
The Visual
Reports –
Create
Report
dialog box.

2. **Click the New Template button.**

Project displays the Visual Reports – New Template dialog box (see
Figure 4-14).

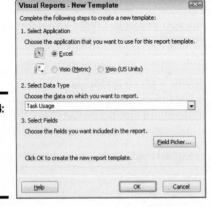

Figure 4-14:
Describe
the new
template
you want
to create.

3. **Choose Excel or Visio as the application that will display the report.**

If you select Visio, choose between Visio (Metric) and Visio (US Units).

4. **Open the Choose the Data on Which You Want to Report list box and select an existing visual report.**

The report you select serves as the foundation for your new report.

To include timephased data on your report, select Task Usage, Resource Usage, or Assignment Usage. *Timephased* data is information that is distributed over time; Project displays this information in Task Usage view or Resource Usage view.

5. **Click the Field Picker button.**

Project displays the Visual Reports – Field Picker dialog box (see Figure 4-15).

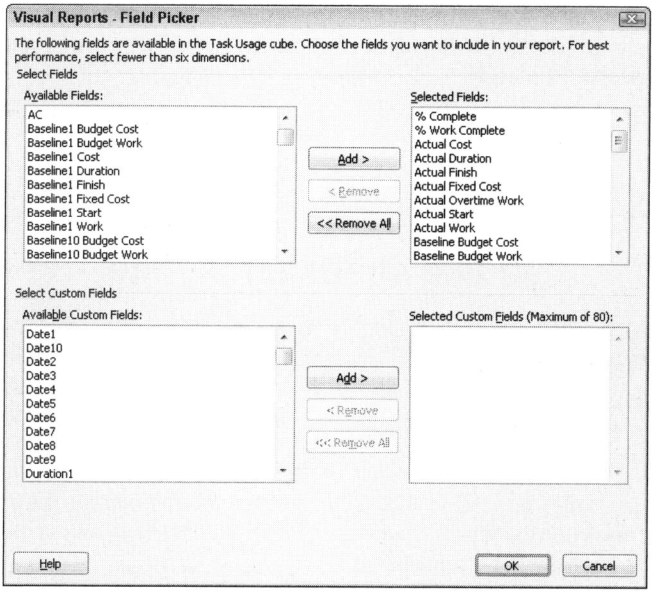

**Book VI
Chapter 4**

**Creating Visual
Reports**

Figure 4-15: Select the fields you want to include in your visual report template.

Visual Reports - Field Picker

The following fields are available in the Task Usage cube. Choose the fields you want to include in your report. For best performance, select fewer than six dimensions.

Select Fields

Available Fields:

- AC
- Baseline1 Budget Cost
- Baseline1 Budget Work
- Baseline1 Cost
- Baseline1 Duration
- Baseline1 Finish
- Baseline1 Fixed Cost
- Baseline1 Start
- Baseline1 Work
- Baseline10 Budget Cost
- Baseline10 Budget Work

Add >
< Remove
<< Remove All

Selected Fields:

- % Complete
- % Work Complete
- Actual Cost
- Actual Duration
- Actual Finish
- Actual Fixed Cost
- Actual Overtime Work
- Actual Start
- Actual Work
- Baseline Budget Cost
- Baseline Budget Work

Select Custom Fields

Available Custom Fields:

- Date1
- Date10
- Date2
- Date3
- Date4
- Date5
- Date6
- Date7
- Date8
- Date9
- Duration1

Add >
< Remove
<< Remove All

Selected Custom Fields (Maximum of 80):

Help   OK   Cancel

6. **On the left side of the dialog box, click a field that you want to appear on the report and then click the Add button.**

Project displays the field on the right side of the dialog box.

The fields that appear in this dialog box change, depending on the report template you selected in Step 4, but the dialog box always functions the same way. The columns on the right show the fields currently included in the report template, and the columns on the left shown the fields available to add to the template. To remove an existing field from the report, click it in one of the right-hand columns and click Remove.

7. **Repeat Step 6 for each field you want to add to the report template.**

8. **Click OK twice.**

   Project builds the report; either an Excel window or a Visio window appears to enable you to establish the PivotTable or PivotDiagram by dragging fields.

9. **Click Office⇨Save As.**

   The Save As dialog box appears.

10. **Navigate to and save the file in the default location where templates are stored.**

    If you use the defaults established by Microsoft Office, navigate to `C:\Program Files\Microsoft Office\Templates\1033`.

    If you save your template in the default location, it appears automatically in the Visual Reports window in Project along with other visual report templates.

Taking a snapshot in time

Company: Software development firm with more than 75 employees.

Project: Upgrade the operating system software on all computers in the firm to Windows Vista.

Challenge: Prepare reports on various phases of the project but be able to reproduce a report prepared at an earlier point in time, including its data.

Solution: To avoid saving hard copies of visual reports, you can save reporting data in an OLAP (On Line Analytical Processing) cube or in a Microsoft Office Access database. Using the cube or the database, you can reproduce the report at any time in Excel or Access. You also can use the data to create other reports. When you save an OLAP cube, you can select the

Project fields you want included in the cube, including custom fields. When you save the data to an Access database, you save all data in the project at the time. On this book's Web site (www.dummies.com/go/project 2007aiofd), you can find CS060401.mpp, a small project that you can use to practice creating an OLAP cube or an Access database.

To create an OLAP cube, follow these steps:

1. **Choose Report⇨Visual Reports.**

   Project displays the Visual Reports – Create Report dialog box.

2. **Click the Save Data button in the lower-left corner.**

   Project displays the Visual Reports – Save Reporting Data dialog box.

3. Select a cube from the first list box.

Project provides six cubes: Task Usage, Resource Usage, Assignment Usage, Task Summary, Resource Summary, and Assignment Summary.

4. Click the Field Picker button.

Project displays the Visual Reports – Field Picker dialog box. The fields available in this dialog box depend on the cube you selected in Step 3.

(continued)

(continued)

5. **On the left side of the dialog box, click a field that you want to appear on the report and then click the Add button.**

   Project displays the field on the right side of the dialog box.

   To remove an existing field from the report, click it in one of the columns on the right and click Remove.

6. **Repeat Step 5 for each field you want to add to the report template.**

7. **Click OK.**

   Project redisplays the Visual Reports – Save Reporting Data dialog box.

8. **Click Save Cube.**

   The Save As dialog box appears.

9. **Navigate to the location where you want to save the cube and click Save.**

   Project saves the cube; the file extension for the cube file is .cub.

10. **Click Close.**

    Project closes the Visual Reports – Save Reporting Data dialog box.

11. **Click Close again.**

    Project closes the Visual Reports – Create Report dialog box.

If you want to save reporting data from your Project file in an Access database, follow Steps 1 and 2. Then click Save Database. Project displays the Save As dialog box; navigate to the location where you want to save the cube and click Save. Project saves reporting data in an Access database file with a file extension of .mdb.

Book VII

Resolving Problems in Your Plan

The 5th Wave   By Rich Tennant

"You ever get the feeling this project could just up and die at any moment?"

Contents at a Glance

Chapter 1: Working with Filters

In This Chapter

✔ **Understanding how filters work**

✔ **Applying a filter**

✔ **Modifying a filter**

✔ **Creating a custom filter**

✔ **Using filters to spot and resolve problems**

✔ **Working with groups**

After you take your best shot at creating your project plan, creating each task, and assigning all your resources, you might think you're ready to start your project. However, that's seldom the case.

Taking the time to review almost any plan reveals some issues that you should resolve before you begin working on your first task. These issues might include a schedule that runs a few weeks past your optimum deadline, a person who is assigned to work on ten tasks on the same day in week 43, or a budget overrun that has no way of making it past your accounting guy.

Even if you don't see any obvious problems in the areas of time, workload, or money, you should still take the time to make sure that your project is as realistic as possible before you commit to it.

Filtering to Spot Resource and Schedule Problems

One of the most helpful things you can do to be sure there are no gotchas in your plan is to look at it from a few different perspectives. It's like walking around a house to be sure you've spotted the mold in the basement and chipped paint on the siding before you head to the closing. Filters help you get that kind of perspective.

Two major problem areas that filters can help you examine at this stage are

✦ **Overallocated resources:** These resources are working more than the number of hours you specified.

✦ **Tasks on a critical path:** A *critical path* consists of the series of tasks in your project that must happen on time for the project to meet its final deadline.

A task that has *slack* — that is, any length of time that it could be delayed without delaying the project's final deadline — isn't on the critical path. If your project has very little slack built in, any delays that occur are likely to cause your project to finish late.

How filters work

Filters allow you to hone in on certain information about your project, weeding out the data that isn't of interest to you at the moment. They can help you spot clues about problems (such as overallocated resources).

You can set a filter to work in one of two ways:

✦ To highlight tasks or resources that meet certain criteria

✦ To remove any tasks or resources from view that don't meet specified criteria

Project provides predesigned filters that you can simply turn on to filter for task or resource criteria, such as

✦ Tasks with a cost greater than a specified amount

✦ Tasks that are on the critical path

✦ Tasks that occur within a specified date range

✦ Milestone tasks (tasks of zero duration)

✦ Tasks that use resources in a specified resource group

✦ Tasks with overallocated resources

Several filters, such as Slipping Tasks and Overbudget Work, help you spot problems after you've finalized your plan and are tracking actual progress. (See Book VIII for more about tracking.)

Applying filters

You can access filters by using the AutoFilter button. When you click this button, you then choose from a list of built-in filters. Filters applied this way remove any tasks from view that don't meet specified criteria.

You can also choose from a list of filters from a drop-down list on the Formatting toolbar. To turn on such filters, follow these steps:

1. **Display a resource view (such as Resource Sheet view) to filter for resources or a task view (such as Gantt Chart view) to filter for tasks.**

2. **Click the Filter drop-down list on the Formatting toolbar and then choose the criteria.**

When no filter is applied, All Tasks or All Resources appears in the Filter drop-down list. If you choose a filter that requires input, you see a dialog box such as the one in Figure 1-1. Otherwise, the filter is applied immediately and removes from view any resources or tasks that don't match your criteria.

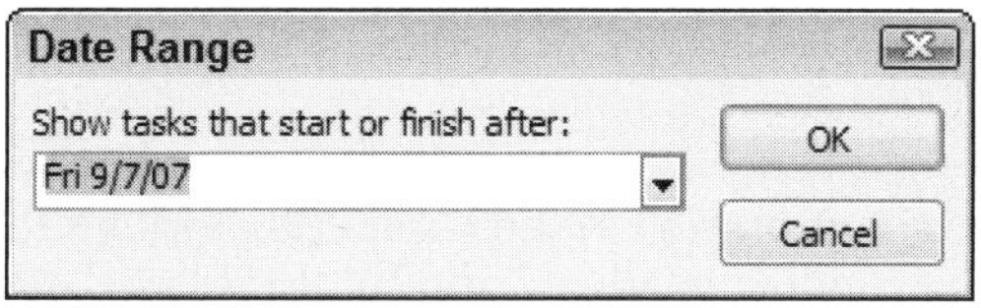

Figure 1-1:
Some filters require that you enter parameters.

Date Range

Show tasks that start or finish after:

Fri 9/7/07

OK

Cancel

3. **If a dialog box is displayed, fill in the information and then click OK.**

The filter is applied.

To display filters and choose whether they highlight tasks fitting the criteria or remove tasks not fitting the criteria, follow these steps:

1. **Choose Project⇨Filtered For⇨More Filters.**

The More Filters dialog box appears, as shown in Figure 1-2.

Figure 1-2:
This dialog box lists all available filters, built-in and custom.

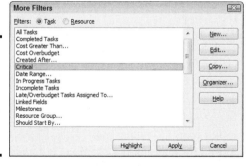

More Filters

Filters: ⦿ Task ◯ Resource

All Tasks
Completed Tasks
Cost Greater Than...
Cost Overbudget
Created After...
Critical
Date Range...
In Progress Tasks
Incomplete Tasks
Late/Overbudget Tasks Assigned To...
Linked Fields
Milestones
Resource Group...
Should Start By...

New...
Edit...
Copy...
Organizer...
Help

Highlight Apply Cancel

2. **Select either the Task or Resource option to specify which list of filters you want the new filter to be included in.**

3. **Click a filter and then click either Highlight or Apply.**

The Highlight choice applies a highlight; the Apply choice removes tasks that don't meet filter criteria.

To redisplay all tasks or resources, click the Filter drop-down list on the Formatting toolbar and then select either All Resources or All Tasks (depending on whether a Resource or Task filter is currently applied).

Letting AutoFilters do the work

You can use an AutoFilter feature that filters on individual fields of data in any view that includes a spreadsheet, such as Tracking Gantt Chart view. When you turn on AutoFilters, drop-down lists of built-in filters appear at the top of each column.

You can use the AutoFilter button on the Formatting toolbar to turn on the AutoFilter feature; when you do, arrows appear at the head of columns in the currently displayed sheet. Click the arrow for the Start Date column (for example), and a list of filter criteria such as Today, Tomorrow, This Week, Next Month, and so on appears.

You can also choose a Custom setting from each of these lists to customize AutoFilter with certain criteria in a context-specific dialog box. For example, the Start area in the Custom AutoFilter dialog box (shown in Figure 1-3) allows you to specify that you want to view tasks with a start date greater than (after) the baseline start date, but less than (before) the actual start date.

Figure 1-3:
AutoFilter choices are specific to each field of information in your sheet.

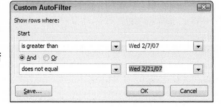

You can save a custom filter definition for future use by clicking the Save button in the Custom AutoFilter dialog box and giving it a name.

Follow these steps to activate and use AutoFilter:

1. **Display the view that contains the fields (columns) you want to filter.**

2. **Click the AutoFilter button.**

Arrows appear at the top of each column.

3. **Click the arrow on the column that you want to filter.**

4. **Click the criterion you want for your filter.**

   For example, if you are filtering for task duration, in the Duration column, you can choose >1 day, >1 week, or a specific number of days (such as 5 days or 10 days). All tasks or resources that don't meet your criteria disappear.

Creating your own filters

You don't have to use predesigned filters: You can get creative and design your own filters. To define a new filter, you specify a field name, a test, and a value.

For example, the following qualifiers filter for any task on the critical path:

Critical (field name) **Equals** (test) **Yes** (value)

You can also include additional qualifiers to the filter. The following qualifiers filter for tasks that are both on the critical path and have a baseline cost of more than $5,000:

Critical (field name) **Equals** (test) **Yes** (value)

and

Baseline Cost (field name) **Is Greater Than** (test) **5000** (value)

Here's how to build your own filter definition:

1. **Choose Project➪Filtered For➪More Filters.**

   The More Filters dialog box appears (refer to Figure 1-2).

2. **Select either the Task or Resource option to specify which list of filters you want the new filter to be included in.**

3. **Click New.**

   The Filter Definition dialog box appears.

4. **In the Name field, type a name for the filter.**

5. **Click the first line of the Field Name column and then click the down arrow that appears to display the list of choices, as shown in Figure 1-4.**

6. **Click a field name to select it.**

**Book VII
Chapter 1**

**Working with
Filters**

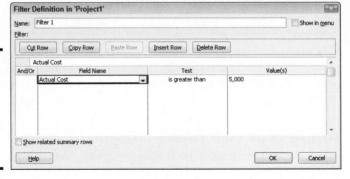

Filter Definition in 'Project1'

Name: Filter 1   Show in menu

Filter:

| Cut Row | Copy Row | Paste Row | Insert Row | Delete Row |

Actual Cost

And/Or	Field Name	Test	Value(s)	
	Actual Cost	is greater than	5,000	

Show related summary rows

Help   OK   Cancel

Figure 1-4:
Give your
new filter a
name that
describes
what it
does.

7. **Repeat Steps 5 and 6 for the Test and Value(s) columns.**

- *Test* is a condition that must be met, such as Does Not Equal or Is Greater Than.

- *Value(s)* is either a value you enter (such as a specific date or cost) or a predetermined value (such as baseline cost).

8. **If you want to enter a qualifier, such as a dollar amount, click the entry box above the column headings and then type the amount at the end of the filter definition.**

   For example, if you choose Cost for the field name and Equals for the test, you might enter the number **5000** at the end of the definition in the entry box.

9. **If you want to add another condition, choose And or Or from the And/Or column and then make choices for the next set of Field Name, Test, and Value(s) boxes.**

   Note that you can cut and paste rows of settings you've made to rearrange them in the list, or you can use the Copy Row or Delete Row button to perform those actions for filters with several lines of criteria.

10. **If you want the new filter to be shown in the list when you click the Filter box on the Formatting toolbar, select the Show in Menu check box.**

11. **Click OK to save the new filter and then click Apply to apply the filter to your plan.**

You can click the Organizer button in the More Filters dialog box to copy filters you've created in one Project file to another file. Just click the filters you want to copy from the file on the left and then click the Copy button to copy them to the file on the right.

Filtering in Action

Book VIII covers tracking in detail, but because we're focused on filtering now, it might be helpful to cue you into some filters that can help you spot problems after your project begins. Especially in larger projects, where it's not always easy to scan hundreds of tasks and notice which are running late or over budget, filters can home in on exactly where your trouble lies.

You can choose to have tasks that don't meet filter criteria removed from your display or simply highlight tasks that meet the criteria on-screen.

Discovering some very useful filters

When things just don't seem to be going the way you'd like, turn to Table 1-1. It lists some filters that are useful when you're trying to identify and solve problems with your schedule.

Table 1-1	Filters to Isolate Problems
Filter Name	*What It Displays*
Cost Overbudget	Tasks that exceed budgeted expenditures
Critical	Tasks in the project that must be completed according to schedule to make your final deadline (critical path)
Incomplete Tasks	Tasks that haven't been marked as complete
Late/Overbudget Tasks	Tasks that are running later than their baseline estimate and are over budget
Overallocated Resources	Tasks with resources assigned that are overbooked at some point during the life of the task
Should Start By	Tasks that should have started as of a specified date
Slipping Assignments	Tasks that involve resource work that should have begun by now
Slipped/Late Progress	Tasks that are running late and have no progress recorded
Update Needed	A task that should have had progress tracked by now
Work Incomplete	Tasks that should have had all their work recorded by now
Work Overbudget	More work hours have been put in on the task than you had estimated

If you don't see all these choices in the More Filters dialog box, remember that you have to enable the Task option to see task-related filters and the Resource option to see resource-related filters.

Identifying the critical path

One of the most useful filters in Project is the one called Critical. This displays or highlights all tasks that are on the critical path. Remember that if a path on the critical path slips, your project end date will slip.

If you're running late, knowing which tasks can't slip helps you identify where there's no room for delay — and, conversely, where you can delay noncritical tasks and still meet your deadline.

You might also use the Critical filter to help you determine tasks that are noncritical; then you can remove some resources from those tasks to put them on other more critical tasks or avoid a resource overallocation scenario.

You can look at the critical path in any Gantt Chart or Network Diagram view. Figure 1-5 shows Gantt Chart view of a project with the critical path highlighted. Figure 1-6 shows Network Diagram view with the same filter applied.

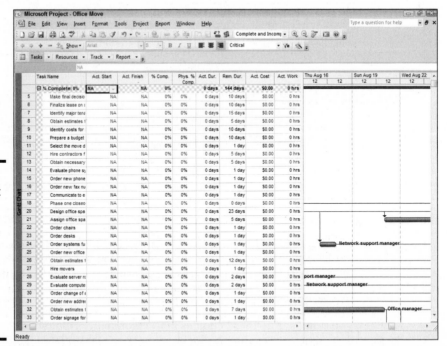

Figure 1-5: Gantt Chart view shows you columns of data and a more precise timescale for each task.

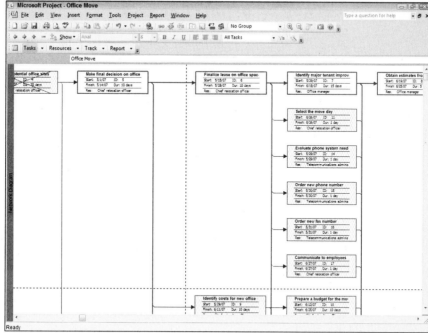

Figure 1-6:
Network
Diagram
view gives
you a feel
for workflow
and depen-
dencies
among
tasks.

Working with Groups

Project lets you group like items together to help you keep track of all the data you enter. The Group feature essentially allows you to organize information by certain criteria.

For example, you can use the Group feature if you want to see resources organized by their hourly rate, or you might organize tasks by their duration or cost.

Organizing tasks or resources in this way can help you identify a potential problem in your project. For example, say that you find that the majority of your resources at project startup are unskilled and that most of the tasks at the end of your project are on the critical path. In that case, you should probably build in more time and money for training, build in more slack, and move out your final deadline.

Like filters, groups come predefined, and you can create custom groups.

Applying predefined groups

Project has some built-in groups that are quick and easy to apply and cover a host of common requirements in projects. These include groups such as Resource Type and Task Constraint Type.

Follow these steps to apply a predefined group structure to your project:

1. **Display either a resource view (such as Resource Sheet view) to group resources, or a task view (such as Gantt Chart view) to group tasks.**

2. **On the Standard toolbar, click the Group By drop-down list and then select a criterion.**

   The information is organized according to your selection. Figure 1-7 shows an example.

To redisplay all tasks or resources in their original order, click the arrow in the Group By drop-down list on the Standard toolbar to display the list and then click No Group. (When no group is applied, the Group By box displays the words No Group.)

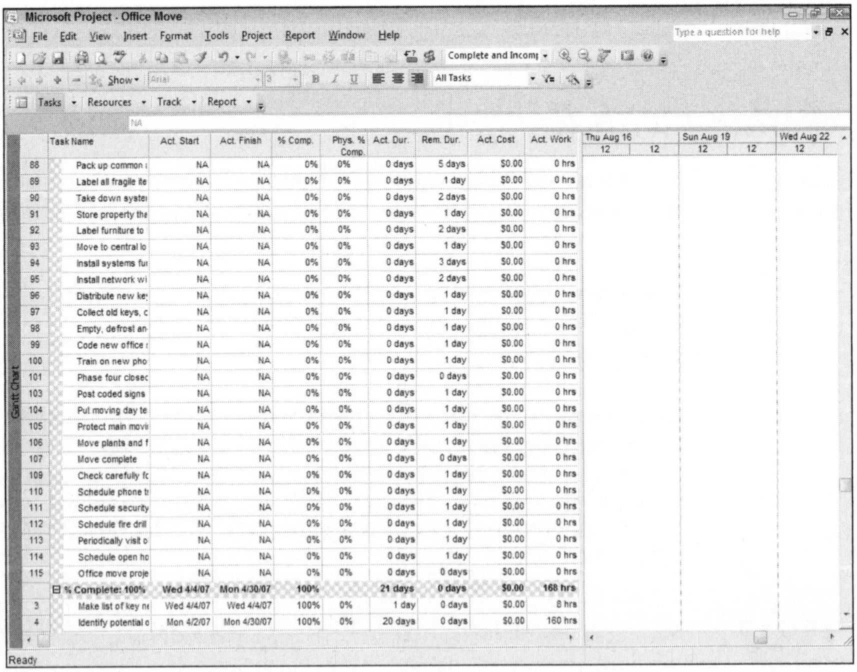

Figure 1-7: Organizing tasks to show only tasks in progress provides this view of your project.

Coming up with your own groups

Custom groups include three elements that you can make settings for: a field name, a field type, and an order. For example, you might create a group that shows the field name (such as Baseline Work) and a field type (such as Tasks, Resources, or Assignments) in a certain order (Descending or Ascending). A group that shows Baseline Work for Tasks in Descending Order would list tasks in order from the most work hours required to the least.

Other settings you can make for groups control the format of the group's appearance, such as the font used or a font color to be applied.

Follow these steps to create a custom group:

1. **Choose Project⇨Group By⇨More Groups.**

The More Groups dialog box appears, as shown in Figure 1-8.

Figure 1-8:
This dialog box is organized by task- or resource-oriented groups.

2. **Select either Task or Resource to specify in which list of groups you want the new group to be included.**

3. **Click New.**

The Group Definition dialog box appears, as shown in Figure 1-9.

4. **In the Name field, type a name for the group.**

5. **Click the first line of the Field Name column, click the down arrow that appears to display the list of choices, and then click a field name to choose it.**

6. **Repeat Step 5 for the Field Type and Order columns.**

Note that if you want the Field Type option of grouping by assignment rather than by resource or task, you must first select the Group Assignments, Not Tasks check box to make that field available to you. Otherwise the Field Type of Task or Resource appears by default.

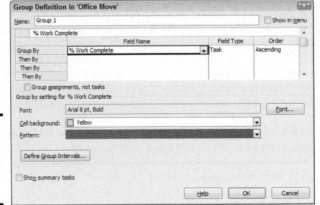

Figure 1-9:
Use your
own groups
to organize
data.

7. **If you want to add another sorting criteria, click a row titled Then By and make choices for the Field Name, Field Type, and Order columns.**

8. **If you want the new group to be shown in the list when you click the Group box on the Formatting toolbar, select the Show in Menu check box.**

9. **Depending on the field name you've chosen, you can make settings for the font, cell background, and pattern to format your group.**

   For example, the font of each duration group heading in Figure 1-7 was determined by making choices from these three lists.

10. **If you want to define intervals for the groups to be organized in, click the Define Group Intervals button.**

    This displays the Define Group Intervals dialog box; use the settings here to set a starting time and an interval. For example, if the Group By criterion is Standard Rate and you select a Group Interval of 1.00, groupings are in $1 intervals (those making $0–$1 an hour in one grouping, those making $11–$20 in another, and so on).

11. **Click OK to save the new group and then click Apply to apply the group to your plan.**

If you want to make changes to an existing predefined group, apply the group and then choose Project⇨Group By⇨Customize Group By. This takes you to the Customize Group By dialog box for that group. This dialog box — whose options are identical to the Group Definition dialog box — allows you to edit all those settings for an existing group.

Chapter 2: Solving Resource Conflicts

In This Chapter

✔ Checking for resource availability

✔ Changing resource assignments

✔ Adding resources

✔ Examining task drivers

✔ Using multiple undo

✔ Using resource leveling

*W*hen you've used all your skills, experience, and data to create what you consider to be a solid plan for your project, you might think you're ready to begin. But it's always a good idea to take a step back and examine your plan before you commit to it and proceed.

Taking the time to review almost any plan reveals some issues that you should resolve before you begin working on your first task. It will be painfully obvious if you have devised a schedule that runs a few weeks past your target deadline, or if you have a budget overrun that puts your project in the red soon after you start. But more subtle problems, such as a person who is assigned to work for 24 hours a day for three weeks, also deserve your attention.

In this chapter, you take a look at your resource planning to make sure that your resource assignments are as realistic as possible before you commit to your Project plan.

Keeping Resources in Line

Before you finalize your plan, you have to take into account your resources' workload. When you assigned resources to tasks in your project, you might have unknowingly created situations where your people were working many more hours on a given day than it makes sense to ask somebody to work. These resource overallocations can mean that nobody short of Superman (or Superwoman) can actually perform the work, and if they can, they might send your resource time budget through the roof.

Your first step in solving these resource overbookings is to spot them. Then you have to act to give those poor, overworked folks some relief.

Checking resource availability

You identify the times during your project when people are working more than you want them to by taking a look at some of the views that focus on resource assignments.

Resource Usage view (shown in Figure 2-1) and Resource Graph view (shown in Figure 2-2) are useful in helping you to spot overbooked resources.

Resources are noted as overallocated in these views based on their assignment percentage and calendars. A resource based on a standard eight-hour-day calendar, assigned at 20 percent to a task, will work eight hours a day on it. If you assign that same resource at 50 percent to another task that occurs on the same day, that resource will be assigned to put in 12-hour days (8 plus 4). When that situation happens, Project marks the resource as overallocated.

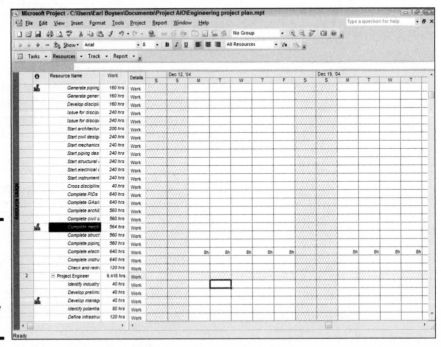

Figure 2-1: Resource Usage view spells out workflow, resource by resource.

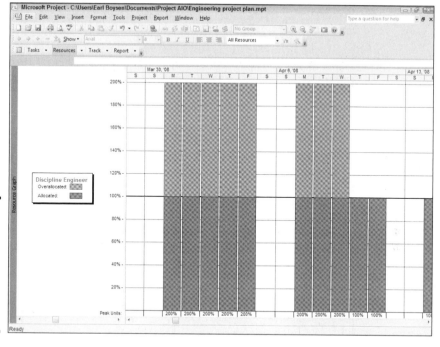

Figure 2-2:
Resource
Graph view
gives you
a visual
clue to
overworked
resources.

If, on the other hand, you create a resource such as a piece of machinery and designate the 24-hour calendar, a 20-percent assignment to a task equals 24 hours of work for a day-long task. If you assigned the same resource at 50 percent to another task the same day, the resource would be working 36 hours in a single day. Even for a piece of machinery, a 36-hour day just doesn't fly.

In Resource Graph view, work is summarized in the Peak Units row. All work in the portion of the bar graphic above the 20 percent mark is displayed in red to indicate the resource is overallocated. All the work below the 20 percent mark is blue and is in line with their calendar and assignment maximum percentages.

In Resource Usage view, all the tasks to which a resource is assigned are listed under the resource name in the Resource Name column. A yellow diamond with an exclamation point in the indicator column indicates an over-allocated resource. The total hours that the resource is working on a selected task is summarized in the Work column.

You can use some of the collaboration features of Project Web Access to get resource availability information online, which can help you resolve resource overallocation problems. See Book II for more about working with Project Web Access.

Picking a method to resolve the conflict

After you review some of Project's views to determine which resources are overbooked, you should resolve the situation before finalizing your plan. What exactly can you do if you discover that some of your resources are as overbooked as an accountant in tax season?

You have a few options:

✦ **Remove a resource from a few tasks to free up some time.**

✦ **Change the Resource calendar to allow the person to have a longer workday (for example, 12 hours).** Keep in mind that this means a 20 percent assignment will have a resource working 12 hours on any one task in a day. If you stretch a resource's workday, you should probably reduce the resource's assignments. For example, if someone frequently puts in 16 hours on two tasks in one day (based on an 8-hour calendar) for two 20-percent assignments, try changing to a 12-hour calendar and 50-percent assignments (6 hours on each of the two tasks, totaling 12 hours a day). However, if the person typically works an 8-hour day and 12- or 16-hour days *are the exception,* you shouldn't change the resource's base calendar because that will have an effect on *all* assignments for that resource.

Keep in mind that the two preceding options might lengthen the tasks that the resource is assigned to, regardless of whether you remove the resource or reduce the resource's assignment.

✦ **Change the resource's availability by increasing her assignment units to more than 20 percent in the Resource Information dialog box.** For example, if you enter **150%** as her available units, you're saying it's okay for her to work 12 hours a day, and Project then considers that she isn't overallocated until she exceeds that 12 hours. The danger here is that you won't get any more alerts when she's working more than 8 hours a day, and most people won't put up with 12 hour days throughout the life of the project.

✦ **Ignore the problem.** This is a real possibility: Sometimes someone working 14 hours *for a day or two* during the life of a project is acceptable. If so, there's no need to change the resource's usual working allocation to make that overwork indicator go away. But if you see that indicator popping up too often, use that notification to make some changes as your project progresses.

See Book V, Chapter 3 for details on exactly how to modify resource assignments.

Finding someone to help

If you find in reviewing your plan that you have resources who are over-booked at various points in time, you have to find a way to cut their work-load down.

One way to help your overbooked resources out is to assign someone to help them on tasks. This can reduce the overbooked resource assignment so that he or she doesn't have to put in as many hours.

By adding resources to some tasks, you may also shorten the task duration. That means you might free up your resource in time, which could eliminate a conflict with a later task in the project. For example, if in the second week of a two-week task you have a resource overallocated, by shortening that two-week task to be completed in one week, you get rid of the overallocation in week two.

Another option is to reduce the resource's work assignment on one or more tasks — say, by reducing 20 percent assignments to 50 percent. You make this change in the Task Information dialog box on the Resources tab, shown in Figure 2-3, or by selecting the task and clicking the Assign Resources tool to open the Assign Resources dialog box.

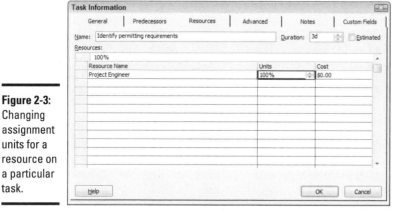

Figure 2-3:
Changing
assignment
units for a
resource on
a particular
task.

Note that you can quickly display a visual representation in the form of a work graph for any resource by clicking the Graphs button in the Assign Resources dialog box.

You can also change the work contour setting for the resource. By default, Project puts a resource to work on a task at the same level of effort for the life of the task. You can modify the work contour to set when the resource works the most and when they work fewer hours. For example, you can set a contour such that a resource puts in the most effort at the start of a task; this frees up the resource's workload later in the life of the task when a conflict with another assignment might exist.

See Book V, Chapter 3 for information about how to apply a work contour to a resource assignment.

Using task drivers to resolve problems

When you give a speech, many factors affect your presentation. You might be getting a cold, the audience might be drowsy from a big lunch, or your equipment might malfunction. In the same way, the timing of every task in your project is likely to be affected by several conditions, which Microsoft Project refers to as task drivers. The Task Drivers feature in Project helps you recognize these conditions, including

+ **Actual Start Date or Assignments:** You've entered an actual start date, or you've made a resource assignment to a task and the resource isn't available.

+ **Leveling Delay:** If you turned on leveling to deal with resource overallocations, that feature might have caused a delay on a task.

+ **Constraints:** You apply a constraint to a task, such as forcing it to finish on a certain date.

+ **Summary Tasks:** Summary tasks' timings are driven by the timings of their child tasks or subtasks.

+ **Dependency Relationships:** A predecessor or successor task can cause changes in a task's timing.

To display task driver information, simply click the Task Drivers button on the Standard toolbar (it looks like a taskbar with an arrow and question mark above it). The Task Drivers pane appears (see Figure 2-4). Here the various conditions driving a task's timing are listed. You can click another task to display its drivers; click the Close button in the Task Drivers pane to close it when you're done.

Change Highlighting

The Change Highlighting feature is useful to help you see how changes you make to fine-tune your project schedule may have an impact on your project. You can click the Show Change Highlighting/Hide Change Highlighting button on the Standard toolbar to toggle this feature on and off. When you turn on Change Highlighting and take any action that changes your project's schedule, a highlight appears on every task that has been impacted by that change (see Figure 2-5).

Task Drivers button

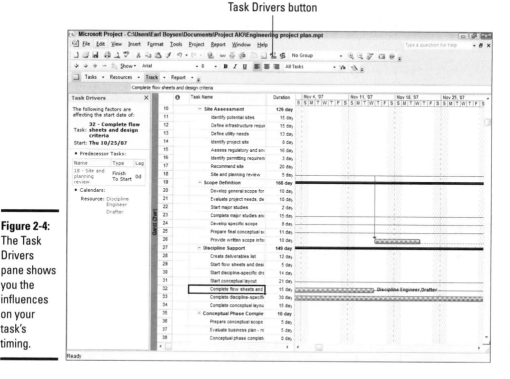

Figure 2-4:
The Task Drivers pane shows you the influences on your task's timing.

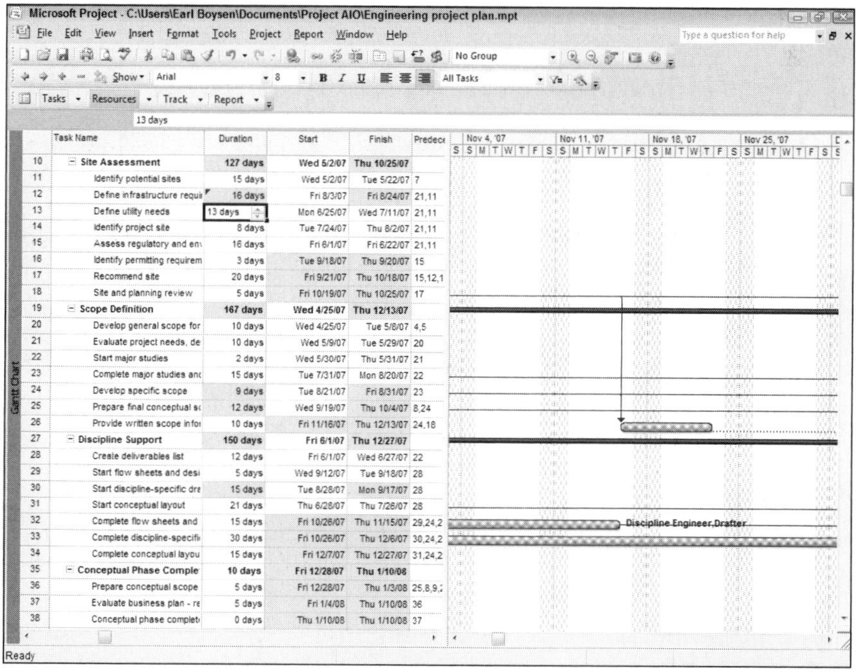

Figure 2-5:
Change Highlighting lets you see what effect your changes have on your project.

Change Highlighting shows you only the results of the last change you made and works only on scheduling changes.

Undoing again and again

Multiple Undo is a long-awaited feature finally appearing in Project 2007. Although you've probably used multiple undo in several other software programs, essentially allowing you to undo a series of actions rather than just the last action, it took time to get this feature to work in Project.

What was the big challenge in implementing this feature? Because of the complex nature of a Project plan with its series of tasks, resource assignments, dependencies, and so on, individual changes to anything in your project plan can have several results. For that reason, undoing several actions in a row was a major technology challenge.

In the past, if you wanted to try out different scenarios that involved several changes to your project, you had to do an action and then undo it, then do the next action and undo it, and so on, which was time-consuming and didn't really allow you to see the cumulative effect of your actions. With Multiple Undo, you can try out several changes and then undo the whole list of changes or only a portion of them. Because you often need to try out several changes when finalizing or making adjustments to a project — for example, changing the timing of several tasks or the hourly rates of several resources — Multiple Undo can be a very useful feature.

How task drivers help pinpoint problems

Company: A Midwestern gourmet food company.

Project: Market research for a new soup product line.

Challenge: To research the potential market and competition for a new line of gourmet soups.

The pivotal phase in this market research project is the generation of a preliminary report for senior management recommending whether the company should proceed with the new product line. Currently the task is finishing two weeks late.

Solution: Before that report can be generated, several other phases (but not all) must be complete. By turning on the Task Drivers feature of Project, you can see the following factors driving the timing of the Generate Preliminary Report summary task:

- Dependencies exist between this task and three other summary tasks: Competitive Research, Market Assessment, and Pricing Analysis.

- There's a constraint on the task to finish no earlier than the last day of the company's third quarter.

Resource leveling has been turned on and is causing a two-day delay of the task.

Glancing at this project, you might surmise that the most likely culprit is the task constraint. This

could force the task to end no sooner than the end of the quarter, which is in fact the current end date. Though the project planner was originally given that target date for the report, the project is ahead of schedule. By forcing the task to end no sooner than that date, Project is actually delaying the end of the task to be two weeks later than it could be if that constraint were removed.

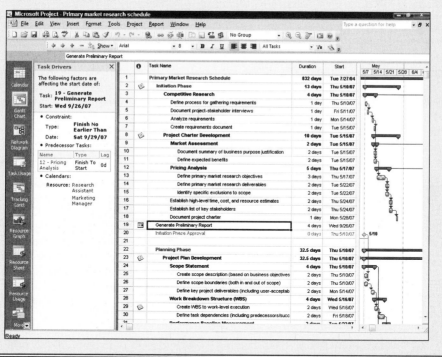

Book VII Chapter 2

Solving Resource Conflicts

You do have to undo all changes in order. For example, if you made seven changes and you want to undo the fourth change, you have to undo changes one through four.

To undo a change or series of changes, click the down arrow of the Undo button on the Standard toolbar and then choose the change you want to undo (see Figure 2-6). That change and all others you performed subsequent to it are undone.

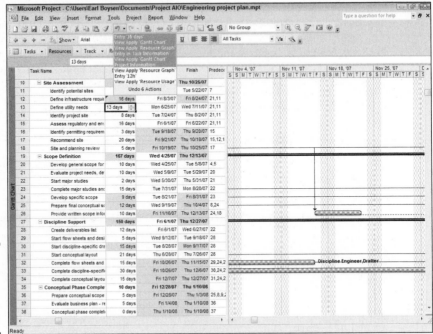

If you choose a high number of Undo operations, it can slow down your computer a tad because it then must keep that many actions in memory.

Leveling to fix resource problems

Resource leveling is a calculation that Project makes to try to resolve resource overallocations in your project. The feature uses two approaches: delaying a task until the overbooked resource frees up, or splitting tasks. Splitting a task stops the tasks at some point, thereby freeing up the resource. The task then resumes at a later time when the resource is available.

You can, of course, make such changes yourself, but leveling is a way to automate the process, leaving the calculation to Project. Here's how leveling works:

1. Project first delays tasks that involve overallocated resources to use up any available slack.

2. When no more slack is available on these tasks, Project makes changes based on any priorities you've entered for tasks, dependency relationships that are affected, and task constraints (such as a Finish No Later Than constraint).

You can turn on leveling to see what changes Project would make and then clear the leveling to reverse those actions if you don't like the results. Or, if you like some of the changes but not others, turn off leveling and manually implement only the changes you prefer. Do be aware that if you leave on the automatic leveling setting mentioned in the following steps, it may make dramatic changes to your schedule that you may or may not notice!

To level the resources in your project, follow these steps:

1. **Choose Tools⇨Level Resources.**

The Resource Leveling dialog box appears, as shown in Figure 2-7.

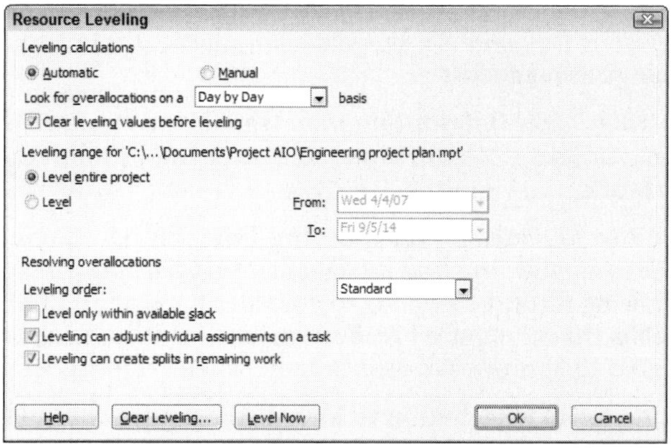

Figure 2-7:
You can control some aspects of the resource-leveling calculation.

Book VII
Chapter 2

Solving Resource
Conflicts

2. **Make a choice between allowing Project to do Automatic or Manual leveling:**

• *Automatic* tells Project to level every time you change your plan.

• *Manual* requires that you go to the Resource Leveling dialog box and click Level Now.

3. **If you choose to level automatically, be sure to enable the Clear Leveling Values Before Leveling check box if you want previous leveling actions reversed before you level the next time.**

4. **Set the leveling range to either**

• *Level Entire Project*

• *Level: <a date range>*

5. **If you chose *Level: <a date range>*, fill in a date range by making choices in the From and To boxes.**

6. **From the Leveling Order drop-down list, click the down arrow and make a choice:**

   - *Standard* considers slack, dependencies, priorities, and constraints.

   - *ID Only* delays or splits the task with the highest ID number; in other words, the last task in the project.

   - *Priority, Standard* uses task priority as the first criterion in making choices to delay or split tasks (rather than using up slack).

7. **Select any of the four check boxes at the bottom to control how Project will level:**

   - *Within Available Slack:* No critical tasks are delayed, and your current finish date for the project is retained.

   - *Adjusting Resource Assignments:* This allows Project to remove or change assignments.

   - *Splitting Tasks Only for Unstarted Work in the Project:* This can put some tasks on hold for a period of time until resources are freed up for work.

   - *Relative to Booking Type:* Booking Type (proposed or committed) relates to how firm you are in using that particular resource. Allowing resource leveling to consider a resource's booking type means that committed resource assignments are considered more sacred than proposed assignments when Project goes about making.

8. **Click the Level Now button to have Project perform the leveling operation.**

It's a good idea to display Leveling Gantt view to see what changes leveling has wrought. If you don't like what you see, to reverse leveling, go to the Resource Leveling dialog box (Tools➪Level Resources) and click the Clear Leveling button.

Combining Solutions

We have one more point to make about all the solutions suggested in this chapter that can help you deal with time, cost, and overallocation problems. In many cases, you'll probably have to use a combination of all of these methods to get to a usable project plan.

Making the leveling choice

Resource leveling has its pros and cons. It can make changes that you might not want it to make — for example, taking a resource off a task where you absolutely need that person to supervise the other resources' work. Leveling frequently delays your project's finish date, which might not be acceptable to you (or your client).

For that reason, the safest setting for Resource Leveling — that is, the one that makes the least drastic changes to your project's timing — is to level only within slack. This setting might delay some tasks, but it won't delay your project completion date.

If you just can't live with everything Resource Leveling did, the capability to turn Resource Leveling on and off is your best ally. You can turn on the feature and look at the things it did to resolve resource problems. When you turn it off, any changes it made are reversed.

Still, if you're absolutely stuck as to how to resolve resource problems in a complex project, leveling can be a handy, quick way to make all those problems go away.

Although you might initially look for one quick fix (you're only human), in reality, the best solution might come through making a dozen small changes. And even then, solving these problems is often a trial-and-error process.

Take the time to find the best combination of solutions for your project to make your plan the best it can be before you launch it.

Chapter 3: Reviewing Timing and Costs

In This Chapter

✔ **Viewing timing information**

✔ **Saving time**

✔ **Saving money**

✔ **Keeping your schedule realistic**

The two key issues for most people when trying to finalize their project plan are time and money. When that finish date is staring back at you, a full three months later than the date your boss gave you, it gives you pause. If the total project costs are 50 percent higher than you'd hoped, you still have some work to do (if costs are lower, count your blessings and send your plan off to your boss right away).

In this chapter we explore some steps you can save to trim time and dollars from your plan before you hand it in to the powers that be.

Timing is Everything

The weekly staff meeting has just ended. As you linger over your last bit of donut, you realize you and your boss are the only two left in the room. Your boss turns to you and asks you, after weeks of planning, if you're finally ready to commit to a final project date. Your palms sweat, you gulp down the last bit of donut, add a week to the last finish date Project gave you to cover yourself, and then you promise to deliver the impossible.

Before you go to your boss and make any promises, make sure you're comfortable with two things: the total time it takes to complete the project and the critical path (the longest series of tasks that must be completed on time in order for you to meet the overall project deadline).

Project allows you to feel much more confident about committing to a timeframe because you can see how long all your tasks will take to complete. You can use a variety of views and tables of data to get as much detail as you like about your task and project timing.

On a macro level, the timing data for your project summary task tells you how long the entire project will take. Just display Gantt Chart view and look at the Duration, Start, and Finish columns for the project summary task (see Figure 3-1).

To get into the details of your task timing, you can examine the chart pane of Gantt Chart view, Task Usage view (shown in Figure 3-2), which shows you the hours of work on tasks week by week, or even Calendar view, shown in Figure 3-3. For many people, seeing tasks laid out on a calendar is the easiest way to visualize how many months or even years a project is taking.

Project summary task

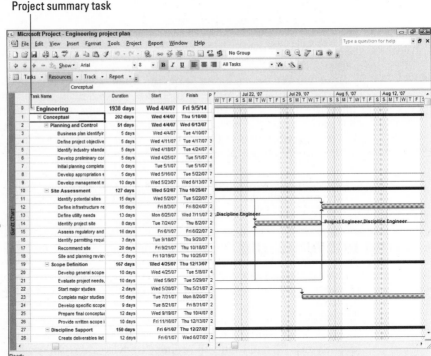

Figure 3-1: The summary task for your project tells you your project length.

Doing It All in Less Time

If you do your homework and make your plan realistic, the price you pay might be that you end up with a really long project. What happens when your project finish date just isn't acceptable to your manager? That's when you have to try a few tactics that might help you keep your schedule under control.

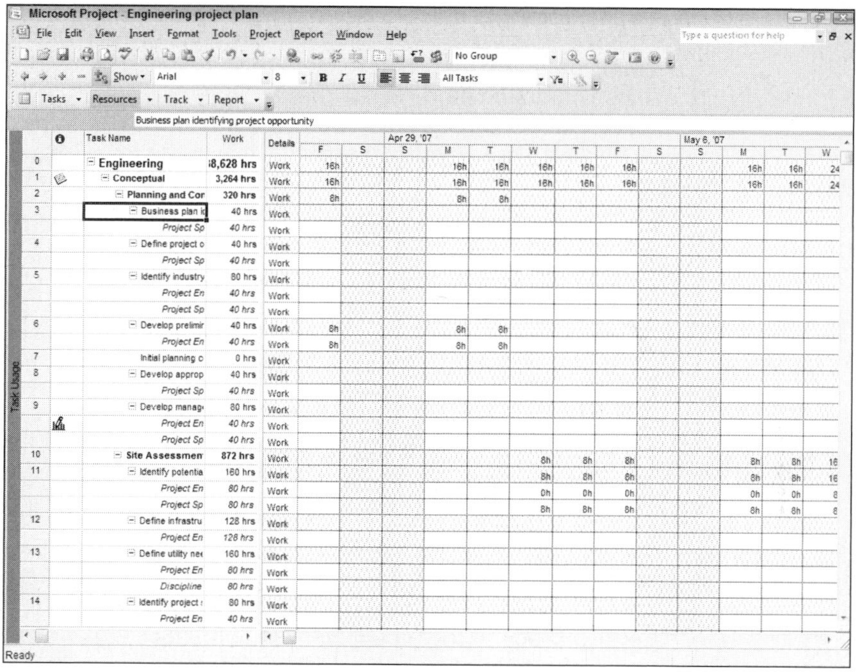

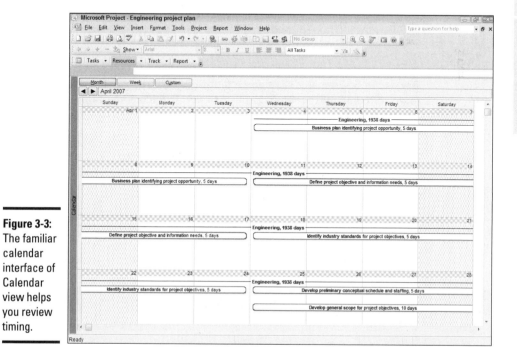

Figure 3-2:
Task Usage view helps you tally the amount of work going on each day of your project.

Figure 3-3:
The familiar calendar interface of Calendar view helps you review timing.

Check your dependencies

The timing of your plan is determined, to a great extent, by the timing relationships you build among tasks: that is, by *dependencies*. When you review your plan to see whether you can save some time, take a look at those dependencies to see whether you built them in the most logical way possible.

Perhaps you didn't start one task until another was completely finished, but could you actually start the second task two days before the end of its predecessor?

Here are some examples of dependencies that could do with some tweaking:

- ✦ You delayed the start of your office move until new office furniture arrived. But could you start moving smaller boxes and supplies three days before all the furniture is in place? Building in that little bit of overlap between these two tasks might save you some time.

- ✦ You created a finish-to-start relationship for the *Do Research* and *Write Speech* tasks, such that you couldn't start writing the speech until your research was finished. But is that true? Can't you do a first draft of the speech when you're three-fourths of the way through the research? Getting a second task going before the first is complete can save you time, especially when you have two different resources working on those tasks.

Use the Task Drivers feature, covered in Chapter 2 of this minibook, to spot what's driving the timing of tasks.

Over the life of a project with hundreds of tasks, adding overlap to even a few dozen tasks might save you a month of time or more! If you have a very large schedule and reviewing all the dependencies is daunting, start by reviewing any dependencies between just the summary tasks and milestones.

You can take a refresher course in creating and changing dependencies in Book IV, Chapter 3.

Rethinking your resource needs

Another factor that drives timing in your project is the availability of resources. Sometimes you set a dependency relationship to deal with the fact that one task can't start before another is over because the resources aren't available until the predecessor task is over. When finalizing your plan, you might find that those provisions for resource schedules are no longer needed or that you can rearrange your resources or call in outside help to save time.

Here are a few things to look for with resource-dependent timing:

✦ Maybe you delayed the start of a task because a resource wasn't available. But can some other resource do the work? If so, switch resources and let the task start sooner.

✦ Project calculates the duration of some tasks (fixed work and fixed units with effort-driven scheduling) according to the number of resources available to do the work. If you add resources to those tasks, Project shortens their duration.

✦ If you assign a more skilled resource to some tasks, you might be able to shorten the hours of work required to complete the task because the skilled person will finish the work more quickly.

✦ Can you hire an outside vendor to handle the work? If you have money but no time or resources, that's sometimes a viable option.

Book V, Chapter 3 covers the mechanics of making and changing resource assignments.

Modifying task constraints

Task constraints have a great impact on a task's timing. By default, all tasks start with the As Soon As Possible constraint, meaning that as soon as all dependency obligations are met, the task will start. Other task constraints, such as No Earlier Than or No Later Than essentially force your task timing to align with a particular date.

Display task drivers and look for any task whose timing is being controlled by a constraint that you might just be able to do without. For example, say you created a task called Publish Annual Report and you set a No Earlier Than constraint such that you couldn't publish the report before you announced your earnings to the press. In reviewing your project, you realize that you can publish the report, but you just can't distribute it. If you ditch that constraint, you might find that the task gets completed earlier, which lets another task finish earlier . . . and so on. The overall impact on timing might surprise you!

Delete the tasks you don't need

If you really have to squeeze your schedule and you can't find anything about the dependencies or resources to help you do it, consider cutting back on tasks. Can you skip that final quality check, the one that occurs after the other three you built in? Would it be okay to hold two focus groups instead of three?

Maybe you can find a new home for some of the tasks. For example, can you get some other project manager to handle some of your tasks for you with different sets of resources? If your buddy has a project that involves the marketing launch for a new printer, can you convince him to also write the in-box glossy assembly instructions, which was your responsibility to begin with? It's worth a shot.

If you think a major shift is necessary to make your project fly, see Chapter 4 of this minibook for information about redefining the project's scope.

Getting It for Less

Here are some tips for trimming that bottom line:

+ **Use cheaper resources.** Do you have a high-priced engineer on a task that can be performed by a junior engineer? Did you assign a high-priced manager to supervise a task that could be handled by a lower-priced line supervisor?

+ **Lower fixed costs.** If you allowed for the travel costs associated with four plant visits, can you manage with only three? Can you book flights ahead of time and get cheaper airfares? Can you find a cheaper vendor for that piece of equipment you allocated $4,000 to buy? Or can you make do with the old equipment for just one more project?

+ **Cut down on the overtime.** Are resources that earn overtime overallocated? Try cutting down their hours or using resources on straight salary for those 14-hour days.

+ **Do it in less time.** Resource costs are a factor of task durations, hourly wages, or number of units. If you change tasks so that fewer work hours are required to complete them, they cost less. However, don't be unrealistic about the time it will *really* take to get the work done.

Making Your Project Timing Realistic

Up till now, we've been talking about reviewing your project to save time or money, but after you've done all that corner-cutting to meet expectations for your project, you should perform a reality check. That means taking a look at the tasks on your critical path and building in some slack to allow for inevitable delays and problems.

Reviewing the critical path

Remember that the critical path is the longest series of tasks in your project that can't be delayed without delaying your end date. If every task in your project is critical, absolutely nothing can change without causing you to miss your target finish date. If, however, you have plenty of noncritical tasks, you have already built some spare time into your plan.

You can use filters and groups to identify the critical path in, for example, Gantt Chart view or Network Diagram view. If you judge that too many tasks are on the critical path, it's wise to add some slack to the plan to allow for inevitable delays (see the section "Giving yourself some slack," later in this chapter).

Figure 3-4 shows Network Diagram view of a project with way too many tasks on the critical path for comfort. (See Book VII, Chapter 1 for more about applying filters such as the one for critical path.)

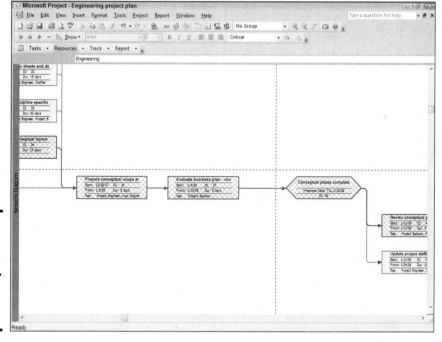

Figure 3-4: With all tasks on the critical path, there's no room for error.

How many critical paths are enough?

A group of settings on the Calculation tab of the Options dialog box concerns how Project handles critical path calculations.

The Inserted Projects Are Calculated Like Summary Tasks option is straightforward. If you insert another project as a task in your project, having this setting selected allows Project to calculate one critical path for your entire project. If you don't select it, any projects you insert are treated like outsiders — that is, they're not taken into account in the master project's critical-path calculations. If an inserted project won't have an effect on your project's timing, you might want to clear this option.

If following one project's critical path is too tame for you, try getting critical with multiple paths. By selecting the Calculate Multiple Critical Paths option, you set up Project to calculate a different critical path for each set of tasks in your project. Doing so can be helpful if you want to identify tasks that, if delayed, will cause you to miss your final project deadline or the goals of a single phase in your project.

Finally, you can establish what puts a task on the critical path by specifying the number of days of slack critical tasks might have. By default, tasks with no slack are on the critical path. However, you can change this situation if you want to be alerted that tasks with only one day of slack are critical — figuring that one day isn't much padding and that these tasks are still in jeopardy.

If you want all the settings on the Calculation tab to pertain to all projects, click the Set as Default button before clicking OK to save the new settings in the Options dialog box.

Giving yourself some slack

How many tasks should be on the critical path in your project, and how many should have some slack — that is, some time that they can be delayed without delaying the entire project? We wish we could give you a formula, but sadly, it's not a science. Ideally, every task in your project *should* have slack because things can come up that you never expected (shortages of vital materials, asteroid strikes, management turnover that places you in an entirely different department). If you add slack to each and every task, however, your project is probably going to go on into the next millennium. Figure 3-5 shows a more typical scenario, with a mix of noncritical and critical tasks.

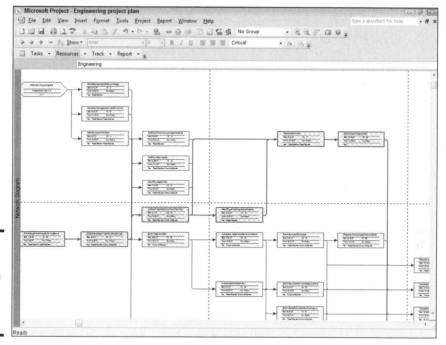

Figure 3-5:
Follow the critical path in Network Diagram view.

Some tasks have slack naturally because they occur during the life of a longer task with which they share a dependency. The shorter task could actually be delayed until the end of the longer task without delaying the project.

Think about this example: You can start installing the plumbing and electrical elements of a new office building as soon as the framing inspection is complete. The plumbing takes two weeks, and the electrical work takes one week. The next task, mechanical inspection, can't happen until both the plumbing and electrical tasks are finished. The shorter of the two (electrical) has a week of slack because nothing else can happen until the dependent task, plumbing, is finished (as in Figure 3-6). However, if electrical runs one week late, the electrical task becomes critical.

Never, we repeat, *never* get rid of all the slack in your schedule. Otherwise, it will come back and haunt you like the Ghost of Christmas Past. Just tell your boss we said so.

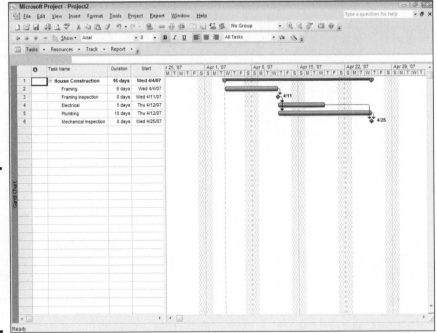

Figure 3-6:
Taskbars
help you
visualize
slack
available to
tasks not on
the critical
path of your
project.

These natural cases of slack occur in any project. In many cases, though, you have to build in slack. Slack can be added in a couple ways.

First, you can simply inflate task durations. Add two days to the duration of all the tasks in your project, or go in and examine each task to figure out the risk of delay and pad each duration accordingly. This method is a little problematic, however, because when changes occur, you might have to go into many tasks and adjust durations to deal with a schedule that's ahead or behind. You also have to keep track of exactly how much slack you built into each task.

The second method of building in slack is the one we like best. You build one slack task or several slack tasks that occur throughout your project — say, one at the end of each phase of the project.

As things slide in your project (and they will, trust us), you'll spot that slack is being eaten up because the slack task is suddenly ending later than the date you'd wanted the phase to end. You can change the duration of the slack task, reflecting the fact that your slack is being used up. The duration of that task gives you a good indication of how much more time you have before the entire phase goes critical.

Slack by any other name

Now, there's one must-do here, even if it seems obvious: Don't call this task *Slack*. Nobody in a position of responsibility would be caught dead approving slack time for anybody. Give slack tasks appropriately respectable names that reflect useful (but admittedly, somewhat generic) activities — say, *Engineering Analysis*, or *Debriefing*, or *CYA Meeting*. Then give the task a duration that provides breathing space for the other tasks in that phase. For example, at the end of a two-month phase of designing a new product package, you might add a task called *Design Debriefing* and make it one week long. (That way, if a sudden mandate for design tweaks comes out of nowhere, you're covered.) Then create a dependency between that task and the last "real" task in the phase. We're not talking dishonesty here — just reality. In the real world, slack is indispensable.

Chapter 4: Putting Final Changes into Place

In This Chapter

✔ **Redefining the scope of your project**

✔ **Breaking off a piece of your project**

✔ **Selling changes to shareholders**

✔ **Cutting corners: Quality versus cost**

*I*n the preceding chapters in this minibook, we explore specific changes you can make to your tasks and resources to fine-tune your Project plan.

In this chapter, we tackle the sometimes-painful, big-picture changes that are occasionally necessary to get to a plan you and your management can live with.

We explore some more comprehensive changes to the scope, timing, and quality of your project, and then we tell you how to pitch your final project and any changes to it to your management.

Getting to a Final Project Plan

Say that you've done everything you can to tweak the timing and costs on your project, and you still end up with a finish date that's one month too late, and you're $10,000 over budget. What can you do on a strategic level to get to a final project plan that you can get buy off on and begin to implement?

You can try several tactics, including redefining your project scope, splitting off a piece of the work to become a different project, and cutting some serious corners on quality of your deliverables.

Redefining the scope of your project

When you've pushed and pulled and tried every single thing you can think of to get your project plan to work, it might be time to revisit the project scope. In essence, you're analyzing whether you bit off more than you can chew and still meet the schedule and budget requirements for the project.

In Book I, Chapter 3 we introduce the concept of a project goal and project scope. In brief, the scope of your project should define both what a project will involve and what it won't involve, and should include specifics about the project budget, timeframe, and deliverables in a scope statement.

So, first revisit a sample scope statement from Book I:

> This project will involve all the steps involved to design and implement a new shopping cart feature (but does not include maintaining or refining it once launched). The cost of the project will not exceed $25,000 and implementation must be completed before October 1st to accommodate holiday sales traffic. The new shopping cart feature should help to increase sales by allowing customers more options to review their orders, give them more frequent opportunities to shop for more items after they have added a product to the cart, and allow them to save their cart contents and come back to complete the sale at a future date. The new feature must function on our existing Web technology infrastructure.

How might you revise this if you find your schedule is running long or you're overbudget? In this case, you have a few options:

✦ Can the project include just design and not implementation of the feature? Or can it include design and a prototype, but not the final implementation?

✦ Could you revise the cost of the project to total $30,000 instead of $25,000?

✦ Can you change the final implementation date from October 1st to December 1st?

✦ Is there one aspect of the new shopping cart feature that you can leave to a future project? For example, what if you didn't include the ability for customers to save contents for future visits but add that on at a later date?

Product scope versus project scope

Projects involve two kinds of scope: product scope and project scope. Here's how they differ:

✦ **Product scope addresses the feature set and quality of whatever it is your project will deliver.** If you can sacrifice a product feature or a bit of quality without any serious impact, you might want to change the product scope.

✦ **Project scope concerns how many tasks you can accomplish.** You might choose to keep the original product scope, but just not get as far in the process as you thought you would, and hence modify project scope. This might mean that you handle the product launch or development or testing, but you leave it to somebody else to handle some other aspect of the project in another timeframe and budget.

Give careful thought to which of these you might want to modify. Either will have an impact on your final result, but one might be more acceptable than the other to you, your management, or your client.

In Project, consider using the linking feature discussed in Book III, Chapter 4 to link any split-off project to your project so you can keep tabs on its progress.

Cutting corners: The quality factor

If you decide that it's product scope you want to change, you're facing the challenge of sacrificing quality. You have decided that to save time and money, you will end up with a lesser product. That product might be a literal product that you manufacture, such as shoes, or it might be a service you provide or a procedure you're performing, such as a new drug test.

Take into account your internal or external client's priorities and any safety or regulatory requirements in taking this path. If the FDA says you have to perform a certain number of tests on a new drug to ensure its quality, skipping a test isn't an option. If your client wants to produce the very best gourmet food on the market, skimping on quality won't meet her needs. If, however, one less focus group or a slightly lower-quality ingredient will do just as well, you might consider modifying product scope.

Breaking off a piece of your project

If you decide that project scope is where you want to cut, you can take a discreet portion of your project, such as the packaging design phase shown in Figure 4-1, and either have somebody else handle it or turn those tasks into another project that you'll deal with down the road. You'll still get everything done, but not within the current budget or time period.

Modifying project scope typically means getting your client's or management's buy-in. They have to agree to more time to deal with a portion of the tasks later on and more money to fund a split-off project.

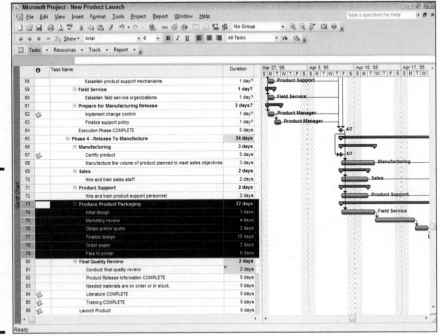

Figure 4-1:
Removing
an entire
phase for
somebody
else to deal
with is
sometimes
a good
solution.

Selling Changes to Shareholders

One of the biggest challenges in making drastic changes to make your project plan workable is selling your solution to your management.

Your task at this point is to document why it's impossible to meet a particular schedule or budget and to suggest alternatives. We hate to say it, but sometimes presented with this evidence, management says do the impossible anyway. Documenting your concerns is your best hedge against that fateful day when you fail. It's a corporate version of "I told you so," but you might find that it has you looking like the smart guy instead of the loser.

The following sections discuss some tools you can use to document your concerns.

Using Project's tools to close the "sale"

Project offers several useful features to help you at this point:

✦ The ability to make changes to a project easily allows you to try out various What If scenarios. Cutting costs by taking resources off of tasks results in a longer schedule. Adding resources to save time costs more, and so on.

✦ Use Change Highlighting (see Figure 4-2) to show how certain changes affect the schedule. If you changed the duration for a certain task in your project, you can highlight how that change had an impact on several others.

✦ Use reports or print views to show your management these various scenarios or alternative project plans (see Figure 4-3). Project Visual Reports can help you make a strong impact on your audience.

✦ Use filters to help your bosses focus on areas such as the critical path (see Figure 4-4). Being able to see the critical path helps you to demonstrate how little spare time your plan provides, and hence how unrealistic forcing you to stick to it might be.

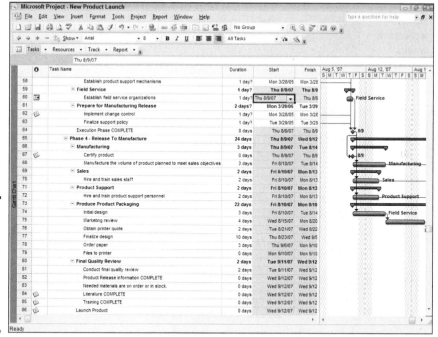

Figure 4-2: Change Highlighting calls attention to the results of changes you make.

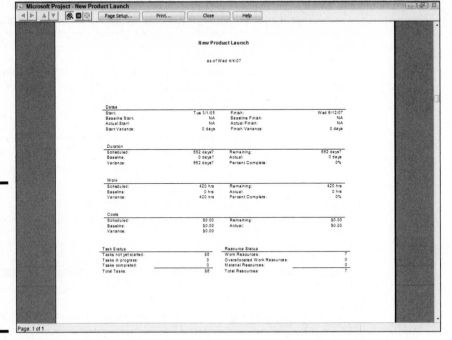

Figure 4-3: Printing your Gantt Chart or another view can help document issues.

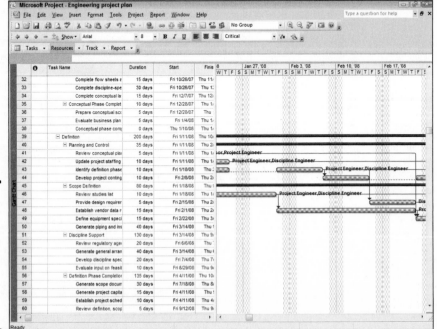

Figure 4-4: Highlighting critical tasks in a project with a tight schedule can be a useful tool.

Creating a compression table

A compression table is a good tool to use when your management has insisted that you save time or money on your project, and you want to show the tradeoffs involved in either action. This isn't a feature of Project, it's just a useful way that project managers have found to document change for your bosses, so it's worth knowing about.

A compression table such as the one shown here might show more aggressive dates alongside the current plan, highlighting the proposed compressed duration for the project and the potential cost savings.

Table 4-1	A Compression Table				
Task Name	*Original Duration*	*Cost*	*Suggested Duration*	*Cost*	*Cost to Compress*
Market Research	2 weeks	$8,000	1 week	$16,000	$8,000
Brochure Design	3 weeks	$15,000	1.5 weeks	$25,000	$10,000
Printing	2 weeks	$14,000	1 week	$20,000	$6,000

A compression table might help everybody see the most logical tradeoff to make. If you need to save a week, and speeding up the brochure design will cost you more than paying a rush fee for printing, it's easy to see that the place to save time is in the printing phase of your project.

Book VIII

Tracking

The 5th Wave   By Rich Tennant

"Why, of course. I'd be very interested in seeing this new milestone in the project."

Contents at a Glance

Chapter 1: Working with Baselines and Interim Plans

Creating tasks, assigning resources, and establishing task dependencies describe the planning phase of creating a project schedule. The planning phase can help you clarify what you need to do and what resources you'll need to do it. But using Project doesn't stop there. When you move into the phase of actually *doing* the project, Project can continue to help you.

If you set a baseline for your project, Project can help you compare your original estimates with what actually occurs and to alert you to shifts in timing. As you see in this chapter, you can set more than one baseline, and you can use interim plans to capture dramatic timing shifts in your project. Finally, you can use the critical path to identify the tasks that will cost you the most, both in time and expense, if they slip.

Understanding Baselines and Interim Plans

As you prepare to track actual progress on a project (discussed in the next chapter of this minibook) you should establish a baseline for your project. The *baseline* is the detailed project plan against which actual work is tracked. Setting a baseline is like taking a picture of your project schedule at the moment your planning is complete but before you begin to record actual information about the progress of your project.

Why set a baseline? Because, by setting a baseline in Project, you give yourself the opportunity, with no added work, to compare the estimates you established during the planning phase of creating your Project schedule with what actually happens as the project progresses. Good project managers use these comparisons to become better project managers. The comparisons present you with the opportunity to learn from your successes and your mistakes — and, face it, none of us is infallible. In our opinion, the worst mistake anyone can make is to not learn from a mistake.

You set a baseline when you finish the planning phase of your project, and, sometimes, you also set a baseline at the end of various phases. The baseline is a set of your project data saved in the same Project file where you track actual progress data.

An interim plan is really very similar to a baseline; the major difference between them is that a baseline stores much more information than an interim plan stores. An *interim plan* stores a set of task start and finish dates that you can compare with another interim plan's start and finish dates or with a baseline plan's start and finish dates, so the focus of an interim plan is to keep an eye on progress or slippage. A baseline, on the other hand, contains much more information; along with start and finish dates, a baseline contains duration, work, and cost information about tasks, resources, and assignments.

Setting a Baseline

You can set up to 11 baselines in your project. Saving baselines increases the size of your Project file; for each baseline you save, Project adds a set of fields to store the baseline information. So, saving 11 sets of baselines can create a really large Project file and slow down Project's calculation of changes to the project schedule.

In addition to slowing down Project's ability to calculate your schedule, saving too many sets of baselines can make the analysis work confusing and more difficult.

That said, when would you need to set more than one baseline? On a shorter project — one that lasts only a few weeks or even a couple of months — you might set one baseline at the end of the planning phase and things might proceed closely enough to your estimates that you won't need any other baselines. On longer projects, you might need to set several baselines along the way, particularly if your original estimate is no longer useful because it differs so much with what's actually taking place. You might want to consider setting a different baseline for each major milestone in your project.

You should always save a baseline at the end of the planning phase of your project, before you start to record actuals. To save a baseline for the entire project, follow these steps:

1. **Complete the planning phase of the project, which includes defining tasks, defining resources (along with resource costs), setting task dependencies, and assigning resources to tasks.**

2. **Save the project.**

You might also want to print the project at this point, before setting the baseline.

3. **Choose Tools⇨Tracking⇨Set Baseline.**

Project displays the Set Baseline dialog box, shown in Figure 1-1.

Figure 1-1:
Use this dialog box to save a baseline.

4. **Click the Set Baseline option.**

5. **Open the Set Baseline drop-down list box.**

6. **Select the baseline that you want to set.**

You can choose from 11 different baselines.

Don't worry about the other options in this dialog box for now; you read about them later in the chapter.

7. **Click OK.**

Project creates the baseline information.

8. **Save your project.**

Project saves the baseline information along with the rest of your project information.

Take a look at a baseline. In Figure 1-2, you see Tracking Gantt view of a project before setting the baseline. In Figure 1-3, you see the same project after setting a baseline. In Tracking Gantt view in Figure 1-3, the bottom bar represents the baseline information and the top bar represents the actual information.

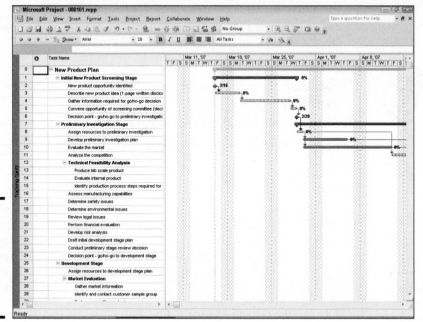

Figure 1-2:
Tracking
Gantt view
of a project
before
setting a
baseline.

Baseline information   Actual information

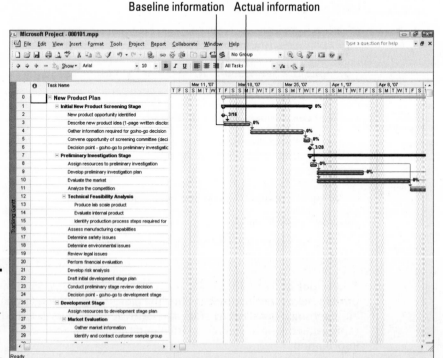

Figure 1-3:
The same
project after
setting a
baseline.

You can compare baseline information with actual information. See the next chapter of this minibook for details.

Saving an Interim Plan

You can use interim plans when the only information you need to track is timing information. You can save up to ten interim plans for your project. Saving interim plans, like setting baselines, increases the size of your Project file. However, setting an interim plan doesn't affect the file size as much as setting a baseline because interim plans store only task start and finish dates, whereas baselines store much more information.

When you save an interim plan, you copy a set of start and finish dates into one of ten other sets of start and finish dates. You can select certain tasks to save in the interim plan, or you can save an interim plan for the entire project. If you want to include only certain tasks in an interim plan — such as future tasks — select those tasks before you start the following steps. To save an interim plan, you follow the same basic steps, with a few changes:

1. **Choose Tools⇨Tracking⇨Set Baseline.**

Project displays the Set Baseline dialog box (see Figure 1-4).

Figure 1-4:
Copy information into an interim plan.

2. **Click the Set Interim Plan option.**

3. **Open the Copy drop-down list box and select the set of data you want to copy to the interim plan.**

4. **Open the Into drop-down list box and select the start and finish fields in which you want to store the interim plan information.**

5. **If you selected tasks before you started these steps, click the Selected Tasks option button; otherwise, click the Entire Project button.**

6. **Click OK.**

Project saves the information in the interim plan fields you selected.

Don't forget to save your project to save your interim plan information.

You can compare interim plan information with actual information. See the next chapter of this minibook for details.

Changing a Baseline or Interim Plan

Sometimes you want to change the baseline or interim plan for some but not all tasks. For example, if you're six months into your project and it's put on hold for three months, you might want to retain the baseline for tasks completed up to this point, modify the timing of future tasks, and reset the baseline only for tasks going forward; that way, you retain the ability to accurately assess, for the entire project, how well you estimated. Or, suppose that you find you need to add a task to the project. For example, you might decide to break one task into two. In this case, you want to save that one task along with the original baseline.

When you add a task to a baseline or an interim plan, you select the task before you open the Set Baseline dialog box. And, Project presents you with some options when you add selected tasks to a baseline. You can choose to roll up baselines to all summary tasks and from subtasks into their parent summary task(s). The relationship between the tasks in the project and the task(s) that you select before you open the dialog box determine the effect of these options.

Suppose that you have a project set up like the one shown in Figure 1-5. Also suppose that you select Task 3, a child of Task 1 and the parent of Tasks 4 and 5, before you open the Set Baseline dialog box. If you select only the From Subtasks into Selected Summary Task(s) check box in the Set Baseline dialog box, Project rolls up the information from Tasks 4 and 5 to Task 3. If you select only the To All Summary Tasks check box, Project rolls up baseline information from Task 3 without regard to the baseline information that is stored for Tasks 4 and 5. Finally, if you select both check boxes, Project rolls up baseline information from Tasks 4 and 5 to Task 3 and then rolls up that information to Task 1.

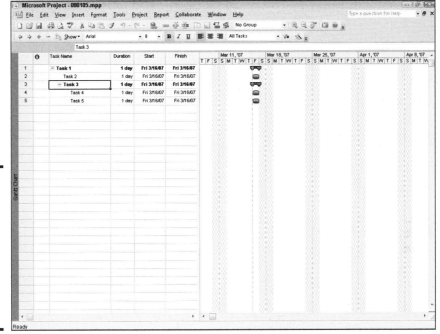

Figure 1-5:
A task's position in the project outline determines baseline information rollup behavior.

You add a task to an interim plan the same way that you add a task to a baseline; since you have additional options to set when you add a task to a baseline, let's look at the steps to add a task to a baseline:

If you want to save changes to an existing task, make those changes and then select the task.

1. **Set up the new task.**

2. **Select the new task.**

3. **Choose Tools➪Tracking➪Set Baseline.**

   The Set Baseline dialog box appears (see Figure 1-6).

4. **From the Set Baseline drop-down list, select the baseline that you want to update.**

5. **Choose the Selected Tasks option button.**

6. **Choose the appropriate Roll Up Baselines settings (described earlier in this section).**

7. **Click OK to save the baseline.**

   The baseline now includes the new task.

**Book VIII
Chapter 1**

**Working with
Baselines and
Interim Plans**

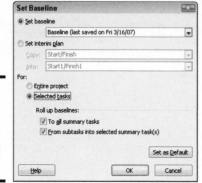

Figure 1-6:
Making
changes to
an already
established
baseline.

If you want Project to roll up baselines or interim plans for selected tasks the same way every time you work with baselines or interim plans for selected tasks, you can select the appropriate rollup setting and then click the Set as Default button.

Clearing Baselines and Interim Plans

Although you really want to try to keep your baselines and interim plans, you might have valid reasons to clear them. For example, suppose that you complete the planning phase of your project, set the baseline, and then receive word that your project is on hold. When you actually start work six months later than you planned, you should set a new baseline so that you'll ultimately have good information for comparison when you review your estimated and actual data.

To clear a baseline, choose Tools⇨Tracking⇨Clear Baseline. Project displays the Clear Baseline dialog box (see Figure 1-7). Using this dialog box, you can clear a baseline plan or an interim plan for the entire project or for selected tasks.

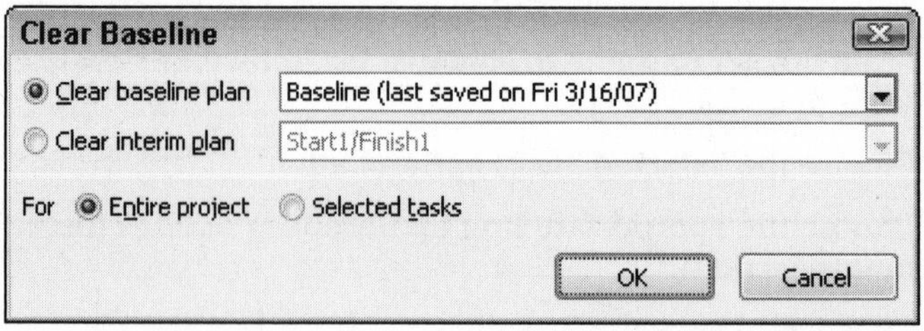

Figure 1-7:
Clear a
baseline or
interim plan
from this
dialog box.

TIP

If you want to clear a baseline or interim plan for only part of the project, select the affected tasks before you open the Clear Baseline dialog box.

Viewing the Critical Path

The *critical path* of your project is composed of those tasks that will cause your project to take longer if any one of the tasks doesn't finish on time. Completing these tasks on time is critical to maintaining the project end date. So, knowing which tasks are critical is important to you as a project manager; you want to monitor those tasks closely.

All Tasks ▾

You can view the critical path of your project in a number of ways; we find filtering Gantt Chart view for critical tasks as the most effective way. In Figure 1-8, you see all the tasks in the project, and in Figure 1-9, we filtered to display only critical tasks. You use the Filter drop-down list box (shown in the margin) on the Formatting toolbar to filter for critical tasks.

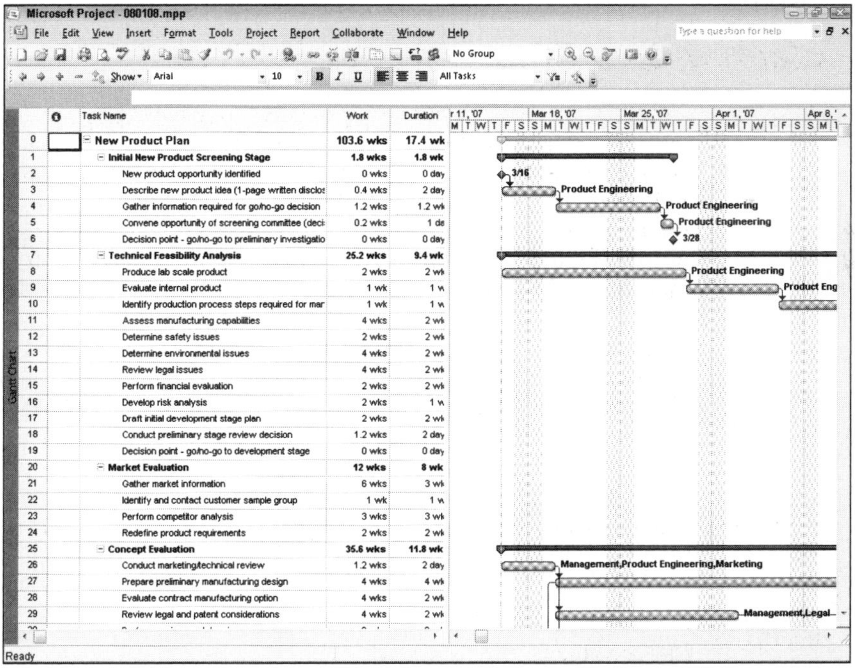

Figure 1-8:
A project before filtering for critical tasks.

Book VIII
Chapter 1

Working with
Baselines and
Interim Plans

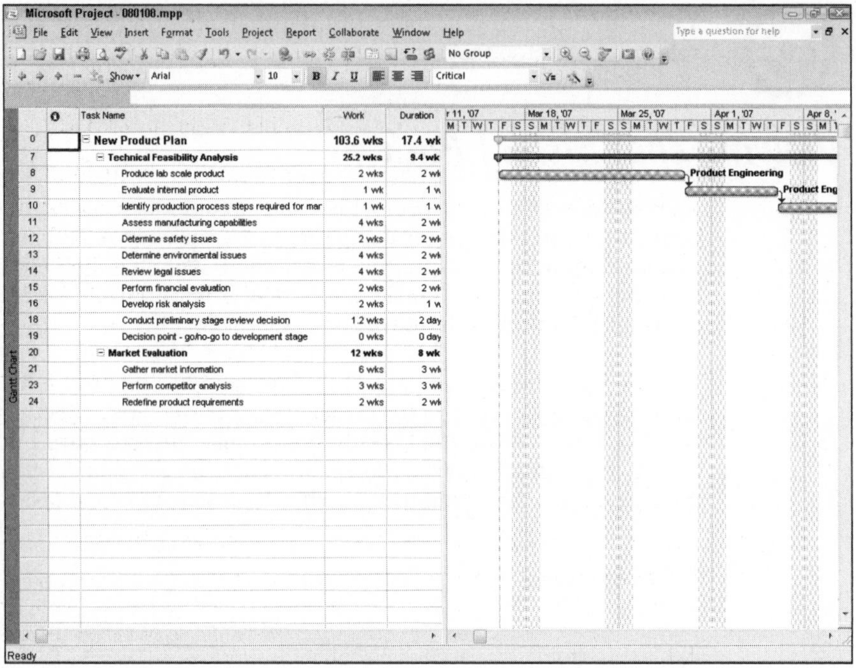

Figure 1-9:
The same
project
filtered to
display only
critical
tasks.

If you like to see all the tasks in your project but want to be able to identify critical tasks, you have a couple of choices:

✦ You can use Tracking Gantt view. In this view, the top bars of critical tasks are red while the top bars of noncritical tasks are blue.

✦ In Network Diagram view, boxes for critical tasks are red, and boxes for noncritical tasks are blue.

✦ You can use the Gantt Chart Wizard, discussed in Book IX, Chapter 2, to color critical task Gantt bars in red in Gantt Chart view.

Noncritical tasks typically have some slack time. *Slack time* is the amount of time that a task can slip before it affects another task's dates or the finish date of the project. Noncritical tasks with slack can start late without affecting the schedule. But remember, a noncritical task can become critical if you use up all of its slack by allowing it to start late or run longer than planned.

Viewing multiple critical paths

Company: Medium-sized firm specializing in managing larger projects.

Project: Manage a larger project with several networks of tasks.

Challenge: Ensure that the project finishes on schedule.

Solution: Larger projects often contain several networks of tasks; within any given network, you can see tasks driving other tasks. The firm can see the project's critical path but has some concerns because the project contains several networks of tasks. From experience, the firm knows that today's task with slack can become tomorrow's critical task.

For this reason, the firm wants to identify not only the project's critical path but also the critical path of each network of tasks. That way, the firm can identify, within a network of tasks, the ones that are critical to finishing the network on time. Finishing a network of tasks on time helps ensure that the project won't slip because a noncritical task becomes critical.

In the figure, you see a project composed of four networks of tasks:

- Network 1: Tasks 1, 2, and 3
- Network 2: Tasks 4 and 5
- Network 3: Tasks 6 through 10
- Network 4: Tasks 11 through 16

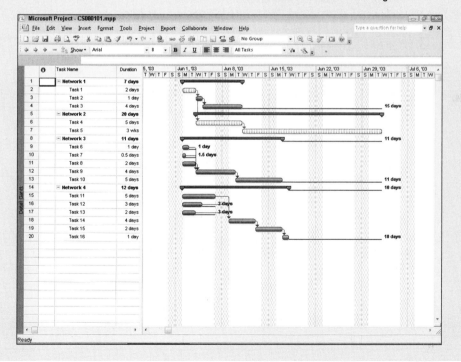

(continued)

(continued)

We've formatted the Gantt bars so that the bars of critical tasks appear with a cross-hatched pattern. (On-screen, they're also red, as you see if you open CS080101.mpp, the Project file for this case study found on this book's Web site.) Notice that the project's critical path involves the tasks in the first two networks.

Although none of the tasks in Network 3 and Network 4 are on the project's critical path, determining which tasks within each network are critical helps you identify the tasks within each network that cannot slip if the network of tasks is to remain on schedule. You can display multiple critical paths — one for each network of tasks — by following these steps:

1. **Choose Tools⇨Options.**

   Project displays the Options dialog box.

2. **Click the Calculation tab.**

3. **Select the Calculate Multiple Critical Paths check box.**

4. **Click OK.**

   Project displays a critical path for each network of tasks.

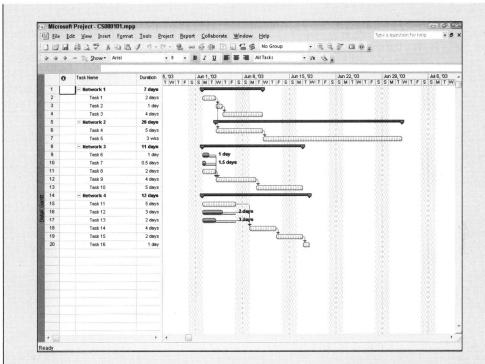

For each task, Project sets its late finish date equal to its early finish date. When a task has no links, it is critical because its late finish is equal to its early finish. If a network of tasks contains slack, like Networks 3 and 4, some tasks are not critical while others are critical. When you view multiple critical paths, you can determine which tasks within a network of tasks must be completed on time to avoid delaying the network.

Chapter 2: Entering Actuals

In This Chapter

✔ **Understanding the tracking process**

✔ **Gathering tracking information**

✔ **Preparing to track**

✔ **Recording actuals**

✔ **Checking the progress**

*A*lthough our book isn't linear in nature, some things about working with projects are linear. You initially identify the project's tasks and set them up, creating dependencies between them and, if necessary, imposing constraints. Next, you work with resources — defining them and then assigning them to project tasks. You typically follow that exercise by focusing on ironing out the kinks in the schedule caused by overallocations or by the schedule predicting that you won't finish on time or within budget. Finally, you hit the magic day when you set a baseline and the project starts.

At this point, you enter a new phase in the project management life cycle that can make you a better project manager. Noting what actually happens during the life of a project — called *tracking* or *recording actuals* — holds the key to obtaining lots of different kinds of valuable information. For example, setting a baseline and recording actuals gives you the ability to compare estimates to actuals. You can use this information to revise your plan to better fit reality, minimizing potential problems or avoiding them altogether. After your project ends, comparing estimates with actuals helps you become a better estimator, and making better estimates makes you a better future project manager.

What's Involved in Tracking?

Mostly, tracking is exactly what you think it is — finding out from those working on the project just where things stand and then entering the information in your Project file. What kind of information do you enter? Well, you enter details such as the actual start date, the actual finish date, and the actual duration of a task. You enter actual time that is worked by resources and actual costs that are incurred. Project uses the information you provide to adjust both the schedule and the project's costs, and you can see the adjustments by using various views. If Project determines that you're running late on a task, you see dependent tasks moved into the future. And, Project adjusts projected total costs using a combination of actual costs and remaining estimates.

You can read more about monitoring progress later in this chapter in the section "Viewing Progress."

After you enter actual information, you can produce reports that show management where your project stands, providing a foundation for requests for more time, more resources, or a shift in strategy if things aren't going as you expected.

Don't wait until the end of a task to enter tracking information. Tracking on a regular basis helps you to identify changes from the estimated schedule. The earlier you spot a delay, the more time you have to make up for it. Wise project managers track activity on a regular basis, such as once a week or every two weeks. Postponing the task of tracking simply makes the task take longer.

You can enter a "Tracking" task in your schedule to help you remember to track. Set it up as a recurring task, and don't forget to estimate the time to collect the tracking information along with the time to enter it.

Collecting Tracking Information

Most of the time, collecting the information isn't a "computer thing." You get tracking information pretty much however you can — having staff meetings, using forms, and getting off-the-cuff updates at the water cooler.

Although it might sound obvious, you should determine exactly what information you need to collect before you dive into collecting information. Information may be power, but too much information is chaos. Besides, if you ask folks for tons of information, you're not likely to get *any* information.

So, how do you decide what information to collect? The information you need to collect depends on the information you need to track. For example, you might need to track only the timeline of a particular project, and therefore you didn't assign resources to tasks. In this case, you need to collect information that identifies how far along a task is — a percent complete value for the task at a given point in time, along with an estimate of remaining work if the task is ahead or behind the original schedule.

In other cases, you might need to manage resources, but you might not need to track whether resources actually perform the amount of work you estimated; that is, you can simply monitor the progress on tasks and let Project assume that the resources assigned to the task split the work evenly. In this case, you can still collect a Percent Complete value for the task at a given point in time, along with an estimate of remaining work if the task is ahead of or behind the original schedule.

But suppose that you need to track exactly how many hours each resource works on a task on a given day to manage resource allocation, to precisely record the work performed, and to determine, at any point in time, whether your project is within budget. In this case, your best bet is to collect time-sheets from resources, along with their best estimates concerning the amount of work remaining to complete a task.

When you exceed your budget on one task, you might be able to make up the difference on another task. So, although you might be overbudget this week, you might be back on track next week.

As you probably expect, Project contains views that make entering actual information easy, regardless of the type of information you collect.

After you identify the information you need to collect, create a short form — the word "short" being the operative word — that asks for the information you need. At a minimum, the form should ask each person whether the task is on schedule and how much of the task is complete. The form should also request a revised estimate of the task's duration and a revised estimate of the work required to complete the task. And, if you need more detail, such as hours worked each day, request a timesheet be attached to your form.

If your organization uses Project Server, each person working on a project can report all this information online, and you can use the information to update your project.

Remember to specify how often you need to receive update information.

Setting Up to Track

Before you start recording tracking information in Project, you should

1. Check your calculation options.
2. Set the status date.
3. Select a tracking view.

The following sections discuss these steps in greater detail.

Checking calculation options

Project contains several calculation options that affect the way Project calculates your project's schedule and costs. You can set these options by choosing Tools⇨Options and, in the Options dialog box that appears, clicking the Calculation tab (see Figure 2-1).

We cover some of these options in other places in the book, so we won't repeat them here. Instead, we focus on the calculation options that affect the way recording actuals affects your project.

You can read about Project's overall calculation options — the first two on the Calculation tab — in Book V, Chapter 4. And, you can read about earned-value calculations in Chapter 3 of this minibook. You can read about critical path calculations in Book VII, Chapter 3, and Book III, Chapter 4 covers inserted projects and how Project calculates them.

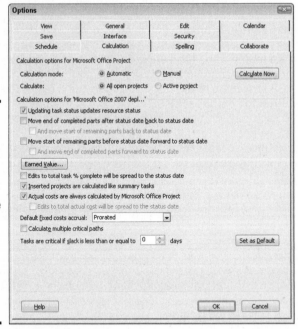

Figure 2-1:
Use the Calculation tab of the Options dialog box to determine the way Project calculates your project's schedule and costs.

Updating resource status using task status

When you select the Updating Task Status Updates Resource Status check box, Project updates the resource status to correspond with any updated task status. This option works in reverse, too. If you update a resource's status, Project also updates the task status accordingly. For example, if you select this check box and update the percentage of completion for a task, Project also updates the % Complete field for the resource and the assignment.

Adjusting task start dates

By default, when tasks begin late or early, Project doesn't change the task start dates or adjust the remaining portions of tasks. You can change this behavior so that Project updates the tasks in relation to the Status Date. The following check boxes affect how Project adjusts for late or early starts:

✦ Move End of Completed Parts after Status Date Back to Status Date

✦ And Move Start of Remaining Parts Back to Status Date

✦ Move Start of Remaining Parts before Status Date Forward to Status Date

✦ And Move End of Completed Parts Forward to Status Date

The first two check boxes work together, and the second two check boxes work together, so we review them as two pairs.

You read about setting the status date in the section "Setting the status date," later in this chapter.

Suppose that you set the Status Date to February 7 and you have a task with a Start Date of February 12 and a duration of 4 days. If the task actually starts on February 5 and you select the *Move End of Completed Parts after Status Date Back to Status Date* check box, Project moves the task start date to February 5, sets the percent complete to 50%, and schedules the start of the remaining work for February 14, creating a split task. If you also select the *And Move Start of Remaining Parts Back to Status Date* check box, Project makes the changes that we just described and moves the start of the remaining work to February 7.

To understand the effects of checking the second pair of boxes, suppose, once again, that the Status Date is February 7 and you have a task with a Start Date of February 1 and a duration of 4 days. Furthermore, suppose that the task actually starts on February 5. If you select the *Move Start of Remaining Parts before Status Date Forward to Status Date* check box, Project leaves the task start date at February 1, sets the percent complete to 50%, and schedules the remaining work to start on February 7 (the status date), again creating a split task. If you also select the *And Move End of Completed Parts Forward to Status Date* check box, Project makes the changes that we just described but also moves the task's actual start date to February 5.

These options apply only when you make total actual value edits, including task total actual work, task actual duration, total percent complete, and percent work complete. These options don't apply when you record actual information on summary tasks or if you use timesheet information from Project Server to update your project.

Spreading changes to Total Task % Complete

By default, the *Edits to Total Task % Complete Will Be Spread to The Status Date* check box is not selected, so Project distributes percent completion changes to the end of the actual duration of the task. If you select this check box, Project distributes the changes evenly across the schedule to the project status date.

Setting cost calculation options

Select the *Actual Costs Are Always Calculated by Microsoft Office Project* check box to have Project calculate actual costs instead of you entering actual costs. If you select this check box, Project overwrites any costs that you enter prior to the task being 100% complete as Project recalculates costs.

You use the Default Fixed Costs Accrual list box to specify the way Project accrues fixed costs for new tasks. Project can accrue fixed costs at the start of a task or at the end of a task, or Project can prorate the costs throughout the duration of the task.

Setting the status date

When you get ready to start recording tracking information, you want to set the Status Date field — the "as of" date for the information you're recording. For example, although today may be March 30, you might want to record information as of March 23.

To set the status date, choose Project⇨Project Information, and Project displays the Project Information dialog box for the current project (see Figure 2-2).

Open the Status Date list box, select the date you want to use when recording actuals, and click OK.

If you don't set the status date, Project uses the current date to recalculate your project when you record actuals.

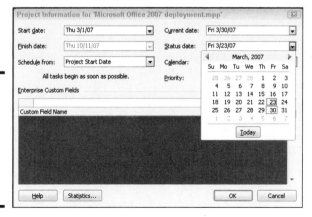

Figure 2-2:
Use this
dialog box
to set the
status date
before
recording
actuals.

Selecting a tracking view

You'll find it easiest to enter actuals in a view that matches the information you plan to record. Earlier in this chapter, in the section, "Collecting Tracking Information," we talk about the kind of information you'll be collecting, and we mention that Project has a view that supports entering actuals, regardless of the information you collect.

You can record actuals by indicating total work or costs for a task or for a resource assignment. The view that you choose depends largely on the level of detail you plan to record.

When you record tracking information for a task, Project allocates the work performed evenly among the resources assigned to the task — even if the resources contributed different amounts of work to achieve the level of completeness you record. To record actuals for tasks without concern for resource assignments, we suggest that you use Task Sheet view with the Tracking table (see Figure 2-3).

You can assign the Tracking table to any task-oriented view. We're using Task Sheet view to keep things simple, but if you like working in Gantt Chart view, that's fine — use the Tracking table in Gantt Chart view.

If you want to record information by task but you also want an accurate record of the amount of work completed by each resource assigned to the task, we suggest that you use Task Usage view with the Tracking table (see Figure 2-4). In this view, Project lists each task and, below the task, displays a line for each resource assigned to the task. You record actual information in the Actual Work column for each resource assigned to the task, and Project calculates and displays the totals for the task in the Actual Work column across from the task name.

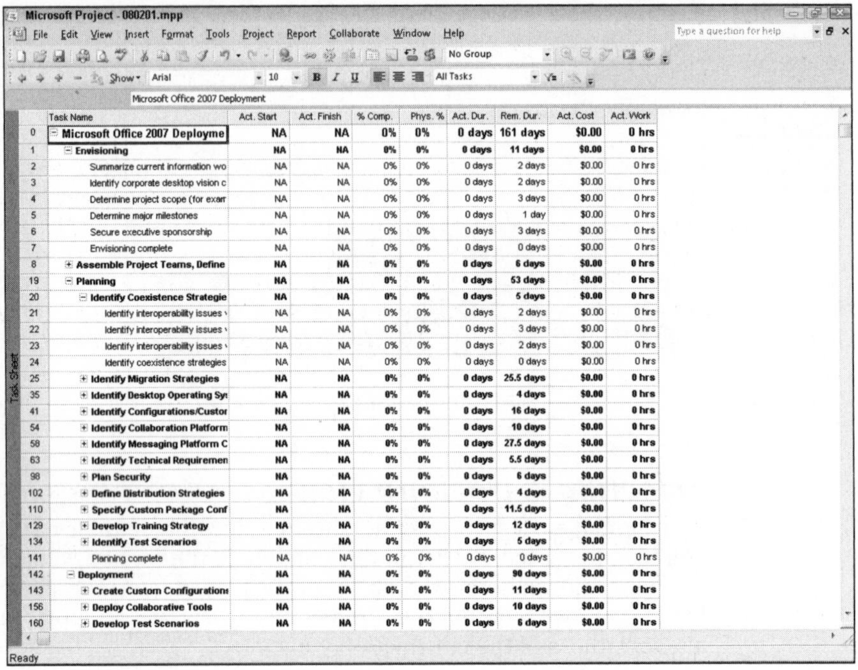

Figure 2-3:
Use Task Sheet view and the Tracking table to record actuals by task.

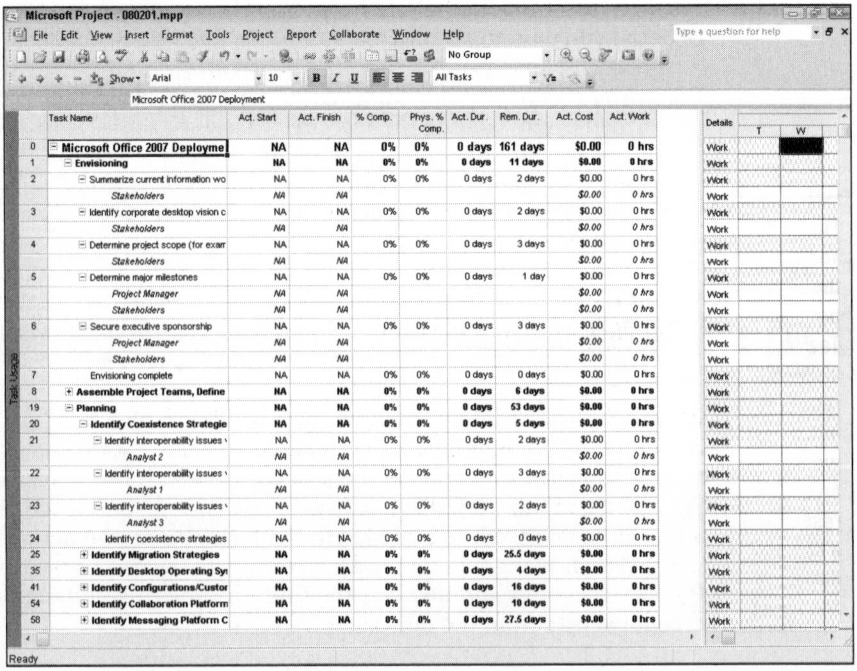

Figure 2-4:
Use Task Usage view to record total actual work by resource.

If you don't care about work by specific resources, you can record tracking information by entering the value on the same row as the task, rather than on the individual rows for the resources. Project divides the actual and remaining work among the resources.

If you want to work from resource timesheets and record hours worked on a task on specific days, you can use Project's *timephased* fields, available on the Details portion — the right side — of Task Usage and Resource Usage views. As you can see in Task Usage view shown in Figure 2-5, these views show, by default, one row — the Work row — along with fields for each day of the week. You can add the Actual Work row to the Details view by right-clicking anywhere on the Details portion of the view and choosing Actual Work from the shortcut menu that appears. Then you can record information on the Actual Work row beside the appropriate resource and in the column of the day on which the work occurred.

In addition to selecting the view and table that best matches your need to enter tracking information, take advantage of the Tracking toolbar (see Figure 2-6). You can display this toolbar by right-clicking in the toolbar area at the top of the screen and choosing Tracking from the shortcut menu that appears.

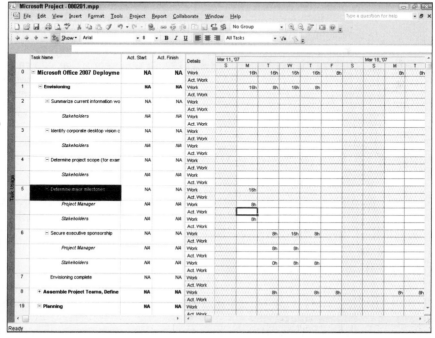

Figure 2-5:
You can use the Details portion of Task Usage view to record actual hours worked by an assigned resource on a specific day.

**Book VIII
Chapter 2**

Entering Actuals

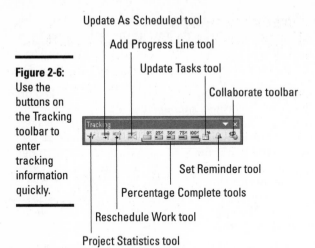

Update As Scheduled tool

Add Progress Line tool

Update Tasks tool

Collaborate toolbar

Figure 2-6:
Use the
buttons on
the Tracking
toolbar to
enter
tracking
information
quickly.

Set Reminder tool

Percentage Complete tools

Reschedule Work tool

Project Statistics tool

Using buttons on the Tracking toolbar, you can display the Project Statistics dialog box, the Collaborate toolbar, and progress lines; you can read more about progress lines later in this chapter, in the section, "Viewing Progress." You can use other tools on the toolbar to mark a task 0%, 25%, 50%, 75%, or 100% complete. When you select a task and click the Update As Scheduled tool on the Tracking toolbar, Project updates the task to the percent complete the task should be based on the status date. The Reschedule Work tool reschedules all tasks that begin after the status date. The Update Tasks tool opens a dialog box that you can use to record tracking information. And, clicking the Set Reminder tool opens a dialog box that you can use to play a sound a specified number of minutes before a task should begin. You might find the sound useful to set a reminder for tasks that represent meetings you need to attend.

Ways to Record Actuals

Project provides you with many ways to record actual information. Typically, when you enter tracking information in one field, Project calculates values for other fields. For example, if you enter a percentage complete for a task, Project calculates and supplies an actual start date, an actual duration, a remaining duration, and an actual work value.

As you record tracking information, Project adjusts your project's cost to reflect the effect of higher-than-expected costs. And, if Project determines that you're running late on a task, it automatically moves dependent tasks into the future.

Estimating the Percent Complete

You can establish the progress of a task by assigning a Percent Complete value to the task. Enter any value less than 100 to indicate that the task is not complete. You can enter a Percent Complete value using Task Sheet view and the Tracking table (see Figure 2-7), and you can use the tools on the Tracking toolbar to enter Percent Complete values.

To display the Tracking table, right-click the Select All button and choose Tracking.

If you prefer to enter the percent of work complete on a task, use Task Sheet view (the one shown in Figure 2-7) but use the Work table instead of the Tracking table, and enter the percentage value in the Percent Work Complete field (see Figure 2-8).

Entering the values isn't difficult; deciding what values to enter is a bit trickier. We typically recommend that you enter your best guess, based on your experience and the information you get from the resources who provide you with information about a task's progress.

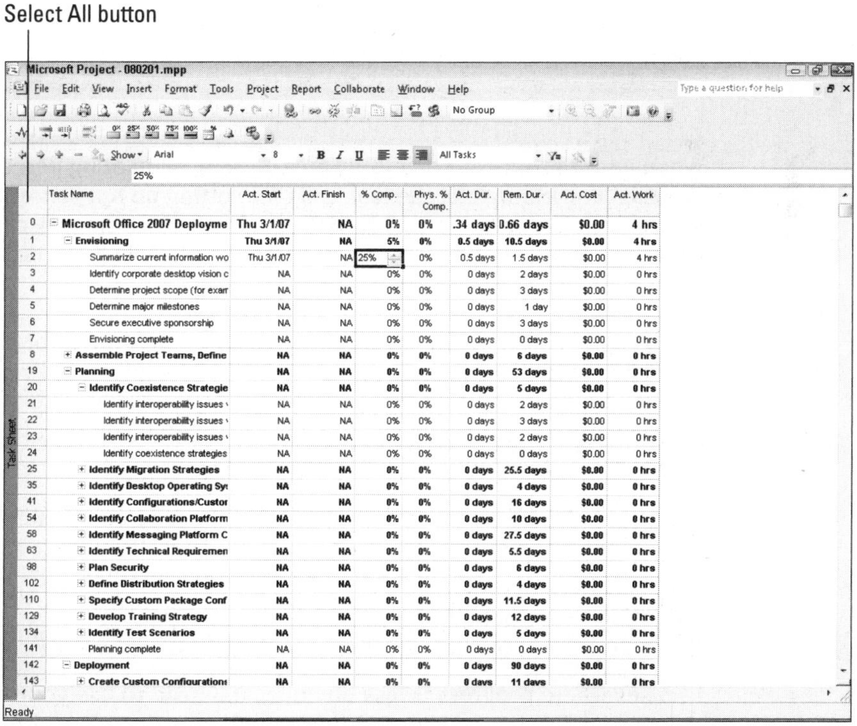

Select All button

Figure 2-7:
You can use Task Sheet view with the Tracking table to enter Percent Complete values.

**Book VIII
Chapter 2**

Entering Actuals

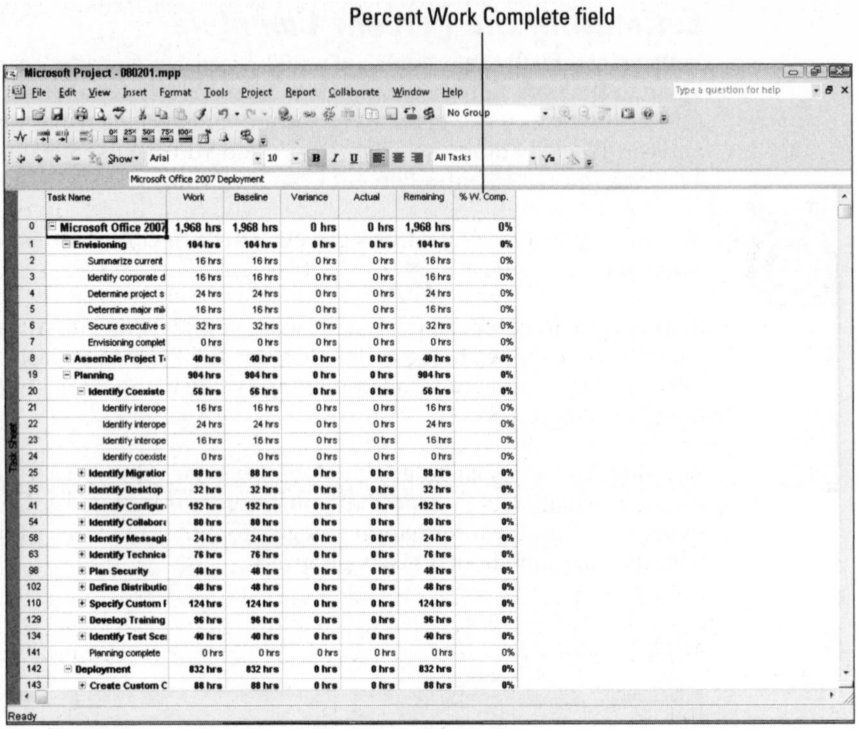

Percent Work Complete field

Figure 2-8:
Enter percent of work complete on a task by using Task Sheet view with the Work table.

When a task produces something measurable, estimating percent complete is easier. For example, if the task calls for setting up ten servers and you've set up five, the task is probably 50% complete. Or, if the task calls for training 100 employees and 75 have completed the training, the task is probably 75% complete.

But sometimes estimating completeness isn't that straightforward. If you estimate that a task should take eight days to complete and your resources report spending two days on the task, the task might be 25% complete, but just because resources have put in 25% of the time you estimated doesn't mean that they've completed 25% of the work.

You might also be tempted to use costs to estimate completeness. If you estimate that two resources assigned to a two-day task will cost $2,000, you might be tempted to estimate that a task is 50% complete when the task's costs reach $1,000. But, once again, just because costs have reached the 50% mark, it doesn't mean that 50% of the work on the task is complete.

In cases where progress is less obvious, you need to use your intuition when you make your estimate. Remember, you didn't get to be a project manager without demonstrating some good management skills.

% Complete versus Physical % Complete

Although they sound like they're related, the relationship is tenuous at best. Project's % Complete field represents exactly what it sounds like — the percentage of a task that is complete. If you don't enter a value in the % Complete field, Project calculates it for you based on Total Duration or Actual Duration values you enter, and Project uses these duration fields to calculate the *budgeted cost of work performed (BCWP),* which is a budget value that you can read about in the next chapter of this minibook.

Project uses the Physical % Complete field as an alternative way to calculate BCWP. The Physical % Complete field is independent of the Total Duration and Actual Duration fields. Use the Physical % Complete field when the % Complete value would not accurately represent the real work performed on a task. You can read more about having Project calculate BCWP using Physical % Complete in the next chapter of this minibook.

What happens when you enter a Percent Complete value? Project assigns an Actual Start Date (unless you entered one previously) and calculates the Actual Duration and Remaining Duration values. If you set Calculation options to update resources when you update tasks, Project also calculates the Actual Cost and Actual Work values.

If you enter 100 in the Percent Complete column, Project assigns the planned finish date to the Actual Finish Date column. If the task doesn't finish on the planned finish date, don't enter a Percent Complete value; instead, enter an Actual Finish Date.

Using start or finish dates

You can update task start or finish dates to record actuals in Project. If you mark a task as 100% complete and don't record an actual start date or an actual finish date, Project assumes that the task started and finished on time.

Because real life rarely matches estimates, you should enter an actual start date if the task didn't start on time so that your schedule reflects actual timing. Similarly, if the task didn't finish on the estimated finish date, you should enter an actual finish date so that your schedule reflects actual timing.

REMEMBER

If you enter an actual finish date that is earlier than the estimated finish date *and* you don't adjust the task duration, Project assumes that the task started earlier than planned.

The Actual Start and Actual Finish fields appear on the Tracking table of any view, or you can use the Update Tasks dialog box, shown in Figure 2-9, to record actual start or actual finish dates.

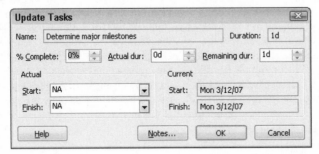

Select the task you want to update and click the Update Tasks button on the Tracking toolbar.

Using Windows selection techniques, you can select more than one task simultaneously. Press Ctrl and click each task you want to select, or, if the tasks appear contiguously in the schedule, click the first task, press Shift, and click the last task you want to select.

In the Actual section, click the Start list box arrow to display a calendar and select the task's start date. When you enter an actual start date, Project changes the task's estimated start date. When you enter an actual finish date, Project changes several fields: the estimated finish date, the Percent Complete field, the Actual Duration field, the Remaining Duration field, the Actual Work field, and the Actual Cost field. If you set only an actual finish date and not an actual start date, Project changes the actual start date also.

Recording actual and remaining durations

You can use Task Sheet view and Tracking Table to record both actual and remaining duration. And, when you record actual and remaining duration values, Project updates the Actual Start, Actual Cost, Actual Work, Percent Complete, and Remaining Duration fields. In some cases, Project also updates the Actual Finish field.

The actual duration of a task is the amount of time that was needed to complete the task. When you record an actual duration, Project calculates a value for the Percent Complete field using this formula:

```
Percent Complete = Actual Duration / Duration
```

and a value for the Remaining Duration field using this formula:

```
Remaining Duration = Duration - Actual Duration
```

When you set an actual duration that's less than or equal to the planned duration, Project assumes that the task is progressing on schedule and sets the actual start date to the planned start date unless you previously set the actual start date. In that case, Project leaves the actual start date alone.

When you set an actual duration that is greater than the planned duration, Project assumes that the task is finished but that it took longer than expected to complete. Project fills in the Actual Finish field using the planned finish date, adjusts the planned duration to match the actual duration, and changes the Percent Complete field to 100% and the Remaining Duration field to 0%.

Suppose that you set calculation options (on the Calculation tab of the Options dialog box) so that Project updates the status of resources when you update a task's status. When you supply an actual duration, Project also updates the work and cost figures for the resources.

The Remaining Duration field shows how much more time you need to complete a task. If you enter a value in only the Remaining Duration field that's higher or lower than the existing figure, Project assumes that you're changing the planned duration of the task instead of tracking actual progress for the task. In this case, Project adjusts the schedule based on the new planned duration.

But, if you enter a value into the Remaining Duration field after entering a value in the Actual Duration field, Project assumes that the work for the task will be completed based on the remaining duration value. Therefore, Project sets the Percent Complete value based on a combination of the remaining duration value that you supplied and the original planned duration. Entering 0 in the Remaining Duration field is the same as entering 100% in the Percent Complete column. Project assigns the planned finish date to the Actual Finish Date field. If this value isn't correct, change the Actual Finish Date.

Project makes a similar adjustment if you enter information into the Percent Complete field and the Remaining Duration field. In this case, Project adjusts the Actual Duration field using a combination of the remaining duration value and the original planned duration.

Recording Actual Work

When you schedule tasks based on the availability of certain resources, tracking progress on a task is easiest if you update the Actual Work field — typically, you use timesheet information to make your entries.

You can record total actual work by resource by following these steps:

1. **Choose View⇨Task Usage.**

   Project displays the Task Usage view.

2. **Right-click the Select All button.**

   A shortcut menu appears.

3. **Choose Tracking.**

   Project applies the Tracking table to the view.

4. **Drag the divider bar almost completely to the right edge of the screen to reveal the Actual Work column (see Figure 2-10).**

5. **Under the appropriate task, find the appropriate resource.**

6. **Enter a value for the resource in the Actual Work column.**

TIP

You can record actual work for the task by entering the value in the Actual Work field on the Tracking table (instead of using the Details portion of the view) and entering the value on the same row as the task, rather than on the individual rows for the resources. Project divides the actual and remaining work among the resources.

Figure 2-10:
Task Usage
view using
the Tracking
table.

Task Name	Act. Start	Act. Finish	% Comp.	Phys. % Comp.	Act. Dur.	Rem. Dur.	Act. Cost	Act. Work	Details	S	M	T
0 ⊟ Microsoft Office 2007 Deployme	NA	NA	0%	0%	0 days	161 days	$0.00	0 hrs	Work		16h	1
1 ⊟ Envisioning	NA	NA	0%	0%	0 days	11 days	$0.00	0 hrs	Work		16h	
2 ⊟ Summarize current information wo	NA	NA	0%	0%	0 days	2 days	$0.00	0 hrs	Work			
Stakeholders	*NA*	*NA*					*$0.00*	*0 hrs*	Work			
3 ⊟ Identify corporate desktop vision c	NA	NA	0%	0%	0 days	2 days	$0.00	0 hrs	Work			
Stakeholders	*NA*	*NA*					*$0.00*	*0 hrs*	Work			
4 ⊟ Determine project scope (for exam	NA	NA	0%	0%	0 days	3 days	$0.00	0 hrs	Work			
Stakeholders	*NA*	*NA*					*$0.00*	*0 hrs*	Work			
5 ⊟ Determine major milestones	NA	NA	0%	0%	0 days	1 day	$0.00	0 hrs	Work		16h	
Project Manager	*NA*	*NA*					*$0.00*	*0 hrs*	Work		8h	
Stakeholders	*NA*	*NA*					*$0.00*	*0 hrs*	Work		8h	
6 ⊟ Secure executive sponsorship	NA	NA	0%	0%	0 days	3 days	$0.00	0 hrs	Work			
Project Manager	*NA*	*NA*					*$0.00*	*0 hrs*	Work			
Stakeholders	*NA*	*NA*					*$0.00*	*0 hrs*	Work			
7 Envisioning complete	NA	NA	0%	0%	0 days	0 days	$0.00	0 hrs	Work			
8 ⊞ **Assemble Project Teams, Define**	**NA**	**NA**	**0%**	**0%**	**0 days**	**6 days**	**$0.00**	**0 hrs**	Work			
19 ⊟ **Planning**	**NA**	**NA**	**0%**	**0%**	**0 days**	**53 days**	**$0.00**	**0 hrs**	Work			
20 ⊟ **Identify Coexistence Strategie**	**NA**	**NA**	**0%**	**0%**	**0 days**	**5 days**	**$0.00**	**0 hrs**	Work			
21 ⊟ Identify interoperability issues	NA	NA	0%	0%	0 days	2 days	$0.00	0 hrs	Work			
Analyst 2	*NA*	*NA*					*$0.00*	*0 hrs*	Work			
22 ⊟ Identify interoperability issues	NA	NA	0%	0%	0 days	3 days	$0.00	0 hrs	Work			
Analyst 1	*NA*	*NA*					*$0.00*	*0 hrs*	Work			
23 ⊟ Identify interoperability issues	NA	NA	0%	0%	0 days	2 days	$0.00	0 hrs	Work			
Analyst 3	*NA*	*NA*					*$0.00*	*0 hrs*	Work			
24 Identify coexistence strategies	NA	NA	0%	0%	0 days	0 days	$0.00	0 hrs	Work			
25 ⊞ **Identify Migration Strategies**	**NA**	**NA**	**0%**	**0%**	**0 days**	**25.5 days**	**$0.00**	**0 hrs**	Work			
35 ⊞ **Identify Desktop Operating Sy**	**NA**	**NA**	**0%**	**0%**	**0 days**	**4 days**	**$0.00**	**0 hrs**	Work			
41 ⊞ **Identify Configurations/Custor**	**NA**	**NA**	**0%**	**0%**	**0 days**	**16 days**	**$0.00**	**0 hrs**	Work			
54 ⊞ **Identify Collaboration Platform**	**NA**	**NA**	**0%**	**0%**	**0 days**	**10 days**	**$0.00**	**0 hrs**	Work			

You can also use this view to enter a resource's work on a task on the day the work occurred; when you use this approach, Project calculates total actual work — the value in the Actual Work column — for you. Follow Steps 1–3 in the preceding list. Then right-click anywhere in the Details portion of the view (the right side) and choose Actual Work from the shortcut menu that appears. In the Details portion of the view, beside the appropriate resource, record tracking information on the Actual Work row in the column of the day on which the work occurred (see Figure 2-11).

You also can use Resource Usage view, shown in Figure 2-12, to enter a resource's work on a task on the day the work occurred. Project automatically displays the Usage table on the left side of the view, but if you're recording actuals from timesheets, this view might work better for you than Task Usage view because it lists resources and then the tasks assigned to them.

Make sure that you record actual work in the Details portion of the view on the appropriate day. Be aware that the Work column in the Usage table on the left side of the view displays *planned* work, not actual work. You can add the Actual Work column to the view and record actuals in that column; if you do, Project assumes that the actual work you record occurred on the days estimated in the baseline plan.

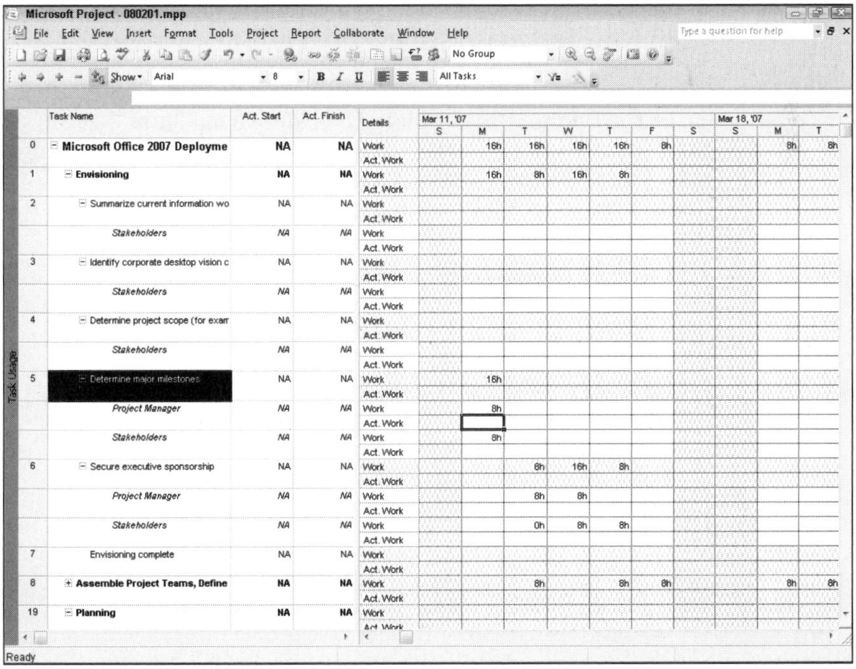

Figure 2-11:
Recording actual work for a resource on a specific day.

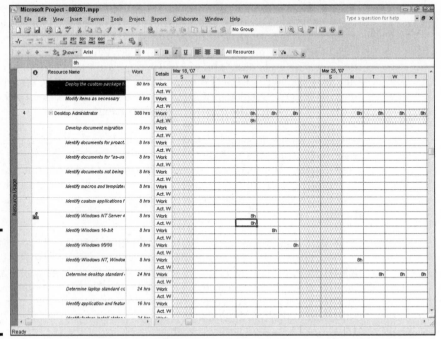

Figure 2-12:
You can record actuals in Resource Usage view.

Speeding up recording actuals

You can update several tasks or even your entire project at one time by using the Update Project dialog box shown in Figure 2-13. To open this dialog box, start in any task-oriented view. If you plan to update only selected tasks, select them before you open the dialog box by choosing Tools⇨Tracking⇨Update Project.

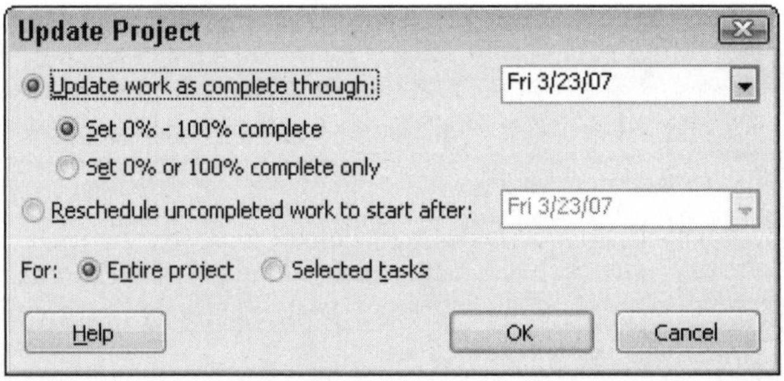

Figure 2-13:
Use the Update Project dialog box to update work on many tasks or your entire project.

Update Project

◉ Update work as complete through: Fri 3/23/07
  ◉ Set 0% - 100% complete
  ◯ Set 0% or 100% complete only
◯ Reschedule uncompleted work to start after: Fri 3/23/07

For: ◉ Entire project   ◯ Selected tasks

Help   OK   Cancel

This technique works well if you have several tasks that are on schedule or were completed on schedule. Select the Update Work As Complete Through option and select a date. Then select an option:

✦ **Select the Set 0% – 100% Complete option** to let Project calculate the percent complete on every task that should have begun by that date. When you select this option, Project assumes that tasks started and progressed as planned.

✦ **Selecting the Set 0% or 100% Complete Only option** tells Project to mark as finished all tasks that the baseline plan indicates would have been complete by the date you selected and to leave all other tasks as 0% complete.

The Update Project dialog box also helps you ensure that no remaining work for partially completed tasks is scheduled for dates that have already passed. Select the Reschedule Uncompleted Work To Start After option and select a date; Project reschedules the portions of tasks that aren't complete to start after the date you selected.

For either option, you can select to update your entire project or only selected tasks. When you update the entire project, Project sets the project status date to the date that you selected in the dialog box.

When you reschedule a partially completed task, Project automatically splits the task between the completed portion and the remaining portion. If the completed portion of the task finished sometime before the remaining portion is scheduled to start, you see a split task on the Gantt chart. In addition, Project places constraints on all tasks you reschedule; you'll see indicators in the Indicators column of many views.

Tracking materials usage

As Book V, Chapter 1 describes, you can create Material resources and assign them to tasks. You update actual work for Material resources the same way you update actual work for Work resources. You can work in Task Usage view and record total work for the Material resource in the Actual Work column. Or, if you want, use the time-phased fields in the Details portion on the right side of the view. Make sure you display the Actual Work row by right-clicking anywhere in the Details portion and choosing Actual Work. Then, on the appropriate day, across from the resource under the appropriate task, record the amount of the Material resource that was used.

Although it might not seem important to track the use of Material resources, they do affect the cost of your project.

Tracking consolidated projects

Book III, Chapter 4 covers inserting and linking projects to create a consolidated project. When you create a consolidated project, you can choose to link the projects. If you link the projects, Project retains, in the subproject files, updates you make when recording actuals in the consolidated project (and vice versa). If you don't link the projects, changes made to the consolidated project don't affect the individual subproject files (and vice versa).

Viewing Progress

Project provides some visual cues when you record tracking information for your project. For example, in Gantt Chart view, a check mark appears in the Indicator column beside tasks that are 100% complete (see Figure 2-14). In addition, a black bar extends inside the Gantt bar of each task that has started, providing a visual cue that represents how far along the task has progressed.

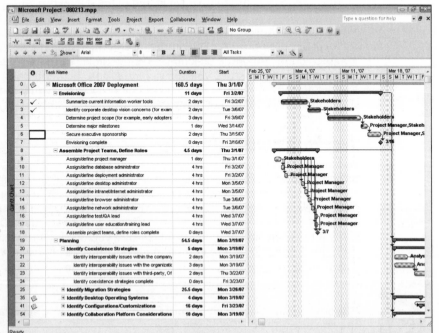

Figure 2-14:
You can identify progress visually in your project.

Using progress lines

You can add progress lines to your project to provide additional information about tasks that have started. A progress line zigzags between tasks, and the direction of the left- or right-pointing line identifies late or early tasks. A progress line that points to the left of a task identifies a task that is running behind schedule, and a progress line pointing to the right of a task identifies a task that is running ahead of schedule (see Figure 2-15).

To add progress lines to your schedule, follow these steps:

1. **Choose View⇨Gantt Chart.**

2. **Choose Tools⇨Tracking⇨Progress Lines.**

Project displays the Dates and Intervals tab of the Progress Lines dialog box.

3. **Select the Display Selected Progress Lines check box.**

The Progress Line Dates list becomes available.

4. **Click once in the Progress Line Dates list.**

Project displays a list box arrow.

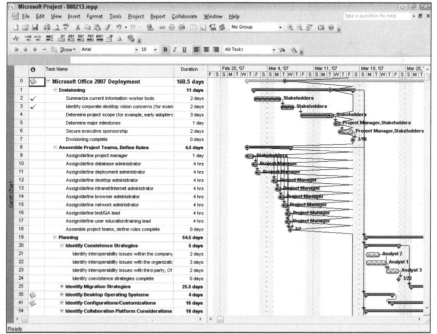

Figure 2-15:
Progress lines provide visual cues to identify tasks ahead of or behind schedule.

5. **Click the list box arrow.**

A small calendar appears (see Figure 2-16).

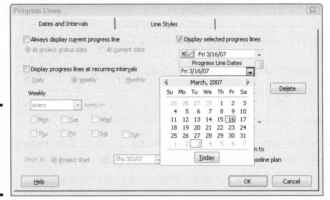

6. **Select a date for the progress line.**

7. **Select either Actual Plan or Baseline Plan in the Display Progress Lines in Relation To section.**

8. **Click OK.**

Project adds the progress line to your Gantt chart (refer to Figure 2-15).

You can use the Line Styles tab of the Progress Lines dialog box to change the shape, thickness, and color of progress lines.

If you decide that you like progress lines, you can display them at varying intervals, in relation to the Baseline plan or the Actual plan, and from the Line Styles tab you can add a date to each progress line. If you display more than one progress line, consider using the Line Styles tab of the Progress Lines dialog box to format the lines so that you can tell them apart.

You can delete any single progress line by selecting it in the Display Selected Progress Lines list and clicking the Delete button. To stop displaying all progress lines, reopen the Progress Lines dialog box and remove the check mark from the Display Selected Progress Lines check box on the Dates and Intervals tab.

Using Tracking Gantt view

After you set a baseline — and maybe even an interim plan — and record actuals, you can compare your baseline or interim plan to what's happening in your project now. You can see the differences between your plans and what's actually happening both graphically, using Tracking Gantt view, and through data that appears in various tables.

Tracking Gantt view helps you view actual progress compared to a baseline estimate. To display Tracking Gantt view, click its icon in the View bar or choose View➪Tracking Gantt.

The default table for Tracking Gantt view is the Entry table, but you can change the table and you can insert and hide fields (columns) to display other information. In Figure 2-17, you see Tracking Gantt view and the Tracking table.

The bars on Tracking Gantt view vary in appearance slightly from the task bars on standard Gantt Chart view; the Tracking Gantt bars indicate progress on tasks in the project. At the top of Tracking Gantt view, you see the summary task for the project, and below it, you see a black-and-white hatched bar. That hatched bar represents progress on the summary task. On Tracking Gantt view, noncritical tasks appear in blue, and critical tasks appear in red.

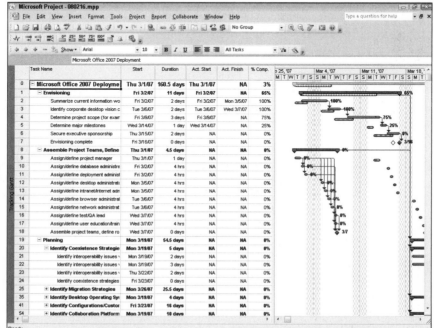

Figure 2-17: Tracking Gantt view presents a visual comparison of your estimates versus actual data.

On all tasks that aren't summary tasks, you see two bars. The top bar represents expected duration based on actuals you enter, and the bottom bar represents baseline duration.

The percentage indicator at the edge of a task bar identifies the percentage complete for that task. Although you have to look very closely, the bars of partially completed tasks are solid on the left and patterned on the right. The solid part represents the completed part of the task, and the patterned part represents the incomplete part of the task.

Using tables to review progress

The Variance, Work, and Cost tables help you review progress by showing you the details associated with your project's progress. The numbers you find in these tables help you determine whether you're on schedule and within budget.

To review these tables, we suggest that you start in Task Sheet view, which lets you focus strictly on table information.

The Variance table

To display the Variance table, follow these steps:

1. **Choose View⇨More Views.**

The More Views dialog box appears.

2. **Select Task Sheet from the list.**

3. **Click Apply.**

Project displays Task Sheet view.

4. **Right-click the Select All button and choose Variance.**

Project displays the Variance table (see Figure 2-18).

The Variance table highlights the variance in task timing between the baselines and actuals. You can easily compare the Baseline Start and Baseline Finish and the actual Start and Finish columns that show actual data for tasks on which you have tracked progress as well as baseline data for tasks with no progress. The Start Variance field shows you how many days late or early the task started, and the Finish Variance field shows you how many days late or early the task ended.

Select All button

Figure 2-18:
The Variance table helps you see that you're ahead of or behind schedule.

	Task Name	Start	Finish	Baseline Start	Baseline Finish	Start Var.	Finish Var.
0	– **Microsoft Office**	**Thu 3/1/07**	**hu 10/11/07**	**Thu 3/1/07**	**Thu 10/11/07**	**0 days**	**-0.5 days**
1	– Envisioning	Fri 3/2/07	Fri 3/16/07	Thu 3/1/07	Thu 3/15/07	1 day	1 day
2	Summarize cu	Fri 3/2/07	Mon 3/5/07	Thu 3/1/07	Fri 3/2/07	1 day	1 day
3	Identify corpor	Tue 3/6/07	Wed 3/7/07	Mon 3/5/07	Tue 3/6/07	1 day	1 day
4	Determine proj	Fri 3/9/07	Tue 3/13/07	Wed 3/7/07	Fri 3/9/07	2 days	2 days
5	Determine maj	Wed 3/14/07	Wed 3/14/07	Mon 3/12/07	Mon 3/12/07	2 days	2 days
6	Secure execut	Thu 3/15/07	Fri 3/16/07	Tue 3/13/07	Thu 3/15/07	2 days	1 day
7	Envisioning co	Fri 3/16/07	Fri 3/16/07	Thu 3/15/07	Thu 3/15/07	1 day	1 day
8	– **Assemble Proj**	**Thu 3/1/07**	**Wed 3/7/07**	**Tue 3/13/07**	**Tue 3/20/07**	**-8 days**	**-9.5 days**
9	Assign/define	Thu 3/1/07	Thu 3/1/07	Tue 3/13/07	Tue 3/13/07	-8 days	-8 days
10	Assign/define	Fri 3/2/07	Fri 3/2/07	Thu 3/15/07	Thu 3/15/07	-9 days	-9 days
11	Assign/define	Fri 3/2/07	Fri 3/2/07	Thu 3/15/07	Thu 3/15/07	-9 days	-9 days
12	Assign/define	Mon 3/5/07	Mon 3/5/07	Fri 3/16/07	Fri 3/16/07	-9 days	-9 days
13	Assign/define	Mon 3/5/07	Mon 3/5/07	Fri 3/16/07	Fri 3/16/07	-9 days	-9 days
14	Assign/define	Tue 3/6/07	Tue 3/6/07	Mon 3/19/07	Mon 3/19/07	-9 days	-9 days
15	Assign/define	Tue 3/6/07	Tue 3/6/07	Mon 3/19/07	Mon 3/19/07	-9 days	-9 days
16	Assign/define	Wed 3/7/07	Wed 3/7/07	Tue 3/20/07	Tue 3/20/07	-9 days	-9 days
17	Assign/define	Wed 3/7/07	Wed 3/7/07	Tue 3/20/07	Tue 3/20/07	-9.5 days	-9.5 days
18	Assemble proj	Wed 3/7/07	Wed 3/7/07	Tue 3/20/07	Tue 3/20/07	-9.5 days	-9.5 days
19	– **Planning**	**Mon 3/19/07**	**Fri 6/1/07**	**Wed 3/21/07**	**Fri 6/1/07**	**-2 days**	**-0.5 days**
20	– **Identify Coes**	**Mon 3/19/07**	**Fri 3/23/07**	**Wed 3/21/07**	**Tue 3/27/07**	**-2 days**	**-2 days**
21	Identify inte	Mon 3/19/07	Tue 3/20/07	Wed 3/21/07	Thu 3/22/07	-2 days	-2 days
22	Identify inte	Mon 3/19/07	Wed 3/21/07	Wed 3/21/07	Fri 3/23/07	-2 days	-2 days
23	Identify inte	Thu 3/22/07	Fri 3/23/07	Mon 3/26/07	Tue 3/27/07	-2 days	-2 days
24	Identify cor	Fri 3/23/07	Fri 3/23/07	Tue 3/27/07	Tue 3/27/07	-2 days	-2 days
25	+ **Identify Migr**	**Mon 3/26/07**	**Mon 4/30/07**	**Wed 3/28/07**	**Wed 5/2/07**	**-2 days**	**-2 days**
35	+ **Identify Desk**	**Mon 3/19/07**	**Thu 3/22/07**	**Wed 3/21/07**	**Mon 3/26/07**	**-2 days**	**-2 days**
41	+ **Identify Conf**	**Fri 3/23/07**	**Fri 4/13/07**	**Tue 3/27/07**	**Tue 4/17/07**	**-2 days**	**-2 days**
54	+ **Identify Colla**	**Mon 3/19/07**	**Fri 3/30/07**	**Wed 3/21/07**	**Tue 4/3/07**	**-2 days**	**-2 days**

If you save several baselines or interim plans, you can view the information in them by adding columns to the table. The baseline fields that appear on the Variance table are associated with the first baseline, which Project calls Baseline. If you saved information to Baseline 1, add the fields for Baseline 1 to the table. To view interim plan information, add information for Start 1 through Start 10.

REMEMBER

Interim plans store only start and finish dates, whereas baselines store much more information, including cost, budgeted costs, budgeted work, duration, and more. For details on interim plans and baselines, see Chapter 1 of this minibook.

To add a field to the table, insert a column. Right-click the column that you want to appear to the right of the column you plan to insert. Then choose Insert Column from the shortcut menu. In the Field Name list, select the field for which you want to add a column and click OK.

For details on adding columns to tables, see Book VI, Chapter 2.

The Cost table

Project contains two versions of the Cost table: the Cost table associated with task-oriented views, and the Cost table associated with resource-oriented views. To view the Cost table associated with tasks (see Figure 2-19), start in any task-oriented view (we like Task Sheet view), right-click the Select All button, and choose Cost.

The Cost table is most useful for pointing out variations in money spent on the project. Project takes the following factors into account when calculating cost variations:

✦ The estimate of resource time still to be expended to complete the task

✦ Actual resource time worked

✦ Actual costs (such as fees and permits) that have been tracked on the task

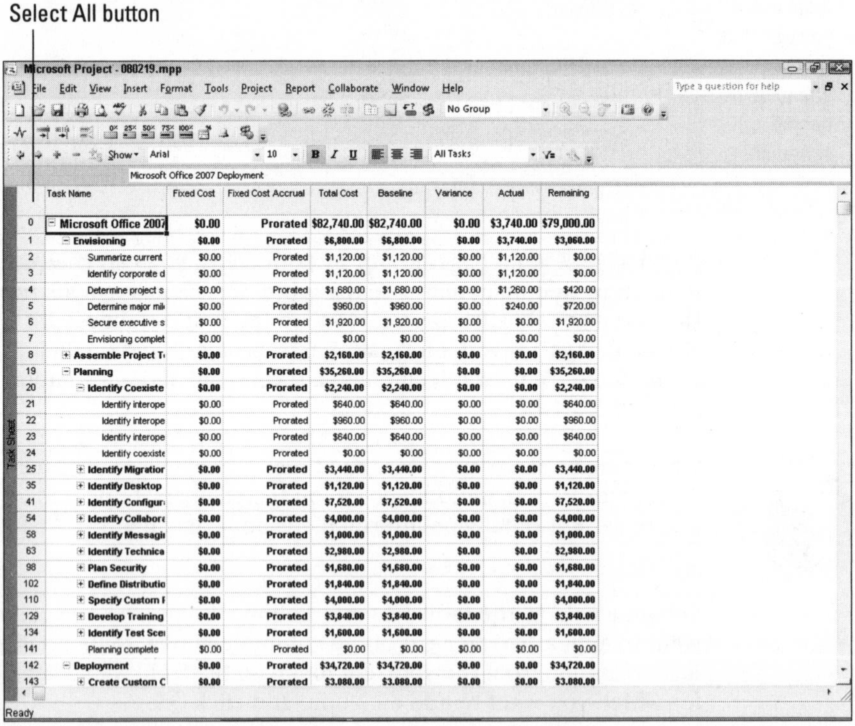

Select All button

Figure 2-19: The Cost table associated with a task-oriented view.

The Cost table for resources is similar to the Cost table for tasks, with the breakdown of costs being displayed by resource rather than by task (see Figure 2-20).

To display this table, begin with a resource view such as Resource Sheet view. Then right-click the Select All button and choose Cost from the shortcut menu that appears.

The Work table

Like the Cost table, Project contains two variations of the Work table — one for tasks and one for resources. You display the Work table for tasks (see Figure 2-21) by starting in a task-oriented view such as Task Sheet view, right-clicking the Select All button, and selecting Work from the shortcut menu. The Work table focuses on the number of work hours put in by resources that are working on tasks. The Variance field shows the difference between the baseline hours of work and the actual hours spent; if the amount in the Variance field is negative, fewer hours were used than were estimated in the baseline.

Select All button

	Resource Name	Cost	Baseline Cost	Variance	Actual Cost	Remaining
1	Project Manager	$17,600.00	$17,600.00	$0.00	$100.00	$17,500.00
2	Database Administrat	$480.00	$480.00	$0.00	$0.00	$480.00
3	Deployment Administr	$8,000.00	$8,000.00	$0.00	$0.00	$8,000.00
4	Desktop Administrator	$13,580.00	$13,580.00	$0.00	$0.00	$13,580.00
5	Intranet/Internet Admi	$2,520.00	$2,520.00	$0.00	$0.00	$2,520.00
6	Browser Administrato	$1,040.00	$1,040.00	$0.00	$0.00	$1,040.00
7	Network Administrato	$7,200.00	$7,200.00	$0.00	$0.00	$7,200.00
8	Test/QA Lead	$12,160.00	$12,160.00	$0.00	$0.00	$12,160.00
9	User Education/Traini	$9,920.00	$9,920.00	$0.00	$0.00	$9,920.00
10	Logistics Managemen	$0.00	$0.00	$0.00	$0.00	$0.00
11	Stakeholders	$6,720.00	$6,720.00	$0.00	$3,640.00	$3,080.00
12	Analyst 1	$2,240.00	$2,240.00	$0.00	$0.00	$2,240.00
13	Analyst 2	$640.00	$640.00	$0.00	$0.00	$640.00
14	Analyst 3	$640.00	$640.00	$0.00	$0.00	$640.00

Figure 2-20:
The Cost table for resources.

The resource version of the Work table (see Figure 2-22) displays work information for resources. You can display the Work table for resources to any resource-oriented view, such as Resource Sheet.

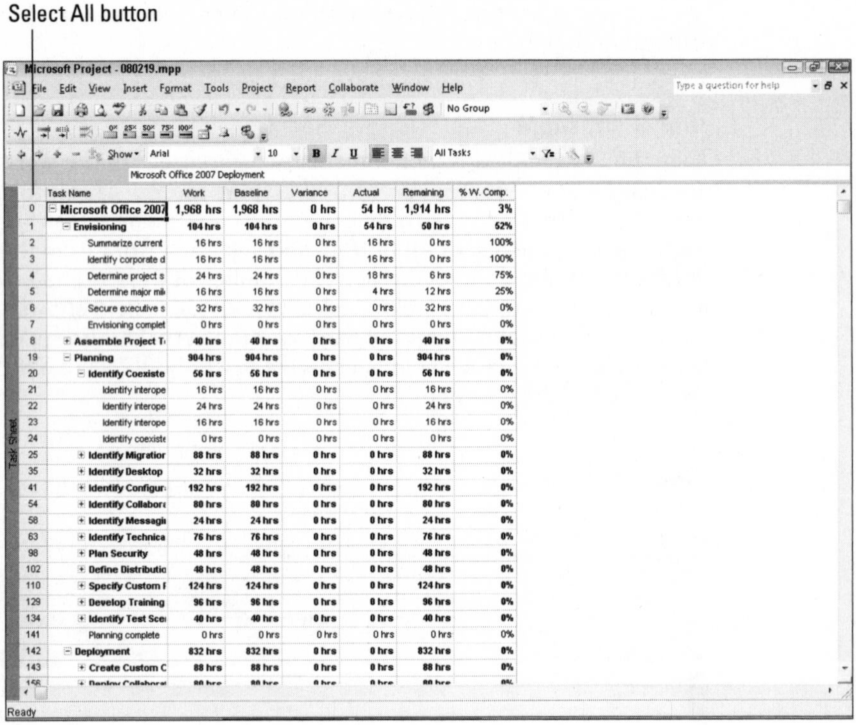

Select All button

Figure 2-21:
The Work table in a task-oriented view.

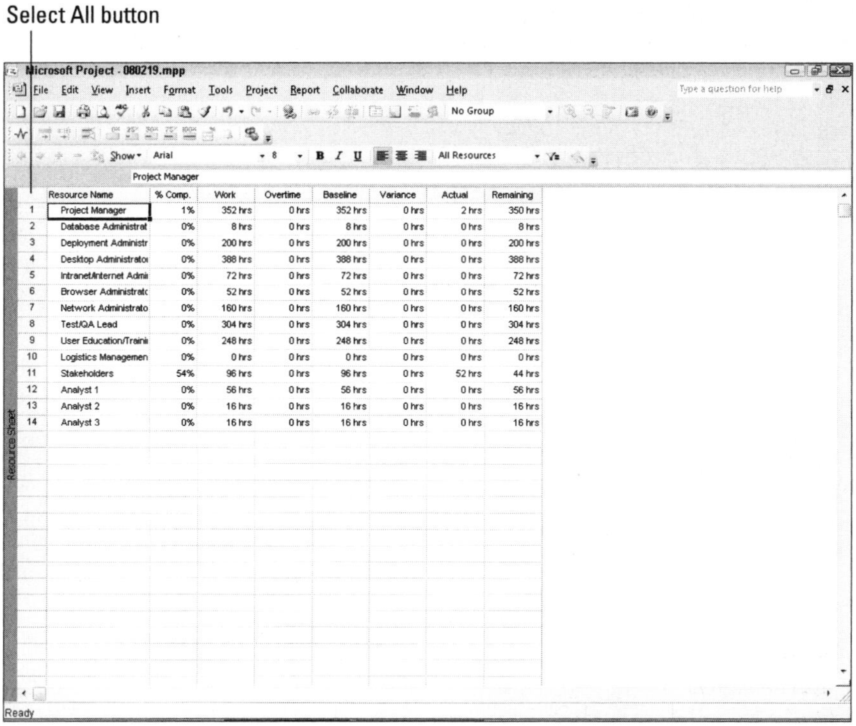

Select All button

Figure 2-22:
The Work
table for
resources.

Chapter 3: Reviewing Your Budget

In This Chapter

✔ **The basics of Earned Value fields**

✔ **Examining cost variance**

✔ **Using Physical % Complete or % Complete in Earned Value calculations**

After you save a baseline for your project, assign resources with costs to tasks in your project, and complete some work on the project, you can begin to analyze the progress of your project based on the costs that you incur — or the *Earned Value* of your project.

Project managers use Earned Value information to measure the progress of a project based on the cost of work performed up to the project status date. Project calculates Earned Value by comparing your original cost estimates to the actual cost of work performed to show whether your project is on budget. This chapter explains Project's Earned Value fields and shows you how to compare budgeted to actual costs.

The Basics of Earned Value Fields

Earned Value fields in Project are currency fields, and Project uses acronyms to represent the various Earned Value fields in tables, but three Earned Value fields are at the heart of the analysis when Project calculates Earned Value:

✦ **BCWS (Budgeted Cost of Work Scheduled):** Measures the budgeted cost of individual tasks based on the resources and fixed costs that are assigned to the tasks when you schedule them.

✦ **BCWP (Budgeted Cost of Work Performed):** Indicates how much of a task's budget should have been spent given the actual duration of the task. For example, suppose that you have a task budgeted at $1,000 and work has been performed for one day. You find that, after one day, 40 percent of the work has been completed. The BCWP for the task at this point is $400.

✦ **ACWP (Actual Cost of Work Performed):** Measures the actual cost that's incurred to complete a task. Before you complete the process, ACWP represents the actual costs for work performed through the project's status date.

In addition to these three Earned Value fields, you also find the following fields:

+ SV (Schedule Variance)
+ CV (Cost Variance)
+ BAC (Budgeted at Completion)
+ EAC (Estimate at Completion)
+ VAC (Variance at Completion)
+ CPI (Cost Performance Index)
+ SPI (Schedule Performance Index)
+ CV% (Cost Variance %)
+ SV% (Schedule Variance %)
+ TCPI (To Complete Performance Index)
+ Physical % Complete

Project calculates BCWS, BCWP, ACWP, SV, and CV through the project status date or through today. SV represents the cost difference between current progress and the baseline plan, and Project calculates this value as BCWP minus BCWS. CV represents the cost difference between actual costs and planned costs at the current level of completion, and Project calculates this value as BCWP minus ACWP. BAC represents baseline cost, and Project calculates this field as the sum of planned fixed costs plus planned costs for all assigned resources. EAC shows the planned costs based on costs that are already incurred plus additional planned costs, and Project calculates this field using the following formula: ACWP + (BAC – BCWP) / CPI. VAC represents the variance between the baseline cost and the combination of actual costs plus planned costs for a task.

You find task fields, resource fields, and assignment fields as well as time-phased versions of each field for BCWS, BCWP, ACWP, SV, CV, and BAC. EAC is a task field only, and VAC is a task field, resource field, and assignment field but there are no timephased versions of this field.

Project calculates CPI, a timephased field, by dividing BCWP by ACWP.

Project calculates SPI, a timephased field, by dividing BCWP by BCWS.

Project calculates CV%, a timephased field, by dividing CV by BCWP and multiplying the result by 100.

Project calculates SV%, a timephased field, by dividing SV by BCWS and multiplying the result by 100.

Project calculates TCPI by using the following formula: (BAC – BCWP) / (EAC – ACWP). This field is not a timephased field.

The Physical % Complete field represents your estimate of the progress of a task, regardless of actual work or time. Project calculates Physical % Complete, not a timephased field, by rolling up BCWP on subtasks to BCWP on associated summary tasks.

The section "Physical % Complete Versus % Complete," later in this chapter, describes the difference between these two fields and how you can use them.

Examining Cost Variance

Project contains four Earned Value tables that you can use to compare your expected costs with your actual costs and evaluate the relationship between work and costs:

✦ Earned Value for tasks

✦ Earned Value for resources

✦ Earned Value Cost Indicators

✦ Earned Value Schedule Indicators

You can use the Earned Value tables to forecast whether a task will finish within the budget based on the comparison of the actual costs incurred for the task to date and the baseline cost of the task.

Using the Earned Value table for tasks (see Figure 3-1), you can compare the relationship between work and costs for tasks and evaluate your budget to estimate future budget needs and prepare an accounting statement of your project.

To display the Earned Value table for tasks, follow these steps:

1. **Start in any task view, such as Task Sheet view.**
2. **Right-click the Select All button and choose More Tables from the shortcut menu that appears.**
3. **In the More Tables dialog box that appears, select Earned Value.**
4. **Click Apply.**

   Project applies the Earned Value table for tasks to the view.

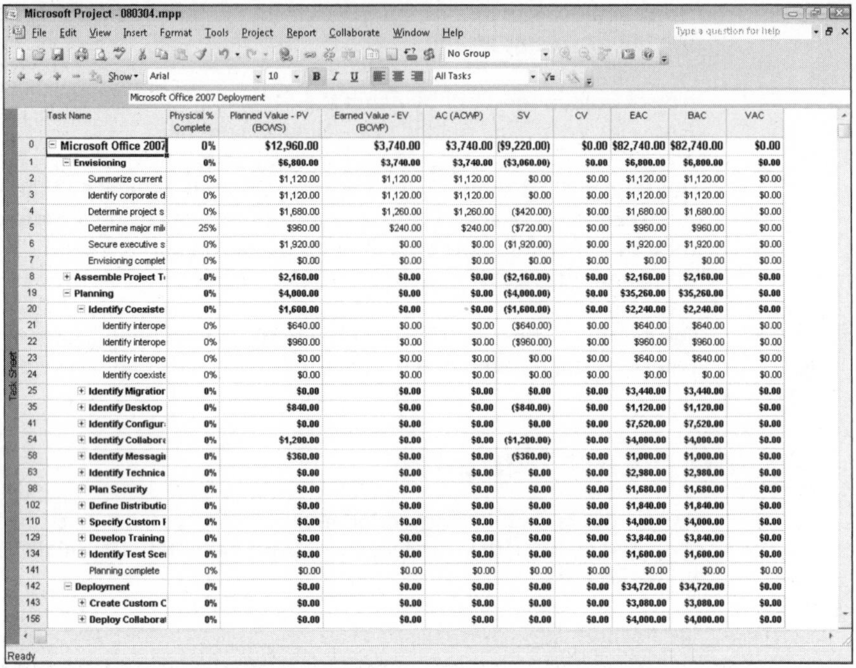

Figure 3-1:
The Earned
Value table
for tasks.

All the fields on this sheet are calculated, except BAC. You can type values into the BAC field to change information in the table.

The Earned Value table for resources (see Figure 3-2) displays the same fields as the Earned Value table for tasks, helping you compare the relationship between work and costs for resources.

To display the Earned Value table for resources, follow the preceding steps, but in Step 1, start in any resource view, such as Resource Sheet view.

The Earned Value Cost Indicators and Earned Value Schedule Indicators tables are similar to their cousin, the Earned Value for tasks table. Using the Earned Value Cost Indicators table (see Figure 3-3) you can compare the various cost factors related to tasks in your project. Using the Earned Value Schedule Indicators table for tasks (see Figure 3-4), you can focus on the effects of scheduling variances on the cost of your project.

To display either table, follow the preceding steps, but in Step 4, select either the Earned Value Cost Indicators table or the Earned Value Schedule Indicators table.

Figure 3-2: The Earned Value table for resources.

	Resource Name	Planned Value - PV	Earned Value - EV	AC (ACWP)	SV	CV	EAC	BAC	VAC
1	Project Manager	$4,000.00	$100.00	$100.00	($3,900.00)	$0.00	$17,600.00	$17,600.00	$0.00
2	Database Administrator	$0.00	$0.00	$0.00	$0.00	$0.00	$480.00	$480.00	$0.00
3	Deployment Administrator	$0.00	$0.00	$0.00	$0.00	$0.00	$8,000.00	$8,000.00	$0.00
4	Desktop Administrator	$840.00	$0.00	$0.00	($840.00)	$0.00	$13,580.00	$13,580.00	$0.00
5	Intranet/Internet Administre	$0.00	$0.00	$0.00	$0.00	$0.00	$2,520.00	$2,520.00	$0.00
6	Browser Administrator	$0.00	$0.00	$0.00	$0.00	$0.00	$1,040.00	$1,040.00	$0.00
7	Network Administrator	$360.00	$0.00	$0.00	($360.00)	$0.00	$7,200.00	$7,200.00	$0.00
8	Test/QA Lead	$0.00	$0.00	$0.00	$0.00	$0.00	$12,160.00	$12,160.00	$0.00
9	User Education/Training Le	$0.00	$0.00	$0.00	$0.00	$0.00	$9,920.00	$9,920.00	$0.00
10	Logistics Management Lea	$0.00	$0.00	$0.00	$0.00	$0.00	$0.00	$0.00	$0.00
11	Stakeholders	$6,160.00	$3,640.00	$3,640.00	($2,520.00)	$0.00	$6,720.00	$6,720.00	$0.00
12	Analyst 1	$960.00	$0.00	$0.00	($960.00)	$0.00	$2,240.00	$2,240.00	$0.00
13	Analyst 2	$640.00	$0.00	$0.00	($640.00)	$0.00	$640.00	$640.00	$0.00
14	Analyst 3	$0.00	$0.00	$0.00	$0.00	$0.00	$640.00	$640.00	$0.00

Figure 3-3: The Earned Value Cost Indicators table.

	Task Name	Planned Value - PV (BCWS)	Earned Value - EV (BCWP)	CV	CV%	CPI	BAC	EAC	VAC	TCPI
0	Microsoft Office 2007	$12,960.00	$3,740.00	$0.00	0%	1	$82,740.00	$82,740.00	$0.00	1
1	Envisioning	$6,800.00	$3,740.00	$0.00	0%	1	$6,800.00	$6,800.00	$0.00	1
2	Summarize current	$1,120.00	$1,120.00	$0.00	0%	1	$1,120.00	$1,120.00	$0.00	1
3	Identify corporate d	$1,120.00	$1,120.00	$0.00	0%	1	$1,120.00	$1,120.00	$0.00	1
4	Determine project s	$1,680.00	$1,260.00	$0.00	0%	1	$1,680.00	$1,680.00	$0.00	1
5	Determine major mil	$960.00	$240.00	$0.00	0%	1	$960.00	$960.00	$0.00	1
6	Secure executive s	$1,920.00	$0.00	$0.00	0%	0	$1,920.00	$1,920.00	$0.00	1
7	Envisioning complet	$0.00	$0.00	$0.00	0%	0	$0.00	$0.00	$0.00	0
8	+ Assemble Project T	$2,160.00	$0.00	$0.00	0%	0	$2,160.00	$2,160.00	$0.00	1
19	− Planning	$4,000.00	$0.00	$0.00	0%	0	$35,268.00	$35,268.00	$0.00	1
20	− Identify Coexiste	$1,600.00	$0.00	$0.00	0%	0	$2,240.00	$2,240.00	$0.00	1
21	Identify interope	$640.00	$0.00	$0.00	0%	0	$640.00	$640.00	$0.00	1
22	Identify interope	$960.00	$0.00	$0.00	0%	0	$960.00	$960.00	$0.00	1
23	Identify interope	$0.00	$0.00	$0.00	0%	0	$640.00	$640.00	$0.00	1
24	Identify coexiste	$0.00	$0.00	$0.00	0%	0	$0.00	$0.00	$0.00	0
25	+ Identify Migration	$0.00	$0.00	$0.00	0%	0	$3,440.00	$3,440.00	$0.00	1
35	+ Identify Desktop	$840.00	$0.00	$0.00	0%	0	$1,120.00	$1,120.00	$0.00	1
41	+ Identify Configura	$0.00	$0.00	$0.00	0%	0	$7,520.00	$7,520.00	$0.00	1
54	+ Identify Collabora	$1,200.00	$0.00	$0.00	0%	0	$4,000.00	$4,000.00	$0.00	1
58	+ Identify Messagi	$360.00	$0.00	$0.00	0%	0	$1,000.00	$1,000.00	$0.00	1
63	+ Identify Technica	$0.00	$0.00	$0.00	0%	0	$2,980.00	$2,980.00	$0.00	1
98	+ Plan Security	$0.00	$0.00	$0.00	0%	0	$1,680.00	$1,680.00	$0.00	1
102	+ Define Distributio	$0.00	$0.00	$0.00	0%	0	$1,840.00	$1,840.00	$0.00	1
110	+ Specify Custom F	$0.00	$0.00	$0.00	0%	0	$4,000.00	$4,000.00	$0.00	1
129	+ Develop Training	$0.00	$0.00	$0.00	0%	0	$3,840.00	$3,840.00	$0.00	1
134	+ Identify Test Scel	$0.00	$0.00	$0.00	0%	0	$1,600.00	$1,600.00	$0.00	1
141	Planning complete	$0.00	$0.00	$0.00	0%	0	$0.00	$0.00	$0.00	0
142	− Deployment	$0.00	$0.00	$0.00	0%	0	$34,720.00	$34,720.00	$0.00	1
143	+ Create Custom C	$0.00	$0.00	$0.00	0%	0	$3,080.00	$3,080.00	$0.00	1
156	+ Deploy Collabora	$0.00	$0.00	$0.00	0%	0	$4,000.00	$4,000.00	$0.00	1

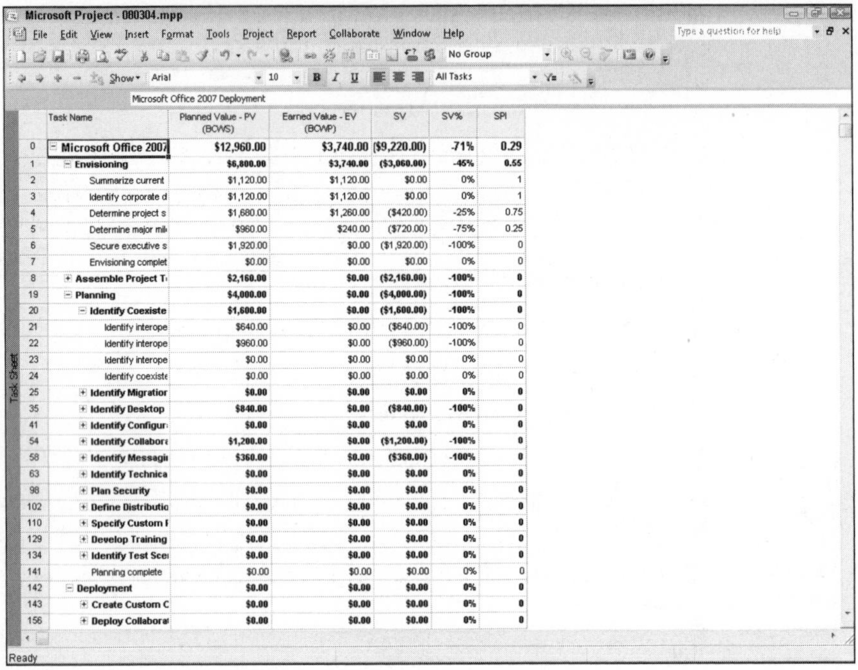

Figure 3-4:
The Earned
Value
Schedule
Indicators
table.

In addition to using Earned Value tables to examine how the costs of your project are progressing, you can use Excel to analyze the data by using the Earned Value Over Time visual report. You also can export your project to Excel and create a PivotTable to analyze the information. See Book VI, Chapter 4 for details on visual reporting, and turn to Book IX, Chapter 5 for information on exporting Project information.

Physical % Complete Versus % Complete

Although % Complete and Physical % Complete sound like they're related, they really aren't. Project's % Complete field represents exactly what it sounds like — the percentage of a task that is complete. If you don't enter a value in the % Complete field, Project calculates it for you by dividing actual task duration by total duration. Project uses % Complete to calculate the budgeted cost of work performed (BCWP).

Physical % Complete is your estimate of where a task stands and has no connection to duration. You enter Physical % Complete estimates, and Project applies Physical % Complete to assignment data or Fixed Costs data for the associated summary task.

You can use the Physical % Complete field as an alternative way to calculate BCWP when the % Complete value wouldn't accurately represent the real work performed on a task.

Calculating BCWP using Physical % Complete

You can set Physical % Complete as the default Earned Value calculation method for all new tasks in your project by following these steps:

1. **Choose Tools⇨Options.**

   The Options dialog box appears (see Figure 3-5).

2. **Click the Calculation tab.**

3. **Click the Earned Value button.**

   The Earned Value dialog box appears (see Figure 3-6).

4. **From the Default Task Earned Value Method list box, select Physical % Complete.**

5. **From the Baseline for Earned Value Calculations list box, select a baseline.**

6. **Click Close.**

   Project redisplays the Options dialog box.

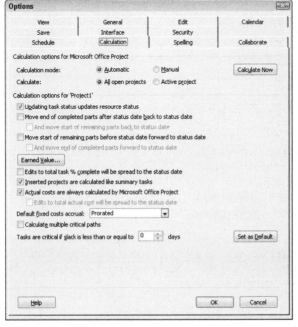

Figure 3-5: Click the Earned Value button to select a method to calculate Earned Value.

Book VIII Chapter 3

Reviewing Your Budget

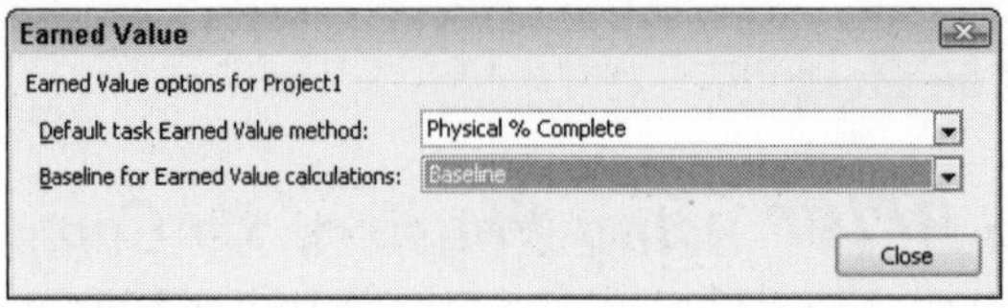

Figure 3-6:
Select an
Earned
Value
calculation
method.

Figure 3-6:
Select an
Earned
Value
calculation
method.

Earned Value	

Earned Value options for Project1

Default task Earned Value method: Physical % Complete

Baseline for Earned Value calculations: Baseline

Close

7. Click OK.

Project saves the settings.

Using Physical % Complete selectively

If your project already contains tasks (or if you want to use the Physical %
Complete method for some but not all tasks), set the Earned Value calculation method on a task-by-task basis using these steps:

**1. Select the task(s) for which you want to set the Earned Value calcula-
tion method to Physical % Complete.**

2. Click the Task Information button on the Standard toolbar.

Project displays the Multiple Task Information dialog box.

3. Click the Advanced tab.

**4. From the Earned Value Method list box, select Physical % Complete
(see Figure 3-7).**

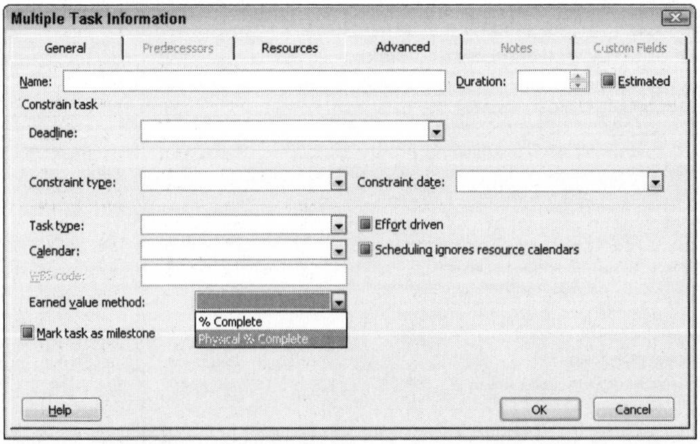

Figure 3-7:
Use the
Multiple
Task
Information
dialog box
to establish
the Earned
Value
method for
selected
tasks.

Multiple Task Information

General | Predecessors | Resources | Advanced | Notes | Custom Fields

Name: Duration: Estimated

Constrain task

Deadline:

Constraint type: Constraint date:

Task type: Effort driven

Calendar: Scheduling ignores resource calendars

WBS code:

Earned value method:

Mark task as milestone   % Complete
                                        Physical % Complete

Help   OK   Cancel

5. Click OK.

Project saves your settings for the selected tasks.

Entering Physical % Complete values

To record Physical % Complete, add the field as a column on a table view; Figure 3-8 shows the field in the Earned Value for Tasks table. Then type in appropriate amounts for tasks. You see other Earned Value fields update accordingly.

To insert a column, click the heading of the column to the right of the column that you are inserting. Then choose Insert➪Column.

You saw when you established Physical % Complete as the Earned Value calculation method that the Earned Value calculation method is associated with a particular baseline, and you can clear baselines. Because the preceding section explained how to enter Physical % Complete values, you might be wondering what happens to your Physical % Complete estimates if you clear a baseline. You can quit worrying; clearing a baseline after entering Physical % Complete values for it doesn't clear the Physical % Complete values.

Figure 3-8:
Record Physical % Complete values by adding the field to a table and then typing the information.

	Task Name	Physical % Complete	Planned Value - PV (BCWS)	Earned Value - EV (BCWP)	AC (ACWP)	SV	CV	EAC	BAC	VAC
0	☐ Microsoft Office 2007	0%	$12,960.00	$3,740.00	$3,740.00	($9,220.00)	$0.00	$82,740.00	$82,740.00	$0.00
1	☐ Envisioning	0%	$6,800.00	$3,740.00	$3,740.00	($3,060.00)	$0.00	$6,800.00	$6,800.00	$0.00
2	Summarize current	0%	$1,120.00	$1,120.00	$1,120.00	$0.00	$0.00	$1,120.00	$1,120.00	$0.00
3	Identify corporate d	0%	$1,120.00	$1,120.00	$1,120.00	$0.00	$0.00	$1,120.00	$1,120.00	$0.00
4	Determine project s	0%	$1,680.00	$1,260.00	$1,260.00	($420.00)	$0.00	$1,680.00	$1,680.00	$0.00
5	Determine major mi	25%	$960.00	$240.00	$240.00	($720.00)	$0.00	$960.00	$960.00	$0.00
6	Secure executive s	0%	$1,920.00	$0.00	$0.00	($1,920.00)	$0.00	$1,920.00	$1,920.00	$0.00
7	Envisioning complet	0%	$0.00	$0.00	$0.00	$0.00	$0.00	$0.00	$0.00	$0.00
8	⊞ Assemble Project T	0%	$2,160.00	$0.00	$0.00	($2,160.00)	$0.00	$2,160.00	$2,160.00	$0.00
19	☐ Planning	0%	$4,000.00	$0.00	$0.00	($4,000.00)	$0.00	$35,268.00	$35,268.00	$0.00
20	☐ Identify Coexiste	0%	$1,600.00	$0.00	$0.00	($1,600.00)	$0.00	$2,240.00	$2,240.00	$0.00
21	Identify interope	0%	$640.00	$0.00	$0.00	($640.00)	$0.00	$640.00	$640.00	$0.00
22	Identify interope	0%	$960.00	$0.00	$0.00	($960.00)	$0.00	$960.00	$960.00	$0.00
23	Identify interope	0%	$0.00	$0.00	$0.00	$0.00	$0.00	$640.00	$640.00	$0.00
24	Identify coexiste	0%	$0.00	$0.00	$0.00	$0.00	$0.00	$0.00	$0.00	$0.00
25	⊞ Identify Migratior	0%	$0.00	$0.00	$0.00	$0.00	$0.00	$3,440.00	$3,440.00	$0.00
35	⊞ Identify Desktop	0%	$840.00	$0.00	$0.00	($840.00)	$0.00	$1,120.00	$1,120.00	$0.00
41	⊞ Identify Configur	0%	$0.00	$0.00	$0.00	$0.00	$0.00	$7,520.00	$7,520.00	$0.00
54	⊞ Identify Collabor:	0%	$1,200.00	$0.00	$0.00	($1,200.00)	$0.00	$4,000.00	$4,000.00	$0.00
58	⊞ Identify Messagi	0%	$360.00	$0.00	$0.00	($360.00)	$0.00	$1,000.00	$1,000.00	$0.00
63	⊞ Identify Technica	0%	$0.00	$0.00	$0.00	$0.00	$0.00	$2,980.00	$2,980.00	$0.00
96	⊞ Plan Security	0%	$0.00	$0.00	$0.00	$0.00	$0.00	$1,680.00	$1,680.00	$0.00
102	⊞ Define Distributio	0%	$0.00	$0.00	$0.00	$0.00	$0.00	$1,840.00	$1,840.00	$0.00
110	⊞ Specify Custom F	0%	$0.00	$0.00	$0.00	$0.00	$0.00	$4,000.00	$4,000.00	$0.00
129	⊞ Develop Training	0%	$0.00	$0.00	$0.00	$0.00	$0.00	$3,840.00	$3,840.00	$0.00
134	⊞ Identify Test Scer	0%	$0.00	$0.00	$0.00	$0.00	$0.00	$1,600.00	$1,600.00	$0.00
141	Planning complete	0%	$0.00	$0.00	$0.00	$0.00	$0.00	$0.00	$0.00	$0.00
142	☐ Deployment	0%	$0.00	$0.00	$0.00	$0.00	$0.00	$34,720.00	$34,720.00	$0.00
143	⊞ Create Custom C	0%	$0.00	$0.00	$0.00	$0.00	$0.00	$3,080.00	$3,080.00	$0.00
156	⊞ Deploy Collabora	0%	$0.00	$0.00	$0.00	$0.00	$0.00	$4,000.00	$4,000.00	$0.00

Book IX

Advanced Project Topics

The 5th Wave   By Rich Tennant

@RICHTENNANT

"Of course graphics are important to your project,
Eddy, but I think it would've been better to
scan a _picture_ of your worm collection."

Contents at a Glance

Chapter 1: Working Your Own Way

In This Chapter

✔ Controlling the Project Guide's behavior

✔ Controlling the levels of undoing actions

✔ Controlling the way you switch between projects

✔ Customizing the way you open and save projects

✔ Customizing toolbars and menus

✔ Sharing elements across projects

You probably feel more comfortable in your own home than any other place. After all, you decorate your home to reflect your personality and make it a comfortable place for you to be. You choose the colors, the furnishings, the carpet, the tile . . . you get our drift.

You can make Project comfortable by customizing it to reflect the way you work. For example, you can choose to display the Project Guide each time you open Project, and you can decide whether you want the Standard and Formatting toolbars to take up one line or two on-screen. You can even build your own toolbars. So, this chapter explores the things you can do to make the Project working environment suit your needs.

Lots of settings can change Project's behavior; in this chapter, we cover the ones we think can help you most and impact your daily work.

Controlling the Project Guide's Behavior

The Project Guide is a tool that can guide you through the process of setting up a project. When visible, the Project Guide appears in a task pane on the left side of the screen (see Figure 1-1). In the Project Guide, you see links that you can click to walk you through actions necessary to set up a project.

When the Project Guide appears on-screen, the Project Guide toolbar also appears; each button on the Project Guide toolbar changes the links that appear in the Project Guide pane to focus on setting up different project information.

When you first start working with a project, having the Project Guide visible can be handy, helping to remind you of the things you need to do. But, as you get into working with a project, you might not want the Project Guide taking up valuable screen real estate. You can control whether the Project Guide appears on-screen from the View menu. Choose View⇨Turn On Project Guide (see Figure 1-2); when the Project Guide appears in the task pane, you can hide it by choosing View⇨Turn Off Project Guide.

For the technically curious, selecting or deselecting the Display Project Guide check box on the Interface tab of the Options dialog box has the exact same effect as using the command on the View menu.

Project Guide toolbar

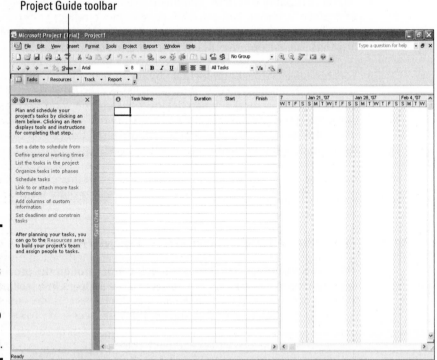

Figure 1-1:
The Project Guide walks you through the process of setting up a project step by step.

How Many Times Can You Undo?

Project fell behind its Office cousins when it came to undoing actions — until Project 2007. Now, Project also has the capability to undo more than just your last action. You can set the number of actions that you can undo to any number between 1 and 99; Project sets the number to 20 by default.

Figure 1-2:
Hide or display the Project Guide by using the View menu.

We can hear you thinking (it was our first thought, too), "Why not set it to 99?" Yes, you're right — there's a reason.

Each action you take while working in Project requires Project to track a relatively large or small amount of data. For example, changing the task names of 20 different tasks isn't really a lot of changes for Project to track. But, tracking the information associated with ten baselines is a much larger set of data.

Project tracks everything in memory, and some processes use more memory than others. By increasing the number of actions to track to 99, you're actually asking Project to use more memory to track your actions, in case you need to undo. If you change the Undo level to 99, Project's performance might go down enough for you to notice.

That said, if you prefer to have Project track more than 20 actions, you can do it. Choose Tools⇨Options and click the General tab. Then change the number that appears in the Undo Levels box (see Figure 1-3).

Undo Levels option

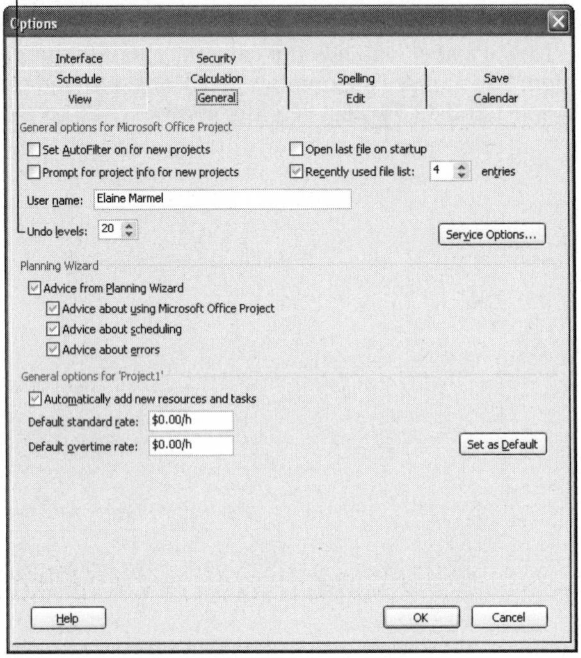

Figure 1-3:
Use the
Undo Levels
option to set
the number
of actions
Project
tracks for
the purpose
of undoing
actions.

Switching Between Open Projects

By default, Project displays a Windows taskbar icon for each open Project (see Figure 1-4). Depending on the number of open files, you might not necessarily be able to identify the file from the icon on the Windows taskbar, but you can see a few letters of the filename on the icon. In addition, if you point the mouse at the icon, you see a ToolTip that shows the entire path and filename.

This behavior works well for people who like to switch between projects by clicking an icon on the Windows taskbar. But, suppose that you're one of those people who places a premium on Windows taskbar real estate and you really don't want to see each project in the Windows taskbar; you prefer to see one icon per open program — not open file — in the Windows taskbar. You can change Project's behavior by following these steps:

1. **Choose Tools⇨Options.**

Project displays the Options dialog box (see Figure 1-5).

Book IX
Chapter 1

Working Your
Own Way

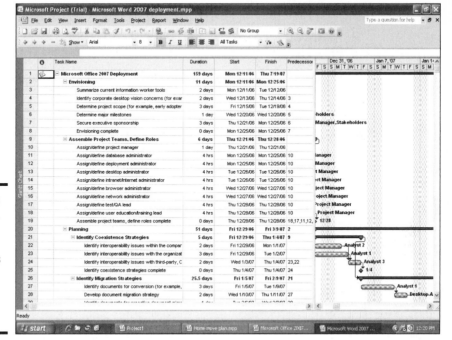

Figure 1-4:
By default,
each open
project
displays its
own icon
on the
Windows
taskbar.

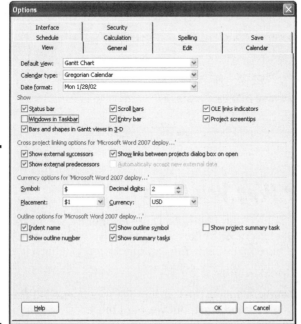

Figure 1-5:
Use the
Windows in
Taskbar
option to
control
Project's
treatment
of the
Windows
taskbar.

   2. **Click the View tab.**

   3. **Remove the check from the Windows in Taskbar option.**

   4. **Click OK.**

   Project saves your changes and closes the Options dialog box.

Project changes the appearance of the Windows taskbar to display only one icon for the project you're currently viewing. But all open projects appear on the Window menu (see Figure 1-6), and in fact, you use the Window menu to switch to a different open project by clicking the name of the project you want to view.

Regardless of the behavior that you choose in the Options dialog box, all open Project files appear at the bottom of the Window menu, and you can use the Window menu to switch among Project files.

Figure 1-6:
Although only one icon for the project you're viewing appears on the Windows taskbar, all open projects appear on the Window menu.

Customizing the Way You Open

This setting is one of our favorites. Quite frequently, we find ourselves working with the last six or eight files we opened. We really like being able to find them quickly to reopen them. You can quickly open a file if it appears at the bottom of the File menu (see Figure 1-7).

By default, Project displays the last four files we opened at the bottom of the File menu. That's a good start, but we want more.

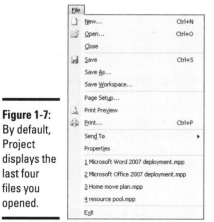

Figure 1-7:
By default,
Project
displays the
last four
files you
opened.

To display more files at the bottom of the File menu, follow these steps:

1. **Choose Tools⇨Options.**

Project displays the Options dialog box (see Figure 1-8).

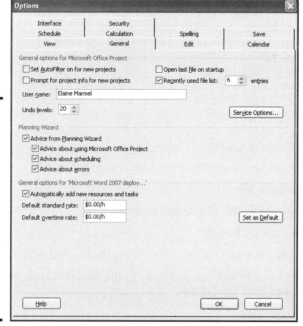

Figure 1-8:
Use the
Recently
Used File
List Entries
box to
specify the
number of
files you
want to see
at the
bottom of
the File
menu.

2. **Click the General tab.**

3. **Change the number in the Recently Used File List box.**

4. **Click OK.**

   Project saves your changes and closes the Options dialog box.

As you open other projects, Project expands the number of files that appear at the bottom of the File menu to display the number of files you chose in the Options dialog box.

Don't forget that you can turn on the display of the project summary task from the View tab.

Customizing the Way You Save

When you set the File Locations option, you actually help yourself when it comes to both saving and opening files because you establish a default folder in which Project saves files. And, when you open a file, Project always looks for it first in the default folder where you save files.

By default, Project saves files to the My Documents folder. Some orderly folks prefer to save Project files in a folder created to store only Project files. Other folks set up folders by subject and store all files related to a particular subject in a folder. So, you might have one or more Project files, Word documents, and Excel spreadsheets in a folder that contains all the information related to a particular project.

Whatever your method of organization, you can set a default folder where Project saves files and then looks when you want to open them by following these steps:

1. **Choose Tools⇨Options.**

   Project displays the Options dialog box (see Figure 1-9).

2. **Click the Save tab.**

3. **Click Projects in the File Types section.**

4. **Click the Modify button.**

   The Modify Location dialog box appears (see Figure 1-10).

5. **Open the Look In list and navigate to the folder where you want to save Project files by default.**

6. **Click OK twice.**

   Project saves your changes and closes the Options dialog box.

Figure 1-9:
Set a default
folder
to store
Project files.

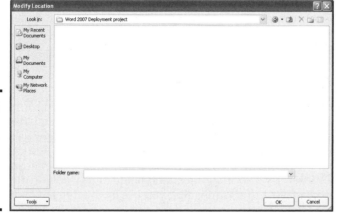

Figure 1-10:
The Modify
Location
dialog box
works like
the Open
dialog box.

A few other options on the Save tab bear mentioning:

+ **Auto Save:** The Auto Save feature is particularly valuable if you tend to
  work extensively and forget to save regularly. By setting the Auto Save
  option, you can avoid becoming a victim of power failures or server

crashes. Select the Save Every check box and specify the number of minutes that should elapse between saves. You also can choose to save only the project you're viewing or all open projects, and you can have Project prompt you before saving.

Although Auto Save works in the background, it can slow down Project's performance with large files.

✦ **Default file format:** You can specify the default file format for each new Project file that you save. This option comes in handy, for example, if you regularly share files with someone who uses another version of Project.

The Project 2007 format is different from Project 2003, Project 2002, and Project 2000, all of which share the same file format. You can no longer save a file to the Project 98 format.

You might lose information if you save a file created in Project 2007 in the format of Project 2000 – 2003. For example, background cell formatting doesn't exist in any version of Project prior to Project 2007. If you apply background formatting to cells in a file and then save the file in Project 2000 – 2003 format, you lose the background cell formatting.

Customizing the Toolbars

Toolbars provide a quick and easy way to avoid opening menus and choosing commands. To make the most of this high-tech tool, you have some options.

One line or two?

By default, Project displays the Standard toolbar and the Formatting toolbar on the same row. On most monitors, you can't see all the buttons on either toolbar because there simply isn't enough room. Initially, Project displays the buttons that Microsoft thinks you'll use most often, and you use the Toolbar Options button to display the hidden buttons when you need to use one of them. As you work, Project personalizes the toolbars to your work habits, displaying the buttons that you use most often and hiding others that you don't use as often.

If you're like us, you want to see all the buttons on each toolbar all the time, and you don't want to bother using the Toolbar Options button. To display each toolbar on its own line, click the Toolbar Options button and choose Show Buttons on Two Rows (see Figure 1-11).

Figure 1-11:
You can display the Standard and Formatting toolbars on two rows instead of one.

Project displays the two toolbars on separate rows and all of the buttons on each toolbar are visible.

Change your mind? Click the Toolbar Options button and choose Show Buttons on One Row.

Creating your own toolbar

Eventually, you'll find that you regularly use certain buttons on a variety of toolbars. You might even come to the conclusion that you'd really like one toolbar that contains all the buttons you use regularly instead of working with a bunch of different toolbars. No problem — create your own custom toolbar.

You can add buttons to an existing toolbar without creating a new toolbar. Perform Steps 1, 5, 6, and 7 in the following list.

You create custom toolbars and add buttons to them by following these steps:

1. **Choose Tools➪Customize➪Toolbars.**

Project displays the Customize dialog box (see Figure 1-12). While the Customize dialog box remains open, Project enables you to add or delete buttons on toolbars and create new toolbars.

2. **Click the Toolbars tab.**

Project displays a list of the toolbars that currently exist.

3. **Click the New button.**

The New Toolbar dialog box appears (see Figure 1-13).

Figure 1-12:
On the Toolbars tab of the Customize dialog box, you see all the toolbars available in Project.

Figure 1-13:
Name your toolbar anything you like.

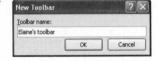

4. **Type a toolbar name and click OK.**

   A small, empty toolbar appears.

   You can drag this floating toolbar to any location on-screen that's convenient for you.

5. **Click the Commands tab of the Customize dialog box.**

6. **From the Categories list, select a category of commands.**

7. **From the Commands list, drag commands from the Customize dialog box onto the new toolbar.**

   Project places the button on the toolbar where you drop it. Figure 1-14 shows the new toolbar we created.

f you're satisfied with your toolbar, click Close to close the Customize dialog box. If you want to make changes to the toolbar, leave the Customize dialog box open and read the next section.

Modifying a toolbar

You can make changes to the appearance of any toolbar — not just one that you created. But, for this example, we focus on the toolbar we just created in the preceding section.

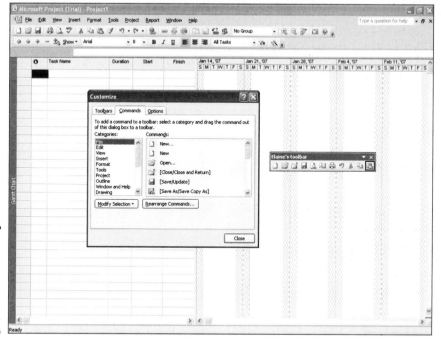

Figure 1-14:
Place
buttons on
the toolbar
in any order
that you like.

IFirst, make sure that the Customize dialog box is open. When this dialog box is open, Project assumes that you're making changes to a toolbar and not trying to use a button on a toolbar to perform a command. If the Customize dialog box isn't open, choose Tools➪Customize➪Toolbars.

The preceding section shows you how to add buttons to the toolbar. Simply follow Steps 5 through 7 in the preceding section to add buttons to toolbars while the Customize dialog box is open.

Changing the position of the buttons on a toolbar is easy. To move a button to a new position on the toolbar, drag it to its new position. And, if you change your mind about a button and want to remove it from the toolbar, simply drag it off the toolbar and drop it on any white space in your project.

You can organize the buttons on your toolbar into groups of buttons by placing dividers — thin gray lines — on either side of the group. For example, you might want to group buttons that perform actions related to printing. Follow these steps:

1. **With the Customize dialog box open and displaying the Commands tab, select the button that you want to place to the right of the divider.**

2. **Click the Modify Selection button on the Commands tab.**

    The menu shown in Figure 1-15 appears.

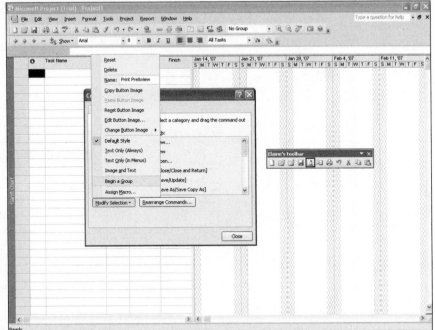

Figure 1-15:
Use this menu to make changes to buttons and toolbars.

3. **Select the Begin a Group command from this menu.**

   Project inserts a divider to the left of the selected button on your tool-bar (see Figure 1-16).

Figure 1-16:
A divider (a thin gray line) helps group buttons on a toolbar.

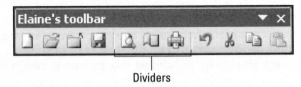

Dividers

4. **Click Close.**

   Project closes the Customize dialog box, enabling you to click the but-tons on all toolbars to perform actions.

To delete a divider, make sure that the Customize dialog box is open. Then, select the tool to the divider's right and click Modify Selection. From the menu that appears, select Begin a Group again to deselect that command.

Messing with button images

Even if you're not particularly adept at drawing, you can personalize a button image by selecting from a set of button image designs that includes everything from smiling faces to musical notes. If you *are* adept at drawing . . . well, first, we envy you, and second, you can change a button's default image to one you personalize.

If anyone else uses your copy of Project, be careful about changing button images. You can confuse even the most advanced user by assigning a well-known button image like the scissors on the Cut button to a button that doesn't perform the well-known action of cutting.

To change the images that appear on tools, follow these steps:

1. **Choose Tools⇨Customize⇨Toolbars.**

The Customize dialog box appears.

2. **If the toolbar containing the button isn't visible, click the Toolbars tab and select the toolbar.**

3. **Click the Commands tab.**

4. **Click a button on any toolbar that you have displayed.**

5. **Click the Modify Selection button.**

6. **Select Change Button Image.**

A pop-up palette of images appears (see Figure 1-17).

7. **Click the image that you want to use.**

8. **Click Close to close the Customize dialog box after you finish.**

ToolTips still work with modified buttons and are a great help in remembering what function a button performs. Just hover your mouse pointer on any tool, and its original name appears.

You can return a button image to its original setting. With the Customize dialog box open and the button you want to restore selected, choose Modify Selection⇨Reset Button Image.

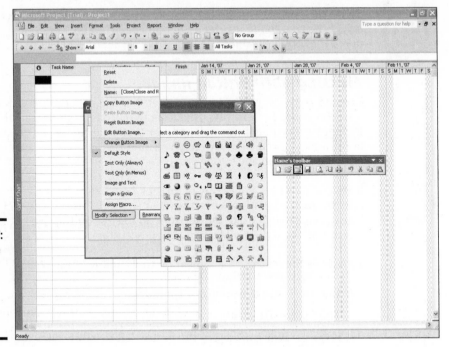

Figure 1-17:
The palette
of button
images
provides
great
variety.

If you're artistically inclined, you can edit an existing button picture by modifying the pattern and colors on it. For example, if two buttons seem similar to you, you can differentiate them by applying a bright red color to either one. Button images consist of many tiny squares called pixels. By coloring in the pixels, you can form an image. You can use a color palette and the individual pixels to modify button images or even draw an entirely new image.

To edit a button image, follow these steps:

1. **Choose Tools⇨Customize⇨Toolbars.**

The Customize dialog box appears.

2. **Click a button on any displayed toolbar.**

If the toolbar containing the button isn't visible, click the Toolbars tab and select the toolbar.

3. **Click the Commands tab.**

4. **Click Modify Selection.**

5. **Select the Edit Button Image command.**

Project opens the Button Editor dialog box (see Figure 1-18).

Figure 1-18:
Use the
Preview
window to
see how
changes to
individual
picture
pixels affect
the button
image.

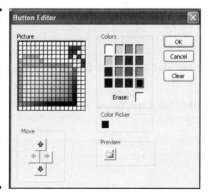

6. **To change a pixel's color, click a color block in the Colors palette and then click an individual pixel.**

7. **To remove color from a pixel, click the Erase block in the Colors palette and then click the pixel.**

You can operate on a large area of pixels, either to color the area or to erase it. Click a pixel and then drag the mouse in any direction to color or erase multiple pixels in one motion. Release the mouse button to stop coloring or erasing the pixels.

8. **To see more of a large button that doesn't fit in the Picture box, click the Move arrows.**

9. **Click OK to save your changes and to return to the Customize dialog box.**

10. **Click Close to return to your Project screen.**

The changes you made appear on the button image.

Customizing the Menus

Okay, so, you're a menu person. You *like* menus. You want to use them. But, you really wish you could set up the menus the way *you* want them so that your menu or menus contain the commands you use and they appear in the order you want them to appear. Once again, no problem. Or, mostly no problem. You can create and customize menus just like you can create and customize toolbars. However, the same caveat applies: If you share your copy of Project with others, be aware that they might prefer to use the menus in Project as they appear by default. Still, that shouldn't stop you from personalizing menu behavior and even creating your own menu that others don't need to use.

Personalizing menu behavior

You have some choices about the way menus behave in Project:

✦ You can have Project display all commands on the menu when you open it.

✦ You can have Project display only the most frequently used commands, and you then take action to display all commands.

✦ You can have Project initially display only the most frequently used commands and, after a pause, display all commands.

When you choose the second option and open a menu, the expand arrows appear at the bottom of the menu (see Figure 1-19).

Figure 1-19:
You can display only the most frequently used commands initially.

When you click the expand arrows, the rest of the commands on the menu appear. The gray bar that runs down the left side of the menu is lighter for commands that don't appear initially than for commands that do appear initially (see Figure 1-20). If you select a command that didn't appear initially, that command becomes a frequently used command and appears on the abbreviated menu the next time you open the menu.

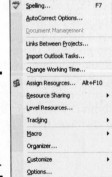

Figure 1-20:
Click the expand arrows to display the entire menu.

When you choose the behavior described in the third option, Project initially displays the most frequently used commands (refer to Figure 1-19), but you don't need to click the expand arrows to see the rest of the commands; if you just wait a few seconds, Project automatically displays them (refer to Figure 1-20).

You can control menu behavior in Project from the Options tab of the Customize dialog box, shown in Figure 1-21. Choose Tools➪Customize➪ Toolbars and then click the Options tab.

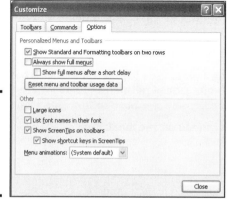

Figure 1-21:
Control
menu
behavior
from this
dialog box.

If you select the Always Show Full Menus check box, Project displays all commands on the menu when you open it — the first bullet option in the preceding list. And, the Show Full Menus After a Short Delay check box becomes unavailable.

If you don't select either check box, Project displays only the most frequently used commands, and you then click the expand arrows to display all commands — the second bullet option.

If you select the Show Full Menus After a Short Delay check box, Project initially displays only the most frequently used commands and, after a pause, displays all commands — the third bullet option.

Creating your own menu

The process of creating a new menu is a three-part process. First, you drag a new, blank menu to the menu bar, then you assign it a name, and finally you drag commands onto it.

Project adds new menus to your Global template file, the default file on which Project bases all files. So, changes that you make to menus or the menu bar affect all files — new or existing — that you create with this copy of Project.

Follow these steps to create a new menu:

1. **Choose View⇨Toolbars⇨Customize.**

Project opens the Customize dialog box.

2. **Click the Commands tab.**

3. **Scroll to the bottom of the Categories list and click the New Menu category.**

New Menu appears in the list of commands.

4. **Drag New Menu in the Commands list up to the menu bar. When the dark vertical line of your mouse pointer appears where you want to place the new menu, release the mouse button (see Figure 1-22).**

Project places the new menu on the menu bar.

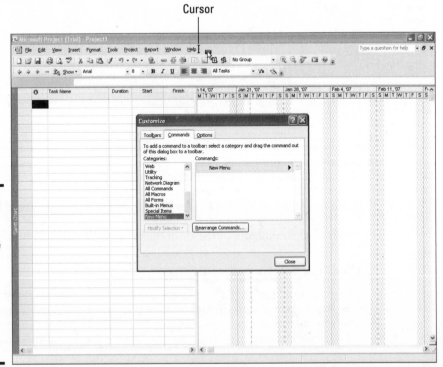

Figure 1-22: When you click New Menu in the Categories list, only one choice appears in the Commands list.

Naming a new menu you created

After you create a new menu, Project gives it the clever name "New Menu," which isn't very meaningful. But, you can name the menu whatever you want by using these steps:

1. **With the Customize dialog box open, select New Menu on the menu bar.**

2. **Click the Modify Selection button on the Commands tab.**

A pop-up menu appears (see Figure 1-23).

3. **Select the text that appears in the Name text box.**

The default name is New Menu.

4. **Type a new name for the menu.**

5. **Click outside the Modify Selection menu to close it.**

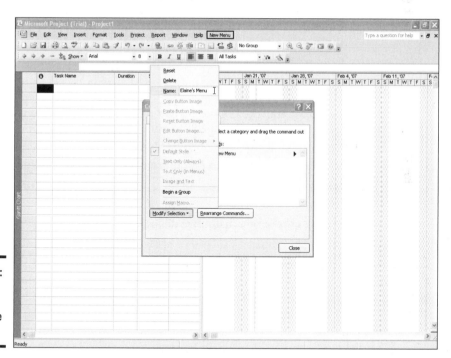

Figure 1-23:
Assign a
meaningful
name to the
menu.

Adding commands to a menu

After you create and name a new menu, you're ready to add commands to it.

You can use the following steps to add a command to any menu — not just a new menu that you created:

1. **With the Customize dialog box open and displaying the Commands tab, select a category of commands that you want to place on the new menu.**

   You can place a macro you created on the menu. Select the All Macros category and then continue with these steps.

2. **Drag an item in the Commands list up to the menu.**

   Project automatically opens the menu. When you drag the first command onto the menu, a small, blank box appears under the menu heading.

3. **Place the mouse pointer in that blank area and release the mouse button.**

   Project places the command on the menu.

   After you place the first command on the menu, commands you previously dragged onto the menu appear. You place a command on the menu by positioning the horizontal bar attached to the mouse pointer where you want the new command to appear. In Figure 1-24, we're adding a command between two existing commands.

4. **Repeat Steps 2 and 3 to add more commands to the menu.**

5. **When the menu contains all the commands you want to add, click Close.**

   Project closes the Customize dialog box.

You can divide the menu into groups of commands the same way that you divide buttons on a toolbar into groups. With the Customize dialog box open and displaying the Commands tab, select the command on the menu that should appear just after the group starts. Then choose Modify Selection⇨ Begin a Group to add a dividing line.

Deleting commands and menus

It's possible that, at some point, you'll want to remove a particular command from a menu or even an entire menu. But, you'd like to make the change without resetting all the menu changes that you've made. Follow these steps:

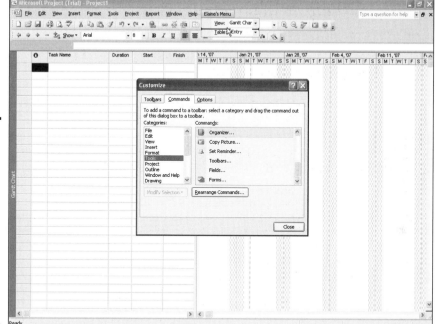

Figure 1-24:
Add new commands to a menu by dragging the commands onto the menu in the position where you want them to appear.

1. **Open the Customize dialog box.**

2. **Click a menu name or open the menu and click a particular command.**

3. **Drag the item off the menu bar and drop it someplace away from any menu or toolbar.**

Project removes the command from the menu or the menu from the menu bar.

4. **Close the Customize dialog box.**

Using the Organizer to Share Project Elements

Using the Organizer, you can share toolbars, the Menu Bar, views, tables, forms, reports, and more among projects. The Organizer makes it easy for you to copy something you customized in one Project file to other Project files or to the Global template so that all new Project files will contain the element you copied.

To display the Organizer dialog box shown in Figure 1-25, choose Tools➪ Organizer.

Figure 1-25:
The
Organizer
window
helps you
share
elements
across
Project files.

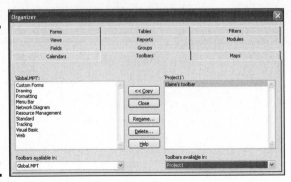

Use the various tabs in the Organizer dialog box to copy elements from the Global template (Global.mpt) to the current project. You also can copy elements from the current project to the Global template or simply between projects.

All elements in the Global template (Global.mpt) file are available to every file that you create based on the Global.mpt file, which is the default file Project uses when you create a new, blank project.

To copy an element between projects, follow these steps:

1. **Open the Project file that contains the information you want to copy.**

2. **Open the Project file into which you want to copy the information.**

3. **Choose Tools⇨Organizer.**

The Organizer window appears.

If you have other files open besides the ones described in Steps 1 and 2, make sure that the names of the files described in Steps 1 and 2 appear in the list boxes at the bottom of each tab.

Global.mpt also appears in both list boxes. If you select it, you can copy an element to the Global template, making the element available to all new files you create.

4. **Click the tab of the element you want to copy.**

5. **Click the element you want to copy.**

6. **Click Copy.**

7. **Repeat Steps 4 to 6 for each element you want to copy.**

You can rename or delete elements using the Organizer and the same steps you use to copy elements; in Step 6, click Delete or Rename.

If you delete an element from the Global template, it won't be available to any project. Deleting is risky at best, and you should avoid it unless you really need to do it. Backing up the Global template before you delete any element is a very wise idea. You can back up the Global template by searching your computer for `Global.mpt` and copying it to another folder.

8. **When you're finished, close the Organizer dialog box, and Project will save your changes.**

You can read about creating custom tables in Book VI, Chapter 2.

Sharing a customized table

Company: Company with more than 75 employees and several project managers using their own copies of Project.

Project: All projects created by the company.

Challenge: Enable all company project managers to use a table created by one project manager without re-creating the table in each copy of Project.

One of the project managers at the subject company has created a customized table that all project managers agree would be an effective one for their organization to use as part of the progress-tracking process. Each project manager can sit down and create the table in Project, but they'd prefer not to reinvent the wheel.

Solution: To meet the challenge, the project manager who created the table provides a copy of the file containing the table to each of the other project managers either via a network, in e-mail, or on disc. Then, each of those project managers follows these steps to copy the table into their individual `Global.mpt` files, which will make the table available in every new project they create. They also can open existing projects in which they want to use the table and copy the table into those projects.

1. **Open the file containing the table.**

2. **Choose Tools⇨Organizer.**

   The Organizer window appears.

3. **Click the Tables tab.**

(continued)

(continued)

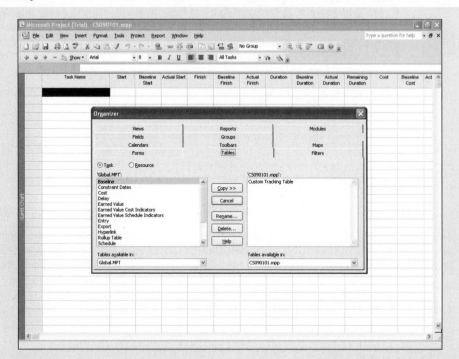

4. **Make sure that Global.mpt appears in one of the Tables Available In lists and the file containing the table appears in the other.**

5. **Click the customized table.**

6. **Click Copy.**

   The customized table appears in the Global.mpt file.

Each project manager then opens an existing project in which they want the table to appear

and follows the preceding steps, making sure, in Step 4, that an existing project appears in the Tables Available In list in place of the Global.mpt file.

On the Web site for this book, you can find the CS0901.mpp file, a file containing a customized table. You can practice copying it into one of your files by using the Organizer.

Chapter 2: Changing the Look of a Project

In This Chapter

✓ Changing fonts in tables

✓ Formatting Gantt Chart view

✓ Formatting Network Diagram view

✓ Formatting Calendar view

You can change the look of a project in a variety of ways. For example, you can use different fonts for task names in views containing tables. And, Project contains special formatting that you can apply to Gantt Chart, Network Diagram, and Calendar views. In this chapter, we look at these different ways to change the appearance of a project.

Changing Fonts

In views that contain tables, such as Gantt Chart view, Task Usage view, and Resource Usage view, you can make changes to the fonts that appear in the table cells to highlight pertinent information. You change font information for selected tasks or for tasks that fall into a particular category, such as external tasks in an inserted project.

See Book III, Chapter 4 for more information on inserting and linking projects.

Don't go overboard with multiple fonts or colors on a single schedule. You can make a project harder to read by using too many fancy fonts. Try to use only one or two fonts or colors in your schedule, and vary the text by using bold or italic between categories. Using too light a color, such as yellow, for a font face can make the text very difficult to read, and in print, the schedule won't look much better. If you really want to use color, set the background color of the cell to any color other than black. Also, try to set up company standards for formatting so that all your project schedules have a consistent, professional look.

Changing fonts for selected tasks

Suppose that you're preparing a report for your boss and you need to call attention to one particular task because you want to focus your boss's attention on that task. You can change the font, font style, point size, and even the font color of that task's name.

You can change other fields besides a task's name. For example, if you want to focus on the number of hours of Work assigned to a task or a resource, select that field.

1. Display a view that contains a table.

In Figure 2-1, we displayed the Task Usage view.

2. Click the name of the task that you want to change.

You can apply the changes to more than one task if you select the tasks. To select a contiguous list of tasks, press and hold Shift while clicking the names of the first and last tasks. To select noncontiguous tasks, press and hold Ctrl while clicking each task.

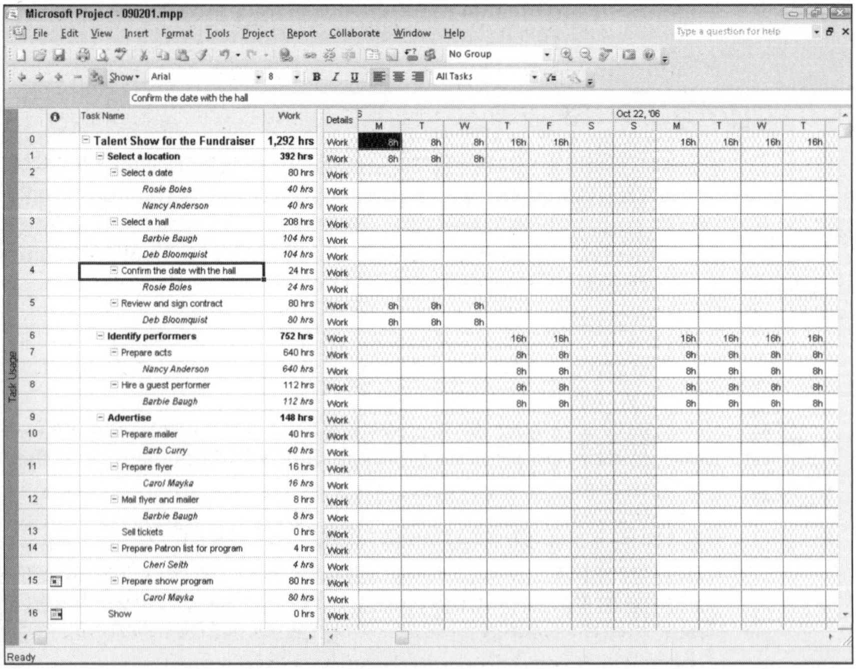

Figure 2-1:
Start in a view containing a table.

3. Choose Format⇨Font.

Project displays the Font dialog box (see Figure 2-2).

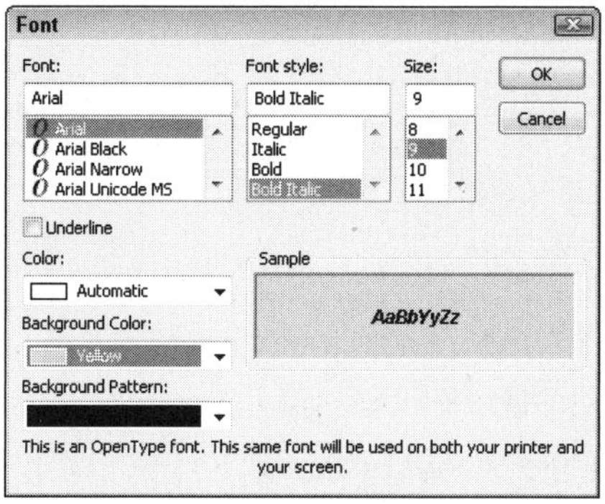

Figure 2-2:
Use this
dialog box
to make
changes to
the fonts for
a field.

4. From the Font list, select a new font.

5. From the Font Style list, select Italic, Bold, or Bold Italic formatting.

The Regular font style applies neither italic nor bold font styles to text.

6. From the Size box, change the font size.

7. Select the Underline check box to apply underlining to text.

8. Select a color from the Color and Background Color drop-down lists.

A preview of your selections appears in the Sample area.

You can apply a background pattern to a cell, but be careful because a background pattern can make text harder to read.

9. Click OK.

Project applies your changes to the selected task name.

 You can click Undo to reverse the results of changes to fonts and other formatting features if you don't like what you see.

Changing fonts for a task category

Suppose that you're preparing slides for a presentation where you want to show all tasks in your project's schedule but call attention to critical tasks. You can, for example, display the names of all critical tasks in bold, red text. To make these changes, follow these steps:

1. **Display a view that contains a table.**

2. **Choose Format⇨Text Styles.**

Project displays the Text Styles dialog box (see Figure 2-3).

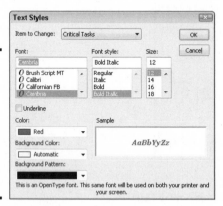

Figure 2-3:
Use this
dialog box
to change
font
information
for a
category of
tasks.

3. **Open the Item to Change drop-down list and select the type of tasks you want to affect.**

We selected Critical Tasks.

4. **From the Font list, select a new font.**

We selected Cambria.

5. **From the Font Style list, select Italic, Bold, or Bold Italic formatting.**

We selected Bold Italic.

6. **From the Size box, change the font size.**

We changed the font size to 12.

7. **Click OK.**

Project applies the changes to the selected category of tasks (see Figure 2-4).

 You can click Undo to reverse the results of changes to fonts and other formatting features if you don't like what you see.

Applying Special Formatting to Gantt Chart View

You can make changes to Gantt Chart view's bars, layout, and gridlines. You can use the Gantt Chart Wizard to format Gantt Chart view, or you can format elements individually.

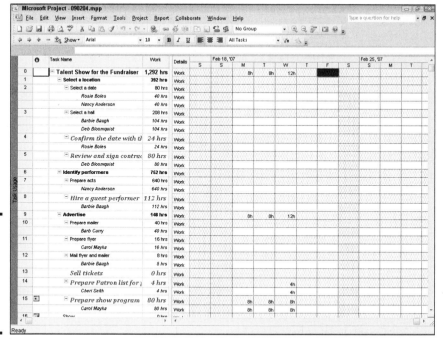

Figure 2-4:
This figure
shows the
changes
made to the
critical task
names.

Using the Gantt Chart Wizard

The Gantt Chart Wizard is an interactive series of dialog boxes that prompt you for information. Project uses your input to modify the appearance of the Gantt chart.

You can use the Gantt Chart Wizard from either Gantt Chart view or Tracking Gantt view. The formatting applied by the Gantt Chart Wizard affects only the Project file you're viewing when you run the wizard. To use the Gantt Chart Wizard to apply formatting to Gantt Chart view, follow these steps:

1. Choose Format⇨Gantt Chart Wizard.

   Project displays the first dialog box of the Gantt Chart Wizard, a dialog box that simply greets you and tells you what the wizard does.

2. Click Next.

   The second wizard dialog box appears (see Figure 2-5).

3. Select an option for the kind of information that you want to display.

   - *Standard* shows blue taskbars, black summary taskbars, and a black line inside the taskbars to indicate progress on tasks.

   - *Critical Path* uses the same settings as Standard, except that critical-path tasks appear in red.

Figure 2-5:
The preview shown in this window gives you an idea of the formatting each option applies to the Gantt chart.

- *Baseline* displays baseline taskbars and progress taskbars separately, rather than displaying progress bars inside taskbars the way that the Standard option does.

- *Other* offers a drop-down list that contains several alternative chart colors and styles for the Standard, Critical Path, and Baseline options, along with some additional styles; you can select each from the list and watch the preview to see its effect.

- *Custom Gantt Chart* enables you to create a highly customized Gantt chart; when you select this option, the Gantt Chart Wizard displays several additional screens.

4. Click Next.

The third wizard dialog box appears (see Figure 2-6).

If you select Custom Gantt Chart, several additional dialog boxes appear before the box shown in Figure 2-6.

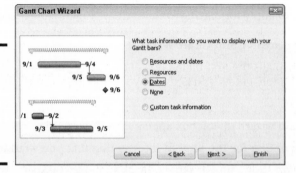

Figure 2-6:
Select the text you want to display alongside taskbars.

5. Select an option to describe the type of task information to display with your Gantt bars.

- If you choose *Resources and Dates,* Project displays resource names to the right of each task and milestone date.

- If you choose *Resources,* Project displays resource names to the right of each task.

- If you choose *Dates,* Project displays the task start date and end date at the beginning and end of each taskbar.

- If you choose *None,* Project displays no information beside taskbars.

- If you choose *Custom Task Information,* Project adds a dialog box to the wizard that prompts you for the type of information you want to display to the left, right, and inside each taskbar.

6. **Click Next.**

Project displays the wizard dialog box shown in Figure 2-7.

Figure 2-7:
Use this
dialog box
to specify
whether to
display link
lines
between
dependent
tasks.

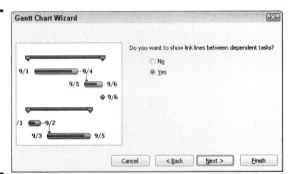

7. **Select an option to show or hide link lines between dependent tasks.**

8. **Click Next.**

Project displays a box that congratulates you on selecting your options. You can use the Back button to go back and make changes.

9. **Click the Format It button.**

Project formats the Gantt chart and displays a final dialog box to tell you that your formatting is complete.

10. **Click the Exit Wizard button.**

Project closes the dialog box and you can see the changes.

If you don't like the changes you made to the project using the Gantt Chart Wizard, you can click the Undo button before you save your project to remove the changes that the Gantt Chart Wizard applies to your project.

Changing individual taskbars

You can change the appearance of a taskbar's shape and its text. When you change the shape of a taskbar, you can control the appearance of the start, middle, and end of the taskbar.

You can apply the changes to more than one task if you select the tasks. To select a contiguous list of tasks, press and hold Shift while clicking the names of the first and last tasks. To select noncontiguous tasks, press and hold Ctrl while clicking each task.

To change a taskbar's appearance, choose Format⇨Bar. Project displays the Format Bar dialog box shown in Figure 2-8.

Figure 2-8:
Use this dialog box to control the appearance of one or more selected taskbars.

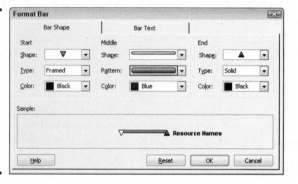

The Format Bar dialog box contains two tabbed sheets called Bar Shape and Bar Text. On the Bar Shape tab, use the Start and End sections to select a shape, type, and color for the beginning and end of the selected taskbar. The shapes you select appear at either end of the taskbar. The Type list contains Dashed, Framed, and Solid choices that affect the appearance of the shape you select. And, of course, the Color list lets you control the color of the shape.

In the Middle section of the Bar Shape tab, you control the shape, pattern, and color of the middle portion of the taskbar. From the Shape list, you can determine the size for the middle of the taskbar; if you make the middle thinner than the default size, you can set the vertical alignment of the taskbar so that it aligns with the top, middle, or bottom of the shapes on either end of the taskbar. From the Pattern list, you can change the selected taskbars from solid colors to a variety of hatched patterns. And, once again, the Color list controls the color of the selected taskbars.

From the Bar Text tab, shown in Figure 2-9, you can select text to appear to the left, right, top, bottom, or inside each taskbar. The Sample area allows you to preview your selection.

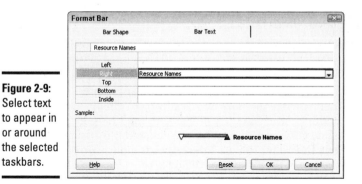

Figure 2-9:
Select text
to appear in
or around
the selected
taskbars.

Changing taskbar styles for categories of tasks

Rather than changing individual taskbars that you select, you can control the appearance of taskbars for categories of tasks. For example, you can set up the taskbars for critical tasks to appear as thin red bars aligned to the center of shapes that appear at the beginning and end of each bar, and display the start and end dates of the task at the beginning and end of each critical bar.

To set the appearance of a category of taskbars, choose Format➪Bar Styles. Project displays the Bar Styles dialog box shown in Figure 2-10.

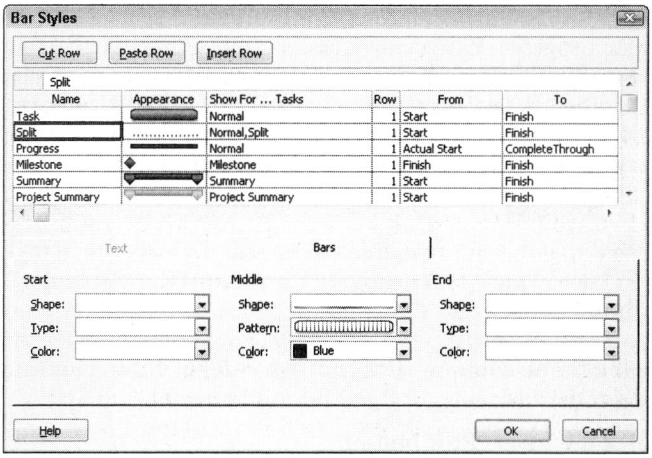

Figure 2-10:
Use this
dialog
box to
control the
appearance
of
categories
of taskbars.

Like its cousin, the Format Bar dialog box, the Bar Styles dialog box has two tabs that you can use to control the appearance of taskbars. On the Text tab, you control the text that appears to the left, right, top, bottom, or inside the taskbar. On the Bars tab, you control the shapes of the beginning, middle and end of taskbars.

The Bar Styles dialog box differs from its cousin because of the table that appears at the top of the dialog box. You select a category of task in the table at the top of the dialog box to display the settings for that category's taskbars, and then you use the Bars and Text tabs to change the settings for the selected category. If the category of task you want to modify doesn't appear in the Name column of the table, you can add it by using the Insert Row button above the table. Table 2-1 describes the purpose of each column in the table at the top of the Bar Styles dialog box.

Table 2-1   Understanding the Table at the Top of the Bar Styles Dialog Box

Column Heading	Purpose
Name	Identifies the taskbar category. This name appears in a legend for your chart when you print it.
Appearance	Displays a sample of the current formatting settings for the bar.
Show For . . . Tasks	Defines the types of tasks that the specified formatting affects.
Row	Indicates how many rows of bars (up to four) that Project displays for each task.
From and To	Defines the time period that is shown by the bar.

It's possible that a particular task can fit into more than one category for which you've defined formatting. For example, a regular (Normal) task can also be in progress. When a task fits into more than one category, Project tries to display multiple formatting settings. If Project can't display the formats together, the category that appears closer to the top of the table in the Bar Styles dialog box takes precedence. To modify the formatting precedence, you can reorder the categories in the table by using the Cut Row and Paste Row buttons to rearrange the rows in the Bar Styles dialog box.

Suppose that you want to define the appearance of critical taskbars — and you don't see critical tasks listed in the table at the top of the Bar Styles dialog box. Follow these steps:

1. **In the Name column, click the task category that you want to appear below the task category you intend to insert.**

2. **Click the Insert Row button.**

   Project inserts a blank row in the table.

3. **Click in the Name column of the blank row and type a name for the category of task you're defining.**

4. **Click in the Appearance column.**

Project displays a default bar style for the new category.

5. **Click the Bars tab.**

6. **Make changes by using the list boxes in the Start, Middle, and End sections.**

7. **Click in the Show For . . . Tasks column of the task category you're defining.**

   A list box arrow appears (see Figure 2-11).

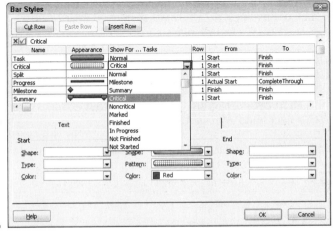

Figure 2-11: Defining the appearance of taskbars for critical tasks.

8. **Select the category of task to affect from the drop-down list.**

   To specify more than one category, add a comma (,) after the first category you select and then select or type a second category. For example, to define critical tasks that are in progress as a new category of taskbar style, choose Critical, type a comma (,), and then choose In Progress.

9. **Click in the Row column for the task category you are defining.**

   A list box arrow appears.

10. **Select the number of rows to allot for the task category you're defining: 1, 2, 3, or 4.**

    If you allot only one row and you show bars for both the baseline timing and progress, the bars might overlap each other. To display two separate bars, allot two rows. You also can add extra rows to accommodate text above or below taskbars.

11. **Click in the From column for the task category you're defining and select, from the drop-down list that appears, a date for the beginning of the taskbar.**

12. **Repeat Step 11 in the To column for the task category you're defining.**

13. **Click the Text tab and add appropriate text to the left, right, top, bottom, or inside of the task category you're defining.**

14. **Click OK.**

Project applies the formatting you defined to tasks that fit into the specified category.

Changing the Gantt chart layout

When you make changes to the layout of a Gantt chart, you can modify the appearance of link lines, date formats displayed near taskbars, the height of taskbars, and how Project displays certain characteristics of taskbars.

In views other than Gantt Chart view, layout changes affect different elements. For example, in Calendar view, layout changes affect the order in which Project lists multiple tasks on one calendar day and how it splits date bars. And, in Network Diagram Chart view, layout changes affect link lines and how Project handles page breaks.

To modify the layout of Gantt Chart view, display Gantt Chart view and then choose Format⇨Layout. The Layout dialog box appears (see Figure 2-12).

Figure 2-12: Use this dialog box to change layout characteristics for Gantt Chart view.

Use Table 2-2 to understand the layout choices you can make in Gantt Chart view; when you click OK, Project applies your choices.

You can click the Undo button to remove changes that Project applies to your schedule when you use the Layout dialog box.

Table 2-2	Layout Options for Gantt Chart View
Option	*Purpose*
Links	Select an option button to specify the link line style or hide link lines altogether. Link lines graphically display dependency relationships among tasks.
Date Format	From this drop-down list, select a date or time format.
Bar Height	Select a height in points for the taskbars in your Gantt chart.
Always Roll Up Gantt Bars	Displays your Gantt schedule by rolling up tasks onto summary bars. If you select this check box, you have the option of selecting the Hide Rollup Bars When Summary Expanded check box, which hides rollup behavior if your schedule is completely expanded.
Round Bars to Whole Days	Displays taskbars in whole day increments.
Show Bar Splits	Displays split tasks graphically on the Gantt chart.
Show Drawings	Project displays drawings that you've inserted in your chart.

Two interesting date formats include a week number (W5/1 and W5/1/02 12:33 PM) of the year and the day of the week. Therefore, W49/2/06 is December 4, 2006 (the second day of the 49th full week of 2006). Your nation's or industry's conventions for numbering weeks might be different from what Project produces.

The Round Bars to Whole Days option works well on longer schedules but not as well on schedules with tasks that tend to run in hourly or half-day increments. If you have a short schedule with many tasks running only hours in length, don't round taskbars to whole days.

Split tasks are tasks that start, then stop for a time, and then start again. For example, if you expect to start creating a mailer for a talent show but not complete the mailer until you receive final confirmation on who will ultimately serve as emcee, you can create a split task. The Show Bar Splits option in the Layout dialog box simply enables you to show the split task as separate taskbars or as one continuous taskbar.

Changing Gantt chart gridlines

Gridlines mark off periods of time, rows and columns, pages in your schedule, and regular intervals in the Gantt chart and the Gantt table. For example, in Figure 2-13, gridlines mark off every other row in the chart portion of the view, helping you read across the page on a long schedule.

To modify gridlines, choose Format⇨Gridlines. The Gridlines dialog box appears (see Figure 2-14).

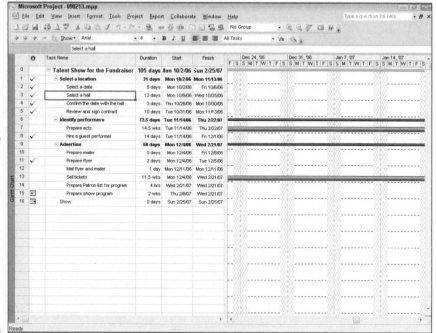

Figure 2-13:
You can
make a long
schedule
easier to
read by
displaying
gridlines in
the chart
portion of
Gantt Chart
view.

Figure 2-14:
Project
offers you
five different
line styles
for gridlines.

In the Line to Change list, the options Gantt Rows, Sheet Rows, and Sheet Columns enable you to set gridlines at regular intervals. For example, the project in Figure 2-13 has the Gantt Rows set to show at an interval of every two rows. You can change the line type and color only (not the interval) for the other choices in the Line to Change list. To modify these settings, highlight the kind of line that you want to change and then select the desired settings from the Type and Color drop-down lists.

You can click the Undo button on the Formatting toolbar to cancel the effects that you apply in the Gridlines dialog box.

Working with the Network Diagram

You can make changes to any view using the techniques described in Book VI, Chapter 1, but the Network Diagram bears some special attention because you can make changes to it in a way that doesn't apply to any other view. The Network Diagram, shown in Figure 2-15, provides a visual representation of your project using boxes — sometimes called *nodes* — to represent each task. Each box contains a variety of information about each task. The box shapes and colors have meaning. For example, square boxes designate tasks, and angled boxes designate summary tasks. Red boxes identify tasks on the critical path, and blue boxes identify noncritical tasks. Lines entering and leaving boxes help you identify dependencies.

You can change much of the information that appears on the Network Diagram. In particular, you can control

✦ The layout of the Network Diagram

✦ The color, line style, and shape of Network Diagram boxes

✦ The contents of Network Diagram boxes, including the style of text, number of fields per node, and the horizontal and vertical alignment of text within the box

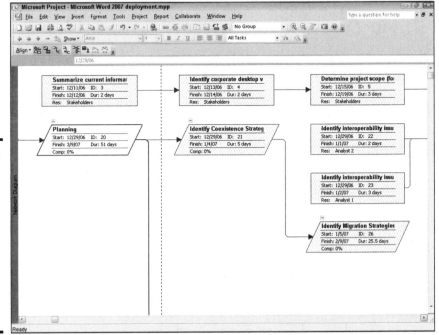

Figure 2-15:
The
Network
Diagram
provides
you with a
graphic
represen-
tation of
your
project's
workflow.

You can use the Network Diagram toolbar (see Figure 2-16) to make many of the changes you read about in this section. To view this toolbar, right-click any toolbar and then choose Network Diagram.

Figure 2-16:
You can use the buttons on this toolbar to make many of the changes described in this section.

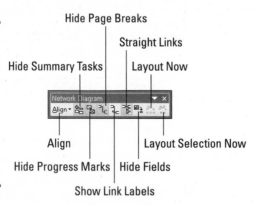

Hide Page Breaks

Hide Summary Tasks | Straight Links

Layout Now

Align

Hide Progress Marks | Hide Fields

Layout Selection Now

Show Link Labels

Suppose that you like the default Network Diagram, but you also find yourself changing it to display other information. Consider creating a second Network Diagram view with different settings. Use the information in Book VI, Chapter 1 to create a copy of the Network Diagram and then apply the techniques in the following sections to the copy.

Controlling the layout of Network Diagram view

Want to change the overall appearance of Network Diagram view? Choose Format⇨Layout to open the Layout dialog box shown in Figure 2-17.

Figure 2-17:
Use this dialog box to change the overall appearance of the Network Diagram.

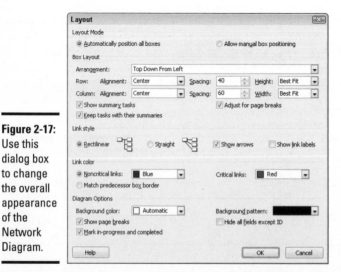

In the Layout Mode section, you can tell Project to let you manually position boxes on the diagram instead of positioning them for you.

In the Box Layout section, you can use the Arrangement drop-down list to change the order in which Project displays the boxes; the arrangement you choose changes the number of pages Project needs to print your Network Diagram. You can arrange the boxes in any of the following ways:

✦ Top Down From Left

✦ Top Down By Day

✦ Top Down By Week

✦ Top Down By Month

✦ Top Down - Critical First

✦ Centered From Left

✦ Centered From Top

In the same section, you can change the row and column alignment and spacing along with row height and column width. Using the check boxes at the bottom of the Box Layout section, you can hide or display summary tasks, keep tasks with their summaries, and tell Project to adjust the Network Diagram for page breaks.

In the Link Style section, you can control the style of the link lines, and you can choose to show arrows and link labels. When you show link labels on the Network Diagram, Project displays abbreviations such as FS, which stands for Finish-to-Start, for the type of link dependency that exists between two tasks.

In the Link Color section, you can select different colors for both critical and noncritical links; by default, Project colors noncritical links in blue and critical links in red. If you select the Match Predecessor Box Border option, Project doesn't color link lines to distinguish between critical and noncritical tasks. Instead, link lines assume the same color as the box of the predecessor task.

Finally, you can use the choices in the Diagram Options section to change the appearance of the Network Diagram as a whole. For example, you can set a background color and pattern for the Network Diagram.

To choose a background color or pattern for individual boxes, use the Format Box or Format Box Styles dialog box described in the following sections.

You can also choose to show page breaks, which appear as dotted lines on-screen in Network Diagram view. A page break appears in Figure 2-15. When you select the Mark In-Progress and Completed check box, Project marks in-progress tasks with half an X and completed tasks with an entire X.

If you select the Hide All Fields Except ID check box, Project eliminates all the information on a box except for the task ID, reducing the size of the boxes on your Network Diagram and the number of pages Project needs to print the Network Diagram. Figure 2-18 shows a Network Diagram that includes link labels and hides all task information except the ID. A page break appears at the right side of the diagram.

If you select the Hide All Fields Except ID check box, you can still view any task's information by pausing your mouse pointer over the task.

Controlling the appearance of Network Diagram boxes

You can change the appearance of Network Diagram boxes, either individually or of a particular category of boxes. Project contains a set of previously defined templates that define the shape, color, and content of each box, based on the type of task the box represents. You can override the settings of these templates.

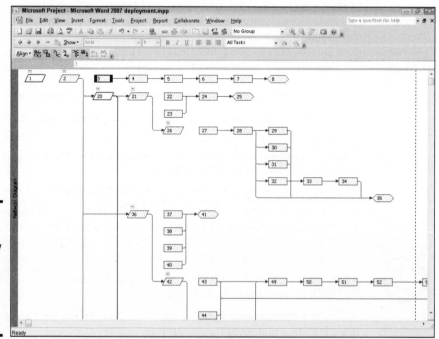

Figure 2-18:
You can dramatically change the appearance of the Network Diagram.

"Controlling the content in Network Diagram boxes," the next section in this chapter, describes how to override the templates to change the content that appears in a Network Diagram box. The information in this section describes how to override the templates to change the formatting and style of Network Diagram boxes.

You can follow these steps to change the formatting and style of an individual box:

1. **Select the box in the Network Diagram.**

2. **Choose Format⇨Box.**

Project displays the Format Box dialog box (see Figure 2-19).

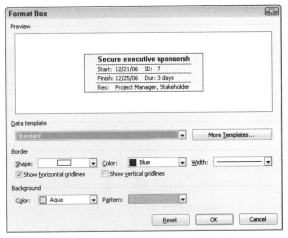

Figure 2-19: You can use this dialog box to modify the appearance of a single box in the Network Diagram.

3. **In the Border section, open the Shape drop-down list to select one of ten shapes for the box.**

4. **In the Border section, open the Color drop-down list to select the color for the lines of the box.**

5. **In the Border section, open the Width drop-down list to select a line representing the width of the box's border.**

You can select the Show Horizontal Gridlines and Show Vertical Gridlines check boxes to display lines that separate each field on the box.

6. **In the Background section, open the Color drop-down list to choose a background color for the box.**

7. **In the Background section, open the Pattern drop-down list to choose a background pattern for the box.**

Project combines the effect of all your changes; watch the Preview to determine their effects.

8. **Click OK to save the changes.**

Formatting box styles one at a time can be lengthy and time-consuming. Instead of formatting boxes one at a time, you might prefer to format all the boxes for a particular type of task, such as all Critical tasks. Follow these steps:

1. **Choose Format⇨Box Styles.**

Project displays the Box Styles dialog box (see Figure 2-20).

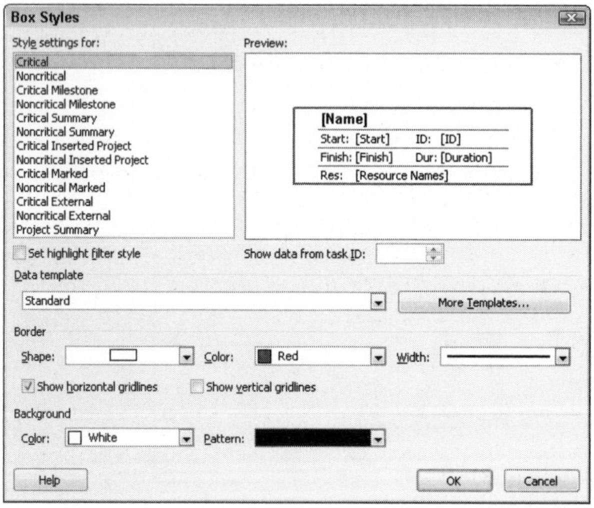

Figure 2-20:
From this dialog box, you can select a category of tasks and format the boxes that represent them.

Box Styles

Style settings for:

Critical
Noncritical
Critical Milestone
Noncritical Milestone
Critical Summary
Noncritical Summary
Critical Inserted Project
Noncritical Inserted Project
Critical Marked
Noncritical Marked
Critical External
Noncritical External
Project Summary

Preview:

[Name]
Start: [Start]   ID: [ID]
Finish: [Finish]   Dur: [Duration]
Res: [Resource Names]

☐ Set highlight filter style

Show data from task ID: [   ]

Data template

[Standard ▾]   [More Templates...]

Border

Shape: [▾]   Color: [■ Red ▾]   Width: [———— ▾]

☑ Show horizontal gridlines   ☐ Show vertical gridlines

Background

Color: [☐ White ▾]   Pattern: [▬▬▬ ▾]

[Help]   [OK]   [Cancel]

2. **From the Style Settings For drop-down list, select the type of task box that you want to format.**

The current appearance of the box appears in the Preview window.

You can display actual task data in the Preview box if you provide a task ID number in the Show Data from Task ID box.

3. **In the Border section, open the Shape drop-down list to select one of ten shapes for the box.**

4. **In the Border section, open the Color drop-down list to select the color for the lines of the box.**

5. **In the Border section, open the Width list box to select a line representing the width of the box's border.**

You can select the Show Horizontal Gridlines and Show Vertical Gridlines check boxes to display lines that separate each field on the box.

6. **In the Background section, open the Color drop-down list to choose a background color for the box.**

7. **In the Background section, open the Pattern drop-down list to choose a background pattern for the box.**

    Project combines the effect of all your changes; watch the Preview to determine their effects.

8. **Select the Set Highlight Filter Style check box (below the Style Settings For list) to select formatting options for the box style when you filter tasks on the Network Diagram.**

    To set filter style information for the type of task you selected in Step 2, select this check box and then repeat Steps 3 to 7.

9. **Click OK to save the changes.**

Controlling the content in Network Diagram boxes

The boxes on the Network Diagram are actually divided into *cells,* and each cell displays the information in a particular field. The following fields appear on the Network Diagram by default:

✦ Task Name

✦ Duration

✦ ID

✦ Start and Finish Dates

✦ Percent Complete

✦ Resource Name, if assigned

You can change the fields that appear on a Network Diagram box, and you can display up to 16 fields of information. For example, to focus on project costs, you might include Task Name, Baseline Cost, Actual Cost, Remaining Cost, and Cost Variance information in the boxes of the Network Diagram. If you're trying to focus on scheduling issues, you might want to include information like Task Name, Critical, Free Slack, Early Finish, and Late Finish in the boxes of the Network Diagram.

Just because you can do something, that doesn't mean you should do it. Although you can display up to 16 pieces of information, providing too much information in a box makes the Network Diagram difficult to understand, and your reader might miss your point.

You can change the information that appears in a box, the font that Project uses to display the information, and the horizontal and vertical alignment of the information. The steps that follow show you how to change the template for a particular type of task.

You can customize a view by making changes to one of the existing views or by making a copy of the view and then changing the copy. The same concepts apply to the templates that define the appearance of Network Diagram boxes: You can change the template or you can copy the template and change the copy. We prefer to copy the template so that we retain the original settings of the template.

So, in the steps that follow, we once again show you a hybrid process that you can use to change the appearance of Network Diagram boxes, by making changes to a copy of an existing Network Diagram box template:

1. **Choose Format⇨Box.**

   Project displays the Format Box dialog box.

2. **Click the More Templates button.**

   Project displays the Data Templates dialog box (see Figure 2-21).

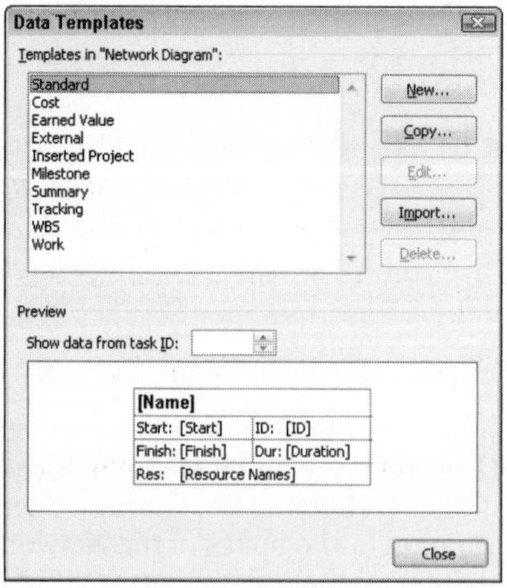

Figure 2-21: Select a template to modify or create a new template.

3. **Select the template that you want to change.**

4. **Click the Copy button.**

   Project displays the Data Template Definition dialog box.

5. **To change the contents of a cell of the box, click the corresponding cell in the Choose Cell(s) section of the dialog box (see Figure 2-22).**

    A list box arrow appears to the right of the cell.

Click here to change the contents of the cells in the box

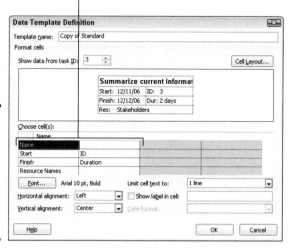

Figure 2-22:
Use this dialog box to change the content of Network Diagram boxes.

6. **Open the list box to choose a field for the selected cell.**

    You can change the font for a particular cell. Select that cell and click the Font button. A dialog box appears from which you can select a new font, font size, and font attributes, such as boldface or italics.

7. **Open the Horizontal Alignment drop-down list and select an alignment for the text within the cell.**

8. **Open the Vertical Alignment drop-down list and select an alignment for the text within the cell.**

9. **Open the Limit Cell Text To drop-down list and select the number of lines for each cell.**

    A cell can have as many as three lines.

10. **Select the Show Label in Cell check box to include an identifier in the cell for the type of information.**

    In Figure 2-22, the cell containing the task's start date also contains the field label.

    You also can change the label text that appears in the box after you click the Show Label in Cell text box. For example, instead of "Start," you can display "Start Date."

11. **To increase or decrease the number of cells in the box, click the Cell Layout button.**

Project displays the Cell Layout dialog box (see Figure 2-23).

The picture at the top of the Data Template Definition dialog box presents a preview of the structure of the box. In Figure 2-22, you see six fields of information, but the box actually contains eight cells; because the top and bottom row of the box each contain only one piece of information, the template merges the blank cells on those rows with the non-blank cells.

Figure 2-23:
Use this dialog box to control the number of cells in a Network Diagram box.

12. **Specify the number of rows and columns and click OK.**

Project redisplays the Data Template Definition dialog box, with the appropriate number of cells available for formatting.

13. **Click OK.**

Project closes the Data Template Definition dialog box.

14. **Click Close.**

Project closes the Data Templates dialog box.

15. **Click OK.**

Project closes the Box Styles dialog box and displays your updated Network Diagram.

Modifying Calendar View

Calendar view in Project 2007 (see Figure 2-24) now looks and acts more like Calendar view in Outlook. Although you can't format the text of individual items in Calendar view, you can use the Text Styles dialog box, described in the section "Changing Fonts" at the beginning of this chapter, to format categories of text. And, you can apply color to the text, but you cannot apply background color to the bars on the calendar.

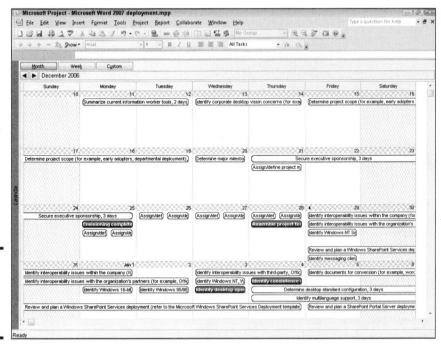

Figure 2-24:
The Month
format of
Calendar
view.

In the following sections, we explore the changes you can make to the layout and entries in Calendar view.

Changing the time period displayed in Calendar view

The Project 2007 Calendar view now supports daily, weekly, and monthly formats, and you can create your own format to focus on the tasks for a specific timeframe.

You can use the three new buttons at the top of the view to see your project a month at a time or a week at a time, or you can create a custom format. Click the Month button or the Week button to view your project in those increments. You can then use the arrows below the buttons to move forward or backward by the selected increment.

In Figure 2-25, we created a custom format that shows two weeks.

To create a custom view, click the Custom button; the Zoom dialog box appears (see Figure 2-26). In the Zoom dialog box, indicate the timeframe to display in Calendar view.

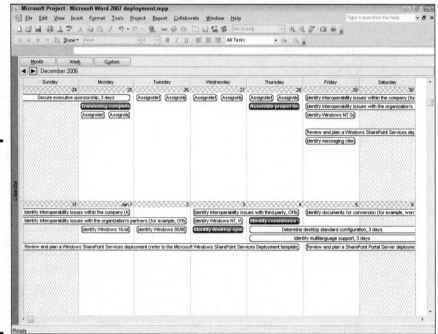

Figure 2-25:
Use the built-in formats to create a custom format in Calendar view to focus on a specific time period.

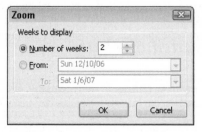

Figure 2-26:
Use the Zoom dialog box to identify the timeframe for a custom Calendar view format.

Changing Calendar view layout

Use the Layout dialog box (see Figure 2-27) to change the layout of tasks in Calendar view. By default, Project displays tasks in Calendar view using the currently sorted order of tasks. To open this dialog box, choose Format⇨Layout.

You can select the Attempt to Fit As Many Tasks As Possible option button to change the sorted order of tasks in Calendar view. Project sorts tasks by Total Slack and then by Duration (longest task first) to try to fit the maximum number of tasks into the rows for a week without overlapping bars.

Figure 2-27:
The Layout dialog box controls the way that Project presents tasks in Calendar view.

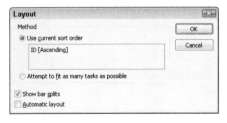

You can read about sorting tasks in Book VI, Chapter 1.

By default, Project identifies split tasks in Calendar view; you can change this behavior if you remove the check mark from the Show Bar Splits check box.

When you select the Automatic Layout check box, Project automatically adjusts Calendar view to accommodate new tasks that you add or tasks that you delete.

Formatting Calendar view entries

When you display Calendar view, entries for tasks appear in boxes that Project calls *bars,* and you can change the appearance of these bars by using the Bar Styles dialog box. For example, you can make all critical tasks appear on the calendar in red. Follow these steps:

1. **From Calendar view, choose Format⇨Bar Styles.**

Project displays the Bar Styles dialog box (see Figure 2-28). From this dialog box, you can assign different font colors to different task types or use a line instead of a bar to represent the task's duration in Calendar view.

2. **From the Task Type list on the left, select a type of task.**

3. **Open the Bar Type drop-down list and identify the way you want to display tasks.**

The choices are Line, Bar, or None. Choosing None hides the selected task type from Calendar view. When you choose Line, Project uses lines instead of bars to represent each task's duration, and the Pattern drop-down list and the Shadow check box aren't available. When you choose Bar, Project displays bars that represent each task's duration.

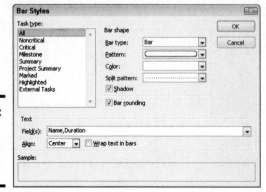

Figure 2-28:
Pull up a
seat at the
Bar Styles
dialog box.

4. **Open the Pattern drop-down list and select a pattern.**

Project displays the pattern inside the bar.

5. **Open the Color drop-down list and select a color for the bar or line.**

6. **Open the Split Pattern drop-down list to choose a pattern for Project to display between split tasks.**

7. **Select the Shadow check box to display a shadow behind a bar.**

This option is available only if you select Bar from the Bar Type drop-down list.

As you make changes in the Bar Shape area and the Text area, watch the Sample window at the bottom of the box for the effects of your changes.

8. **Select the Bar Rounding check box to tell Project to draw the bar or line for tasks that take less than one day so that the task's duration is implied.**

Bar rounding works well for tasks with durations of less than one day. For these tasks, Project draws a bar that extends that portion of the day that represents the task's duration. If you don't use bar rounding, Project doesn't imply the duration of the task by the length of the bar.

9. **In the Text area, open the Field(s) box to include Project fields for each task type.**

To include more than one field, separate fields with a comma (refer to Figure 2-28).

10. **From the Align drop-down list, select an alignment for the text.**

You can select Left, Center, or Right.

11. **If you chose Bar as the bar type in Step 3, you can select the Wrap Text in Bars check box.**

When you select this check box, Project wraps text so that it fits within the bar. So, for shorter tasks with longer names, wrapping text enables you to read all the displayed information about the task. But, the task takes more than one row when it appears on the calendar. If you don't select the Wrap Text in Bars check box, Project displays only as much information as it can fit in a bar that's sized to match the task's duration.

12. **Repeat Steps 2 to 11 for each item in the Task Type list that you want to format.**

13. **Click OK.**

Project saves your settings and redisplays Calendar view using them.

Chapter 3: Using Macros

*M*acros help you save time. And anything that helps you save time is worth discussing. So, this chapter explains what macros are, how to create them, and how to use them.

Understanding Macros

A *macro* is a small program that helps you save time whenever you need to perform a repetitive task. For example, suppose that you use the Delay table fairly often. You've already added the Delay table to the menu using the steps you found in Book VI, Chapter 2, but suppose that you're a toolbar button kind of a person, and it annoys you greatly to have to display the Delay table by going through menus. What you *really* want to do is just click a button on a toolbar to display the table. You can create a macro that selects the Delay table and then assign the macro to a toolbar button — and then you can just click a button on a toolbar to display the table.

Don't let the word "program" scare you, because you won't actually have to write any program code to create a macro.

The more you use Project, the more you'll notice the things you do over and over, and those things are candidates for macros. For example, we create macros for every combination view we use regularly that involves views that don't appear automatically when we split the view.

See Book VI, Chapter 1 for details on combination views.

Creating a Macro

You can easily create a macro by having Project memorize the steps you take to complete any repetitive action. See — no programming required. You just do whatever it is you want Project to do. Project then converts the actions you take into Visual Basic statements and stores the statements in a macro. Later, when you want to take that action again, you run your macro, which you read about in the next section.

Knowing your macro's steps

Before you record a macro, we suggest that you run through the steps that you want to take and maybe even write them down. That way, you gain a clear idea of what you're going to do, and you'll be less likely to make (and record) mistakes.

We suggest that you *not* include a step in a macro that saves your project. If you do and the macro causes unexpected results, you won't be able to undo the effects of the macro.

These steps walk you through displaying the Delay table to give you a clear idea of the steps you're going to record:

1. **Open the View menu.**

2. **Point at Table.**

3. **Click More Tables.**

Project displays the More Tables window.

4. **Click Delay.**

5. **Click Apply.**

Project displays the Delay table.

If your repetitious steps involve using a particular view, select that view as your first step of your macro. That way, when you run your macro, it forces Project to start by displaying that view, regardless of the view that you were using before you ran your macro.

Recording the macro

When you know what you're going to record, use the following steps to record the macro:

1. **Choose Tools➪Macro➪Record New Macro.**

Project opens the Record Macro dialog box (see Figure 3-1).

2. **Type a name for the macro in the Macro Name text box.**

Figure 3-1:
The Record
Macro
dialog box.

You can't include a space in a macro name, so try capitalizing the first letter of each word or using an underscore character as a word separator.

The first character of the macro name must be a letter, but the other characters can be letters, numbers, or underscore characters.

3. **Type a description of the function that the macro performs in the Description box.**

   This description appears whenever you run the macro from the Macros dialog box, so it can help you remember the purpose of a macro.

4. **If your macro selects rows and columns, make appropriate choices in the Row References and Column References sections.**

   See the information that appears after these steps for an explanation of these options.

5. **Click OK.**

   Project redisplays your project. You don't notice any differences, but Project is now recording each action that you take.

6. **Take all the actions that you want to record.**

7. **Choose Tools⇨Macro⇨Stop Recorder (see Figure 3-2).**

   Project stops recording your macro.

Some notes about recording a macro:

✦ **Using keyboard combinations:** You can run a macro by using a keyboard combination that you define. In the next section, we explain more about using a keyboard combination, including how to set one up after you've recorded a macro.

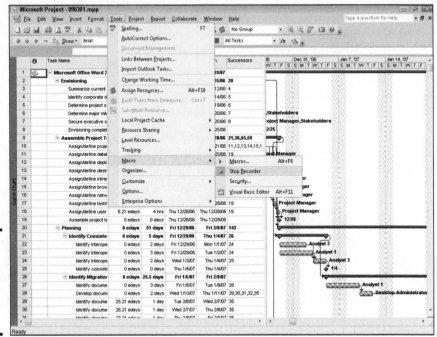

Figure 3-2:
Use this
command
to finish
recording a
macro.

✦ **Storing macros:** You can store macros in any Project file, but storing them in the Global File — also called the Global Template file — makes the macro available to all projects.

✦ **Selecting rows and columns:** The options in the Row References and the Column References sections control the way that the macro selects rows and columns. By default, a macro always selects rows in relation to the position of the cell selected when the macro begins. If you want a macro to always select the same row, regardless of which cell is selected when you start the macro, select Absolute (ID). For columns, the macro, by default, always selects the same column each time you run the macro, regardless of the cell that's selected when the macro begins. If you want a macro to select columns in relation to the cell that is selected when you run the macro, select Relative in the Column References section.

Effectively, these two options combine to determine where the cell pointer will appear when the macro begins. To always start the macro in a specific cell, select that cell before you start recording the macro and then select Absolute in both the Row References and Column References sections.

Using a Macro

To use a recorded macro, you run it. You have four ways that you can run a macro. You can

✦ Use the Macros dialog box.

✦ Assign a keyboard shortcut to the macro.

✦ Assign a menu command to the macro.

✦ Assign a toolbar button to the macro.

In the following sections, we look at each of these methods of running a macro.

Running a macro from the Macros dialog box

Before you run a macro, it's a good idea to save your project, especially if the macro makes substantial changes to your project. Although unlimited Undo capabilities let you undo a macro's effects, we don't think you'd find that fun. Closing the project and reopening it would be much easier. To run a macro from the Macros dialog box, follow these steps:

1. **Open the project that contains the macro.**

If you stored the macro in the Global template file, you can open any project.

2. **Choose Tools⇨Macro⇨Macros.**

Project displays the Macros dialog box (see Figure 3-3).

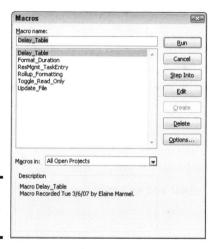

Figure 3-3:
The Macros
dialog box.

3. **Select the macro that you want to run from the Macro Name list.**

4. **Click Run.**

   Project performs the steps that you recorded in the macro.

In most cases, your macro finishes before you have a chance to stop it. But, if your macro is long enough and you want to stop it while it's still running, press Ctrl+Break.

Using a keyboard shortcut to run a macro

Suppose that you decide that you really want to run your macro from a keyboard shortcut and you didn't set a shortcut when you created the macro. Follow these steps to add a keyboard shortcut to the macro after you create it:

1. **Open the project that contains the macro.**

   If you stored the macro in the Global template file, you can open any project.

2. **Choose Tools➪Macro➪Macros.**

   Project displays the Macros dialog box (refer to Figure 3-3).

   You can also press Alt+F8 to display the Macros dialog box.

3. **Highlight the macro to which you want to add a keyboard shortcut.**

4. **Click the Options button.**

   Project displays the Macro Options dialog box (see Figure 3-4).

Figure 3-4:
You can set a keyboard shortcut for an existing macro from the Macro Options dialog box.

5. **Click in the Shortcut Key text box and type a letter.**

   You can assign any letter key on your keyboard except a number or a special character.

6. **Click OK.**

If Project isn't using the combination that you selected, Project displays the Macros dialog box again. If Project is using the combination that you selected, even for another macro, Project asks you to try a different combination.

7. **Click Close.**

Project closes the Macros dialog box.

To run a macro to which you've assigned a keyboard shortcut, press and hold Ctrl while pressing the key that you assigned.

Using a menu command to run a macro

You might want to use a menu command to run a macro. And, you can assign a hotkey to the menu command so that you can choose the command by using the keyboard. If you plan to assign a hotkey, open the menu on which you intend to place the command and take note of all underscored letters on the menu. You *should not* choose one of those letters as the hotkey for your command; if you do, the hotkey won't work.

If you have lots of macros, you might want to create a menu just for macros and then set up commands on that menu for all your macros. To create that menu, see Chapter 1 of this minibook.

Follow these steps to add a command that runs a macro to a menu:

1. **Choose View➪Toolbars➪Customize.**

Project displays the Customize dialog box.

2. **Click the Commands tab (see Figure 3-5).**

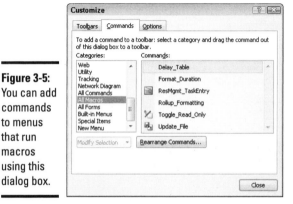

Figure 3-5:
You can add commands to menus that run macros using this dialog box.

3. From the Categories list, select All Macros.

Project displays a list of macros in the Commands list on the right.

4. Drag the macro that you want to add to the desired menu (see Figure 3-6).

As you drag, the mouse pointer image changes to include a small button and a plus sign (+). As you move the mouse pointer over a menu, the menu opens. On the mouse pointer, a large horizontal insertion point marks the location where the menu command will appear when you release the mouse button.

5. Release the mouse button.

The macro appears on the menu (see Figure 3-7).

6. To change the name of the macro on the menu, click Modify Selection in the Customize dialog box.

Project opens a pop-up menu (see Figure 3-8).

7. Type the name in the Name box, exactly as you want it to appear on the toolbar button.

When you type this name, you can include spaces in the command's name.

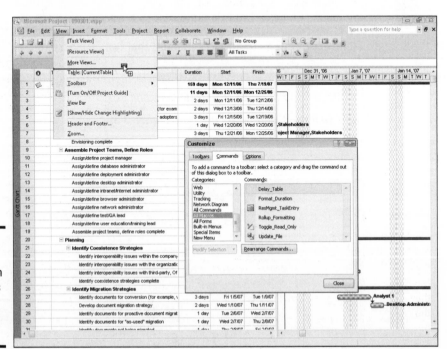

Figure 3-6:
The mouse pointer icon changes as you drag a macro onto a menu.

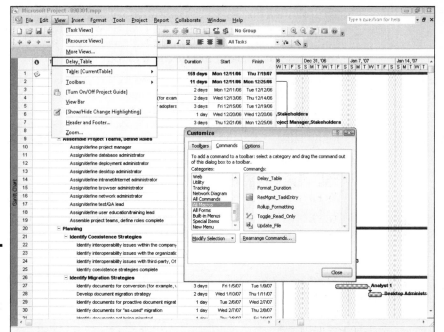

Figure 3-7:
A macro appearing on a Project menu.

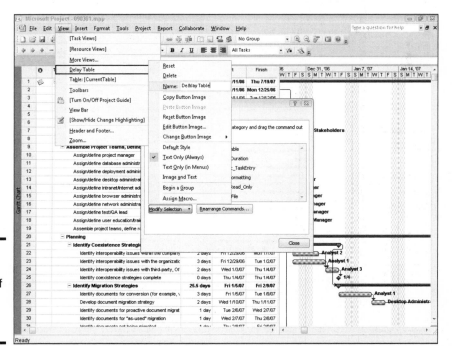

Figure 3-8:
Modifying the name of the macro on the menu.

8. To provide a hotkey character for the new command, place an ampersand (&) immediately before the character that you want to be the hotkey, making sure that Project isn't using the letter you select for some other command on the same menu.

Hotkey characters contain underscores on menus, and you can choose the command by using the keyboard letters for the command. In Figure 3-8, we placed an ampersand before the l in Delay. To use the hotkey in our example, we can press Alt+V+L. Alt+V opens the View menu, and L selects Delay Table, the item in the View menu with L as the hotkey.

9. Press Enter.

The pop-up menu disappears, and Project renames the menu command. As Figure 3-9 shows, the command includes your hotkey if you added an ampersand.

10. Click Close.

Project closes the Customize dialog box.

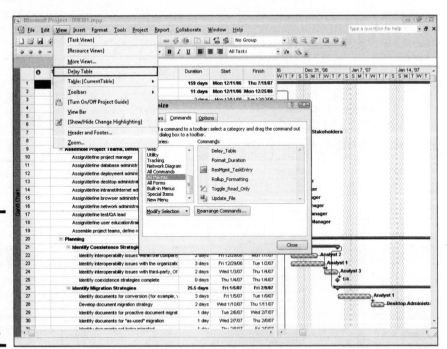

Figure 3-9:
The command after renaming it and assigning a hotkey to it.

When you add a command to one of the default menus, Microsoft Project saves the command and the menu in your Global template file. Any other project file that you open on your computer using that Global template file contains the new menu command.

You can remove the command from the menu by opening the Customize dialog box and then simply dragging the command off the menu and dropping it anywhere on your project. The command disappears, but the macro is still available.

Using a toolbar button to run a macro

Earlier in this chapter, we suggest that you might be a fan of toolbar buttons, and you'd like one for a macro you've created. Follow the steps in this section to add a button for a macro to a toolbar.

You also can add toolbar buttons for macros to a custom toolbar that you create. Chapter 1 of this minibook explains how to create a custom toolbar.

1. **If the toolbar to which you want to add a button doesn't appear on-screen, display it by right-clicking any toolbar button and choosing the toolbar from the shortcut menu that appears.**

   If the toolbar already appears on-screen, skip this step.

2. **Choose View➪Toolbars➪Customize.**

   Project displays the Customize dialog box.

3. **Click the Commands tab.**

4. **Scroll down the Categories list, and select All Macros.**

   Project displays a list of macros in the Commands list on the right side of the dialog box (see Figure 3-10).

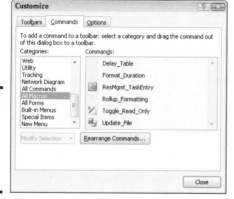

Figure 3-10: Use this tab to add macros as buttons to toolbars.

5. **Drag the macro that you want to add onto the desired toolbar (see Figure 3-11).**

   As you drag, the mouse pointer image changes to include a small button and a plus sign. As you move the mouse pointer over a toolbar, a large vertical insertion point marks the location where the button will appear when you release the mouse button.

6. **Release the mouse button.**

   A new button, using the name of your macro, appears selected on the toolbar (see Figure 3-12).

7. **To change the name of the toolbar button, click Modify Selection in the Customize dialog box.**

   Project opens a pop-up menu (see Figure 3-13).

Mouse pointer

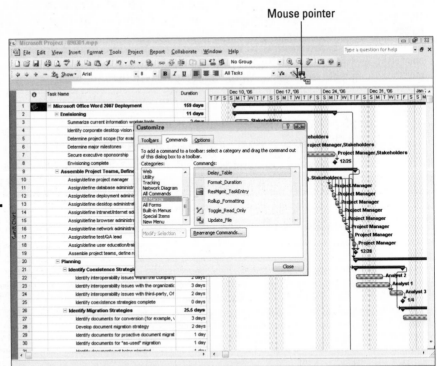

Figure 3-11: The appearance of the mouse pointer icon changes as you drag a macro onto a toolbar.

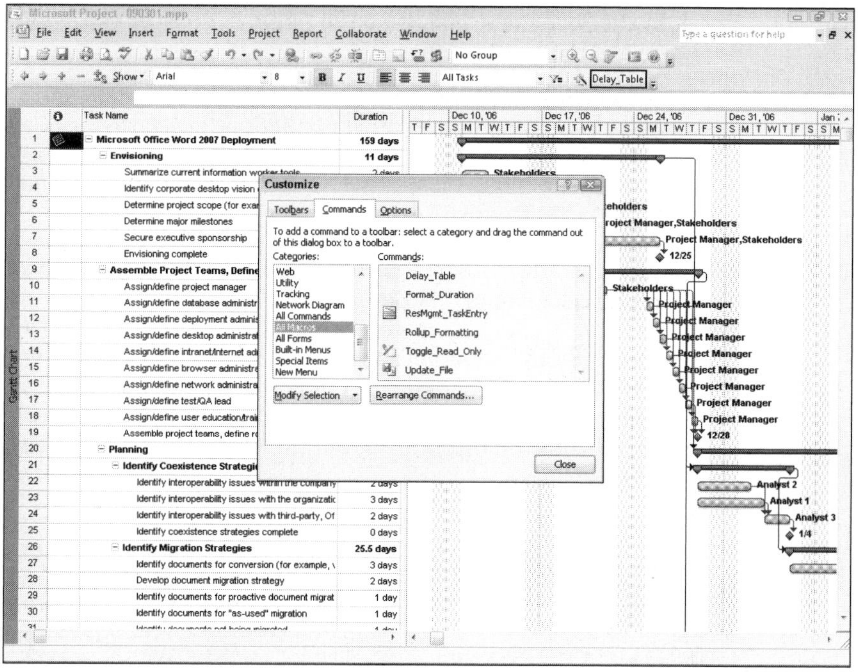

Figure 3-12:
The new
button after
dropping it
on the
toolbar.

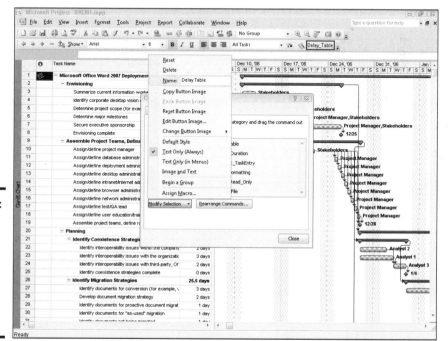

Figure 3-13:
Use this
pop-up
menu to
change a
macro
toolbar
button's
name.

8. **In the Name text box, type the name exactly as you want it to appear on the toolbar button.**

You can include spaces.

9. **Press Enter.**

The pop-up menu disappears, and Project renames the macro toolbar button (see Figure 3-14).

10. **Click Close.**

Project closes the Customize dialog box.

If you decide that you don't want the button on the toolbar, you can remove it. Follow Steps 1 and 2 in this section to open the Customize dialog box. Then simply drag the button off the toolbar and drop it anywhere on your project. The button disappears, but the macro is still available.

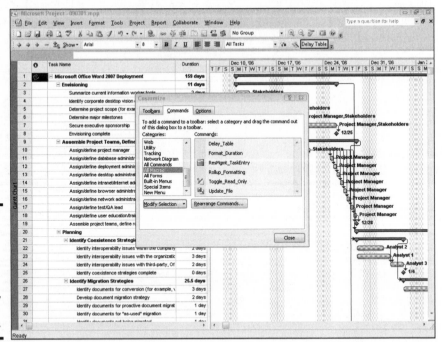

Figure 3-14:
We renamed the toolbar button Delay Table, without the underscore.

CASE STUDY

The Rollup Formatting macro

Company: Local Theater Group.

Project: Organize and present a talent show.

Challenge: View a summary of the project schedule that helps focus on important task dates.

A local theater group is putting together a talent show and has created a project schedule to manage the tasks associated with presenting the talent show. In addition to viewing task details, the group members would like to view the project in a summarized format, with some way of identifying tasks along the summary bars.

Solution: Each copy of Project ships with some built-in macros, and the Rollup Formatting macro meets this need. To use the Rollup Formatting macro, you must identify the tasks in your project that you want to roll up and display as summary tasks. Typically, you roll up subtasks only. Then, when you run the macro, you select the way you want rolled up tasks to appear and Project formats the schedule so that you get a summarized view.

To identify tasks to summarize, follow these steps:

1. **Select tasks in Gantt Chart view.**

    Typically, you select subtasks, not summary tasks.

2. **Click the Task Information button on the Standard toolbar.**

    Project displays the General tab of the Multiple Task Information dialog box.

(continued)

(continued)

3. Select the Roll Up Gantt Bar to Summary check box.

4. Click OK.

Now that you've identified the tasks you want to roll up onto summary bars, you can run the Rollup Formatting macro. Choose Tools⇨ Macros. In the Macros dialog box, click Rollup_ Formatting and then click Run. You see a dialog box that asks you whether you want rolled up tasks to appear as bars or as milestones. In the Project file for this case study — found on this book's Web site — we formatted rolled up tasks as milestones, and Project displays the project using the Milestone Rollup view.

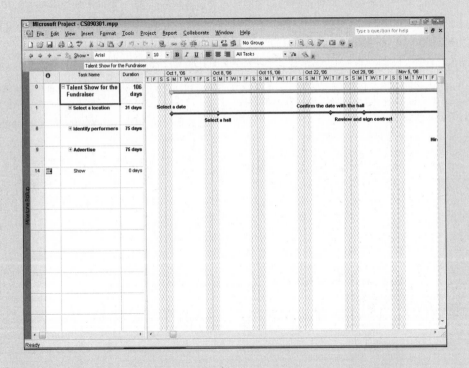

After you run the macro, you can use two other views to view rolled up information: Bar Rollup view and Milestone Date Rollup view. Choose View⇨More Views to switch to either of these views.

When you use the Rollup_Formatting macro, you might run into an issue. The macro displays task names for rolled up tasks above and below the summary bars, and often the text for the names overlaps, making the names unreadable. You can see an example of this in the case study file if you choose the Milestone Date Rollup view. You can remove the text that appears on the bars by using the Bar Styles dialog box: Choose Format⇨Bar Styles and select Rolled Up Task in the Name list at the top of the box. Then, on the Text tab at the bottom of the box, delete Name wherever it appears;

in the case study file, it appears in the Top box. For more information on using the Bar Styles dialog box, see Chapter 2 of this minibook.

To remove rollup formatting from your project, click the Show button and then select All Subtasks. Then repeats Steps 1–4.

Chapter 4: Importing Information into Project

In This Chapter

✔ Using graphic objects in a project

✔ Importing tasks from Outlook's Task List

✔ Importing Excel and Access information into Project

✔ Importing Project Exchange files

✔ Importing text or comma-separated files

*W*hen you import information, you bring information created by another program into a Project file. In addition to importing information from Outlook, Excel, and Access into Project, you can insert drawings and objects into a Project file. In this chapter, we look at how you insert graphic images such as photos, illustrations, and diagrams into various parts of a Project file, and then we cover how to import information from Outlook, Excel, and Access.

Using Graphic Objects in Project

Images can reinforce the information about your project and lend a professional look to your reports. For example, you might want to add your company logo to the header of your schedule. Or, if a particular task involves a schematic or diagram of a product, you might want to place a copy of the diagram in the task notes for reference. You might even consider adding photographs of each resource in his or her resource note to help you get to know all the team members in a large-scale project so that you can address them by name when you see them.

Placing graphics in a schedule makes your file larger. Bigger Project files need more time to calculate.

To insert an object into a header, footer, or legend, choose File➪Page Setup and click either the Header tab or the Footer tab. Then click the Insert Picture button to open the Insert Picture dialog box (see Figure 4-1); you can use this dialog box to navigate to the picture file you want to insert. When you find the picture, select it and click Open to insert it in the header of your project schedule.

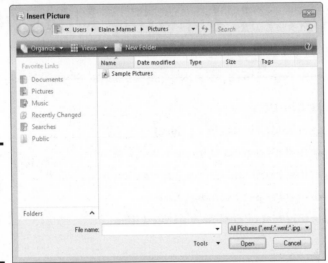

Figure 4-1:
Navigate to
the location
containing
the picture
you want
to insert.

Suppose that you have Visio diagram that provides information that you
need for a task involving resource assignments. You can insert a graphic
image of your Visio file on the Notes tab of the Task Information dialog box
for the task. Follow these steps:

1. **Double-click the task to which you want to add the graphic object.**

Project displays the Task Information dialog box.

2. **Click the Notes tab.**

 3. **Click the Insert Object button.**

The Insert Object dialog box appears (see Figure 4-2).

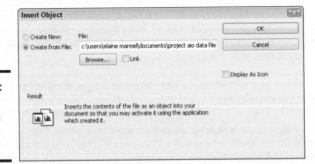

Figure 4-2:
Use this
dialog box
to select
a file.

Getting Tasks from Outlook **605**

Book IX
Chapter 4

Importing
Information into
Project

4. **Select the Create from File option.**

5. **Click the Browse button to select the file.**

6. **Click the OK button.**

   The information appears as a graphic on the Notes tab (see Figure 4-3).

Figure 4-3:
Project
inserts the
information
in the file as
a graphic
object on
the Notes
tab of the
Task
Information
dialog box.

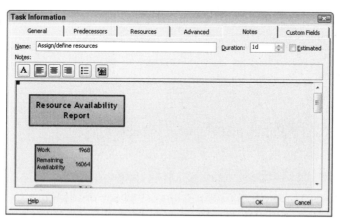

 You can place any image directly on the Gantt chart. Don't open the Task Information dialog box. Instead, copy the image to the Windows Clipboard, switch to Project, and click the Paste button. You can also use the Copy and Paste method to import Microsoft Office Word information into Project.

Getting Tasks from Outlook

Okay, it happens: You're diligently recording tasks in Outlook's To-Do List when you realize that your list of tasks is really a project, and you need the scheduling and cost features in Project. Good news — you don't need to start over. You can import the Outlook Task List into Project by following these steps:

1. **Open Project.**

   If you want the tasks to appear in an existing project, open that project. If the tasks make up a new project, use a blank Project file.

   Outlook doesn't need to be open.

2. **Choose Tools➪Import Outlook Tasks.**

   Project displays the Import Outlook Tasks dialog box (see Figure 4-4).

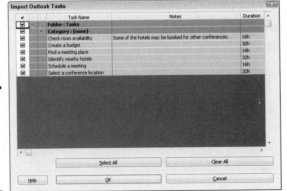

Figure 4-4:
Mark the
tasks that
you want to
import into
Project.

3. **Select the tasks that you want to import.**

4. **Click OK.**

The tasks appear in Project (see Figure 4-5).

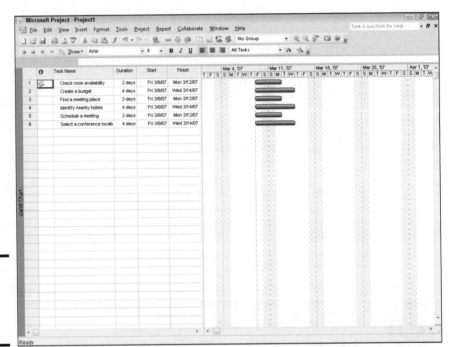

Figure 4-5:
Tasks
imported
from
Outlook.

If the open project was blank, the tasks appear starting on Row 1. If the open project already contained tasks, Project adds the Outlook tasks to the bottom of the Project file's Task List.

If you assign Total Work values to the tasks in Outlook, Project imports those values as durations. If you don't assign Total Work values, Project imports the tasks with an estimated duration of one day.

If you included notes in the Outlook tasks, Project includes those notes when it imports the tasks, and an icon appears in the indicator column for tasks with notes.

Importing Excel and Access Information into Project

You can import information from Excel or Access into Project by using an import/export map, which helps you match fields from Excel or Access with fields in Project.

If you're importing information from Excel and you know in advance that you're starting a Task List in Excel with the intent of moving the information to Project, use a special template in Excel to create the Task List (as we discuss later).

You can import all or part of an Access 2003 database or an earlier database into Project, and the process to import an Access database is the same as the process we describe to import an Excel file. You can import Excel files into Project 2007 as long as you aren't trying to import an Excel PivotTable into Project and as long as you save the Excel file in Excel 97–2003 file format.

To import either type of file, you need to set Project's security settings to allow importing files from versions of Office earlier than Office 2007 or files that don't use the Project file format; the steps for this task appear in the next section.

Changing Project's security settings

By default, Project doesn't allow you to import Excel files from Excel 97–2003. But, Project also can't read the new format of Excel files in Excel 2007. So, you need to change settings in Project to permit importing Excel 97–2003 files. To set Project's security settings, follow these steps:

1. **Choose Tools⇨Options.**

Project displays the Options dialog box (see Figure 4-6).

2. **Click the Security tab.**

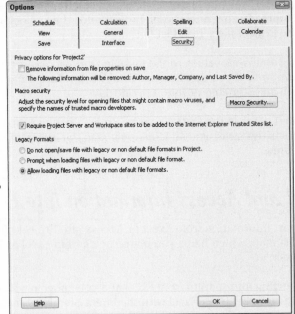

Figure 4-6:
Set options
in Project
to permit
loading files
in formats
older than
Office 2007.

3. **Select the Allow Loading Files with Legacy or Non Default File Formats option.**

4. **Click OK.**

   Project now permits you to import non-Project files in formats older than Office 2007.

Using an import map

You're an Excel person. Your friends call you "guru." You do everything in Excel, even when you probably should use some other software program. So, you started a Task List in Excel that you now realize is really a project. If you save the Excel file as an Excel 97–2003 file, you can import the tasks into Project using Project's Import Wizard. This process works with Access databases, too; just save your Access database in Access 2002/2003 format or Access 2000 format.

Project uses import/export maps that define the information that you want to import or export and help you match the information in the other program's file with the fields in a Project file. Using an import/export map as a template, Project can correctly translate information from one program to another.

Be sure that you save your Excel file in Excel 97–2003 format and complete the steps in the section "Changing Project's security settings," earlier in this chapter, before you begin the following steps.

For this example, use these steps to import an Excel 97–2003 file into Project:

1. **In Project, choose File⇨Open.**

The Open dialog box appears.

2. **Click the list box beside the File Name box and select Microsoft Excel Workbooks.**

3. **Use the Previous Locations list box to navigate to the folder that contains the Excel workbook that you want to import.**

4. **Select the workbook and click Open.**

Project starts the Import Wizard.

5. **Click Next.**

The Map dialog box of the Import Wizard appears (see Figure 4-7).

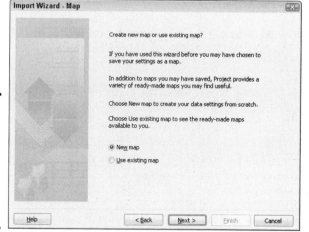

Figure 4-7: Decide whether to create a new map or use an existing map.

6. **Select New Map and click Next.**

The Import Mode dialog box of the Import Wizard appears.

7. **Select the As a New Project option.**

Choosing this option tells Project to place the information in the Excel file in a new, empty Project file.

8. Click Next.

The Map Options dialog box of the Import Wizard appears (see Figure 4-8).

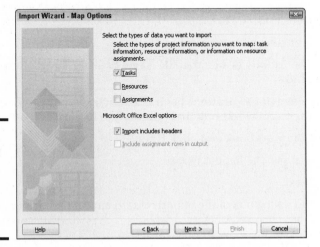

Figure 4-8:
Select the types of data and other mapping options.

9. Select the check boxes for the types of data you want to import and specify whether the Excel file contains headers.

10. Click Next.

The Task Mapping dialog box of the Import Wizard appears (see Figure 4-9).

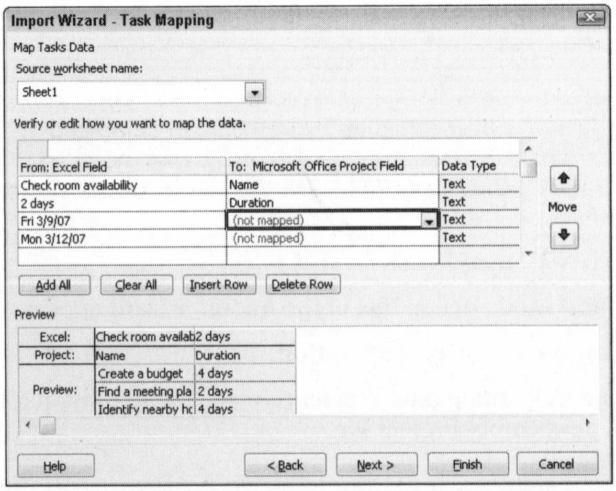

Figure 4-9:
Use this dialog box to map Excel worksheet information to Project fields.

11. **Open the Source Worksheet Name list and select the Excel worksheet that contains the data you want to import.**

The dialog box updates to show each field in the Excel worksheet. In the To: Microsoft Office Project Field column, "(not mapped)" appears in red.

12. **Click in the To: Microsoft Office Project Field column and select a Project field to represent the information in the Excel worksheet.**

As you match fields, the Preview portion of the dialog box compares Excel fields to Project fields. Repeat this step for each field.

13. **Click Next.**

If you selected the Resources and the Assignments check boxes in the Map Options dialog box (shown previously in Figure 4-8), the Import Wizard displays additional dialog boxes that are almost identical to the Task Mapping dialog box so that you can map these data types.

14. **Click Next.**

The End of Map Definition dialog box appears and gives you the opportunity to save your map. If you expect to import Excel files in this same format on a regular basis, click Save Map, supply a map name, and click Save. In most cases, you don't need to save the map.

15. **Click Finish.**

Project imports the Excel file information into a new Project file (see Figure 4-10).

The tasks in the imported file all contain a Start No Earlier Than constraint that you probably want to change to As Soon As Possible when you start working with task dependencies.

Creating a Task List in Excel using a Project-related template

You can start a project Task List in Excel and then import it into Project at the point where you begin to need Project's scheduling and project management tools. To make the job easy in both programs, use a specially designed Excel template to create your Task List. Follow these steps to create your Task List in Excel:

1. **In Excel, click the Office button.**

2. **Click New.**

The New Workbook dialog box appears (see Figure 4-11).

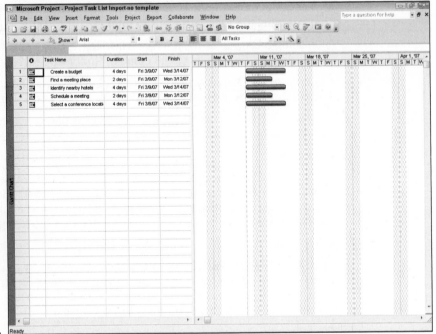

Figure 4-10:
An Excel file that used no template imported into Project.

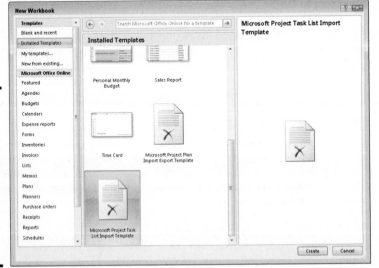

Figure 4-11:
Use this dialog box to select a template to use to create a list of tasks you intend to import into Project.

3. **Click Installed Templates in the list on the left.**

4. **Scroll down the center list and click the Microsoft Project Task List Import Template.**

5. **Click Create.**

   Excel formats a workbook suitable for recording tasks you intend to import into Project (see Figure 4-12).

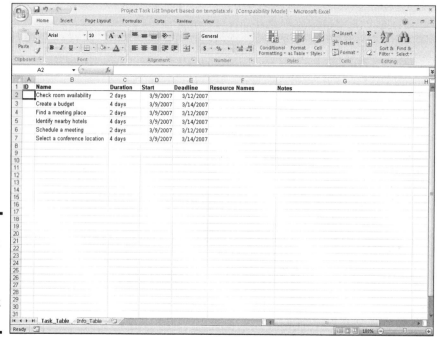

Figure 4-12:
A workbook designed to help you build a Project Task List.

6. **Create your Task List.**

7. **Save your workbook as an Excel 97–2003 workbook.**

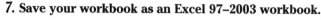

   Project 2007 cannot import an Excel 2007 workbook, but it can import an Excel 97–2003 workbook.

Importing the Excel Task List into Project

After you've saved your Task List in Excel 97–2003 format in Excel, importing it into Project is a fairly simple matter. You first need to tell Project that you want to be allowed to import files from earlier versions of Office or files that don't use the Project file format. Then, you can use the Import Wizard to import the Task List into a new project or an existing project. Follow these steps in Project:

1. **Choose File⇨Open.**

The Open dialog box appears (see Figure 4-13).

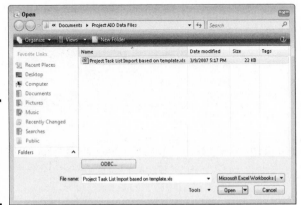

Figure 4-13:
Use this
dialog box
to open an
Excel
97–2003 file.

2. **Click the list box beside the File Name box and select Microsoft Excel Workbooks.**

3. **Use the Previous Locations list box to navigate to the folder that contains the Excel workbook that you want to import.**

4. **Highlight the workbook and click Open.**

Project starts the Import Wizard.

5. **Click Next.**

The Data Type dialog box of the Import Wizard appears (see Figure 4-14).

6. **Select Project Excel Template and click Next.**

The Import Mode dialog box of the Import Wizard appears.

7. **Select the As a New Project option.**

Selecting this option tells Project to place the information in the Excel file in a new, empty Project file.

8. **Click Finish.**

Project imports the Excel file information into a new Project file (see Figure 4-15).

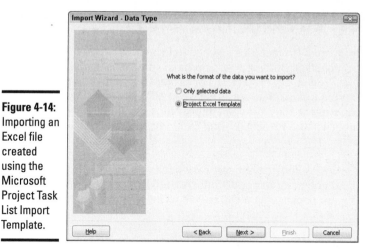

Figure 4-14:
Importing an
Excel file
created
using the
Microsoft
Project Task
List Import
Template.

The tasks in the imported file all contain a Start No Earlier Than constraint that you probably want to change to As Soon As Possible when you start working with task dependencies.

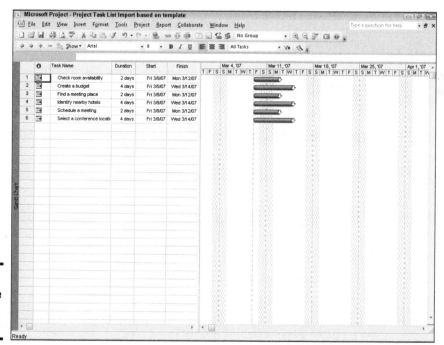

Figure 4-15:
An Excel file
imported
into Project.

Importing Project Exchange Files into Project

You can simply open Project files created in Project 98, Project 2000, Project 2002, and Project 2003. But suppose you have some files from older versions of Project, like Project 4.0, Project 4.1, or Project 95, that you want to use in Project 2007. Or suppose that you created an MPX file in Project 98 that you want to use in Project 2007. You can import files using the MPX file format — used by Project 4.0 and Project 4.1 and available in Project 98 — into Project 2007.

Some other project management software packages also support the MPX file format, so if you need to import information from another project management software package, you can save it as an MPX file and import it into Project.

Importing an MPX file is similar to opening any project. Follow these steps to import an MPX file:

1. **Choose File⇨Open.**

The Open dialog box appears.

2. **Click the list box beside the File Name box and choose MPX.**

3. **Use the Previous Locations list box to navigate to the appropriate file.**

4. **Click Open.**

The currently recommended file format for exchanging Project data with other products is XML.

Importing Text or Comma-Separated Files into Project

Project can read text (tab-delimited) and comma-separated value (CSV) files. If you have project data in a program that can create either a text file or a comma-separated value file, you can import information from that program into Project. Using the other program, save the information that you want to import into Project as either a text file or a CSV file. Then follow these steps in Project to let the Import Wizard walk you through the process. If the map that you need doesn't exist, you need to create it.

Follow these steps in Project to import the information:

1. **Choose File⇨Open.**

The Open dialog box appears.

2. **Click the list box beside the File Name box and choose Text (Tab delimited) (*.txt) or CSV (Comma delimited) (*.csv).**

3. **Use the Previous Locations list box to navigate to the folder that contains the file that you want to import.**

4. **Select the file.**

5. **Click Open.**

   Project starts the Import Wizard.

6. **Click Next.**

   The Map dialog box of the Import Wizard appears.

7. **Select New Map and click Next.**

   The Import Mode dialog box of the Import Wizard appears.

8. **Select the As a New Project option.**

   Selecting this option tells Project to place the information in the text or comma-separated file in a new, empty Project file.

9. **Click Next.**

   The Map Options dialog box of the Import Wizard appears (see Figure 4-16).

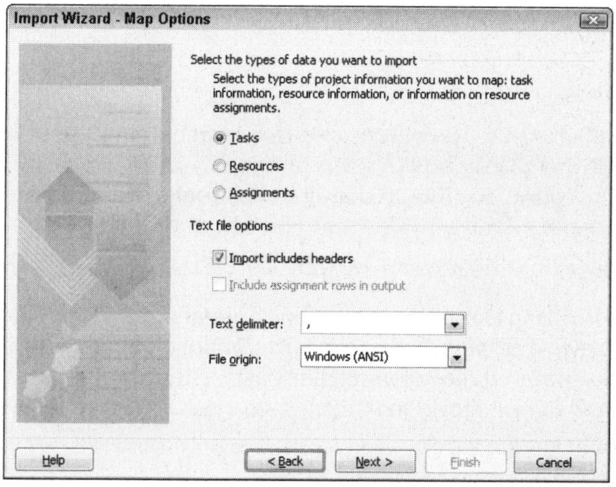

Figure 4-16:
Select the types of data and other mapping options.

10. **Select the check boxes for the types of data you want to import and indicate whether the text or comma-separated file contains headers.**

11. **Click Next.**

   The Task Mapping dialog box of the Import Wizard appears (see Figure 4-17).

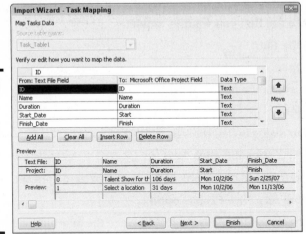

Figure 4-17:
Use this
dialog box
to map text
or comma-
separated
file infor-
mation to
Project
fields.

12. **Click in the To: Microsoft Office Project Field column and select a Project field to represent the information in the text or comma-separated file.**

   As you match fields, the Preview portion of the dialog box compares the text or comma-separated file fields to Project fields. Repeat this step for each field.

13. **Click Next.**

   If you selected the Resources and the Assignments check boxes in the Map Options dialog box (shown previously in Figure 4-16), the Import Wizard displays additional dialog boxes that are almost identical to the Task Mapping dialog box so that you can map these data types.

14. **Click Next.**

   The End of Map Definition dialog box appears and gives you the opportunity to save your map. If you expect to import similarly organized text or comma-separated files on a regular basis, click Save Map, supply a map name, and click Save. In most cases, you don't need to save the map.

15. **Click Finish.**

   Project imports the file information into a new Project file.

   The tasks in the imported file all contain a Start No Earlier Than constraint that you probably want to change to As Soon As Possible when you start working with task dependencies.

Chapter 5: Exporting Project Information

In This Chapter

✓ Copying pictures into Office programs

✓ Saving visual reporting information for use in other programs

✓ Exporting Project data to Excel

✓ Exporting Project data to text files

You can export Project information in a variety of ways so that you can use it in Microsoft Office applications. You also can export some Project information to graphic images that you can use in a graphics program or as an image on a Web page. And you can export information to XML, text (.txt) files, or comma-separated value (.csv) files.

Although you can't export Project data directly into Word, you can copy images from a Project Schedule into Word, as you see in the next section. You can copy table information from Project to Word using the Windows Copy and Paste commands. When you copy the columns in any table to a Word document, they appear as tab-separated columns. Using Word's Convert Text to Table feature, you can convert the columns into a Word table.

Copying Pictures into Office Programs

Here's the situation: You've just written a great report in Microsoft Word about your project and you really want to include your Gantt chart in the report. Although you can print the Gantt chart on a separate page and manually insert it in the appropriate place in the report, you'd really rather include it as part of the report file in Word. Using the Copy Picture to Office Wizard, you can send an image *and* fields you select to Word, PowerPoint, or Visio.

The Copy Picture to Office Wizard button appears on the Analysis toolbar, along with the Adjust Dates button and the PERT Analysis button, but the

Analysis toolbar doesn't appear by default in Project. You need to jump through some hoops to make it appear. Follow these steps:

1. **Click Tools⇨Customize⇨Toolbars.**

The Customize dialog box appears.

2. **Click the Commands tab.**

3. **In the Categories list on the left, click All Commands.**

4. **In the Commands list on the right, drag COMAddInsDialog to any existing toolbar (see Figure 5-1).**

Commands appear in alphabetical order.

5. **Click Close to close the Customize dialog box.**

6. **Click the COM Add-Ins button you just added to a toolbar.**

The COM Add-Ins dialog box appears (see Figure 5-2).

7. **Remove the check marks beside Adjust Dates, Copy Picture to Office, and PERT Analysis.**

The Compare Project Versions Utility uses its own toolbar; if you want the utility available, deselect the Compare Project Versions Utility check box along with the other options in the COM Add-Ins dialog box.

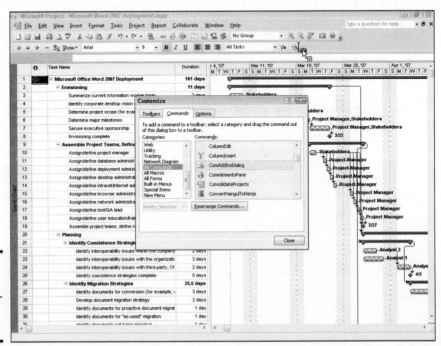

Figure 5-1:
Drag
COMAddIns-
Dialog onto
any toolbar.

Figure 5-2:
Use this
dialog box
to create
the Analysis
toolbar,
which
contains
buttons for
each of the
add-ins
listed in the
dialog box.

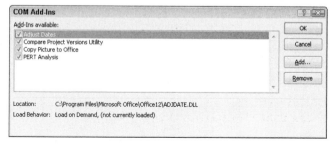

8. **Click OK.**

9. **Repeat Steps 6 to 8, but, in Step 7, select the check boxes you previously deselected.**

Project generates the Analysis toolbar, and when you display the toolbar, buttons appear for Adjust Dates, Copy Picture to Office Wizard, and PERT Analysis.

If you included the Compare Project Versions Utility check box both times in Step 7, then Project also generates the Compare Project Versions toolbar.

You can remove the COMAddInsDialog button from the toolbar by reopening the Customize dialog box and then dragging the button off the toolbar.

Now you're ready to use the Copy Picture to Office Wizard; follow these steps:

1. **Right-click any toolbar.**

   A list of available toolbars appears.

2. **Click Analysis.**

   The Analysis toolbar appears.

3. **Click the Copy Picture to Office Wizard button.**

   The wizard begins.

4. **Click Next.**

   The Step 1 screen of the wizard appears (see Figure 5-3).

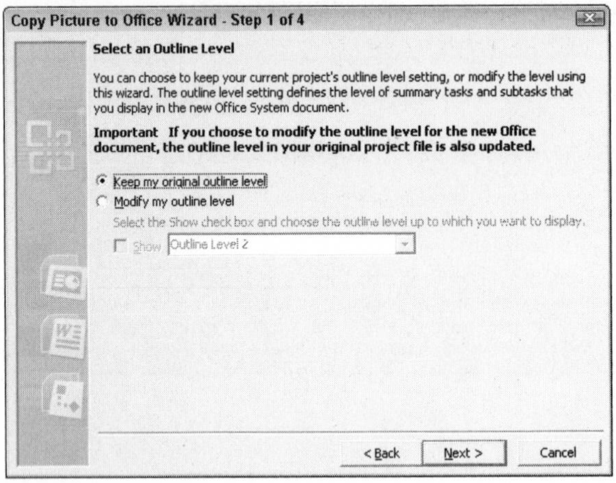

Figure 5-3:
Tell the
wizard how
to handle
your outline
level.

5. **Identify the method you want the wizard to use when handling your outline level and click Next.**

6. **Select the options you want Project to use while creating the image (see Figure 5-4) and click Next.**

   You can select the rows and portion of the timescale to copy and the size of the image.

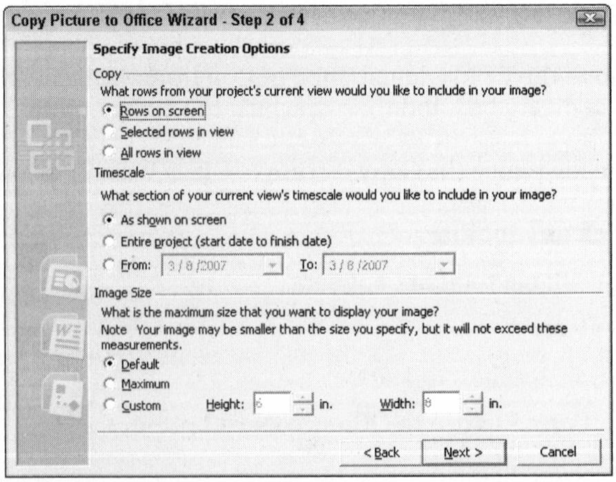

Figure 5-4:
Set the
options for
the image.

7. **Select the Office application to which you want to send the picture and the orientation of the picture and click Next (see Figure 5-5).**

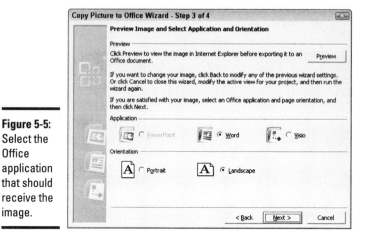

Figure 5-5:
Select the
Office
application
that should
receive the
image.

8. **Select the Project fields you want to include with the image (see Figure 5-6).**

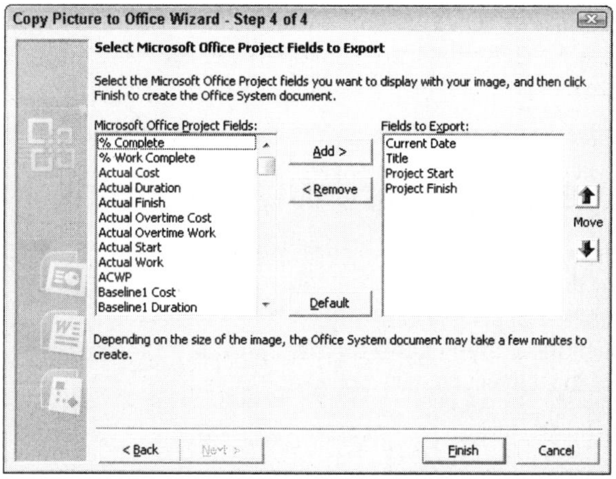

Figure 5-6:
Identify
Project
fields to
include with
the image.

9. **Click Finish.**

Project creates an Office document.

10. **Click Close.**

The document opens in the appropriate Office program (see Figure 5-7).

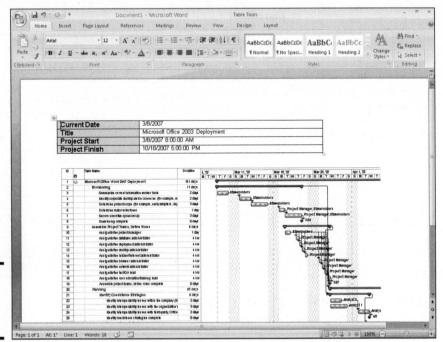

Figure 5-7:
A Project
schedule in
Word.

Copying a picture without fields

Using the Copy Picture command, you can copy your Project schedule to the Windows Clipboard and then paste it into any application as a graphic image if you use the Copy Picture command. When you use this command, you copy only a picture without Project fields.

Click the Copy Picture button on the Standard toolbar or choose Edit⇨Copy Picture to display the Copy Picture dialog box.

To copy the picture to the Windows Clipboard, select the For Screen option button in the Render Image section and click OK. If the image that you're copying will fit well into another document, Project simply copies the picture to the Windows Clipboard. But, if the picture that you're copying is particularly large, Project warns you and displays a dialog box that gives you the opportunity to scale the picture before saving or pasting it.

After you've copied the picture, simply switch to another program in which you want to place the picture and click the Paste button in that document to place a graphic in your document.

To create a graphic image file that you can use on a Web page or in a document, select the To GIF Image File option in the Copy Picture dialog box.

When you render the image for a printer, Project copies the image to the Windows Clipboard but formats the image by using your printer driver. If you have a black-and-white printer, the image appears in shades of gray rather than in the colors that you see on-screen. If you have a color printer, the image appears in color, like it looks on-screen. You can view the image by pasting it into another application.

Saving Visual Reporting Information

Book VI, Chapter 4 describes how to create Visual Reports in Project — reports that use Project data to create reports in Excel or Visio. When Project generates the data for these visual reports, Project temporarily creates OLAP (On Line Analytical Processing) cubes and an Access database. You don't have direct access to the data, and when you close your project, Project automatically deletes these OLAP cubes and Access databases.

OLAP cubes help answer analytical queries that are up to six dimensions in nature. Two-dimensional data typically appears in rows and columns. To analyze more than two dimensions, think "cube"; each dimension that you analyze is assigned to one face on the cube. For example, you can use an OLAP cube to evaluate the sales data of three items for five stores located in four different regions over a period of several years — and you still haven't used up all the sides of the cube.

You can save the OLAP cube and the Access database information and use it outside of Project. Follow these steps in Project:

1. **Open a project and choose Reports⇨Visual Reports.**

The Visual Reports – Create Report window appears.

2. **Click the Save Data button.**

The Visual Reports – Save Reporting Data dialog box appears (see Figure 5-8).

Figure 5-8:
Use this
dialog box
to create an
OLAP cube
or an
Access
database by
using visual
reporting
information.

3. Open the first drop-down list to select the type of OLAP cube you want to create.

You can create six different OLAP cubes: Task Usage, Resource Usage, Assignment Usage, Task Summary, Resource Summary, and Assignment Summary.

4. Click the Field Picker button.

Project displays the Visual Reports – Field Picker dialog box (see Figure 5-9). The fields available and already selected in the Field Picker dialog box depend on the type of cube you selected.

5. Click a field in the Available Fields list or the Available Custom Fields list.

6. Click Add.

Project displays the field in the appropriate list box on the right side of the dialog box.

To remove a field from the cube, select it in the appropriate list on the right and click the Remove button.

7. Repeat Steps 5 and 6 for each field you want to add.

8. Click OK.

Project redisplays the Visual Reports – Save Reporting Data dialog box (refer to Figure 5-8).

9. Click Save Cube.

Project displays the Save As dialog box.

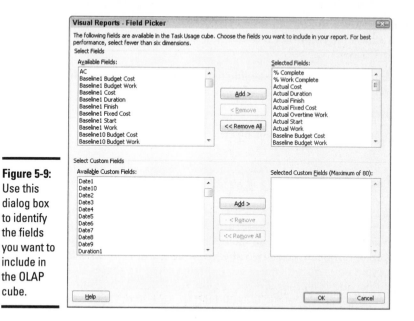

Figure 5-9:
Use this
dialog box
to identify
the fields
you want to
include in
the OLAP
cube.

10. **Navigate to the location where you want to save the cube, assign it a
name if you don't like the default name provided by Project, and click
Save.**

Project redisplays the Visual Reports – Save Reporting Data dialog box,
builds the cube, and saves it.

11. **Click Close twice.**

Project redisplays your project.

Creating an Access database file follows basically the same procedure, but
it's a bit less complicated because you don't select a cube or fields; instead,
the database file will contain all reporting information in your Project file.
Follow these steps:

1. **Open a project and choose Reports⇨Visual Reports.**

The Visual Reports – Create Report window appears.

2. **Click the Save Data button.**

The Visual Reports – Save Reporting Data dialog box appears (refer to
Figure 5-8).

3. **Click the Save Database button.**

Project displays the Save As dialog box.

4. **Navigate to the location where you want to save the database, assign it a name if you don't like the default name provided by Project, and click Save.**

   Project saves the database file and redisplays the Visual Reports – Save Reporting Data dialog box.

5. **Click Close twice.**

   Project redisplays your project.

Exporting Project Data to Excel

You can export Project information — tasks, resources, and assignments — to Excel workbooks using the Export Wizard. You can export the information to an Excel workbook or to an Excel PivotTable. When you export to an Excel PivotTable, Project creates two sheets in the Excel workbook for each type of data that you export. One sheet contains the data that is used in the PivotTable, and the other sheet contains the PivotTable. Project uses the last field in each map as the default field for the PivotTable, and all the other fields appear as rows in the PivotTable.

The Export Wizard lets you export specific Project data or all data in your Project file using an Excel template. The Excel template approach makes it easy to export Project data to Excel and then send it back again to Project, and the steps that follow show you how to use the Excel template:

1. **Open the Project file that contains the information that you want to export.**

2. **Choose File⇨Save As.**

   Project opens the Save As dialog box.

3. **In the File Name text box, type a name for the file that you want to export.**

4. **In the Save As Type drop-down list, select Microsoft Excel Workbook or Microsoft Excel PivotTable.**

5. **Click Save.**

   Project starts the Export Wizard.

6. **Click Next.**

   The Data screen of the Export Wizard appears (see Figure 5-10).

7. **Choose Project Excel Template.**

8. **Click Finish.**

   Project creates the Excel file using the settings you provided.

Figure 5-10:
To export the entire Project schedule to Excel using a predefined format, use the Project Excel Template.

You can open the file in Excel; the Excel workbook that Project creates resembles the one shown in Figure 5-11. Notice that the workbook contains four worksheets: one for each type of data you can export from Project to Excel and, on the fourth tab — the Info_Table tab — you find a brief advertisement of Project's purpose.

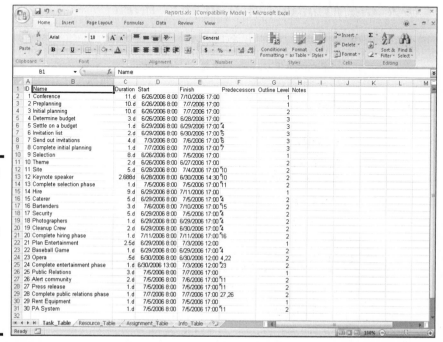

Figure 5-11:
A sample of the workbook that Project creates when you select the Project Excel Template.

If you want to start your project in Excel and later export it to Project, use the Microsoft Project Plan Import Export Template in Excel. That template contains all the fields shown in Figure 5-11.

If you choose to export specific Project data (and not use the Excel template), you can find the steps you need in the next section because exporting specific Project data to Excel is very much like exporting Project data to a text file. You can find only a few differences:

✦ You can simultaneously export task, resource, and assignment data to an Excel workbook; you can export only one type of data at a time to a text file. If you choose to export more than one type of data, the Export Wizard displays Mapping dialog boxes for each type of data.

✦ While mapping fields, you can specify the name of the destination worksheet.

✦ Although you can quickly add all the fields in the Project file by clicking the Add All button, be aware that you can export a maximum of 255 fields to Excel for each type of data. Project contains over 700 task fields and over 400 resource or assignment fields. So, if you choose Add All, you'll have to delete some of the fields before Project will allow you to proceed to the next step in the wizard.

Exporting Project Data to Text Files

You can use Project information in any program that can open either text (.txt) files or comma-separated value (.csv) files by exporting Project schedule information using the Export Wizard.

Follow these steps to export information to a text or comma-separated value file:

1. **Open the Project file that contains the information that you want to export.**

2. **Choose File⇨Save As.**

Project opens the Save As dialog box.

3. **In the File Name text box, type a name for the file that you want to export.**

4. **In the Save As Type drop-down list, select Text (Tab Delimited) (*.txt) or CSV (Comma Delimited) (*.csv).**

5. **Click Save.**

Project starts the Export Wizard.

6. **Click Next.**

7. **Choose New Map or Use Existing Map.**

If you choose Use Existing Map, you see the Map Selection dialog box, from you which can select a predefined set of Project fields to export to Excel. If you choose New Map, the Map Selection dialog box doesn't appear. In this example, we use the New Map option.

8. **Click Next.**

The Export Wizard displays the Map Options dialog box.

9. **Select the type of data to export (see Figure 5-12).**

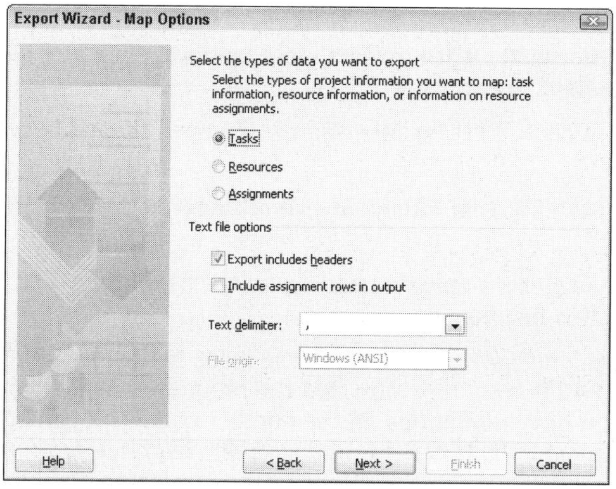

Figure 5-12: Select the type of data to export in the Map Options dialog box.

Export Wizard - Map Options

Select the types of data you want to export

Select the types of project information you want to map: task information, resource information, or information on resource assignments.

○ **Tasks**

○ **Resources**

○ **Assignments**

Text file options

☑ Export includes **headers**

☐ **Include assignment rows in output**

Text **delimiter:** ,

File **origin:** Windows (ANSI)

Help   < Back   Next >   Finish   Cancel

To include assignments that are listed under tasks or resources, similar to Project's Task Usage or Resource Usage views, select the Include Assignment Rows In Output check box.

10. **Click Next.**

One of the Mapping dialog box appears (see Figure 5-13).

11. **Use the Export Filter drop-down list to select the tasks that you want to export.**

By default, Project assumes that you want to export all tasks, but you can export, for example, only critical tasks.

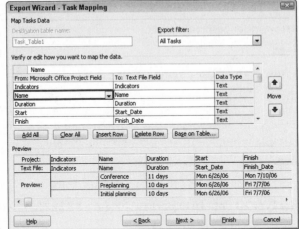

Figure 5-13:
As you add fields, a preview of the file that you're creating appears at the bottom of the dialog box.

12. **In the Microsoft Office Project Field column, click any blank cell to select a field to export.**

After you click, a list box arrow appears; open the list to select a field.

13. **Click in the To: Text File Field column next to the field that you added.**

Project suggests a column heading for the field in the text file; you can change this heading.

Although you can quickly add all the fields in the Project file by clicking the Add All button, be aware that the program to which you are exporting might have limitations on the number of fields it can hold. Project contains over 700 task fields and over 400 resource or assignment fields, and exporting all of them could create a very large file that would take a long time to open.

14. **Repeat Steps 12 and 13 until you've selected all the fields you want to export.**

15. **Click Next.**

The final box of the Export Wizard appears.

16. **If you expect to export the same data frequently, click the Save Map button to save your map settings.**

Project displays the Save Map dialog box (see Figure 5-14).

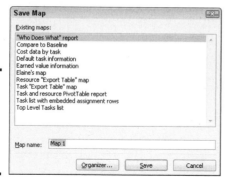

Figure 5-14:
Use this
window to
save your
export map
settings.

17. **In the Map Name text box, provide a name for the new map and click Save.**

Project redisplays the last screen of the Export Wizard.

18. **Click Finish.**

Project creates the text file using the settings you provided.

Book X

The Basics of Project Server

The 5th Wave   By Rich Tennant

FELDMAN NOVELTY ITEMS

"We monitor our entire operation from one central location. We know what the 'Wax Lips' people are doing, we know what the 'Whoopee Cushion' people are doing, we know what the 'Fly-in-the-Ice Cube' people are doing. But we don't know what the 'Plastic Vomit' people are doing. We don't want to know what the 'Plastic Vomit' people are doing."

Contents at a Glance

Chapter 1: Understanding Project Server

In This Chapter

✓ Discovering Project Server

✓ Determining whether you need Project Server

✓ Planning the implementation of Project Server

*B*ecause you're reading this book, we can safely assume that the products or services your organization provides are best accomplished in a project environment. We can also safely assume that you have a limited staff available to complete all your projects. In an organization where most of the work happens in a project environment using the same resources, the organization needs to manage the management of projects to maximize productivity and profit.

Enter Project Server. Project Server answers the needs of an enterprise to manage multiple projects that draw their resources from a common resource pool. This chapter describes the basics of how Project Server functions and how to approach using Project Server.

What Is Project Server?

Project Server provides your organization with one central database, located on a Web server or in a server farm on your company's *local area network* (LAN) or intranet, in which you store all projects and all resources for your organization. Using Project Server, you can

✦ View a project's Gantt chart

✦ Enter and view timesheet information

✦ Update assignments with progress and completion information

✦ Send status reports to the project manager

✦ Receive notices about task status

✦ Receive, refuse, and delegate work assignments

✦ Manage resource allocation across your organization

✦ Carry out basic issue and risk management

✦ Attach supporting documentation, such as budget estimates or feasibility studies, to a task or project

Although Project Server works in conjunction with Project Professional, only project managers need to install Project Professional; the project manager uses Project Professional to create projects using the techniques we've described throughout this book. In the Project Server environment, your organization can create projects that use identical custom settings to help you manage projects in a consistent manner because Project Server uses the Enterprise Global template the same way that Project uses the Global.mpt template file. The Enterprise Global template contains all the fields, maps, views, tables, reports, filters, forms, groups, and calendars that are stored in the Global.mpt template file that's included in Project Professional, along with additional enterprise-only fields. You can define whether fields are required, and you can create look-up tables and value lists for fields.

In addition to setting up the Enterprise Global template, use Project Professional to create a resource pool that contains all the resources available in your entire organization using the same techniques described in Book III, Chapter 4. Because the resource pool contains all the resources available in your entire organization, it's aptly named the Global Resource Pool in Project Server.

You then publish (that's "upload" in Project Server lingo) the resource pool and all the organization's projects to the Project Server database. To work with the information in the Project Server database, you can use Project Professional or Project Web Access, an Internet Explorer browser-based client-side interface that installs when you install Project Server. Figure 1-1 shows you a typical home page in Project Web Access.

The way in which you use the Project Server database depends on your role in your organization, because different people have different needs for project information. For example, project team members can use Project Web Access to see the assignments that they've received, enter time spent on various project tasks, update work assignments, send status reports to the project manager, and even set up to-do lists. Chapter 4 of this minibook describes how a team member might use the Project Server database.

Project Server can exchange information with Outlook. Resources can import tasks from Project Server and export work information from Outlook to Project Server.

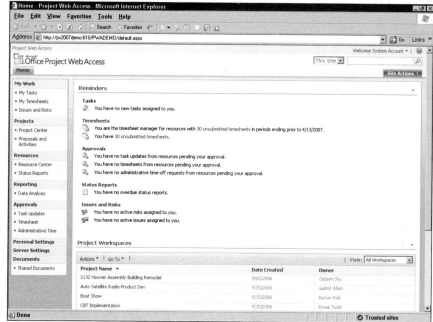

Figure 1-1:
A typical
Project Web
Access
home page.

Project managers can receive updates to tasks and status reports from team members. Project managers also can use the Global Resource Pool when assigning resources while setting up new projects or tasks within an existing project. The Global Resource Pool helps project and resource managers avoid overallocating resources and also contains a matching feature you can use to match the skills you need for a task to a person in the resource pool with those skills. Chapter 3 of this minibook describes how a project manager might use the Project Server database.

Clearly, security becomes a serious issue when you decide to place all the information about your organization's work into a central repository. Not only do you need to secure the LAN or intranet from the outside world, but you also need to secure the various projects within the Project Server database because everybody doesn't need to see everything. In fact, two team members working on the same project might need access to different information. Along with other jobs, the Project Server administrator sets up the Project Server database security. The Project Server administrator doesn't typically decide that John gets to see financial data and Mary doesn't; instead, the Project Server administrator works with others within the organization to develop security profiles that describe the varying levels of security needed in your organization. And, the Project Server administrator sets up new users in the Project Server database with the privileges that organization management deems appropriate. The next chapter of this mini-book describes the role of the Project Server administrator in more detail.

Do You Need Project Server?

You might have been managing multiple projects for a long time now, and you might have been managing them effectively, too. So, the question might arise, "Do I really need Project Server?"

To determine whether Project Server can help you, ask yourself the following questions:

+ Has your organization identified a need to track projects more accurately or use resources more efficiently?

+ Does your organization manage many different projects using the same resources?

+ Has your organization determined that the time of project managers and resources would be used more efficiently if resources could record their time directly in the project schedule instead of providing it to the project manager, who then updates the schedule?

+ Do your users need access to project data anywhere in the world?

If you answered yes to any of these questions, Project Server can help you. The more "yes" answers you gave, the more likely it us that your organization can benefit from using Project Server.

Planning the Implementation of Project Server

To successfully implement Project Server, you need to plan for the needs of your organization. You need to assess where your organization is today and where it plans to go. You need to identify the players, their needs, and their roles in the process. You need to figure out what needs to be done, who has the skills and availability to do it, when it needs to be done, and what else depends on it getting done.

To summarize, implementing Project Server is a project. You should treat it as such, identifying the tasks that you need to accomplish, estimating the work needed to accomplish them, identifying task dependencies, and assigning resources to the tasks.

To successfully implement Project Server, you should treat the project the same way you would treat an information technology project. You should assess requirements, design the system, and develop an implementation strategy.

Defining requirements

When you assess requirements for an information technology project, you focus on determining your organization's direction and needs; the Project Server design ultimately depends on the information that you gather.

On the team you set up to implement the system, you need people who are good at gathering information, making design decisions, and managing implementation. You'll find it helpful to include people who are experienced in using enterprise project management systems. You need a mix of business people and technical people to address the various facets of implementing Project Server. The business people should include senior project managers and staff with experience using Project. The technical people should include those who are experienced in your company's network architecture and hardware configuration. To customize or automate Project Server functions, you should include a technical person with skills in developing object models for Project. Everyone on the team should be familiar with your company's standards.

Book X
Chapter 1

**Understanding
Project Server**

The team needs to set milestone dates and task durations for each of the following activities:

+ Identify the people who will approve the Project Server design

+ Identify staff members to interview

+ Create a requirements definition questionnaire

+ Conduct interviews

+ Calculate return on investment

As with any project, it's important to identify the decision-makers as soon as you start. If possible, include one or more of them on the team so that they are a part of the process and they feel ownership for the system that you ultimately design.

For interviews, identify staff members who fill the following roles:

+ **Administrators:** People who manage changes and access to the Project Server database. The people who start the administrator job might ultimately phase out of the job because the job functions change over time. Initially, the administrator installs and sets up Project Professional, Project Server, and SQL Server and may use both Project Server and SQL

Server tools to meet the needs of users. Eventually, the administrator role migrates to a maintenance function, where knowledge of Project Server administrative functions is the only prerequisite.

✦ **Executives:** People who view reports on projects and resources.

✦ **Portfolio managers:** People who are familiar with company standards and can manage the Enterprise global template.

✦ **Project managers:** People who prepare project plans and monitor project progress.

✦ **Resource managers:** People who delegate work to team members and monitor project progress and resource utilization.

✦ **Team members:** People to whom work is assigned.

To effectively interview, the team should create a questionnaire that focuses on obtaining information about how people work. To gather information for your questionnaire, evaluate the reports that your company currently uses to record project performance. Analyze these reports to identify the resources and projects that are or should be included on the report. Evaluate how tasks, projects, and resources are categorized on the reports and note who uses each report.

When you conduct interviews, make sure that you include more than one person in each role because two people filling the same role do things differently and potentially have different needs.

Implementing Project Server will require software and role-based training for resources, and it might also require investments in hardware. Because of the investment required to implement Project Server, you should calculate your return on investment to assess the costs and benefits of implementing Project Server.

Designing the system

Using the information that you gathered while defining requirements, you should be able to identify the features in Project Server that you want to implement. In addition, the implementation team must also address issues that aren't directly related to the design of the Project Server database. For example, the team should

✦ Evaluate the technology environment

✦ Address special needs

✦ Establish and/or enforce organizational standards

✦ Plan for training

The team must evaluate the organization's technology environment because Project Server requires certain software, and the hardware that you use affects the performance of Project Server.

The requirements definition might highlight some special needs. For example, your organization might want to use Windows SharePoint Services, which comes with Project Server, to build and maintain document libraries for projects and deal with issues in a collaborative way.

The team should customize the Enterprise Global template to reflect the standards of your organization so that everyone uses the same terminology and applies the same processes and procedures to their projects. In the Enterprise Global template, you can create custom fields, outline codes, views, and calendars. The team can also set up the Enterprise Resource Pool so that your organization can share resources between projects and identify conflicts between assignments in different projects.

We can't stress strongly enough how important training is. Suffice it to say that without proper training for those who will use Project Server, implementation will fail.

Developing an implementation strategy

Because the scope of implementing enterprise project management affects your entire organization, doing it "all at once" is very risky. Using a phased approach reduces the risk considerably and increases your chances for success.

Start by creating a prototype of the system. Identify a few projects and project teams to participate in the prototype test, making sure that you select users who represent all the various roles that the team identified so that you can fully test the system. Also, select projects that don't depend on other projects that won't be a part of the prototype. Design and develop the prototype system and demonstrate it to the project teams that will use it. Make modifications to the prototype design based on input from these project teams and demonstrate the prototype to senior management, once again, making changes as needed.

Then develop training materials and begin a pilot phase. Reset the Project Server database and load the pilot projects that include users who represent all the various roles that the team identified. During this pilot phase, you should include at least one project that has external dependencies to another project to test that aspect of using Project Server, and then you can make adjustments as needed. Train the pilot group and allow the group members to use Project Server for at least four reporting cycles. Solicit feedback and address all the issues that arise.

When you're satisfied that you've ironed out any kinks identified during the prototype and pilot phases, expand the user base of the system again, adding projects to the Project Server database, and train the new group that is to begin using the system. Allow each new group of users to work through at least three reporting cycles before you add more projects and users.

Reviewing software needs

As you'd expect, Microsoft has established certain basic software and hardware requirements needed to support Project Server. On the software side, you need to meet requirements for both client machines and server machines.

Client machines used by the project manager need Project Professional and Internet Explorer 6.0 or higher. The client machines of other resources need only Internet Explorer 6.0 or higher. And, if you intend to exchange task information with Outlook, client machines also need Outlook 2007.

Servers that will host Project Server need, at a minimum, Windows Server 2003, Standard or Enterprise Edition, 32-bit or 64-bit, with Service Pack 1 or later. You need to enable Microsoft Internet Information Server (IIS) 6.0 or above, and for the Project Server database engine, you need SQL Server 2000 with Service Pack 3 or higher or SQL Server 2005. If you want to use the portfolio modeling features that are available in Project Web Access, you need SQL Server Analysis Services and SQL Server Reporting Services, which are included with SQL Server but must be installed separately. In addition, Project Server depends on the Windows SharePoint Services 3.0 (WSS) platform, which comes on the Project Server 2007 CD and installs automatically when you install Project Server. To use e-mail notifications, both the server and client machines need Internet SMTP/POP3, IMAP4, or MAPI-compliant messaging software.

Reviewing hardware needs

Microsoft recommends that each client machine have, at a minimum, a 300-MHz processor, have 192MB of RAM, and use Windows XP Professional as the operating system. The minimum processor on a client machine is a Pentium 133-MHz. Each client machine should have a Super VGA (800 x 600) or higher resolution monitor with 256 colors and a Microsoft Mouse–compatible pointing device.

Typically, you install Project Server on your company's server or in a server farm. If you're planning to use the bare-minimum hardware, you should load only Project Server on that computer. Other components, such as SQL Server, should run on separate computers to help you balance the load.

You can read more about load balancing in the next section.

Microsoft recommends that you install Project Server on a computer with a minimum Pentium III processor that runs at 700 MHz and has 1GB of RAM, a DVD-ROM drive, a Super VGA (800 x 600) or higher resolution monitor, and a Microsoft Mouse–compatible pointing device.

To install Project Server, you need 200MB of available hard drive space. To install WSS, you need another 70MB of hard drive space and a minimum of 256MB of RAM, but 512MB of RAM is recommended.

To install SQL Server 2000, you need 250MB of hard drive space and 128MB of RAM. If you also intend to install SQL Analysis Services, you need another 130MB of hard drive space and another 128MB of RAM.

You might want to plan to upgrade your network infrastructure. The amount of traffic that you can expect on your network is directly related to the total number of users, the number of concurrent users updating the Project Server databases, and the number and size of projects that you store in the Project Server database. Using older network architecture (10Base-T) in a heavily trafficked environment will undoubtedly result in complaints that the system is slow.

Considering software and hardware configurations

The overall performance of Project Server is affected by the features of Project Server that you want to use, the total number of users and concurrent users, and the number of projects that you want to store in the Project Server databases.

As you read earlier in this chapter, you're loading a lot of software to use Project Server. But, because Project Server 2007 depends on Windows SharePoint Services 3.0, you have some choices about how you configure the hardware on which you will load the software, and your choices will affect the performance of Project Server. You can use a single server or a server farm.

If you use a single server, you load all the software that Project Server needs to run onto that one server. But, if you choose to use a server farm, you can place various components and services on several networked computers to balance the load. The server farm has a few advantages. Using a server farm improves your ability to easily expand to meet growing needs while simultaneously limiting the impact created when a single component or service fails.

You can set up Project Server 2007 in a small farm, a medium farm, or a large farm. There are many ways that you can set up each server farm size, and Microsoft makes some recommendations about the various server farm configurations. In each of these configurations, Microsoft classifies the servers in the farm as Web front-end servers, application servers, and SQL servers and recommends placing different components of Project Server on the different classifications of servers. Typically, here's how things work:

✦ You place Windows SharePoint Services and Project Web Access on Web front-end servers.

✦ You put applications such as the Project Server Interface, Project Server business objects, and Project Server reporting and queuing services on application servers.

✦ You place Project Server SQL databases, SQL Analysis Services, and SQL Reporting Services on SQL servers.

In a small server farm, you load everything on two servers. You designate one computer as the SQL Server, placing SQL 2000 or SQL 2005 and SQL Analysis Services and SQL Reporting Services on that computer. Then use the other computer as both a Web front-end server and an application server, where you install Project Server and Windows SharePoint Services. This configuration separates database processing from other processing and typically improves performance.

In a medium server farm, you use three tiers of servers, installing each Project Server component in a separate Web front end, application, and database server tier. This approach works well when you need to accommodate more users because you can add more Web front-end servers, application servers, and, if necessary, database servers.

In the large server farm configuration, you use three tiers and install each component in a separate tier like you do in the medium server farm. In the large server farm configuration, you might also be using other services available through SharePoint Server 2007, such as Search, Index, or Excel Calculation Services. In this case, you set up each of these services on its own server.

Chapter 2: The Project Server Administrator

In This Chapter

✔ Understanding the structure of the Project Server database

✔ Working with users, views, the Enterprise Global template, custom fields, and calendars

✔ Setting up the Enterprise resource pool

✔ Loading projects into the Project Server database

✔ Managing timesheet and task settings

✔ Customizing Project Web Access

✔ Managing information in the Project Server database

*I*nitially, the Project Server administrator needs information technology (IT) skills to install Project Server. When the design and implementation processes described in Chapter 1 of this minibook are complete, setting up the Project Server database for use in your organization requires both IT skills and the skills of a person familiar with project management and your organization's needs while managing projects. This chapter describes the administrative tasks involved in customizing the Project Server database.

Understanding the Structure of the Project Server Database

Using the term "Project Server Database" is a bit misleading because each installation of Project Server actually consists of four databases: the Draft database, the Published database, the Archive database, and the Reporting database.

We continue to refer to the collection as "the Project Server database" throughout this book, just to make things easier.

You can think of the Draft database as a holding tank area where project managers can store projects created in Project Professional that they don't yet want the general public to view. Only users of Project Professional can view draft projects.

Projects that are available to Project Web Access users reside in the Published database. For these projects, team members can update timesheets, update project information, and view reports, based on their Project Web Access credentials.

The Archive database contains older and backed-up versions of published projects.

Project Server uses the Reports database, which holds the data used in reports, to generate reports and OLAP cubes. Project Server updates the information in the Reporting database almost as soon as information changes.

Reviewing Defaults

The Project Server database contains many useful default values and settings that you can double-check, using Project Web Access, to make sure that they're right for your organization.

Launch Project Web Access by starting Internet Explorer and entering the URL for your Project Server database.

Your organization can set up access to the Project Server database by using one of two types of authentication: Windows authentication or Forms authentication. If your organization uses Windows authentication, you see the Project Web Access home page of the account you used to log onto the computer. If your organization uses Forms authentication, you're prompted to log onto Project Web Access by supplying a username and password.

The Quick Launch pane runs down the left side of the Project Web Access home page, and the Project Web Access home page for the administrator contains an additional link in the Quick Launch pane: the Server Settings link. When the Project Server administrator clicks the Server Settings link, Project Web Access displays the Server Settings page (see Figure 2-1) from which the Project Server administrator can manage and customize the Project Server database and Project Web Access.

By clicking the Additional Server Settings link in the Operational Policies section of the Server Settings page, you can make changes to a variety of features available for use in Project Server. For example, the Project Server administrator can confirm whether your organization will allow projects to use a local base calendar instead of the Enterprise base calendar. Also from this page, the Project Server administrator can change settings that help manage the size of the reporting database.

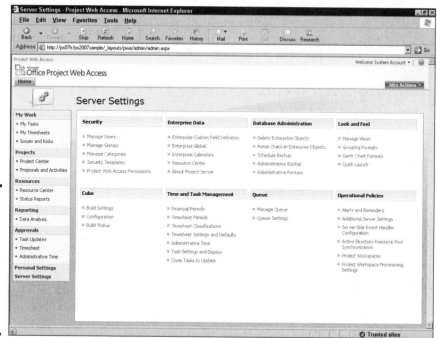

Figure 2-1:
Use this
page to
manage
most of the
Project
Server
database
settings.

Project Server uses Windows SharePoint Services technology as its foundation, and the Project Server administrator can manage Windows SharePoint Services settings by clicking the Site Actions tab in the upper-right corner of the Project Web Access window and choosing Site Settings to display the Site Settings. For example, you can set your time zone, select a calendar type, define your workweek, and select a time format.

To manage security settings, Project Server uses security templates, groups, and categories.

Security templates are sets of permissions; you use security templates to assign a set of permissions to a user or a group of users. Groups are collections of users, such as administrators, project managers, and team members. And, using categories, you can map users and groups to the projects, resources, views, and custom fields the users and groups can see in Project Web Access.

The Project Server database contains default security templates, groups, and categories; you can modify any of these security elements or create your own. To add or modify security templates, click Security Templates in the Security section of the Server Settings page. To add or modify groups, click the Manage Groups link in the Security section of the Server Settings page.

You can create a new category or modify any of the existing categories by clicking the Manage Categories link in the Security section of the Server Settings page.

Working with Users

People in your organization can't open the Project Server database until you add them to it as users. From the Server Settings page, click the Manage Users link in the Security section of the Server Settings page to display the Manage Users page (see Figure 2-2). From this page, the Project Server administrator can add, modify, or deactivate user accounts. In addition, the administrator can merge two usernames into one account if a user appears twice in the Log On list under two different names.

To add a user, click New User at the top of the list of users. To edit a user, click the user's name. When you add or edit a user, you see a page on which you specify the user's name and other identification information, the type of authentication to use (Windows Authentication or Forms authentication), the user's assignment attributes, resource custom fields, security groups, security categories, global permissions, group fields, team details, and system identification data. In Figure 2-3, you see the top of the Edit User page.

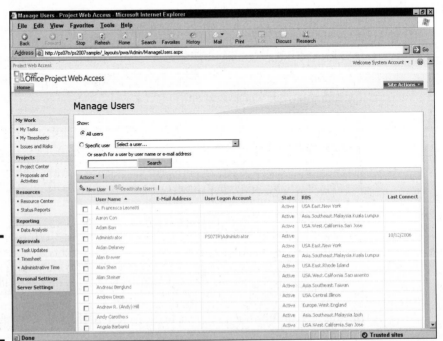

Figure 2-2:
Use this page to add a new user or select a user to edit.

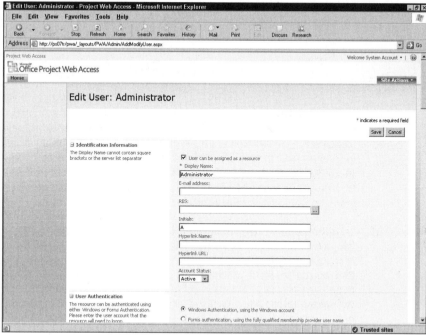

Figure 2-3:
At the top of the page, supply basic user identification information.

Working with Views

Views enable users to examine project information in different ways, because a view contains a set of fields and filters that Project Web Access uses when displaying project information. Through views, the administrator controls what you see in Project Web Access.

As you'd expect, the Project Server database contains many default views, and the Project Server administrator can use the Manage Views page to create new views and modify or delete existing views. To display this page from the Server Settings page, click the Manage Views link in the Look and Feel section of the Server Settings page.

You can specify the type of view, the view name, the tables and fields that you want to appear in the view, view format options, including outline levels, grouping and sorting options, filter options, and security categories. The type of view that you select determines the choices that appear as you create the view. For example, for some views, you can choose a Gantt Chart format that isn't available for other views.

We suggest that you load a project into the Project Server database before you create a view or if you want to modify an existing view. With a project in the database, you can view that project using each default view that

Microsoft provides, and you might find that the view that you want or one close to it already exists.

Working with the Enterprise Global Template

The Enterprise Global template and the Global template in Project Professional serve the same purpose. They store all the default settings used by projects across your organization. The Project Server administrator customizes the Enterprise Global template to set up the custom fields and calendars that meet the needs of your organization. When you customize the Enterprise Global template, it opens in Project Professional (note the title bar in Figure 2-4), where you can customize fields, groups, and filters, just to name a few elements.

To open the Enterprise Global template from the Server Settings page in Project Web Access, click the Enterprise Global link in the Enterprise Data section to display the Configure Project Professional page. Click the Configure Project Professional button.

When you finish, choose File⇨Close. You'll be prompted to check in the Enterprise Global template. Click Yes to save your settings and make the Enterprise Global template available in Project Web Access.

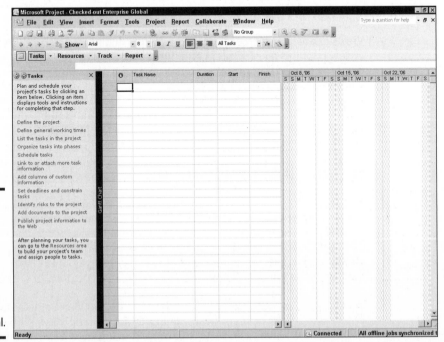

Figure 2-4:
You customize the Enterprise Global template using Project Professional.

Creating Enterprise Custom Fields

You can use Enterprise custom fields for many purposes. For example, if your organization opts to use generic resources and wants to be able to match the skills of a generic resource with a real resource that possesses those skills, you can create a custom field and establish a value list for the field where each value represents a set of skills. After you assign the appropriate value to each resource by using the custom field, you can use the custom field to match skills that are required by generic resources with skills that are possessed by real people when project managers run the Team Builder.

You set up enterprise custom fields essentially the same way that you set up Project custom fields, but you use Project Web Access. On the Server Settings page, click the Enterprise Custom Field Definition link in the Enterprise Data section of the Server Settings page. The Custom Fields page (shown in Figure 2-5) lists all custom fields that currently exist in the Enterprise Global template. Below the list of custom fields, you also see a list of defined lookup tables; you can identify the lookup table assigned to a given custom field in the Lookup Table field at the right edge of the Enterprise Custom Fields table.

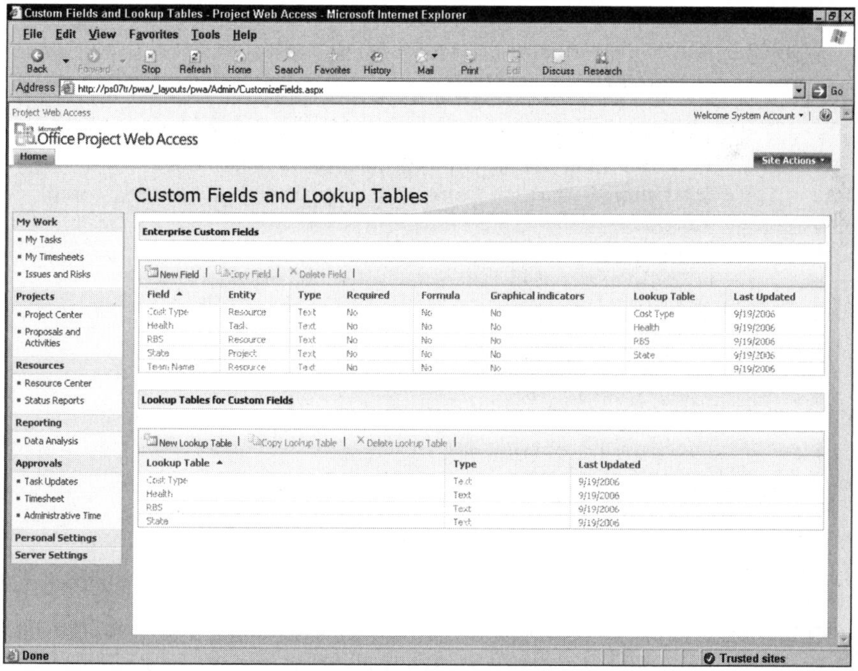

**Book X
Chapter 2**

The Project Server Administrator

Figure 2-5:
The list of existing custom fields.

You can edit an existing field by clicking its name. To create a new custom field based on the definition of an existing custom field, click anywhere on the row of the existing custom field and then click the Copy Field button that appears above the list of fields. Or, you can click the New Field button to create a new custom field.

Establishing Enterprise Calendars

When you assign a calendar to the Enterprise Global template, you establish common workdays and work times across all projects. Resources in the Enterprise Resource Pool can use the calendar in the Enterprise Global template unless you override that calendar by assigning a resource-specific calendar.

You set up the calendar for the Enterprise Global template the same way that you set up a calendar for a project, but you start in Project Web Access. On the Server Settings page, click the Enterprise Calendars link in the Enterprise Data section. The Enterprise Calendars page appears, listing the calendars defined in the Enterprise Global template.

You can edit an existing calendar by clicking anywhere on the line where its name appears and then clicking the Edit Calendar button above the list of calendars. If you want to create a new calendar based on an existing calendar, click anywhere on the row of the existing custom field and then click the Copy Calendar button. Or, you can click the New Calendar button to create a new calendar. When you edit or create a calendar, Project Web Access opens the Change Working Time dialog box in Project Professional (see Figure 2-6).

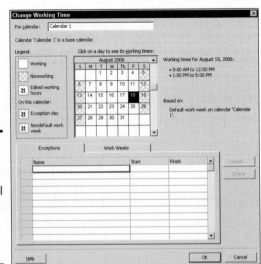

Figure 2-6:
You work in Project Professional to create or edit an enterprise calendar.

For details on making calendar changes, see Book II, Chapter 4.

Working with Enterprise Resources

The Enterprise Resource Pool is a single repository that project and resource managers can use when assigning resources to their projects. To assign a resource to a project, a project manager *checks out* the resource from the Enterprise Resource Pool (much like checking a book out of a library).

**Book X
Chapter 2**

You can easily create the Enterprise Resource Pool using a project that contains the resources that you want to store in the Enterprise Resource Pool. Make sure that the project containing the resources is closed or checked in, and then follow these steps to create the Enterprise Resource Pool:

The Project Server Administrator

1. **Open Project Professional and connect to the Project Server database by logging in.**

2. **Choose Tools⇨Enterprise Options⇨Import Resources to Enterprise.**

   The Open dialog box appears.

3. **Select the project that contains the resources and click Open.**

4. **If you've set up any custom fields for resources, click the Map Resource Fields link in the Project Guide pane.**

   The Map Custom Fields dialog box appears, and you can match custom fields that you've set up for resources to enterprise resource fields.

5. **Click Continue to Step 2 in the Project Guide.**

6. **Identify the resources that you want to upload to the Enterprise Resource Pool by choosing Yes in the Import column (see Figure 2-7).**

7. **Click Validate Resources in the Project Guide pane.**

   Project compares the selected resources to those in the Enterprise Resource Pool and displays any errors.

8. **Correct the errors and click Save and Finish in the Project Guide pane.**

   Project sends the resources to the Enterprise Resource Pool in the Project Server database. In the Project Guide pane, Project Professional gives you the opportunity to optionally set booking types — Proposed or Committed — for selected resources.

9. **Click Done.**

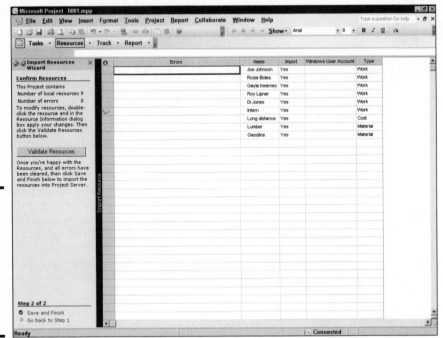

Figure 2-7:
Identify
resources
that you
want to
store in the
Enterprise
Resource
Pool.

After you have stored a resource in the Enterprise Resource Pool, you can make a change to that resource by checking it out, making the change, and then checking it back in. While resources are checked out, others can't make and save changes to the resources. Follow these steps to check out resources from the Enterprise Resource Pool:

1. **Open Project Professional and connect to the Project Server database.**

2. **Choose Tools⇨Enterprise Options⇨Open Enterprise Resource Pool.**

Project displays a temporary project called Checked-Out Enterprise Resources that lists the resource pool; notice the title bar in Figure 2-8.

3. **Place a check mark next to the resource(s) that you want to edit.**

4. **Click the Edit Details button above the list of resources.**

The Edit Resource window appears.

5. **Make changes to the resource.**

6. **Click Save and Continue.**

Project saves your changes to the Enterprise Resource Pool.

7. **Click the Save button on the Standard toolbar to check the resource back in to the Enterprise Resource Pool.**

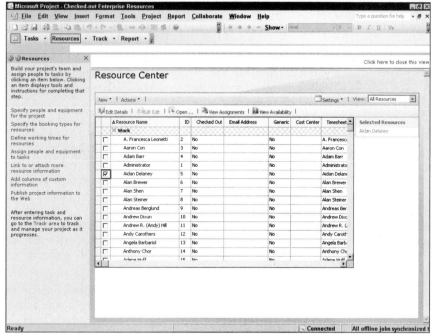

Figure 2-8:
The
Enterprise
Resource
Pool open
in Project
Professional.

Project closes the Edit Resource window and redisplays the Resource Center window in Project Professional.

8. **Choose File⇨Exit.**

Project Professional closes.

Loading Projects into the Project Server Database

You will, no doubt, have projects already created and in progress that you want to load into the Project Server database. You can use the Project Guide in Project Professional to walk you through loading these projects. While connected to the Project Server database, choose Tools⇨Enterprise Options⇨Import Project to Enterprise. Use the Open dialog box that appears to navigate to the .MPP file that you want to import into the Project Server database. Project opens the project and displays the Import Project Wizard, a five-step process, in the Project Guide pane. As a part of the process, you

✦ Map resources in the project to resources in the Enterprise Resource Pool

✦ Validate the resources in the project

✦ Match local task custom fields to Enterprise task custom fields

✦ Confirm the tasks that Project will import to Project Server

✦ Save the project to the Project Server database

When you close the project in Project Professional, you see a dialog box that asks you if you want to save changes to the project and if you want to check the project in to Project Server. Save the changes and check in the project so that others can use it.

Managing Timesheet and Task Settings

Project Server contains a variety of timesheet and task settings that you can manage through Project Web Access. For example, you can

✦ **Establish fiscal periods** that match your business's fiscal periods from the Fiscal Periods page. To display this page, click the Financial Periods link in the Time and Task Management section of the Server Settings page.

✦ **Create reporting periods** for timesheet entries from the Timesheet Periods page. When users want to record time spent on project tasks, they select a time period. You can create 52 weekly time periods, 26 biweekly periods, 12 monthly periods — create periods that match the way project managers want users to report time spent. To display the Timesheet Periods page, click the Timesheet Classifications link in the Time and Task Management section of the Server Settings page.

Ways to record actual work

Project offers three possible ways for users to record actual work in Project Server:

✔ **The Percent of Work Complete method** is the fastest way for resources to record time, but it's also the least accurate because it's based on the resource's estimate of the total amount of work to be done, along with the amount that's actually completed. Resources enter the percentage amount.

✔ **The Actual Work Done and Work Remaining method** is the "middle of the road"

method because it's both moderately fast and moderately accurate. Resources enter the amount of work done and the amount of work remaining to be completed in hours, days, weeks, and so on.

✔ **The Hours of Work Done per Time Period method** is the most accurate method but also the most time-consuming. Resources enter the actual hours worked on each task for a specified time period, such as a day.

+ **Set up classifications** that match account codes or cost codes that your company uses in its general ledger so that you can match lines that appear on timesheets with account codes or cost codes in your general ledger to help you track project costs. To display the Edit or Create Line Classifications page, click the Timesheet Classifications link in the Time and Task Management section of the Server Settings page.

+ **Set a variety of default settings** related to timesheets, such as whether users enter data against projects or against assignments. To display the Settings and Defaults page, click the Timesheet Settings and Defaults link in the Time and Task Management section of the Server Settings page.

+ **Set a variety of options** that control the way tasks function and display in Project Web Access. For example, you can set the default tracking method for projects that are published to the Project Server database and permit project managers to select different tracking methods when creating their projects. To display the Task Settings and Display page, click the Task Settings and Display link in the Time and Task Management section of the Server Settings page.

The sidebar, "Ways to record actual work," describes each method and its pros and cons.

+ **Lock down tasks** so that resources cannot report time for those tasks. To display the Close Tasks to Update page, click the Close Tasks to Update link in the Time and Task Management section of the Server Settings page.

+ **Set up administrative time categories** that users can use to record administrative time on timesheets. These categories represent reasons why a resource might not be available for work, such as vacation, sickness, jury duty, or bereavement. To display the Edit or Create Administrative Time page, click the Administrative Time link in the Time and Task Management section of the Server Settings page.

Customizing Project Web Access

The administrator can customize Project Web Access. For example, from the Edit Quick Launch page (see Figure 2-9), you can control the appearance of the Quick Launch pane. To display this page, click the Quick Launch link in the Look and Feel section of the Server Settings page. Working in the Quick Launch pane default behavior, all choices appear in each section. You can change the behavior to display only the main headings. Then, if you click a main heading, the subordinate headings for that section appear. You also can reorganize or hide default menu items in the Quick Launch pane, and if you click the New Link button, you can add a new menu item to the Quick Launch pane.

TIP

You also can choose to hide or display menu items from Windows SharePoint Services in the Quick Launch pane. Simply select or deselect the check box that's aptly named Show Menu Items from Windows SharePoint Services.

The Project Server administrator can control the appearance of Gantt taskbars on the timescale of Gantt charts for some or all Gantt charts that team members and managers view in Project Web Access using the Gantt Chart Formats page. To display this page, click the Gantt Chart Formats link in the Look and Feel section of the Server Settings page.

Finally, using the Grouping Formats page, the Project Server administrator can format the appearance of grouped information on the timesheet and define the appearance of up to ten groups for views in the Projects Center and the Resource Center. To display this page, click the Grouping Formats link in the Look and Feel section of the Server Settings page.

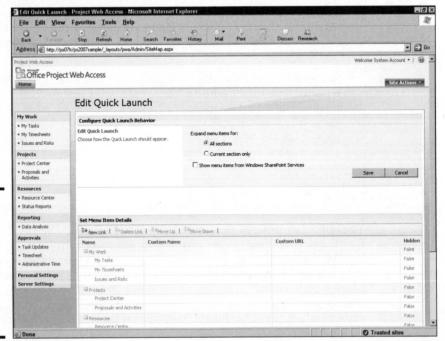

Figure 2-9:
Use this page to customize the appearance of the Quick Launch pane.

Checking in Enterprise Projects and Resources

When a project manager works on an enterprise object (like a project) stored in the Project Server database, Project Server checks out that enterprise object to the project manager. While the object is checked out, nobody else can make changes to it.

If somebody leaves work without closing a checked out object and you need to perform some maintenance on the Project Server database, you need to check in the object, and you can do that from the Force Check-in Enterprise Objects page (see Figure 2-10). To display this page, click the Force Check-in Enterprise Objects link in the Database Administration section of the Server Settings page.

From this page, you can check in Enterprise projects, resources, custom fields, calendars, lookup tables for Enterprise custom fields, and resource plans. Use the drop-down list at the top of the page to select the type of object you want to check in. Then check the object and click the Check-In link.

**Book X
Chapter 2**

**The Project Server
Administrator**

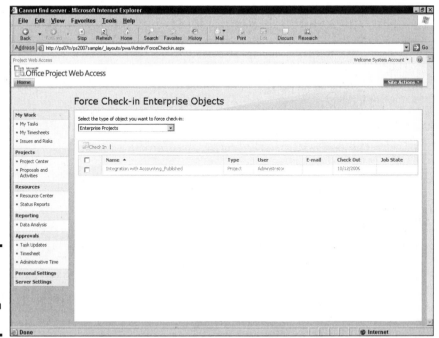

Figure 2-10:
Check in Enterprise objects from this page.

Managing Information in the Project Server Database

Response time from the Project Server database increases as the database grows in size. Therefore, periodically, the Project Server administrator should delete old information from the Project Server database using the Delete Enterprise Objects page (see Figure 2-11). To display this page, click the Delete Enterprise Objects link in the Database Administration section of the Server Settings page.

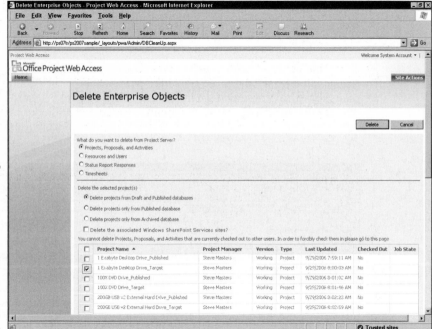

Figure 2-11:
Reduce the size of the database and speed the processing in the database by deleting old information.

Backing Up and Restoring

Backing up and restoring the Project Server database is one of the most important actions you can take to protect your data. The backups you create in Project Web Access are item-level backups designed to work with SQL Server database backups — not in place of SQL Server database backups.

From the Daily Backup Schedule page (see Figure 2-12), you can set up a schedule for backing up items in the Project Server database, and you can specify the number of versions of the backup you want to keep. Project Server stores the backups in the Archive database, and the more versions you keep, the larger the Archive database becomes.

To display this page, click the Schedule Backup link in the Database Administration section of the Server Settings page.

Alternatively, the Project Server administrator can back up items in the Project Server database outside of the daily schedule by using the Backup page. To display this page, click the Administrative Backup link in the Database Administration section of the Server Settings page. Select the items you want to back up and click the Backup button.

Use the Restore page to restore a backup. To display this page, click the Administrative Restore link in the Database Administration section of the Server Settings page. From the Item drop-down list, select the type of object you want to restore. If you want to selectively restore projects, click a project and then click the Restore button.

Figure 2-12:
Identify the items to back up and the number of backups to retain.

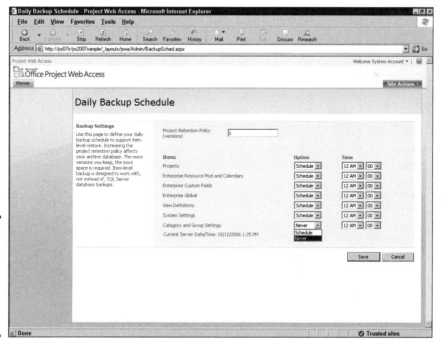

Managing the Queue

To improve performance, Project Server uses a service to queue work requests until the server becomes available to act on the request. You can control the behavior of the queue. Using the Queue Settings page, you can establish or change settings for the Project queue or the Timesheet queue. To display this page, click the Queue Settings link in the Queue section of the Server Settings page.

Using the Manage Queue Jobs page (see Figure 2-13), you can view the current status of queued jobs and, if you want, retry or cancel jobs. To display this page, click the Manage Queue link in the Queue section of the Server Settings page.

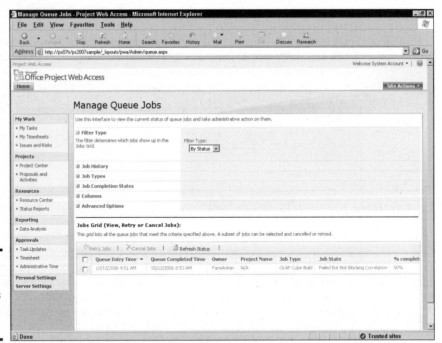

Figure 2-13:
Manage queued jobs from this page.

Chapter 3: Project Server and the Project Manager

In This Chapter

✔ Logging onto Project Server

✔ Working with Web-based projects

✔ Setting up status reports

✔ Receiving updates

Although the project manager can use Project Web Access, typically, the project manager uses the Project Server database in conjunction with Project Professional. This chapter describes how the project manager logs into the Project Server database while using Project Professional and then how to create and work with projects that you load into the Project Server database.

You can't use Project Standard with Project Server. You must use Project Professional.

Logging onto Project Server

You can work with a project as though you weren't connected to the Project Server database, or you can connect to the Project Server database and work with the project. You make that choice when you start Project Professional. To be able to make that choice, however, you need a Project Server account to connect to the Project Server database. You can create a Project Server account by using Project Professional after your Project Server administrator gives you the URL for your Project Server database. To create a Project Server Account, follow these steps:

1. **Start Project Professional.**

2. **Choose Tools⇨Enterprise Options⇨Microsoft Project Server Accounts.**

   The Project Server Accounts dialog box appears (see Figure 3-1).

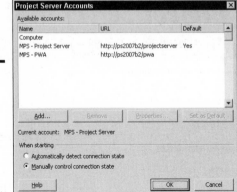

Figure 3-1:
Use this
dialog box
to log on to
an existing
Project
Server
account.

3. Click the Add button.

The Account Properties dialog box appears (see Figure 3-2).

Figure 3-2:
Use this
dialog box
to create a
new Project
Server
account.

4. In the Account Name text box, type a name for the account.

You must use a name that doesn't already appear on your computer. There are no other rules about this name, so your own name is a good choice, or, if your company uses multiple servers, you could assign the name of the server to help you identify the server to which you are connecting.

5. In the Project Server URL box, type the URL for the location of your Project Server database.

You can click the Test Connection button to ensure that you type the URL correctly.

6. In the When Connecting section, choose the type of connection that your organization uses; your Project Server administrator can tell you the type of connection:

- Use your Windows logon information by selecting the Use Windows User Account option button.

- Use your Project Server account, which uses Forms authentication, by selecting the Use a Project Server Account option button. In the User Name text box, type your name.

7. Click OK.

The Project Server Accounts dialog box reappears.

8. At the bottom of the box, choose whether you want to log on automatically or manually control the connection state.

- If you choose the Automatically Detect Connection State option button, Project attempts to detect the Project Server when you open Project in the future.

- If you choose the Manually Control Connection State option button, a Login dialog box appears when you open Project in the future, and you'll have the opportunity to choose the account that you want to use to log on to Project Server.

Book X
Chapter 3

Project Server and the Project Manager

REMEMBER

You also can choose to make this account the default account for logging on to Project Server.

Working with Web-based Projects

Building the project schedule for a project you intend to work on with Project Server database isn't all that different from setting up any project. You use Project to create the schedule and make assignments to team members to track their activities pretty much the same way we describe in the other minibooks, with two new tasks: You need to set the project's options to use Web communication, and you need to *publish* the project to the Project Server database. *Publish* is Project Server lingo for "upload and make the project visible to other Project Server users."

To set a project's options to use Web communication, log on to the Project Server database, open the project for which you want to set Web-based options, and choose Collaborate➪Collaboration Options. Project displays the Collaborate tab of the Options dialog box (see Figure 3-3).

To review a project's options for Web communication, use the Collaborate tab in the Options dialog box. Choose whether resources can delegate tasks in Project Web Access.

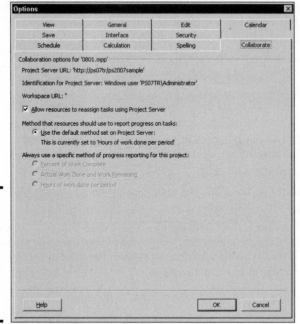

Figure 3-3:
Use this
dialog box
to set Web
communi-
cations
settings for
a project.

If your organization didn't select a tracking method for you, you can select a tracking method. If your organization has locked down the tracking method in Project Server, none of the options will be available. If the options are available, you can choose to use the default method set up in Project Server or you can select a method for the current project:

✦ **The Percent of Work Complete method** is the fastest way for resources to record time, but it is also the least accurate because it is based on the resource's estimate of the total amount of work to be done, along with the amount that is actually completed. Resources enter the percentage amount.

✦ **The Actual Work Done and Work Remaining method** is the "middle of the road" method because it is both moderately accurate and moderately fast. Resources enter the hours, days, weeks, and so on of the amount of work done and the amount of work remaining to be completed.

✦ **The Hours of Work Done per Time Period method** is the most accurate method but also the most time-consuming. Resources enter the actual hours worked on each task for a specified time period.

Before you can place a copy of a project into the Project Server database for public consumption, you need to save a draft version of it to the Project Server database. You can continue to work with the draft project in Project

Professional and modify it, and the project won't be visible to other users. To save a draft version, open Project Professional and log on to Project Server. Then open the project that you want to store in the Project Server database and choose File➪Save As. The Save to Project Server dialog box appears (see Figure 3-4); any custom fields stored in the Enterprise Global template appear at the bottom of the box. Click the Save button, and Project Professional uploads the project to Project Server.

Figure 3-4:
Use the Save to Project Server dialog box to save a draft project to the Project Server database.

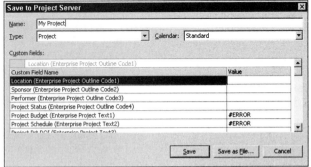

When you want the world see your project, you publish it. Choose File➪ Publish; the Publish Project dialog box appears (see Figure 3-5). If your organization uses the Windows SharePoint Services features that help manage documents, issues, and risks associated with projects, you might want to select the Create a Workspace for This Project option button. Project fills in all the information for you, and there really isn't any reason to change any of it. Click Publish, and you can watch the status bar to monitor progress while Project updates Project Server.

If you choose not to create the project workspace, the Project Server administrator can create it later.

Figure 3-5:
This dialog box appears when you choose to publish a project.

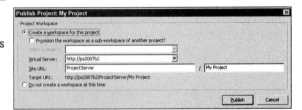

Lightweight projects

No, these aren't inconsequential projects. Instead, they might be ideas for future projects or lists of things you don't want to slip through the cracks. But, you know that you don't need the full capabilities of Project Professional yet. You can use Project Web Access Proposals or Activity Plans to manage these simple lists. To create a proposal or activity plan, click the Proposals and Activities link in the Quick Launch pane of Project Web Access.

There isn't a lot of difference between a proposal and an activity plan, unless your organization uses Microsoft Office SharePoint Server (MOSS). In this case, MOSS enables you to set up workflow values such as "Proposed," "Accepted," and "In Progress" that MOSS assigns automatically to a Project Server

proposal. In this way, you can monitor the state of a proposal's workflow; otherwise, proposals and activity plans are the same.

If your organization doesn't use MOSS, you can still use workflow states for proposals; you simply need to manually assign them.

For both proposals and activity plans, you can set up tasks, identify them as milestones if appropriate, and link the tasks to each other. You also can attach a document to a proposal or activity plan and even assign resources using the Team Builder in Project Web Access.

When the time comes, you can convert both activity plans and proposals into projects and then use Project Professional and Project Web Access to manage them.

At this point, two versions of your project reside in the Project Server database — the draft version and the published version. You can continue to work with your project in Project Professional; typically, you'll work with the draft version and ultimately republish it to update the version that everyone else sees.

Opening and closing a project

You can open the original project schedule stored on your hard drive, or you can open either the draft version or the published version stored in the Project Server database. Click the Open button on the Standard toolbar. You see the Open dialog box (see Figure 3-6).

 The first time you display the Open dialog box, no projects appear in it. Instead, you see only one item — the Retrieve the List of All Projects from Project Server item — because you haven't opened a project stored in the Project Server database yet. The situation we're about to describe sounds very much like trying to answer the question "Which came first — the chicken or the egg?" (and makes our heads hurt).

Figure 3-6:
You can open an original .mpp file or open the draft or published project stored in the Project Server database.

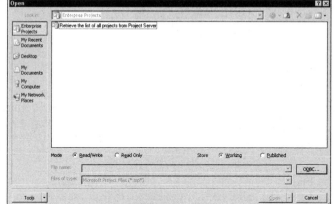

When you're connected to the Project Server database and you open a project in Project Professional, Project Professional stores a copy of the project in the local cache; the local cache is new to Project 2007 and serves the purpose of improving performance when exchanging information between Project Professional and the Project Server database. The Open dialog box lists projects stored in the local cache. So, you won't see any projects listed in the Open dialog box until you've opened a project. And, the next time you display the Open dialog box, that project will appear in the list, along with the Retrieve the List of All Projects from Project Server item. See what we mean about the chicken or the egg?

So, to open the original Project .mpp file, use the buttons on the left side of the dialog box to navigate to the location where you stored the .mpp file on your hard drive, click the file, and then click Open.

To view all the draft or published projects in the Project Server database, double-click the Retrieve the List of All Projects from Project Server entry in the list. The Store options and Mode options at the bottom of the Open dialog box affect both the projects that appear in the Open dialog box and the way in which you can work with those projects, and these options work together.

The Store options determine whether you open a draft version or a published version of a project. When you select the Working option, draft projects appear in the Open dialog box. When you select the Published option, published projects appear in the Open dialog box. By default, Project displays draft projects in the Open dialog box.

If you don't see any difference between the two lists, all draft projects have been published.

The Mode options, in combination with the Store options, determine whether you can save changes to a project you open. When you select Working as the Store option, you can choose either Read/Write or Read Only as the Mode option. But, when you select Published as the Store option, you can select only the Read Only option for the mode. That means that you can save changes only to a project stored in the draft database, which is the default database from which to open projects. To save changes to a published project, make the changes to the draft project, save it, and then publish it.

So, why bother opening a published version if you want to change it? Well, you can use a published version to create a draft version with which to work. Open the published version, which will be a read-only copy, and then save a draft version using the same filename as the published version.

You can use the same technique to create a local .mpp version of a draft or published project. Open a draft or published project from the Project Server database and, then choose File⇨Save As. In the Save to Project Server dialog box, click the Save as File button.

When you open a Web-based project, you check it out (Project Server term). While a project is checked out, nobody else can open it in Project Professional and work on it. So, when you close the project, Project Professional prompts you to check the project in, and you should check it in.

Managing the local cache

The local cache is new to Project 2007 and streamlines the process of updating the Project Server database with changes from Project Professional. You can manage the local cache from Project Professional. Choose Tools⇨Local Project Cache⇨Cache Settings to display the Cache Settings dialog box (see Figure 3-7).

Figure 3-7:
Use this dialog box to establish the size and location of the local cache.

Cache Settings	☒
Cache size limit: 511 ÷ in (MB)	
Cache location: C:\Documents and Settings\FarmAdmin\Application Data\Microsoft\MS Project\Cache\	Browse
Help	OK Cancel

Choose Tools⇨Local Project Cache⇨View Status to view the status of updates you sent to the Project Server database from the Status tab of the Active Cache Status dialog box (see Figure 3-8). If errors occur, they'll appear on the Errors tab.

Figure 3-8:
Monitor the status of updates you send from Project Professional to the Project Server database from this dialog box.

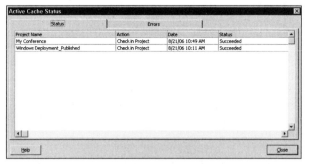

Book X
Chapter 3

Project Server and the Project Manager

If you clean up the local cache, you can free up cache space and improve performance between Project Professional and the Project Server database. Choose Tools⇨Local Project Cache⇨Clean Up Cache to display the Clean Up Cache dialog box (see Figure 3-9).

Figure 3-9:
Use this dialog box to remove projects from the local cache.

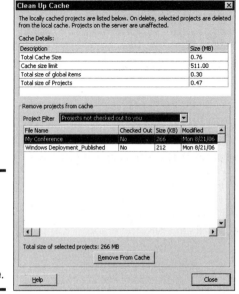

By default, Project displays projects in the local cache that aren't checked out to you; you can open the Project Filter list box and change the view to projects that are checked out to you.

To remove a project from the cache, click it in the bottom portion of the window and click Remove From Cache. When you finish, click the Close button.

Adding Enterprise resources to a project

When you're ready to add resources to a Web-based project, you can use the Build Team dialog box to view the resources in the Enterprise Resource Pool and assign them to your project. In Project Professional, choose Tools➪ Build Team from Enterprise. Project displays the Build Team dialog box (see Figure 3-10).

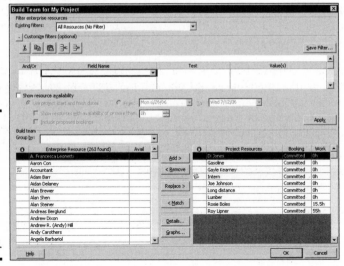

Figure 3-10: Select resources from the Enterprise Resource Pool to assign to your project.

By default, you see all resources you have permission to view, but you can apply filters to limit the resources that you see. Use the Existing filters drop-down list and click the plus sign (+) that appears next to Customize Filters to choose fields by which to filter. Figure 3-10 shows the additional space for selecting filters. You also can filter by available hours to work for a given time period.

After you select resources and click OK, the resources appear on the Resource Sheet of your project, and you can assign tasks to them. When you republish your project, the Enterprise Resource Pool is updated to reflect the assignments. At a minimum, the team members receive announcements of new or updated assignments on the home page in Project Web Access. If your organization chooses, team members may also receive e-mail notifications of assignments.

Replacing generic resources with real resources

Think of generic resources as job descriptions rather than people. When you use a generic resource, you're really using a set of skills, and it's possible that, in your organization, you have several people with the required skills. So, you can take advantage of the Team Builder feature, which helps you match the skills defined for a generic resource in your project to a real resource that has the same skill set of the generic resource.

To use the Team Builder feature, your organization must create a custom field with a value list where each value in the list represents a set of skills. Then the outline code must be assigned to each resource in the Enterprise Resource Pool, with the appropriate value from the value list selected, so that each resource's skill set is described. Project can then match generic resources with specified skills to real resources in the Enterprise Resource Pool with the same skills.

Book X
Chapter 3

Project Server and the Project Manager

To replace generic resources with real resources, use the Team Builder to filter the Enterprise Resource Pool so that it displays only those resources that match the generic resource. Follow these steps:

1. **In Project, open the published version of the project containing generic resources that you want to replace.**

2. **Choose Tools⇨Build Team from Enterprise.**

   Project displays the Build Team dialog box.

3. **In the list on the right side of the dialog box, click the generic resource for which you want to search for a replacement.**

4. **Click the Match button.**

   On the left side of the dialog box, Project displays those resources that match the selected generic resource.

5. **Click the resource that you want to use in your project from the list on the left.**

6. **Click the Replace button.**

   Project replaces the resource in the Team Resource list with the Enterprise resource that you selected.

7. **Click OK.**

   Project also updates the project by replacing the generic resource with the one that you selected.

Using the Resource Substitution Wizard

When you have available more than one resource that can do a particular job, you want to try to set up work assignments so that you minimize over-allocations. In a smaller environment, you probably know off the top of your head that both John and Mary are qualified to do the job. So, you simply review John's schedule and Mary's schedule to determine who has the most time available for the assignment.

But, in a larger environment, with many resources and many projects, it's harder to determine who has the skills and the availability. But the Resource Substitution Wizard can help you smooth assignments.

The Resource Substitution Wizard can use different criteria to substitute resources. For example, the wizard can simply consider the resources in the projects that you select and reallocate them to better utilize their time. Or, the wizard can use the custom field that represents skill sets to match skills required by resources that are already assigned to tasks and then substitute other resources with the same skill set.

To run the Resource Substitution Wizard, open the project(s) for which you want to substitute resources and choose Tools⇨Substitute Resources. The Resource Substitution Wizard begins.

As you walk through the wizard, you select the project(s) that you want the wizard to consider — the wizard displays all open projects, and you select the ones you want to use. You also select the resources for the wizard to consider, and you specify options for the wizard to use, such as substituting resources from the Enterprise Resource Pool or simply shuffling resources already on the project.

After you run the wizard, a grid of proposed assignments that the wizard has changed appears (see Figure 3-11). You can review the results, and if you want, back up and change the wizard's options to try again.

You can let Project update the projects with the wizard's proposed changes.

Assigning resources using Project Web Access

As a resource manager, you might not have Project Professional, but you can manage resources, including building a team for your project, using Project Web Access. Log on to Project Web Access. In the Quick Launch pane on the left side of the page, click Project Center. Then click the link of the project for which you want to build a team. Project Web Access displays the Project Details page for the project in the Project Center, which closely resembles Gantt Chart view in Project Professional.

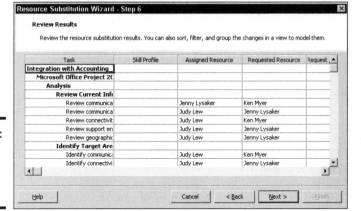

Figure 3-11:
The wizard
displays
proposed
changes.

To begin building a team for a project, click the Build Team button above the list of tasks. On the left side of the Build Team page, Project Web Access displays the list of resources that you have permission to view (see Figure 3-12). On the right side of the page, you see resources that already work on your project.

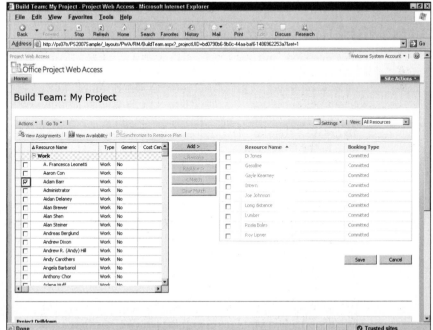

Figure 3-12:
Use Project
Web
Access to
build a team
for a
project.

In the list on the left, select the resources that you want to add to the project and click the Add button. You can create a filter to find resources with specified skills by clicking the Settings button at the top of the page and choosing Filter to display the area where you can use enterprise outline codes to define and apply a filter.

You also can replace generic resources. Select the generic resource on the right, and then click the Match button. On the left side of the page, Project Web Access displays real resources with the same skills as the selected generic resource. To replace the generic resource, select it on the right side of the window and select the real resource that you want to use on the left side of the window. Then click the Replace button.

You can view an availability graph of a resource before you add it to your project. Place a check mark beside the resource in the list on the left and then click the View Availability button. Project opens a separate page to display the Resource Availability graph. You also can view the resource's assignments by placing a check mark beside the resource in the list on the left and then clicking the View Assignments button. Project Web Access again opens a separate page that shows all the selected resources' assignments.

To assign a resource, click the Save button on the Build Team page.

Creating Status Report Layouts

As a manager, you can use Project Web Access to create the layout for the status report that you want to view from your team members. You can specify how often you want status reports, when reporting should begin, which resources should report, and the sections you want included in the report.

To create a standard layout for a status report, log on to Project Web Access and, in the Quick Launch pane, click the Status Reports link to display the Status Reports page, which lists existing status report layouts and status reports you need to submit.

Click the New button and then click New Request. The Status Report Request page appears. On the top of the page, you assign a name to the status report, establish a frequency and a start date, and identify the resources you want to submit the report (see Figure 3-13).

At the bottom of the page, select the sections that should appear in the report. You can create a new section by clicking the Insert Section button. Project Web Access adds blank lines in which you type the section names. Click Send when you finish, and Project Web Access creates the status report and sends a skeleton of the status report to the selected team members, requesting a status report. The team members can then use the skeleton to fill in the information that you want to see.

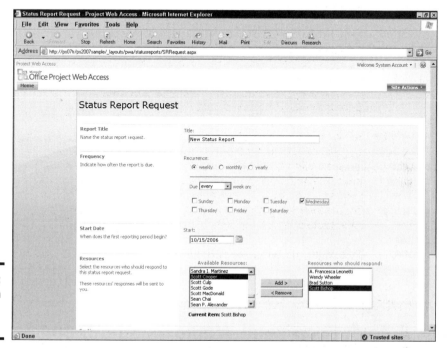

Figure 3-13:
Setting up a
status
report.

Receiving Task Updates from Team Members

If you approve the time reported by resources and you don't use Project Professional, you'll see the number of task updates from resources that await your approval when you log on to Project Web Access; the information appears on the Project Web Access home page in the Approvals section.

To view the task updates, you can click the link in the Approvals section or you can click Task Updates in the Approvals section of the Quick Launch pane. The Task Updates page appears (see Figure 3-14).

Accept or reject any update by clicking in the leftmost column to select an update. Then click the Accept button or the Reject button above the list of updates. If, after reviewing updates, you want to accept all updates you received, you can click the Select All button and then click the Accept button.

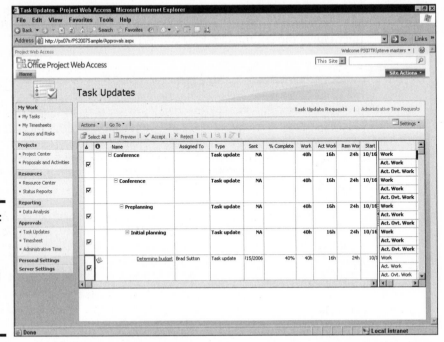

Figure 3-14:
From this
page, you
can view
and accept
or reject
the task
updates.

Project Server and Windows SharePoint Services

Windows SharePoint Services provides a way for users to share information and collaborate. As the foundation for Project Server, your organization might decide to take advantage of Windows SharePoint Services to manage issues, risks, and deliverables through Windows SharePoint Services. In this case, the project manager or the Project Server administrator can create the Windows SharePoint Services workspace for the project, where collaboration takes place. Project workspaces appear at the bottom of your home page.

Issues are unexpected things that occur on projects. They might be problems, or they might be opportunities. When they arise, you can create an issue, let others on the team review the issue, assign the issue to someone to address, and monitor the progress of the issue.

Risks are possible events or conditions that could negatively impact a project. Essentially, a risk is an issue before it happens.

Deliverables are, typically, work products that you deliver as a function of completing a task or a project. Deliverables can be documents such as financial reports or the birthday cake for the CEO's retirement party. Because the deliverables of one project can affect another project, deliverables need to be tracked and possibly even linked to tasks. After you have published a project and created a workspace for it, you can set up its associated deliverables in Project Professional and manage their dependencies.

You can set up rules to automatically accept changes from selected users for selected projects. Click Task Update in the Quick Launch pane. Then click the Actions button and choose Manage Rules.

Project managers can view updates and approve them in Project Web Access or in Project Professional. When you open Project Professional, you see a message indicating that updates are awaiting approval and asking whether you want to review the updates. If you choose Yes, Project opens the project and displays the updates in Project Professional using the same Task Updates window that appears in Project Web Access. Using the information that appears in the Project Guide pane on the left side of the screen, you can preview the updates, accept or reject the updates, and apply the updates to the plan.

Just like the Task Updates window that appears in both Project Web Access and Project Professional, you can view the Project Web Access Project Center and the Resource Center without leaving Project Professional. Open the Collaborate menu and choose either Project Center or Resource Center.

Book X
Chapter 3

Project Server and the Project Manager

Chapter 4: Project Server and the Team Member

In This Chapter

✔ Working with the Project Web Access home page

✔ Working with your tasks

✔ Working with your timesheet

✔ Integrating Outlook and Project Web Access

✔ Reporting status

*T*he way in which you use Project Server and Project Web Access depends on your role in the project. Chapters 2 and 3 of this minibook describe how the Project Server administrator and the project and resource manager use Project Server and Project Web Access, respectively. This chapter describes how the team member uses Project Web Access to work with project tasks, submitting work information on either tasks or timesheets and report status. You also read about how you can integrate Outlook 2007 and Project Web Access to exchange project information between these programs.

Understanding the Project Web Access Home Page

To log on to Project Server by using Project Web Access, you need the URL for the Web database, and your project manager or the Project Server administrator can give you the URL. In addition, if your organization uses Forms authentication, you need the username and password that the Project Server administrator set up for you.

If your organization uses Forms authentication, you see a page you use to log on to Project Web Access after you type the URL. If your organization set up Project Server to use Windows user account logons, the logon page doesn't appear; instead, your Project Web Access home page appears immediately.

To log on to Project Server, open Internet Explorer and, in the Address box, type the URL of the Web database.

TIP

Save the URL in your Favorites list, or if you use Project Web Access more than any other Web page, set it up as your home page so that Project Web Access appears when you open Internet Explorer.

The Project Web Access home page serves the same introductory function as most home pages on the Web (see Figure 4-1). In the Reminders section, you see summary information such as the number of new tasks that have been assigned to you and the number of unsubmitted timesheets and over-due status you have.

Use the Quick Launch pane that appears on the left side of the screen to navigate to other areas of Project Web Access and to Windows SharePoint Services support tools for Project Server if your organization uses these tools.

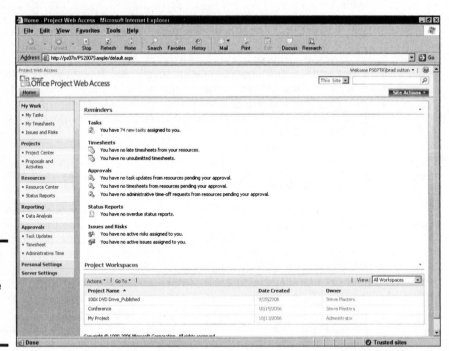

Figure 4-1:
A typical home page in Project Web Access.

Customizing the Home Page

You can customize the appearance of your Project Web Access Home page either temporarily or permanently by using the Web Part menu that appears on the Home page beside each part. Each Web Part menu is a small downward-pointing carat at the right edge of a section on the Home page; in Figure 4-2, the mouse pointer is pointing at a Web Part menu.

To temporarily close a section of the Home page, click the section's Web Part menu and choose Minimize. To redisplay the information, click the Web Part menu and choose Restore.

If you want to remove a section from the Home page on a more permanent basis, click the Web Part menu and choose Close.

You can edit or add sections to the Home page. To edit a particular section, click the section's Web Part menu and choose Modify My Web Part. Project Web Access displays the Home page in Edit Mode with the details of the section you want to change appearing in the pane on the right side of the screen (see Figure 4-3).

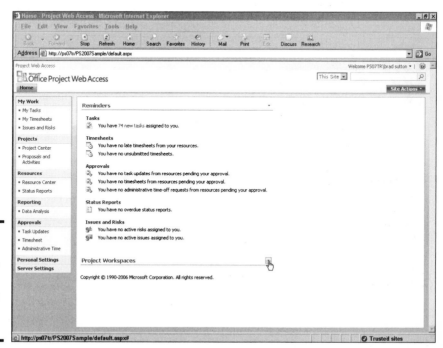

Figure 4-2:
You can temporarily hide sections on the Home page.

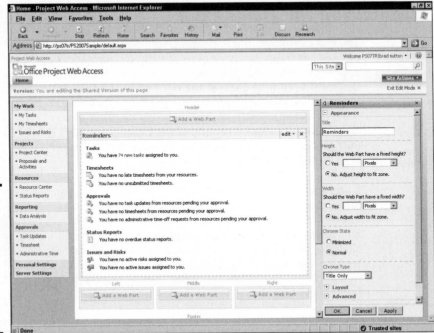

Figure 4-3:
The Home
page in Edit
Mode with
details
available
for the
Reminders
section.

If you want to reorganize Home page elements, drag the title of a section to a new location.

Make changes in the right pane and click OK at the bottom of the pane; Project Web Access exits Edit Mode and redisplays your home page, incorporating the changes.

If you change your mind and don't want to make any changes, click the Exit Edit Mode command just above the right pane.

To add a Web part, click the Add a Web Part button in the area where you want to add the Web part. For example, you can add a Web part above Reminders or below Reminders; if you add a part below Reminders, you can add it on the left, in the middle, or on the right side of the page. When you click Add a Web Part, Project Web Access displays a dialog box showing you the parts you can add (see Figure 4-4).

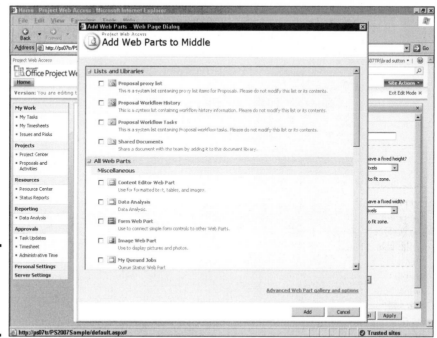

Figure 4-4:
Select a
Web part to
add to the
Home page.

Working with Your Tasks

You can record work you've performed using either the My Tasks page or
the My Timesheets page; the difference between the methods is simply a
matter of focus. Using the My Tasks page (see Figure 4-5), which you display
by clicking My Tasks in the Quick Launch pane, you select tasks to record
work performed. Using the My Timesheets page, described later in this chapter in the section "Working with Your Timesheet," you select a timesheet and
then record work on tasks for the selected time period.

If you use the My Tasks page to record work, you can import the work values
to your timesheet by clicking the Import Tasks button on the My Timesheets
page.

You probably work on more than one project at a time, and you'll see each of
your projects, indented, and each task assigned to you on the project. Beside
each project, you'll see either a plus or a minus sign; you can click the symbol
to toggle between hiding and displaying the tasks for a particular project.

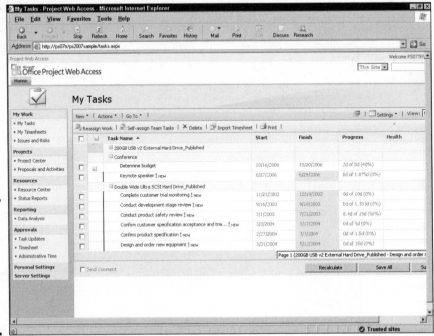

Figure 4-5:
The Task
Center lists
your task
assign-
ments, both
new and
existing.

Recording time

If you click a task name, Project Web Access displays the Assignment Details page (see Figure 4-6). From this page, you can see the details of the task, including the planned work, and, if you scroll down the screen, any transaction comments and task history, attachments, contacts, related assignments, and notes.

Use the Attachments section to attach a document, an issue, or a risk to a task.

Above the grid that displays planned, work, and overtime hours, a set of dates with arrows pointing in either direction appears. Click the arrows to display the timeframe that you want to update. Then click in the cell that represents the intersection of the date that you worked and the type of hours you want to record — typically work hours — and type the hours you want to record. Click the Recalculate button to refresh the page. When you click Save, Project Web Access saves your updates and redisplays the My Tasks page.

If you use the My Timesheets page to record work, you can import the work values from your timesheet to tasks by clicking the Import Timesheet button on the My Tasks page.

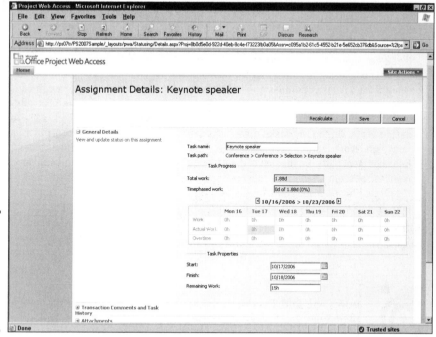

**Book X
Chapter 4**

**Project Server and
the Team Member**

Figure 4-6:
Record time
you spent
on the
Assignment
Details
page.

Saving a task update doesn't send it to the project manager. The My Tasks page provides a visual cue — an exclamation point beside the task title — when you've recorded work but haven't yet submitted the update. If you point the mouse at the exclamation point, a tip appears, indicating that you haven't yet submitted the update. To submit the update, click in the leftmost column beside the task to select it and then click the Submit Selected button. In the Submit Changes dialog box that appears, you can type a comment to the project manager. Click OK, and Project Web Access sends your updates.

You can send several task updates simultaneously without selecting them if you click the Save All button.

Adding a task

Suppose that you discover that what you're doing requires more work than the manager anticipated and probably calls for tasks that the manager didn't assign to you. If you have sufficient Project Web Access privileges, you can add a task from the My Tasks page. Click the New button and choose Task. Project Web Access displays the Add Task page, where you describe the new task (by identifying the project associated with the task), supply a task name and estimated start and end dates, and optionally add a comment about the task. If you want, you can assign the task to yourself. When you finish, click the Submit button and Project Web Access adds the task to your My Tasks page.

Reassigning work

If you can't possibly complete everything that you've been assigned and as long as your Project Web Access permissions permit, you can reassign some of your tasks and keep your project manager informed of the change in assignments. On the My Tasks page, click the Reassign Work button to display the Task Reassignment page. On the line of the task you want to reassign, in the last column, select a resource. Provide a start date for the new task and, if you want, any comments about the assignment. Then click the Submit button.

When Project Web Access redisplays the My Tasks page, the reassigned task still appears in your task list, but it appears with a line drawn through it. Select the task and click Submit Selected or simply click Save All to send the reassignment to your project manager. After the project manager approves the reassignment, the reassigned task appears on the My Tasks page of the affected recipient and remains on your My Tasks page, but you can delete the task if your permissions allow you to delete.

Select the Add Task to Timesheet check box to make the task appear on your timesheet.

To notify the project manager about the additional work, you need to select the task on the My Tasks page and click the Submit Selected button, or you can click the Save All button, which submits all updates you've recorded in the Task Center.

Working with Your Timesheet

You can record the time you work on tasks by using a timesheet. Timesheets for appropriate periods appear on the My Timesheets page, which you can see if you click the My Timesheets link in the Quick Launch pane (see Figure 4-7).

If you don't have any timesheets in progress, click the Click to Create link beside the appropriate timesheet period. Otherwise, click the In Progress link. Project Web Access displays the timesheet for the period you selected (see Figure 4-8).

If your organization set up administrative time for you, it appears on the timesheet, as do any tasks planned for the timesheet working period. Depending on your organization's defaults, you might be able to view planned time for the task. If you click the task name, you see the Assignment Details page shown earlier in Figure 4-6.

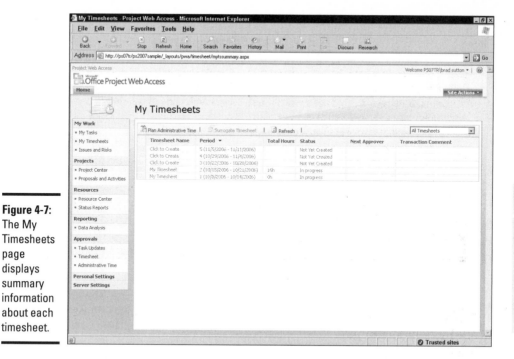

Figure 4-7:
The My
Timesheets
page
displays
summary
information
about each
timesheet.

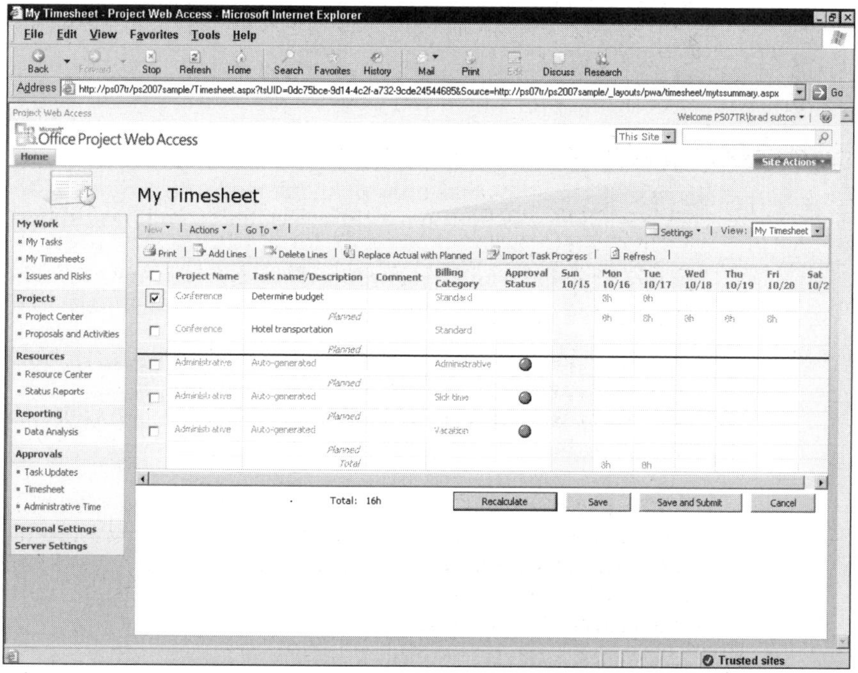

Figure 4-8:
A timesheet.

Administrative time

You can plan administrative time off from work if you're aware in advance that you need the time. For example, suppose that you were just selected for jury duty and you're scheduled to work on a project at the same time. From the My Timesheets page, click the Plan Administrative Time button to display the Administrative Time dialog box. From the Category list, select the type of administrative time, such as sick leave, vacation, or jury duty, and, from the Period list, select the appropriate period. Then, identify the days and hours of planned or committed time.

To report actual administrative time that you take, use the pre-established administrative time tasks that appear on your timesheet; you fill in these tasks the same way you report work you performed on a task.

You can enter time manually, or by replacing actual with planned time, or by importing task progress.

To record time manually, click in the box that represents the intersection of the date for which you want to record work and the task on which you want to record work. Then type the number of hours you want to record.

You can replace actual work values with planned work values for an entire row. Select the task by clicking in the leftmost column. Then click the Replace Actual with Planned button.

Finally, you can import work values you entered on the My Tasks page. Select the task for which you want to import work values and click the Import Task Progress button.

If you don't see the tasks on which you need to report on your timesheet, click the Add Lines button to add a new line to your timesheet.

You don't typically finish recording all information on a timesheet at one time. You can click the Save button on the Timesheet page to save your entries but keep the timesheet available for further updating; you'll want to take this approach as long as your working dates fall in the period covered by the timesheet. When the timesheet period no longer covers your working period, click the Save and Submit button to save your work and submit your timesheet for approval.

Integrating the Outlook Calendar with Project Web Access

If you use Outlook 2003 or later, you can get a better handle on all the things you need to do by viewing them all in one place if your Project Server administrator has enabled Outlook integration. With Outlook integration enabled, you can import assignments from Project Web Access to your Outlook calendar. You can choose to import assignments automatically at regular intervals, or you can import them when you choose. And, when you work on tasks, you can record the information in Outlook and then upload the information to Project Web Access.

You can exchange information between Project Web Access and either the Outlook Task List or the Outlook Calendar.

You'll notice some visual changes in Outlook if Outlook integration is set up. The Project Web Access toolbar appears in the main window, and on the Tools menu you see a menu for Project Web Access. In Figure 4-9, we've moved the Project Web Access toolbar so that you can see it; it typically appears anchored below the Standard toolbar.

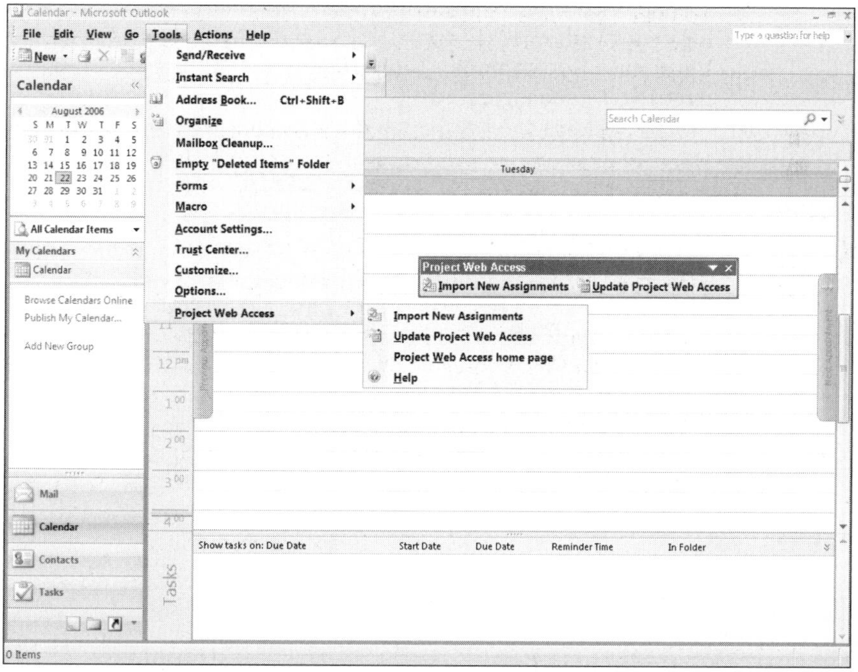

**Book X
Chapter 4**

**Project Server and
the Team Member**

Figure 4-9:
When Outlook is integrated with Project Web Access, you see the Project Web Access menu and toolbar in Outlook.

Enabling integration

To enable integration between Project Web Access and Outlook, open Project Web Access. Then, click the My Tasks link in the Quick Launch pane; once the My Tasks page appears, click the Actions button and click Set Up Outlook Sync. Project Web Access displays the Synchronize Your Tasks with Outlook page. Click the Download Now button. When the File Download dialog box appears, click Run. If an Internet Explorer security warning dialog box appears, click Run. When prompted to proceed with the installation, click Yes. Then click the Install button and, when the integration finishes, click OK.

You might need to edit your Project Web Access logon information in Outlook. In Outlook, choose Tools⇨Options. On the Project Web Access tab, click the Advanced Options button. In the Advanced Options dialog box that appears, click the Enter Login Information button to display the Enter Login Information dialog box, where you supply the URL for your Project Server database and select a connection method.

You have some choices about the way that updating occurs. By default, you control all the information exchange, manually importing all assignments from Project Web Access to the Outlook To-Do List and all updates from Outlook to Project Web Access. You can import assignments to the Outlook Calendar, choose to import for a specific time period, and set up the updating process to occur automatically by changing your Assignment Import settings. In Outlook, choose Tools⇨Options and then click the Project Web Access tab (see Figure 4-10).

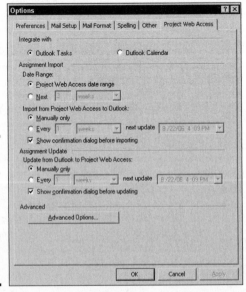

Figure 4-10:
You can set up the information exchange between Outlook and Project Web Access.

Sending Project Web Access assignments to Outlook

While you're working in Outlook, you can launch Project Web Access by choosing Tools⇨Project Web Access⇨Project Web Access Home Page.

When you have assignments in Project Web Access and you click the Import New Assignments button on the Project Web Access taskbar in Outlook, you see a dialog box similar to the one shown in Figure 4-11.

Figure 4-11:
This dialog box appears when you import assignment information from Project Web Access to Outlook.

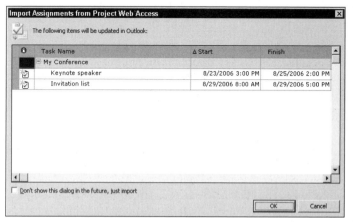

If you import the assignments to your calendar, they appear on your calendar on the start date of the assignment, but not associated with a particular time. If you import the assignments to the Outlook task list, they appear as dated list items, and Outlook imports both the start and due dates of the assignment.

Sending Outlook information to Project Web Access

You record work on a task that you imported to Outlook from Project Web Access by double-clicking the task in Outlook to open a dialog box similar to the one shown in Figure 4-12.

As you fill in time worked in the grid, Outlook saves the updates and updates the status of the task, but you need to click the Save to Project Web Access button to transfer your updates to Project Web Access. You can, simultaneously, submit the updates to the project manager if you leave the And Submit to Project Manager check box selected. If you deselect this check box, Outlook transfers the updates to your Project Web Access timesheet but doesn't send them to the project manager.

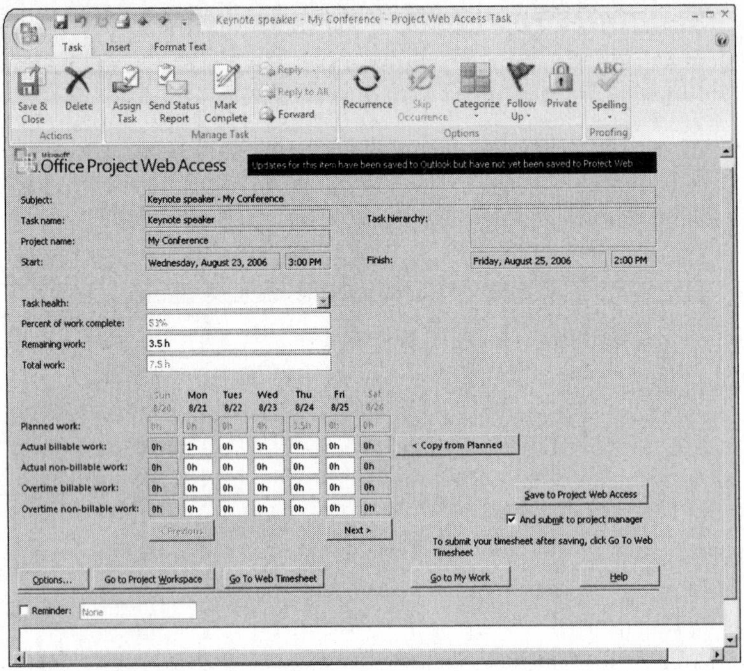

Figure 4-12:
A dialog box
like this one
appears
when you
open a task
imported
from Project
Web
Access.

Reporting Status

Your project manager sets up, in Project Web Access, a status report that describes the information your project manager wants and the frequency you should use to submit the information. These status reports encourage collaboration and help things continue to run smoothly on your project.

You can create an issue or a risk if you've run into something unexpected that you want to report; other team members, as well as your project manager, can see and comment on the issue or risk. You can attach the issue to a specific task or to the project in general.

Click the Status Reports link in the Quick Launch pane. The Status Reports page lists status reports requested by your project manager.

To open and fill out the report, click the status report link; the Status Report Response page looks like the page shown in Figure 4-13. If you need to include information that doesn't fit in any of the existing sections, you can add a section at the bottom of the report. When you're ready to submit the report, click the Send button at the bottom of the page.

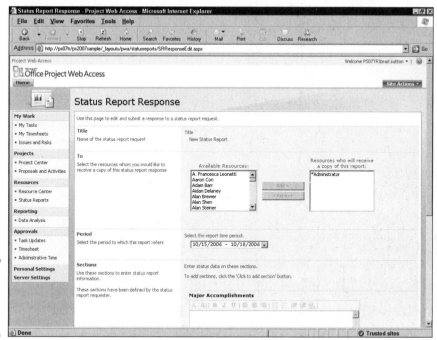

**Book X
Chapter 4**

**Project Server and
the Team Member**

Figure 4-13:
A typical
status
report page.

If you want to submit a status report that your project manager didn't set
up, click the Submit Unrequested Report button on the Status Reports page.
Then fill in the Unrequested Status Report page, which strongly resembles a
requested status report except that you select the report recipients and
define the report sections. You can use an unsolicited status report as a
simple way to communicate with other members of your team.

Glossary

Actual: The cost of the percentage of work that has been completed on a task.

Actual Cost of Work Performed: *See* ACWP.

ACWP (Actual Cost of Work Performed): Cost of the actual, real work done on a project to date, plus any fixed costs.

ALAP (As Late As Possible): A constraint put on a task's timing to make the task occur as late as possible in the project schedule, taking into account any dependency relationships. *See also* dependency.

ASAP (As Soon As Possible): A constraint put on a task's timing to make the task occur as early as possible in the project schedule, taking into account any dependency relationships. *See also* dependency.

BAC (Budget at Completion): The sum total of all costs involved in completing a task. *See also* baseline cost.

base calendar: The default calendar on which all new tasks are based, unless a resource-specific calendar is applied.

baseline: The detailed project plan against which actual work is tracked.

baseline cost: The total planned costs for a project's tasks, before any actual costs are incurred.

BCWP (Budgeted Cost of Work Performed): Also called *earned value,* this term refers to the value of work that has been completed. For example, a task with $1,000 of costs accrues a baseline value of $750 when it's 75 percent complete.

BCWS (Budgeted Cost of Work Scheduled): The percentage of the plan that's completed multiplied by the planned costs. This calculated value totals a task's completed work and its remaining planned costs.

booking type: A category for resources that specifies whether they are committed to the project or simply proposed to be involved.

budget at completion: *See* BAC.

budgeted cost of work performed: *See* BCWP.

budgeted cost of work scheduled: *See* BCWS.

calendar: The various settings for hours in a workday, days in a workweek, holidays, and nonworking days on which a project schedule is based. You can set Project, Task, and Resource calendars.

Change Highlighting: A feature that highlights the most recent change you make in your project and any other changes that action caused in your schedule.

circular dependency: A timing relationship among tasks that creates an endless loop that can't be resolved.

collapse: To close a project outline to hide subtasks from view.

combination view: A Project view with task details appearing at the bottom of the screen.

constraint: A parameter that forces a task to fit a specific timing. For example, a task can be constrained to start as late as possible in a project. Constraints interact with dependency links to determine a task's timing.

cost: The amount of money associated with a project task when you assign *resources,* which are equipment, materials, or people with associated fees or hourly rates.

Cost resource: A type of resource whose total cost doesn't depend on the amount of work on a task or the task's duration. Airfare or lodging are examples of Cost resources.

critical path: The series of tasks that must occur on time for the overall project to meet its finish date.

critical task: A task on the critical path. *See also* critical path.

crosstab: A report format that compares two intersecting sets of data. For example, you can generate a crosstab report showing the costs of critical tasks that are running late.

cumulative cost: The planned total cost to date for a resource's effort on a particular task. This calculation adds the costs already incurred on a task to any planned costs remaining for the uncompleted portion of the task.

cumulative work: The planned total work of a resource on a particular task. This calculation adds the work completed on a task to any planned work remaining for the uncompleted portion of the task.

current date line: The vertical line in a Gantt chart indicating today's date and time. *See also* Gantt chart.

CV (Cost Variance): The difference between the baseline costs and the combination of actual costs to date and estimated costs remaining *(scheduled costs)*. The cost variance is either positive (overbudget) or negative (underbudget).

deadline date: A date you assign to a task that doesn't constrain the task's timing. However, if a deadline date is assigned, Project displays an indicator symbol if the task runs past the deadline.

demote: To move a task to a lower level in the project outline hierarchy.

dependency: A timing relationship between two tasks in a project.

dependency link: Causes a task either to occur before or after another task, or to begin or end at some point during the life of the other task.

detail task: *See* subtask.

duration: The amount of calendar time it takes to complete a task.

duration variance: The difference between the planned (baseline) task duration and the current estimated task duration, based on activity to date and any remaining activity still to be performed.

EAC (Estimate at Completion): The total planned cost for resource effort on a specific task. This calculation combines the costs incurred to date with costs estimated for a task's remaining work.

earned value: A reference to the value of work completed. A task with $1,000 of associated costs has a baseline value of $750 when it's 75 percent complete. *See also* BCWP.

earned-value cost variance: *See* CV.

effort-driven: A type of task that requires an assigned amount of effort to be completed. When you add resources to an effort-driven task, the assigned effort is distributed among the task resources equally.

elapsed duration: An estimate of how long it will take to complete a task.

enterprise custom fields: Custom fields stored in a global file; these fields can be used to standardize Project plan content across an organization.

enterprise resources: A feature that allows you to save all resource information for resources used across an organization in one location.

estimated duration: A setting that indicates that you're using a best guess of a task's duration. When you enter an estimated duration for a task, a question mark appears next to the duration in the Duration column. You can also apply a filter to displays only tasks with estimated duration, which reflects the fact that they have questionable timing.

exception: A specified date or date range that isn't governed by the default working time calendar.

expand: To open a project outline to reveal both summary tasks and subtasks.

expected duration: An estimate of the actual duration of a task, based on work performance to date.

external task: A task in another project. You can set links between tasks in your project and external tasks.

finish date: The date on which a project or task is estimated to be completed.

finish-to-finish relationship: A dependency relationship in which the finish of one task determines the finish of another task.

finish-to-start relationship: A dependency relationship in which the finish of one task determines the start of another task.

fixed cost: A cost that doesn't increase or decrease based on the time a resource spends on a task. A consultant's fee or permit fee are examples of fixed costs.

fixed date: A task that must occur on a certain date. Fixed-date tasks don't move earlier or later in the schedule because of dependency relationships.

fixed duration: The length of time required to complete a task remains constant no matter how many resources are assigned to the task. A half-day seminar is an example of a fixed-duration task.

fixed-unit: A type of cost for which the resource units are constant; if you change the duration of the task, resource units don't change. This is the default task type.

fixed-work: A type of task for which the number of resource hours assigned to the task determine its length.

float: *See* slack.

Gantt chart: A standard Project view that displays columns of task information alongside a chart that shows task timing in bar chart format.

gap: *See* lag.

generic resources: A type of resource that allows you to make skill-based assignments based on a skill/code profile.

grouping: The organization of tasks by a customized field to summarize costs or other factors.

ID number: The number automatically assigned to a task by Project based on its vertical sequence in the project list.

indent: To move a task to a lower level of detail in the project's outline hierarchy.

lag: The amount of downtime that can occur between the end of one task and the beginning of another. Lag is built into a dependency relationship between tasks when you indicate that a certain amount of time must pass before the second task can begin.

leveling: A calculation used by Project that modifies resource work assignments for the purpose of resolving resource conflicts.

linking: (1) To establish a connection between tasks in separate schedules so that task changes in the first schedule are reflected in the second. (2) To establish dependencies among project tasks.

Material resources: The supplies or other items used to complete a task (one of three resource categories; the other categories are Cost and Work resources).

milestone: A task of zero duration, which marks a moment in time or an event in a schedule.

Network Diagram: An illustration that graphically represents workflow among a project's tasks; one of the Microsoft Project standard views.

node: In Network Diagram view, a box containing information about individual project tasks.

nonworking time: The time when a resource is not available to be assigned to work on any task in a project.

outdent: To move a task to a higher level in a project's outline hierarchy.

outline: The structure of summary and subtasks in a project.

overallocation: When a resource is assigned to spend more time on a single task or a combination of tasks occurring at the same than that resource's work calendar permits.

overtime: Any work scheduled beyond a resource's standard work hours. You can assign a different rate than a resource's regular rate to overtime work.

percent complete: The amount of work on a task that has already been accomplished, expressed as a percentage.

PERT chart: A standard project management tracking form indicating workflow among project tasks. This is a Network Diagram in Project. *See also* Network Diagram.

predecessor: In a dependency link, the task designated to occur before another task. *See also* dependency link *and* successor.

priorities: A ranking of importance assigned to tasks. When you use resource leveling to resolve project conflicts, priority is a factor in the leveling calculation. A higher-priority task is less likely than a lower-priority task to incur a delay during the leveling process. *See also* resource leveling.

progress lines: Gantt Chart View bars that overlap the baseline taskbar and allow you to compare the baseline plan with a task's tracked progress.

project: A series of tasks that achieves a specific goal. A project seeks to meet the triple requirements of timeliness, quality, and budget.

project calendar: The calendar on which all new tasks are based; the built-in project calendars are Standard, 24 Hour, or Night Shift, though you can create custom calendars.

Project Guide: A wizardlike help feature that takes Project users through various steps to build a Project schedule.

project management: The discipline that studies various methods, procedures, and concepts used to control the progress and outcome of projects.

Project Server: A server-based companion product of Microsoft Project.

Project Web Access: A component of Project Server that enables team members to enter information about their tasks into an overall project schedule without having Project installed on their own computers.

promote: To move a task to a higher level in a project's outline hierarchy.

recurring task: A task that occurs several times during the life of a project. Regular project team meetings or quarterly inspections are examples of recurring tasks.

resource: A cost associated with a task. A resource can be a person, a piece of equipment, materials, or a fee.

resource contouring: Changing the time when a resource begins work on a task. You can use contouring to vary the amount of work that a resource does on a task over the life of that task.

resource driven: A task whose timing is determined by the number of resources assigned to it.

resource leveling: A process used to modify resource assignments to resolve resource conflicts.

resource pool: (1) Resources that are assigned as a group to an individual task, such as a pool of administrative workers assigned to generate a report. (2) A group of resources created in a centralized location that multiple project managers can access and assign to their projects.

resource sharing: A feature that allows you to copy resources you created in another project to your current plan.

Resource Substitution Wizard: A wizard that replaces an unavailable resource with another of similar skill and cost.

roll up: The calculation by which all subtask values are *rolled up* — summarized — in a single summary task.

Shared Workspace: A feature of Windows SharePoint Services in which you can share documents online that were created with various Microsoft Office 12 applications.

slack: The amount of time that you can delay a task before the task becomes critical. Slack is used up when any delay in a task will delay the overall project deadline. Also called *float*.

split tasks: Tasks that have one or more breaks in their timing. When you split a task, you stop it part way and then start it again later.

start date: The date on which a project or task begins.

start-to-finish relationship: A dependency relationship in which the start of one task determines the finish of another task.

start-to-start relationship: A dependency relationship in which the start of one task determines the start of another task.

subproject: A copy of a second project inserted in a project. The inserted project becomes a phase of the project in which it is inserted.

subtask: A task detailing a specific step in a project phase. This detail is rolled up into a higher-level summary task. Also called a *subordinate task*. *See also* roll up.

successor: One task in a dependency relationship, in which there is always a predecessor (often, but not always the earlier task) and a successor (often, but not always, the later task). *See also* dependency.

summary task: In a project outline, a task that has subordinate tasks. A summary task rolls up the details of its subtasks and has no timing of its own. *See also* roll up.

task: An individual step performed to reach a project's goal.

template: A format in which a file can be saved. The template saves elements such as calendar settings, formatting, and tasks. New project files can be based on a template to save the time involved in reentering settings.

timescale: The area of Gantt Chart view that displays units of time; when placed against those units of time, taskbars graphically represent the timing of tasks.

tracking: Recording the actual progress of work completed and the costs accrued for a project's tasks.

Value List: An alternative to entering data manually; a customizable feature of Project that allows you to create a list of values in a field from which a user can choose.

variable rate: A shift in resource cost that can be set to occur at specific times during a project. For example, if a resource is expected to receive a raise or if equipment lease rates are scheduled to increase, you can assign variable rates for those resources.

WBS (work breakdown structure): Automatically assigned numbers that designate an outline structure for each project task. Government projects often require WBS codes.

work breakdown structure: *See* WBS.

Work resources: The people or equipment that perform work necessary to accomplish a task. *See also* Material resources.

workload: The amount of work that any resource is performing at any given time, taking into account all tasks to which the resource is assigned.

workspace: A set of files and project settings that you can save and reopen together so that you pick up where you left off on a set of projects.

Index

D

F

U

BUSINESS, CAREERS & PERSONAL FINANCE

0-7645-9847-3

0-7645-2431-3

Also available:
- Business Plans Kit For Dummies
  0-7645-9794-9
- Economics For Dummies
  0-7645-5726-2
- Grant Writing For Dummies
  0-7645-8416-2
- Home Buying For Dummies
  0-7645-5331-3
- Managing For Dummies
  0-7645-1771-6
- Marketing For Dummies
  0-7645-5600-2

- Personal Finance For Dummies
  0-7645-2590-5*
- Resumes For Dummies
  0-7645-5471-9
- Selling For Dummies
  0-7645-5363-1
- Six Sigma For Dummies
  0-7645-6798-5
- Small Business Kit For Dummies
  0-7645-5984-2
- Starting an eBay Business For Dummies
  0-7645-6924-4
- Your Dream Career For Dummies
  0-7645-9795-7

HOME & BUSINESS COMPUTER BASICS

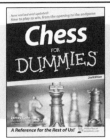

0-470-05432-8

0-471-75421-8

Also available:
- Cleaning Windows Vista For Dummies
  0-471-78293-9
- Excel 2007 For Dummies
  0-470-03737-7
- Mac OS X Tiger For Dummies
  0-7645-7675-5
- MacBook For Dummies
  0-470-04859-X
- Macs For Dummies
  0-470-04849-2
- Office 2007 For Dummies
  0-470-00923-3

- Outlook 2007 For Dummies
  0-470-03830-6
- PCs For Dummies
  0-7645-8958-X
- Salesforce.com For Dummies
  0-470-04893-X
- Upgrading & Fixing Laptops For Dummies
  0-7645-8959-8
- Word 2007 For Dummies
  0-470-03658-3
- Quicken 2007 For Dummies
  0-470-04600-7

FOOD, HOME, GARDEN, HOBBIES, MUSIC & PETS

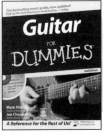

0-7645-8404-9

0-7645-9904-6

Also available:
- Candy Making For Dummies
  0-7645-9734-5
- Card Games For Dummies
  0-7645-9910-0
- Crocheting For Dummies
  0-7645-4151-X
- Dog Training For Dummies
  0-7645-8418-9
- Healthy Carb Cookbook For Dummies
  0-7645-8476-6
- Home Maintenance For Dummies
  0-7645-5215-5

- Horses For Dummies
  0-7645-9797-3
- Jewelry Making & Beading For Dummies
  0-7645-2571-9
- Orchids For Dummies
  0-7645-6759-4
- Puppies For Dummies
  0-7645-5255-4
- Rock Guitar For Dummies
  0-7645-5356-9
- Sewing For Dummies
  0-7645-6847-7
- Singing For Dummies
  0-7645-2475-5

INTERNET & DIGITAL MEDIA

0-470-04529-9

0-470-04894-8

Also available:
- Blogging For Dummies
  0-471-77084-1
- Digital Photography For Dummies
  0-7645-9802-3
- Digital Photography All-in-One Desk Reference For Dummies
  0-470-03743-1
- Digital SLR Cameras and Photography For Dummies
  0-7645-9803-1
- eBay Business All-in-One Desk Reference For Dummies
  0-7645-8438-3
- HDTV For Dummies
  0-470-09673-X

- Home Entertainment PCs For Dummies
  0-470-05523-5
- MySpace For Dummies
  0-470-09529-6
- Search Engine Optimization For Dummies
  0-471-97998-8
- Skype For Dummies
  0-470-04891-3
- The Internet For Dummies
  0-7645-8996-2
- Wiring Your Digital Home For Dummies
  0-471-91830-X

* Separate Canadian edition also available
† Separate U.K. edition also available

SPORTS, FITNESS, PARENTING, RELIGION & SPIRITUALITY

0-471-76871-5

0-7645-7841-3

Also available:
- Catholicism For Dummies
  0-7645-5391-7
- Exercise Balls For Dummies
  0-7645-5623-1
- Fitness For Dummies
  0-7645-7851-0
- Football For Dummies
  0-7645-3936-1
- Judaism For Dummies
  0-7645-5299-6
- Potty Training For Dummies
  0-7645-5417-4
- Buddhism For Dummies
  0-7645-5359-3

- Pregnancy For Dummies
  0-7645-4483-7 †
- Ten Minute Tone-Ups For Dummies
  0-7645-7207-5
- NASCAR For Dummies
  0-7645-7681-X
- Religion For Dummies
  0-7645-5264-3
- Soccer For Dummies
  0-7645-5229-5
- Women in the Bible For Dummies
  0-7645-8475-8

TRAVEL

0-7645-7749-2

0-7645-6945-7

Also available:
- Alaska For Dummies
  0-7645-7746-8
- Cruise Vacations For Dummies
  0-7645-6941-4
- England For Dummies
  0-7645-4276-1
- Europe For Dummies
  0-7645-7529-5
- Germany For Dummies
  0-7645-7823-5
- Hawaii For Dummies
  0-7645-7402-7

- Italy For Dummies
  0-7645-7386-1
- Las Vegas For Dummies
  0-7645-7382-9
- London For Dummies
  0-7645-4277-X
- Paris For Dummies
  0-7645-7630-5
- RV Vacations For Dummies
  0-7645-4442-X
- Walt Disney World & Orlando
  For Dummies
  0-7645-9660-8

GRAPHICS, DESIGN & WEB DEVELOPMENT

0-7645-8815-X

0-7645-9571-7

Also available:
- 3D Game Animation For Dummies
  0-7645-8789-7
- AutoCAD 2006 For Dummies
  0-7645-8925-3
- Building a Web Site For Dummies
  0-7645-7144-3
- Creating Web Pages For Dummies
  0-470-08030-2
- Creating Web Pages All-in-One Desk
  Reference For Dummies
  0-7645-4345-8
- Dreamweaver 8 For Dummies
  0-7645-9649-7

- InDesign CS2 For Dummies
  0-7645-9572-5
- Macromedia Flash 8 For Dummies
  0-7645-9691-8
- Photoshop CS2 and Digital
  Photography For Dummies
  0-7645-9580-6
- Photoshop Elements 4 For Dummies
  0-471-77483-9
- Syndicating Web Sites with RSS Feeds
  For Dummies
  0-7645-8848-6
- Yahoo! SiteBuilder For Dummies
  0-7645-9800-7

NETWORKING, SECURITY, PROGRAMMING & DATABASES

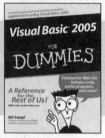

0-7645-7728-X

0-471-74940-0

Also available:
- Access 2007 For Dummies
  0-470-04612-0
- ASP.NET 2 For Dummies
  0-7645-7907-X
- C# 2005 For Dummies
  0-7645-9704-3
- Hacking For Dummies
  0-470-05235-X
- Hacking Wireless Networks
  For Dummies
  0-7645-9730-2
- Java For Dummies
  0-470-08716-1

- Microsoft SQL Server 2005 For Dummies
  0-7645-7755-7
- Networking All-in-One Desk Reference
  For Dummies
  0-7645-9939-9
- Preventing Identity Theft For Dummies
  0-7645-7336-5
- Telecom For Dummies
  0-471-77085-X
- Visual Studio 2005 All-in-One Desk
  Reference For Dummies
  0-7645-9775-2
- XML For Dummies
  0-7645-8845-1

HEALTH & SELF-HELP

0-7645-8450-2

0-7645-4149-8

Also available:
- Bipolar Disorder For Dummies
  0-7645-8451-0
- Chemotherapy and Radiation
  For Dummies
  0-7645-7832-4
- Controlling Cholesterol For Dummies
  0-7645-5440-9
- Diabetes For Dummies
  0-7645-6820-5* †
- Divorce For Dummies
  0-7645-8417-0 †

- Fibromyalgia For Dummies
  0-7645-5441-7
- Low-Calorie Dieting For Dummies
  0-7645-9905-4
- Meditation For Dummies
  0-471-77774-9
- Osteoporosis For Dummies
  0-7645-7621-6
- Overcoming Anxiety For Dummies
  0-7645-5447-6
- Reiki For Dummies
  0-7645-9907-0
- Stress Management For Dummies
  0-7645-5144-2

EDUCATION, HISTORY, REFERENCE & TEST PREPARATION

0-7645-8381-6

0-7645-9554-7

Also available:
- The ACT For Dummies
  0-7645-9652-7
- Algebra For Dummies
  0-7645-5325-9
- Algebra Workbook For Dummies
  0-7645-8467-7
- Astronomy For Dummies
  0-7645-8465-0
- Calculus For Dummies
  0-7645-2498-4
- Chemistry For Dummies
  0-7645-5430-1
- Forensics For Dummies
  0-7645-5580-4

- Freemasons For Dummies
  0-7645-9796-5
- French For Dummies
  0-7645-5193-0
- Geometry For Dummies
  0-7645-5324-0
- Organic Chemistry I For Dummies
  0-7645-6902-3
- The SAT I For Dummies
  0-7645-7193-1
- Spanish For Dummies
  0-7645-5194-9
- Statistics For Dummies
  0-7645-5423-9

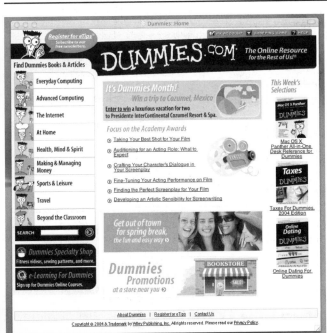

Get smart @ dummies.com®

- **Find a full list of Dummies titles**
- **Look into loads of FREE on-site articles**
- **Sign up for FREE eTips e-mailed to you weekly**
- **See what other products carry the Dummies name**
- **Shop directly from the Dummies bookstore**
- **Enter to win new prizes every month!**

* Separate Canadian edition also available
† Separate U.K. edition also available

Available wherever books are sold. For more information or to order direct: U.S. customers visit www.dummies.com or call 1-877-762-2974.
U.K. customers visit www.wileyeurope.com or call 0800 243407. Canadian customers visit www.wiley.ca or call 1-800-567-4797.

Do More with Dummies

Instructional DVDs • Music Compilations
Games & Novelties • Culinary Kits
Crafts & Sewing Patterns
Home Improvement/DIY Kits • and more!

Check out the Dummies Specialty Shop at www.dummies.com for more information!

 WILEY